KATONAH

The History of a New York Village and its People

SPECIAL CENTENNIAL FACSIMILE EDITION

Frances R. Duncombe

And other members of the Historical Committee

Katonah Village Improvement Society

KVIS

KATONAH, NEW YORK

1897-1997

FOREWORD TO THE CENTENNIAL EDITION

The 100th anniversary of the move to New Katonah has been a much anticipated event in the community. It was a very happy coincidence that we found ourselves in need of a new supply of this book at the same time. We were presented with a fine opportunity to give this edition a new look for the occasion.

We of the Katonah Village Improvement Society wish to thank the Katonah Village Library Board of Trustees for its generous support of this printing. Without that help we would have been unable to republish this in time for the Celebration.

It is with great pride that we present this Centennial Edition of Katonah's history.

MARY M. TSCHORN, President
Katonah Village Improvement Society

The Hamlet of Katonah is about to celebrate its centennial, and at the same time this volume is about to enter its third printing. One reflects on a community rich in its tradition, as mindful of its past as it is of its future, and populated by a citizenry zealously involved in civic issues. A population so steeped in community pride, values and spirit, that the Supervisor one hundred years from now will echo these same thoughts as he or she prepares for that celebration, and yet another printing.

JOHN R. DININ
Supervisor
Town of Bedford

FOREWORD TO THE 1978 EDITION

Rarely in any community is there found a group so dedicated to the accomplishment of a project as the Historical Committee of the Katonah Village Improvement Society. With unselfish devotion they have worked together for five years to produce this historical and genealogical record of our village and vicinity. Further, they have amassed valuable supplementary material which has been made part of the reference collections of the Katonah Village Library and the Westchester County Historical Society, White Plains. By their efforts they have made Katonah's past accessible to those of us who live here and to students of a wider area.

We of the Katonah Village Improvement Society are indebted to all who have had a part in the making of this book, which we take much pride in publishing.

JOHN W. RUGER, President
Katonah Village Improvement Society

"Perhaps the most sincere compliment to the Historical Committee and the work represented by this book is the rate at which the original supply was exhausted. It is therefore a special pleasure to make a second printing available as part of the centennial celebration of the Katonah Village Improvement Society. The names of Hoagy B. Carmichael, Sylvia Finlayson, Philip J. McGovern, Phillip J. Raneri, and Donald H. Streeter are gratefully added to the original list of people making this reprint possible. Some errors in the first printing are listed on p. 470ff. otherwise the book remains the same.

We hope that this book and the special events and exhibits of the centennial will bring enjoyment to all our friends, and inspire those who will write the next chapters of the history of Katonah.

George S. Almasi, President
Katonah Village Improvement Society.

Historical Committee of the Katonah Village Improvement Society

Miss Julia A. Mead, Committee Chairman
F. Everett Abbott
Mrs. Alexander Addis, Cochairman for Organization Materials
Mrs. Arthur S. Bailie
Arthur I. Bernhard, Chairman for Maps
Robertson T. Barrett, Consultant
Mrs. F. C. Bonny
Miss Elizabeth Bonny
Mrs. Charles S. Brown
Mrs. N. E. Derecktor
Mrs. Philip de Young,* Chairman for Photographs
Miss Janet Doe, Technical Editor
Mrs. Herbert S. Duncombe, Jr., Main Author
Mrs. Benjamin F. Finch, Jr., Cochairman for Organization Materials
Mrs. Leonard H. Hall
C. H. Hendrickson, Publicity Chairman
Mrs. C. H. Hendrickson
Coleman W. Hoyt, Production Chairman
Dr. & Mrs. Thomas H. Jameson
Mrs. James R. Jarman
Mrs. William A. Kelly, Chairman for Genealogies
Richard G. Lucid, Chairman for Military Materials
Mrs. Clifford P. Morehouse
Mrs. E. H. Portsch
Mrs. Kerr Rainsford
Miss Madelon Ryan
Mrs. Paul E. Stuckert
Mrs. Gilbert L. Thurston
Mrs. Oliver U. Todd
Miss Helen M. Towey
Mrs. William G. Weist

* Mrs. de Young's death in 1960 was a great loss to the Committee.

INTRODUCTION

A need for a history of Katonah became apparent several years ago when real estate development brought many new families here. The term "Old Katonah" was often heard, as were references to the village having been transplanted. Newcomers wanted to know what all this meant, and frequently sought information from the Katonah Village Library. Two small booklets had been written, one in 1896 and the other in 1900, but the few precious copies extant were for reference only and could not be borrowed. Our librarian urged the Historical Committee of the Katonah Village Improvement Society to take on the project of writing a new history.

On a Saturday afternoon in March, 1956, the project began in the home of the Committee chairman. Several ladies who had known Old Katonah since childhood were there to give us the wealth of their memories. Mr. Robertson T. Barrett, Bedford's Town Historian and author of *The Town of Bedford, a Commemorative History, 1680-1955,* was master of ceremonies, drawing out through well directed questions information which we preserved on tape. This provided a wonderful point of departure from which to proceed to our historical investigations. We realized, however, that working funds would be needed, and temporarily put aside historical studies to publish *The Katonah Directory.* This netted us a sufficient amount so that we could proceed with confidence.

In the fall of 1957 we took up the history again. Mr. Barrett, a continuing help and source of encouragement, was unavailable to us as author. We found one in Frances Duncombe who has written the major narrative and taken over-all charge of writing. We found other writers among members of our own enlarged Committee. Katharine Barrett Kelly accepted responsibility for our genealogical section and Janet Doe became our technical editor. The Committee's chairman acted throughout as coordinator of work and liaison between the various groups. Subcommittees were formed on maps, pictures, publicity, and one wrote up accounts of our churches, organizations and other subjects of community interest.

Two years ago, when the writing had carried the narrative up through the creation of the reservoirs, groups re-formed into what we called "decade writers," each group taking a decade from 1907 through the 1950's, doing the research and writing a chapter on it. As work progressed, the manuscript was offered for evaluation to all Committee

vii

members and to the elder generation who knew Old Katonah. From this review came tremendous help in revision. At last our manuscript neared completion. Then Coleman W. Hoyt stepped in as "architect," solving the many problems of production and taking the book through its final stages. We should like to acknowledge our debt to him and to the *Reader's Digest* who have most kindly allowed us to make use of their facilities.

Outside the Committee and in some cases outside the community, individuals and organizations have given to the project valuable and generous assistance in various fields. Among these, too many to mention each by name, our special gratitude is due the following:

for contributing the fruits of their personal research,
> Miss Mildred G. Black, Mrs. Robert A. Chambers, Mrs. J. Harold Crane, John Gemmill, the Rev. Bruce Moss, Lewis C. Rubenstein, and Matt Savage Walton, Jr.;

for giving use of old newspapers, inherited documents and family scrapbooks,
> Mrs. Charles M. Allen, Edward Percy Barrett, the late Miss Elizabeth N. Barrett, Clinton S. Benedict, Mrs. James G. Bonacorda, Mrs. Stephen Brown, Frank B. Ginnell, Mrs. Henry F. Haight, Mrs. John R. Holmes, the late C. Fayette Lawrence, Mrs. Alfred G. MacKenzie, Mrs. Henry D. Miller, Miss Annie O'Neill, Mrs. Jonathan T. Rorer;

for allowing use of hitherto unpublished material from their private collections,
> Arnold S. Askin, Columbia University, Nathaniel E. Stein;

for making photographs in their possession available,
> Miss Ella Avery, Harvey and Holly Avery, Mrs. Mildred Banks, Edward Percy Barrett, Bedford Historical Society, Bedford House (Home of John Jay), Clinton S. Benedict, Arthur I. Bernhard, Mrs. James G. Bonacorda, Howard F. Bowles, Mrs. Carl L. Breuninger, the late Mrs. Herbert S. Chapman, Clark Associates, Inc., the County Trust Company, Mrs. William Curran, Mrs. John L. Dorsett, William J. Doyle, Jr., Mrs. Herbert S. Duncombe, Jr., Fahnestock & Company, Mrs. Charles Ferguson, Mrs. George C. Haas, Mrs. Leonard H. Hall, Katonah Village Library, A. Elliott Kellogg, Mrs. William A. Kelly, the late C. Fayette Lawrence, Ralph E. Mayers, Mrs. Charles G. Mead, Mrs. David R. Mead, Mrs. Henry D. Miller, John J. Miller, Mrs. John D. Morgan, *New York Herald Tribune,* Edgar Newman, Carl J. Noe, H. Halsted Park, Jr., *Patent Trader,* Frank Pinchbeck, Col. Allan M. Pope, Mrs. Kerr Rainsford, R. Benson Ray, Walter and Lucie Rosen Foundation, Cyrus W. Russell, St. Luke's Episcopal Church, St. Mary's Church, Mrs. Theodore Taylor, James R. Thomson, Miss Helen M. Towey, Mrs. Matthew J. Towey, the Misses Josephine

and Margery Van Tassel, Westchester County Historical Society, *Westchester County Publishers,* William M. Will, Mrs. Frederick H. Williams;
for their contribution in preparing photographs for reproduction,
George A. Aarons and Edward G. Carman;
for aid in cutting and editing,
Miss Dorothy Hinitt and Clifford P. Morehouse;
for their personal recollections given in interviews or writing,
Miss Ella Avery, Enoch Avery, Mrs. Mildred Banks, Mr. and Mrs. Edward Percy Barrett, the late Miss Elizabeth N. Barrett, Robertson T. Barrett, Mrs. Albert Burt, Walter T. Chace, the late Mrs. Herbert S. Chapman, Mrs. Cassie Hoffman, the late Morris Holmes, Ferdinand T. Hopkins, Robert D. Knapp, David McClure, Mrs. Charles G. Mead, Mrs. David R. Mead, the late Adrian L. Quick, Robert B. Ryan, Miss Millie Smith, Miss Helen M. Towey, William Travis, the Misses Josephine and Margery Van Tassel, William M. Will, Mrs. Frederick H. Williams;
for their courteous attention to the needs and requests of our historians,
Hon. Douglas L. Barrett, Supervisor, William J. Millmore, Town Clerk, and Mrs. Helen R. Hancock, Assistant Clerk of the Town of Bedford, Hon. Cyrus W. Russell, Supervisor of Lewisboro, Hon. Patrick V. Ryan, Supervisor of Somers, Henry C. Strippel and Mrs. Amos Struble of the Westchester County Historical Society, Mrs. Carl Cnobloch of the Bedford Historical Society, Morgan H. Seacord of the Huguenot and Historical Association of New Rochelle, Miss Greta Cornell and Mrs. Laurence D. Redway of the Ossining Historical Society, William M. Will of the Bedford Farmers' Club, Miss Edith T. Parker of the Westchester County Department of Public Welfare, Miss Eleanor Fair of the Metropolitan Life Insurance Company Library, the staffs of the Katonah Village Library, New York Academy of Medicine Library, New York State Library, New-York Historical Society Library, Library of Congress, Princeton University Library, Special Collections Library of Columbia University, and the Westchester Academy of Medicine Library; also the New York City Board of Water Supply, New York Telephone Company, New York State Engineers Office, Westchester County Division of Land Records; the *Patent Trader* and the *North Westchester Times*; also, Dr. Joseph Epstein, Mrs. Edward M. Fielder, Dr. John P. Lambert, and Russell L. Snow;
for genealogical help and information,
Mrs. J. Harold Crane, Grenville C. Mackenzie, the New York Genealogical and Biographical Society, the New York Public Library, and present day representatives of families listed;
for research in aid to our writers,

Charles W. Graydon and Mrs. Philip G. Stratton;
for providing material on organizations from which our summaries were made,
Eli Antonecchia, Mrs. Elmer D. Appleby, Mrs. John I. H. Baur, Arthur R. Covey, Don Friend, Edwin T. Ganung, C. H. Gifford, Mrs. William R. Kellogg, Paul Lang, the late C. Fayette Lawrence, Mrs. Constance M. Meyerson, Mrs. Hugh H. F. Morton, Mrs. Paul A. Noe, Mrs. William A. Paddock, Walter L. Raith, R. Benson Ray, Miss May Jean Robins, Dr. William H. Smith, George C. Williams, Mrs. W. W. Woodcock;
for design of chapter headings,
Paul Orban, Miss Gloria Strang;
for aid in publicity,
Henry Jacobs, Henry J. Slesar, Katonah Girl Scouts Troop No. 244;
for legal advice,
Miss Ione P. Barrett, Arthur R. Covey;
for assistance in seeing the manuscript through the press,
Mrs. Mary Porter;
for advice on special typographic problems,
Veto Varlotta;
for cataloging and filing,
Mrs. Lewis A. Benedict;
and last but not least, for volunteer typing,
Miss Alden Finch, Mrs. Richard G. Lucid and Mrs. Thomas J. Newton.

As to the hours spent in writing the history—in committee meetings, over typewriters, on the telephone, poring over old newspapers, deciphering the handwriting in ancient letters, deeds and minute books —the number is astronomical! This account of work done is not to give the impression that we have felt it a burden. On the contrary, it has been a project filled with excitement and infinite interest. This common concern has kept our very large group of collaborators working together with never-ending pleasure and complete satisfaction.

The Historical Committee
JULIA A. MEAD, Chairman

CONTENTS

APPENDIXES

LIST OF ILLUSTRATIONS

LIST OF MAPS

PREFACE

This book is about the village of Katonah which lies in Bedford Township, Westchester County, New York. It is also about the adjoining Bedford districts of Cantitoe and Mt. Holly and areas now submerged by the Muscoot and Cross River Reservoirs.

The information gathering and also the writing represents the work of a great many people. Some of us are still living; some of us have been gone a long time. The bond we share and hope to share with you is our fascination with the past and our conviction that on it are founded our present and future.

We will let Elizabeth Ann Robertson express this feeling for us. Born at Cantitoe in 1826, she wrote while still a very young girl:

> History is the narration of things that are past. It is one of the greatest blessings that is bestowed on the human family. Without it we should have been ignorant of things that have taken place in days that are past; we should have been ignorant of the Creation of the World, and all things therein, and of the existence of God, the Creator of the World. . . . [History] gives an account of many other interesting transactions. It gives us an account of the discovery of America, and of those by whom it was inhabited when discovered . . . of some of the most renowned men of our own country and of others, which is very interesting. O! how pleasing, interesting and useful is history to the human family. Without it how ignorant we should have been! How grateful we ought to be to our Creator for our many blessings.*

* Letter in possession of Mrs. W. A. Kelly, Katonah, N.Y.

Being a true account of the Times, the Temper,
the Growth of this town and its Environs
in Northern Westchester from the early 1600's
to the present; with sixty-four definitive
Illustration & Maps; authentic Letters, Diaries,
Deeds, Waybills, Advertisements and Memorabilia;
and Genealogies of fifty-eight village families

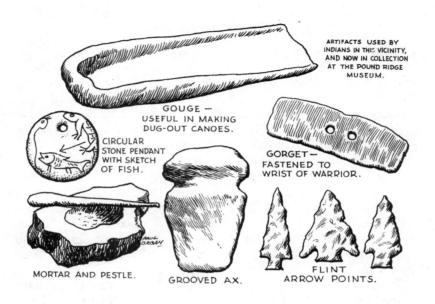

GOUGE —
USEFUL IN MAKING
DUG-OUT CANOES.

ARTIFACTS USED BY
INDIANS IN THIS VICINITY,
AND NOW IN COLLECTION
AT THE POUND RIDGE
MUSEUM.

CIRCULAR
STONE PENDANT
WITH SKETCH
OF FISH.

GORGET—
FASTENED TO
WRIST OF WARRIOR.

MORTAR AND PESTLE.

GROOVED AX.

FLINT
ARROW POINTS.

CHAPTER I
EXPLORERS, SETTLERS, INDIANS

IT ISN'T possible to give either date or location to the founding of Katonah. The village we know today did settle in its present site in 1897, but actually Katonah had existed in a different location under the same name—and under many of the same roofs—for forty-five years prior to that date. Some of its people had lived together as a community, in various places with various names, long before that. To find reasons for their coming together and for being the sort of individuals they were, we must reach back into township and general history.

We know very little about our first human families in this region, but there had existed here Indians of an older and more primitive culture than the Mohegans encountered by the first settlers of our Bedford Township in 1680. Tools and pottery of these earlier Indians have been found in nearby rock shelters buried well below the possessions left by the Mohegans.[1] What these early men were called, when they came, and from where, we don't know. We only know they had gone long before the coming of the whites. It was not with them that men from European countries bargained for land in this hemisphere.

In the early days of European migration to this country, for-

1

eign nations wanting land but unready to fight one another for it came to a practical agreement. Discovery of land by subjects of any European monarch gave that monarch the sole authority to dispose of it. This was done by a system that allowed individuals or groups, not outright ownership, but the exclusive right to obtain ownership from the Indians "by purchase or otherwise." The Indians, according to this same agreement, were prohibited from selling land to any other persons.[2]

From the first the French were undisputed in Canada and the English in Virginia, but there was a conflict of claims along the Atlantic Coast and Long Island Sound between the 40th and 45th parallels. The Dutch claimed discovery by Adrian Block, who sailed up through the Sound in 1614. The English had already claimed this territory and two patents had been issued in 1606 by James I that included it.[3]

In this confusion of claims and interests, it was the migrant colonizers and not the adventurous voyagers who really determined who should live where in the new land. At Plymouth the Pilgrims began English possession in 1620. Governor John Winthrop, the real founder of the Massachusetts Bay Colony, arrived with eleven ships at Salem in 1630. By 1633 other English groups had spread west and south into the Connecticut valley. In 1638, Theophilus Eaton with the Rev. John Davenport planted a colony at New Haven,[9] Bedford's grandparent colony.

Meanwhile the Dutch were establishing themselves in the adjacent territory. Their first permanent settlers bought Manhattan Island in 1626 and subsequently patroonships were granted northward along both sides of the Hudson River.[4] In the year 1640 (April 19) the Dutch States General bought from the Siwanoy Indians all lands located in the southeast portion of Westchester running as far eastward in Connecticut as the Norwalk River.[5]

In July of 1640, the British colony at New Haven bought much of this same land from different Indians.[10] The deciding factor again was colonization, not claims. Nathaniel Turner, agent for the New Haven Colony, purchased from the sagamores, Ponus and Wascussue, a tract of land described on the deed rather loosely as "all the ground belonging to the said sagamores except a piece of ground which Ponus reserved for himself and the other Indians to plant upon." Later, however, a deed of confirmation gave it the more definite boundaries of "sixteen miles north of the town plot of Stamford and two miles still further north for the pasture of their cattle; also eight miles east and west." Within these boundaries lay the land which later became Bedford Township.[13]

The same year that the New Haven Colony (which included Windsor, Hartford and Wethersfield) bought this land, they resold it to a group from Wethersfield for £33. The Wethersfield men, under the leadership of the Rev. Richard Denton, proceeded immediately to establish the Town of Stamford.[14] Stamford was Bedford's parent colony.

Forty years after its founding, twenty-two Stamford inhabitants felt a desire to strike out on their own. They came inland until they found land good for farming near the Mianus River on which to erect a mill. This land they originally called the "Hopp Ground" because of the wild crop they found there; but in 1682, when they secured a license from the General Court at Hartford, it was noted that the plantation was henceforth to be called Bedford.[18]

The six-mile square which now comprises the Township of Bedford was obtained from the Indians between the years 1680 and 1722 in eight pieces. All of this land had already been bought by the New Havenites from Ponus.[15] However, Chief Katonah— also written Catoonah, Cattonah, Katoona, Catonah, according to various phonetic renderings—who had fallen heir to much of Ponus' domain since the Turner purchase of 1640, either didn't understand this or chose to ignore it. The white men who were moving into his home territory evidently thought it politic to ignore it also. They paid again for each separate piece.

As we use Katonah's name for our village and its surrounding area, it would be satisfying to have an authentic description of the man himself. But the best we can do is to piece together what clews existing documents, history and legends give us. Indian titles generally, though not necessarily, passed down by blood lines; so Katonah, inheriting from Ponus, was probably a descendant.[19] Just when he became "Sagomore and cheef proprietor of ye lands about Bedford," as he is styled in the Cross's Vineyard confirmation of 1702,[21] it is hard to say; but he was certainly an important man in these parts by 1680 when his name preceded those of the other Indians who signed with him on the first Bedford deed.[22] Later, in 1708, in a conveyance for a tract of land at Ridgefield, Connecticut, he is given the truly impressive title of "Sachem of Ramapoo Indians . . . within her majesties province of New York in America."[16]

The strata of Indian social structure were many and sometimes confusing, but as we understand it, the Ramapo Sachemdom was part of the Tankiteke Chieftaincy of the Wappinger Confederacy. The Wappingers were Mohegans who in turn belonged to the great Algonquin race.[25]

One confusion here, on the lowest rung of the ladder, is that the lands claimed as Ramapo by Katonah agreed in description with those of Ponus and Wascussue, who were called sagamores of Toquam and Shippan. We won't try for an explanation on this, but Katonah's inheritance of territory already disposed of by the above sagamores and his assumption that it was his right to dispose of it again have an explanation that is unusual but not too complicated.

The Indians and the white men did not have the same concept of land sale. To the whites, it meant ownership; to the Indians, it meant the right of use co-existent with their own use. This right, according to their views, terminated by non-use and could be transferred at a price and by other deeds to a different group of whites. For those who feel that the coats, blankets, cloth and wampum mentioned as consideration in the early sales were poor compensation, this may clarify the Indians' acceptance of them.[2]

Katonah's name appears on eight deeds or confirmations for Bedford land between 1680 and 1704,[23, 26] on one confirmation to the inhabitants of Stamford in 1700[17] and on one Ridgefield deed in 1708.[16] This is the last year we hear of him by documentary evidence.

Legend gives Katonah a wife, sometimes called Cantitoe and sometimes Mustato. In the Cohamung purchase deed, May 2, 1683, the wording suggests that Katonah had a son named Papiag, though lack of punctuation allows two interpretations here.[24] Legend supported by reasonable deduction gives him another son, Wackemane, also spelled Wackemone and Wackamawa, whose name follows Katonah's on the later Bedford deeds and supplants it on the last one in 1722,[27] by which time the former "cheef proprietor of ye lands about Bedford" may be presumed to have moved on to the Happy Hunting Ground, where he may also have become "cheef proprietor."

Legend buries Katonah beside his wife and sometimes a child in the woods southwest of Cantitoe Corners, which, accordingly, have been named "Katonah's Wood." Large boulders mark their supposed last resting place. Because the legend is part of our village heritage, we quote a few lines of a poem on this subject by William Will:

Katonah

The village of Katonah in a masque-like quiet lay,
Where it sweltered in the torture of a sultry, humid day.
Not a sign of life was stirring—round the wigwams droned
    the fly
And the dogs were lapping water as the Beaver Dam rushed
    by.

The sun, a disk-shaped, reddish mass was sinking toward
    the west,
Its shadows, cool, refreshing, stirred the savages at rest.
Then at length there came the thunder in a deep and grum-
    bling tone—
The Great Spirit was unrestful in the Land of the Unknown.

Chief Katonah from his deerhide rose and rubbed sleep laden
    eyes,
And Cantitoe, his squaw-wife, soothed her papoose from its
    cries.
In a curt, stern voice he told her that he would not tarry long
For he went to hold a council with the chieftain Aspetong.

The Great Spirit rose in fury, sent the rain in hissing moan,
The giant oaks were swaying as the wind passed with its
    groan,
When the lightening fell asunder as it split a mighty tree
It glided through the smoke-vent of Katonah's lone tepee.

Now the storm has passed to northward leaving cooler air
    and clear
As Katonah hastened homeward, on his shoulder a limp deer.
At the door he laid his burden and went in with noiseless
    tread,
And the scene that lay before him snapped his heart strings—
    left him dead.

On the deerskin in the corner, Cantitoe sat as in rest
As she'd closed her eyes forever with her papoose at her breast.

Since no sign of life was stirring, in the morning came the
   braves,
And they buried them together with three boulders on their
   graves.[28]

And this is absolutely all, to the best of our knowledge, that
history, documents or legends have to say about Katonah as an
individual.

Collected in the Pound Ridge Museum are agricultural tools
that indicate Katonah's people were adequate farmers. Stone
axes and hoes made from the shoulder blades of deer may seem
a bit awkward to us but they did the job of clearing land and
cultivating crops of corn, sieva beans and pumpkins.[11] Our
Indians' main interest, however, was in hunting and fishing and
here they exercised ingenuity at a high level. In the Kitchawan
(Croton River) near where the Peppeneghek (Cross River) flowed
into it, they constructed stone weirs, through which the unwary
fish swam into basket-like nets woven of willow. These weirs
were so staunchly built that before they were covered by the
damming of the river, they remained for the children of Whitlockville and Old Katonah to use in summer at low water as
stepping stones.[29]

In Pound Ridge, Katonah's people, taking advantage of the
natural leading together of the ridges, built a barrier or palisade
of logs, rocks and brush to form a corral into which they drove
and impounded hundreds of deer and other animals to be
slaughtered for food and clothing. And of course, they trapped
small animals. The number of beaver caught along the streams
was sufficient to bring John Jacob Astor here later to trade.[30]

Arrowheads have been found and are still being found throughout the fields and woods in and around Katonah. The heads
themselves, however numerous, do not indicate a settlement—
just good hunting. But when flint chips are found, it means a
village or camp, because the Indians did not stop to manufacture
arrowheads when they were in active pursuit of game.[12] As the
Indians traveled far in their hunting and for pleasure, their feet
beat out paths, some of which we still use today, such as Muscota
Path, our Cherry Street, Potiticus Path, our Maple Avenue, and
others.

Near Bedford Village, there were native villages at Indian Hill
and Noname's Hill. In our own locality, there is said to have been
one on the Croton River near the fish weirs. This last village

was believed by Thatcher T. P. Luquer to be the site of the famous Bedford Massacre of Christmas, 1644, when Captain John
Underhill marched eighteen miles up from Greenwich and
wiped out an entire Indian settlement in reprisal for the murder
of Anne Hutchinson by a different tribe of Indians on the
Sound.[31] Most other historians, however, place this massacre at
Indian Hill.

In the woods north of Old Katonah and of great interest to
children of the late eighteen hundreds was a "rocking stone"
which they believed had been used by the Indians to call one
another. According to Miss Margery Van Tassel, it "could be
made to teeter back and forth and make a deliciously thrilling
thud of a noise as it hit the underlying rock bed." [29]

Nearby was another spot of interest to the adventurous children of the day. Again we quote Miss Van Tassel:

> Across the gully to the north from the stone is the site of a
> supposed-to-be Indian burial ground. They say that when the
> railroad was put through, the workmen dug up human
> bones.[29]

As no local scribe of the sixteen hundreds has left us a description of the Indians found in Bedford, we have to assume they
resembled the Indians described by Adriaen Van der Donck, a
Westchesterite from Yonkers. In a book published in 1653, he
wrote at length of the native inhabitants in order "that after the
Christians have multiplied and the natives have disappeared and
melted away, a memorial of them may be preserved." Selected
from Van der Donck's writing, but of necessity much condensed,
are the following observations:

> Their appearance and bodily form, as well of the men as of
> the women, are well proportioned . . . varying little from the
> common size. Their limbs are properly formed, and they are
> sprightly and active. They can run very fast for a long time,
> and they can carry heavy packs. To all bodily exertions they
> are very competent, as far as their dispositions extend; but
> to heavy slavish labour the men have a particular aversion,
> and they manage their affairs accordingly, so that they need
> not labour much. . . . The men and women commonly have
> broad shoulders and slender waists. Their hair, before old
> age, is jet black, sleek and uncurled, and nearly as coarse as

a horse's tail. . . . The colour of their skin is not so white as
ours; . . . they have a yellowish colour like the Tartars. . . .
Their yellowness is no fault of nature, but it is caused by the
heat of the scorching sun, which is hotter and more power-
ful . . . than in Holland. . . .

In eating and drinking the Indians are not excessive, even
in their feast-days. They are cheerful and well satisfied when
they have a sufficiency to . . . satisfy hunger and thirst. . . .
Their common drink is water from a living spring or well.
. . . Brandy or strong drink is unknown to them, except those
who frequent our settlements, and have learned that beer and
wine taste better than water. . . . Their common food is meat,
and fish of every kind. . . . For bread they use maize, or Turkey corn, which the women pound fine into meal. . . . Their
common food . . . is *pap, or mush.* . . . When they intend
to go a great distance on a hunting excursion, or to war,
where they expect to find no food . . . they provide themselves severally with a small bag of parched corn meal, which
is so nutritious that they can subsist on the same many
days. . . . When they are hungry, they eat a small handful
of the meal, after which they take a drink of water, and then
they are so well fed, that they can travel a day. . . .

The males until they are twelve or thirteen years old, run
nearly naked in summer. The females when they are able to
run about, wear a little covering. They are all accustomed
to wear a leathern girdle, which is usually ornamented
with . . . wampum (zewant) . . . When the men can procure duffels cloth, then they wear a piece of the same half
an ell wide, and nine quarters long, which they gird around
their waists, and draw up a fold to cover their nakedness,
with a flap of each end hanging down in front and rear. . . .
When it [duffels cloth] is not to be had, they wear a dressed
skin cut in a proper form. . . . The women also wear a cloth
around their bodies, fastened by a girdle which extends down
below their knees, and is as much as an under-coat; but next
to the body, under this coat, they wear a dressed deer-skin
coat, girt around the waist. . . . The wampum with which
one of those skirts is ornamented, is frequently worth from
one to three hundred guilders. The men and women usually
wear a plaid of duffels cloth of full breadth, and three ells
long. This is worn over the right shoulder, drawn in the form
of a knot about the body, with ends extending down below

the knees. This plaid serves them for a covering by day, and for a blanket by night. Stockings and shoes (moccasins) made of deer and buffalo skins, are worn by both sexes; some of those they ornament . . . with wampum. . . . They also make shoes out of corn husks. . . . Some of them purchase shoes and stockings from us, which they find to be most comfortable. The men usually go bare-headed, and the women with their hair bound . . . in a club about a hand long, in the form of a beaver's tail; over which they draw a square cap, which is frequently ornamented with wampum. . . . Around their necks they wear various ornaments, which are also decorated with wampum. . . . They also wear hand-bands, or bracelets, curiously wrought, and interwoven with wampum. . . . In winter, when the weather is cold, the women and children do not go abroad much, and when they do, they cover themselves with duffils and other articles. The men, to defend themselves against the cold, grease themselves with bear and racoon fat. They also wear clothing made of weasel, bear, deer, and buffalo skins. . . . To white linen they formerly were strangers, but now many begin to wear shirts, which they buy from our people, and those they frequently wear without washing until the same are worn out.[32]

The wampum (or zewant) mentioned so frequently by Van der Donck was the Indian's money as well as his decoration and measured by the pound or by the fathom (the arm spread of a man, about a six-foot length). White zewant was made from the stem or stock of the periwinkle, a small marine shell. Black or purple zewant, made from quahog shells, was called suckauhock, from which the Indian trail derived the name which later the Englishmen turned into Succabone, according to Bolton.[20]

The homes in which the Indians of Westchester lived have been described by historians of the nineteenth and twentieth centuries in various ways: as bowl-like, teepee-like, and as long narrow houses. Again, the only account written at the time which we have found comes from the pen of Van der Donck, who possibly only saw those houses nearer to Yonkers. He wrote:

Sometimes they build their houses above a hundred feet long; but never more than twenty feet wide. . . . They place long slender hickory saplings in the ground, having the bark stripped off, in a straight line of two rows. . . . Those sapling

poles are bent over towards each other in the form of an arch,
and are secured together. . . . The sapling poles are then
crossed with split poles in the form of lathing. . . . For covering they use the bark of ash, chestnut, and other trees, . . .
laying the smooth side inwards, leaving an open space of about
a foot wide in the crown, to let out the smoke. . . . From
sixteen to eighteen families frequently dwell in one house. . . .
The fire being kept in the middle, the people lay on either
side thereof, and each family has its own place. If they have
a place for a pot or a kettle, with a few small articles, and a
place to sleep, then they have room enough. . . . Such is
the construction of an Indian dwelling in every place, unless
they are out on fishing and hunting excursions, and then they
erect temporary huts or shanties. . . . For the erection of
. . . castles, or strong holds, they usually select a situation
on the side of a steep high hill, near a stream or river. . . .
Their castles and large towns they seldom leave altogether.
From other situations they remove frequently, and they seldom remain long at other places. In the summer, and in the
fishing seasons, many come to the water sides and rivers. In
the fall and winter, when venison is best, they retire to the
woods and hunting grounds. Sometimes towards the spring of
the year, they come in multitudes to the sea shores and bays,
to take oysters, clams, and every kind of shell-fish, which they
know how to dry, and preserve good a long time.[32]

A present-day Indian who visits this locality believes that our
early Bedford Indians had winter homes built in the shelter of
cliffs, lean-tos constructed against rock which retained the heat
of Indian fires for many hours.[33]
    Concerning the religious patterns of our Westchester Indians
we have found very little. If they worshipped idols, they left
none behind them that have been found. Van der Donck says
they believed

there is a God in heaven from all eternity, who is almighty.
But they say God is good, kind, and compassionate, who will
not punish or do any injury to any person, and therefore takes
no concern himself in the common affairs of the world,
nor does he meddle with the same, except that he has ordered
the devil to take care of those matters.[32]

A later source states that they believed in a good, all-wise spirit called Cantantowit and an evil spirit called Hobbamocko, but the imaginative ceremonies of the Indians of the southwest evidently had no counterpart here. In civil life, this source continues, their institutions were mostly democratic, though the title of sachem (ruler) usually remained hereditary in the family despite the fact that the people reserved the right to election. The sachem was assisted in governing by several chiefs, who were elected by the people. They carried on their affairs in councils, which were convened by a chief who was called a "runner" and was chosen for that purpose.[6]

We are particularly grateful for Van der Donck's "memorial" of 1653, as, within fifty-odd years, what he had foreseen had already begun to happen. In a letter dated January 9, 1708, to the Venerable Society for Propagating the Gospel in Foreign Parts in London, the Rev. George Muirson, rector of Rye and Bedford, paints an unhappy picture of the Indian families in his parish:

> As to the Indians, the natives of the country, they are a decaying people. We have not now in all this parish twenty families; whereas, not many years ago, there were several hundreds. I have frequently conversed with some of them, and been at their great meetings of *powowing,* as they call it. I have taken some pains to teach some of them, but to no purpose; for they seem regardless of instruction; and when I have told them of the evil consequences of their hard drinking, etc., they replied that Englishmen do the same: and that it is not so great a sin in an Indian as in an Englishman; because the Englishman's religion forbids it, but an Indian's does not. They further say they will not be Christians, nor do they see the necessity for so being, because we do not live according to the precepts of our religion. In such ways do most of the Indians that I have conversed with, either here or elsewhere, express themselves.[34]

Apparently, in spite of differences our remaining Indians got along well enough with the English, co-existing with them for some time. There is no mention in our township history of early settlers putting an Indian off the land they had bought. When later descendants of those settlers determined to become a nation independent of England, Westchester Indians fought beside them in battle and, according to Washington, conducted themselves "with great propriety and fidelity." [7]

It was the white man's use of the Indian hunting grounds for agriculture and the general changes due to increased civilization that prompted those of our Indians who survived rum and the Revolution to move from this locality. Most of them went to Stockbridge, Massachusetts, and from there on were known as "Stockbridge Indians," though later they moved to Wisconsin.[8] A few, however, remained as long as the middle eighteen hundreds. The late Adrian Quick told us shortly before his death in 1958 that in his father's boyhood a family of Indians still made their home on Muscoot Mountain and used to bring baskets to Cherry Street to sell.

References

1. Harrington, M. R. Rock shelters of Armonk, N.Y. In: *American Museum of Natural History, Anthropological Paper,* 1909, v. 3, pp. 125-37.
2. Shonnard, Frederic & Spooner, W. W. *History of Westchester County.* New York, 1900, pp. 30-33.
3. *Ibid.,* pp. 59-62.
4. *Ibid.,* pp. 110-11.
5. *Ibid.,* p. 84.
6. *Ibid.,* pp. 41-45.
7. *Ibid.,* p. 37.
8. *Ibid.,* p. 38.
9. Scharf, J. T. *History of Westchester County.* Philadelphia, 1886, v. 1, p. 25.
10. *Ibid.,* v. 2, p. 578.
11. *Ibid.,* v. 1, p. 13.
12. *Ibid.,* v. 1, pp. 14-15.
13. Huntington, (Rev.) E. B. *History of Stamford, Conn.* Stamford, 1868. Quoted by Robert Bolton, *History of the several towns . . . of Westchester.* New York, 1881, v. 1, p. 2.
14. Hurd, D. H. *History of Fairfield County, Connecticut.* Philadelphia, 1881, p. 692.
15. *Ibid.,* pp. 699-700.
16. *Ibid.,* p. 631.
17. *Ibid.,* p. 701.
18. Cour. Col. Rec. Hartford, v. 3, fol. 131-34. Quoted by Robert Bolton, *History of the several towns . . . of Westchester.* New York, 1881, v. 1, p. 19.
19. Bolton, Robert. *History of the several towns, manors, and pattents of the County of Westchester.* New York, 1881, v. 1, p. 3.
20. *Ibid.,* v. 1, p. 5.
21. Bedford (N.Y.) Town Book I, 1680-1704, p. 141. MS. (At Bedford Town House)
22. *Ibid.,* p. 129.
23. *Ibid.,* pp. 115, 129, 139, 141, 160, 170, 181.
24. *Ibid.,* p. 115.
25. Bolton, R. P. *New York City in Indian possession.* New York, 1920, p. 246.
26. Deed from Katonah and Wackemane to Zachariah Roberts, Sr., May 5, 1703. MS. (In possession of Mr. & Mrs. Arnold S. Askin, Katonah)
27. Bedford (N.Y.) Town Book II,

1708-41, fol. 110ᵛ-111ʳ. MS. (At Bedford Town House)

28. Will, William. Katonah. In: *Katonah Record*, Mar. 9, 1917.

29. Van Tassel, M. H. Something about Indians. In: *Katonah Record*, May 20, 1932.

30. Barrett, R. T. *The Town of Bedford*. Bedford, N.Y., 1955, p. 15.

31. Luquer, T. T. P. The Indian village of 1643. In: *Quarterly Bulletin of the Westchester County Historical Society*, April/July 1945, v. 21, no.2/3, pp. 21-24.

32. Van der Donck, Adriaen. *Description of the New Netherlands*. New York, 1841 (Collections of the New-York Historical Society, Second Series, v. 1), pp. 190-216.

33. McClure, David. Cross River, N.Y. Oral communication, quoting an Indian friend, Wally Fanton.

34. Muirson, George. Letter to the Secretary of the Venerable Propagation Society, Rye, N.Y., Jan. 9, 1707-08. In: Robert Bolton, *History of the Protestant Episcopal Church in the County of Westchester*. New York, 1855, pp. 180-81.

From Bedford Town Book I.

CHAPTER II
OUR TOWNSHIP'S FIRST YEARS

HAVING DISPOSED of our Bedford Indians by turning them into Stockbridge Indians, let us go back to our white men. Although the original proprietors of our Township came from Stamford, they were soon joined by men from other localities. From 1639 on, much land changed from red hands to white throughout Connecticut and on both sides of the Sound. These settlements are of interest to us because from each, indirectly, some family came to us in the 1700's.

Men from the New Haven Colony had begun settlements at Stratford and Fairfield in 1639. In 1640, land was purchased at Greenwich and Norwalk.[1] In 1644, a group from Stamford under the leadership of the Rev. Richard Denton made a settlement across the Sound at Hempstead,[3] from which some went on to Jamaica. There were already settlements at Southhold, Southampton, and Easthampton from Connecticut and Massachusetts;[2] and in the 1650's, families from Rhode Island began to settle in and around Oyster Bay.[4]

It is our habit to think of all of the early landowners of Bedford Township as English, and of landowners across the Croton River as Dutch. Actually, this was not so. Jacobus Van Cortlandt who became the largest landowner in the Township of Bedford was just as Dutch as his brother Stephanus whose manor lay north of the Croton.[5] Descended from Jacobus was John Jay, considered by the world at large as Katonah's foremost citizen. Between 1680 and the first ownership by Jacobus, however, Bedford was entirely owned by Englishmen of the New England variety and character, who had their center at Bedford Village.

Joseph Barrett covered these initial years delightfully in a speech he made at the old village of Katonah July 4, 1876. On

14

These boulders in Katonah's Wood, Cantitoe, are said to mark the graves of Chief Katonah and his squaw.

(1)

At a Town meeting held in Bedford October 4th 1701
The Town by major vote Doth Order the Comitte to proceed
wth ye Indians about purchasing ye Lands to estward
of the old purchase & now mark the old purchase formerly bought
of the Indians. —

At a Town meeting November 3. 1701 in Bedford aforesd
The Town by major vote doth Agree that ye Land westward of
the first purchase shall be paid by heads and every head that
payeth ye Indians for it shall have every one of them an
Equal share according to what they pay —

The Town by major vote doth Chuse Zachariah Roberts
Senr John Holmes Junr & Jonathan Pollot for their Comitte
and Giveth them full power to take Care in ye Towns behalf
to see the Indians satisfied for ye Land they formerly
bought of the Indians which is west of our first purchase
and every man that hath Land in the Town hath Liberty
to put in a head and they are to pay Twenty Shillings
to ye purchase and to defray Charges. — — —

At a Town meeting in Bedford September 28th 1702
The Town by major vote Agrees that in the first place
there shall be Convenient high ways laid out in ye last
purchase and then fifty Acres laid out to a Lot to the
Number of Thirty Six Lots, and the Comitte appointed to
lay out the high ways & the Lots and if the Land will hold
out then Sixty Acres to a Lot, The Comitte Chosen by
the Town to lay out the above sd high ways & Lots are
Zachariah Roberts, John Copp, Stephen Clason, Nathan
Clark, John Miller Junr Jonathan Miller, John Wascot &
Richard Wascot these or any three of them have power
to lay out and what Lots want in Quallity to make them
up in Quantity

The Town by major vote Agrees that the Comitte shall
have five Shillings a Lot for Laying out Lots & ye high way

The above are true Copys Transcribed out of ye
book of Records of Town Acts in Bedford:

16   First page of John Copp's records of New or West Purchase 1701-40.

Courtesy of New York State Library

Census of Westchester, 1712, shows Town of Bedford as having 172 inhabitants. (N. Y. Colonial MSS. v. 57, p. 179 b)

Stanford

Know these presents that wee whose names are hereunder written: namely: Lahtorah:
Rockahoe: Sepotah: Joris: Tohmacoyoh: yanaoyt: Lahoxond: wee doe for our selves
our officers executors administrators and assignes: and for and in behalfe of all
others proprietors off of land comonly called of Hogg ground: wee set our hands doe
alienate assigne and set over from us our heires executors administrators and
assignes all certaine parsell of rylands and meadow: comonly called and knowen
by name of the Hoggpound which land lyeth at of northend of Stanford bounds
as it is already bounded with markt trees: onely the most westerly lyne to be
extended southward untill it still meet with of southmost lyne drawen
from three markt notable stones they prove neere together of southeast
corner of of Island: wee of above named doe for us our heires administrators and
from us and ours of land above signifyed with all of rights and privileges thereunto belonging

for us our heires
Richard Ambler Abraam Ambler Joseph Ashad: Daniell Neck
Isazar seazon John Bostol: Jonathan postil Johon Cross Johon Mitchlo: Miccolo Webster: Richard
Jacob William Clarke Jacob Seel: Jacob Strusis Daniell Joris Thomas Hanover
for Hom for Boniamien Storions: from theire heires executors administrators and assignes: for our

quitt shall equally to possess and injoy without molestation or disturbance by us or ours or by any of our meanes
Land subway or procurement: moreover wee the above named Lahtorah: Rockahoe: Sepotah Joris
now three Tohmacoyoh yanaoyt Lahoxond our bargaine and sale grant full and free libertie
Jorah killow of Laindes and privileges forevermore: upon our present bargaine and sale wee doe
our heires our heires acknowledge to have received full satisfaction for of land above said
  will of such our heires cause said the bill of sale to be made and fully set our

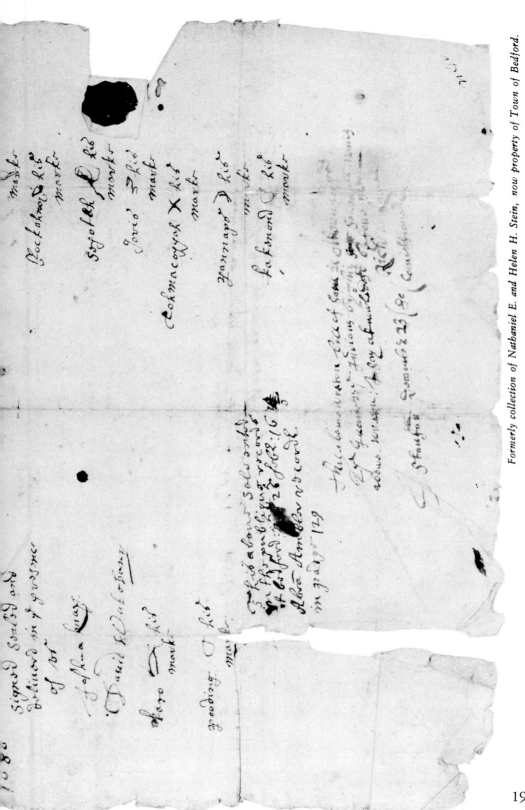

Formerly collection of Nathaniel E. and Helen H. Stein, now property of Town of Bedford. First Indian deed for Bedford land, the Hopp Ground, 1680.

19

Tax List of Cherry Street area taken from 1779 list of Westchester County, Bedford Township. Headings rearranged as necessary to understanding of content.

Coppy of a Tax List of the County of Westchester made on the Seveveral Freeholders and Inhabitants Living in the Deftricts herein mentioned in the Said County purfuant to an act of the Legiflature of the State of New York. pafsed the 2d Day of March 1779

Coppy of a Tax lift for the Town of Bedford taken 31 march 1779

Isaac Bafset	412	20	12	810	20	5
Ezakiel Griffin				533	13	6
Adam Griffin	800	40		482	12	1
John Borent 3rd	640	32		446	11	3
Caleb Akerly	480	24		398	9	9
James Morshall	300	15		492	12	6
Ezekiel Griffin	400	20		820	20	10
John Williamfon				300	7	14
	181	**12**		**106**	**14**	

	Real	£	s	Pers	£	s
		181	12		106	14
Enoch Honywell	675	33	15	844	21	2
John Myers	140	7				
William Brown	404	20	4	344	8	14
Samuel Brown	400	20		188	4	14
Michael Basset	560	28		306	7	16
Samuel Buckbee	100	5		500	12	10
Elijah Miller	540	27		774	19	7
Michael Basset Jr	425	21	5	438	11	2
Nehemiah Merrit	450	22	10	310	7	15
Aman Fowler	480	24		328	8	4
Elijah Buckbee	759	37	19	752	18	16
Zephaniah Miller	304	15	4	146	3	13
Samuel Palmer	885	43	15	784	19	12
Gershom Griffin	448	22	4	684	17	2
Abraham Berrit	210	10	10			
Bethuel Berrit				450	11	5
William Williamson	168	8	8	35		
Timothy Miller	232	11	12	336	8	8
Silas Miller	480	24		774	19	7
James Clerk	195	9	15	32½	8	2
Moses St John	315	15	15	700	17	10
Gabriel Smith	600	30		722	18	1
Ezekiel Harris	590	29	10	628	15	14
Lemuel Light	256	12	16	316	7	18
Gibbeat Write	700	35		58	14	12
Justus Lyon	300	15		564	14	12
Timothy Ketchum	500	25		552	13	16
		695	14		413	19

21

The Henry Robertson home at Cantitoe. On site purchased by William Robertson in 1744, possibly some part of this house was of that date. In picture are Elizabeth N. and Robertson T. Barrett, grandchildren of Henry Robertson. House burned around 1915.

The Buckbee House, Cherry Street. The older part was built around 1750 by Elijah Buckbee. Now owned by Douglas L. Barrett. House stands on Harris Road west of tracks, once part of Cherry Street

22

Courtesy of Mrs. William A. Kelly

Built by John Silkman in 1751, this house stands on Route 35 at Holly Branch Road. Now owned by Mr. and Mrs. Alfred Wells.

Courtesy of Mrs. Theodore Taylor

Home of David and Elizabeth (Wetmore) Haight soon after the Revolution. The site, then Cherry Street, is at intersection of present Bedford and Harris Roads. Property now owned by Mrs. Reginald Vockins.

23

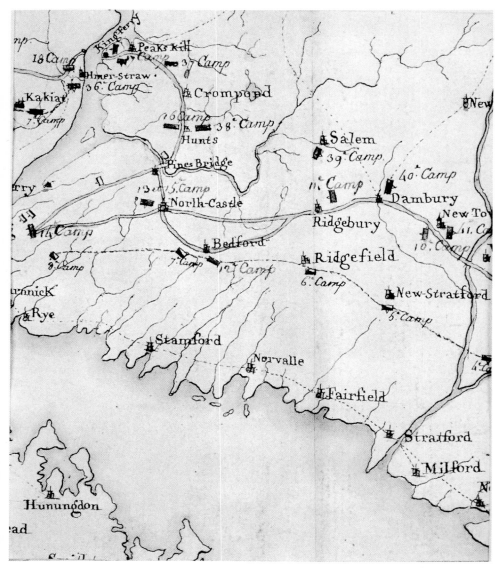

FRENCH CAMPS, BEDFORD AND NORTH CASTLE AREAS, 1781-82

Camps 10-18 and 36-41 show the Bedford area portions of the French army
routes between New England and Yorktown, Va. The dotted line of 4-8
indicates the Lauzun Legion's march protecting the main body.
Section of map from the Rochambeau papers.

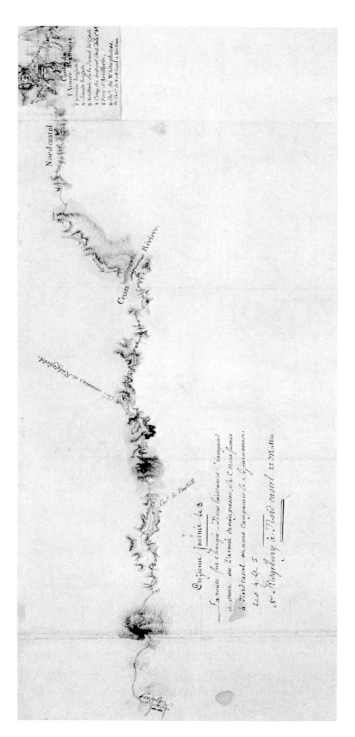

Courtesy of Princeton University Library

ROUTE OF THE FRENCH ARMY THROUGH BEDFORD, 1781

The French army under Rochambeau marched from Rhode Island to join forces with Washington on this side of the Hudson, and later proceeded to Yorktown, Va., where the combined armies defeated Cornwallis. During these marches Alexander Berthier prepared maps of the routes. This map traces the march of 22 miles from Ridgebury, Conn., to North Castle Camp (now Mt. Kisco), N. Y., on July 3, 1781.

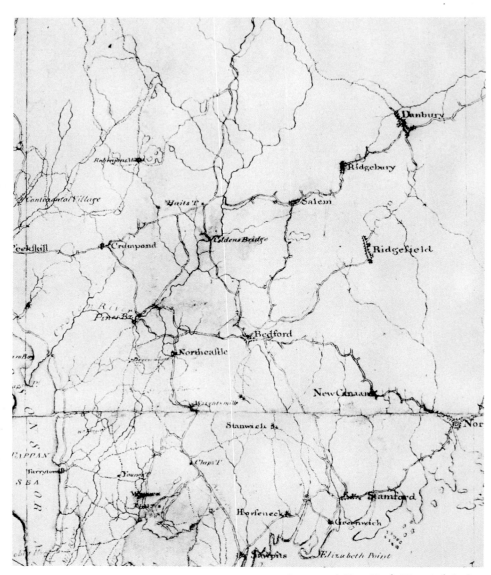

AMERICAN MILITARY ROUTES, BEDFORD AREA, 1779

Robert Erskine, a geographer and surveyor general, 1777-1780, to the American army in the Revolution, was responsible for many maps in the Erskine-Dewitt series. This portion of his map No. 102 shows military routes in the Bedford area between Connecticut and Peekskill on the Hudson.

26

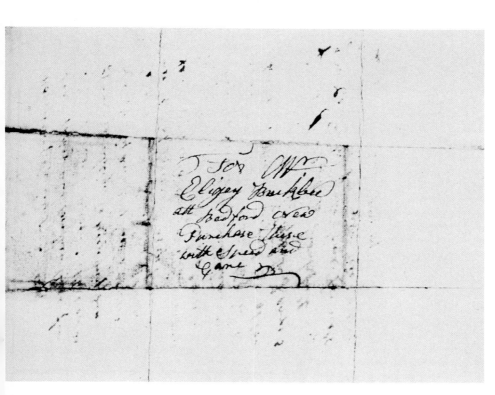

Courtesy of Mrs. Henry F. Haight

Letter from Elizabeth Harris to her father, Elijah Buckbee, written April 2, 1783.

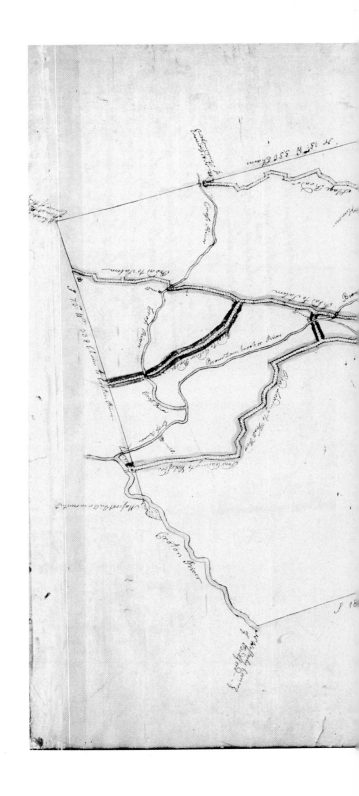

28

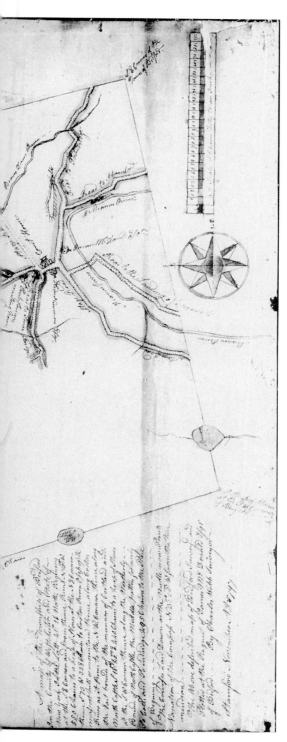

Courtesy, Office of the New York State Engineer

BEDFORD VILLAGE AREA, ROADS EAST AND NORTH

Of particular interest is the "Road to Veals Ford," now Harris Road and Cherry Street. Map drawn by Charles Webb at request of James McDonald of Bedford, November, 1797.

29

Courtesy of Bedford Historical Society

This schoolhouse on Mt. Holly may have existed in 1792
prior to the founding of our public schools

Courtesy of R. Benson Ray

Hoyt's Mills in the Mt. Holly area were on the north side of the Cross
River and below the bridge at the junction of the Cantitoe to
North Salem and the Katonah to Cross River Roads

that hundredth anniversary of our nation's Declaration of Independence, the President had asked that each town should include in its celebration an historical sketch of the town from its foundation. Joseph Barrett was petitioned to be our spokesman, and for his material he drew freely and faithfully from our first Township records. We feel that he, not we, should tell of these early years:

The twenty-two "propriators of ye hopp-ground" whose names are given in the first Indian deed of 1680, began their settlement by holding a meeting at Stamford (whence they came) on the tenth of March, 1681, to "chuse and appoint and fully impower Jos. Theale, Abra. Ambler, John Miller, Daniel Jones, and John Cross to lay out the house lots" and also "one lotment to every proprietor in the field on the east side of the plaine," "and it shall be in the discresion of these men to make each mans lot proportionable in quantity what it wants in quality," but "noe mans house lot shall be less than three acres."

So on March 17 the committee made the division by drawing lots, and on the 23rd of March the "propriators agree that wt the committee had done shall stand"—"and the meeting house shall be set upon the comman so layd out, namly, the rock called Bates his hill." At this same meeting John Bates and Nathaniel Cross were received as "propriators" they paying their share of the charges, and new men are from time to time taken in on the same basis.

The first official notice or recognition of the settlement, that I know of, is the grant from the general court of Connecticut Colony, at Hartford, a copy of which has been preserved among the old papers of John Holmes, one of the original pioneers. I think it has not been published hitherto. It is as follows:

At a generall court held at Harford May 12th, 1681. This court being moved to grant liberty to erect a plantation upon the hoppground & aiacent lands about Twelve miles to ye northwards of Stanford doe grant their request & appoynt Captain Richard Olmsteed Lieut. Jonath Bell Lieut. Jonathan Lockwood and Mr Joseph Theal to be a committee to entertain shuch parsons as shall plant there & to manage, order & dispose of ye affays of that planta-

tion according to their best skill so as may best aduance ye
wellfar and groth of ye said plantation & they ear to tacke
care yt there be a sutable loot laid out for the first minister of ye place & a loot for ye ministry to be and belong
to ye ministry forever. This is a trew coppy tacken out of
the Records of Harford.

Vera Copia

Hartfrd   Test, Eleazar Kimberly
Janry 21st 1696   Secretry

At this time it was supposed that Bedford lay within the
bounds of Connecticut, by the colonial lines of 1664. Soon
after the settlement was effected the matter was again opened,
and after a long discussion between Governors of both Colonies the difficulty was settled in 1700, by the General Court
of Connecticut releasing Bedford from all allegiance and a
copy of this release is in the town records.

The first meetings of the proprietors were numerous and
the records are carefully entered in paragraphs like sermons,
from "1stly" as far as the case required. The minutes of a
meeting on Oct. 11, 1681, extend to "14ly" and are chiefly
rules about laying out of lands and cartways. The settlers
seem to have feared the accumulation of large tracts of land
in the hands of single individuals. Hence each man had a
home lot of three acres which was to be forfeited if not built
on in three years, "in the town," where Bedford village now
is, and a lot in the "east field" or the "great northe plaine,"
and also some meadow land. From this time forward the
town records contain a wealth of quaint and curious history. . . . These people were Dissenters who came to the new
world to escape religious persecution and to worship God in
their own way. So one of their first acts was to provide as we
have seen, for a meeting house, and in December, 1681, they
called "mr. Priddon of Gemeco" (Jamaica, L.I.) to be their
minister, and when the sacred office was vacant, as occurred
from time to time, we find them appointing some of their
own number to "carry on the Lord's day." This was the
origin of the First Presbyterian Church of Bedford. In 1693
a few adherents of the Church of England came in, and in the
next dozen years a church was organized, of which St. Mat-
thews of Bedford is the outgrowth.

In December, 1681, Samuel Barrett, Zachariah Roberts and Thomas Canfield were received as inhabitants. This Roberts was soon chosen town clerk, afterward Justice of the Peace and for many years appears prominent in nearly all the affairs of the town. He seems to have been a very dissenting Dissenter. He had a quarrel with the Rev. Thomas Pritchard, the first church of England Rector, in 1705. . . .

In "december 1681 Joshua Webb is reseived an Inhabitant, in case they shall agree with him to build a Grist mill in ye place." A committee was appointed to confer with Joshua, and a mill and dam were built by him and the town jointly, he to furnish the iron work and the town to cart and furnish the timber and millstones . . . "and the said Joshua doth binde himself: and his: to finde the towne at hop-ground with good meale they finding good corne: the tole as in the law is expressed."

This mill stood on Mianus river about a quarter of a mile above where James Miller's mill now stands. In 1701 the town "doth agree to buy" the mill of Richard Webb, son of Joshua, for the use of the town, for the sum of 15 pounds. Another mill seems to have become necessary at this time, for in November, 1701, "the town by a maigor uote doth agree that their corn mill shall be set upon beuer dam Riuer at the first conueniant place below davids broock: and that there shall be thirty acres of land layed out to the mill and to lye to it for euer that the lawfull oners of the mill shall enioy the said thirty acres of land for euer, not else." And very stringent "artickells of agreement" were entered into with John Dibell to build the mill, he as in the former case to "finde ye town with good sofisiant meall, they finding good and sofisiant corne" and he to have both mill and "thirty acres of land" forever. This was on the site where Cox's mill now stands [now Matthew's Mill]. . . .

The following will serve as a sample of the vote by which new settlers were received into the colony. The date is "december 1681. They give unto william Sturdeuant upon his acceptance and submitting to their order of reseuing Inhabitants: they give him a house lott containing three Accres, and six Accres of land in the east feild: and three accres of meadow: he paying twenty shillings to ye company and to take twenty rod of fence in ye coman field for euer."

There was for many years after this date a great extent of common or town land, where the people pastured their cattle. It is probable that they also pastured lands not yet bought of the Indians. A brander for the town was therefore appointed and the cattle were marked with the owner's mark and such entries as the following begin to appear on the town records. "Zackariah Roberts maketh entry of his ere marck for his marckeble creatures, namly a swalow forck on ye toop of each ere." "John Miller senr macks entry of his ere marck for his marckable creatures namly one half penny on the under sid of the offe ere & a slit on the toop of the neer ere." These marks are found on record as late as 1813.

In "ienwary 1687-8" there were 18 men at a town meeting who voted "that every one here presant at the town meeting shall have a pees of land containing four akers aded unto theyr former diuidens for theyr faithfulness at the attending of towne meetings." These men of two hundred years ago were not so far behind the age, after all.

In 1690 the town voted a bounty on wolves. The annual meeting in March shows a "clark, two sezars" (assessors), two fence "vewars" and two "souairs" (surveyors). In 1691 they made "chois of Daniell Simkings for head man for ye town of Bedford to end any contrauercy between indians and inglish acording to the best of his skill."

In 1697 they sent the inevitable Zach. Roberts to confer with Governor Treat of Connecticut about being settled under the colony, and paid him 3 shillings a day "for himself and his hors, and paid halfe his expence." After his return Roberts had another town meeting and got an allowance for back-pay in the shape of an assessment of two pounds of flax on each man in the town.

There is abundant legislation about the minister and his "yearley reate" and who shall "geather it for him."

In 1699 the town votes to exchange with Stephen Clason 4 acres of swamp and give him 4 acres of upland if he will "beat the Drum untill this day twelve month," the town to keep the drum in repair. It was in this way the people were called together at church or town meeting or in any emergency.

In November 1699 the town received a great acquisition in Mr. John Copp, of Norwalk, a surveyor and quite a scholarly man for that time. He was at once given a "home loot, twenty acres of out land, sixteen of plow land and four acres of medow land." He was also to have "the use of ye towne loot and ye towne land and medow in ye feild this next yeare, without they want of it for a minestar." The next month "the town by a maigor uot chuse Mr. John Copp to put things to uote in theyr town meetings if he is presant."

They also bought of "ye said Copp" a "grindle stone" for which they paid the modest price of "six acres of pastur land." For a while he quite eclipsed Zachariah Roberts. The next week. they elected him town Treasurer, and put him on a "committy" to agree with the Indians for the land westward of the town. This committee arranged with the Indians for the "west purchase" included in the deed of Sept. 6, 1700, and it may have been incident to the negotiations that we find this entry on "Aprell 15, 1700. The town by a maigor vote doth agree yt if they fortify, it shall be John Holmes senrs hous, and ye house yt was Joshua Webb's desesed." It does not appear that it became necessary to fortify.

The west purchase was made and "every man yt hath land in ye town hath liberty to put in a head," or share. There were 36 of these head rights, of which Col. Jacobus Van Cortlandt had 8, Zach. Roberts, 3, John Copp, 2, John Holmes, Jr., 2, and the rest one. The land was then surveyed by Copp and laid out into 36 lots of 50 acres each (for the small field plan seems to have become exploded) which were subsequently drawn for by lot. One of the town books consists of the records of this "west purchase" or "new purchase," and is in the neat hand-writing of Copp—Proprietors Clerk. . . . The division of the "west purchase" was not fully concluded until 1738. In 1700, after the decision which left the town within the province of New York, the people began to again agitate the matter of getting their patent confirmed and sent John Thomson and Zach. Roberts to New York, which was then the capital, on that mission, but nothing came of it until May 14, 1702, when they empowered "Mr. Capt. Peter Mathews to git our patent and privileges confermed to us the town of Bedford as soon chep and easy as may be," and they promised Mathews a "gratetude of land" for his services. So the next year they gave him 300 "akers on the south sid of the road that goeth from bedford to hutsons Riur and so by

the place whair Wampas wigwam was." Upon this the enterprising Roberts got the town to vote him a large tract near the
west boundary, "on condision that he goeth to New York and
ioynes with, and is helpful to Captain Peter Mathews." It
appeared that Zack. helped "git" the patent and got his land,
and in "Ogust" of that year Mathews asked for and obtained
700 acres more, and in 1707, 200 more, making 1200 acres in
the south west corner of the patent, that is, in the vicinity
of Mt. Kisco. The patent was granted to the township of
Bedford in Westchester County dated 3d April, 1704, at £5
per annum. This sum was the Quit Rent paid to the Crown,
and mention of its being levied and collected is occasionally
found in the minutes of the town meetings. It was thus paid
until 1767. In 1703 the town granted John Thomson, formerly
a London merchant but lately of Stamford, a tract of land on
condition that he should pay forty shilling "and to bring
up four hundred sheep and lambs next summer and let them
to ye inhabitance of ye town for two bits in money, or one
pound and halfe of flees wool as the sheep afords it yearly."
Whether this was the first importation of sheep into the colony
I do not know, but probably it was not.[6]

Mr. Barrett's speech goes on to cover later days but these selec-
tions give the character of our Township's first proprietors, their
New England town meeting form of local government and their
general way of life.

References

1. Hurd, D. H. *History of Fairfield County, Connecticut*. Philadelphia, 1881, p. 65; 279.
2. *Ibid.*, p. 366; 482.
3. Mills, S. H. *Samuel Mill's ancestry*. [Denver, Colo., 1958], p. 2.
4. Carpenter, D. H. *History and genealogy of the Carpenter family in America*. Jamaica, N.Y., 1901, p. 32.
5. Bolton, Robert. *History of the several towns . . . of Westchester*. New York, 1881, v. 1, p. 36.
6. Barrett, Joseph. Historical sketch of the Town of Bedford, delivered at the Fourth of July celebration at Katonah, 1876. In: *Recorder*, Katonah, N.Y., July 7, 1876.

From Bedford Town Book I.

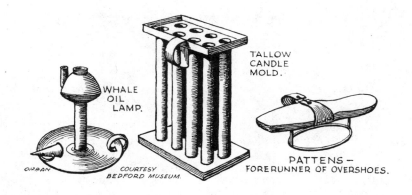

WHALE OIL LAMP.

TALLOW CANDLE MOLD.

PATTENS — FORERUNNER OF OVERSHOES.

COURTESY BEDFORD MUSEUM.

CHAPTER III

EARLY FAMILIES AND WHERE THEY LIVED

ALTHOUGH full coverage has been given by other historians to the early days of the southern part of our township, very little has been written about the northern part in which lie the areas of our especial interest. These areas were much later in their community development but all had passed from Indian ownership by 1722. The answer to the slower development of our northern section appears to lie in one man, Colonel Jacobus Van Cortlandt. Unlike other Bedford real estate investors of the time such as Zachariah Roberts, John Dibell, and Joseph Seely, he bought to hold, not to sell,[1] except in rare instances.

Jacobus, born 1658, was the son of Oloff Stevense Van Cortlandt who emigrated from Holland in 1638[2] and became an important figure politically during the Dutch government of New York City. Oloff's eldest son, Stephanus, born in 1643, began land-collecting along the Hudson about the time the men from Stamford came to Bedford. By 1697 all of the present townships of Cortlandt, North Salem, Somers, and Yorktown, as well as a large part of Lewisboro, were his by Royal Charter.[4]

Jacobus, the younger brother of Stephanus, set about acquiring acreage in a less spectacular way. Bedford to the south of the Croton River and of his brother's vast holdings attracted him and he already had contacts there. On October 4, 1702, the Town of Bedford, having no wish to be joined with Mamaroneck and Rye as an Episcopal parish, had voted they desired "mr. Jacobus Van Cortlandt to present theyr desire e pertision to the generall assembly e ye town is willing to satisfie sd Cortland for his trouble." [5] Van Cortlandt had been a member of the Assembly frequently since 1693 and had just been elected to the new Assembly that year[31] and was therefore in a good position to help the Bedford townsfolk, had such been possible.

Jacobus's first acquisition of Bedford land was in March, 1703, when he bought from John Dibell a tract known as Cross's Vineyard which the Town had purchased from the Indians in 1700 and sold to Dibell two years later.[8] On this tract stands "Bedford House," the retirement home of Van Cortlandt's grandson, John Jay.

The next real estate venture, in July of 1703 and in conjunction with Zachariah Roberts, was the only one in which Van Cortlandt had direct dealings with the Indians. By deed from "Catonah Sagemor and Wockemone cheef proprietors of the lands about Bedford" the two white partners became owners of the Northwest Corner.[9] Previously, on May 5th, Roberts had reserved this same tract to himself in a document which stated he had paid "10 peeses of eight, . . . 6 shirts, 4 Dazell cots, 2 blanckets, 1 brodcloth cot, 4 hatchets, 4 pound powder and 2 galons of rum." [17] This then, was the original price for the 2800 acres, more or less, of land which includes much of our present village of Katonah.

Roberts was out for a quick turnover. In 1705 he sold about 300 acres of his share and a few in the New Purchase for one hundred pounds sterling.[18] The buyer was none other than the same Mr. Thomas Pritchard with whom he had dissented so violently only a few months before that he had persuaded the Town to pass an act "enjoining upon the people not to pay Mr. Prichard anything"! [24]

Unlike Roberts, Van Cortlandt retained all of his Northwest Corner acreage and he began acquiring more land from John Dibell as well as head rights. Included in the land was all that tract, except for 420 acres, which Dibell had bought from the Indians in 1703, lying to the east of Cross's Vineyard[19] and known as the Dibell Purchase. Thus, eventually, Van Cortlandt came to own almost the entire south shore of the Cross River.

In 1708, when thirty-six 50-acre lots were laid out in the "New or West Purchase" of 1702, Jacobus Van Cortlandt secured eight of them on rights he had acquired from John Dibell.[10] To these holdings more was later added[25] and in 1717 he bought around 300 acres from Zachariah Roberts, Jr., and his wife Elizabeth.[20]

Van Cortlandt was not through yet. The Northeast Corner

sold to Joseph Seely in 1722 by Wackemane had been quitclaimed
by Seely to the proprietors of Bedford, and in 1736, with the
assistance of surveyor Samuel Purdy, this land north of the Cross
River was divided into "29 lots, accordingly the number of ye
Pattentees." [11] In this division Jacobus acquired a 105-acre piece
and a 55-acre piece.[25] For some reason Van Cortlandt's Dibell
Purchase land south of the Cross River was also apportioned to
the patentees this same year as "undivided land." However, in
1738, each and every patentee released his share back to Van
Cortlandt!

To finish with our real estate collector, he kept almost all of
his Bedford land until 1738. Then he turned it over undivided
to his three daughters and their husbands and to his son.[19] The
map drawn by the surveyor Purdy for the purpose of dividing
the property among them totals the acreage divided at 4,393 acres
and shows it as including Cantitoe, about half of the Cross
River Reservoir basin, much of our present village area and a
good bit of Mt. Holly, as well as land in other parts of Bedford.
This then is one very good reason why history is comparatively
silent about the Katonah-Cantitoe-Mt. Holly vicinity until Van
Cortlandt heirs began to sell their inheritances or use them.

There were tenants living on Van Cortlandt farms, but so far
as we know Jacobus was never a resident of Bedford and his
grandson, John Jay, was the first of his descendants to make a
home in our area. Under the provisions of his father's will, John
had first choice of Peter Jay's property when it was divided in
1784.[21] He elected to take 287 acres at Cantitoe, to which was
added 171½ adjoining acres on the death of his aunt, Ann Chambers. It wasn't until 1801, however, after his retirement from
public life, that John Jay came to live in Bedford on this Cantitoe
property.

While Jacobus Van Cortlandt was busy accumulating property,
the smaller landowners of the township were also busy collecting and trading acreage. The system of granting rights in new
purchases to existing landowners was rather similar to the issuing
of rights to stockholders of present-day corporations, and without
the aid of IBM machines it seems to have defeated the town
clerks at times. Especially when Queen Anne's dues of quitrent
needed collecting did the Town become worried by the fact that
it didn't know just who owned just what. In the minutes of the
Town Book for April 18, 1708, there is entry of an act passed
requiring all the inhabitants and proprietors to bring in an

account of all the lands in their possession and their rights of commonage. "Commonage," a term often employed in the early minutes, meant the undivided land held by the Town as a whole and used for pasturage of those "marckable creatures" belonging to the inhabitants whose brands are found registered in the records.

It must have been difficult for the landowners themselves to keep track of the scattered bits of real estate they had collected here and there. To us it is utterly confusing. Just as soon as a document seems to place a man in one area, he turns up in another! Eventually though, most families began to consolidate their holdings into single tracts. The desirable land of course was near water or "highways."

The land north of Cross River was divided by lot in 1736, but it is not probable that many homes were built there in the first half of the eighteenth century. We only know that at some period prior to 1748 the 55-acre lot on the northeast of the present North Salem and Cross River highways was occupied by Samuel Lyon as tenant,[23] and that further east toward the Lewisboro line there were three houses indicated by deed or family record. These were the homes of John Rundle, John Silkman and Daniel Hait.[13] Rundle's house was just this side of the Lewisboro line, Silkman's still stands at the foot of Holly Branch Road on Route 35, and Hait's was to the southwest of Silkman's.

For our earliest inhabitants in the vicinity of our present village we turn to the land along Cherry Street, which was described as the "Indian Path which leads to Moschatach" in a deed of 1705 and as the "Muscotow Path" on a map drawn by Samuel Purdy in 1748. Both Zachariah Roberts and the Pritchards owned property along this path in 1705. We don't know if the Pritchards ever lived there themselves as he died in 1705,[7] but when the widow sold the property in 1750, it was well developed, containing houses, outhouses, barns, gardens and pastures.[22]

Our other probable residents prior to 1750 were in the "Zachariah Roberts house" marked on the Purdy map as being on the east side of the path and about opposite the junction of our present Croton Lake Road and Cherry Street. Zachariah, Sr., died in or before 1708.[8] Zachariah, Jr., lived for the most part in Stamford. Perhaps neither of them ever occupied it but a house indicates occupants of some sort.

The first permanent landowner residents of which we have record in the area were the Buckbees and the Fowlers. In 1750,

Elijah Buckbee bought, along what we now call Harris Road, land "laid out to John Holmes in the last Division," and another lot "laid out to John Holmes and Joseph Seely deceased, in partnership." For this land, part of which is now owned by Douglas L. Barrett, he paid £738.[14]

Ammon Fowler bought further north on Cherry Street in 1762. Part of this was land bought by the Pritchards from Zachariah Roberts.[22] The present home of Clifford Morehouse on Lily Pond Lane is a Fowler house of very early date if not that of the first Ammon. Until after the Revolution, however, it is not certain that Ammon was a full-time resident, as records would indicate that for a part of the time at least he remained in North Castle.[26]

Families that established themselves early in our northern section of the Township, other than the ones mentioned, were in the Cantitoe section. In 1736 Jonathan Miller gave his grandson Jonathan "for love and affection" a piece of land at a place called Cantitoe[15] and in 1744 Daniel Merritt sold property to William Robertson,[16] thereby bringing into our community as residents, two men through whom several prominent Katonah families are descended. Both of these farms were just south of Van Cortlandt's holdings.

Unlike the first settlement at Bedford which was made at one time by families migrating together from Stamford, our northern part of the Township drew its earliest men from various places. They came in from Greenwich, Rye, Eastchester and North Castle for the main part. One migrant was John Silkman who came by way of Greenwich from the Palatinate in the exodus caused by religious persecution of German Protestants.

Now that we have brought a few families into our district, it would be nice to know how they got along. What we know of their personal lives is written in our genealogies. As to the conditions that contributed to their comforts and hardships, we don't know too much.

Taking hardship first: in the Hoyt family book[27] there is a picture of life as the Haits found it about 1740:

> the descendants of Daniel suppose him to have been one of the first settlers in the north part of Bedford, when the forest was unbroken. Some stories are still extant of the hardships himself and family endured: the depredations of the bears, taking their only pig, living entirely on game.

In the middle seventeen hundreds there were not many conveniences around Cantitoe, Cherry Street and Mt. Holly. There
were no churches, public schools, doctors, inns, newspapers, general stores or post offices. There were very few white neighbors
and of the social relations between whites and Indians we have
no records. A census taken in 1712[28] (given on p. 17) shows
the entire population of the Township as only 172 souls. Of
course this increased yearly but we may be certain that most of
the population was located around Bedford Village.

Real estate in our areas varied in price, apparently at the
whim or shrewdness of seller and buyer. Prices ranged from
a pound to five pounds an acre, and whether land was developed
with houses, barns and orchards or uncleared didn't seem to
affect the price.

There were at least two roads connecting us with Bedford
and, by the middle of the century, "highways" connecting us
with Salem and North Castle. In eighteenth century times North
Castle included that part of Mt. Kisco which now lies in New
Castle.

Church of England people and Presbyterians could find places
to worship if the will was strong enough, and for schooling there
was that "silly Quaker-woman" in North Castle and the "enthusiastic Methodist" at Bedford, mentioned in a 1744 letter
written to the secretary of the parish of Rye by three Bedford
men,[6] Lewis McDonald, Daniel Smith and Arthur Smith. In
reply to this letter an Episcopal preacher-teacher also was supplied to them. Long before this, in the very early seventeen
hundreds, Bedford had enjoyed a school master four months
during the year, sent out by the Society for the Propagation of
the Gospel. This man apparently instructed Indians and Negro
slaves as well as whites.[29] There was a school in Cherry Street
as early as 1750.[32]

According to all Township historians our population was
made up almost entirely of farmers, but by 1763 a scattering of
artisans had come into the Township, riding from farm to farm
practicing their trades. In the list of freeholders eligible for jury
duty published that year, there were eighteen artisans mentioned
and we have no way of knowing how many others there were who
were not included because they did not meet the land and financial requirements.[30] Their listed professions are an indication of
what sort of help was welcome in a very self-dependent era and
society. There were four weavers, three blacksmiths, two masons,

two joiners, one cooper, one taylor, one millwright, one merchant and three cordwainers. A cordwainer, in case anyone meets it in a crossword puzzle, is one who works with leather.

Two wars occurred before the Revolution in which Bedford men fought for England. John Silkman was one who served in the first conflict known as "King George's War," 1744-48. James Holmes of the Hook Road area distinguished himself in the French and Indian War, 1755-63.

The minutes of the Bedford town meetings are missing between the years 1722 and 1784, so we have no way of knowing what part our local men took in civic affairs and to what offices they were elected. So little is written about this period that we are tempted to reconstruct from the only town documents that remain to us, the land records. One gives in its boundary description, "Sd land to begin at a rock near the corner of a field where Jonas sowed wheat." [12] With a little imagination we could enlarge on that one both from the angle of agriculture and surveying.

We are not going to do it. We will leave Jonas and his wheat and a great big hole in time that we can't fill in and go on to the time of the Revolution.

References

1. Scharf, J. T. *History of Westchester County.* Philadelphia, 1886, v. 1, p. 762.
2. *Ibid.,* v. 1, p. 128.
3. *Ibid.,* v. 2, p. 589.
4. Bolton, Robert. *The history of the several towns . . . of Westchester.* New York, 1881, v. 1, pp. 94-95.
5. *Ibid.,* v. 1, p. 59.
6. *Ibid.,* v. 1, p. 64.
7. Bolton, Robert. *History of the Protestant Episcopal Church in the County of Westchester.* New York, 1855, p. 146.
8. Bedford (N.Y.) Town Book I, 1680-1704, p. 152 & 167. MS. (At Bedford Town House)
9. *Ibid.,* p. 170.
10. Bedford (N.Y.) Town Book II, 1708-41, fol. 1. MS. (At Bedford Town House)
11. *Ibid.,* p. 137.
12. *Ibid.,* p. 133.
13. Bedford (N.Y.) Town Book III, 1727-1882, p. 133. MS. (At Bedford Town House)
14. *Ibid.,* p. 124.
15. *Ibid.,* p. 78.
16. *Ibid.,* p. 104.
17. [Indian deed transferring land in the Northwest Corner of Bedford to Zachariah Roberts, Sr.] May 5, 1703. MS. (In possession of Mr. and Mrs. Arnold S. Askin, Cross River Rd., Katonah)
18. Westchester County. Division of

Land Records. Deeds, Liber G, p. 491. MS. (At County Office Building, White Plains, N.Y.)

19. *Ibid.*, Liber G, p. 294.
20. *Ibid.*, Liber G, p. 540.
21. *Ibid.*, Liber I, p. 283.
22. *Ibid.*, Liber I, p. 337.
23. *Ibid.*, Liber K, p. 87.
24. Barrett, R. T. *The Town of Bedford*. Bedford, N.Y., 1955, p. 37.
25. Purdy, Samuel. [Map of the Van Cortlandt properties. Bedford, N.Y.] 1748. MS. (At N.Y. State Library, Albany. Photostat at Katonah Village Library)
26. North Castle (N.Y.) Minute book of the Town, 1736-1848, p. 35. MS. (At North Castle Town House)
27. Hoyt, D. W. *A genealogical history of the Hoyt, Haight, and Hight families*. Providence, 1871, p. 342.

28. List of the inhabitants and slaves in the County of Westchester, 1712. In: *New York colonial manuscripts*. Albany, bound 1919, v. 57, p. 179b. MS. (At N. Y. State Library, Albany)
29. Fox, D. R. *Caleb Heathcote, gentleman colonist*. New York, 1926, pp. 230-32.
30. Becker, E. M. The 801 Westchester County freeholders of 1763. In: *N.Y. Historical Society Quarterly*, 1951, v. 35, pp. 283-321.
31. Lamb, M. J. *History of the City of New York*. New York, 1877-80, v. 1, pp. 409, 416, 435, 465, 489.
32. Westchester County. Road Commissioners. Record of highways. [New York?] 1714-95, p. 62. MS. (At the Westchester County Clerk's Office, Court House, White Plains, N.Y.)

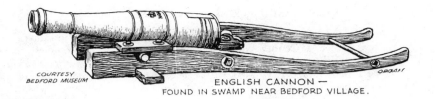

ENGLISH CANNON —
FOUND IN SWAMP NEAR BEDFORD VILLAGE.

CHAPTER IV

THE DAYS OF THE REVOLUTION

IN THE DAYS before the Revolution, travel by land was so difficult that we, living in the interior of the country, were very slow
in getting news current along the Hudson and the Sound. Also
we were less affected by acts that roused the ire of those who
lived near water and led more sophisticated lives. The Stamp
Act really didn't bother us because the legal documents to which
the stamps had to be affixed were rarely used here. To get stirred
up when the Townsend Act levied duties on glass, lead, paper
and tea was academic: the price of their transportation inland
already made them prohibitive to our farm population. When
the port of Boston closed in retaliation for the Tea Party, it did
not affect the economic lives of our families. Each home from
the first had manufactured its own necessities and we were not
used to luxuries. The ports on the Hudson and Sound were
several hours away by fast riding when the roads were passable;
so was White Plains. In winter they were formidable journeys.
So our communities were isolated both by distance and self-
sufficiency.[1]

Either no beat of town drum announced the caucus held in
White Plains in April of 1774 or few listened. This meeting to
consider calling a Congress of *all* the colonies to discuss general
welfare was only sparsely attended. John Jay, who was asked
at the caucus to represent Westchester as well as the City of New
York at the first Continental Congress, was not a neighbor living at Cantitoe until many years later. His world and that of
our local farmers were far apart at this time.

When the first Continental Congress met at Philadelphia September 5, 1774, the series of papers it prepared all advocated continued but less restrictive union with Great Britain on a constitutional basis.[2] None expressed a desire for independence.
Jay's own paper, the "Address to the People of Great Britain,"

46

asked only for a return to the basis of 1763, though it did contain the stirring words:

> But if you are determined that your ministers shall wantonly sport with the rights of mankind; if neither the voice of justice, the dictates of law, the principles of the constitution, or the suggestions of humanity can restrain your hands from shedding human blood in such an impious cause, we must then tell you that we will never submit to be hewers of wood or drawers of water, for any ministry or nation of the world.[19]

Today, of course, Jay's words would make headlines in every local paper. Most likely our farm families never heard them. Neither those families who later became Patriots nor those who remained Loyalists wanted war. If any of the controversial pamphlets issued during 1774 and 1775 found their way to Cherry Street, Cantitoe, and the Northeast Corner, possibly the pro-Loyalist ones signed "A Westchester Farmer" seemed more in accord with the farming interests of our local families.[3]

The first Continental Congress despite its moderate words had not pleased even the moderate Loyalists, and a convention in White Plains to elect members to the second Continental Congress brought strong opposition. The Loyalists refused to cast their ballots and departed to Hatfield's Tavern singing:

> *God save great George, our King,*
> *Long live our noble King, etc.*

Those on the other side of the fence remained and elected delegates, but they ended *their* meeting with "three Huzzas for our gracious Sovereign!"[4]

It was still not yet necessary to make an irrevocable choice of sides, though the document signed April 11, 1775, at Hatfield's Tavern by 300 Westchester freeholders and inhabitants, resolving "to support the King and Constitution"[20] would appear rather definite. One who signed this paper was David Haight who married James Wetmore's daughter and came later to the foot of Cherry Street to live.

Before the second Continental Congress met in May, 1775, the battles of Lexington and Concord had been fought (April 19, 1775). Congress resolved on a national army and our New York Provincial Congress was called on to raise four regiments. One of these, the 4th, contained three companies from Westchester. Congress also asked that the Militia of New York be armed and trained,[5] and accordingly, two companies were raised from Bedford. Volunteering for a Regiment of the Line or for the Militia was a declaration against the King, but failure to volunteer did not stamp a man as a Tory. There were many on both sides who did not sign up. But from this time on, it would have been difficult for any farmer, however isolated, to remain unaware that a choice would soon be forced upon him. The Westchester delegates to the Continental Congress in Philadelphia were writing back, asking how to vote on independence.[6] When the Declaration of Independence was read from the Court House steps in White Plains on July 11, 1776,[7] no one on either side could have been unprepared for it.

In October the British marched into the County. The battle of White Plains, on the 28th, brought active war near us for the first time.[8] When war was an actuality, most of our men joined up on the Continental side. A few joined the United States service in the New York 4th Regiment of the Line. More joined the Militia which could only be sent out of the state for three months at a time. It had another advantage also: men serving in it were called out when needed but allowed to go home and attend to their farms when not needed. Many of our men served in several different Militia regiments during the war years, including those which in 1781 began offering a bounty of "land rights" as an inducement. We also had a few men in the "Associated Exempts," volunteers over sixty for the most part, and in the Levies, which were drafts from various Militia regiments and also direct drafts on the people. A man in the Levies could be called on to serve outside the State during his entire term of service.[22] Listed in Appendix No. 30 are those men from our area whom we have been able to place in New York regiments.

The life of an American soldier was not organized in those days so that his bodily needs were cared for or his worries eased. The Militia had even to supply its own arms and ammunition.[5] In neither army nor Militia was the pay sufficient for a soldier to provide for his family. The Colonies, which had broken away from England mainly because of taxation, neglected or were unable to tax themselves adequately. In 1779 our township was taxed 23 pairs of shoes and 27 pairs of stockings for the soldiers in the field.[9] The only tax in money our Westchester supervisors were willing to levy was on the Quakers, who refused to do military service because of religious convictions. The five Bedford Quakers were taxed £300, a substantial help to the war they deplored.[10]

Our soldiers in the field endured cold and hardship and also an ever present worry not shared by the army as a whole, for Bedford Township lay in what was called the "Neutral Ground." This territory between the British positions north of the Harlem River and the American lines north of the Croton was supposedly not molested by the military of either side, but its inhabitants were preyed on by the lawless of both.[23] In '77 Bedford petitioned Gov. Clinton against Rogers' Rangers (see App. 20). In '79 British Capt. Patrick Ferguson described conditions:

> Most of the houses are thoroughly and indiscriminately plundered, the beds cut up, the furniture and windows broke to pieces, the men rob'd of their watches, shoe buckles and money, whilst their wives and daughters have their pockets and clothes torn from their bodies, and the father or husband who does not survey all this with placid countenance is beat or branded with the name of traitor or rebel.[27]

Actually, our northern section of Bedford suffered less than many other places within the "Neutral Ground" because of our proximity to the Croton River. The "Westchester Lines," a sparse string of outposts defended by various units of the Continental Line, afforded us some measure of protection. These lines swayed back and forth, sometimes as far south as a Tarrytown-Rye line, but in 1780 they moved back north of the Croton, which became their permanent boundary.[28]

Although no engagements or even skirmishes took place in our Katonah area so far as we know, our people became well accustomed to the sight of troops and small contingents of light horse. We were surrounded by a network of military roads, and Veal's Ford at the foot of Cherry Street was a crossing surely as familiar to American raiding parties as to the British colonel, Banister Tarleton. Tarleton used it on his raid on Crompond (Yorktown), June 24, 1779, when with a body of light horse, he "came up by a circuitous route, going up the Croton above Pines Bridge one mile and a half or more, crossed at Vail's ford, advanced upon Crompond from the east."[29] This route to the ford undoubtedly brought Tarleton to Cherry Street by our present Croton Lake Road, which, unnamed, appears on a map bearing Tarleton's signature.[31] Apparently raids by small parties of Patriots, even when conducted for plunder, were sources of pride and satisfaction to our farm families so long as the farms raided were those of Tories. Said Mrs. Martha Griffen, then aged 77, in an interview with John M. McDonald in 1847, "Capt. Yaup Vermille lived in Cherry Street and was very good at plundering." [30]

North of us in the Titicus River valley lay an important wartime highway from Boston to Philadelphia. The main route ran almost on a straight line to Peekskill, but between Danbury and Crompond there were alternate routes to the south, meeting in Bedford, which were frequently used in its stead. One of these ran through Ridgefield, east of South Salem, and over the Old Stone Hill Road. The other route came via Ridgebury, North Salem and Cross River. Joining, the combined route passed through Bedford Village and proceeded to Crompond and Peekskill by Guard Hill Road, North Castle Church and Pines Bridge. From Bedford Village this combined road also served as a connection with a military route to White Plains.

On July 2 and 3, 1781, our Mt. Holly families would have had good opportunity of watching the colorful French regiments march through Cross River on their way from Ridgebury, Connecticut, to Bedford Village when Washington, planning a surprise attack on the British forts at the head of New York Island, sent changed orders to the Comte de Rochambeau to assemble his regiments at the North Castle camp.[32] With Rochambeau on July 2nd came the 1st Brigade, white-uniformed Bourbonnais and the Royal Deux-Ponts in white breeches and blue coats with brilliant yellow facings and cuffs. On July 3rd on a forced march came the 2nd Brigade, the Soissonnais in white and rose and the Saintonge in white and green.[34] What a gay and heartening sight they must have been in comparison with our own ragged army!

Another important military road in our area ran north on the far side of the Croton River. Veal's Ford and Golden's Bridge both led to this road which joined the Titicus valley route.

In proximity to these roads, the following points of strategic importance were in our nearby vicinity.

Goldens Bridge. There was a passable crossing over the Croton River at this point, heavy traffic fording the river beside the Bridge. In his memoirs, Major General William Heath notes in 1779:

July 10. About 6 o'clock, P.M. our General [Heath] received orders from Gen. Washington to march, with the two Connecticut brigades, by the way of Crom Pond, toward Bedford. The next morning, although rainy, the first brigade marched to the Village [Continental?].

July 12. The storm ceasing, the tents (although as wet as water could make them) were struck, and the troops took up their line of march, reaching Amawalk about sunsetting. A report having been spread in the fore part of the day, that the enemy were at or near Pine's Bridge, our General ordered the baggage-wagons, under proper escort, to file off to the left and pursue a road running parallel with the one on which the column was moving, thereby keeping the column between the enemy and the wagons. Both arrived on the ground of encampment within a few minutes of each other. The troops lay on their arms, without pitching their tents. The enemy continued their depredations at the Sound, and burnt some houses at Norwalk.[35]

This would indicate that the wagons crossed at Dean's Bridge, went on towards Salem, and approached Bedford from the northeast. The army, consisting of two Connecticut Brigades, would have turned south to Goldens Bridge and entered Bedford from the northwest. One year previously, Washington used Goldens Bridge as a headquarters, in the late summer and fall of 1778,[36] while he supervised the withdrawal of army units from White Plains and their relocation north of the Croton.[43] While at Goldens Bridge, Washington arranged with the farmers of that place, and probably with those in the whole general area, for supplies for the men who were going into winter quarters at Fishkill, Fredericksburg, and Danbury for 1778-79. The house used by Washington in Goldens Bridge, designated on the Beers map, 1868, was moved to the present village when the reservoir system took over the original site, and is occupied at present by J. J. Palmer.

Bedford Village. Possibly the first troops seen in Bedford during the Revolution were on Guard Hill. According to a story handed down through one of Bedford's oldest families, Nehemiah Lounsbury, who in 1740 built what is now known as the Kirby house on Guard Hill Road, gave it over to the American Army following the retreat from White Plains in 1776. Soldiers posted at the top of Guard Hill could see the whole countryside, from which is said to have come the hill's name.[44]

The story of Tarleton's raid and the burning of Bedford Village has been told so well by so many that we will here quote only from the notes of General Heath, who had taken command of the "Westchester Lines" June 23, 1779:

> July 2, 1779. About 360 of the enemy's light horse and light infantry came out from Mile-Square, and attacked Col. Sheldon's light horse, who were posted at Poundridge, about 90 in number. The superior force of the enemy obliged our horse, at first, to retreat, but, being reinforced by the militia, they in turn pursued the enemy. Our loss was one Corporal, one Trumpeter, and eight privates wounded; three Sergeants, one Corporal, and four privates missing; and 12 horses missing. The standard of the regiment being left in the house where the dragoons suddenly turned out, was lost. Of the enemy, one was killed, four taken prisoners, four horses taken, and one horse killed. The enemy set fire to and burnt the meeting-house and Maj. Lockwood's house; they also burnt Mr. Hay's house, at Bedford.[35]

Tarleton in his report to Clinton stated that the round-trip march covered 64 miles in 23 hours.[24]

A few weeks after this raid, according to Samuel Barrett, there was another enemy raid in which a counterattack was made by an American company. Barrett, a member of another of Bedford's oldest families, had enlisted about May, 1779, in Captain Moseman's company, for his fourth term of duty. His affidavit for a pension in 1832 says that a few weeks after Tarleton's raid on Bedford Village,

> the enemy advanced as far north as Crompond and took about forty of the Militia guard prisoners. We attacked them at Croton River Bridge, took four of the enemy's horsemen, made a second attack on their outguards. We lost one taken prisoner. Thus continuing our guards and patrols alternately to repel the Enemy whose lines were near the west part of Bedford untill the month of November, 1780.[45]

Before this, on June 29, 1779, Moylan's light horse and Armand's legion were assigned from New Jersey to Bedford.[31] On

July 10, 1779, General Heath was ordered by Washington towards Bedford with two Connecticut brigades to deter the British along the Sound from moving inland from Stamford. This is the troop movement referred to above under Goldens Bridge. After making a march towards Stamford, Heath took up a strong position on July 15th between Bedford and Ridgefield.[35] During the months of September, October and November, 1780, Lt. Col. Jameson's 2nd Light Dragoons, to which Washington's chief of intelligence, Major Benjamin Talmadge, was attached, were assigned to the Bedford–North Castle Church–Pines Bridge area. Information of the enemy was secured through many sources and passed on through "the Relay," an underground system from one farmhouse to another, from forward observers in lower Westchester to the intelligence officer on the "Westchester Lines." [12]

On December 31, 1780, Captain Pritchard of the 5th Massachusetts Regiment was posted at Bedford with a company of Continental troops and repelled an attack by 150 men of De-Lancey's corps, pursuing them past North Castle Church.[38] Through Heath's entries of the next few months run sentences such as: "Brigadeer General Huntington advanced as far as Bedford"; "Enemy out towards Bedford"; "Enemy makes excursion from Morrisania towards Bedford."

On Rochambeau's maps (Library of Congress) showing the route of the French army from Providence, R.I., there are marked two Bedford camps, No. 12 and No. 7. Camp No. 12, which can be seen on map p. 26, was occupied by Rochambeau with the 1st Brigade on the night of July 2, 1781.[46] The 2nd Brigade, following by a day, could not take time to stop there and marched straight through to North Castle Church.[47] A story handed down from that time quarters the cavalry of Rochambeau in the western fields of Jabez Robertson's Cantitoe farm.[21] The horses are said to have "girdled" the trees, from which this area received its name, Girdle Ridge. We cannot vouch for this tale but it could very well be true.

Camp No. 7, indicated on the same map, was a mile nearer New York. It was occupied briefly some time during the day of July 2nd by the legion of the Duc de Lauzun, which had marched to the left of the 1st Brigade and met it at Bedford,[46] most probably where the old Stone Hill Road met with the road from Cross River. That same evening, Lauzun, who had been covering the left flank of the French army continuously since June 20th, standing between it and the Sound,[48] left it and proceeded to

Eastchester which he reached early on the morning of July 3rd. This parting of the ways was to have resulted in a surprise attack by Lauzun's legion, in company with Sheldon's dragoons and Waterbury's Connecticut troops, on DeLancey's Refugees near Kingsbridge.[33]

North Castle Church. In the vicinity of our present Northern Westchester Hospital, Mt. Kisco, and at the meeting point of roads from Pines Bridge, Bedford, Tarrytown and White Plains, this area was one of strategic importance from the first. It is referred to in the journals of von Closen and Berthier of the French army simply as "North Castle" but the maps of Berthier leave no doubt as to its location. Its name came from St. George's Episcopal Church, built there in 1761, which, abandoned as a place of worship, served our troops as a hospital immediately after the Battle of White Plains and continued to serve both Americans and French as a hospital and for other military purposes. From October, 1776, on, the camp at North Castle Church formed a vital link in the intermittent line of defense extending from White Plains to the Croton River and beyond. It was an overnight stopping-place for General Heath moving his division from the battlefield to Peekskill, November 9, 1776.[39] General Charles Lee, ordered to secure the supplies left behind at White Plains and to guard the approaches to the strong points to the north, distributed his men from Wright's Mills in Armonk through North Castle Church and Bedford to Pines Bridge. He spent the month following the battle in superintending operations from headquarters at North Castle Church, from the White Plains camp and the Philipsburg (Dobbs Ferry) camp until in December, 1776, his division joined Washington in New Jersey,[49] at which time Heath's division from Peekskill took over this guard duty. In January, 1777, this area was used by Colonel Frost's regiment and General Scott's militia.[40]

On July 3, 1781, the 1st Brigade of the French army moved from Camp No. 12 at Bedford to Camp No. 13 at North Castle Church.[11] The following is a translation from the *Journal* of Alexander Berthier:

> July 3rd, the 2nd brigade left Ridgebury at 3 a.m. and arrived at North-Castle—22 miles—at 1 hour after dinner and joined the first, who had just arrived from Bedford. The 4th division, who had marched the 92 miles from East-Hartford without stay, did this last 22 miles march under excessive heat, and

with a courage and a gaiety very characteristic of French ardor.[47]

In Berthier's *Journal* also, the strategic importance of this camp is described:

> This camp was in a very advantageous position, having its left protected by marshes and closed by mountains and woods, able to march to the enemy in three columns and retreat in two, one towards Pines Bridge, where the Croton is crossed four miles away, and the other towards Ridgebury and Bedford at 22 and 5 miles. It is easy to be well protected in this country since troops are obliged to follow the roads, and cannot leave them without running into woods, mountains, and a thousand unsurmountable obstacles, particularly for a considerable body of troops.[47]

On August 19, 1781, an attack on New York having been given up, the French moved from North Castle Church to Pines Bridge and then across the Hudson at Kings Ferry en route to Yorktown, Virginia.[41] "All Westchester County was again alive with the tramp of troops, the gleam of arms, and the lumbering of artillery and baggage wagons along its roads." [50]

Pines Bridge. A little north of where it stands today, the original Pines Bridge was so necessary to the American army that one of the greatest blunders of the British is considered to be their failure to secure it before it was finally protected and fortified by the American army. On October 30, 1776, Washington ordered three Maryland regiments under the command of General Beall to the heights south of the Croton commanding its approaches.[13] From then on, it was always guarded by our troops, who on some occasions even removed its planks at night. André crossed Pines Bridge on the morning of his capture, September 23, 1780.[14] Two of the most prominent members of the "Westchester Guides" lived in this area, John Pine and his brother, Peter.[25]

It was from Pines Bridge that a daring and successful American raid on DeLancey's Camp at Morrisania was launched by 600 men, commanded by Lt. Col. William Hull, January 21, 1781.[15] It was at the Davenport house, a short distance from Pines Bridge, that Col. Christopher Greene, of the First Rhode Island Regiment, commanding the "Westchester Lines," was surprised and killed by DeLancey's forces, May 13, 1781.[16]

Our experiences during the war years were of ceaseless forays. Crops were planted and harvested by men between tours of duty. Sometimes these crops fed our own army, sometimes the British. Sometimes they were burned.

After seven long and bitter seasons of sowing and reaping, the war ended. The preliminary treaty of peace, negotiated by John Jay, John Adams, and Benjamin Franklin, was signed at Paris November 30, 1782.[17] In May of 1783 the last of the British army left Westchester, and on November 25th New York City was evacuated.[18]

To all of our families some sorrow remained. For those whose members had been divided in their loyalties it was the hardest. Ammon Fowler's oldest son, Weedon, was banished to Canada, where he died. Col. James Holmes for years could not return to his home on the Hook Road south of the Cross River.[26] To the Harris Road end of Cherry Street came a sad little letter addressed "for Mr. Elijey Buckbee, att Bedford New Purchase. There with Speed and Care." It was from his daughter living within the British lines at Morrisania, now the Bronx, and despite the notation, it might have taken weeks for the letter to reach its destination. It read:

> Morreseney April ye 2d—1783
> Deare father and mother—these few Lines Leaves me in a poor Sittuation as I am now obliged to keep my Bead Constantly and my husband worse taken Prisener ye 14th Day of March and is not Returned as yet. Dear father Please to Come or Send me Some Relief or Else Eye must Suffer Soon I give my Love to my Dear father and mother and Childe and all friends there from your Dutifull Daughter
> Elizabeth Harriss
> further I Should Be thankfull if you Could bring me Some fennell Seed and Rutz Licorise Seed Spignard and hartshorn and Comfery [See p. 27]

Referring to this period which led to the establishment of our nation and had such an impact on world history, an injunction occurring more than once in the memoirs of Major General William Heath is fitting for us who reap the benefits of Westchester's years of trial: "Remember these things, ye Americans, in future times!"[42]

References

1. Barrett, R. T. *The Town of Bedford*. Bedford, N.Y., 1955, p. 40.
2. Hufeland, Otto. *Westchester County during the American Revolution, 1775-1783*. White Plains, N.Y., 1926, pp. 12-13.
3. *Ibid.*, pp. 18-20.
4. *Ibid.*, pp. 62-63.
5. *Ibid.*, pp. 65-66.
6. *Ibid.*, p. 69.
7. *Ibid.*, p. 72.
8. *Ibid.*, p. 140.
9. *Ibid.*, p. 441.
10. *Ibid.*, p. 442.
11. *Ibid.*, p. 385.
12. *Ibid.*, p. 283.
13. *Ibid.*, p. 147.
14. *Ibid.*, p. 348.
15. *Ibid.*, pp. 374-75.
16. *Ibid.*, pp. 378-82.
17. *Ibid.*, pp. 424-25.
18. *Ibid.*, p. 438.
19. Bancroft, George. *History of the United States*, v. 7, p. 149. Quoted by Hufeland, p. 13.
20. Scharf, J. T. *History of Westchester County*. Philadelphia, 1886, v. 1, p. 248.
21. *Ibid.*, v. 2, p. 600.
22. New York State. Comptroller's Office. *New York in the Revolution as colony and state*. 2. ed. Albany, 1898, p. 10.
23. McDonald, J. M. *Papers;* ed. by William S. Hadaway. White Plains, N.Y., 1926-27, v. 2, p. 3.
24. *Ibid.*, v. 2, p. 48.
25. *Ibid.*, v. 1, p. 68.
26. *Ibid.*, v. 2, p. 69.
27. *Short history of New York State:* David M. Ellis, James A. Frost, Harold C. Syrett, Harry J. Carman. Ithaca, N.Y., 1957, p. 105.
28. Patterson, E. L. *Peekskill in the American Revolution*. Peek-
skill, N.Y., 1944, p. 100.
29. McDonald, J. M. Papers. 1846-47, v. 4, pp. 552-53. MS. Statement by Thomas Strang. (In possession of the Hufeland Memorial Library, Huguenot and Historical Association, New Rochelle, N.Y.)
30. *Ibid.*, 1847-48, v. 5, p. 641. MS. Statement by Mrs. Martha Griffen.
31. Tarleton, Banister. [Map of North Castle Church area. 1779?] MS. (At the University of Michigan Library, Ann Arbor, one of the British headquarters maps used by Sir Henry Clinton, 1775-1782)
32. Keim, DeB. R. *Rochambeau*. Washington, D.C., 1907, p. 397.
33. *Ibid.*, p. 399.
34. The Army of Louis XVI of France. In: *The American Heritage Book of the Revolution*, New York, 1958, pp. 174-75.
35. Heath, William. *Memoirs;* new ed. New York, 1901, pp. 191-92.
36. *Ibid.*, p. 179.
37. *Ibid.*, p. 190.
38. *Ibid.*, p. 248.
39. *Ibid.*, p. 75.
40. *Ibid.*, p. 98.
41. *Ibid.*, p. 279.
42. *Ibid.*, p. 207.
43. Burt, Miss Helen, of Goldens Bridge (1859-1958). Oral communication to Richard Grady of Goldens Bridge, reporting information from her parents and grandparents.
44. Waller, Mrs. T. M. Fall pilgrimage to Bedford Township September 26, 1959. In: *Westchester Historian*, Oct./Dec., 1959, v. 35, pp. 90-92.
45. Barrett, Samuel. [Affidavit for

Revolutionary War pension.]
Oct. 3, 1832. MS. (Photostat in
possession of Mrs. W. A. Kelly,
Katonah)

46. von Closen, Ludwig. *Revolutionary journal, 1780-1783.*
Chapel Hill, N.C., 1958, p. 88.

47. Berthier, Alexander. *Journal de
la campagne d'Amérique 10
mai 1780-26 août 1781.* [Princeton, N.J.?] 1951, p. 63.

48. *Ibid.,* p. 60.

49. Lee, Charles. *The Lee papers.*
New York, 1872-73, v. 2, pp.

267-329. (Collections of the
New-York Historical Society
1871-72)

50. Irving, Washington. *Life of
George Washington,* v. 4, p.
388. Quoted by Patterson, pp.
151-52.

51. Harriss, Elizabeth. Letter to
Elijah Buckbee, Morris
Heights, N.Y., April 2, 1783.
MS. (In possession of Mrs.
Henry F. Haight, P.O. Box 162,
Dixon, Calif. Photostat at Katonah Village Library)

Chapter 4 written by Richard G. Lucid assisted by Frances R. Duncombe and Janet Doe

John Jay,
First Chief Justice
of the United States

ORBAN

CHAPTER V

AFTER THE REVOLUTION

WHEN THE WAR ended, the Township of Bedford began the business of picking up and going forward. The Westchester County Board of Supervisors started to function again as a representative body. County Courts, which had been forced to move from place to place during the war, returned to Bedford in 1785, meeting in the rebuilt Presbyterian Church until the new courthouse was finished in 1787.[1] Town meetings were continued as the basis of local government and were conducted much as they had been in colonial days. In 1784, which is the first year for which we have minutes after the blank period following those of 1722, the Town was still "making choice of" damage prisers, fence viewers and pounders.[2] A new office appears in these minutes, however, which was not mentioned in the earlier ones. There were thirty-one highway or pathmasters chosen. (See Appendix No. 21.)

Commissioners of roads had charge of new construction and major repairs of roads and bridges. For these purposes, Town money was provided. Current maintenance was carried out without funds under supervision of the pathmasters. There was one appointed to each stretch of road, and it was his job to get the neighbors living along it to put in so many days of work a year, which they were assessed in lieu of money.

"Pathmaster" appears to have been an honorary position and the honor was shifted frequently from one landowner to another, probably with a sigh of relief each time. The highways were rough dirt roads, mud bogs in spring and deep snow in winter: no Town snowplows in those days, and no Town gravel. Privately owned teams of oxen hitched to stone boats or carts did the jobs of today's Town trucks. Each farmer used his own equipment and his own muscles.

There was only one motion passed in this 1784 meeting which marks it definitely post-Revolutionary. It was voted "that No Persons that have been Over to the Enemy Shall Come into town to Reside if Any have all Ready come in they are to be Imedietely Drove out." [2] To make sure this resolution was carried out, a committee of twelve was chosen. How many *were* "drove out," we have no way of knowing.

Three years later, another law was passed [2] which also had its reason in the Revolution. This one aimed to curb the practice of inoculating against smallpox, which had been done with some success in the army, but had the civilian population up in arms. It was "VOTED: That no person enocolate any person within 80 rods of any Public Highway under the forfeiture of 10 pounds for the person enochalateing and the same for the person enocholated and the money so to be raised to go for the use of the Poor."

Running through all the early post-Revolution minutes is mention of various provisions for the poor. If the disposal of them seems callous to us, we must remember there were not as yet any county homes for them nor any welfare agencies. Tax money, generally from fifty to a hundred pounds a year, was given to the poormasters for their relief. With this they boarded them out singly in private families whenever possible and occasionally attempted a community shelter. The vote in 1787 "that the poor be sold to the lowest bidder from the first of May till the first of May next year" [2] came only after a try at a local poorhouse had failed.

In 1786, eighteen hundred pounds were appropriated by the County for erection of courthouses and jails at White Plains and Bedford.[3] In the town minutes of Bedford, we find much about the proposed courthouse and no mention of a jail being built. Perhaps Town of Bedford men preferred to employ more active treatment for their transgressors. In 1796, the annual meeting "VOTED: To raise three pounds and four shillings for to build a stocks and whipping post." [2] And it is probable that each constable had a "lock up" in or behind his own house for drunks and mild offenders.

Also at the 1796 meeting, four school commissioners were

chosen and these offices continued to be filled until 1799, when we hear of them no more until 1812. Apparently, Bedford was studying the State's "Act for the Encouragement of Schools" passed in 1795[3] and trying to decide whether to accept State aid at the price of putting up half the amount received themselves.

Post-Revolutionary town meetings were augmented by new arrivals in the township and new names began to appear on all our pathmaster lists. Shortly before and after the end of the war, Van Cortlandt heirs began selling property at Cantitoe and along the east side of Cherry Street. March 20, 1773, Margaret De Peyster Axtell, granddaughter of Jacobus Van Cortlandt, sold to Arnell ("Arnold" on deed) Dickinson, of North Castle, his first piece of property at Cantitoe,[5] and brought into our midst one of our most influential and civic-minded families.

At the north end of Cherry Street, running east to the Cross River, Augustus Van Cortlandt and Frederick Van Cortlandt sold land in 1793 to Timothy Ketcham[8] and to John Thorpe and Nathan Price.[9] Daniel Smith, already a Bedford Township man, bought his first acreage in our immediate neighborhood in 1789 from Augustus Van Cortlandt.[10] Across the Lower Salem line in the angle between the Cross and Croton Rivers, John Van Cortlandt was selling property which later became part of the short-lived community of Whitlockville. One piece went to Thaddeus Whitlock himself in 1792.[11]

Into other parts of our Katonah area new families were coming also. In 1791 or '92, David Haight and his wife Elizabeth Wetmore, moved from Rye to land which is now the corner of Bedford and Harris Roads. This is interesting in relation to the town vote of 1784 concerning those who had "been over to the enemy." David, as you will remember, signed the article of April 11, 1775, supporting the King,[4] and his descendants believe him to have remained a Tory.[13] Memory and bitterness are short-lived after the end of hostilities always. He was not only accepted among us but given many Town offices.

Up in the rugged and hilly section of the Northeast corner, Jonah Holly came to make his home and give the name of Mt. Holly to the whole area. His name appears as pathmaster in the 1795 list.

In the post-Revolutionary records of Lower Salem (now Lewisboro) several families that we later identify with Katonah are mentioned in the 1780's. In 1784, we find John Quick elected an overseer of the poor; and in 1786, there is a notation "To Dr.

William Wood, for a visit to James Brown, a transient person
£0/3/2." [14]

By 1800, the name "Cherry Street" had come into use. In a
mortgage given by David Olmsted at that date,[15] his land on
the north end of it (now the home of Mr. and Mrs. Arthur I.
Bernhard) is described as "land in Bedford, situate in Cherry
Street by the road leading from Veals Ford to Bedford." The
use of the word "in" rather than "on" is important. It designates
Cherry Street as a place rather than a road.

With the first mention of Cherry Street as a locality, we have
at last caught up with Mrs. Ophelia (Todd) Avery, whose *Historical Sketch of Katonah,* published in 1896, is one of our most
valued sources of information concerning the beginnings of our
village. Writing her article before the birth of our present Katonah, she calls Cherry Street the "grandparent Village," which
makes it our great-grandparent, with Whitlockville and Old
Katonah succeeding it. She does not date the hamlet other than
to say "during the palmy days of Cherry Street—the Revolutionary War was still fresh in the memory of its inhabitants" but
we would place the beginning of its life as a center of rural
conveniences in the seventeen-nineties, with four men at the
core of its development. They were Dr. William Wood, Thaddeus Whitlock, David Olmsted and David Haight.

The importance of the Cherry Street hamlet to us today is
that it established a center independent of Bedford Village and
gave us a village of our own in the northern part of the township.
The reason we have picked Wood, Whitlock, Olmsted and
Haight as our village great-greatgrandfathers is that they sired
our first generation of merchants in a locality purely agricultural
before that time.

Thaddeus Whitlock and David Olmsted were already brothers-in-law when they emigrated from Fairfield County in 1790
and '97. Their children began marrying with each other and
with the offspring of Wood and Haight in the early 1800's. Mr.
Squire Wood, son of Dr. William, married Mary Whitlock,
daughter of Thaddeus and Grace Burr Whitlock, in 1800. John
Burr Whitlock, son of Thaddeus and Grace, married his cousin,
Rachel Olmsted, in 1808. Betsey Whitlock married Caleb Haight,
son of David and Elizabeth Wetmore Haight, sometime after
1811.[12]

Other Whitlock, Olmsted, and Haight children began marrying up and down Cherry Street and into the valley to the east

Courtesy of Harvey and Holly Avery

The Holly Homestead, Mt. Holly. The oldest part was built in the 1790's by Jonah Holly. House is now occupied by his descendants, Harvey and Holly Avery.

Courtesy of the Westchester County Historical Society

"Bedford House," Cantitoe, the residence of Chief Justice John Jay, from an engraving in *Historical Collections of the State of New York* by J. W. Barber and Henry Howe, New York, 1841.

63

The Whitlock Homestead, Whitlockville. To this Lewisboro side of th
Cross River, Thaddeus and Grace (Burr) Whitlock came from Connecticut in 179.

The Olmsted House on Cherry Street now owned by Arthur I. Bernhar
Original part was built by Major David Olmsted about 179

Courtesy of Edward Percy Barrett

Saw and gristmills originally owned by Squire Wood and John Burr Whitlock. Whitlockville Road in foreground built in 1817 to connect them with Cherry Street. Mills later were known as Cox's Mills.

Courtesy of Mrs. Mildred Banks

Road from Whitlock farm, Whitlockville. The team is approaching the small bridge over the Cross River going towards Woods Bridge.

65

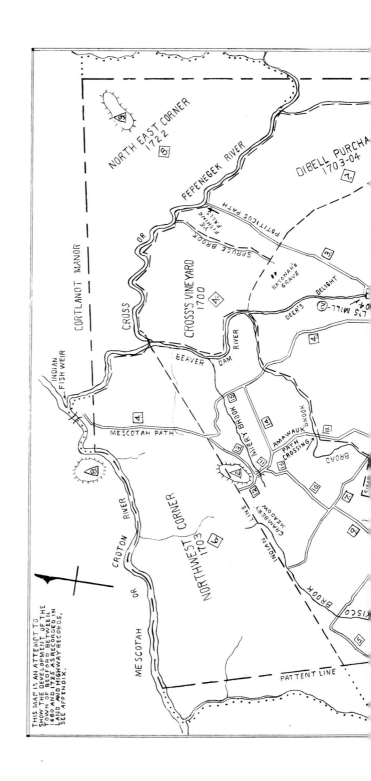

THIS MAP IS AN ATTEMPT TO
SHOW THE DEVELOPMENT OF THE
TOWN OF BEDFORD BETWEEN
1680 AND 1725 AS RECORDED IN
LAND AND HIGHWAY RECORDS.
SEE APPENDIX.

NORTH EAST CORNER
1722 ⑧

⑨

FEPENEGEK RIVER

DIBELL PURCHA
1703-04
⑦

POTTICUS PATH

SPRUCE BROOK
OR
FISHING
FALLS

③

KATONAH'S
GRAVE

DEER'S DELIGHT

⑩ O'S MILL

CROSS'S VINEYARD
1700 Ⓐ

CORTLANDT MANOR

CROSS

BEAVER DAM RIVER

④

INDIAN FISH WEIR

④

MESCOTAH PATH

⑤

④

AMAWAUK BROOK

⑪

PATH CROSSING

⑬

WIERY BROOK

⑥

BROAD

Ⓐ②

⑫②

⑩

⑧

⑫

⑨

CROTON RIVER
OR

⑧

CRANBERRY MEADOW

NORTHWEST CORNER
1703 ⑥

INDIAN LINE

ISCO BROOK

MESCOTAH

PATTENT LINE

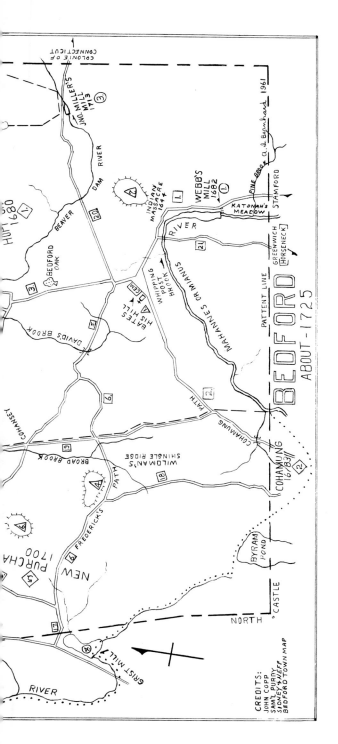

BEDFORD TOWNSHIP ABOUT 1725

Drawn from highway and land records of the time by
A. I. Bernhard. For explanation, see Appendix 15.

67

Katonah Advertiser.

EVERETT BENEDICT, - Editor,

PUBLISHER AND PROPRIETOR.

THURSDAY, NOVEMBER 5th, 1874.

OUR GRANDFATHERS' NEWSPAPERS.

No change in the manner of doing anything, more strongly marks the peculiar genius of this time, than the metamorphosis (scarcely an exaggeration to call it so) of newspapers. Looking at the old issues we see no head-lines! No special correspondence! No personals! No Jokes! No reports of amusements! much less criticism; much less puffs; much less book notices! much less market reports! much less court decisions. O, easy-going, non-news-devouring, low pressure long ago. O, lolling, lazy, limp, luxurious, lounging anti-telegraphic days. How many exhausted editors and gorged readers sigh for your return, and long to exchange at least for one short day (say Monday), the same old bliss of ignorance for this overburdening load of universal intelligence. They are like bees caught in the rain, overloaded with honey; and such honey!

Katonah Advertiser.

THURSDAY, NOVEMBER 5th, 1874.

LOCAL & GENERAL.

Revolution.

Now kill quails.

We are glad it is over.

A terrible famine in Nevada.

Boston is again seizing liquor.

Try the new 25 cent Coffee at Benedict's.

Three murderers hang on November 12th.

Why does all creation sneeze twice, Mr. Tyndall?

Mr. Horace Todd has our thanks for a basket of fine eating apples.

The President has recommended November 26, as a day of Thanksgiving.

The banking house of Henry Clews & Co. is in the hands of the Sheriff.

And now the Rev. T. T. Merry, of Machias, Maine, is on the ragged edge.

The total eclipse of the moon began at 11:45 p. m. on the 24th inst. and ended at 4:18 a. m. on the 25th.

Katonah was attended with more than usual drunkeness on election night, the occasion of the gathering of politicians and others, to learn the result of the vote.

RESULTS BEFORE RETURNS. We would thank the parties who left their undigested election suppers on our store steps, to call around or we shall avail ourselves of the civil damage act.

It is suggested that while sojourning at the Falls, the Irish team might have won the gratitude of the nation by picking off a few hackmen at 1000 yards or less.

MARRIED--On November 4th, at the residence of the brides' parents, Gideon Avery of Cross River, to Marietta Holly of Mt. Holly, Bedford, the Rev. Mr. Slater tying the knot. The guests numbered about 60, who enjoyed the occasion with the usual zest.

Courtesy of Mrs. James G. Bonacorda

The Cherry Street schoolhouse near Lily Pond Lane is now the home of Ralph E. Lent. This picture taken around 1880 shows "Uncle" Weedon Fowler on horse, and among children, Emma (Fisher) Mead.

Coming to Cherry Street in 1829, Dr. Seth Shove built this house in 1837 opposite Whitlockville Road.

until practically the whole community became one of brothers- and sisters-in-law.

The merchants who first set up in business were Squire Wood, John Burr Whitlock and Moses Marshall, husband of Lavinia Haight. Marshall was a saddler; Wood and Whitlock were part- ners in merchandising and tavern-keeping. Mrs. Avery tells us that their store and tavern were in a large building which also contained a town hall and that it stood on the west side of Cherry Street just south of the house built later by Dr. Seth Shove. According to her account, courts of justice were held in this hall and it was also used for "General Training" of the Militia and social gatherings.

It was here probably that polling took place. Elections in those days, as described by Mrs. Avery, took three days. The ballot box came to Cherry Street on the morning of the first day and was taken to Cantitoe in the afternoon. The second day, it travelled to Bedford Four Corners, then to Bedford Court House, where ballots were inspected and counted on the third day. One of David Olmsted's first important town offices after he moved to Cherry Street was that of inspector of elections from 1803 to 1807.[16] These elections were for other than local offices. Fence viewers, assessors, justices of the peace, etc., were still being elected at town meetings.

Mrs. Avery tells of a blacksmith's shop on Cherry Street owned by Daniel Park, and of a young man named Hiram Oysterbanks who was engaged in a transportation business of sorts. There were not many bridges across the Croton at this period. Pines Bridge was about five miles downstream, and the one at Goldens Bridge a mile or so upstream. The only crossing we had was at Veals Ford, which was shallow but fairly wide. Across this, the enterprising young Mr. Oysterbanks ferried foot passengers on his horse—fare, sixpence a trip. We think Hiram's family lived on the Reyburn property, possibly in the present Stanton house.

Another interesting enterprise mentioned by Mrs. Avery was the wool-carding mill of Harry Haight. On high ground far from any water, the mill machinery was powered by a horse hitched to a capstan bar. As he walked round and round, the bar turned the mill shaft. Unfortunately, Mrs. Avery does not date this mill for us and we have not run into any mention of it in town records.

There were two water-operated mills available to Cherry Street residents that we can date, and a third that we speculate about.

In 1795, William Miller asked the Town to lay out a private road for the use and benefit of his mills. The Commissioner granted his request and laid it out as follows:

> Begining at the Bedford Road that leads to Vail's [Veal's] Ford at the corner of the land belonging to Daniel Smith, thence running easterly by the said Smith's land and to extend northerly two rods in width till it comes to a ledge of rocks, then to extend in width to John Thorp's fence as it now stands and going round the rocks to go still by Daniel Smith's line and to extend two rods in width till it passes the house of William Wood, then to take the said Wood's bowns [bounds] for the north bowns of the sd. mill path and follow the said Woods bowns to the Cross River to the Common Riding Place.[17]

The second water-operated mill is mentioned prior to 1810. It belonged to Squire Wood, antedating the one he owned in partnership with John Burr Whitlock.[22] The third, which is problematic as to continued use at this time, could have been operating on "Hezekiah Robert's mill pond" which is mentioned in a deed of 1789[10] as lying east of Cherry Street.

By 1795, Cherry Street had a doctor, William Wood, who had been a surgeon's mate in the 4th N.Y. Regiment during the Revolution. If the 1750 school[23] was still functioning, it had some form of education. The hamlet lacked a church but it had religion brought to its doors. Methodist preachers on horseback began to visit Cherry Street soon after the Revolution. Called back to England during the war because their allegedly pro-Loyalist sentiments and their distribution of Wesley's pro-King tract, "A Calm Address to our American Colonies," made them unwelcome,[24] the Methodists returned to this country when war ended. Thomas Ware was sent out in 1786 by the central body in New York City to examine the possibilities of extending a circuit from New Rochelle throughout the northern part of the county. He rode as far northwest as Peekskill and was probably the earliest circuit rider to pass through this vicinity. The route outlined by Ware was established as the New Rochelle Circuit by the 1787 Methodist Conference. Soon thereafter, such men as Peter Moriarty, Albert Van Nostrand and Lemuel Smith began to preach in the homes of our farm families.[25] Of the early Methodists, the Rev. Thomas LaMonte, pastor of the Katonah

Methodist Episcopal Church from 1872 to 1875, wrote in the 1878 issue of the *Feast of Lanterns:*

> These faithful itinerants penetrated to nearly all parts of the county, entering every open door, preaching and organizing classes, which were the germs of future churches. . . . In the latter part of the last century, Moriarty and his colleagues on the New Rochelle circuit began preaching on week day evenings once in five or six weeks at Enoch Honeywell's and Elijah Buckbee's. Soon a class was formed and regular meetings held at Honeywell's, Buckbee's, Joseph Griffin's, Mrs. Halstead's, Silkman's (towards Cross River), Moseman's, and in some other neighborhoods. This class was the nucleus of what afterwards became the Cherry St. class, the Moseman class, the New Castle class, and perhaps the Cross River class.[26]

While Cherry Street was enjoying village life, Cantitoe and Mt. Holly remained more rural. They had, however, some of the same advantages. According to a deed of 1792 there was a school on Mt. Holly as well as at Cherry Street. This from description was on the east side of the North Salem Road near present Route 35.[7] There were also mills in this northeast section of the township, and as places for the exchange of conversation, produce and currency, our old-time mills took the place of club, store and bank.[27]

In convenient distance to Mt. Holly was John Rundle's mill on the Cross River near Bedford's eastern boundary. This was built prior to 1783.[18] Further west on the Cross River just below the bridge on the Cantitoe-North Salem road, there were other mills. These, known as Hoyt's Mills in their last years, were operated at an even earlier date. Before 1781 they belonged to John Rall but thereafter they changed hands so frequently that the farmers patronizing them may well have wondered to whom they would belong on their next visit. In 1781 John Rall conveyed them to Jesse Holly, as "mills and lands hereafter mentioned, Griss Mill, Saw Mill, Oyl Mill and Fulling Mill, all standing on or near the Fishing Falls."[6] Apparently they returned to Rall and in 1792 he sold them to John Jay who at this time had in mind the improvement of the Cantitoe farm, inherited in 1782, on which there were outbuildings and at least one house. The deed contains the following description of the mill parcel:

with . . . dwelling house, grist mill and saw mill and all other buildings and tenements thereon, . . . on the northerly side of Cross River and on the westerly side of the . . . highway which passing over the bridge near the said dwelling house leads towards North Salem, which said lott . . . John Rall purchased of John Osburn and confirmed his right to the Falls on which the Mills are erected by an act or vote of the Town.[7]

Thereafter these mills became known as Jay's, Powell's, Collyer's, Hallock's and finally, Hoyt's.

Mills were centers for social and business activities.[27] Churches served as centers to a wider extent, but as yet we had none in our northern part of the township. That did not mean however that our families deprived themselves of the opportunity for worship or neglected the social and civic responsibilities of parish life. They traveled miles in springless farm wagons to churches in other areas. There was the Baptist Church in Bedford Center and later in 1789 its offshoot at Cross River, which began its meetings in private homes. There were Presbyterian churches at Bedford and South Salem. There was a Quaker meeting-house at North Castle. Some of our families attended Christ Church of Salem and some, St. George's Episcopal Church at North Castle.

Episcopal services were brought nearer to us with the church at Bedford Center, later called St. Matthew's. This was consecrated in 1810. Our Cherry Street families were active in this church from the beginning. David Haight, Nicholas Haight and David Olmsted had all been vestrymen of St. George's and continued as such at St. Matthew's. Platt Bennett of Cherry Street and Samuel H. Miller and John B. Whitlock in the valley to the east served on the vestry within the first ten years. David Olmsted was on the building committee with William Miller and Peter A. Jay of Cantitoe.[28] John Jay, though not on this committee, showed a vital interest in the church and loaned money which made possible the purchase of land in connection with it.

John Jay after retirement from public life had come to Cantitoe in May, 1801, moving with his daughter, Ann, into the old and previously existing portion of what became "Bedford House." Mrs. Jay in delicate health waited at the home of her brother for its enlargement and renovation.[29] For three years Jay had been striving to expedite the enlargement of this house and of a smaller one, the "brick house," thwarted, it would seem, as much by the inactivity of his manager Major Lyon as by difficulties in securing materials and labor. To his father, then Governor of New York State, Peter Augustus Jay wrote on March 16, 1799:

> The Major has made but small progress towards building. . . . The Boards are not yet brought from Coscob. No Lime has been procured and only about 20,000 Brick drawn. All the Necessary Timber has been drawn to the Saw mill but not sawed. Two Carpenters of whom the Major has a good Opinion have given him an Estimate of the Sum for which they will undertake the House amounting to £93. Upon a careful Calculation we supposed that it was worth no more than £60. . . . I wished to conclude if possible a bargain with them immediately, but he supposed that [he] could negociate more advantageously alone. . . . There are but few Masons in the County and they but indifferent Workmen. Of Carpenters there are many. I endeavored to hasten the Majr. and he promised to agree with the Carpenters and contract for Lime immediately after my departure and that the Stone for the Cellar shall be drawn as soon as the weather will permit.[30]

On April 20th Peter Augustus reported with more optimism. The Major was "now persuaded you intend to reside at Bedford and I hope this belief will persuade him to be more active."

In July Mrs. Jay visited the Cantitoe farm and she too was optimistic. She wrote her husband of the embellishments she contemplated and of her anticipation of a life of social virtue and intellectual bliss in the country.[31] Her anticipations, unfortunately, were not to be realized. There were more years of procrastination on the Major's part. In the fall of 1800 the Brick House was completed but work on the larger house still dragged. When Jay was free to supervise matters himself there were still many problems to be overcome. When finally in the autumn of 1801, Bedford House, though not yet entirely finished was deemed comfortable enough for Mrs. Jay to join her husband there, the poor lady had only a few more months to live.

Because a recent tale depicts Mrs. Jay as haunting the Brick House, we wrote her great-great-granddaughter, Eleanor Iselin Wade, for information. From Libby, Montana, Mrs. Wade replied that she had never heard mention of a ghost in connection with any house on the place except Bedford House itself, where she grew up. We quote from her letter:

There *is* an old family story of a gray shade of a lady which was seen by my great-grandmother, Mrs. William Jay, in the bedroom over the dining-room in Bedford House, and was also seen by two guests at a wide interval of time. There has never been any conjecture as to who she was. I have never seen with my eyes anything of this kind, but I have, since I was tiny, felt and heard very unusual presences. . . . I've always felt that all those great personalities who lived there, and some who only visited, have left their lasting spell, which in a subtle way the house has absorbed—even the gardens, barns and farms.[32]

Turning from such nebulous matter as ghosts to the more concrete matter of facts and votes, we set down a few as a condensed record of the way we lived in early post-Revolutionary days and as clews to later developments.

In 1785, April 5th, at the annual town meeting, it was Voted that from the 20th Day of August to the first Day of November No Ram shall run at Large. Any Person or Persons finding any Ram at Large within the said times may Geld the same att the Risque of the Owner. Voted that any Stone Hors that may be found Loose or at Liberty in the fields or highways from the first of April to the first of September may be Lawfully Put in Pound and kept in by the Pounder untill the owner Pay ten Shillings to the Person Pounding the same.[2]

In 1786, on the first Tuesday of April at the annual town meeting it was

Voted that the overseers of the poor bind out Leah Lock and Jonah Linsey on Tuesday Next and if they find any such stragler or Idle Person in the Course of the year they shall do the Like to them as to the above Named Persons.[2]

In 1790 the first United States census was taken, a report of which appears following that of a 1791 Bedford town meeting. It gives for the Township of Bedford a total of 2,470 souls, of which 38 were slaves.[2]

In 1790, March 18, we find the first mention of indenture in our town records. In this, James Burrell bound himself to Samuel Peck.[19]

In 1795, there is a record of the voluntary freeing of "Sarah Negro woman Slave belonging to Caleb Sands of the Town of Bedford . . . under fifty years of Age and of Sufficient Ability to provide for herself." [10]

In 1802, a Negro boy was bought from Benjamin Hays of Bedford for $200.00. His new masters, two gentlemen from Scarsdale, agreed to give him his freedom in ten years.[21]

In 1805, among the Town's expenditures for the poor were these items:

To: Sylvanus Reynolds [for keeping] John Indian—$10.50
To: Cornelius Miller for making a Coffen for J. Indian—$1.00
To: Joseph Miller for digging his Grave—$.60.[33]

References

1. Shonnard, Frederic & Spooner, W. W. *History of Westchester County.* New York, 1900, p. 526.
2. Bedford (N.Y.) Town Book IV, 1784-1841 (unpaged). MS. (At Bedford Town House)
3. Scharf, J. T. *History of Westchester County.* Philadelphia, 1886, v. 1, p. 474.
4. *Ibid.,* v. 1, p. 248.
5. Westchester County. Division of Land Records. Deeds. Liber I, pp. 268-69. MS. (At County Office Building, White Plains, N.Y.)
6. *Ibid.,* Liber I, pp. 219-20.
7. *Ibid.,* Liber L, p. 452.
8. *Ibid.,* Liber L, p. 394.
9. *Ibid.,* Liber L, p. 392.
10. *Ibid.,* Liber M, p. 120.
11. *Ibid.,* Liber X, pp. 367-68.
12. *Ibid.,* Liber X, pp. 369-70.
13. Taylor, Mrs. Theodore, Rowley, Mass. Personal communication.
14. South Salem (N.Y.) Town Book, 1784-1837, p. 106. MS.
(At the Westchester County Historical Society Library, White Plains, N.Y.)
15. Westchester County. Division of Land Records. Mortgages. Liber G, pp. 164-65. MS. (At County Office Building, White Plains, N.Y.)
16. Bedford (N.Y.) Voting records, 1799-1841 (unpaged). MS. (At Bedford Town House)
17. Bedford (N.Y.) Town Book III, 1727-1882, p. 202. MS. (At Bedford Town House)
18. *Ibid.,* p. 154.
19. *Ibid.,* p. 194.
20. *Ibid.,* p. 203.
21. *Ibid.,* p. 213.
22. Somers (N.Y.) Highway Commissioners' Reports. Undated entry between that for Mar. 26, 1806, and that for Mar. 27, 1810. In: Somers (N.Y.) Town Clerk's Book, 1788-1868. MS. (At Somers Town House)
23. Westchester County. Road Commissioners. Record of high-

ways. [New York?] 1714-95, p. 62. MS. (At the Westchester County Clerk's Office, Court House, White Plains, N.Y.)

24. Luccock, H. E. & Hutchinson, Paul. *The story of Methodism.* New York, 1949, pp. 153-55.

25. Moss, (Rev.) A. B. Letter to Mrs. H. S. Duncombe, Brooklyn, N.Y., Apr. 15, 1960. MS. (At the Katonah Village Library)

26. LaMonte, (Rev.) Thomas. Historical sketch of Katonah M. E. Church. In: *Feast of Lanterns,* Aug. 15, 1878.

27. Sloane, Eric. The mills of early America. In: *American Heritage,* October 1955, v. 6, pp. 104-07.

28. Luquer, T. T. P. *An historical sketch of St. Matthew's Church, Bedford, N.Y., 1694-1938.* [Katonah? 1938?] (unpaged).

29. MS notes taken by Mr. Lewis C. Rubenstein, Curator of History, Jay House, Katonah, from original MS letters as follows:
a. Jay, Peter A. Letter to his sister, Sept. 8, 1800.
b. Jay, John. Letters to his wife, May 17, 1801, and June 16, 1801.
c. Jay, John. Contract made with carpenters, Dec. 13, 1800. (In possession of the Special Collections Library, Columbia University)

30. Jay, Peter A. Letter to his father, New York, Mar. 16, 1799. (In possession of the Special Collections Library, Columbia University)

31. MS notes taken by Mr. Lewis C. Rubenstein, Curator of History, Jay House, Katonah, from the original MS letter from Sarah Livingston Jay to her husband, John Jay, July 21, 1799. (In possession of the Special Collections Library, Columbia University)

32. Wade, Mrs. C. Wanny. Letter to Mrs. H. S. Duncombe, Libby, Montana, June 18, 1959. MS. (In possession of Mrs. Duncombe, Katonah)

33. Bedford (N.Y.) Accounts of moneys expended for the maintainance of the poor, 1787-1845 (unpaged) MS. (At Bedford Town House)

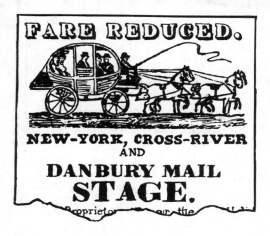

From advertisement of Gideon Reynolds in *Westchester Herald & Gazette,* Oct. 13, 1829. Collection of Mrs. Leonard H. Hall

CHAPTER VI

THE EARLY 1800'S

THE EARLY 1800's brought some innovations that connected our very self-contained rural areas with the world outside. One of these was the expansion of the postal system. At first the post came to northern Westchester by boat via the Hudson or the Sound and from there afoot or on horseback. After 1787 it began to go by stage. "Way mail" was picked up by the post rider along his route, at two cents a letter, and turned in to the next post office. At unofficial offices, often in stores, the letters might be kept in a box on the counter, to be gone through by people looking for their own mail or their friends'. The post office at Cherry Street doubtless began in this way. Squire Wood was appointed postmaster when it was officially recognized April 10, 1826.

Our earliest post office had been the one established in Bedford Village shortly before January 1, 1798, only the fourth post office in Westchester. Bedford was on the important highway between New York and Danbury, and a mail route was run on this during 1814-17 by S. Sellick, for which he received $119 quarterly for one round trip a week. Later on, 1828-32, Gideon Reynolds of Cross River carried this mail, operating post coaches six times a week and extending the service in 1832-36 to daily trips in four-horse coaches. Hachaliah Bailey of Somers, also with four-horse coaches, served Cherry Street and Whitlockville once to three times a week during 1832-36 on the Sing Sing to Somers route. Cantitoe received and sent mail once a week on a route from

79

Bedford to Southeast (now Brewster) operated by Edward Stears of Mt. Pleasant.

Postage in early days was high, and folk wrote only when necessary. Rates were based on the number of sheets and the distance travelled. An envelope constituted an additional sheet, and so it did not come into use till after 1845. Postal rates varied: in 1816 a single letter could be sent 30 miles for 6¢. Over 400 miles, the cost was 25¢. These rates continued until 1845.[1]

Another enlargement of our outlook came through increased publication and wider distribution of newspapers. The *Westchester Gazette & Peekskill Advertiser,* started in 1808, and the *Somers Museum,* started in 1809, brought to our doors a medium for advertising and an opportunity to read what was going on locally and, to a surprising degree, nationally and internationally. Carried over the new turnpike by a "good, faithful and active Post Rider,"[2] several of the *Museum's* 37 issues are still cherished in Katonah today.

The turnpikes came in answer to necessity if the interior of the county and state were to prosper. Along the Hudson and Sound there were docks. But to reach the market sloops that plied between these docks and New York City, miles of sometimes entirely impassable terrain had to be overcome. Quite a few township roads, especially those to the mills, had been constructed or improved after the war, but for lack of money they were given no surface except the dirt and mud which were also their bottom. County and state did little better. And so, except in fine weather it was often impossible to transport anything heavier than mail carried in saddle bags.

To alleviate this situation and also in the hopes of profit, no doubt, private turnpike companies began to spring up with the blessing and under the authority of the State Legislature. Groups of business men took over existing roads whenever possible, made connecting links between them and surfaced the whole. They charged toll at gates set at intervals along the routes.[7] The Croton Turnpike organized in 1807[8] passed near us, less than a mile from Veal's Ford at the foot of Cherry Street. From that time on until the coming of the railroad in 1847 we did a brisk trade with the sloop captains at Sing Sing through which the Turnpike ran. Some of our young men even bought sloops of their own, among them the Lyon brothers.[11]

Connecting Cherry Street with the Croton Turnpike were

a new bridge and road. From the Somers town clerk's book come the following entries:

> 1802, April 6th. voted for at Town Meeting for to raise fifty dollars to build a bridg across Croton River at Veal's ford now Grifen's ford.

> [Undated, except that it occurs between 1806 and 1810 entries.] A new [Highway] district beginning at the Turnpike runing easterly through the land of James Van Corland to the new bridg leading to Squire Wood's Mill.[27]

These two items interest us. They seem to indicate we had a bridge across the Croton prior to Woods Bridge and that Squire Wood was an independent mill owner before he went into partnership with John Burr Whitlock on the Cross River.

There was also a turnpike company organized in Bedford Township. Application was made to the State Legislature by two groups in December of 1809. The first group, consisting of Benjamin Hays, David Hobby, David Hobby, Jr., Robert Eames, Nathan Lockwood and Jesse Holly, proposed a turnpike beginning where the Post Road intersected the west line of the town of Ridgefield, running "to or near the Court House in Bedford from thence to the north line of the town of Greenwich in Conn., southerly of Col. David Hobby's house." [3]

The second group, Samuel B. Isaacs, Amos Canfield, Aaron Read, John Smith and Henry V. Kleeck, announced their intended application for a route "from Ridgefield line where the New York Stage Road leads into Salem" to Bedford Court House—past the house of Josiah Woolsey—to the house of Joseph Lyon in North Castle, thence down the Stage-Road to house of Jonathan Lyon, the school house by Daniel Tripp's, houses of John Smith and David Dayton to or near where the same Stage-Road leads into the corner of Conn.[4] This latter application apparently won out and by March 20, one sixth of the shares of the capital stock of the Bedford Turnpike Company was subscribed to, and a meeting of stockholders called. There we lose track of the Bedford group.

Turnpikes and news ended our era of almost complete self-dependence. True, women still spun and wove and farmers still produced for their own needs, but extras could be brought in from outside and surplus could be sold. Material things available to our small-income farmers increased. Now that roads were better, carriages "made in the latest style" and "elegant Riding Chairs" were advertised. Crockery and even nails could be sold reasonably. Mahogany was available to our local cabinet makers.[2]

A shadow thrown across this picture of increased comfort was that of impending war. Any farmer who subscribed to the *Museum* could read the latest Washington letter on international affairs from a member of Congress to a gentleman of Somers. He could read of the complex quarrels abroad which were bringing war nearer and nearer to our shores.

Ships arriving at New Orleans, Norfolk, Boston and New York brought from far places such as Rotterdam, Lisbon, Cadiz, Bayonne and London, news which could now be discussed around kitchen tables at Cherry Street, Cantitoe and Mt. Holly. Was Napoleon really insane as rumor had it? Would war, when it involved us, be against France or England? On a national level, what about the practical use of the torpedo for submarine explosion that was being considered?[5]

The growing tensions that led to the second war with England, unlike those that led to the Revolution, were well publicized in the homes of our inland farmers. They read on January 24th, 1810:

> A Bill has this day been introduced into Congress providing for equipping for immediate service our Navy; to raise 20,000 Volunteer Troops and to organize 100,009 militia, to be ready at a moment's warning. It is not the object of Congress to make war now, but to prepare in good earnest for an event which may very soon happen.[4]

John Jay at Bedford House, hoping still that war could be avoided, wished perhaps that the inflammatory words used at a Republican meeting at New Castle in March, 1810, had not so readily found print. Condensed they were as follows:

> Lawless violence and mercantile cupidity attempt to crush or confine our enterprise and industry, or insidiously attack our sacred independence. . . . This election will . . . show

. . . whether we are sunk so low as to crouch to the cruel disposition that attacks our sovereignity murders our citizens
and insults our government.[6]

The *Museum* ceased publication shortly thereafter but the
Westchester Gazette and Peekskill Advertiser and the *Westchester
and Putnam Gazette* remained [12] to carry news of continued
interference with our commerce, impressment of our seamen,
attacks on our frigates, "Chesapeake" and "President," and the
declaration of war. Between 1812 and 1814 the news was dis-
heartening for the most part, redeemed by the great naval vic-
tories of 1814.

Whether the war was necessary is not a conjecture for local
historians. Henry Clay felt it was, saying "England would do
everything to destroy us. Resolution and spirit are our only security." [18] Jay felt otherwise. To a friend he wrote, "In my opinion
the delaration of war was neither necessary, nor expedient, nor
seasonable." [19] Our conjecture and also our concern must remain
strictly on the local level.

War never came near enough to harass our civilian population,
but according to Joseph Barrett, "The war of 1812 found two
uniformed companies in town, one of cavalry and one of artillery. These both went, with drafts of the three militia companies
of the town, to the defense of the City of New York, then threatened by the British fleet, and were stationed at Brooklyn for
several months." [9]

We have tried without success to identify the cavalry and artillery companies. Our militia regiments were the 33rd, the 38th,
and the 139th of the 15th Brigade, Brigadier-General Pierre Van
Cortlandt commanding. The 38th attracted more of our northern
township men than the other two. It was to this that Abijah
Harris, Squire Wood, Stephen Newman, William Lyon, Caleb
Haight, David Olmsted, Jr., and John Burr Whitlock all belonged as officers at various times.[20] In 1817 Squire Wood became lieutenant-colonel of this regiment and thereafter the regiment was wont to meet at his home on Cherry Street for drill and
recreation.

To be realistic, we seem to have suffered little personal loss
and gained quite a few benefits from the War. Our greatest
gains stemmed from apprehensions felt by the State in the many
years of warning we had preceding it. The hazardous condition

of commerce influenced the Legislature to encourage domestic manufacture and agriculture by liberal patronage, loans and bounties.[13] Thus encouraged, our farm and mill products increased. Economically transported now via turnpike and water to city markets at New York, they brought excellent prices. Foreign competition was no longer a factor.

Along with encouragement to agriculture and industry, the State concerned itself with building a free, strong population. To this end it provided for a gradual freeing of slaves in the State[21] and became increasingly insistent on public education. The first attempt at this latter made in 1795 had failed, but in 1802 Governor George Clinton took up the matter again urging that one failure should not discourage further attempts.[14] Governor Morgan Lewis succeeding him was even more insistent on public education. In his message of November 6, 1804, he said,

> Common schools under the guidance of respectable teachers should be established in every Village and the indigent be educated at the public expense.[15]

In 1805 he went further, advocating a fund to support colleges as well as common schools by selling "unappropriated lands" which still existed in this state to the extent of 1,500,000 acres.[16] This apparently was done. In 1810 Governor Tompkins stated that the funds appropriated for common schools already produced an income of about twenty-six thousand dollars annually.[17]

When in 1812 State aid was again offered to any township provided it would put up an equal amount with the State,[10] The Town of Bedford decided to accept and elected as their school commissioners Benjamin Isaacs, Aaron Read and our own David Olmsted from Cherry Street.[22] As outlined in their report of August 27, 1813, these three gentlemen proceeded to divide the township into eleven school districts, and thus our common schools were established.

The cost of public education in the Township of Bedford for the year 1814 is given in the following notations:

> Feb. 7: by cash received from Ezra Clark, Collector, $144.78.
> April   by cash received from William Barker, Esq. given
>   by State, $144.78.[23]

The only district figures we have on hand for 1814 are those of District #7, Cherry Street. The amount reported by its trustee, John Banks, as spent that year was $12.27.[24]

Costs of public education were split. The Town's share was divided. Taxes on each district as a whole provided for building and repairs. The parents of attending children paid all costs of tuition.[25]

The regulations in the hiring of teachers were hazy on scholastic requirements, though undoubtedly respectability was a requirement. Sometimes these schools set up in 1813 may have been good, sometimes not, but at least they were with us to stay. Even indigent children, whose tuition costs had to be paid by the solvent parents of their classmates, had the opportunities and privileges of education. Attendance however was not compulsory until much later.[26]

References

1. Gemmill, John. Our post offices. Baldwin Place, N.Y., 1959. MS. (At the Katonah Village Library)
2. Somers Museum, Dec. 6, 1809.
3. Ibid., Dec. 20, 1809.
4. Ibid., Jan. 24, 1810.
5. Ibid., 1809-10.
6. Ibid., Mar. 21(?) 1810.
7. Griffin, E. F. Westchester County and its people. New York, 1946, v. 2, pp. 178-79.
8. Scharf, J. T. History of Westchester County. Philadelphia, 1886, v. 2, p. 472.
9. Ibid., v. 2, p. 600.
10. Ibid., v. 1, p. 474.
11. Advertisement by Stephen Lyon, Westchester Herald, Mt. Pleasant, N.Y., Apr. 6, 1819.
12. Redway, V. L. Short history and bibliography of Ossining newspapers, 1797-1951. Tarrytown, N.Y., 1951, pp. 21-22.
13. New York State. Governor. Messages from the Governors. Albany, 1909, v. 2, p. 658.
14. Ibid., v. 2, p. 512.
15. Ibid., v. 2, p. 551.
16. Ibid., v. 2, pp. 556-57.
17. Ibid., v. 2, p. 660.
18. Lossing, B. J. Pictorial field book of the War of 1812. New York, 1868, p. 223.
19. Monaghan, Frank. John Jay, defender of liberty. New York, 1935, p. 434.
20. New York State. Council of Appointment. Military minutes, 1783-1821. Albany, 1901-02, v. 2, pp. 1019; 1152; 1489; 1507.
21. French, A. P. History of Westchester County, New York. New York, 1925, v. 2, p. 834.
22. Bedford (N.Y.) Town Book III, 1727-1882, p. 7. MS. (At Bedford Town House)
23. Ibid., back section, p. 13.

24. *Ibid.*, back section, p. 12.
25. New York State. Superintendent of Common Schools. *Report made to the Legislature,
April 13, 1840.* Albany, 1840,
pp. 5; 10.
26. *Katonah Times,* Nov. 1, 1901.

27. Somers (N.Y.) Highway Commissioners' Reports. Undated
entry between that for Mar. 26,
1806, and that for Mar. 27,
1810. In: Somers (N.Y.) Town
Clerk's Book, 1788-1868. MS.
(At Somers Town House)

CHAPTER VII ·

CHERRY STREET, MECHANICVILLE, WHITLOCKVILLE

IT IS GENERALLY held that 1812 marks the decline of Cherry Street as a village and the reason given is that Wood and Whitlock, to enlarge their business, moved down the hill to the Cross River valley and established a store and mills there. Actually, this is oversimplification. The move down the hill did not seriously affect Cherry Street for many years after that.

Squire Wood and John Burr Whitlock were in business for a time together on Cherry Street and for a time they were partners in the mills on the Cross River, but jointly and singly they engaged in many other ventures. They were not the inseparables we are prone to consider them. Prior to his merger with Whitlock, Squire Wood owned a mill and also a store. An 1808-09 ledger[1] of the latter business carries the names of Cherry Street residents although the flyleaf is inscribed "Squire Wood, Mt. Pleasant." Soon afterwards Whitlock must have joined Wood in this Cherry Street store. The following advertisement dated Bedford, April 4th, appeared in the *Somers Museum* of April 25, 1810:

> In the meantime they would suggest to those persons who are indebted to them, the propriety of closing their Accounts previous to the time of their removal; as the Books and Papers

87

will be removed to Mount Pleasant, as also the Accomptant
who wrote them.

N.B. The Business will hereafter be conducted at the Stand
formerly occupied by Wood & Whitlock under the Firm of
P. and C. Haight, where those who are indebted to the Firm
of Wood and Whitlock, can be attended to for settlement
until the first day of May next.[2]

In 1811, possibly to bring son and son-in-law back from Mt.
Pleasant, Thaddeus and Grace Burr Whitlock deeded them land
east of Cherry Street in the valley of the Cross River on which
they built their mills. There was a new mill dam already on the
property and a bridge across the Cross River.[3] A good sound
business venture it must have seemed to the older generation,
as indeed it turned out.

There was no holding our young men to just one line of business however. Squire Wood was in a side business on Cherry
Street in saddling and store-keeping with Caleb Haight and
Moses Marshall until 1819.[4] He was part owner of two market
sloops that plied between Sing Sing and New York in 1822.[5]
Wood and Whitlock were jointly involved with Henry Harris
in a partnership at Sing Sing that wasn't terminated until 1818,[4]
at which time creditors were asked to settle accounts with Wood
and Whitlock at the store of Whitlock and Smith at Mechanic-
Ville! [6] This was the original name of the new little settlement
that grew up around the mills.

The mills, because they had steady customers coming to them,
attracted other enterprises to settle nearby, but this did not mean
a general exodus from Cherry Street. The two settlements co-
existed amiably, the older remaining the more important for
many years. When, in 1826, a post office was first established in
our northern part of the township, it was located at and named
Cherry Street. It had as first postmaster Squire Wood and was
used by both settlements until 1832.[13] In July of '32 the hamlet
down the hill, still known as Mechanicville as late as 1830,[14]
was given a post office as "Whitlocks." This name was changed
to "Whitlockville" in November.[13] William Silkman, its first postmaster, had moved from Cross River in the 1820's and set up a
hat business in this growing young community.[15] The Cherry
Street post office was discontinued in 1837, so we may presume
that by that date its volume of business no longer warranted one.
While we are on the subject of post offices, we may as well men-

tion that Cantitoe was given one in 1834, which continued till 1846. Samuel Lyon was its first postmaster, succeeded by Arnell F. Dickinson.[13]

Because Mrs. Avery was the first to write of Whitlockville-née-Mechanicville in any detail, we should like to republish parts of her description of it:

> In 1812, Wood & Whitlock, determining to enlarge their business operations, came down the hill from Cherry Street to the Cross River Valley and built a grist mill, now the property of Cox, Todd & Avery. Two carpenters from Newburg named Hutchings were employed upon the building. It has proved to have been well and substantially built. The site is an admirable one, the dam setting back the water for nearly a mile, forming one of the finest water powers in the county. . . . The dwelling known as the Warren Whitlock house was the old Whitlock homestead, and the lane leading to it was part of the old road. Years before the advent of the mill, a store had been built for a son of 'Squire Olmsted of Cherry Street, in the yard on the place now occupied by Horace Searles by Judge William Miller. This property was then owned by him, and was the home of his son Samuel. His grandson John A., father of Joseph O. Miller, afterward sold it to Gideon Reynolds. About the same time, the store was moved to Whitlockville and was a part of the old Whitlock store. A new store was built later, which is still standing and in a good state of preservation. . . .
>
> After the founding of the mill, the road was cut through from Cherry Street and a bridge built over the Croton by Col. Wood. The business outlook was promising. Farmers "went to mill" and with their wives and daughters came from "far and near" to trade at the store. It was said that Whitlock "kept everything from a cambric needle to a crowbar." In time, like a great many other old-fashioned country stores, it became a place of resort where all sorts of subjects, both national and local, were discussed. . . .
>
> Among the early settlers was Noah Smith, who built a house about half way up the hill. For a while, he was in partnership with Whitlock, the firm being known by the name of Whitlock & Smith. Then, severing his connection with the business, he went upon the hill and built a store opposite his residence. After his son Harvey became of

sufficient age to enter into business, a new building was
erected on the corner opposite Whitlock's, which for many
years displayed the sign, "N. Smith & Son." The store on the
hill was converted into a dwelling, and it is now the property
of Mrs. C. Flewellyn. After the death of Harvey W. Smith,
his store was moved a few rods west and has since been the
residence of Mrs. McCall.[16]

By " 'Squire Olmsted" we presume Mrs. Avery meant Major
David Olmsted, as his son was a brother-in-law of Samuel Miller.[17] The road "cut through from Cherry Street" is our present
Whitlockville Road. As laid out in 1817[18] it continued down a
steep hill from where it now ends at Woods Bridge Road and
bridged the Cross River just below the falls and mills at a spot
now deep under the water. By "a bridge built over the Croton
by Col. Wood," Mrs. Avery meant of course Woods Bridge. The
iron bridge which we use today at approximately the same spot
is at least the third built there. In 1904[19] it replaced the bridge,
which was constructed in 1869, also of iron,[20] which in turn had
replaced a wooden one. Because most of the old bridges are given
birth dates in town records, we became stubborn about docu-
menting the original bridge when we found no mention of it in
Bedford, South Salem or Somers records. No town money was
voted for it by any of the adjacent townships benefiting from
its use. Therefore we believe with Mrs. Avery that it was a private
enterprise on the part of Squire Wood, later a lieutenant-colonel
of the 38th Regiment Militia.[21] As for its date, both Somers and
South Salem (now Lewisboro) altered roads or built new ones
in late 1814 or early 1815 that would have been necessary to
the use of it. The Somers road, approved July 20, 1814, ran from
the Turnpike to the Croton River "30 rods above the place
called Vail's Ford."[22] The South Salem alteration completed by
May 4th, began "oposit the Intended Butment of the Intended
New Bridge."[23]

Across this bridge Squire Wood carted freight from Sing Sing
for John Jay on October 18, 1817, and Ebenezer Mead carted
three kegs of nails for the store on the 27th. It was over it in
reverse that Jacob Dickinson carted buckwheat flour from the
mill to the Hudson on November 11th.[24]

The accounts of the mill and store were kept in the same ledger
and Wood and Whitlock charged and credited themselves as
well as their customers in it. As people's living habits are re-

flected in what they buy and sell, we should like to enlarge on Mrs. Avery's "from a cambric needle to a crowbar." Items on the debit side of the ledger include crockery, buttons, Crawley steel, shoes, nails, children's spelling and instruction books, candles, almanacs, harness, Nicaragua wood, laudanum, indigo, flour, tobacco, rum, beer, brandy, silk thread, pearl-ash, goose feathers, eggs, mackerel, gingham, muslin, cambric, powder, shot, jews harps, medicine, smoothing irons, window glass and window papers, shovels, tongs, paregoric, paint, flax seed, tea, and milling charges.

On the credit side are items bought from the farmers of the neighborhood: flax seed, mustard seed, rye, buckwheat, corn, cider, eggs, butter, potatoes, apples, meat, peaches, chestnuts, walnuts, goose feathers, muskrat and mink skins, fish and stockings. On the credit side also are many notations of cartage money due those bringing items from Sing Sing to the store and one very interesting entry that puzzles us. On October 21, 1817, John B. Whitlock credits himself as follows:

C. by boarding Workmen since 3rd July 1815 328 days @ 2/ to 26, Sept. 1817, 32-6-0.

We do not wish to draw a conclusion from this but we wonder if these men could have been working on the construction of the mills?

The ledger kept by Jabez and Henry Robertson at their store at Bedford Center in 1815-16[25] shows about the same type of merchandise with the addition of one Parkinson's hymn book and quinine. Both ledgers show an amazing amount of liquor sold, the Robertson one carrying almost two pages headed "Liquor for the Meeting House." Both ledgers indicate that slaves were still owned: "By his black boy" followed many an entry. Both ledgers show that the stores acted in the capacity of banks on occasion. There is even one entry in the Robertson book: "Squire Wood, D. To cash lent $24.00."

These early stores led to a new form of enterprise called the "market wagon." After his marriage in 1822, Henry Robertson ran one to Tarrytown and Cos Cob.[26] The Lyon brothers, John, William and Stephen, were also in the market wagon business. Stephen had his own dock and sloop at Sing Sing.[7] Undoubtedly local produce also went to Squire Wood's sloops, the "General Delavan" and "Volunteer" at Sing Sing.[5] The procedure was for the driver to pick up farm produce and poultry all along his route for shipment to New York. Chickens and geese hung squawking and honking in baskets beneath the wagons; butter and eggs traveled inside. On his return journey, the driver left off articles that he had been commissioned to buy or that had been ordered from New York. There must have been excitement in the heart of many a farm wife while she waited the return of the market wagon and wondered if the city finery she'd ordered would be worth the butter and eggs that were its price.[27]

We have very little record of social affairs of this period. There was a "Horse and Watch Fair" held at the "Store of Andrew Heister, near Squire Wood's" September 4, 1819,[8] and Cherry Street planned a Fourth of July celebration in 1820.[9] There were doubtless similar celebrations in our other areas but we haven't come across them in print.

As material needs show themselves up in store ledgers and spiritual needs in church records, civic needs record themselves in organizations. Those drawing members from our northern part of the township prior to 1820 were the following:

> Society for the Suppression of Horse Stealing[10]
> Westchester Auxiliary Bible Society[11]
> Society for Suppression of Vice[28]
> Westchester Agricultural Society.[12]

References

1. Wood, Squire, & Co. [Ledger] Bedford, N.Y. Oct. 3, 1808-Mar. 29, 1809. MS. (In possession of Mrs. Lucy Brady Brown, Goldens Bridge, N.Y.)
2. *Somers Museum,* Apr. 25, 1810.
3. Westchester County, Division of Land Records, Deeds. Liber X, p. 370. MS. (At County Office Building, White Plains, N.Y.)
4. *Westchester Herald & Farmers Register,* Mt. Pleasant, N.Y. Feb. 17, 1818; *Westchester Herald,* Mt. Pleasant, N.Y. June 16, 1818; May 18, 1819.
5. *Westchester Herald,* Mt. Pleasant, N.Y., June 25, 1822.

6. *Ibid.,* Nov. 17, 1818.
7. *Ibid.,* Apr. 6, 1819.
8. *Ibid.,* Aug. 24, 1819.
9. *Ibid.,* June 20, 1820.
10. *Ibid.,* Nov. 10, 1818.
11. *Ibid.,* Apr. 20, 1819.
12. *Ibid.,* Mar. 30, 1819.
13. Gemmill, John. Our post offices. Baldwin Place, N.Y., 1959. MS. (At the Katonah Village Library)
14. *Westchester Herald and Putnam Gazette,* Mt. Pleasant, N.Y. Feb. 23, 1830.
15. Kelly, K. B. Silkman family. Katonah, 1959. MS. (At the Katonah Village Library)

16. Avery, O. T. *Historical sketch of Katonah*. Katonah, 1896. (Unpaged)

17. Westchester County. Surrogate's Office. Wills. Liber K, p. 324. MS. (At the County Court House, White Plains, N.Y.)

18. Bedford (N. Y.) Town Book III, 1727-1882, p. 221, recto. MS. (At the Bedford Town House)

19. *Katonah Times,* June 24 and Nov. 25, 1904.

20. *Republican,* Sing Sing, N.Y. Oct. 14, 1869.

21. New York State. Council of Appointment. *Military minutes, 1783-1821.* Albany, 1901-02, v. 2, p. 1814.

22. Somers (N.Y.) Highway Commissioners. Reports, 1797-1865. July 20, 1814. MS. (At the Somers Town House)

23. South Salem (N.Y.) Record Book, 1784-1837. May 4, 1815. MS. (At the Westchester County Historical Society Library, White Plains, N.Y.)

24. Whitlock, John Burr. Store ledger. Salem, N.Y., 1817. Oct. 18, Oct. 27, Nov. 10, 1817. MS. (In possession of Mr. C. S. Benedict, Katonah)

25. Robertson, Jabez & Henry. Store ledger. Bedford, N.Y., 1815-16. MS. (In possession of Mrs. W. A. Kelly, Katonah)

26. Scharf, J. T. *History of Westchester County*. Philadelphia, 1886, v. 2, p. 591.

27. French, A. P. *History of Westchester County*. New York, 1925, v. 2, p. 645-46.

28. Tuckerman, Bayard. *William Jay and the constitutional movement for the abolition of slavery*. New York, 1893, p. 10.

FROM NEW YORK TO PEEKSKILL,
AND INTERMEDIATE PLACES.
Fare from New York to Peekskill, 50 cents
To all intermediate places, 37 1-2
The new & elegant low pressure steamboat

John Jay,

Advertisement, *Westchester Herald,* June 29, 1830.
Collection of Mrs. Leonard H. Hall

Advertisement in *Hudson River Chronicle*, 1838.
Collection of Mrs. Leonard H. Hall

CHAPTER VIII

DAYS BEFORE THE RAILROAD

BEGINNING IN the eighteen twenties and thirties, several coming events threw their shadows before them, giving warning that they were about to change our lives.

The movement against slavery wasn't exactly a new idea to the Jays of Cantitoe. Although John Jay owned slaves, he had long been an opponent of the system and had served as president of an abolition and manumission society formed in New York in 1785.[1] In New York State, the law of 1817 urged by Governor Tompkins, provided that every "Negro, mulatto or mustee within this State, born after the 4th day of July, 1799, shall, from and after the 4th day of July, 1827, be free."[2] From 1817 on, manumission became a general practice around here but it wasn't just a question of turning a slave loose. An owner was liable for his support unless freed of the responsibility. In the *Westchester Herald and Farmers Register* of Mt. Pleasant, the following notice appeared June 23, 1818:

94

Notice: The estate of Nicholas Haight, late of Bedford, deceased, being liable to support a certain black man by the name of Amos, who is apt to wander from said estate— therefore all persons are forbid harboring said negro man.[4]

James Raymond of Bedford in freeing his man Prince had to have the approval of the overseers of the poor, who certified:

Now therefore we do hereby certify in pursuance of the said Act that we have inspected said servant and that he appears to be over the age of twenty-one years (to wit) of the age of twenty-three years and eight months and of sufficient ability to provide for himself. Witness our hands this thirteenth day of March one thousand eight hundred & twenty-seven.

Joseph Barrett
William Fowler[5]

In 1835, William Jay's *Inquiry* was published. From then on, the fight was never abandoned in this township until national abolition was accomplished.

New York City's need for water was not a new development either. In pre-Revolutionary times, New Yorkers got their water from wells dug in their streets. In 1776, a reservoir was built but it didn't take care of the needs of an increased population. The Revolution halted a search for a better supply but at its end, spurred on by epidemics, the search was resumed. In 1798, the Bronx and Passaic rivers were considered as sources but discarded.[6]

In 1832, De Witt Clinton recommended the Croton River saying:

This supply may be considered as inexhaustible, as it is not at all probable that the city will ever require more water than it can provide.[7]

These words doomed the flourishing little village of Whitlockville, the not-yet-born village of Old Katonah, and the prosperous farms and mills in the river basin above the present Cross River dam.

An act to provide for supplying the City of New York with pure and wholesome water was passed on May 2, 1834, and in 1835 New Yorkers voted to bring the water of the Croton to

New York.[8] In 1837, construction began on Croton Dam. The building of this dam was not entirely without incident as can be seen from the letter of John Silkman, of Cross River, to his brother, dated January 11, 1841:

> Yours of the 28th came to hand last evening. It has been a long time on way in all probability this will be as long as there has been a grate freshit in this country and carryd off almost all of the bridges the damage on the croton river is immense perhaps from 3 to 5 hundred thousand dollars it has swept of almost every bridge from John Owens to the hudson. . . . The dam they made 2 or three miles below for rises was finished about 2 months since and ponded within ½ of a mile of Woods bridge Grate part of the water was very deep from 10 to 50 feet in Common times and you must think how that large pond froze over very thick and then a sudden change of weather and 2 days of rain and the last ½ day after the snow got all reddy to run which was about 2 feet on the level the wind blew very heavy gale from the south which hasend it still more the river being full of ice. . . . Bridges came down on this large pond which is said to be about 5 miles long and a way went the dam and guess what followed houses and mills, wire factory, and bridges swept clean to the hudson it is reported that 3 lives were lost a woman one that was taken of a tree and 2 men clim one tree and the ice broke the tree and they were lost. . . . Reynolds had to leave his house the water being most to the chamber flore. . . . The dam gave way about 3 at nite and people was thare watching and ran and gave notice to the mill. . . . He thought his house would stand it was in bed I believe sick but they tuck him right out by forse and his house and mill went in 5 minutes with 500 dolars in specie in the house nothing saved of course.[11]

However, despite setbacks, on July 4, 1842, Croton water flowed from Croton Lake into the reservoir on Murray Hill.[3] There was a big celebration and everyone was happy. Cherry Street and Whitlockville, about six miles to the northeast of the dam, probably forgot the whole thing in the course of months. New York had its water. We had ours. There seemed no conflict. The only hardship felt perhaps by Whitlockville folk was the loss of shad which before the erection of the dam had come up the Croton to that point.[12] If anyone had told them that around fifty-five years later, their beautiful little village would be drowned in a further quest for city water, they probably wouldn't have listened. As for the village of Old Katonah, it was still just a cinder in the eye of the New York and Harlem Railroad.

In the late eighteen-twenties, there were several railways operating for short distances in other states. In New York City, two companies became interested in running tracks north. The New York & Albany had the more ambitious plan of connecting those two cities. The plan of the New York & Harlem was less far reaching. In fact, it reached only from 23rd Street to the Harlem River and its locomotion was horsepower. The New York & Harlem was incorporated in 1831; the New York & Albany, in 1832. Both ran into structural and financial difficulties. As this is a local history and not one of railroading, let us just quote that in 1838, the New York & Albany, "unable to carry out the provisions of its charter . . . surrendered its rights in Westchester County to the New York & Harlem Company." [13] This latter company, overcoming its difficulties and extending its original intentions, began to push its tracks up towards us.

While railroads, reservoirs and the Civil War were creeping closer, daily life went on as usual. Children were born and old people died. Over at Cantitoe, Arnell Frost Dickinson was born in 1818, and William Henry Robertson in 1823. Former Chief Justice John Jay died in 1829, and his grandson, John Jay, was born in 1817. In Whitlockville, old Thaddeus Whitlock died in 1823. Major David Olmsted of Cherry Street followed him the next year.

On the west end of the Mt. Holly Road, Stephen Holly Miller was born in 1823. On the top of the hill the second Jonah Holly, his cousin, was born in 1824. In 1823 Increase Miller, on the North Salem Road at the northern boundary of Bedford Township, gave land just over the line in Salem that year for a Methodist church, later known as Herman Chapel, a graveyard and a school.[14] It was in this graveyard that many Merritts and Millers living in the Northeast Corner were buried thereafter.

The first church in our northern area was the Methodist Episcopal Church built on the Whitlockville-to-Cherry Street Road in 1837. In his "Historical Sketch" the Reverend Thomas LaMonte, the pastor from 1872 to 1875, wrote:

> In the summer of 1836, a school house was built in Whitlockville. In November the few Methodists in the place began to hold Thursday evening prayer meetings in it. About the

same time, two zealous Methodist laymen from Peekskill, Thomas Miller and Abraham Ellis, were visiting some friends in the neighborhood. On Sunday morning, they attended a prayer meeting in Cherry Street, which was a season of spiritual power. At the close of the meeting, it was decided to hold another in the Whitlockville school house in the evening. Of this meeting these two visiting brethren were leaders. The Divine presence was greatly felt, and an opportunity was given to sinners to seek Christ. Some six or more at once embraced the opportunity, and Walter Lyon, who was present, said, "Now I think we shall get a Church here." This was the beginning of "The Great Revival," at it was called, and it deserved the name, for it was probably the greatest religious revival, everything considered, the place has ever known.

These two laymen remained and continued the meetings for a few evenings until the circuit preachers, Alonzo F. Silleck and George L. Fuller, who had been notified, came and entered upon the good work, which they prosecuted with great zeal for several weeks. The whole region was deeply moved, and more than one hundred and fifty professed conversion; the larger part of whom joined the M.E. Church. Some fell away; probably less than one hundred were ever received into full membership.

The principal workers in this revival were Walter Lyon, Ozias Nash, Norman W. Miller, Samuel Benedict, Warren Whitlock, and some others worthy of mention.

Towards the spring of 1837, the question of building a church in the place began to be seriously discussed. Preliminary meetings were held in the school house, and in an upper room of Warren Whitlock's mill. At length an organization was formed and the first board of trustees was elected, consisting of the following: Walter S. Lyon, Norman W. Miller, Joseph Wilson, Joel W. Miller and Noah Smith. A subscription was started and headed by Walter S. Lyon and Joseph Wilson with a hundred dollars each. A site was procured; the contract let; and the M.E. Church built in the summer and fall of 1837. Its total cost is said to have been not far from two thousand dollars.[15]

Fare was reduced on the New York, Cross River and Danbury mail-stage in 1829. Sloops on the Hudson were in competition with steamboats. Harvey Wood, son of Squire, was running a lottery and exchange office at Cherry Street in 1826. This was a "Literature Lottery." His advertisements asked:

> What can be more transporting than for a person to pay only five shillings and obtain more than two thousand dollars!! [16]

In 1829, Dr. Seth Shove of Warren, Connecticut, was traveling through our countryside on horseback. Engaged to be married, he was looking for a place to start a practice. At Cherry Street, he stopped at the house of Squire Wood, listened to Wood's often quoted remark about that village being "the hub" of the surrounding countryside,[23] and decided to settle there. Dr. Shove became a dearly beloved figure as doctor and dentist[24] and public-spirited friend. His fees were modest, the distances he traveled, long. Two and a half dollars was his usual price for delivering a baby. A visit near home was fifty cents, one at a distance, seventy-five. We often hear about "horse and buggy doctors." Dr. Shove sometimes galloped cross country to a patient in emergency! Many young men studied under him. Among them were Dr. J. Francis Chapman, who married his daughter, Irene, and Dr. Jared G. Wood, great-grandson of Dr. William Wood. Dr. Shove became a member of the County Medical Society and later the Croton Medical and Surgical Union. He gave continuous valuable service to each, as well as to the State Medical Society.[25] The need for this organization was great. Previous to its founding, there had been no license necessary for the practice of medicine in New York. Thereafter, the required licensing was implemented through county societies and in 1813, their legal corporate status was established "for the purpose of regulating the practice of physic and surgery in this state." [25] It was high time and we fear our own society was not strict enough. Laudanum was sold with no more ado than goose feathers by Messrs. Wood and Whitlock.

From a cultural standpoint, the "Franklin" or "Whitlockville Literary Association" founded in 1841 was nearest Dr. Shove's heart. After four years, when this organization began to die of inertia, he tried to keep it alive, putting such thought and energy in his effort that had it been a human patient, it would surely have survived. He even procured for it an "Electrical Machine." [25]

This society fostered lectures, subscribed to periodicals, had a committee on literature and started a small museum, "its collection of the rare and curious consisting of upwards of 100 different specimens." [26] Except for Arnell F. Dickinson and John A. Lyon, of Cantitoe, this society drew its members mostly from the Cherry Street and Whitlockville areas.[23]

Over near Cantitoe, young William H. Robertson promoted the Literary Fraternity of Union Academy in 1840. He was then seventeen years old. This society went in for debating and the subjects of discussion show what the young were concerned with in that era. We list a few:

Were the whites justified in taking possession of America, as they did?

Has Congress a right to abolish slavery in the District of Columbia?

Should the application lately made by the Roman Catholics to the common council of the city of New York for their proportion of the common school fund have been granted?

Has the love of money greater influence over the mind of man than the love of women?

Was Great Britain justifiable in banishing Napoleon to the Island of St. Helena?

This society came to an end in March, 1841. The division of its members on the subject of admitting ladies seems to have led to discord. At the meeting of March 10, most of the minutes concern the expulsion of members.[27]

In October of the same year, the Cantatoe Lyceum was founded, with Robertson again secretary. Its object was "the obtainment of useful knowledge." Its charter members were Arnell F. Dickinson, William H. Robertson, Hezekiah Miller and John A. Lyon. This society met in the schoolhouse in District No. 6. Its last minutes are dated February 28, 1842.[28]

Our social conscience in the eighteen-thirties and forties was strong. Temperance as well as abolition had a champion in William Jay. Temperance and reform of the almshouses were the particular concerns of Arnell F. Dickinson. Both men were interested in the advancement of agriculture and the betterment of schools as well.

Temperance organizations formed were:

Westchester County Temperance Society, 1829.[29]
Temperance Societies formed in our local School Districts in 1834.[30]

Drink was considered such a directly contributing factor to pauperism that tavern license fees and fines went to the support of the poor[31] and an amendment was proposed to a bill being introduced in the Senate making it penal to sell intoxicating drinks to paupers.[32]

While slavery was at an end in our state as of 1827, a practice not very different from slavery continued. This was that of taking children from the County Almshouse to work on farms. We are told by his granddaughter that until Arnell F. Dickinson became county overseer of the poor in 1845 and initiated a reform, children sent to the almshouse were not registered.[33] They were taken out by anyone wanting unpaid labor and their names and those of the families taking them were lost forever. That a county aroused about Negro slavery had unconcern about the far less responsible ownership of white children seems incredible, but it was so.

Dickinson's interest in our schools was also constructive. One improvement he made in his own district was the purchase of chairs and desks to replace the old-time benches.[34] He also lent support to a Teachers Association which died for lack of interest on the part of others.[35] We were not ready yet for such a forward-thinking plan. Special training for teachers was still nonexistent. In fact, the State superintendent of common schools in his report to the Legislature in 1840, stated he saw no use or profit in the establishment of normal schools.[36]

A typical teacher's certificate of the time is the one that follows:

> I do hereby certify that I have examined Elizabeth A. Robertson and do believe that she is well qualified in respect of moral character, learning and ability to instruct a common school in this town for one year from the date hereof.[37]

This was signed by John S. Bates, "Town Supt. of Common Schools." Miss Robertson, daughter of Town Supervisor Henry D. Robertson, sister of William H. Robertson, and future wife of Arnell F. Dickinson, was twenty years old at the time. She walked the two and a half miles from her home at Cantitoe to teach at the Mt. Holly School and was paid the magnificent sum of two dollars a month. She saved all this and bought a teapot. As an example of school management and budgeting, we will use District No. 8, the school she taught. In 1843, its trustees were Stephen Holly, Daniel Bouton and James Miller. Their budget provided $26.88 for payment of teachers, which they exceeded by $1.12, and $6.71 for the school library.[38] Heat, light, janitor service, buses, etc., were not items on the budget, nor were text-books, which were supplied by the parents.

For $34.71 fifty-two children received schooling that year for varying lengths of time as their parents could spare them from farm work. The term was forty-four weeks, but five pupils attended less than eight months, twelve less than six months, twenty-four less than four months, and eleven less than two months. Figuring the total time put in, we reach a ten-month year attended by an average of twenty-three children at $1.52 per head. As an interesting comment only, and not as a comparison, in 1961-62 the cost of educating one child in Union Free School District No. 1 for the school year will be $974.00.

In the years that the Committee on Literature of the Franklin Society was recommending such books as *Philip in Search of a Wife* by a "Gentleman Butterfly," and frowning on *Barnaby Rudge* and *Nicholas Nickleby*,[23] it is interesting to note what the children of School District No. 8 had in their library in 1842. These are a few of the volumes:

Life and Works of Dr. Franklin
The Farmer's Instruction
The Persuits of Knowledge under Difficulties
Animal Magnetism and Philosophy
The Elephant and her Existence in a Moral State
Applications of the Science of Mechanics
An Attempt to Reach the North Pole by W. E. Parry
Life of Oliver Goldsmith
Life before the Mast
History of Lost Greenland
Napoleons Expedition to Russia[38]

Outside our local areas but of interest to them during these years were the following:

1822 The New York and Sharon (Conn.) Canal Company gave notice they intended to apply to the State Legislature for permission to make a canal from Sharon, Connecticut, to the City of New York or the tidewaters of the Hudson River at or near Sing-Sing. In our area, this was to run from Goldens Bridge

This covered railroad bridge spanned the Cross River
south of Old Katonah after 1847.

This Old Cantitoe Schoolhouse stood on east side of Route 22 south of Cantitoe
Corners. A later schoolhouse on same site is now the property of Furman V. Gaines.

Courtesy of Mrs. Charles G. Mead

CIVIL WAR VETERANS

Picture taken at a G.A.R. reunion, about 1915. Identified are: bottom row from left, first Asbury Elliott; middle row from left, second James Tuttle, fourth Edgar Hitt, seventh Charles Fisher; top row from left, second Jerry Turner, fifth E. Wilton Brown, M.D.

River Road, Old Katonah, led west to Whitlockville.
The Cross River in foreground and A. F. Avery's house in background.

Palmer Avenue, Old Katonah, ran north from the River Road.
Left to right: residence of Dr. J. F. Chapman, Presbyterian Manse,
residence of Dr. W. J. Carpenter.

Presbyterian Church on left and Methodist on right
seen from Old Katonah looking southwest across the Cross River

St. Mary's Roman Catholic Church, Old Katonah, was on a rise above
the Cross River, west of the southern end of Railroad Avenue

Courtesy of R. Benson Ray

South Street School, west of the Cross River was occupied in 1862. As shown here it is remodeled into home of F. W. Gorham who is seen on porch with his wife.

Courtesy of Katonah Village Library

Palmer Avenue School, Old Katonah, was built in 1883 and burned in 1893.

The Titicus Cycle Club was active around 1890.
Mrs. Charles A. Whitlock, woman on extreme right in front row.
Mr. Whitlock, center of rear row, 4th man from left

Summer boarders at the A. F. Avery home on River Road, Old Katonah,
enjoying the popular game of croquet in the 1880's.

Station platform, Old Katonah.

Courtesy of Mrs. F. H. William

The Searles' boarding house, one of the Whitlockville's most hospitable homes, was moved to Valley Road in New Katonah. Torn down in 1957, its site is now occupied by St. Mary's new elementary school. Left to right: Horace E. Searles, Agnes Searle Collard, Mrs. Searles, Edwina Searles (Mrs. F. H. Williams), Mr. Jardin (a boarder), Miss Anna Waterbury. Child, Wallace Searles

Courtesy of Katonah Village Library

In 1890 the Katonah Silk Company, a ribbon mill located east of the tracks in Old Katonah

to the junction of Cross and Beaver Dam Rivers and then proceed southwesterly along Muddy Brook. The canal was never constructed, although interest in this and alternate routes went on for several years.[17] In 1825 railways were suggested as more practical and cheaper.[18]

1823 Notification was made on January 7 by James Fish, Tyler Fountain, Oliver Green, Stephen Ferris, Henry Clark, Squire Wood, Stephen Knowlton, that they intended to apply to the State for an act "to sell and dispose of Court House and Jail in White Plains and Court House in Bedford and for the erection of a single Court House, Jail, and Fire Proof Clerk's Office (at or as near the centre of said County as a site can conveniently be obtained)." [19]

This move did not meet with unanimous favor. An opposition meeting was held in the town of North Castle on February 5.[20] The two county seats were continued until 1870.[41]

1825-29 State Prison erected at Sing-Sing, using prison labor.[40]

1828 County Almshouse opened at Knapp's Corners.[9]

1839 The Farmers' and Drovers' Bank of Somers was organized. This was the first bank to serve our area.[21]

1839 Notice dated Bedford, December 21, tells of the intended application to the Legislature for passage of a law dividing the County of Westchester into two counties, the division to be made at the southern boundary lines of the towns of Mount Pleasant and North Castle.[22] This plan failed.

1840 The name of our neighbor township, South Salem, was changed to Lewisboro in honor of John Lewis who gave $10,000 to establish a fund in maintenance of the town's public schools.[10] As in 1836 a new school district, combining No. 11 of South Salem and No. 7 of Bedford, had been made,[39] this fund was beneficial to Bedford also.

Of interest to us, and undoubtedly to their parents, were the births of Joseph Barrett and Ophelia Todd Avery in 1840. It may have been coincidence or it may have been the stars that made them both historians of this area.

During this period, we find many references to the "General Training" days of the Militia. The boys really seem to have enjoyed themselves. As Colonel A. H. Lockwood wrote in urging Arnell F. Dickinson to accept the post of sergeant major: "the expence of equipping is but a trifle and the Staff is the most pleasant way of doing military duty." Their officers for 1836 were:

Alsop H. Lockwood, Colonel
C. M. Ferris, Lieutenant Colonel
Samuel Gardner, Major
Joseph Brundage, Adjutant
Alfred B. Mead, Quartermaster
C. W. Seeley, Paymaster
Seth Shove, Surgeon[42]

Mrs. Avery's *Sketch* tells of a choir at Whitlockville and of donation parties where people traveled for miles to bring offerings to the parsonage. On July 4th, 1842, the Whitlockville Literary Association held a "purely intellectual repast" in the "Oaken Grove" belonging to Anthony M. Merritt, with the Society's new banner floating overhead and the Sunday School singing an original national hymn prepared for the occasion.[43]

We also come across accounts of a few purely social activities. As a glimpse of the social doings and vocabulary of the younger set, we give the following letters. In fairness to the writers, who did not intend to become our collaborators, we have deleted names. The first is from a youth at Cantitoe to a friend at the Quaker Hill Boarding School:

Cantitoe January 31st 1837

Most Esteemed
Sir
It is with pleasure that I now Find yours of the 16th at Hand which was not received untill the 24th and now take this oppurtunity to announce to you that so Far from Having forgotten or weaned my affections from you sir while absent from our social circle that it has Been with sentiments of Deep regret when in company with the rest of our good Friends to not find you saiten like there also. . . . I am pleased to Hear that You and numbers of others are endeavouring to improve the mind and hope that your efforts may be crowned with success—— And as to shine up it Has got to Be so much the fashion that I often times am put to my trumps For the want of Your assistance—— the next time

you see Sue For me pray ask Her How Do-Doe. Give her my
Best respects a little Bit of Love and then Shine up Shine
up Shine up. . . . As for weddings about these times they
are getting few and scarce most are just upon the point of
making preparations shining up &c &c and I cant say But
that Miss R"'d is in the act too and peradventure to some
one unknown to Mr. M—— and if He would take my advice
He would return Home and attend to Miss R——, But alass
undoubtably a correspondence has long since found its way
Betwene quaker Hill and Cross river ++ and as for my
weding By the eternal as the Old General says you shall have
knowledge of it and on the same princaple I shall consider myself entitled to Yours as to your letter Sir I Beg
you not to make any excuses to me—— the Ball if nothing
unforseen occurs to prevent I shall Be one of the number. your
letter agreeable to your request I have not exhibited to any
one But far from Burning it as it is worthy of Being kept in
long remembrance of a Respected Friend.

My Respects Pleas accept and present un-
feighned—with sentiments of High Respect I
cherefully subscribe

Yours

A.————[44]

A party tomorrow night
at Mr. Hortons and then we
will Shine up.

From an 1838 letter from a young man in Fairfax County,
Virginia, to the same young gentleman at Quaker Hill, we take
one paragraph:

I saw by the Courier and Enquirer that you have had a wedding in the neighborhood and I almost fancied I could see
you kimboing about amongst them eating cake & drinking
wine. . . . I have not heard of any more weddings in old
West Chester but do really hope someone of the 19 old maids
that was at E.H's. that evening has leap'd from old maidish
darkness into the light an liberties of a married State.[45]

The last letter is from a cousin at Goldens Bridge to one at
Cantitoe in July 1842. In a postscript he writes:

CONFIDENTIALY—J.S. and J. are making quite a stir concerning the riding party to Lake Mahopac. All kinds of storys afloat. Perhaps you have heard some of them, if not prepare for a *North-Wester*.[46]

This last fascinates and also haunts us because we found no follow-up on that North-Wester. It shows, however, that neither gossip nor young people have changed too much in the last hundred years.

References

1. Tuckerman, Bayard. *William Jay and the constitutional movement for the abolition of slavery.* New York, 1893, pp. 20-23.
2. French, A. P. *History of Westchester County.* New York, 1925, v. 1, p. 133.
3. *Ibid.*, v. 1, p. 348.
4. *Westchester Herald and Farmers Register,* Mt. Pleasant, N.Y., June 23, 1818.
5. Raymond, James. [Release of black servant Prince.] Bedford, N.Y., 1827. MS. Loose sheet laid in Town Book I, 1680-1704, between p. 159 and p. 160. (At Bedford Town House)
6. Griffin, E. F. *Westchester County and its people.* New York, 1946, v. 2, pp. 501-02.
7. *Ibid.*, v. 2, p. 503.
8. Smith, Henry T. *Manual of Westchester County, past and present.* White Plains, N.Y., 1898, p. 23.
9. *Ibid.*, p. 112.
10. *Ibid.*, p. 206.
11. Silkman, John. Letter to William Silkman, Jan. 11, 1841. MS. (In possession of Mrs. Eltinge S. LaBar, 249 Belmont Avenue, Hawley, Penn. Copy at the Katonah Village Library)
12. Bolton, Robert. *The history of the several towns . . . of Westchester.* New York, 1881, v. 1, p. 81.
13. Shonnard, Frederic & Spooner, W. W. *History of Westchester County.* New York, 1900, p. 547.
14. Westchester County. Division of Land Records. Deeds. Liber 26, pp. 84-86. MS. (At the County Office Building, White Plains, N. Y.)
15. LaMonte, (Rev.) Thomas. Historical sketch of Katonah M. E. Church. In: *Feast of Lanterns,* Aug. 15, 1878.
16. *Westchester Herald,* Mt. Pleasant, N.Y., July 18, 1826.
17. *Ibid.*, Sept. 3, 1822.
18. *Ibid.*, June 14, 1825.
19. *Ibid.*, Jan. 21, 1823.
20. *Ibid.*, Jan. 28 or Feb. 4, 1823.
21. *Ibid.*, Mar. 26, 1839.
22. *Ibid.*, Jan. 7, 1840.
23. Avery, O. T. *Historical sketch of Katonah.* Katonah, 1896. (Unpaged)
24. Robertson, W. H. Diary. Katonah, May 17, 1848. MS. (In possession of Mrs. W. A. Kelly, Katonah)
25. Doe, Janet. Medicine in Katonah. Katonah, 1959. MS. (At the Katonah Village Library)
26. Whitlockville Literary Association. Executive Committee. Report, Nov. 4, 1842. Katonah, 1842. MS. (In possession of Mrs. W. A. Kelly, Katonah. Copy at the Katonah Village Library)

27. Literary Fraternity of Union Academy. Bedford, N.Y., 1840-41. MS. (In possession of Mrs. W. A. Kelly, Katonah. Copy at the Katonah Village Library)
28. Cantatoe Lyceum. Minutes. [Katonah?] 1841-42. MS. (In possession of Mrs. W. A. Kelly, Katonah)
29. Westchester County Temperance Society. Book of records. 1829-48. MS. (Copy at the Katonah Village Library)
30. Temperance society formed in School Districts No. 6, 8, and 10 in 1834. MS. (In possession of Mrs. W. A. Kelly, Katonah.

Copy at the Katonah Village Library)
31. Hillery, H. E. *Putnam County history "workshop."* Patterson, N.Y., 1954-57, v. 3, p. 111. Mimeographed.
32. Westchester County. Superintendents of the Alms House. Letter to A. F. Dickinson, Tarrytown, N.Y., 1857(?). MS. (In possession of Mrs. H. D. Miller)
33. Miller, Mrs. Henry D. Katonah. Oral communication.
34. Dickinson, A. F. Diary. Bedford, N.Y., Dec. 23, 1848. MS.

Advertisement, *Westchester Herald and Putnam Gazette,* Oct. 18, 1831. Collection of Mrs. Leonard H. Hall

(In possession of Miss Rhoda B. Lawrence, 455 E. 14th St., New York 9. Copy in the Katonah Village Library)

35. *Ibid.,* Oct. 4, 1848.

36. New York State. Superintendent of Common Schools. *Report made to the Legislature, April 13, 1840.* Albany, 1840, p. 12.

37. Bates, John S. Teaching certificate of Elizabeth A. Robertson, Bedford, N.Y., April 2, 1846. MS. (In possession of Mrs. H. D. Miller, Katonah)

38. Bedford (N.Y.) School District No. 8. Report for 1842 to the School Commissioners. Bedford, 1843. MS. (At Bedford Town House, at present in attic)

39. Bedford (N.Y.) Town Book III, 1727-1882, p. 100. MS. (At Bedford Town House)

40. Scharf, J. T. *History of West-* *chester County.* Philadelphia, 1886, v. 1, p. 478.

41. Barrett, R. T. *The Town of Bedford.* Bedford, N.Y., 1955, p. 49.

42. Lockwood, A. H. Letter to A. F. Dickinson, Pound Ridge, N.Y., Aug. 16, 1836. MS. (In possession of Mrs. H. D. Miller, Katonah)

43. Whitlockville Literary Association. Minutes, July 4, 1842. MS. (In possession of Mrs. H. D. Miller, Katonah)

44. Letter, Cantitoe, N.Y., Jan. 31, 1837. MS. (In possession of Mr. John Gemmill, Baldwin Place, N.Y.)

45. Letter, Fairfax County, Va., July 8, 1838. MS. (In possession of Mr. John Gemmill, Baldwin Place, N.Y.)

46. Letter, Lewisboro, N.Y., July 21, 1842. MS. (In possession of Mrs. H. D. Miller, Katonah)

A typical train of early days, 1839-49.

CHAPTER IX

THE RAILROAD

IN THE LATTER part of 1844, the New York and Harlem Railroad opened its road to Tuckahoe and White Plains and this remained its extent until 1846 when cars began running to Pleasantville.[1] In the interim the Company had been busy purchasing land from farmers who for the most part had never seen a train and understandably felt apprehensive.[2] When sales in our own vicinity were concluded in November, 1845, Whitlockville knew it was to be bypassed and doubtless felt relief. The road was to run to the east through the flat sandy lands of Elisha and Gideon Reynolds.[6]

Boarding-houses—actually crude shanties, some without floors —were put up along the line of track-laying, and Irish workmen moved in. They were paid $.75 a day and board.[3] So far as we know, these were the first Irish to come into the Katonah district.

In certain parts of New York City, horses were still used to draw the cars,[4] but five-ton, wood-burning, "screeching, spiteful looking little engines" took their places in the country.[2] By June 1847, the road was completed as far north as Croton Falls[5] and the cars stopped for the first time at "Whitlockville Station," a houseless, stationless field, later the center of our first Katonah so named. An eyewitness account is the following, published in 1879:

> Away back in the dim vista of the past I recollect standing, one soft Spring morning, upon the crest of a grand bank where the hotel is, with scores of my neighbors, and watching and waiting for a certain portentious event. As we stood watching we heard the thundering and screaming of a locomotive rushing through the Dowburg cut, and before our eyes glided the first passenger train that ever traversed West-

117

chester county since the world began. We congratulated each
other, and expressed the hope that it was a sight we might
behold if we chose each day, so long as we lived, and that like
the rising of the sun it should be a matter of course for all
future time. Such it has been thus far, with one notable excep-
tion. During the Southern Rebellion, there came a day when
the dark shadow of war hung over our own dwellings. New
York city was in the grip of the enemy and for forty eight
hours the Harlem road sent no passenger trains over its track.
But my memory reaches still farther back into antiquity. I
took a round trip on the Harlem Railroad when its northern
extremity was the Harlem River. The good citizens of New
York flocked to it for a ride to Harlem and back, as they
would get into an anchored balloon for a trip of a thousand
feet into the air, and indeed with about the same sense of
adventure and danger. There were then but two railroads
on this Continent besides, and they scarcely longer than this.[7]

In 1848 there occurred to the north of us what may have been
a new form of action at that date. On May 16th, William H.
Robertson wrote in his diary:

> The Irish on the part of H. R. [the Harlem Railroad] in
> Putnam County had a "strike" for hours today. . . . They
> were paid off and discharged.[8]

The coming of the railroad caused immediate economic change
for the whole area. Perishables such as milk, that could not survive the overland trip to the Hudson and thence by boat to New
York City, could now reach the City in a few hours via the
nightly milk train. The market sloops, already feeling the competition of steam, were hard hit. In the *Westchester Herald*
of June 18, 1850, Captain Jenks of the "Sea Gull" advertised:

> So it goes! Things Upside Down! Steamboats and Railroads
> all bearing against Individual Enterprise! Powerful Monop-
> olies! Yet I venture again, (soliciting a share of public patron-
> age) in the marketing business.[12]

Because of the trains, our farmers turned to dairying and for
many, many years thereafter this was dairy country. The railroad put an end to the market wagon business but it fostered

a new type of service, the milk wagon. Some farmers brought their own cans to the station at night, but some found it convenient to have them picked up at the door. The convenience went beyond milk evidently. To his brother, Stephen Holly Miller wrote in 1851, May 7th:

> We have been ploughing against time. I ploughed seven acres in four days, and done it good, besides milking night and morning in time for the milk wagon. I have ploughed fifteen acres and sold twelve hundred quarts of milk from four cows. . . . If you will send me word what time you will be at Whitlockville, I will meet you with a carriage. If you cannot send word, you can ride any night in the milk wagon. Mr. William Miller stops at my door. He starts at Whitlockville about eight o'clock or a little before.[13]

The biggest change brought by the New York and Harlem in our area was of course the creation of a new village. A station was built to the west of the tracks, just about opposite the present junction of Deer Park Road and new Route 22. Around the station a village grew up and roads were laid out.

It is still possible to walk through most of Old Katonah. When the property was taken over for a reservoir, buildings far back of the proposed water level were condemned for reasons of sanitation, but the streets still remain. They are shaded by the now lofty trees that were planted as saplings to make the little village beautiful. Under the pavement of new Route 22 and east of it lies the site of the across-the-tracks part of the old village.

On both sides of the tracks, and parallel with them, ran Railroad Avenue. It is quite overgrown now but still recognizable as a former thoroughfare. Railroad Avenue formed one side of the "Triangle," as the business section was called. Running at right angles with this, west from the railroad crossing, was Main Street, forming the second side of the "Triangle." It is still clearly defined and easily passable. A couple of hundred yards from their junction, these two roads were connected by the river road which bordered the river and formed the third side. This street is now difficult walking, being in some places submerged. At its midpoint, a bridge once led over Cross River to an extension of the village on the far bank.

Much easier and pleasanter walking is North Street, parallel to the railroad and a block west. It runs north, wandering be-

tween the two charming little ponds, Lake Lovely and The
Dowburg where happy children once delighted to skate. Outside
the old village limits it meets the Dowburg Road—on some maps
called Croton Avenue. The Dowburg was a much traveled highway running between Veal's Ford and Weeks Street in Lewisboro long before the building of Woods Bridge or the coming of
the railroad. It is even now a good road and well marked by
stone walls and stately trees.

From the northwest angle of the "Triangle" a road still partly
above water led west along the river bank. This was the main
route to Whitlockville, Mrs. Avery's "road laid out to the west."
Between and connecting this road and the Dowburg, is Palmer
Avenue which formed the new residential section of the village.
Continuing west either by the river or by the Dowburg, one
comes to Whitlockville, or what remains of it above water. If
the walker looking across the reservoir sees Whitlockville Road
rising to the south and mounting towards Cherry Street, he can
be sure he is in the vicinity of the former mills.

All of this wild and beautiful land belongs now to New York
City. Except for a few cellar holes, a sidewalk in front of the
former Hoyt Brothers' store, one small brick building erected by
the reservoir authorities on former Benedict land, an occasional
rosebush or hedge of lilacs, there is nothing to indicate the busy
life that once went on there.

Quoting Mrs. Avery again, we return to the first days of Old
Katonah village:

> The erection of the depot building, was rapidly followed by
> others. A hotel was built by Haight & Lyon, occupied by
> Cyrus Miller, and a small building for an eating saloon by
> John W. Peck. This was afterwards enlarged and converted
> into a dwelling house, and was for a number of years the
> home of M. S. Benedict. In later times, it has been occupied
> by E. S. Folsom as a residence and picture gallery.
>
> Mercantile pursuits very soon obtained a foothold in the
> place. Horton & Seaman, abandoning their store in Whitlock-
> ville, came to the new settlement and built the store after-
> wards owned by E. J. Purdy, occupying it for a number of
> years as merchants. W. H. Dickinson also built a store on the
> east side of the railroad track; it is now used as the village
> library and reading room.
>
> Zeno Hoyt removed a house from a field about half a mile

north of I. D. Gregory's and placed it a little north of Dickinson's store. He afterward erected beside it, the three-story building, still standing, and the smaller house was subsequently torn down. The third floor of the new house contained a hall which was used as an Odd Fellows Lodge; also for lectures and political meetings. A house was also removed from Whitlockville by W. M. Beyea, who occupied it as a residence. He added another building to the east side, in which he kept a clothing store. The place is now owned by J. E. Horton.

In the rear of the buildings on the street now known as Railroad avenue, a large tank, or reservoir, was constructed for the storage of water brought in a pipe from a spring on a neighboring hill. This was the water supply, and continued in use for many years. Some of the citizens had also their own wells and cisterns.

In the Spring of 1851, a select school was established at the foot of the sand bank and fronting on Main street, in the basement of a small, one-story building, the upper part of which was a milliner's shop, kept by Miss Jane Haight. This structure, greatly changed and enlarged, is now occupied by Edgar Hoyt as an ice cream and eating saloon. The school was taught by Miss M. M. Wilson of Somers, (afterwards Mrs. Yates Ferguson,) and gave great satisfaction to its patrons. Among the youth who enjoyed its advantages, were Dr. J. G. Wood, Mrs. James T. Green, Mrs. Norman Merritt, Mrs. I. D. Gregory, William Nelson, Nathaniel Lyon and others.

A blacksmith's shop, built by Stephen Purdy, stood for many years where the post-office now is. At one time there was a rival shop across the street, where business was carried on by Warren Light. Adjoining Purdy's blacksmith shop, was a wheelwright establishment owned and kept by Norman Miller. All these have long since disappeared, and their sites covered with earth on which are buildings whose foundations are several feet higher than those of the former ones.

About 1851, the row of houses in the alley was built by Stewart Haight; also a bridge over the Cross River, which stream had until this time been a boundary of the little settlement. The bridge was built by J. W. Hanford who owned land on the other side of the river. He also removed his furniture and undertaking business from the old village into his

wareroom on the east side of the railroad track, which was the
germ of the elegant furniture establishment now owned by
Hoyt Brothers.

Soon after, Horton & Seaman sold their store to E. J. Purdy
whose property it still is, and who, for many years, carried
on the mercantile business.

In 1853 M. S. Benedict came to the village and began business as a jeweler. He has now the distinction of being the
oldest business man in town.[14]

The name of the post office which had been transferred from
Whitlockville to the village on the railroad was changed to
"Katonah" on July 22, 1852. Mail now came daily, except Sunday, by rail, and a mail-stage ran three times weekly between
Katonah, Cross River, Boutonville, and South Salem. Postal rates
had gone down: in 1845 it cost 5¢ to send a ½ oz. letter up to
300 miles and 10¢ beyond that. By 1863 it was 3¢ a ½ oz. for
any distance.[15]

While the new village was building, so was the war between
the states, and many were well aware of it. In his diary, Arnell
F. Dickinson of Cantitoe wrote:

> This book was bought Mch 4, 1850 in New York and for
> the purpose to which it is now devoted—a Diary— . . . a
> daily acct. of events, impressions, feelings, etc., etc. . . . Here
> upon these pages, as the wheel of time passes on, are to be
> left some of its traces, o'er which I shall probably look with
> mingled feelings of pleasure and pain in time to come. . . .
> At this time amid the conflict between the North and the
> South upon the subject of the extension of slavery into the
> newly acquired teritory and the threatening of a disolution
> of the Union, the admonitions of Washington, are remem-
> bered and reiterated with a most happy effect. May their
> influence never cease to be felt.[16]

Against this background of mounting apprehension each
man conducted his daily life according to his own lights. The
young Cantitoe lawyer, William H. Robertson, set up an office
at Whitlockville Station from where he conducted a varied practice. On February 9th and 10th of '48 he toured the countryside
with Zener Haight. As this type of business was probably common
to many young lawyers of the time, we will give you these entries
from his diary:

Feb. 9: Wednesday. In compliance with a former promise to accompany Zener Haight, the late carrier of the Hudson River Chronicle, on an excursion to collect some of his debts. Early in the morning I started from Whitlockville and walked to Stephen Frost's, a distance of two miles. After a short conversation there, I got into a sleigh with Mr. Haight and we moved north, keeping east of Croton Falls. . . . Three miles we find good sleighing; when we strike upon the Somerstown & Danbury turnpike. . . . Next we left the turnpike and went south a short distance where we found a carpenter by name Bloomer, he paid us a dollar, promising to pay the rest shortly. We are now on our way to Carmel. We called on a shoemaker by the name Bailey, Had no money, but promised to make a pair of boots for the debt. Called on Widow Crosby whose father-in-law, Enoch Crosby, was Washington's spy who under the garb of a peddler did much good to the American cause. Her daughter and sister were present. We were urged very strongly to return and spend the night. Sleighing quite good from this place to Carmel. Saw Asa Cole, and after three hours conversation came to a settlement by throwing off one half of it. We go east about three miles to Abraham Scott's and after a long talk and repeated examinations of his old papers, he pays his claim: his wife, by way of variety, saying occasionally that she would throw the money in the fire, before she would pay one cent. We now go east again till we come to Anson Crane's. . . . Here we conclude to spend the night. . . .

Feb. 10: Thursday. Borrowed a waggon of Major A. Crane, and went easterly about a mile, met Mr. Fowler with a yoke of oxen in the street, who upon learning the amount of his debt, paid it like a gentleman. Called on Mr. Paddock, with some reluctance he paid it. Went through Monkeytown to a black man by name Hutchins, took his note. Called on Mr. Crosby, who paid his bill. Went to Sodom Corner, and then east to a Mr. Baker, took his note. Returned to Major Crane's, took dinner. . . . Most of the subscribers would first dispute the bill, then say they had received the papers very irregularly, and finally assert that the paper was good for nothing, that it contained nothing but blackguardism. It is worth one's time to see the different ways that people settle their affairs. Came down to North Salem, good sleighing. Called on Mr. Bailey who paid his account. Came thence to Stedwell Frost's.

No sleighing from Salem to Frosts. Walked from Frost's on
the track to Whitlockville. Cold.[9]

Later in February, Robertson represented a wife and daughter accused of murder and sat in on the post mortem made by
Dr. Shove. He wrote of this experience in his diary:

> First, the doctor began to cut through the scalp about a
> half an inch above the eyes and ears. There were two lacera-
> tions on the scalp on the right side of the head and one on
> the back part of the head. Skull was fractured on the right
> side of the head. Then, he sawed off the skull about an inch
> above the place where he cut the scalp. Then he cut the right
> lobe of the brain horisontally and then longitudinally and so
> with the left lobe. The jury brought in a verdict "that . . .
> death was caused by blows inflicted upon his head with a club
> by his wife."[10] The Coroner gave a written permission to bury
> the body.

Every day thereafter Robertson seemed engaged in some different
type of legal problem, many of them pertaining to the Town. He
attended a Teacher's Convention, an Agricultural Fair and a
Whig Convention at the "Rail Road House, Whitlockville," all
in the month before his twenty-fifth birthday. It is not surprising
with this energy and ability that he should have won the nomination for the Legislature at the Whig County Convention on October 19, 1848, nine days after his birthday. He was elected on
November 7th.[11]

While Robertson was engaged politically, four young men of
Cherry Street were engaged adventurously. These were Hosea,
Harvey, William and James Wood, the sons of Alfred and Electa
(Fountain) Wood. They walked to the gold fields of California
in 1849. Three of them remained there. Only Hosea returned.[22]

The second John Jay, sharing his father's and grandfather's
abhorrence of slavery, was acting as counsel for many fugitive
slaves in the years preceding war. In 1855 he took a leading part
in organizing the state Republican Party on the issue of non-
extension of slavery.[23] Jay was in sympathy with the efforts of
John Brown in behalf of the slaves and gave him moral and
financial assistance. Two days before his execution in 1859,
Brown wrote in a letter to his wife:

I have just received from Mr. John Jay of New York a draft for $50 Fifty Dollars for the benefit of my family & will enclose it made payable to your order. . . . Should you happen to meet Mr. Jay, say to him that I fully appreciate his great kindness to me and my family. God bless all such friends.[30]

William Jay, John's father, was devoting more and more time to agriculture in his last years. Over seventy in 1850, he was still on the alert for improvements in machinery. A trial of a new type of mowing machine sent up from New York was held on the ridge in front of his home.[17] In the autumn of 1851, he presided over a meeting at the Bedford Court House, at which Dr. R. T. Underhill spoke on improved agriculture and the cultivation of fruit. Dr. Underhill was president of the Westchester County Agricultural Society and so it was natural that his address should inspire the farmers of Bedford to form an agricultural society on the town level. Arnell F. Dickinson, vice-president of the County Society, and Oliver Green were interested enough to call a meeting in late February of '52 at Warren Collyer's Hall at Katonah.

The Bedford Farmers' Club, the oldest organization still functioning in Bedford, was organized at this meeting. Arnell F. Dickinson was elected president, Oliver Green, secretary, and William H. Robertson appointed to draft a constitution.[24] At the first regular meeting, held at the Dickinson home, Dr. Seth Shove presented a paper on "Agriculture and Horticulture." The second meeting was held at Dr. Shove's home at Cherry Street and the subject, the seeding of grass. In 1854 efforts were started to establish a "Farmers' Library and Reading Room" at Katonah Station. Seventy volumes and many agricultural periodicals were pledged but no suitable room was found, so shares* were sold to raise $300 for a building.[25] As an estimate in library costs, this is probably our first.

The Bedford Farmers' Club sponsored a market fair on October 17, 1860. The event was held at Katonah and its object was to create a local market for the sale and exchange of home products. Such fairs were successful in England and the Club was a forward-thinking organization. Arrangements were made east of the railroad tracks to accommodate several hundred head of

* Share-holders were: A. F. Dickinson, N. C. Lyon, O. Green, Jr., I. H. Green, D. Putney, John Jay, Wm. Jay, Jr., Jonathan S. Holmes.

cattle and suitable space was provided for other livestock, farm produce and manufactured goods.[26] It was an ambitious undertaking for a small community to play host to such a large adjacent farm area. We only wish we had an eyewitness account of the hustle and bustle and mooing and bleating and crowing that must have turned the little village topsy-turvy in a holiday gaiety. On the committee for the Club were John Jay, II, A. F. Dickinson, John D. Haines, Joseph Banks, John Miller and John J. Wood. All communications on the affair were to be addressed to Arnell F. Dickinson.

Dickinson was a very busy man in these pre-war days. He seemed to expend himself in all directions. Besides holding civic and town offices, he was the member of Assembly from this district in 1857. As such, he served as chairman of the Committee on Agriculture and secured the passage of a bill which ended forever the good old custom of pasturing horses, cattle and swine on the highways.[24] And, no matter what duties engaged him, he never ceased to fight for temperance and better schools. His life wasn't all work and no play however. In November of 1850 he went with the Board of Supervisors to New York to hear Jenny Lind[18] and on October 19, 1852, he was married to Elizabeth Ann Robertson[19] and became co-owner of the teapot.

There are two other entries from his diary that we should like to set down here. The first is for those like us who have been wondering all along how land was measured and maps made in those days.

May 6, 1850
    A man engaged by some publisher in Philadelphia passed the house east with instruments surveying the roads and sketching the places intended for a map of West Cheste County. The instrument was in the form of a wheel barrow which he rolled before him, the wheel marking the distance in perches on an index at the side of it & in front of him and just between the handles rose a staff upon which was placed his compass. He gave me the distance from the [Whitlockville] Depot to [Cantitoe] Corner as 2½ miles & 23 perches. He was an Irishman but he appeared well qualified for his business. He took a sketch of the principle places and the names of the principle proprietors.[20]

The other entry is eight months later.

Feb. 4, 1851

[At Poor House.] Brought [home] with me little boy named James Mullin 7 years old to bring up if we thought at the expiration of 30 days he would answer.[21]

This was not the first child that the Dickinsons had taken from the almshouse. But to us the transaction is of more importance than the others because James in 1861 becomes one of our collaborators.

By 1855, events had become tense all over the nation. In Bedford, Town Assessors Winthrop Raymond, Charles G. Betts and Stephen H. Miller made a roll of those liable for military duty.[27] Each year, the hope of peaceful settlement between the states became less. The Lincoln-Douglas debates kept the slavery controversy and its impact on politics, law and government before the eyes of every man who could read.

In October of '59 came John Brown's raid, deplored by conservative northerners and inflammatory to the South. Secession threats became open. In the presidential campaign of '60 the Democrats split according to their views and left the way open for the Republicans to elect Lincoln.[28] Lincoln was not popular with all in Westchester County but he seems to have found supporters in Bedford. William H. Robertson, then County judge, was a member of the Electoral College and cast his vote for Lincoln.[29]

References

1. Hyatt, E. C. *History of the New York & Harlem Railroad*, n.p., 1898, p. 14.
2. *Ibid.*, p. 33.
3. *Ibid.*, p. 17.
4. *Ibid.*, p. 13.
5. *Ibid.*, p. 15.
6. Westchester County. Division of Land Records. Deeds. Liber 117, pp. 142-43. MS. (At County Office Building, White Plains, N.Y.)
7. Parley, Peter, Jr., pseud. [Rev. Richard Wheatley]. Katonah in days gone by. In: *Feast of Lanterns*, Aug. 26, 1879.
8. Robertson, W. H. Diary. May 16, 1848. MS. (In possession of Mrs. W. A. Kelly, Katonah)
9. *Ibid.*, Feb. 9 & 10, 1848.
10. *Ibid.*, Feb. 29, 1848.
11. *Ibid.*, Oct. 19 & Nov. 7, 1848.
12. *Westchester Herald*, Mt. Pleasant, N.Y., June 18, 1850.
13. Miller, S. H. Letter to his brother, Alfred Miller, Bedford, May 7, 1851. MS. (In possession of Mrs. Oliver U. Todd,

Goldens Bridge, N.Y. Copy at the Katonah Village Library)

14. Avery, O. T. *Historical sketch of Katonah*. Katonah, 1896. (Unpaged)

15. Gemmill, John. Our post offices. Baldwin Place, N.Y., 1959. MS. (At the Katonah Village Library)

16. Dickinson, A. F. Diary. Feb. 22, 1850. MS. (In possession of Mrs. H. D. Miller, Katonah)

17. *Ibid.*, July 2, 1850.

18. *Ibid.*, Nov. 19, 1850.

19. *Ibid.*, Oct. 19, 1852.

20. *Ibid.*, May 6, 1850.

21. *Ibid.*, Feb. 4, 1851.

22. More Westchester men in the Gold Rush. In: *Westchester County Historical Bulletin*, 1949, v. 25, pp. 90-91.

23. *Dictionary of American biography*. New York, 1943, v. 10, p. 10.

24. Wood, James. *History of the Bedford Farmers' Club*. Bedford, N.Y., 1895, pp. 2-3.

25. [Statement concerning efforts to establish a "Farmers' Library and Reading Room" at Katonah Station.] Katonah, Dec. 1, 1854. MS. (In possession of Mrs. H. D. Miller, Katonah)

26. Howe, H. B. *Yorkshire to Westchester: a chronicle of the Wood family*. Rutland, Vt., 1948, p. 172.

27. Bedford (N.Y.) Military roll. Bedford, 1855. MS. (At Bedford Town House)

28. Morris, R. B. *Encyclopedia of American history*. New York, 1953, p. 227.

29. Barrett, R. T. *The Town of Bedford*. Bedford, N.Y., 1955, p. 58.

30. St. Matthew's Church in Bedford. *A sesquicentennial history of St. Matthew's Protestant Episcopal Church, Bedford, New York*, by members of the Parish family. [Bedford, N.Y., 1960,] p. 40.

Mott's Patent Revolving Cast-Iron Chair, installed by Arnell F. Dickinson in our common schools. Tracing of original advertisement by Gloria Strang.

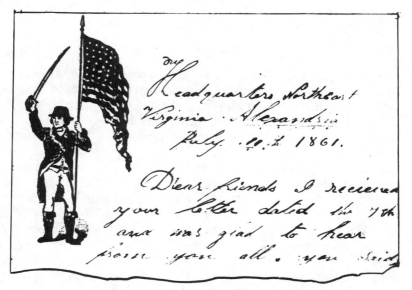

Portion of letter to Arnell F. Dickinson family.
Collection of Mrs. Henry D. Miller

CHAPTER X

CIVIL WAR DAYS

O N APRIL 15, 1861, three days after Fort Sumter had been fired upon, President Lincoln issued a proclamation calling for seventy-five thousand militia volunteers to serve three months. New York's quota was 13,280. The State met the emergency by passing an act to furnish not only the militia asked for but also thirty thousand volunteers to serve two years.[1]

We believe our first two-year Katonah volunteers to be those who enrolled in the 2nd Regiment Scott Life Guards. This was a company assembled by the eighteen-year-old Croton Falls Yale student, Gerard Crane Brown, in April of '61.[3] In May, when it moved to the City, it became Co. G, 38th Regiment. The men from Katonah and adjacent areas who on April 15th signed a petition to form this company were: Horace Miller and Henry Hedge of Bedford, George W. Kniffin of Goldens Bridge, Oscar L. Dearborn and Jesse Hoyt of Katonah.[3] As of April 30th, in addition to the above, William Quick of Bedford, William N. Kniffen of Goldens Bridge, George Lohn, Orville Dingee and Benjamin Lockwood of Katonah were members.[4] On May 5th David Avery and James Mullin enrolled in New York City.[5,16]

In April of '61 young Dr. Jared Green Wood, immediately on

129

graduation, had applied for an assistant-surgeoncy and was assigned first to the 6th Artillery.[6] In February, 1862, seven companies of the 4th New York Heavy Artillery, Col. Doubleday's Regiment, left the state as three-year volunteers.[7] In Company A of this regiment were over seventeen men who enlisted from Katonah (see Appendix No. 30).

Later in the year, as more men were needed to fill quotas, Governor Morgan appointed a Union Defense Committee for the 8th Senatorial District to which we belonged. From our locality members were William H. Robertson, John Jay and Hezekiah D. Robertson. In September of '62, this Committee raised eight companies of artillery in support of the 135th New York Volunteer Infantry Regiment. These eight companies with two additional ones were mustered in three months later at Fort McHenry as the famous 6th New York Heavy Artillery. Many local men joined this regiment, among them Charles Fisher, Enoch and Elisha Avery and David Moulton.[2] Besides the regiments mentioned above, we had men in various other regiments, including those of other states.

The first Union Defense Committee had been organized in New York City April 20, 1861, when all rail and telegraph communication with Washington had ceased, and money had to be found to equip militia and volunteers and send them to defense of the capital. This original committee continued its activities beyond the initial emergency and all the New York State regiments in which our local men were enlisted benefited by it. As of the report of April 30, 1862, the Committee had spent $5,099.42 on the 38th Regiment; $4,003.16 on the 4th; $1,234.30 on the 6th.[8]

On the home front, aid societies were formed as soon as war was declared and on August 16, 1861, the ladies of Katonah put on a "Soldier's Fair" of which Mrs. Seth Shove and Mrs. John Burr Whitlock, Jr., were directoresses. They took in $350. At the fair, Judge Robertson read an extract from a letter from Mrs. Lincoln thanking the Soldiers Aid Society of Katonah for havelocks they had already sent to the army.[9] Groups of women met at each others' homes and scraped lint to be used in dressings instead of cotton which was naturally hard to procure. A notice of one of these meetings is the following:

> Mrs. Jay will be glad to see Mrs. & the Misses Robertson on Tuesday next punctually at 2 o'clock to assist at a meeting for making lint and bandages, etc., for our soldiers. Mrs.

Jay begs that Mrs. Robertson will bring any of her friends who would like to assist at the meeting.

The Jay Homestead Saturday morning[10]

In many cases the families of early volunteers were helped financially by home town organizations. This system was superseded by the town bounty system. Unfortunately, we do not have Bedford town minutes for these years but we have those for Lewisboro which read in part:

A public meeting . . . was called for, in anticipation of a draft being ordered and made, to procure soldiers to assist in putting down the rebellion . . . which was held the 21st day of August 1862. . . . Resolved that sum of [blank] be raised . . . for the purpose of procuring the quota of volunteers for said town under the last two calls of our Government without resorting to a draft.

This same meeting resolved to pay $50.00 bounty to each volunteer on enlistment and $25.00 monthly to his family.[11] That Bedford gave similar help is indicated by the following paper:

Detachment 6th N.Y. Arty
Maryland Heights, 27 May 1863

This is to certify that Enoch H. Avery is in the United States Service, thereby entitling his wife to relief money from the Town of Bedford.

Edward Jones
Capt Comd Detch 6th N.Y.A.[12]

The burden of these bounties became so heavy on the towns that they had to be met by bonds. In 1872 Bedford paid off four bonds issued in 1864.[13]

In 1862, anticipating a draft, individual men sought to have themselves declared exempt for health or other reasons. In some cases, a justice of the peace swore to their ineligibility. In other cases, Drs. Shove and Slawson certified them unfit. Beginning July 15, 1862, there are many certificates of exemption in our Bedford records. The reasons given for ineligibility are varied. Four men in one family were exempt. One declared himself forty years of age and suffering from disease of the kidneys; one had "an old weakness of the chest"; one had lost the sight of his right eye, and one was a deputy post master! [14]

By 1863, it was apparent that volunteers could not fill the quotas. On March 3rd a Conscription Act was passed making all men between twenty and forty-five liable to military duty. William H. Robertson was draft commissioner for Westchester. Service could be avoided, however, by paying $300 or procuring a substitute. Many men adopted this procedure, especially those who were married. To those unable to pay, the system naturally seemed unfair and draft riots ensued in New York City and lower Westchester. [15]

This is not a history of the Civil War but a chapter about our local people who took part in it, both at home and in the field. Among our young soldiers whose letters have been preserved are Charles Fisher, Zener Haight, George Kniffin, David Moulton and James Mullin. James, the child that Arnell F. Dickinson had taken from the almshouse in 1851 was supposed under the terms of his indenture to serve Mr. Dickinson "faithfully, obediently and honestly" until the age of twenty-one. [16] In enlisting at seventeen and a half, he gave his age as eighteen and his name as James Muller. Each soldier was provided with a "Descriptive List" and that of James Muller may be of interest, in contrast to present-day army papers:

DESCRIPTIVE LIST OF PRIVATE JAMES MULLER
CO. G 38th REGT. N.Y.S.V. COM. BY MAJ. WM. H. BAIRD

NAME	JAMES MULLER	REMARKS: Last paid
AGE	18	by Maj. Fessenden to
WHEN ENROLLED	MAY 5/61	Feb. 28, 1862.
WHERE EN-		Clothing acct. cannot
ROLLED	N.Y. CITY	be furnished as the
BY WHOM EN-		Books were left at
ROLLED	LIEUTENANT BROWN	Alexandria for want
HIGHTH	5 FT. 6 IN.	of transportation.
COMPLEXION	FAIR	
COLOR OF EYES	BLUE	
COLOR OF HAIR	SANDY	
NATIVITY	WESTCHESTER [CO.,]	Albert A. Terrille,
	N.Y.	Capt.[17] Co. G, 38 Rt.
OCCUPATION	FARMER	N.Y.

From available letters we have chosen those parts that seem best to reflect the experiences and feelings of our local men. Inaccuracies have undoubtedly resulted from difficulties in deciphering handwriting and from the men's own spelling.

James Muller to Arnell Frost Dickinson[18]
From Washington, June 21, 1861

Dear friends,

I arived at Washington last night about midnight and took up quarters in the Greenwich Church. It is very hot here. We will be reviewed today by Gen. Scot and the cecratary of war. This morning I took a walk through the city and saw the capitall, city hall, patent office, and the White House. I think we will see the President to day.

I enlisted in the 38 ridgement company G, Captain Brenton commanding. We left East New York on Wednesday 12 o'clock noon and marched to the peets slip ferry. We took 3 days ration with us, then we crossed and landed in New York, marched down Broadway. There was a brilliant display along the sidewalks and chearing evry step we took. Crossed over to Jersy City and took the new Jersey Central R.R. to Harisburg. Traveled all night on the cars from Harisburg, we took the Baltimore and Ohio R.R. to Baltimore. There was a great crowed in Baltimore but no displays. We went through Baltimore with our muskets loaded and buaonet fixed. The police where out in full forse. Great enthusiasm was shone all along the route. . . .

Thier is a great many boys in this company that I know. I supose you are very angry with me for leaveing the way I did. I am as well as ever thank Good. We recieved our muskets the same day that I enlisted, a deadful instrument of deat. . . .

I supose if this reaches you it will be the last you will ever have from me. Give my respects to all that I knew. I remain yours most afectionately,

JAMES MULLER

P.S. Farewell. Tell Enoch that David is well. Please excuse bad writing and spelling and let Edwin and Enoch see this letter. My love to all. Good by

James Muller

James Muller to Arnell F. Dickinson
From Alexandria, July 25, 1861

I mentioned in my last letter to you about haveing an engagement before long. We left camp soon after for Fairfax. The route was a very hard one. It was hard for the horses to draw the bagage and canon. They had 12 horses to one gun. The rebels got wind of our coming and when within 10 miles of town we found the roades blockaded by fallen trees witch made it very tiedous. The day was exceedingly hot. The roade was finaly opened, the charge then made. They fled leaveing everything behind them. The[y] had breastworks thrown up very extensively and might have given us a warm reception if they had stad thier ground. They set fire to the Rail Road wood before they left. By the apearance of things they where prepareing to eat thier diner. The camp fires was burning when we entered the town we took 15 prisoners. The place was in bad condishion when we took posesion they where nine thousand strong. They ockupied two churches for hospitals. Disease seam to have prevailed. They left a dead man in one of the churches. We encamped thare and stayed thare untill 3 o'clock the next day. Then started for Centerville whare they had the battle at Bull Run, 3 miles west of Centerville.

We was to late for the fun. . . . We went into camp thare for two days, then started for Manasass Junction whare we had the battle in ernest. We fought for nine hours. Our Regiment and the Zuaves stood under the hotest fire. We charged on the batery and drove them out of it completely. The rebels then retreat to another batery and was reinforsed. Our men was so exausted that we had to retire from the field. Our horses whare all killed so we had to disband our canon so they fell in the hands of the rebels. A number of the boys are missing. Our lieutenant, Thomas Hamlin, is wounded and taken prisoner. Tell Jared D. Powell that Benjamin Taylor was badly wounded twice in the arm once in the sholder. When the bore him off the field he said 'Oh boys, I can't go any farther with you.' I have two of his ambrotypes and would like to send them to his father in York but don't know whare he lives. . . . Tell Enoch that David is well. He was knocked down by a spent ball but soon recovered. I gave him a drink of water. We came very near being taken prisoners by the rebels.

We marched 60 miles and fought 8 hours without refreshing. The rivers had to be waded, the bridges were all burnt. In wading the rivers we got all wet and our feet sore. . . .

From Muller to Dickinson
From Camp Scott, Near Alexandria, Virginia
August 7, 1861

I wrote to you immeately after the retreat from Bull Run. . . . The regiment is badly broken up. A number of the oficers have resined. They returned from the field titled with the name of a coward. Our Captain has resined and Lieutenant Hamlin was wounded and taken prisoner. He was a brave young man and done his duty to the last, so did poor Ben. Tell Jared D. I gave his ambrotypes to his cousin with the 14 regiment. Major Poter is taken prisoner with Dr. Griswold and quartermaster Murphy. Colonel Ward has gone to New York on business. . . .

I supose you are well posted of the various movement as I am. The next time the oficers and wire pulers will wait for General Scott's orders. Had they not been in such a hury, they might have saved the lives of many and not disgraced the Army. . . .

I have sent a note to Washington to Zeno Haight. As yet have had no answer. Wright Banks of Croton Falls has command of the company now. . . . Give my love to Grandma and the children, My best respects to you all.

I remain yours most truly
James Muller

From Zener Haight to James Muller
From Washington City
August 19, 1861

Dear Sir, I received your wellcom letter of the 30th of July ownly a few days since. I have been verry sick ever since the unlucky Battle of Bulls Run. We traveled all night and in the rane next day and I got verry wet both Body and Feet. I toock a verry heavy cold and have been sick ever since. I am getting better. . . .

From Muller to Dickinson
From Camp Scott
November 6, 1861

The report is now that Rosecrans has surounded Floyd and the fleet landed of Charleston, but I think it is to good to be true.

The camps were in an uprore last nigh when the news reached us. Scott has retired and McClellan taken his place. You have no idea what a number of troops there is around here. They have a very fine apearance and are favered with good health. . . .

The troops are well feed and clothed. They have everything, even to gloves. The clothes are of a good material. The soldiers are kept very buisey. They have company drill in the morning. Brigade drill in the afternoon. It would be worth your coming to Washington this winter to see the Army thare is here. . . .

From Muller to Dickinson
From Camp Scott
November 26, 1861

We have new tents. They are the first class with stoves in them. We have had our review. Everything past of very pleasantly. The day was cole and the troops marched well. You have seen the perticulars in the paper. . . .

Muller to Dickinson
From Alexandria, Virginia
January 20, 1862

The roads are almost impassible and will not permit any forward movement for sometime yet to come. We where in hopes of haveing an engagement sone as the Burnside expedition was ready for action. . . . Last week we were out on picket near Mount Vernon. . . . I had an opertunity to see Washington's estate and some of his breastworks. A detachment of the reserve went out on a scout beyond Pokick Church and arested a symphythiser of secesia. The church is a very old building. The pew Washington ocupied remains yet to be seen. We could by the aid of glass plainly see the Rebel camp fires along the rear of Centreville. . . .

From Muller to Dickinson
From Alexandria, Virginia
March 6, 1862

The time has arived for a forward movement. The sick
are being sent to the general hospital and all those that can't
march. We have just recieved our new rifles and are ready for
the advance. The rebels have deserted Centreville and fallen
back to Manasass. . . .

From Muller to Dickinson
From Camp Segwick, Fortress Monroe, Va.
April 2, 1862

We are moveing out towards Big Bethell and Yorktown.
They keep us stiring now. We only stay a day or so in a place.

We have no tents with us but have ruber blankets, so when
we make a halt we stick our rifles in the ground and with the
aid of a few strings we sone have a tent. There is no rebels
near Bethell. I cannot tell how sone we may have an engagement. We have a very large force here. This is a healthy
place.

Yesterday I went to Newport News and saw George Cusno.
He is as talkative as ever and saw the corse the Merimac took
in the late fight. The rebels appear to be stiring about Croney
Islan. I guess they begin to smell a rat seeing so many troops
coming in every day. . . .

From Geo. W. Kniffin, Camp Winfield Scott, Fair Oak, Va.
To James Muller (then at home on sick leave, June, 1862)

We have had another battle. I suppose Miller has given
the poticulares. Col. Ward had command of the brigade. On
Saterday Gen. Birney had command but he failed to carry
out the orders given to him: so Gen. Heintzlemon put him in
arrest and Ward on Sunday won honors to himself and
Brigade. We drove the rebs about a mile at the point of the
bayonet.

Baxter and Sorlesom was wounded. Baxter died the next
day; we buried him deasently and marked well his grave.

Give my respects to all of the boys about Katonah who are
acquainted with me, they are not many however. You had
better go up and call upon my folkes when you receive this.
There is two or three young ladies up there: one is a school

teacher who bords there. I would like for you to go up there and tell me when you do what kind of a gal she is. I never saw her.

All is Well.

Write Soon

Geo. W. Kniffin

From Muller to Dickinson
From Fortress Monroe
August 16, 1862

Transports are loading with artilery, amunition, and camp equipage. Contraband are employed in removeing all lose articles. I think they have fallen back as far as Williamsburg or Yorktown. Today we will return to Fort Monroe. The James River is quite a large stream, nearly as large as the Patomac. A portion of Burnside's force has left here for Washington to reinforce Pope as Jackson gave him a warm reception for the first time. Pope will see some diferent fighting to what he saw in Missuria. But I believe in his moto, 'Nothing ventured, nothing had'. I think the Army will move next in the direction of Fredericksburg and co-operate with Pope. As I write the transports are coming in with the sick and wounded, the stemer John Brooks has on board 900 sick and wounded that have had nothing to eat for the last 48 hours. The[y] present, a pittiful sight, poor creatures, I can appreaciate thier situation. It is very warm and sultry hear. I have not had a good drink of water since I left home. . . .

From Muller to Dickinson
From Fortress Monroe, Va.
August 20, 1862

The Army is moveing down here. Porter's and Peck's Corps arrived here yesterday. They keep comming in all the time. . . . The horses and men are completely exausted.

I have talked with a number of the men. They seam to have lost all confidence in McClellan and say that he might have gone into Richmond if he wanted to. Yesterday I spent the day in going about to see what I could see. I went to the different hospitals and among the soldiers' graves. . . .

Some of Porter's Corps have already embarked from New Port News for Acquia Creek and Fredericksburg . . . Do you think they will draft or not? I hope they won't for it is a disagreable way of geting troops in the field. The last account I heard that they where trying to get an extension of time for recruting. . . .

As I write, a great excitement prevails about here. It [is] reported that McClellan is hotly pursued by the rebels. They are advancing on Yorktown with the intentions of retaking it, but it is of no importance to either side just now for the guns are all removed and the earthworks distroyed. I see the North has been decieved in regard to the strength of the South, but one thing is certain, they will never be any stonger. . . .

As for the Army of the Potomac, they are worth but very little until the[y] get rested they had better remain idle till fall. . . .

From Muller to Dickinson
From Alexandria, Va.
August 26, 1862

There has been a great deal of mistery of late in regard to the late movements of McClellan. . . . Before anny one was aware of it, his main Army had shiped to reinforse Pope. Heintzelman's Corps are at Worenton and how the[y] got there so sone it is a mistery to me.

Porter's Corps shipe for Acquia Creek and then took the rail road to Fredericksburg. We are here now so hurra for the Shenandoa Valley. Probably you will not hear from me again verry sone, but all I can do is to hope for the best. I will assure you that we have a hard task before us. To say the rebels will not fight is a mistake. It is thier only hopes and they must fight. . . .

Gen Lee trying to draw us as near his base of operations as he can and Hallock trying to draw them out of ther strongholds. Let me know when you answer this letter if thier would be any chance to get a position in anny of those new regiments geting up about thare. Speak to Judge Robertson about it. If thier should be I would be wiling to pay anny one to assist in procuring it for me. I am willing to serve in the position I am in but while the war lasts if I can get a position it would open the way for future development and be a great help to one that has no inflence. . . .

D. Moulton to Arnell Dickinson[19]
Sept. 24, 1862

We was one day and two nights a coming from Yonkers to Baltimore, it was a Sunday morning that we arived in town for our breakfast. Then they gave us our guns and equipage for to fight the Rebels with, then we got dinner there. Then we strung our napsacks on our backs for to march about two and a half miles to camp. For a while we had to lay on the ground with just our blankets that night. Next day our tents came for us, or rather hen coops. That is the right name for them. Well, the best of all was that at twelve o'clock at night the news came for to seize our guns in defence of our lives, that the rebels was on to us. You better think that there was some get up and getting our napsacks on and guns to a shoulder for to fight. A few moments the capt. told us to go quite to bed again and sleep for in the morning we had to march for this camp one and a half miles to Camp Willington. . . .

E. H. Avery is well and hearty and so am I. . . .

Muller to Dickinson
From Monocacy, Md.
October 2, 1862

You seam to think the chances wher not verry good to get a commission in the new regiments. Perhaps many would think that I was folish as my time is so short to serve, but my chances would be better for the future in the new regiments than in the old ones. . . .

This week one of the boys in Company H went home and is out in the 126th NY as Captain. . . .

Muller to Dickinson
From Polesville, Md.
October 16, 1862

As I write, heavey fireing is heard in direction of Harper's Ferry. . . . Earley this morning a party of covelery and infantry where ordered across the river to reconnoitre in the direction of Winchester. They will not return untill tomorrow.

We are all verry anxious for an advance rather than go in winter quarters and be subject to such raids as this late one. . . . thare never was better weather for active operation.

Col Ward has been appointed Brigadier General and command this brigade formerly Birney's Brigade. The 38th has recieved 138 recruits since the last call. . . . Stragling has been practiced to much of late but thare has been an order issued to prevent it. To do so they have a large number of men detailed as provost gourds to erest every man that fall out. I am *Corporal* of Provost at these Head Quarters.

If it is not to much trouble for you I would like to have some shirts made and sent to me for it would be much cheaper tham to buy them here. I can not get a good shirt her less than 3 dollars. . . .

Muller to Dickinson
From Headquarters near Whites Ford
October 26, 1862

I would like to have another pair of boots if it will not be to much trouble for you. Have Arnold make them the same size that those shoes where he made before I left home. Tell him to make them of calv's skin with middling thick soles worth about $5.00 dollors. The kind of boots here are miserable things to march in but in the meantime I do not want to make any unnecessary trouble for you.

I see by your letter that Westchester has not her quota full yet. It think it is shame that the men will hang back in such times as these. When the old troops enlisted the[y] done it under many disadvantages only 11 dollars per month and no bounty. Now they have to be bought to come and thier families provided for. They are no better men and the[y] ought to be compeled to come. But the old troop will overlook all this and when the war is ended they can say with a proud concians that they where not bought to fight for thier country.

I have already seen some of the new regiments and it is not an uncommon occurance while pasing each other that the inquirey will be made the 120th N. York or some other new regiment—the next thing from the old regiment—Bought Men. A[ll of] witch is rather a hard nut for them to crack. . . .

All the boys ere well. David Avery is in the Convalesant Camp neare Alexandria. Hobby and Honly are well. I think Nate has reformed for he cant get anything here.

I have just received the Baltimore Cliper that announces that vigerous measures are to be taken to put down the rebeian.

If the war has to be put down by those measures it will be an everlasting war.

Thurlow Weed in Washington so the city must be safe or he would not be there. . . .

Muller to Dickinson
From Camp near Waterloo, Virginia
November 14, 1862

We had allready ocupied the south bank of the Rapohonoc almost in sight of a large portion of the rebel army when it was announced to our regret that little Mac was superceded, witch is a great dissatisfaction to the army of the Potomac.

This was the golden opertunity and will result verry seriously as Lee will no dout make the most and best of his time in removeing his army to the south side of the Rapidan and with the river for his front, his position will be quite formidable. . . .

Burnside is a soldier every inch of him, but it is douted as to his capability of handling this immece army. I hope we may be successful in all our future movements and success to our new commander. We are willing to do almost anny thing to bring the war to an end.

Had McClellan been left alone I am certain that he would have routed the army in frunt of him and driven them to wall.

If the politicians in Washington are agoing to carry on this war they ought to be ordered out and let the soldiers go home. After the battle of Manasas when the armys where defeated and hurled back to Washington allmost demoralized McClellan took them in one week after and went up to Hagerstown Heights and whiped them on ground of thier own choseing. . . .

You mentioned about Zeno Haight. After the battle of Bull Run No. 2, I went to Washington for the purpose of finding him. The best way to do that was to go to the city directory. I went there but could not find his name enrolled thare so I think it verry probable that he is dead. . . .

Muller to Dickinson
From Falmouth, Va.
January 7, 1863

On Monday we had a grand review by Major Gen Burnside. The General was recieved verry colely. Did not recieved

Courtesy of Bedford House, Home of John Jay

"Katonah's Wood," Cantitoe. This stone house purchased from W. H. Schieffelin was the home of H. E. Pellew from 1874 to 1891.

Courtesy of William M. Will

Bought in 1892 by Clarence Whitman, "Katonah's Wood" was enlarged and remodeled. It burned in 1939 while the home of Robert A. Chambers.

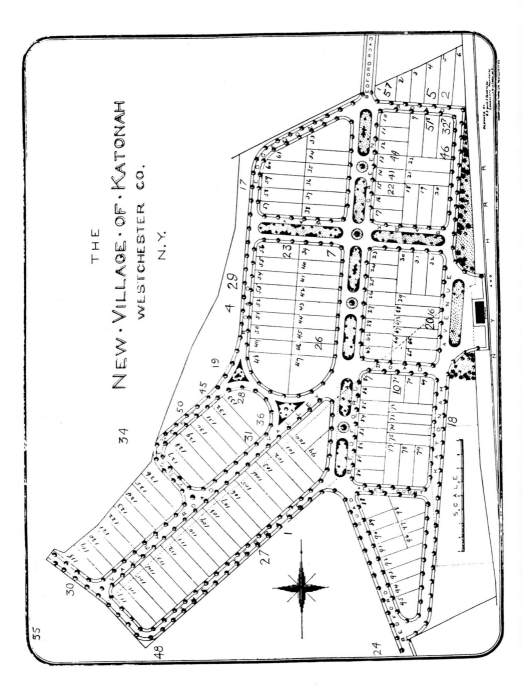

PLOT PLAN FOR NEW KATONAH

Prepared in 1895 by B. S. and G. S. Olmstead, landscape architects, and published in 1896 in O. T. Avery's *Historical Sketch of Katonah*. See Appendix 28 for key to the numbered houses. House numbers by K. B. Kelly.

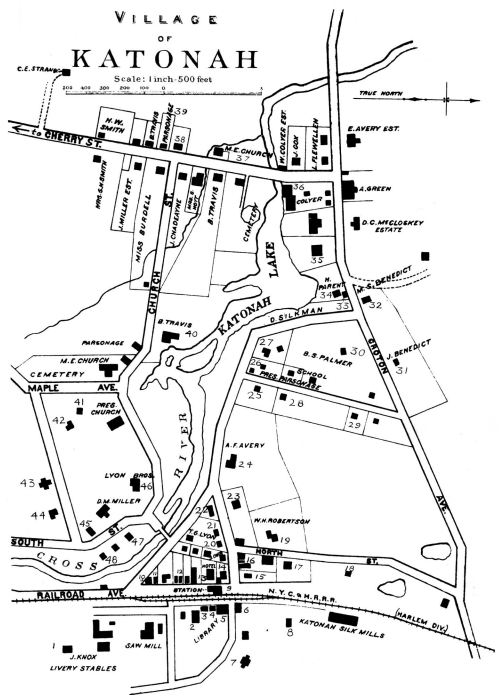

VILLAGE

OF

KATONAH

Scale: 1 inch-500 feet

500 400 300 200 100 0

TRUE NORTH

C.E. STRANG

to CHERRY ST.

H. W. SMITH

B. TRAVIS

PARSONAGE 39

38

M.E. CHURCH 37

MRS. S. N. SMITH

J. MILLER EST.

MISS BURDELL

CHURCH ST.

J. CHADEAYNE

MRS. S. HOYT

B. TRAVIS

CEMETERY

KATONAH LAKE

W. COLYER EST.

J. COX

L. FLEWELLEN

E. AVERY EST.

36 COLYER

A. GREEN

D. C. McCLOSKEY ESTATE

35

M. ST. BENEDICT

B. TRAVIS 40

D. SILKMAN

H. PARENT 34

33

32

PARSONAGE

M.E. CHURCH

CEMETERY

MAPLE AVE.

27

26

PRES. PARSONAGE

B. S. PALMER

30

SCHOOL

CROTON AVE.

J. BENEDICT 31

25

28

41 PRES. CHURCH

42

29

RIVER

A. F. AVERY

24

43

46 LYON BROS.

D. M. MILLER

44

45

23

22

21

T. G. LYON

20

W. H. ROBERTSON

19

SOUTH ST.

47

48

CROSS

16

NORTH ST.

17

18

19 11

12

HOTEL 14

13

15

STATION 9

N. Y. C. & H. R. R. R.

RAILROAD AVE.

3 4

2 LIBRARY 5

6

KATONAH SILK MILLS

8

(HARLEM DIV.)

1

J. KNOX

SAW MILL

7

LIVERY STABLES

OLD KATONAH AND WHITLOCKVILLE, 1893

This map is the latest available before abandonment of the two old villages before
their flooding. Map by Julius Bien & Co., with three minor correction of fact.
See Appendix 28 for key to the numbered houses. Numbers by K. B. Kelly.

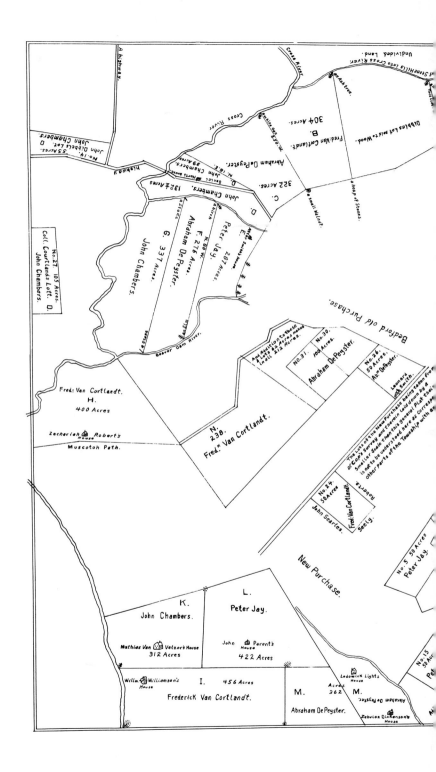

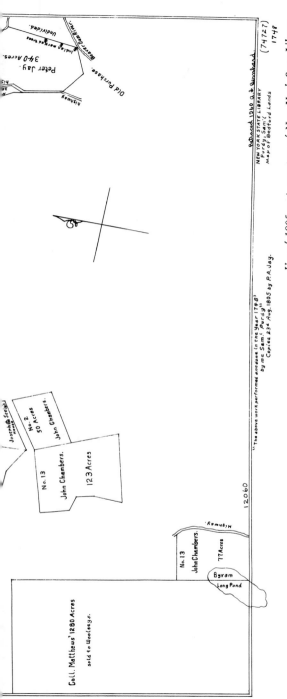

Use of 1805 map, courtesy of New York State Library

HOLDINGS OF VAN CORTLANDT HEIRS

Originally prepared in 1748 by Samuel Purdy to show the Bedford lands owned by heirs of Jacobus Van Cortlandt. The plan of the lands in the center area (New Purchase), taken by Purdy from an original map by John Copp, are on a different scale than Purdy's map. Copp's map has not been found to date. Copied by P. A. Jay, 1805, and traced and relettered by A. I. Bernhard.

Business District, Old Katonah. Railroad Avenue was divided into east and west sides by the tracks.

The row of stores is on the west side, facing the tracks

Courtesy of Katonah Village Library

Main Street, Old Katonah. In the distance, west, it became the road to Whitlockville.

Courtesy of Katonah Village Library

North Street, Old Katonah, looking south toward Main Street.
Left to right: millinery shop, bakery, *Katonah Times* office, and the barber shop.

149

On the north side of Main Street, Old Katonah, Hoyt Brothers' stor
faced the west end of "The Triangle

Auction in Old Katonah. One of the buildings on east e
of Main Street up for sale before exodu

a single cheer, a thing that never occurd while McClellan was in command.

The Gen tryed to look cheerful but the loss of fifteen thousand of our brave comrades must have rested heavily on his heart. As the colum past in review I had a verry good opertunity to see him as he sat on a dark bay and spirited horse with his hat off to pay the honor to the old veterans with thier torn and tatered banars as they past. Nevertheless, we respect him as a good soldier but think this disaster was brought unnesesaraly upon us. . . . Thus far the campaigne in Virginia is a failure while the armys in the southwest gain victory after victory.

I do not think we will make another move. If we do, it will be in the direction of Alexandria.

The express came on Monday last. I looked long and anxiously for my box but it was not thare. I have not recieved any letter from you lately. I wish you all a happy New Year and tell Arny and Hannah that I am comming home next May to see them. The first thirty eight regiment's term expire about that time. Unless they offer some inducement thare will have to be another call for troops. The enemy picket along the apposite bank of the river but the main body of the rebs have fallen back to thier second line of intrenchment. Thier camp fires are visible everry night. The[y] seam to have taken a strong position on our right and have completed the bridg at Rapahanoc Station.

You have doutless heard of the late raids in our rear by the rebel Stuart. He has showed us some good examples but the secratary of the war has not the ambition enough to check these moves but won't untill a more successful one is made. . . .

Muller to Dickinson
From Hd. Quarters near Falmouth, Virginia
January 30, 1863

On the twentieth we started. . . . Moved in the direction of Warenton. . . . The artilary and pontoons where sent to the front. . . . Marched about 12 miles then moved towards Scott's Mills or Bank's Ford and encamped for the night. Commenced raining hard. We managed to weather it through the night as thare was plenty of trees. We considered our-selvs the favored ones to have a tree to lean against.

Birney's Division Stoneman's Corps where selected to lay

the pontoons and open the ball but it was raining. Still the most of the pontoons are on the ground and the rebels are aware of what is going on and are seen moveing to meet us. We could not cross that day, so we are obliged to lay in camp and began to look at it as a failure. Before night the enemy where in sight on the aposite side of the river and had a board nailed to a tree in sight incribed thare-on Burnside Stuck in the Mud, whitch was verry disgusting. We where obliged to come away without an opertunity to fire a shot at the miserable creaturs who are constantly makeing fun of our Generals.

This last move was the worst one the army ever witnessed. Am sorry to say it, but the cuntry is full of stragglers and deserters. The men are completely discouraged and say thare is no use of fighting anny longer. But little Mac, whare is he now? If the people only knew the army loved him thay would send him back at once. We are now in our old camp and Hooker in command. . . .

From Chas. H. Hill to John C. Holmes[20]
From Camp 8th Conn. Vols, Bermuda Hundred, Va.
August 29, 1864

I suppose there is not much use of my telling you what is going on down here as you see the paper every day and they do sometimes get things in as they are but seldom if we win a Small Victory they will get that in but if we get Defeated they keep that stillit seems to me as though we do not gain much but perhaps we do not know there is one thing that I do know we never knew what soldiering was untill this summer. We have found out now if I had known what I know now last Dec. when I took that bunty I think I should let some one else took it but never mind it will all come out right in the end. . . .

We are now at Bermuda We came here on Saturday so now I think we shall have pretty easey time and I think it is about time for our corps is nearly half sick now we have lain in the trenches in front of Petersburg since the 21st of June and it uses up men faster than going in to a fight now and then there was over a week before we left that we were wet through every day it rained nearly all the while and we were under fire all the while if we were in camp they would shell us out so we did not have much peace we have lost 30 men

in Killed Wounded & Missing out of our camp this summer
we have got 76 men that belongs to the comp and only 28
present and we have 13 recruits At that some of them has
returned that was wounded in the first fight I am the only
non commishioned Officer that is left in the Comp. . . .

Charles Fisher to Anna Hallock[21]
From Bermuda Front, Va.
Jan. 31, 1865

Everything is quiet here today. A few rebels deserters
came in last night, and if they keep on so till spring there
will be no rebels to fight. Today is very warm and pleasant
and the troops are at work on the breast-works, and the
Johnnys are at work on theirs too and they are yelling and
making fun of each other like so many School boys. I shall
be on picket tonight and I hope a good many will come in
along my posts.

Anna I often think of the contrast between now and when
I lived to Aunt Elisa's. Then I could go to bed and sleep in
quiet and security from all danger, and get up in the morning
and engage in healthy and honest toil. Now I am obliged to
keep wide awake all night long in the cold and rain sometimes,
without the least bit of shelter, and not knowing what minute
we are to be attecked, and then if we are, our duty is to kill
all the men that we can, and stand a good chance of getting
wounded or killed ourselves.

It is a hard thing to look at, but it is right and just on our
side. . . .

Besides these letters written during the Civil War, a few personal recollections have come down to us. The Rev. D. H. Hanaburgh, who came to Katonah as Methodist minister in 1893,[22] told
in a church lecture of his experiences while confined in Anderson-
ville Prison. He recalled the hunger of the prisoners and that once
he had eaten soup made from a mouse and that nothing had ever
tasted so good.[23] April 4th was Lincoln's second inauguration.
The 9th was the surrender at Appomatox Court House. On April
14th Lincoln was assassinated. Edgar Hitt, who was later to establish himself in Old Katonah as blacksmith, wheelwright and
inventor, was at the theater that night.[24]

For a list of men from Katonah and nearby who served in the
Civil War, see Appendix No. 30.

References

1. Shonnard, Frederic & Spooner, W. W. *History of Westchester County.* New York, 1900, p. 594.
2. *Ibid.,* pp. 596-98.
3. Scott Life Guard. Application for company organization. Putnam County, Apr. 15, 1861. MS. (In possession of Mrs. Jonathan T. Rorer, Mahopac, N.Y.)
4. Scott Life Guard. Record of two-year enlistments. n.p., Apr. 30, 1861. MS. (In possession of Mrs. Jonathan T. Rorer, Mahopac, N.Y.)
5. 38th N.Y. Regiment, Co. G, George Britton, Capt. [Preliminary muster sheet.] New York, May 5, 1861. MS. (In possession of Mrs. Jonathan T. Rorer, Mahopac, N.Y.)
6. Wood, J. G. [Civil War documents.] 1861. MS. (At the National Archives, Washington, D.C. Copies at the Katonah Village Library)
7. Phisterer, Frederick. *New York in the War of the Rebellion, 1861 to 1865.* 3. ed. Albany, 1912, v. 2, p. 1293.
8. Union Defense Committee of the Citizens of New York. *Reports, resolutions and documents.* New York, 1862, pp. 98-99.
9. Barrett, R. T. Westchester women in the Civil War. In: *Westchester County Historical Bulletin,* 1952, v. 28, pp. 112-15.
10. Jay, Eleanor Field (Mrs. John) Letter to Mrs. Henry Robertson, Bedford, N.Y., n.d. (but during the Civil War). MS. (In possession of Mrs. L. H. Hall, Katonah)
11. Lewisboro (N.Y.) Book No.

27, election of town officers and minutes of meetings, 1830-1879. South Salem, 1830-79. MS. (At Lewisboro Town House)
12. Jones, Edward. Enoch H. Avery certificate, Maryland Heights, May 27, 1863. MS. (In possession of Mrs. H. D. Miller, Katonah)
13. Bedford (N.Y.) Supervisor. Account book. Bedford (N.Y.), 1856-73. MS. (Unpaged) (At Bedford Town House)
14. Bedford (N.Y.) [Civil War exemptions.] Bedford, 1862. MS. (At Bedford Town House)
15. Morris, R. B. *Encyclopedia of American history.* New York, 1953, p. 239.
16. Westchester County. Superintendents of the Poor House. Indenture of James Mullin to A. F. Dickinson. White Plains, N.Y., Feb. 3, 1851. MS. (In possession of Mrs. H. D. Miller, Katonah)
17. Baird, W. H. Descriptive list of Private James Muller, Co. G, 38 Regt., N.Y.S.V. 1862(?) MS. (In possession of Mrs. H. D. Miller)
18. All correspondence of James Muller, 1861-63, MSS. in possession of Mrs. H. D. Miller.
19. Moulton, D. Letter to A. F. Dickinson, Sept. 24, 1862. MS. (In possession of Mrs. H. D. Miller)
20. Hill, C. H. Letter to John C. Holmes, Bermuda Hundred, Va., Aug. 29, 1864. MS. (In possession of Mrs. L. H. Hall, Katonah)
21. Fisher, Charles. Letter to Anna Hallock, Bermuda Front, Va., Jan. 31, 1865. MS. (In possession

of Mrs. E. F. Mead, Katonah)
22. Hanaburgh, D. H. Historical sketch of Katonah Methodist Episcopal Church. In: Avery, O. T. *Historical sketch of Katonah.* 1896. (Unpaged)

23. Mead, (Mrs.) E. F., Katonah. Oral communication.
24. Kelly, K. B. The Hitt family of Old Katonah. Katonah, 1959. MS. (At the Katonah Village Library)

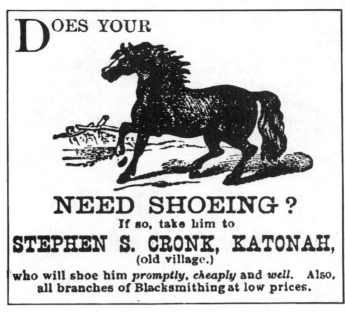

NEED SHOEING ?
If so, take him to
STEPHEN S. CRONK, KATONAH,
(old village.)
who will shoe him *promptly, cheaply* and *well*. Also,
all branches of Blacksmithing at low prices.

Advertisement in the *Feast of Lanterns,* August 11, 1880.
Collection of Mrs. James G. Bonacorda

CHAPTER XI

POST-BELLUM DAYS

THE YOUNG men who came home from the war didn't find too
much change in our rural areas but the villages had grown. In
1865 Katonah had 185 inhabitants and Whitlockville 127.[1]

Dr. Shove was still our only doctor and his nephew, Dr. Wickware, our only dentist, but a new public school had been added.
Miss Margery Van Tassel wrote of it in 1932:

> When the "depot" part of Katonah became a real village
> a school in that section became a necessity. The one in the
> "old village" could not be stretched to accomodate the grow-
> ing population. Then, too, the treasurer of the district had
> moved away and the treasure had been found to have moved
> also. This incident brought about much dispute and dis-
> sension over the question of whether or not the taxpayers
> ought to reimburse the district for its loss. A division of the
> district resulted and in 1862 the new district purchased from
> Mary Miller a building that had been used to house a private
> school.[2]

156

From 1866 on, Katonah began to expand in earnest. Fortunately Irene, one of Dr. Shove's daughters, brought into the community a second doctor by marrying a young man who had just been mustered out of the army. This was J. Francis Chapman, who began his study of medicine with his father-in-law, and remained to practice here for the rest of his life.[3]

From a cultural standpoint Whitlockville still outshone the newer village, holding a very popular series of lectures at its Methodist Church with Horace Greeley as one of the lecturers.[4] Katonah, however, did not lack for entertainment. In 1867 Stephen Holly Miller wrote his brother:

> The depot improves very fast. Saturday night 4 Indians was exhibited there. Benj and S. S. went . . . in the Odd Fellows room but it was crowded so full they had to retreat to the lower part of the building under the hardware store.[5]

The stores as well as the hotels had "halls" for meetings on their upper stories.

A letter from Arnell F. Dickinson to James Muller, in the same year, gives further news of the village:

> Stephen Lyons two boys, Penn and Jere, have bought out the John B. Whitlock store and are doing a good business there, while the Hoyt Brothers, sons of James Hoyt, have the Putney store, and together with the undertaking, furniture and tailoring, are doing a very large business.[6]

Both Miller and Dickinson gave news of their own rural areas as well. There was a debating club at the Mt. Holly School, and taking part was none other than that enthusiast who had started debating societies from the age of seventeen up, William H. Robertson. The question "Resolved that the desire to seek happiness is stronger than the desire to avoid misery" is reminiscent of questions chosen by the Literary Fraternity and the Cantatoe Lyceum of which he had been a leading spirit in his youth. Others taking part in the debate were Messrs. Green, Holly, Merritt and Reynolds. Stephen Holly Miller was president and J. Goldsmith, vice-president.[5] At Cantitoe, Dickinson was milking forty cows a day, Hannah was away at school in Bedford, Arney, a stout boy of eight, was reading a new book entitled "Facts for Farmers," and Lizzy, the baby of two years, was making the house resound with her clatter.

Though not mentioned in Dickinson's letter, Cantitoe had been having as much trouble with poachers as our outlying districts have today. In October of 1866 a group of neighbors got together and had an ultimatum printed.

HUNTERS TAKE NOTICE!

Having suffered much annoyance and damage, the undersigned respectfully give Notice, that from and after this date

SHOOTING AND HUNTING

on their premises are expressly forbidden. Violations of the Law will be Prosecuted!

J. W. Tompkins	Huey Wescott	Wm. Newman
Jere A. Miller	Mrs. L. Robertson	J. D. Powell
John Miller	Gilbert W. Miller	Oliver Green
Hackaliah Miller	Henry Robertson	Jared H. Green.[7]
	A. F. Dickinson	

In the sixties a new residential district was developed in Katonah village. This was on "Blacksnake Hill," a beautiful rise to the north of the river road to Whitlockville. Alfred F. Avery, who in 1866 married Ophelia Todd, our historian, and William H. Robertson were among the first to settle there.[4,8]

Increased population brought increased facilities. Among the innovations were newspapers of our own. On August 20, 1873, the *Katonah Sentinel* started publication. Young William A. Miller and O. H. Miller were the proprietors. The issue of October 2nd carried under County news a rumor that Vanderbilt, whose New York Central and Hudson River Railroad Co. had rented our New York and Harlem Railroad in April for 401 years,[9] intended to build a branch railway from Kensico to Danbury to cut out the "North Housatonic Project." On a map in Beer's atlas of 1867 this New York Housatonic & Northern Railway cuts blithely across the township running through Bedford Village and thence northeast through the village of Cross River in Lewisboro. Actually it never existed.

The October 2nd issue of the *Sentinel* noted further that the Farmers' Club was soliciting members, and that E. S. Folsom and Mrs. Lizzie Lawrence had been married. It is thanks to Mr. Folsom that we have many of the excellent photographs in this book. Advertisers on this date were H. C. Smith, Katonah Pharmacy; Hoyt Brothers; M. S. Benedict, Watches & Jewelry; Arnold, Shoes; A. M. Van Tassel, Mutton, Lamb & Veal; and Alsoph

Green, Proprietor of the Katonah Hotel, with Bar, Billiard Room and Livery Stable.[10]

In 1874 the *Sentinel* became the *Recorder*, with William A. Miller still one of its editors, the other being J. T. Lockwood. Also circulating at this time was a small two-leaf news sheet called the *Katonah Advertiser*, editor and proprietor Everett Benedict (shown on p. 68). It was a sprightly sheet paring news to the bone and leaving us hungry for more. Its advertisers included Miss L. F. White, a dressmaker who gave "Mrs. Doctor Shove" and "Mrs. Doctor Chapman" as references, H. S. Smith who advertised a washing machine, and Lyon Brothers, who advertised sewing machines. In Katonah the "do-it-by-hand" day was coming to an end.

Other papers of great interest were published once a year in connection with church fairs. The Ladies' Aid of the Methodist Episcopal Church published the *Feast of Lanterns* and that of the Presbyterian Church the *Blue Light*. The advertising money of the first was added to the building fund for the new Methodist parsonage, and that of the second went to decrease the Presbyterian Church debt which was paid off in 1877.[11]

The Presbyterians had come together as a very small group in 1871, holding their first services on May 2nd in the third floor hall of C. W. Avery's hardware store. Here they continued to meet until it was destroyed in the great fire and thereafter met in the small hall of Zeno Hoyt's building east of the railroad tracks.[13] For the first few years, services were held by various ministers, notably Mr. Hazeltine of North Salem. The congregation was small, only seven members when organized November 17, 1872, but energetic.[12] They decided to build a church. This they did with considerable debt, and it was finally completed across the river from the "Triangle" and dedicated December 21, 1874. The parsonage, built later, was on the newly developed Palmer Avenue. In April of 1875, John H. Eastman, a young theological student from Union Seminary in New York, was invited to preach at the church and in May he became its pastor, remaining as such for twenty years, dearly beloved by the whole community.[13]

The second church built in Old Katonah was the Methodist. The congregation moved from Whitlockville and erected a new building just across Anderson Road from the Presbyterian Church. This was dedicated on January 21, 1875.[14] Beside it was the Katonah Cemetery, still identifiable by the stones, a great many of which still remain in the thicket on the corner of Anderson Road and Woodsbridge Road, though the bodies were removed at the coming of the reservoir.

It is interesting to note that John Eastman and Thomas La-Monte, who were our Katonah Presbyterian and Methodist ministers in 1875, both had sons who became very well known nationally and internationally. While a member of J. P. Morgan and Co., Thomas William Lamont, with H. P. Davidson, developed and carried out the plans for financial help to Great Britain and France prior to our entry into World War I, and in 1919 he served on the American Commission to Negotiate Peace.[15] Joseph Bartlett Eastman served from 1916-19 on the Massachusetts Public Service Commission, thereafter as a member of the Interstate Commerce Commission, and 1933-36 as Federal Coordinator of Transportation. During World War II he was Director of Defense Transportation.[16]

The third church to be built in Katonah, St. Mary's, began, like the Presbyterian, in a hall. From 1867 until 1890 Mass was celebrated in Green's Hall in Old Katonah.[17] Katonah belonged to St. Joseph's Parish in Croton Falls when, in 1889, its rector announced Bishop Corrigan's desire that the people of Katonah build a church. The parishioners hailed the news with delight, and though possessed with but a small share of this world's goods, set to work with a will and raised $1900. With $400 of this they bought land south of the depot on a hill overlooking the Cross River. On October 14, 1890, the church was dedicated.[18]

Even before the Presbyterians and the Catholics began holding services in Katonah, Episcopalians were active. Apparently they did not have a church building but met in private homes or in a hall. In 1855 Robert Bolton wrote:

> Mr. Partridge [of St. Matthews, Bedford] has also organized St. Marks Church, Katonah where there is a good congregation every other Sunday afternoon.[19]

Beginning in 1857, there is mention of this church in other sources. The Vestry Minutes of St. Matthew's Church yield the following:

> 11 Oct. 1857.
> A communication from Vestry of St. Mark's, Katonah, asking for the services of Rev. Mr. Boggs every Sunday afternoon.

Ordered that the communication lay on the table till the next meeting of the Vestry.

18 Oct. 1857.

The Vestry resumed the consideration of the application from St. Mark's Church, Katonah &

Resolved that it is the desire of this Vestry that during the winter Rev. Mr. Boggs should perform service in *this* church every alternate Sunday afternoon.

17 April, 1860

Resolved: That John Jay Esq. & Rev. E. B. Boggs be a committe to confer with the Church at Katonah as to having Services there, and the amt that could be obtained towards the salary.

3 June, 1860

The Com. appointed to confer with the Church at Katonah *reported* that they had only obtained subscriptions to the amount of about $60.00.[20]

In 1867 the *Living Church Quarterly and Annual* began listing St. Mark's Church in Katonah as under the care of the Rev. L. Luquer of Bedford, but in 1879, the only year in which the name of a priest-in-charge is listed, the Rev. C. Brassington Mee of North Castle was the incumbent. The listing continued each year until 1887, shortly after which it seems to have disbanded. John Jay II had in mind resuscitating this church when in 1888 he made a codicil to his will:

Third. Among my assets is a certificate of the Bank of America for Five Hundred Dollars. This certificate, which includes a small amount subscribed in cash towards the erection of an Episcopal Church at Katonah in the parish which was organized under the name of St. Mark's and which was after abandoned, I give to the Parochial Fund of the Diocese of New York to be held in trust and accumulated until such time as in the opinion of the trustees of said parochial fund, after consultation with the rector of St. Matthew's Church, Bedford, and of the person who may then be the chief representative of the Jay family at Bedford . . . it can be advantageously and permanently invested or employed . . . for the benefit of the Episcopal Church in or near the Village of Katonah.[21]

When he died in 1894, however, for some reason the legacy was not put to this use. In 1898 William Jay, son of the donor, deemed that the fund income should go to St. Matthew's Church at Bedford Center instead. It wasn't until the spring of 1961 that vestrymen of St. Matthew's discovered papers that indicated John Jay's true purpose and advised St. Luke's parish in Katonah immediately of their intention to turn over the use of the fund to them.

In the field of medicine there were many new developments in the 1870's and our local doctors kept well abreast of the times. Physicians of the region forming the Northern Westchester and Eastern Putnam Medical Association met often in Katonah. Our Doctors Shove and Chapman served variously as officers. At a meeting April 7, 1874, at the Katonah Hotel, Dr. Lewis Pelton of Mt. Kisco presented interesting facts relating to the habit of opium-eating as practiced in this vicinity.[22] The action of morphine was not yet well known, and it was only in that year that a German physician was emphasizing its dangers.[28]

Entertainment, except for those "4 Indians" who sound imported, was of the homemade variety and highly inventive. Plays were written for local production by the gifted in the community. One play, found among the papers of Mrs. O. T. Avery, written in careful and legible script, begins in "a parlor nicely furnished."

> Sophia (pulling out her watch), Eight o'clock! And no one has arrived yet. Really! this is tiresome.
> Mrs. Tinkle. Indeed! My love, you forget that in fashionable society no one would think of arriving sooner. How horridly vulgar it would be! [29]

It goes on in a vein as gently ironic as Jane Austen.

A group called the "Katonah Musical Association," functioning during the years 1871-1872, began in Avery's Hall and moved to Green's because of a disagreement on price. Its officers were J. F. Chapman, C. E. Wickware, Joseph Barrett, James E. Hoyt, A. M. Van Tassel and S. B. Hoyt, who was its musical director. Among the out-of-village members was Mrs. W. P. Holly.[30]

On the less cultural side there was never failing entertainment at the Katonah Driving Park, of which Henry N. Parent was manager. Weekly trots took place there for purses of fifty dollars or so. Admission was twenty-five cents. Judges were men such as W. J. Horton, Alsoph Green, Bernard Travis; and among the popular local horses were Henry Parent's Gray Jack, William Nelson's Brown Kitty, and Seth Hoyt's Copper Bottom.

One of the most exciting races occurred in October of 1874 when a Stamford lady, Mrs. Libbie Taff, driving her own horse Whitefoot, competed with Mr. Seth Hoyt driving Copper Bottom. Lady drivers were an uncommon sight and the audience cheered her victory wildly.[23] A few lines from a poem of the day are the following:

> *On Thursday afternoon, it was,*
> *The Thirtieth of July,*
>
> *That vehicles of various kinds,*
> *Well filled, were passing by.*
>
> *I stopped a man, and asked him, why*
> *The cause for such display.*
>
> *He answered me, in hurried tones,*
> *"The Trot takes place today."*
>
> *"What trot?" I asked—he looked surprised,*
> *At my being in the dark;*
>
> *"Why, for the fifty dollar purse,*
> *At Katonah Driving Park."* [24]

The 1876 Fourth of July celebration was a humdinger that lasted two nights and a day. The bells of the churches rang; those of the new fire apparatus joined in. Seth Hoyt mounted a bell on his wagon and drove around town with it pealing wildly. The Katonah Home Guards, commanded by J. G. Miller, fired volleys, and marched about to the beat of drums. There were Chinese lanterns and a calcium light hitched up to a gas jet. Pictures, including those of George and Martha Washington, were thrown on a large outside screen.

Calthumpians in costume (this one defeats us), some forty of them on horseback, marched to Whitlockville and then Cherry Street, passing around Dr. Shove's house. They returned to give three cheers at Judge Robertson's house and stay to breakfast.

The Fire Department paraded and was given a flag by Mr. Travis. An exhibition drill took place at Green's Hotel. Then, after mid-day, came the raising of the 75-foot flag-pole, surmounted by a handsomely gilded weather vane and compass. The pole of hemlock wood was donated by the Honorable John Jay, grandson of the Chief Justice, the 19-foot hemlock splice, by

Captain J. J. Reynolds and his sister, Mrs. Whitman. Henry Robertson raised the flag while the "Star Spangled Banner" was played.

In the afternoon there was band music, prayer and a reading of the Declaration of Independence.[25] Then in compliance with a proclamation of the President of the United States recommending that a historical sketch of each town be part of centennial celebrations, Joseph Barrett gave his now famous speech. A petition asking him to prepare and deliver the address was signed by thirty-six Katonah citizens.[31]

Two of our present-day organizations had their birth in the eighteen-seventies. Our Fire Department was formed as the result of the fire that had swept through the "Triangle" on the night of November 19, 1874, burning eight buildings at an estimated loss of $31,500. It was the general belief that the fire was the work of an incendiary. The old hotel, unused by changing owners, had been occupied by squatters until a new owner ordered them out. There were threats made by one occupant to burn the building and it is thought he did.

Besides the hotel, Avery's buildings went. In the main building there was a gunpowder explosion that terrified the village and could be felt two miles away. From the *Recorder* of November 20, 1874, we take the following:

> Water pipes located in different parts of the village were brought into requisition and with an army of men, women and children with pails, excellent service was done; carpets were procured from Lyon Bros., and thoroughly saturated with water, and suspended to the side of the building, were very successfully used.
>
> At this place fully two hours of the hardest labor was accomplished. Those stationed on the icy roofs and ladders were frequently in great danger. Many were almost exhausted by overexertion and excitement. . . .
>
> The large reservoir of the Katonah Water Co. was particularly serviceable throughout the fire; finally when the flames were entirely under control, there was a large supply. This institution which has frequently been pronounced worthless, is now highly prized, and will no doubt be kept in perfect order to meet any emergency.[26]

Soon after the smoke had cleared, about sixty citizens of Katonah got together and formed three companies, the Alert

Hose Co., the Hope Hook and Ladder Co., and Engine Company No. 1.[32] An interesting document reads:

> We the inhabitants & freeholders of Katonah Depot feeling desirous of securing the said depot from damage by fire do hereby agree whose names are hereafter subscribed that they will pay in proportion to their assessment on the property each owns in said Depot for the procuring of an Enjine and hose sufficient for taking the water from Cross river to any buildings in the bounds of said subscribers and also to erect a suitable building at some suitable place hereafter designated by said subscribers for the safe keeping of the said enjine.

David Putny	Warren Collyer
M. B. Silkman	Harvy Smith
John Knox	S. B. Hoyt
Charles E. Wickware	Zeno Hoyt
E. J. Purdy	George Van kleek[33]
Mark Harris	
Thos. D. Lyon	
John Chadeayne.	

The Katonah Village Improvement Society, first called the Katonah Village Improvement Association, was organized as the result, not of disaster, but of ever growing needs. At a meeting of the Bedford Farmers' Club, held at the home of Mr. Pellew in August of 1878, a committee was appointed to look into the establishment of a town improvement society or individual societies in the separate villages and railway stations of the town. Committee members were: John Jay, Chairman, Bernard Travis, James Wood, Col. Robert Leonard, A. Mead Clark, James Lounsberry, H. E. Pellew.[34] There were already many improvement associations in New England, and in nearby Ridgefield trees planted by their society were considered as enhancing the property value of the town. At the next month's meeting of the Club it was agreed to recommend separate associations for the villages and the committee chosen for Katonah was William H. Robertson, Bernard Travis, and Col. William Jay.[35]

Katonah acted quickly. On October 21st, William H. Robertson presided at a meeting at the Methodist Church. Henry E. Pellew, an English gentleman married to William Jay's daughter, was elected president. Vice-Presidents were John Jay, W. H. Robertson, B. Travis, Rev. Philip Germond, Rev. J. H. Eastman;

treasurer was Oliver Green, and secretary, J. Benedict. The Executive Committee was J. W. Anderson, Col. William Jay, J. E. Hoyt, J. F. Chapman, M.D., J. D. Powell, Jere M. Lyon, Joseph Barrett, A. F. Dickinson, H. C. Smith, J. H. Cox, Mrs. G. Chadeayne, Mrs. Sarah F. Fowler, Mrs. Ophelia Green, Miss M. M. Hoyt, Miss Venie Green. Thirty-nine people were enrolled at this meeting.[36]

When the Executive Committee met three days later, they sprang into action and elected subcommittees on Members, Tree Planting, Nuisances, Sanitary Reform, and Roads and Side Walks.[38] At their next meeting, they voted $25.00 for trees, $10.00 for gravel sidewalks, and elected a special committee to suggest sanitary improvements on the premises of two neighbors.[39] A reading room and library were soon established. The running expenses for 1882 were:

Rental of rooms for Library	$15.00 per month
Janitor	4.00 per month
Miss Devoe, the Curator	6.00 per month[37]

Conditions in Katonah at this time were well and frankly described by Lord Exmouth, son of Mr. Pellew, in a letter to Miss Elizabeth Barrett in 1928:

One subject which, from the beginning, had interested and perplexed him [Mr. Pellew], was how to improve the appearance of and the living conditions in and around, the railroad station and village of Katonah. Every time that he drove to or from the station, he passed through a depressed, muddy . . . stretch alongside of the track, ornamented chiefly with old tomato cans, and refuse and garbage of all sorts and kinds. The village as a whole was ragged and unsightly but that particular bit was not only ugly and smelly but might easily be dangerous to the health of the village community.

On talking the matter over, it appeared that the trouble was mainly due to politics. In the early 70's, the Civil War had not long been over, and political feelings ran high! The animosities of national politics were carried down into local affairs and even into families. . . .

In this little place, Katonah, the dividing line between Republicans and Democrats was so marked, that they and their families would hardly do business with each other. I remember there was one department store kept by a prominent family of Republicans, and nearby was a rival store of the Democrats; and it was a matter of principle for the loyal members of one party not even to buy their shoes or groceries from their opponents' store. . . .

The Katonah Village Improvement Society was organized, and at once began its work. The streets and sidewalks were cleaned and repaired, the street lamps put in and kept bright and clean, back yards were looked after, flowers and shrubbery appeared at corners and in vacant spaces, and were carefully tended, replacing dumps of stones and rubbish. Not only the outward appearance of the village improved enormously, but also its sanitary conditions, which in part at least, sadly needed attention.

But the most important work of the Society, and one for which I think its first president was largely responsible, was the growth and development of the Community Spirit.[40]

On September 30, 1879, a third organization was founded in Katonah, the McKeel Post, No. 120, of the Grand Army of the Republic. The commander was E. B. Newman and its charter members E. B. Newman, J. T. Lockwood, E. S. Folsom, S. S. Austin, Clark See, W. L. Hull, A. S. Knapp, E. A. Teed, Charles Fisher, Edgar Hitt, J. B. Turner, Charles Corbyn, E. H. Avery, C. W. Varian, A. P. Quick and James A. Tuttle.[41] A building was erected on the east side of the railroad tracks near the present home of the late James Lawrence. Dr. Chapman made the dedication speech and the flag was raised fluttering in the breeze. From this hall thereafter on Memorial Day each year the village gathered and marched to the Katonah Cemetery, where veterans decorated the graves of their comrades.[42]

Of this era are the following notes from newspapers and leaflets:

1873　Teachers' Institute held at Sing Sing. Board of Education & Trustees (ours included) asked to induce their teachers to attend. New methods of teaching illustrated on class of children present with teacher.[43]

1874　It is now stated that the Prohibitionists at the recent election in this State, polled about 11,000 votes for their candidate for Governor.[26]

1877　Mrs. H. F. Wood advertised lessons in Piano or Thorough Bass, and at commencement of the fall session, a French conversation class according to methods of M. Louis Pujol.[11]

1878 Katonah and Peekskill Mail Route. Seth Hoyt, Proprietor. Stage leaves Katonah on Tuesdays, Thursdays and Saturdays, at 8 A.M. . . . Fare . . . $1.00.

City Boarders while staying in the country will please leave their orders for papers and magazines at the Katonah Post Office.

City people wishing a nice, quiet place for the summer will do well to visit the Farm-House of S. H. Miller, two miles east of Katonah. Beautiful Drive, Fine Lawn, Plenty of Shade and Croquet . . . Piano . . . Terms moderate.[44]

Of the fifty million of our population, the ten millions who are heads of families are taxed less than ten cents a day for the support of the Federal Government.[27]

1879 Hoyt Bros. advertised for sale COOLEY CORK CORSETS.[45]

References

1. Asher & Adams. *New topographical atlas and gazetteer of New York. 1871.* Quoted from Westchester County Emergency Work Bureau, Historical development of Westchester County. [White Plains, N.Y.,] 1939, v. 1, p. 551. MS. (At Westchester County, Dept. of Planning, County Office Building, White Plains)

2. Van Tassel, M. H. Old Katonah schools. In: *Katonah Record,* July 29, 1932.

3. Doe, Janet. Medicine in Katonah. Katonah, 1959. MS. (At the Katonah Village Library)

4. Avery, O. T. *Historical sketch of Katonah.* Katonah, 1896. (Unpaged)

5. Miller, S. H. Letter to his brother, Alfred Miller. Bedford, N.Y.(?) Oct. 12, 1867. MS. (In possession of Mrs. Oliver U. Todd, Goldens Bridge, N.Y.)

6. Dickinson, A. F. Letter to James Muller, Katonah, Jan. 17, 1867. MS. (In possession of Mrs. H. D. Miller, Katonah)

7. Printed notice, Bedford, Oct. 25, 1866, in E. P. Barrett's scrapbook. (In possession of Mr. E. P. Barrett, Katonah)

8. Kelly, K. B. The Robertson family. Katonah, 1959. MS. (At the Katonah Village Library)

9. Hyatt, E. C. *History of the New York & Harlem Railroad.* N.p., 1898, pp. 25-26.

10. *Katonah Sentinel,* Oct. 2, 1873.

11. *Blue Light,* Katonah, Aug. 1, 1877.

12. *Ibid.,* Aug. 7, 1878.

13. Barrett, Joseph. Katonah Pres-

byterian Church. In: O. T. Avery, *Historical sketch of Katonah*. Katonah, 1896 (unpaged)

14. Hanaburgh, D. H. Katonah Methodist Episcopal Church. In: O. T. Avery, *Historical sketch of Katonah*. Katonah, 1896 (unpaged)
15. *Encyclopedia Americana*. New York, 1953, v. 16, p. 678.
16. Obituary of Joseph Bartlett Eastman. *N.Y. Herald Tribune,* Mar. 16, 1944.
17. Lucid, R. G. *St. Mary's Parish Golden Jubilee, 1908-1958.* Katonah, 1958 (unpaged)
18. Doyle, W. J. St. Mary's Roman Catholic Church. In: O. T. Avery, *Historical sketch of Katonah*. Katonah, 1896 (unpaged)
19. Bolton, Robert. *History of the Protestant Episcopal Church in the County of Westchester.* New York, 1855, p. 627.
20. St. Matthew's Church in Bedford. Vestry minutes. Bedford, N.Y., 1796-1876. MS. (At St. Matthew's Parish House, Bedford)
21. *Patent Trader,* Mt. Kisco, N.Y. June 15, 1961.
22. *Recorder,* Katonah, Apr. 24, 1874.
23. *Ibid.,* Oct. 23, 1874.
24. *Ibid.,* Aug. 7, 1874.
25. *Ibid.,* July 7, 1876.
26. *Ibid.,* Nov. 20, 1874.
27. *Ibid.,* Mar. 1, 1878.
28. Garrison, F. H. *An introduction to the history of medicine.* 4. ed. Philadelphia, 1929, p. 855.
29. Avery, O. T. [Play.] Katonah(?) n.d. MS. (In possession of Mrs. James G. Bonacorda, 4351 Edson Ave., New York 60, N.Y.)
30. Katonah Musical Association. Constitution and minutes. [Katonah, 1871-72.] MS. (In pos-

session of Mrs. L. H. Hall, Katonah)
31. Petition requesting Joseph Barrett to give the address at Katonah's celebration of July 4, 1876. MS. (In possession of Mrs. W. A. Kelly, Katonah)
32. Barrett, H. R. The Katonah Fire Department. In: Katonah Village Improvement Society, *Sketches and views of Old and New Katonah.* Katonah, 1900 (unpaged)
33. Katonah (N.Y.) Fire Department. [Agreement for securing and housing a fire engine.] Katonah, n.d. MS. (Photostat at the Katonah Village Library)
34. Bedford Farmers' Club. Minutes for August 1878. In: *Recorder,* Katonah, Aug. 30, 1878.
35. *Ibid.,* September 1878. Cutting from newspaper. (In possession of Mr. William Will, Katonah)
36. Katonah Village Improvement Society. Minutes. Oct. 21, 1878. MS. (At the Katonah Village Library)
37. *Ibid.,* Mar. 29, 1882.
38. Katonah Village Improvement Society. Executive Committee. Minutes. Oct. 24, 1878. MS. (At the Katonah Village Library)
39. *Ibid.,* Oct. 31, 1878.
40. Exmouth, C. E. Pellew, 7th Viscount. Letter to Miss E. N. Barrett, Sept. 12, 1928. MS. (In possession of Mrs. W. A. Kelly, Katonah)
41. Scharf, J. T. *History of Westchester County.* Philadelphia, 1886, v. 1, p. 512.
42. Mead, Mrs. E. F. Katonah. Oral communication.
43. Westchester County. School Commissioners. *Teachers' institute.* n.p., 1873. (Printed circular in possession of Mrs. H. D. Miller, Katonah)
44. *Feast of Lanterns,* Katonah, Aug. 15, 1878.
45. *Ibid.,* Aug. 26, 1879.

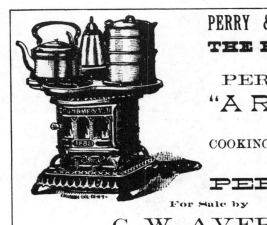

Advertisement in the *Feast of Lanterns*, August 16 and 17, 1882.
Collection of Mrs. James G. Bonacorda

CHAPTER XII

THE GAY EIGHTIES AND NINETIES

THE "Gay Eighties and Nineties" had color and drama. These were the days of village improvement and pride in the community; days of wealth in the rural areas, where Colonel William Jay was driving a four-in-hand with éclat.[1] Towards their end, these were also days of uprooting and heartache.

Much of the village gaiety of this era came from the yearly influx of summer boarders. Even before the eighties, the Whitlocks, Browers, Benedicts,[2] Mrs. Charles Adams,[3] the Stephen Holly Millers,[4] and possibly others, had begun to take city boarders for the summer. They became an important social addition to the community, as well as bringing a certain income to their hosts. Bernard Travis, who certainly didn't lack for anything, took summer guests, and his high stepping beautiful horses were turned out in the latest style to meet them at the train. The A. F. Averys, also in the upper financial bracket, took boarders at their home on the hill where they held weekly dances, an occasional straw ride, and croquet games that went on almost without ceasing from morning to night.

The Benedict's house in Whitlockville was described as follows in a brochure put out by the Railroad:

170

MAPLE LAWN BOARDING HOUSE. 8 minutes' walk; accommodate 25 to 30; 16 rooms, adults $6.00 to $8.00; children according to age; pleasantly situated, on high ground, with well-shaded lawn; fruit, vegetables, milk, eggs, pure water, and plenty of ice, good trout, bass and pickerel fishing in Croton Lake and Cross River; boats free; good gunning—woodcock, partridge, quail, etc.; good livery; churches of various denominations convenient. References exchanged.[5]

How could anyone in New York resist taking the next train, ticket in one hand and exchangeable references clutched in the other?

Up on Cherry Street Mrs. Sarah Shove Barrett ran her father's house, "The Mountain Homestead," as a boarding house after his death.[6] Down at Silkman's Corners near Whitlockville, Mrs. Horace Searles also kept boarders and her guests seem often to have been chosen for inability rather than ability to pay!

Elizabeth Eastman, daughter of the Presbyterian minister, writing of her childhood in later years said:

> Across the hill behind our house was the Searles place, a boarding-house, but much more than that. Maggie Searles had the biggest heart in the whole country-side. In her big, old-fashioned kitchen, you could find cripples, human misfits of all kinds who found refuge with her. Sometimes their families, if they had any, paid her—very little—but that didn't matter. She was not a modern social worker with hard and fast theories but in reality the most successful mender of broken lives. She was a mother to everyone, her husband and her own children, her boarders and those derelicts she harbored. I loved her. So did the whole village, young and old.[7]

The whole community enjoyed the guests and the recreational facilities of the boarding-houses. One delightful occasion seems to have been a concert held at "Maple Lawn" where Miss Sniffin, Miss Jelliff and Mrs. Harriet Avery Lewis were the artists.[8] Mrs. Lewis, the daughter of the John Burr Whitlock, Jrs., had a magnificent voice and sang professionally throughout the country. She was singing with the Clara Louise Kellogg Opera Company in 1889 when she married Edward Strakosch, her second husband, who was also with the company.[10]

Other recreations, not centered in the boarding-houses, were cycling, horse-racing, and events sponsored by the churches and the Village Improvement Society. Around 1890, the Titicus Cycle Club was active, very active, in the community. It was the pleasure of its members to pedal to New York quite frequently, though on the return journey they were wont to weaken and board the train for Katonah.[11]

There were many fine horses in the countryside during this era. Among the men who bred more than a few were Bernard Travis, George and William Nelson, and George Green. Travis raised trotters that he raced at Goshen, more as a hobby than business, but the others went into it on a large scale.

The Nelsons, who were dairymen, had trotting stables and a race track across the Croton River on the flats below Woods Bridge.[6] George Green, owner of the Hotel Metropole and the Green Line Cars in New York, raised champion hackney ponies at Forest View Farm. This elaborate establishment was a millionaire's dream. It spread over ninety acres, now mostly at the bottom of the Cross River Reservoir, and in its heyday accommodated nearly three hundred horses. It had six barns and four training tracks and was the last word in luxury.[12]

There were many others who delighted in raising a good colt or two and racing wasn't confined to the tracks. Almost every man believed he had a horse that could outstep his neighbor's and almost any flat stretch of road served to settle these friendly rivalries.[13]

An affair that a present day church might imitate was the "Bonnet Sociable" held at the home of Stephen Holly Miller in 1892. It was the gentlemen who competed for the prizes in bonnet trimmings! [14]

High on the list of enjoyable events were the lectures and concerts begun in 1881 by the Village Improvement Society. These were in aid of the reading room which had been opened in the autumn of 1880. Among the subjects presented were the travelogs, "A trip up the Rhine" by James Wood and "A Horseback ride through Palestine" by the Rev. George Clarke. A frequent and much enjoyed speaker was Jahu DeWitt Miller. Popular on the lighter side were "Mrs. Jarley's Waxworks" under the direction of Mrs. Shove and Mrs. Chapman in 1884,[15] and Mr. George Green's contribution, "An Evening with the Phonograph," in 1891.[16] In 1894, Mr. Edward Wegmann, Jr., division engineer of the Aqueduct Commission, gave an illustrated lecture on the "Construction of the New Croton Aqueduct." [17]

The river was a continual source of joy and recreation at all seasons. Mrs. Avery described it so beautifully in her poem, "The Diverted Village," that we can do no better than use some of her lines:

> *The quiet river, rippling 'neath the shade*
> *Of oak and bending willow, once surveyed*
> *By dusky dwellers of another race*
> *Gone and forgot with but a name, as trace.*
> *The meadow by it where in placid mood*
> *The contemplative oxen, chewing, stood,*
> *The bridge, whose rough and loosely boarded floor*
> *Sounded afar the clattering wagon's roar,*
> *Where strollers loitered and a youthful row*
> *Stood dropping pebbles in the stream below,*
> *The plash of oar, the merry roundelay*
> *From rustic river craft at close of day,*
> *The milldam's distant rumble, thro' the still*
> *Sweet summer twilight air, the pond, the mill*
> *The clear, shrill call of some lone whippoorwill. . . .*
>
> *When leafless woods and ice o'er lake and stream*
> *Grown thick and smooth, proclaimed the sway supreme*
> *Of Arctic king, then all the air without*
> *Resounded with the joyous skater's shout.*
> *How oft beneath the moon's entrancing light*
> *Far up the "Cove" they glided out of sight!*
> *Then back in graceful curves; in dismal plight*
> *Sat some, to watch the rest contented quite.*
> *Around the crackling fire, discreetly built,*
> *Upon the frozen edge, with easy tilt*
> *And fearless glide, they gathered jestingly*
> *Perching on ledge or log or fallen tree;*
> *Then off again like birds across the pond*
> *That smoothly blent with snowy hills beyond.*[18]

The young had other amusements and excitement as well. Nearby Somers was the birthplace of the circus in this country, and Van Amburgh and Stone brought their shows to the old village and pitched their tents south of the village on the flats.[6] Then there was the hide-and-seek game that went on in the streets of the "Triangle" every summer evening until the whistle of the 9:30 milk train announced it was time for all children to return home. As older children in a family outgrew this sport, the younger ones took it up and the dusk was filled with shrieks of excitement.[19] The children from Cantitoe and Mt. Holly, accompanying their fathers to the depot in farm wagons filled with milk cans, joined in these games with zest.

South of Old Katonah, on land that later became our present village, three families of children were growing up in the early eighties. They played in the flat sandy fields near the tracks where rushes for scouring kitchen sinks and tables grew, and they played in the meadows and woods on higher ground. These were the Fisher, the Hunt and the Tompkins children. It was the Hunt family for whom our Huntville Road is named, and the road follows what was in those days the drive to their home from "the lower road," as Bedford Road was called.[20]

Between Cherry Street, which still had a general store, a shoe-making shop and a school, and Bedford Road, which had no buildings except Mr. Knowlton's big barn, the only connecting link was a farm lane, part of which was later incorporated into Valley Road. The Tompkins farm extended from our present New Street to the railroad south of the brook that runs down Valley Road. The Knowlton farm on which the Fishers lived ran from Cherry Street to the railroad, north of the Tompkins place. The Knowlton and Hunt houses are gone but the farm-house on Terrace Heights, in which Margaret Tompkins, now Mrs. Albert Burt, grew up, still stands. As a child, she attended the Cherry Street school. Her teacher, Miss Ella Mills, walked every day from Bedford.[21]

Emma Fisher, now Mrs. Charles Mead, had many farm chores as a child on land now ill adapted to them. One was picking potato bugs from plants in the middle of today's intersection of Valley and Bedford Roads. When she had time, she loved sitting on top of the board fence by the single track at train time. Sparks from the wood-burning engine flew out of the smoke stack and made a fine sight until engine and cars disappeared in the covered bridge to the north.[6]

Several new industries made their appearance in this era, and some existing ones enlarged to important proportions. A home industry was that of shirt-making. Advertised in our local papers were the "New Home Sewing Machine" sold by Miller and Lent, the "New Remington" sold by the Hoyt Brothers, and the "Singer" sold by Chadeayne's.[22,23] Naturally, every woman wanted a machine, and paid for it by making up shirts cut out in the city. The pay was $1.25 to $2.00 a dozen and the sound of humming machines was as loud in the streets of Katonah and Whitlockville as the humming of thousands of bees.[6]

The American Lens Company was a very successful industry of the time. In 1880, William Wilson, looking for a likely spot for the grinding of glass, which he contemplated engaging in with D. Fletcher Gorham, took over the mill and iron foundry property of Jacob Hanford.[9] The buildings had been part of the old Wood and Whitlock mills, another part of which was still used as a gristmill by Mr. Cox.[24]

We find the lens factory mentioned in "An Annual Walk Around Katonah" in the *Feast of Lanterns*, 1883:

> But what adjectives can do justice to the possible park that will be in front of the property owned by the American Lens Manufacturing Company? As we don't know what the park will look like, of course we can't say anything about it. But judging from the resplendently new attire of Cox's grist mill, and of the factory—old and new—(40 X 36 feet have just been added), it will be something that would make Katonah open his eyes, if he could throw off his great boulder bed quilt. George E. Todd and Alfred F. Avery brought money and push into the Lens Manufacturing Company when they bought out Henry N. Parent's interest last winter. May it yield golden returns—as it promises—out of its object magnifiers, convex and concave colorless lenses, neutral blue and smoked lenses.

Speaking of the station, the same commentator wrote:

> Just across the way [from the station and east of the tracks], in a neat building owned by the Cheeryble Brothers [he thus referred to the Lyons], is the Library and Reading Room of the Katonah Village Improvement Society. . . . It is just the spot for a leisure hour. . . . Provision is also made for a timely ablution; and a handy brush and comb will reduce the most perverse hair to comparative decorum. By the way—don't young ladies use cyclones instead of hair brushes?

Our commentator walked about the villages of Whitlockville and Old Katonah and noted everywhere progress in making

them pleasant, clean and worthy of pride. A. F. Avery had built
an excellent stone wall. Judge Robertson had a new fence of
delicate evergreen. Sidewalks were extending. Roses grew on
the roof of Uncle David and Aunt Laura Silkman's piazza. Dr.
Chapman was taking patients in his spacious and beautiful house.
Mrs. Chapman was a practical and effective assistant. Dr. Carpenter, the other local doctor, was also eminently skillful, careful and
successful but, "like a bee in a nectar cup, he dwells in single
blessedness" near the depot.[23] (Incidentally, Dr. Carpenter, who
had moved to Katonah in 1878, gave up his "single blessedness"
in April, 1884, to marry Venie Green.)[25]

Of the slaughter-house and the grain pit, our commentator
disapproved:

> Barley grain depot! That's what it is. There's been considerable
> litigation about it, but how much improvement your *cicerone*
> cannot say. It is an odorous subject.[23]

We feel perhaps he was a little critical there. In spite of new
industry—a ribbon-mill also established itself in Katonah[26] in
1890[27]—we remained primarily an agricultural community until
the inundation, as the Misses Van Tassel remember:

> Tuesdays and Thursdays were freight days. On Tuesdays cars
> were made up of livestock. There were pens near the track to
> the north of the station where the farmers put the cows and
> calves to be shipped to the city. When the cars came through
> from points further north to pick them up, they already had
> a load of mooing animals and could be heard while still up
> the track. Thursday's farm produce such as apples, potatoes,
> pears, nuts and popcorn were shipped. Farmers came in on
> freight days and did shopping and visited. Wives and children
> came along. At nine-thirty in the evening, the milk train
> stopped. Katonah at one time shipped two carloads a day. . . .
> At the south of the village, there was a pit by the tracks where
> mash from city breweries was unloaded. George Todd bought
> this in New York and the Nelsons and also the Hopkins used
> to feed this to their livestock.[33]

Telephones were a new thing. Just as "crystal sets" challenged
men of scientific bent before the days of moderately priced commercial radios, so in the eighties did the telephone. Private lines

were run between houses of relatives and friends. *The Recorder* of February 19, 1880, notes:

> We notice the construction in town of several lines of telephonic communication. Messrs. Hoyt Brothers have their stores connected; Mr. W. E. Clarke has a wire from his drugstore to his residence and Doctor Chapman has communication from his office with that of Dr. Wickware. This modern convenience is certainly growing more and more into popular use and favor.[28]

An early line installed by Seth Shove Barrett connected the Shove-Barrett house on Cherry Street, Dr. Chapman's residence, Andrew Van Tassel's meat market and Fletcher Lent's livery stable.[19] In some places where a person was willing to tend a switchboard, several subscribers would pay for the service. Sarles Drug Store in Mt. Kisco was one of these centers and connections were made between it and Dr. Carpenter's office in Katonah in 1889.[29] In 1897, Palmer Lewis of Bedford tried to arrange a local system in Mt. Kisco with the central in Sarles Drug Store.[30] Mr. Lewis was extending his line in all directions.

These early lines were doubtless a boon on occasions but also an aggravation, as they were not a twenty-four-hour service by any means. The subscriber got through at hours convenient to the switchboard tender and then only if the tender was not doing something else more important or enjoyable.

Dr. Carpenter evidently felt connecting with a switchboard was an advantage but it must have had its drawbacks too. In the old days, a patient had to be really sick for a member of his family to rouse a doctor from his sleep if he had to be summoned personally rather than by phone. This was no deterrent in real emergency, however. In the blizzard of '88, the husband of a woman in labor not only fought his way to Dr. Chapman's door but carried him on his back to deliver his wife![34] Perhaps it was this grateful husband who delivered the following letter from the otherwise snowbound doctor to an equally snowbound patient:

Katonah
Tuesday, Mar. 13, 1888

Dear Mrs. Van Tassel:

Well! What a state of things! When shall we be able to get out into the world again? Irene [Mrs. Chapman] snow-bound somewhere in Armonk with no means of hearing from her, or of her knowing anything of our well-being; Charlie, somewhere this side of, or in, New York, with 25 cents to subsist upon for two or three days—and not a word of intelligence since he left at seven o'clock yesterday morning. Coal bin empty and no way to get a bushel from the yard—"So near and yet so far." I guess the Oldest Inhabitant will not be far out of the way if he declares this to be "the very worst snow-storm within my recollection."

Last night—I can truly say—I pulled the drapery of my couch about me and lay down, if not to pleasant dreams, at least in a consciousness that no mortal being could drag me out into the night—its storm and its darkness—for no one could get to me; however much they might want to. How long I am to be thus isolated depends on the weather and the road breakers. Let us hope both will be favorable to speedy release. You must know, too, that we are a bit lonesome with our family thus scattered and out of touch.

I am awfully sorry that you are ill again. I hope the hot water and flaxseed will relieve your pain. I have no material at hand to put some medicine for you—and Gorham [drug store] is snow-bound too. The drops will help along, I trust. I will call just as soon as I am at liberty. Hoping you will be better soon, I remain, as ever,

Dr. James Francis Chapman[35]

On March 14th, snowed in on the farm at Cantitoe, Elizabeth Barrett described the blizzard in a letter to her brother:

Wednesday, 8:30 P.M.
Katonah, N.Y.
Mar. 14, 1888

My dear Brother,

. . . As you will perceive before I get on much farther with my letter, we are snowed up, sure enough, and have been ever since Monday. . . . Monday morning there was a dreadful storm, but papa [Joseph Barrett] thought it was his duty to go, and of course he did. Will went with him to Katonah and in spite of the wind and snow, papa's train was only a little behind time. Well the storm kept getting worse all day and by afternoon mama and I were in a high state of figit, as to how Will and papa would get home. About five o'clock Will came pounding through the snow riding Kitty. The drifts in some places were nearly up to her back and she and Will were both wet and cold but you may believe we were glad to see them. Will said at four o'clock the 9 A.M. train had got to Mt. Vernon, and that is the last we've heard from it or papa. Can you imagine our being three days without seeing or hearing a word from papa? Still we have not worried for we felt sure he would get along someway. Of course no one has been to Katonah. I wish you could see our road. Some of the drifts are higher than the gate posts, and for three days we have not seen a mortal, outside of our own family, except yesterday I caught sight of Cousin Will feeding his chickens. It was a welcome sight. This morning he came up to see if we were alive and well. Willie has been up at Arnell's all day helping him and a few other neighbors dig out Sally Anne. Her house was nearly snowed up. Jack went down yesterday just as she was putting in her last stick of wood. From Sally Anne's they went over to the Lyon farm to get some barley grains as Arnell has nothing to feed his cows. The roads were so bad however that they could not get through them and had to go in the lots. Tomorrow we hope the people below here will turn out with the oxen and break the road from here to the corner, anyway Percy and Uncle E. have been busy most all day, digging a ditch through an immense snow bank that has piled itself up against the barn door. We are very comfortably situated, however, and get on very well. Many people have hard work to feed and water their cattle. We will hope to get a letter from you tomorrow night.

Lovingly, E.N.B.[36]

From the time of Dr. Shove's death in 1878 until 1896 when Dr. Jared Green Wood married the widow Newman and moved to her home on the present Legion property there were only three doctors in Katonah. These were Dr. J. F. Chapman, Dr. Carpenter and Irene Shove Chapman, who was called "Doctor" by affection and courtesy though she had only completed one year of medical school. She specialized in delivering babies and there were many who preferred her to her colleagues. It is said that she never lost a case and she assumed far more than the usual medical care. If it seemed necessary, she often moved right into a home and stayed days before the baby came, knitting little garments and giving encouragement and help to the expectant mother.[34] She was called "Aunty Chapman" by little Bessie Eastman and probably by innumerable other children. She practiced up to the time of her death in 1906, one of her last babies being Jacqueline, daughter of Mr. Winston, the young engineer in charge of the Cross River Dam.[37]

In the 1890's when there were no hospitals within feasible radius and few women in the township who had trained as nurses except Ellen Morris Wood and Helena Todd,[38] Dr. Irene's extra care was invaluable. She could not begin to fill the need, however, and in many, many cases of sickness, families nearly always relied on the untrained but practical care of their neighbors such as the Browns, mother and daughter, and Mrs. Andrew Van Tassel.[19] In contrast to our present day attitude that young children should be shielded from contact with sorrow and death, they were taught in those days that it was part of life. When only eight, Margery Van Tassel was taken by her mother to a home where a baby had died and she ironed its little funeral dress and picked flowers to put in its hands for burial.[19]

Katonah was fortunate in its doctors but its dentists were a different matter. Between the death of Dr. Wickware in 1884 and the coming of Dr. Frederick H. Williams in 1899, a series of men came and went. Dr. Chauncey Lane was the first. Drs. Smith, Mayer, Baldwin, and Weeks followed in such quick succession that it would almost seem as though none stayed long enough to fill a tooth.[39]

Our public schools, which appear to have been so sorry in the late seventies and early eighties that even children of nonwealthy parents were sent to private ones,[2] now took an upward turn. In 1889, a Teachers' Institute lasting three days was held at the Mt. Kisco Opera House, with an art exhibit in the Armory Hall. Our Katonah teachers apparently were eager to take advantage of the opportunity. Attending were Willis J. Shields, Annie E. Van Tassel, Elizabeth Dickinson, Wilhelmina Wood, and Clara L. Clark.[31]

In December of 1894, J. Francis Chapman, Henry W. Kellogg and Andrew M. Van Tassel, trustees of School District No. 10, Towns of Bedford and Lewisboro, distributed an interesting little booklet. It published extracts from the *Code of Public Instruction of the State of New York*, Chapter 671, entitled "AN ACT to provide for the compulsory education of children," passed May 12, 1894, to take effect Jan. 1, 1895. Apparently, they expected opposition both from parents and children and appealed to them in conclusion as follows:

> We shall look for a willing obedience to the laws above quoted, and to other enactments of the Code which makes a MISDE-MEANOR of any MUTILATION or wilful MARRING or INJURING of any part of the School building, furniture, apparatus or any property belonging to the district.[40]

In any event their fears were premature. Compulsory education between the ages of eight and fourteen was not actually effected until 1901.[41]

Schools, important and exciting as they are, have a way of going dead in the telling when we stick to documents and statistics. Just so our readers will know how alive they really were, we reprint this description of the Palmer Avenue school built in 1883, written by Miss Margery Van Tassel:

> The grounds were level on the "boys' side," which seemed to include the front as well. A steep bank composed the part reserved for the girls' playground. This was always plotted out by stones and pieces of moss and some broken glass into a playhouse. The best times were when girls and boys played hide-and-seek together and there were no playground boundaries and fences were ignored. Sarleses barn on the adjacent lot was the favorite hiding place. It was also the secret meeting place of the elite who there indulged in cubebs or Sweet Caporals. Even girls rolling their own with dried corn silk.
>
> The school house had an inestimably delightful feature—a large front porch. We were sometimes allowed to take our arithmetics and study out there. Sometimes we lingered there when we were not allowed to and with other diversions than MacVicker's arithmetics. We ate our lunches in its pleasant protection, sitting on the steps if little and on the several benches from the old school house if big enough to command one. Choice places on the railings were available only to the first to arrive. . . .
>
> The huge double doors swung inward to let us pass into the large foyer hall. The right-hand door met the wall at an angle that made a lovely hiding place in the corner behind it; big enough to accommodate several little boys or girls. It became our Star Chamber where dire and dreadful schemes were

plotted, usually of a vengeful nature. In this foyer stood a double desk brought from the former school house and used to hold two granite iron pails of water and two decidedly unsanitary and dilapidated wash-basins. Once, two dippers completed the outfit, but that was before the Broadened Course of Study took effect. If you were a real or a tom boy, you could shinny up the big doors and climb through a scuttle into the attic. Only the reals explored that mystic place, for tales of rats and mice and what not restrained the more timid tom boys from venturing beyond the scuttle itself. The bell hung overhead and curfew was never more unfailing in ringing out the call to duty. . . .

An ell was added in 1893 containing another class room and a fair sized library where the older students were privileged to study. Since apples had been found an efficacious aid to the task of acquiring knowledge from books, we laid in a winter's supply back of the books on the library shelves. Fire broke out on December 20th, 1893, and the building burned to the ground. We rescued the books but the apples were consumed either by fire or by the youthful volunteer firemen and women. Total loss and no insurance. School was resumed, after the fire and Christmas vacation, in the silk mill where the looms crashed gloriously over our heads on the floor above.[43]

As the last days of the two old villages drew near, their inhabitants went about their daily lives as though time would stand still, and a young man from up-state even had the temerity to move into Katonah and buy the printing office and newspaper. The year was 1894, the paper, the *Katonah Times*, and the young man, Robert D. Knapp. Before this date he'd had no experience whatever in running a paper but he had energy and imagination. He bicycled to the Farmers and Drovers Bank in Somers when he needed a loan. Imagination prompted him to buy a kerosene engine to run his presses, an innovation that most of the village came to see installed. Finding that it wasn't needed all of every day for printing purposes, he cut a hole through the wall to Edgar Hoyt's ice cream parlor and ran a long belt to Hoyt's freezer where the engine froze ice cream in slack hours.[44] Among Mr. Knapp's most valued news-gatherers and typesetters during the life of the *Times* were Miss Josephine Van Tassel and Dudley Thomas.[45]

Courtesy of Fahnestock & Company

"Girdle Ridge," the Cantitoe home of William H. Fahnestock, was built in the early 1900's and demolished in 1940.

Courtesy of John J. Miller

Forest View Stock Farm. Here George Green raised champion horses.

Courtesy of Katonah Village Library

Site of New Katonah. This view to the north across the open fields shows the North Street School built in 1894.

Courtesy of Katonah Village Library

In the move from Old Katonah, houses were transported along tracks such as these.

Courtesy of Katonah Village Library

Lined up for moving, these four houses have reached the mid-point of their migration to the new village.

Dr. J. Francis Chapman's house en route to 22 The Terrace in New Katonah.

Lakeside Inn, Greenville. This hotel belonging to Thaddeus Green was moved from Old Katonah to Anderson Road.

New Katonah in the late nineties seen from the junction of present North Street and Greenville Road.

First Library and Reading Room in new village, 21 Edgemont Road
At shelves is librarian, Miss Mary Augusta Horton, later Mrs. Howard L. Van Norden

Sleighride in New Katonah. This gay group is starting off
in front of the new Library February 18, 1899.

Courtesy of Katonah Village Library
North Street School, 1895, the first school in New Katonah.
Now the Vogler residence.

Courtesy of Katonah Village Library
Bedford Road School, 1907, Katonah's first high school.
It housed elementary grades also.

189

First Railroad Station in New Katonah, built 1897.
Picture taken between 1902 and 1910 when it was replaced.

Early automobiles in New Katonah. From left to right: first car driver James McMin
LeRoy Ganung; middle row, Bertram Hoffman, Cornelius Prona
back row, Joseph Towey, Arthur Reynolds, Joseph Barrett, John Towe
second car driver William Ballard; back row, James Lanning, George Nelso
Charles Flewellin; third car back row, Matthew R. Towey, right, Frederick W. Myer

We were then a farm community, with Cox's and Hoyt's mills still grinding our home-grown grain into good flour. We had industry also using the swift waters of Cross River for power. We had Judge Robertson to keep us up with state and national affairs, and Chauncey Depew, his friend and frequent guest, to visit and give stirring speeches in the village.[19] We also had some commuters to White Plains and New York such as: the "traveled" and eccentric Dr. D. D. C. McCloskey,[6] a druggist, who went in to his New York store daily; Joseph Barrett, who commuted to the custom-house; and Judge Robertson, who had an office in White Plains.[19]

Temperance societies were advocating the passage of the Raines Liquor Law,[42] but liquor flowed freely none the less during our last days at "the old stand." Sometimes it was promoted in devious ways, as in this advertisement:

1873, Oct. 2, *Katonah Sentinel*
        Bininger's Old London Dock Gin.
        Especially designed for use of the
        Medical Profession and the Family. . . .
        Indispensable to Females. Good
        for Kidney Complaints. A delicious
        Tonic.[32]

Other advertisements of this era were the following:

1882, Aug. 16, 17, *Feast of Lanterns*
        A Quarter of a Million
        FIFTH EDITION
        Thirty-Second Thousand
        WITHOUT A HOME
        by E. P. Roe . . .
        Dodd, Mead & Co.
        Publishers, New York[22]

1882, *Ibid*.
        The Great Travel Number
        THE AUGUST
        ST. NICHOLAS
        For Young Folks . .
        The Century Co. New York[22]

1883, Aug. 8, 9, *Feast of Lanterns*
>Oh My Tooth, My Tooth!
>Where is DR. LANE?
>You will find him at Katonah
>every Saturday, but his office
>has been moved to the building
>next to Lyon Brothers'. . . .
>*Those wishing to take ether*
>will please make engagements in
>advance. . . . Dr. C. B. Lane, Dentist[23]

and from the Nineties:

1896, Dec. 11, *Katonah Times*
>THE
>GREAT AMERICAN
>T
>E
>A
>COMPANY
>Wanted; Competent Club Agents,
>(Women, Men, Girls, or Boys) in every
>town in the U.S. to get orders for
>our celebrated goods. Liberal terms;
>Good incomes; Big presents with
>every sale.

From the fashion notes of the same issue of the *Times,* we culled the following hint:

>jewelled gloves are the newest addition
>to the . . . toilet. . . . It isn't good form
>to wear rings outside one's gloves.[42]

References

1. Newspaper clipping dated Oct. 22, 1880, from unknown paper in Mrs. Lea Luquer's scrapbook. (At the Bedford Hills, N.Y., Public Library)
2. Hoffman, Mrs. Cassie, Newtown, Conn. Oral communication.
3. Adams, Mrs. Charles. Advertisement in *Blue Light,* Aug. 7, 1878.
4. Miller, S. H. Advertisement in *Feast of Lanterns,* Aug. 15, 1878.
5. Central & Hudson River Railroad. *Summer homes on the*

Harlem Railroad. New York, 1890, p. 62.

6. Mead, Mrs. Emma F., Katonah. Oral communication.

7. Eastman, Elizabeth. The village that was drowned. [Washington, D.C.] n.d. MS. (In possession of Mrs. W. A. Kelly, Katonah)

8. *Mount Kisco Weekly,* Aug. 31, 1888.

9. *Ibid.,* Dec. 25, 1880.

10. Kelly, K. B. The Whitlock family. Katonah, 1959. MS. (At the Katonah Village Library)

11. Banks, Mrs. Mildred. Mt. Kisco, N.Y. Oral communication.

12. Fiss, Doerr & Carroll Horse Co. [Booklet advertising Forest View Stud Farm.] New York (?)1902(?) (In possession of Mr. John J. Miller, Katonah)

13. Van Tassel, Misses Josephine and Margery H. Katonah. Oral communication.

14. Newspaper clipping from *Mount Kisco Recorder,* 1892, in S. H. Miller's scrapbook (In possession of Mrs. Oliver Todd, Goldens Bridge, N.Y.)

15. Katonah Village Improvement Society. Minutes. July 24, 1884. MS. (At the Katonah Village Library)

16. *Ibid.,* Aug. 31, 1891.

17. *Ibid.,* Aug. 9, 1894.

18. Avery, O. T. The diverted village. Katonah, [1903]. MS. (In possession of Mrs. James G. Bonacorda, 4351 Edson Ave., New York 60, N.Y.)

19. Van Tassel, Miss Margery H., Katonah. Oral communication.

20. Mead, E. F. Hunt family. Katonah, 1959. MS. (At the Katonah Village Library)

21. Burt, Mrs. Albert, Katonah. Oral communication.

22. *Feast of Lanterns,* Katonah, Aug. 16 & 17, 1882.

23. *Ibid.,* Aug. 8 & 9, 1883.

24. *Blue Light,* Katonah, July 30 & 31, 1884.

25. Carpenter, W. T. Carpenter family of Old Katonah. White Plains, N.Y., 1959. MS. (At the Katonah Village Library)

26. Katonah Silk Co. By-laws. Katonah, n.d. (In scrapbook of Mr. E. P. Barrett, Katonah)

27. *Mount Kisco Recorder,* June 12, 1891.

28. *Ibid.,* 1880. Quoted in: *Katonah Record,* Feb. 19, 1932.

29. *Ibid.,* Nov. 29, 1889.

30. *Ibid.,* Feb. 5, 1897.

31. *Ibid.,* May 10, 1889.

32. *Katonah Sentinel,* Oct. 2, 1873.

33. Van Tassel, Josephine & Margery H. Remembered about Old Katonah. Katonah, 1958. MS. (At the Katonah Village Library)

34. Doe, Janet. Medicine in Katonah. Katonah, 1959. MS. (At the Katonah Village Library)

35. Chapman, J. F. Letter to Mrs. Ella Van Tassel, Katonah, Mar. 13, 1888. In: *Katonah Record,* Mar. 11, 1938.

36. Barrett, E. N. Letter to Henry R. Barrett, Katonah, Mar. 14, 1888. MS. (In possession of Mrs. W. A. Kelly, Katonah)

37. Adams, Mrs. J. Donald, 444 E. 57th St., New York 22, N.Y. Oral communication.

38. Kelly, Mrs. W. A., Katonah. Oral communication.

39. Doe, Janet. Dentistry in Katonah. Katonah, 1959. MS. (At the Katonah Village Library)

40. Bedford (N.Y.) & Lewisboro (N.Y.) School District No. 10. *An abstract of the compulsory education law.* Katonah, 1894.

41. *Katonah Times,* Nov. 1, 1901.

42. *Ibid.,* Dec. 11, 1896.

43. Van Tassel, M. H. Old Katonah schools. *Katonah Record,* Aug. 5, 1932.

44. Knapp, R. D. Old and New Katonah. Katonah, 1958. MS. (At the Katonah Village Library)

45. Knapp, R. D. Remembered about Old Katonah days. Katonah, 1958. MS. (At the Katonah Village Library)

LYON BROS.,

GENERAL DEALERS IN

DRY GOODS, CLOTHING,

CARPETS, OIL CLOTHS,

GROCERIES,

Flour, Feed and Grain,

PAINTS, OILS, Etc.. Etc.

KATONAH.

———

We would announce to the public that as

FURNISHING UNDERTAKERS

we are now prepared to supply every requisite for funerals in all respects equal to the best, and our charges very reasonable.

Advertisement in the *Feast of Lanterns,*
August 16 and 17, 1882.
Collection of Mrs. James G. Bonacorda

Advertisement in Ophelia Todd Avery's
Historical Sketch of Katonah, N.Y., 1896.

CHAPTER XIII

DAYS OF TRANSPLANTING

In telling of the transplanting of Whitlockville and Old Katonah, we have to go back in years and south to the City of New York. Fifteen years after the first water from the Croton flowed into the reservoir on Murray Hill and rejoicing was made, a new survey was begun to find an even greater supply to meet increased city needs.[1]

Mrs. Ophelia (Todd) Avery wrote that civil engineers were stationed in Katonah as early as 1875 and that rumors were rife of a new Croton dam.[2] Extensive surveys were being conducted along the various branches of the Croton even before that time. In 1873, a new reservoir was constructed on the West Branch at Boyd's Corners. A reservoir on the Middle Branch near Brewster

195

was finished in 1878. From surveys made in 1877 on the East Branch, Sodom and Bog Brook Reservoirs resulted in 1892.[3] It was obvious that a larger Croton Dam would be needed.

In the fall of '82, the Board of Supervisors, anticipating a larger dam and a consequently higher water level, appointed a committee to urge the Legislature to protect the rights of the people. This committee, with several citizens of the Katonah area, went to Albany and secured a provision that all highways and bridges made necessary by the new dam should be built and maintained by the City and that legislation dealing with the health hazard from exposed muddy bottoms when water was drawn off should be worked out to the approval of the State Board of Health.

The site of the new dam had not been determined as late as '84 but it was expected to be at Quaker Bridge. The answer to the sanitary problem in our own front yard was a secondary dam across the Croton at the foot of Muscoot Mountain to hold a constant water level above it.[5]

The Aqueduct Commission was apparently quite willing to discuss proposed changes with our inhabitants. Col. B. S. Church spoke at the annual meeting of the Village Improvement Society in July of '84 and also gave an interview to the *Blue Light*. From that paper we take the following:

> Through the kindness of a resident of this town who served on the supervisors' Committee and who has maintained very intimate relations since that time with the city authorities, the Blue Light has in its possession a map of Katonah and vicinity, showing the high water line as it will be if Quaker Dam should be erected. This map, by courtesy of our geography editor, was examined by some of our citizens at the annual meeting of the Village Improvement Society on Thursday last, and may be inspected by any one interested on application at this office. The entire aspect of the country here will be changed. All the houses from the Methodist parsonage to Dr. McCloskey's will disappear. The water will come nearly up to David Silkman's house, cross the road and cover part of the lawn at Horace Sarles', encroach on Dr. Chapman, the Presbyterian parsonage and Miss Clark, covering the highway in front of A. F. Avery's, and nearly up to Hoyt Brothers' store, and, of course, covering it deeply from Dr. Wickware's, past Carr's shop, nearly down to the hill by the railroad bridge. (The

statement which appeared in a paper a few days ago, to the effect that it would cover the railroad track and necessitate raising it, is nonsense.)

On the opposite side of the river, it comes up into the road at the Presbyterian Church, covers it in front of J. M. Lyon's, prevents any future drought in J. G. Miller's garden, and covers the road near Leemon Brundage's. The valley of the Beaver Dam river, where Jay's meadows and the low land on the Walter Lyon farm are, will be covered. Following up the Cross River Valley, we find that the lake would extend much beyond the bridge near Daniel Smith's, though a longer bridge would probably be necessary there. West of the old village, all the road from Dr. McCloskey's to the high ground beyond Wood's bridge will be submerged. The Croton Valley northward becomes a lake of varying width, as far north as the vicinity of Croton Falls, and the Muscoot forms a lovely lake above Nelson's Mill. The race track of course disappears.

It is understood, that in places where the highway, like that in front of the Presbyterian parsonage, can be preserved by raising it and thus keeping the water from encroaching upon the lands beyond, that plan will be adopted. This will provide a level, pleasant road, like that along the north side of Croton Lake, near Pine's Bridge. It would not be feasible on all roads, however, and in such places other means will be adopted of restoring the highway or substituting another route for it.

Opinions differ very much among our people as to whether all this is desirable from our point of view. Some of us, perhaps, have houses and lands which we would not object to sell to the city of New York for a fair price. Some think an extensive lake would be a great improvement in the landscape, and indulge in visions of steam yachts, sail boats, and possibly college boat races, Courtney-Hanlan contests, and other luxuries. Our conservative folk are satisfied as things always have been and hope the lake won't come. . . . We see, however, that New York must have water, and more water, especially if she should follow the example of our town and quit drinking other beverages, and it is generally thought that to get water in abundance the Quaker Dam plan is the thing.

The statement made by Chief Engineer Church at the annual meeting of the Katonah Village Improvement Associa-

tion, last week, that at all points where the banks of the lake
are not abrupt, its margin will be *beached*, that is, covered
with gravel, preventing the growth of vegetation, will remove
many of the fears expressed in regard to the effect of the lake
upon the health of the surrounding country.[5]

Years of inaction followed in which we seemed to forget the
possibility of inundation and continued the building up and
beautifying of our villages on the Cross River. Col. Church was
still around however. In the *Mt. Kisco Weekly* of August 31,
1888, was the social item:

Mr. and Mrs. H. E. Pellew, last week entertained Chief
Engineer Church of the Croton Aqueduct and his wife.[6]

In 1889, Col. Church spoke again before the Village Improvement Society. He regretted that the promises of his previous
talk had not all been fulfilled.[7]
In 1891, the location of the new dam was finally settled:[3]
three and a quarter miles above the mouth of the Croton River
and three miles below the Old Croton Dam. Ground was broken
for the Cornell Dam September 20, 1892.[4]
We realized now that our situation was serious, especially when
in December of that year Mr. Edward Wegmann, Jr., division
engineer, moved into the community, renting rooms from M. S.
Benedict.[9] *The Recorder* of September 22, 1893, asked in headlines,

WILL KATONAH BE DESERTED?

and answered, also in headlines,

When Cornell Dam is Completed, the Site of the Present
Village will be Submerged. New York will Compensate the
Residents Liberally for the Loss of their Homes.

This article was published subsequent to a meeting of aroused
citizens presided over by Judge Robertson. They had learned that
a hundred homes must be vacated—those in the "Triangle"
being the first—and that their worth would be appraised by
three commissioners. Questions at the meeting were those of
when and where a move must be made. The inhabitants were

only certain of one thing, that they wanted to keep together. Judge Robertson, Henry W. Kellogg and Joseph Benedict were appointed a Citizens' Committee to find out just when the residents of the "Triangle" would have to vacate. As to where they would go, a level tract of land a half mile south of Old Katonah was already under consideration.[11]

The Committee wrote the Commission on September 20, 1893, but not until June 18, 1894, was a reply sent and even this by oversight was delayed in the mailing. It did not reach Katonah until August 2, 1894. The answer when it arrived was curt. It set May 1, 1895, as the deadline for removal and imposed many conditions concerning sanitation, the payment of taxes, etc. It ended:

> I have heard of the intention of some of the citizens to remove in a body to a certain location south of the present depot, and I can only say that this new place would be subject the same as any other to the rules and regulations established for preserving the purity of the river.

The signer was A. Fteley, chief engineer.[10] It must have been bewildering and disillusioning to be so treated by an impersonal pen after all the hospitality and friendship lavished upon Col. Church and Mr. Wegmann.

On November 23, 1894, *The Recorder* carried the following article:

> A new school-house and four or five dwellings, more or less aged, are the only buildings now standing on the site of the proposed new Katonah. The buildings mentioned are near the northern boundary line of the area shown on the Whitman map. Mr. Whitman is the projector of the new village scheme and first secured options on the farming lands of Mr. Wm. H. Ashbee, one mile south of the village railway station. The lands are not of comely grade, but by cutting off the sand knolls and filling in swails and brook courses, the entire tract will be well suited for village purposes. The old highway between Katonah and Bedford runs parallel with the railroad directly through the village. On the map the street is laid out 100 feet in width. The intention is to have a center strip devoted to flowers, and a wagon path upon either side. Paved and curbed gutters, flagging for the sidewalks, and rows of

trees are to be among the other improvements. The old highway will be known as Bedford Ave. A street 300 feet in
length, running east from Bedford avenue, will lead to the
Harlem depot. It will be known as Katonah avenue,* and will
be the business street of the village.

On the south side of this street, on the corner nearest the
railway station, Edgar Hoyt, the baker, will erect a handsome
building to be used as a bakery, and for other business in his
line. The lot secured for this purpose was sold for $600 and
has a frontage of 50 feet on Katonah avenue, and is 150 feet
deep. Next to Mr. Hoyt a Mr. Barrett will erect a building
for offices, then comes Kellogg, the hardware man, each using
50 feet. The 150 feet beyond Kellogg will be devoted to a town
hall, reading room, etc. The main entrance to that building
will be on Bedford avenue, and the lot will have a frontage
of 100 feet on that thoroughfare.

Opposite Mr. Diehl, on the north side of Katonah avenue,
will be the general merchandise store of Hoyt Bros., having a
frontage of 100 feet. Next to them will be Gorham, the druggist, using 50 feet. A. F. Avery has purchased a lot 100 feet
on Katonah avenue by 150 feet on Bedford avenue, and will
erect thereon a first class hotel or boarding house. Judge
Robertson will use three lots for a residence on Bedford
avenue. Hoyt Bros., the Methodist Society, and others have
lots near by. All told about 50 lots have been sold.[12]

Clarence Whitman, who had moved to the former Pellew
house at "Katonah's Wood" in 1891, is generally considered the
leading spirit of the new village. Actually, there was a syndicate
involved. Its original members were: Clarence Whitman, Joseph
Barrett and William Henry Robertson.[13] In 1898 this was incorporated as the Katonah Land Co., with directors: W. H. Robertson, Samuel B. Hoyt, Albert Hoyt, and Clarence Whitman.[14]
In the village planning much thought had been given to
making it a pleasant place to live and restrictive covenants were
imposed to that end. A typical example is the sale to Oliver Hubbard in December, 1895. By its terms, he could erect no building
at a cost less than $2,500.00. He could not build a slaughter
house or a manufactory of gun powder, soap, candles, starch,
glue, vitriol, ink or turpentine. A structure for tanning skins was

* It will be obvious that what is called "Katonah Avenue" here became instead
"The Parkway," while the street paralleling the railroad became "Katonah
Avenue."

barred, so was a brewery or distillery. The selling of liquor was not to be allowed nor the keeping of swine, vicious dogs or poultry.[15] The ban against liquor still holds in our business area except on land formerly held by the New York Central which never was included. Here a package store now operates. We haven't heard of anyone manufacturing ink lately, but there do seem to be a few vicious dogs . . . no poultry. (See Appendix No. 28.)

There were really two problems that confronted many of the people who were moving into the new village. In more than a few cases money owed by the City for their condemned property was necessary to the purchase of land, moving or building. Generally speaking, the values set by the commissioners were not satisfactory and the settlement of claims dragged on for months and in some cases years. Fortunately, the May 1st deadline of 1895 had been modified and when the final exodus took place in 1897, most claims had been adjusted. The City of New York wanted water and a protective surrounding area to insure its purity, but it wasn't particularly concerned with what became of the houses. Robert Knapp, who was editor and owner of the *Katonah Times* during this period, recalls for us:

> Nearly all the buildings in the Village were sold at public auction and the best of them moved to Katonah's new site. I believe that Nathan Voris of Golden's Bridge was the auctioneer on all of them. I did the printing of all the Auction Bills, sometimes three or four a week.
>
> Quite often in those days one would see three or four houses in a row moving toward the New Village and at times the families would be living in them. A special temporary bridge was made for them to cross over at the Cross River.[16]

Not only did the families live in their houses, they continued their normal social lives. One of the first events attended by Dr. F. H. Williams when he came to Katonah was an on-the-move wedding at which he was best man.[17] Children went to school in the morning and found their houses in different places when they returned.[18]

Some buildings were torn down and rebuilt but for months the sight of houses on the move was a familiar one. So many people have shown interest in the technique of house-moving in the 1890's that we give it here. First, each house had to be lifted from its foundations by jacks and two heavy carrying-timbers made fast crosswise under its house beams. A tow rope was then attached to both ends of the front timber and secured to the main towing rope which extended somewhat beyond a capstan placed out ahead of the house and to which the house was to be drawn.

The house was pulled along over a track made of two long timbers, sturdy and smooth, starting under the raised house and extending toward the capstan. To keep these timber tracks nearly level, their elevation had to be controlled by cribbing under them. The timbers, very long and straight, were cut from Georgia pine trees, as no trees around here yielded planks good enough. To enable the house to move easily and smoothly, the track timbers were lubricated with ordinary yellow laundry soap. As soon as one set of timber rails had been passed over, they were picked up and moved ahead to make another section of track.

Horse-power was used to draw the house. A horse hitched to the far end of a long pole attached to the top of the capstan circled round and round, winding up the towing-rope on the capstan and drawing the house forward. After about three turns had been laid around the capstan, the forward end of the rope was pulled out ahead towards what would be the next position of the capstan. When the house reached the capstan, capstan and horse were moved ahead another lap and the process began over again.[19]

Moving buildings across water on temporary bridges was quite a feat, and due to the contours of the Cross River, some had to make more than one such crossing.[20] So far as we know, none met with disaster. While most of the houses marched straight on to the new village, some stopped short before they reached its limits and restrictions. Such a one was the hotel of Thaddeus Green, son of Alsoph. He bought a field from Mr. Travis, set down his building and continued the sale of liquor. It is still there and still doing business under the name of Teddy's Lakeside Inn at Greenville. In Old Katonah, liquor had flowed all too freely. On this account, liquor restrictions were urged for the new village by the Hoyt brothers, Lewis Miller, Clarence Whitman, and Joseph Barrett. They were imposed in all deeds to Syndicate property, later owned by the Katonah Land Company.[13] (See Appendix No. 28.)

If a definite date can be given to the birth of the new village of Katonah, it is April 5, 1897. On that day, the train first rushed by the old station without stopping and pulled up at the new.[2]

On the same day Postmaster Elbridge Arnold began handing out mail in our present village.

The minutes of the Village Improvement Society on its sixteenth anniversary in 1894 end with the following words by its secretary, J. H. Eastman:

> We can only say we are ready to do all we can for old Katonah, so long as the present village endures. And we are equally ready to hail the new Katonah, when the alternative is NO KATONAH or NEW KATONAH and to devote ourselves with unflagging zeal to her development and best interests in all respects.[8]

Despite this brave front, it must have been very hard for those who had grown up in Whitlockville and Old Katonah to leave them. Even those of us who never saw the beautiful water-edged hill-rimmed villages feel nostalgic about their loss.

References

1. *Short history of New York State:* David M. Ellis, James A. Frost, Harold C. Syrett, Harry J. Carman. Ithaca, N.Y., 1957, p. 296.
2. Avery, O. T. The new village: its early years. In: Katonah Village Improvement Society, *Sketches and views of Old and New Katonah,* Katonah, 1900 (unpaged)
3. Griffin, E. F. *Westchester County and its people.* New York, 1946, v. 2, p. 505.
4. *Ibid.,* v. 2, p. 507.
5. *Blue Light,* Katonah, July 30, 1884.
6. *Mount Kisco Weekly,* Aug. 31, 1888.
7. Katonah Village Improvement Society. Minutes. Aug. 12, 1889. MS. (At the Katonah Village Library)
8. *Ibid.,* Aug. 9, 1894.
9. New York City. Aqueduct Commissioners. *Minutes, 1892.* New York, 1893, v. 8, p. 183.
10. *Ibid., Minutes, 1895.* New York, 1896, v. 11, p. 39.
11. *Recorder,* Mt. Kisco, N.Y., Sept. 22, 1893.
12. *Mount Kisco Recorder,* Nov. 23, 1894.
13. Barrett, Mr. E. P., Katonah. Oral communication.
14. *Katonah Times,* June 24, 1898.
15. Westchester County. Division of Land Records. Deeds. Liber 1422, pp. 199-202. MS. (At County Office Building, White Plains, N.Y.)
16. Knapp, R. D. Old and New Katonah. Katonah, 1958. MS. (At the Katonah Village Library)

17. Williams, Mrs. F. H., Katonah. Oral communication.

18. Mead, Mrs. E. F., Katonah. Oral communication.

19. Chace, Walter T. Mechanics of moving to New Katonah, as told to Ella Weist. Katonah, 1960. MS. (At the Katonah Village Library)

20. Van Tassel, Miss Margery H., Katonah. Oral communication.

New Styles

Edison -- Victor

Columbia

New Records

J. A. CLARK,

Office in Hoyt Bros. Co's.

Katonah, N. Y.

CHAPTER XIV

SETTLING THE NEW VILLAGE

THE NEW village of Katonah was busy from the first. In fact it was busy before it became a village. In 1894 thirty-seven acres of land [1] had been purchased and put on the market, and soon afterwards a large company of Italian workmen were brought in to level and grade it. A stone-crusher was noisily busy. B. S. and G. S. Olmstead, noted landscape architects, were engaged as consultants in laying out the new town. They gave us our wide streets with parks running through the center, a decidedly "new look" in those days and a blessing today. [5] All this was going on before a move was made from Old Katonah.

The school, by forethought, had been built on a hill at the north end of the new site when fire in 1893 made replacement of the Palmer Avenue School necessary; and so it was there to welcome the homes that were built in the next few years and the old ones that moved down from above.

In 1895 the first building, Edgar Hoyt's "Pioneer House," was erected. It still stands on the south corner of the Parkway and Katonah Avenue. It was large and modern and its turrets considered very tasty. Other early buildings were those constructed by Hoyt Brothers on the north corner of The Parkway and Katonah Avenue; by Henry Kellogg on The Parkway; and by Harry Barrett also on The Parkway. It was in this last building, in an apartment above the office now occupied by Mr. Andres, that Cornelius J. Pronay, the first baby of the new village, was born November 1, 1897. In 1896 the Van Tassel building was dismantled and rebuilt on a new site on the southwest corner of Valley Road and Katonah Avenue and enlarged.

Although we gave April 5, 1897, as a birth date for New Katonah, the old town kept alive well beyond that date. Through 1897 and 1898 the *Katonah Times* carried news items such as:

> 1897, Feb. 5—Parent & Wright have the four buildings which they are moving all out of sight. They are now on the hill, ready to be placed on the foundations awaiting them.

> 1898, Jan. 14—James Clark has Dr. Chapman's house and the Manse across the river for the last time, and today is sliding them slowly toward the new village. Fremont Ganung has his row of houses close to the river all ready to be pulled across.

> 1898, Mar. 18—The lot for the engine house has at last been located in the new village. It is opposite A. M. Van Tassel's Katonah Provision Store, and is 40 x 95 feet. . . . Work on the building will soon commence. The contract has been awarded to Jaycox & Son for $1,200.

> 1898, Apr. 1—Mr. C. J. Pitman, the asphalt side walk man, is in town again this week. He has the contract for some more walk work about town. They pitched their tent down near the sand bank.

> 1898, Apr. 8—A. F. Avery's men are piling up the stone in preparation for a fine stone cottage on Bedford Road.

1898, Apr. 15—Horace Searles has started his cellar on Edgemont Road and the carpenters have commenced to
take down the Searles' house in the old village. It will
be remodelled and put up again as a boarding house.
Dr. J. F. Chapman and family have moved into their
house in the new village. . . . They expect to get their
house on the foundation before many days.

1898, May 20—There will be another auction sale of buildings . . . next month. . . . A number of the residents
in the old village have been ordered out by the fifteenth
of next month.

1898, June 10—James Clark has arrived in Katonah with H.
W. Kellogg's house and barn. They are now sliding
down Bedford Road and in another week will be near
their foundation next the residence of E. B. Newman.

1898, Aug. 26—Horace Searles new house has been completed
and is now well filled with summer boarders.

1898, Sept. 2—Mr. Thos. S. Smith has let the contract for
tearing down and rebuilding the H. W. Kellogg house
on Palmer avenue, which he purchased at the last auction, to Mr. Westcott, of Danbury. His new house will
be located on Edgemont road, next to Hoyt Bros.' tene-
ment house.

1898, Sept. 16—Mr. Michael Towey has purchased a large lot
from the Katonah Syndicate, nearly opposite the residence of Grace Searles, & will put up a residence there.

1898, Nov. 4—About a dozen men have been appointed as
laborers . . . at $2.00 a day . . . filling up the old
cellars, grading and cleaning up the land taken by the
city.

The old churches were sold for other purposes than worship.
The Presbyterians erected a temporary building on the front of
their new site at Valley and Bedford Roads. The Methodists put
up their present building at Edgemont and Bedford Roads, the
new organ being installed in February of 1900,[6] and the church
bells, in March.

Even beyond 1898 a few houses were being moved. The John
Wes Hallett house was moving down Bedford Road in 1901.[22]

Not only were buildings being transferred but all cemeteries in the watershed were being vacated and the bodies re-interred in neighboring burying grounds.[8]

It took a few years for Katonah to look as though it belonged on its new site. The two hundred and eight trees planted in 1897 by the Village Improvement Society[2] needed time to make them look like more than buggy whips, as did further plantings along the village streets in 1904 and 1905. These latter trees were a donation by the Aqueduct Commission of a quantity of nursery trees growing on land acquired by the City and formerly the property of Doyle Bros.[3]

Social life was far less affected by the move. It continued in much the same pleasant pattern established in the old villages. Always enthusiastic about singing, the Choral Club employed Professor Arthur Hallam to be their teacher and leader. Their first meeting in the new village was in November of '98 in the temporary chapel erected by the Presbyterians. Boarding-houses continued to be social centers. The Searles House, barely settled on its new foundation, gave a "Mother Hubbard Hallowe'en Party." Both men and women dressed in mother hubbards and mistakes in identity apparently caused much hilarity. About seventy of Katonah's "400" were there. In the summer, guests at the Searles House were taken for picnics on the grounds it had occupied at Whitlockville. The other houses were equally alive in entertaining. Outings were planned to the Mt. Kisco Opera House, Lake Waccabuc and other points of interest. Fremont Ganung, who had bought the thirty-two-room "Avery House," set it on top of Bell Hill, now Oak Hill, and kept it as full of guests as had its former owners.

There were horse races at the Nelsons' track, and bicycle races in the village. The course of the bicycle races may have been upsetting to some of our residents. It began at Hoyt Brothers' corner, went down Katonah Avenue to Valley Road, west to Bedford Road, up to Edgemont, and back down Katonah Avenue to the place of beginning. A minute and thirty-eight seconds was the record time.[9]

The Village Improvement Society continued its courses of lectures. Willis Fletcher Johnson entertained members with "Landmarks" and that perennial favorite, Jahu De Witt Miller, gave them an enjoyable talk on "Love, Courtship and Marriage."

There was a camera club started in the new town and also a field club and some young married social clubs such as the "Jolly

Ten." Other forms of recreation mentioned in the papers were crokinole games, phonograph and military band concerts, dancing classes, theatricals, and lawn parties.

Intruding on this gay social whirl was calamity. In May of 1902, occurred the first big fire in New Katonah. It started in the livery stable of Louis W. Elliott at the south end of the village and before it was brought under control by heroic action on the part of Fire Department and citizens, it destroyed or damaged many other buildings in the heart of the business district. The financial loss was great and felt by about every family in the village. The one bright spot in this calamity was the proof of value of the new gasoline pumping engine, which had only recently been installed.[10]

There was sadness also in the first days of the new village. Many old and dearly beloved faces were missing. The Eastman and Pellew families had left Katonah before the move was made. Others were taken soon after by death. Judge Robertson and "Uncle Weedon" Fowler died in 1898. Mrs. Arnell Frost Dickinson, Robertson's sister, died in 1905 and "Mrs. Doctor Chapman" in 1906.

The younger generation was growing up in their footsteps, however. The Chapmans' son, Charles, graduated from the College of Physicians and Surgeons in 1890. Weedon Fowler's grandson, William, was building many of the houses in the new village. Robertson's young nephew, Edward Percy Barrett, made his first entrance into political life in 1905. Barrett's great admirer, Robert D. Knapp, wrote in the November 10th issue of his paper:

> The hardest fight ever witnessed in the Town of Bedford was that last Tuesday over the election of a Supervisor. Isaac W. Turner has held the office for many years. . . . E. P. Barrett . . . made a hustling canvas against great opposition. . . . The slanderous articles printed by Drumgoole [Editor, Mt. Kisco paper] did not injure the reputation of Mr. Barrett.[11]

And on November 17th he wrote:

> The people went to the polls and elected a clean, honest young man to look after the town. It was and will be Barrett for Bedford all the time.[12]

The new town enjoyed several conveniences not known in the old. Electric lighting was one of these. Juengst & Son of Croton Falls put this in many houses and stores. Their charge was $15.00 for a single street light for one year and $6.00 apiece for house lights in quantities of six or more.[13]

There had been some telephones in Old Katonah but now nearly everyone had them. The Hudson River Telephone Company raised its poles in Katonah in June of 1900 and found many subscribers.[14] These were warned, however, not to call the operator out of bed at night "unless you have something important." [15]

The Katonah Water Company had been supplying water from a tank on the hill and in 1906 they enlarged their capacity. One of the directors of the company was Dr. Carpenter.[16]

The community's health had been attracting public attention ever since the District Nursing Association of Northern Westchester was founded in Mt. Kisco in 1898. Serving the population of fourteen villages, this first rural public health nursing organization in the United States aimed at providing instruction in the care of the sick and the best possible nursing facilities. Among the many earnest Katonah women working for it with unfailing enthusiasm were Miss Elizabeth N. Barrett and Mrs. William H. Robertson.[23]

Another welfare undertaking, the Jennie Clarkson Home for Children, admitted its first five youngsters in 1898 and had twenty-four in 1902. Established in the Ammon Fowler farmhouse on Cherry Street, the Home outgrew its quarters by 1906 and moved to Valhalla. During its stay here, Dr. J. F. Chapman looked after the children's health, and local teachers, Miss Hattie Purdy and Miss Margery H. Van Tassel, taught in its school.[24]

Katonah took to automobiles with interest and a spirit of adventure. There were even some do-it-yourself enthusiasts among our numbers. On September 22, '99,[17] Robert Knapp wrote in his paper:

> There was an automobile in town this morning. It was owned by Mr. Chamberlain of Croton Falls. Although these vehicles of locomotion are quite common in and about New York, they are quite uncommon on our country roads. There is a factory located at Tarrytown and by another year we expect the horseless carriages will be very numerous.

They didn't become familiar sights on our streets quite that soon but Dr. Carpenter ordered one in August of 1900 and was driving it the next spring at the really fast clip of 20 miles an hour. Horses were a little slower than their masters to accept this new monster. One morning Dr. Carpenter was called on the phone by a lady who wanted to know if he was driving out in her direction. "I want to go to Katonah, but I don't want to meet you!" she explained.[25]

The automobile made at Tarrytown claimed forty miles an hour, and that it held water enough for 150 miles and gas for 1000. The cost of the trip from Tarrytown to New York City was estimated at 5¢!

In 1904 cars were being sold as near as Bedford and thereafter many items appeared in the paper concerning purchasers:

> Mr. E. P. Barrett has been running his new automobile this week. He seemed to have mastered the machine in a very short time, and is now able to spin about the country at a lively rate. Mr. George Nichols has an exceedingly large fine automobile which he will use this summer in place of horses. Horses are becoming more accustomed to these machines.
>
> Mr. John Thomas has purchased the gear and body for a new automobile and has sent for a steam engine which he intends placing on the body.

This was quite a long article, and technical. It ended by quoting Mr. Thomas as saying he thought this would be better than any made by manufacturers. We surely hope he wasn't disappointed.

Motor cars were obviously increasing. In 1906 Katonah was to have a fire-proof garage for "private machines" where Maxwell cars would also be sold.

Roads were becoming better. As early as 1899 we find in the minutes of the Village Improvement Society, "The streets, being macadamized, are not difficult to keep in order."[2] In 1906 thirteen miles of macadam road, sixteen feet wide, to cost $200,000, were voted by the Town Board of Bedford.[18] Not cheap, but the cost was felt warranted as an attraction to increased population and wealth.

As new homes were built, additional village roads became necessary. In 1899 Valley Road was extended to Cherry Street.[19] There were, of course, lanes to dwellings on the hills above the village, but the Town did not take them over till much later; the lower end of Huntville Road about 1919[26] and its extension to Cherry Street in 1931.[27] At that time, too, New Street was taken over and connected with The Terrace.[28] A new and modern Woods Bridge was built over the Croton River in 1904, replacing the little old bridge.[20]

Wealth and population seemed to be on the upswing. Both school and station had become inadequate to take care of our fast growing community.[4] Wealth in great quantity was already with us, and, like gold, was found in the hills. Extremely wealthy city men had discovered that our hills were beautiful and our climate healthy, just as the city boarders had discovered years before. The day of the "Hill Topper" was with us. They brought so much money into the community that by 1905 the Board of Trade, founded in '98, was discussing the advantages of starting a national bank in Katonah. The fifteen members present at the meeting in March of 1905 were all in favor of the idea. They said:

> The Bank would be a great convenience, as the wealthy people who live around Katonah pay their employees largely by check, and these people come to the stores in the village to get them cashed and do their trading and as the checks are numerous and often large there is hardly enough money to meet the demand.[21]

A committee composed of Joseph Barrett, H. W. Kellogg, Albert Hoyt, and Lewis H. Miller were appointed to investigate the matter.[29] A bank did not result at this time but the need was registered.

References

From Chapter 14 on, social affairs will not be documented, but may be found for the most part in the contemporary local papers.

1. Katonah Village Improvment Society. Minutes. Aug. 21, 1895. MS. (At the Katonah Village Library)
2. *Ibid.*, Jan. 19, 1899.
3. *Ibid.*, Jan. 11, 1905.
4. *Ibid.*, Mar. 27, 1906.
5. Avery, O. T. *Historical sketch of Katonah.* Katonah, 1896 (unpaged).
6. *Katonah Times*, Feb. 23, 1900.
7. *Ibid.*, Mar. 23, 1900.
8. *Ibid.*, Apr. 25, 1902.
9. *Ibid.*, July 1, 1898.
10. *Ibid.*, May 23, 1902.
11. *Ibid.*, Nov. 10, 1905.
12. *Ibid.*, Nov. 17, 1905.

13. *Ibid.*, Feb. 5, 1897.
14. *Ibid.*, June 29, 1900.
15. *Ibid.*, Jan. 13, 1905.
16. *Ibid.*, July 20, 1906.
17. For this and later data on automobiles see *Katonah Times:* Sept. 22, 1899; Aug. 10, 1900; Apr. 6, 1900; May 20, 1904; May 12, 1905; May 25, 1906; Sept. 21, 1906.
18. *Ibid.*, Mar. 30, 1906.
19. *Ibid.*, June 16, 1899.
20. *Ibid.*, Nov. 25, 1904.
21. *Ibid.*, Mar. 24, 1905.
22. *Mount Kisco Recorder,* Dec. 6, 1901.
23. Doe, Janet. District Nursing Association of Northern Westchester County, Katonah Branch. Katonah, 1959. MS. (At the Katonah Village Library)
24. Doe, Janet. The Jennie Clarkson Home for Children. Katonah, 1959. MS. (At the Katonah Village Library)
25. Doe, Janet. Medicine in Katonah. 1959. MS. (At the Katonah Village Library)
26. Bedford (N.Y.) Town Board. Minutes. Feb. 7, 1919. MS. (At Bedford Town House)
27. *Ibid.*, Sept. 1, 1931.
28. *Ibid.*, Aug. 4, 1931.
29. Newspaper clipping pasted in Miss Annie O'Neill's scrapbook, at present loaned to Mrs. H. S. Duncombe, Jr., Katonah.

CHAPTER XV

MUSCOOT AND CROSS RIVER RESERVOIRS

THERE WERE other wealthy newcomers with us in the early years of the twentieth century but they did not expect our stores to act as cashiers for them. These were the big construction companies working on the Muscoot and Cross River Dams.

The Muscoot Dam was the first of Katonah's dams to be built and, as the community felt it was necessary to health in assuring a constant water level and thereby preventing an expanse of mud flats, its construction was welcomed. Towards the middle of May in 1901 men and machinery began moving into Katonah to work on this two-million-dollar project, the contract for which had been let to Williams and Shelborne of New Jersey. The *Katonah Times* informed its interested subscribers that the dam at the foot of Muscoot Mountain was to be a heavy stone barrier twenty-five feet high, stretching two thousand feet across the valley, and would be submerged by several feet when the new Cornell Dam

214

was at high water level. An important part of the Croton water system, it was designed to treasure up the flood waters from above and distribute them at an even rate when needed in the dry seasons.[1] On June 7th the *Times* reported:

> The contractors . . . now have a large gang of men. . . . Almost every train brings in a load of Italians. . . . We see very little of them. . . . They have turned in just this side of the large Croton bridge [Woods Bridge] and have run the new road through the fields and woods to the site of the dam. . . .
>
> A large commissary building has been constructed. . . . The old optical factory building and old houses nearby are now the scene of much life.[2]

Workers were also living in huts on the side hill off Cherry Street. These were the first Italians to establish themselves in our immediate area and they were regarded both with interest and apprehension.

Two months later an interesting headline appeared: "CONTRACTOR AT MUSCOOT DAM SKIPS WITH MONEY." A sub-contractor, whose job was that of putting the footbridge across the river, skipped town leaving his workmen unpaid. Said the *Katonah Times*:

> Last Saturday, Kalback received his money from the contractors, and the men were on hand to be paid off, but by some dexterous moves, having made an excuse that he would be back in an hour, he was driven away by a man by name of Elbert Kaler. Kalback owned a horse and carriage, and with his wife and three children boarded at the Bedell House on Cherry Street.[3]

The footbridge didn't last much longer than Mr. Kalback. It was washed away in the fall. All along, weather played a delaying role in the building of Muscoot Dam. In February of 1902 the *Katonah Times* told its readers:

> Work at the Muscoot Dam, west of Katonah, has been practically at a standstill for the last six weeks, nothing having been accomplished since the first of January when Contractor Williams laid off the large gang of Italians until the weather became more settled.

Before work was suspended in December, large quantities of rock were blasted from the west bank of the river and thousands of tons more are still embedded there which will be used in building the foundations. The rock is of first class quality with a strain of granite running through it.

The foot bridge, which was washed away in the freshet of last Fall, has not been replaced and the only way to cross the river is to use the little skiff kept for that purpose, as the river never freezes over except in the coldest of weather, owing to the swift current.

With the first of March Mr. Williams expects to put a gang of Italians and skilled mechanics to work, and gradually increase the force until the number employed reaches 500 along in the summer.[4]

William Travis, then a boy of ten, remembers watching these workmen spear fish.[28]

For a small dam, the Muscoot took a long time to build and before it was finished the welcoming attitude of the neighborhood had changed somewhat. There were incidents of disorderly conduct and sometimes violence on the part of the men working on it.

There was a report in November of 1904 that the gates of the new Croton or Cornell Dam were closed but this apparently was just a rumor;[5] perhaps a purposeful one. In December the following news item appeared:

The watershed authorities are now hustling the people out who still remain on their property. Thad K. Green was given three days to get his two houses on Bedford Road off the city property.

The Nelson house we understand is being torn down, and a few other houses are being burned.[6]

By May of 1905, only a small opening in the dam remained to be closed.[7] On December 8th Katonah read with relief the following words in the *Times*:

A big force of men are now at work clearing off the lowlands, mowing and burning the grass and bushes and getting things in readiness to turn down the gates at the Muscoot Dam.[8]

Just when water began to be stored permanently behind Muscoot Dam is not certain. Flooding the reservoir was put off because of lack of roads in the valley, but apparently even children were working hard for their completion, driving the dumpwagons that hauled rock from river bed to stone-crushers.[28]

In the spring of 1906 both gates were closed down and the lake commenced to rise rapidly, beginning to cover the flats about Katonah when for some reason one gate was opened and the water commenced to go again.[9] Meanwhile the Croton Dam had been finished in March of 1906.[10] By September 1907 the enormous basin behind the Croton Dam was filling up fast and water was running over the Muscoot Dam to a depth of five or six inches.[11] People watched the incoming water with great interest, going out to see how far it had reached from time to time. No special celebration was held or notice taken when it was finally full. According to Miss Margery Van Tassel the strongest reaction was the eeriness people felt when they went boating on the new lake and passed over the old landmarks.[29]

Though the building of the Muscoot made problems, its result was desired. Not so with the Cross River Dam. Among engineers, even, there were many against it and the hope was that it would never be built. Miss Helen Towey, a member of one of the families living in the area, wrote:

> The city decided to buy the farm and there was much worrying about how much they would pay us and great anger when we were told to evict our tenant from the little house, although we did not know what we would get for the place and therefore could not decide where to go. They burned down our little house and sold the larger one in which we lived to someone from Long Island.[30]

In October of 1904 the following was printed in the *Katonah Times*:

> We understand that engineers have arrived here and are to bore down to see about a foundation for the Cross River dam. Mr. George Welsche has charge of the work. There has been some doubt for a long time as to whether the dam would be built. The subject is now coming up again.[12]

Hope still remained when the paper said on November 25th:

A force of surveyors and engineers are still at work making soundings for the new Cross River dam. This dam, if built, will be just beyond the watering trough on the road to Hoyt's Mills. There seems to be many indications that this structure will be built, notwithstanding the fact that many engineers claim that the Croton Watershed is already overworked and the dam already built will never fill.[13]

Westchester as a whole was tired of New York City's thirst. In late 1904 Assemblyman Apgar prepared a bill shutting New York City out of Westchester County for its water supply. It wiped out the Webster Bill giving New York City the right to condemn lands for extending their water supply. Mr. Apgar also made known he would introduce a bill similar to the Smith Bill of Dutchess County, which would exclude New York City from all streams in Westchester.[14]

The bill was introduced on January 25, 1905. The City moved fast. On February 3 the *Katonah Times* said:

A corps of city engineers are now at work near this village drilling for a foundation for the new Cross River dam. For some time they worked just a short distance this side of Hoyt's Mills, but we understand that a good rock foundation was not found.

The engineers now have a little shanty put up within sight of the village and are at work drilling.[15]

By February 8 the Aqueduct Commission had approved maps and plans. They were sent to the Corporation Counsel requesting that he advertise them at once with the Supreme Court of Westchester and ask for a Commission to condemn the land. A hearing was held which was attended by Col. William Jay and about twenty other Westchester men.[31]

The City had won. Bids on the plans were in by June 2nd and by June 23rd the contract had been awarded to the MacArthur Brothers' Co. and Winston & Co. firms. Their bid of $1,246,000 was not the lowest but their experience was by far the greatest. They were at the time just completing the dam at Clinton, Massachusetts, said to be the second largest in the world.[16]

Late in June the contractors, losing no time, moved in. They started construction of a narrow gauge railway known as the "Boutonville Express," that brought supplies from a spot near

Elliott's lumber yard in Katonah to the dam.[17] The frequency with which the locomotive toppled over earned the little railroad a place of amused affection in the hearts of Katonah townspeople. Two carloads of mules and Negro drivers arrived and were put on the former George Green farm. Two shifts of men worked day and night.[18]

Mr. Winston chose one of the larger houses on the farm for himself and brought his wife and two little boys up from Louisa County, Virginia. Being a sporting gentleman as well as a fine construction engineer, he also brought along his fighting cocks. In Katonah his third child, a daughter, was born, delivered by Irene Shove Chapman.[32]

Work was delayed by an injunction. A suit brought by Frederick Walters, a taxpayer, in behalf of Bart Dunn, a disappointed bidder on the project, was upheld by Justice Bischoff.[19] However, a decision was handed down in October by the Supreme Court of New York which allowed work to continue.[20]

Some 200 Italian workmen were employed, camping in shanties near Katonah. Every Sunday morning passengers on the Harlem Railroad had a startling glimpse of them in deshabille, kneeling beside tubs at the river's edge, scrubbing away at their brilliantly colored but grimy attire.[21] There were numerous complaints of sanitary conditions among the workmen and a typhoid epidemic was involved.

In 1906 events took a frightening turn. The Italian Mafia moved in, and in terrorizing the workmen, frightened the community as well. From April to October there were frequent killings.[22] Most of the attacks took place in the vicinity of Mt. Holly Road where apparently there were shanties close to the building dam.

On September 21st Doc Kesler, a cop, sometimes described as four feet high and sometimes as five, was shot at on the Mt. Holly Road, at the spot where the Italian, Jumbo, had recently been killed.[23] Kesler, whatever his height, was a man with courage and brought in more than one assassin.

In the October 5th issue of the *Katonah Times* was the following story:

> Mounted Police patrol Westchester watershed. Acting under authority from the Supervisor's [office] Sheriff James S. Merritt last week opened a police headquarters in the New York city watershed where four men are detailed for the purpose of protecting industrious Italians from Black Hand brigands

and blackmailers. The station is in charge of James Clark, of Tuckahoe, who acts as captain, and his force is composed of three uniformed officers who will patrol the region on horseback, horses having been furnished for this purpose by Winston & Co. The station is at the Cross River dam and it is equipped with a telephone system so that Captain Clark can reach the other police of Westchester county and New York city in a hurry. . . .

Sheriff Merritt is determined to break up the Black Hand gang and as the result of his efforts eight bandits, all charged with murder, are now confined in the White Plains jail.[24]

Thereafter we hear no more of the Black Hand in this area.

Work was progressing fast. By the end of October it was half completed.[25] On August 7, 1907, the gates were closed and water started accumulating behind them.[26] The last stone was laid in the Cross River Dam on October 26, 1907, by the president of the Aqueduct Commission, John F. Cowan, using a silver trowel. Speeches were delivered atop an oil-barrel placed on the driveway over the dam. One of the best was that given by our supervisor, E. P. Barrett. In spite of a six months' delay because of the injunction, the dam had been completed August 30th, within the time called for by the contract.[27] The colored men left with their Louisa County mules. Italians departed from their boarding-houses below at Hoyt's Mills. The Winstons went on to Kingston to build the Ashokan Dam.[32]

Katonah, Mt. Holly, and Cantitoe were left to themselves again. One reminder of those times is the "No Trespassing" signs, still posted on some of our trees, printed both in Italian and English. Other reminders are the fine Italian families who remained with us after the dam was completed. The most constant reminder is the Reservoir itself, one of the beauty spots of our area.

References

Social affairs will not be documented, but may be found for the most part in the contemporary local papers.

1. *Katonah Times,* May 31, 1901.
2. *Ibid.,* June 7, 1901.
3. *Ibid.,* July 19, 1901.
4. *Ibid.,* Feb. 14, 1902.
5. *Ibid.,* Nov. 4, 1904.
6. *Ibid.,* Dec. 30, 1904.
7. *Ibid.,* May 19, 1905.
8. *Ibid.,* Dec. 8, 1905.

9. *Ibid.*, May 25, 1906.
10. *Ibid.*, Mar. 23, 1906.
11. *Ibid.*, Sept. 13, 1907.
12. *Ibid.*, Oct. 21, 1904.
13. *Ibid.*, Nov. 25, 1904.
14. *Ibid.*, Jan. 13, 1905.
15. *Ibid.*, Feb. 3, 1905.
16. *Ibid.*, June 23 & July 7, 1905.
17. *Ibid.*, June 30, 1905.
18. *Ibid.*, July 14, 1905.
19. *Ibid.*, Sept. 22, 1905.
20. *Ibid.*, Oct. 13, 1905.
21. *Ibid.*, Oct. 27, 1905.
22. *Ibid.*, Apr. 6, 1906, ff.
23. *Ibid.*, Sept. 21, 1906.
24. *Ibid.*, Oct. 5, 1906.
25. *Ibid.*, Oct. 26, 1906.
26. *Ibid.*, Sept. 6, 1907.
27. *Ibid.*, Nov. 1, 1907.

28. Travis, William. Old Katonah as remembered. Largo, Fla., 1960. MS. (In possession of Mrs. W. A. Kelly, Katonah. Typed copy at the Katonah Village Library)
29. Van Tassel, Miss Margery H., Katonah. Oral communication.
30. Towey, Helen M. Reminiscences of life in the basin of the Cross River Reservoir. Katonah, 1959. MS. (At the Katonah Village Library)
31. New York City. Aqueduct Commissioners. *Minutes, 1905.* New York, [1906,] v. 21, p. 55.
32. Adams, Mrs. J. Donald, 444 E. 57th St., New York 22, N.Y. Oral communication.

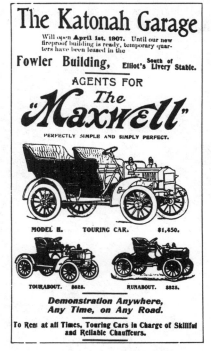

Advertisement in the *Katonah Times,*
August 2, 1907.

THE LAST HALF CENTURY

As WE COME into our last fifty-odd years, it is hard to judge what will be considered of importance to Katonah's history by future generations. We are too close to the picture and time has not yet done its job of weeding out the irrelevant. And so we believe the most useful thing we can do is to set down a chronological record of what has taken place in each decade of our existence since the completion of the Cross River Dam. Those historians who follow us can decide which of these many events have had lasting significance.

222

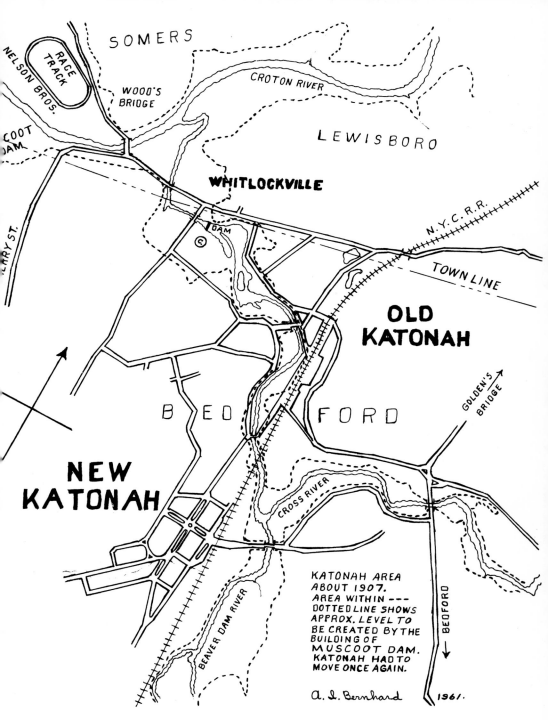

SOMERS

RACE TRACK

NELSON BROS.

WOOD'S BRIDGE

COOT DAM

CROTON RIVER

LEWISBORO

MARY ST.

WHITLOCKVILLE

DAM

N.Y.C.R.R.

TOWN LINE

OLD KATONAH

B ED FORD

GOLDEN'S BRIDGE

NEW KATONAH

CROSS RIVER

BEAVER DAM RIVER

KATONAH AREA
ABOUT 1907.
AREA WITHIN ---
DOTTED LINE SHOWS
APPROX. LEVEL TO
BE CREATED BY THE
BUILDING OF
MUSCOOT DAM.
KATONAH HAD TO
MOVE ONCE AGAIN.

BEDFORD

a. I. Bernhard   1961.

Courtesy of the New York City Board of Water Supply

THE CROSS AND CROTON RIVERS BEFORE FLOODING

This section of an Aqueduct Commissioners' map of the New Croton Reservoir System, made in 1907, shows the Katonah, Woods Bridge and Whitlockville areas and the Nelson Brothers' race track. Traced by A. I. Bernhard.

Muscoot Dam. Construction started 1901 and gates closed 1906. Its purpose was t maintain a constant level of the Muscoot Reservoir in Katonah are

Present Woods Bridge, built 1904, above the one it replaced whe flooding of the Croton Valley necessitated a longer spa

Cross River Dam. Started 1905, gates closed 1907. Behind crane in foreground can be seen tracks of the "Boutonville Express" which brought material from the New York Central Railroad to the Dam.

BEDFORD TOWNSHIP, 1851

Section of Sidney and Neff map of Westchester County.

227

Courtesy of Edward Percy Barrett

Katonah Fire Department, early 1900's. Front row: Princey Lyon, O. Wendell Green, James Williams, Frank Gumboldt, Wilfred Keeler, George H. Covey, J. Franklin Ryan, George Gregory, Elbridge Arnold, Herbert S. Chapman, George S. Ray, Lewis H. Miller, William B. Newman, William G. Barrett. Back row: Melville Allen, William Daniel, Louis Haight, William Lent, E. P. Barrett, Peter Gruber, Robert D. Knapp, Thomas Doyle, DeWitt Benedict, Daniel I. Smith, Frank Westcott, David Doyle, William I. Doyle,

Calamity of 1902. Fire starting in Elliott's Livery Stable destroyed block between Katonah Avenue and Bedford Road. Running toward center distance is The Terrace.

Looking north on Katonah Avenue after fire of 1902, showing Elliott's Livery Stable rebuilt on a new site.

229

Courtesy of Edward Percy Barrett

Katonah Baseball Team, "The Lakesides," taken about 1912-14. In front row, left to right: George Nelson, Mascot; James Brundage, Robert Lent, George Marler, Frank Gumboldt. Back row: Clarence Wanser, Leroy Gregory, George Jones, Horton Dennis, John Miller, Wallace Searles, Robertson T. Barrett, Manager (standing).

Advertisement in the *Katonah Times,*
December 6, 1907.

CHAPTER XVI

1907–1916

IN KATONAH the period 1907 to 1916 was one of great wholesomeness with no thought of juvenile delinquency and practically no major crimes. The local churches set up a high moral code which in some aspects was almost puritanical. The Katonah Village Improvement Society was a strong body, providing many local advantages without the burden of taxes. The Republican party was then, as now, of great influence in Katonah. It was the strong majority party of the community and in power nationally until Teddy Roosevelt and his Bull Moosers caused the split which brought about the election of Woodrow Wilson. At the end of this era the Great War ensued and the way of life we are to relate never completely returned.

In 1907 Katonah was well settled down after the great tearing up and moving, although it was not until 1909 that the last three dwellings were auctioned off and removed.[1] The cooperative spirit was very strong and there was great enthusiasm for any worthy object. Suspicion of the motives of the New York City water authorities was easy to arouse, and great and quick objections were made when the level of the reservoir lake was lowered too much to suit the village leaders.

We note the influence on the community of the local churches. At first the churches had the only spaces suitable for public assembly and were in constant use by civic and social organizations as well as by church groups. The Village Improvement Society used one or the other of these meeting places for its annual meeting and for fund-raising functions. Beginning in 1907, the assembly room of the new school on Bedford Road, built that year,[2] was also available for the use of local groups but the church meeting-rooms continued in great demand. In this period the Protestant churches were drawn closely together by the struggle against the "Demon Rum," and were united in the fight which was to result in the adoption of the eighteenth amendment. Sad to say, there was bitter feeling against the Italian immigrant and he was blamed locally for participation in the illegal liquor traffic. We are happy to add that this feeling changed and in 1910 night classes in English were established for them.

Katonah had a Civic League and for some years it acted as a vigilante committee for the community. It did so well that while it was functioning the Law and Order Committee of the Village Improvement Society had little business to report at the annual meetings. One year they did report that boys had been playing ball in the streets but that the practice had been stopped after words of warning.

In November of 1908 the Civic League led a posse of Sheriff's men from White Plains on successful raids on three liquor-selling places in Greenville. Greenville at this time was a community quite apart from the village proper. Miss Elizabeth Barrett in an account of the informal Bible classes held there by herself and Mrs. A. F. Avery gave us the following description:

> When Old Katonah moved to its new site, the hotel of Thaddeus Green did not follow the majority of the buildings to the restricted land near the station where the selling of liquor was prohibited. Instead, it was set down midway in the orchard formerly belonging to Bernard Travis.
>
> Around the hotel grew up a little community that became known as Greenville and in the early days its population was

mostly Italian. It had a ball field and Green's saloon as centers of its social life and the people who lived there kept pretty much to themselves.[5]

Miss Barrett and Mrs. Avery, finding the children of Greenville eager to listen to the Bible stories that no one had told them, decided to take on the assignment.

> Every Sunday afternoon for more than a year we returned. In fine weather we met in the ball park. On rainy days and during the winter some mother would invite us to use her kitchen. We taught the children hymns and told them stories from the Bible and we all became such very good friends that we had much happiness together. We shared sorrow together also at times. A baby died and its mother asked us to sing a hymn and say a prayer so we all went to the room where it lay. We took flowers and sang "Jesus Loves Me" which I had taught the children and also a hymn in Italian which they had taught me.
>
> Mrs. Avery and I were always careful to keep our class undenominational. . . . We never tried to make Presbyterians out of [the children]. We only taught them to know and love God, and also to brush their teeth and comb their hair.[5]

It would be our guess that Miss Barrett and Mrs. Avery, continuing these classes into the 1920's, were far more effective than a dozen vigilante committees!

In the new village of Katonah proper there was much progress in the decade 1907-1916. The new station with its *two* waiting rooms, which had been proposed in 1906, was finally ready in March of 1910.[6] Travel both by rail and motor increased. The automobile came into such general use that World War I was largely mechanized. The automobile posed many attendant problems such as the need for more surfaced roads, licensing, a motor vehicle law and local control of speeding. In 1907 in White Plains, a driver was sentenced to ten days and a fine of $100 for travelling at nearly 30 miles an hour. In 1908 the automobile association favored a state tax on automobiles of two to five dollars each, to yield an estimated $250,000, an amount that could provide scant funds for road improvement. But nothing could stop the attraction of the automobile and each year more advertisements appeared of more makes, strange to us now but appearing very dependable and certainly eye-catching.

In 1916 the Katonah Fire Department purchased its first piece of motorized equipment, a Garfield, for the sum of $3150; and in that year in Westchester County 11,808 motor vehicles were registered. The gas-buggy was here to stay. In Katonah, however, it did not displace the horse for many years. When on May 25, 1909, the livery stable of Fletcher H. Lent burned and eleven horses perished, he rebuilt his stables and business and was soon meeting all trains again.[4]

More and more people were installing electricity, and in 1910 the Katonah Lighting Company advertised that it was securing one new customer a day. Astute merchants, seeing the writing on the wall, advertised sales of oil lamps in an effort to clear their shelves of this doomed item. The telephone was considered more of a luxury and at first was used mostly by business places and doctors. However, as early as 1916 the telephone company's advertising pushed the idea of more than one telephone to a home.

There was mention of a possible need for incorporation of Katonah village during this decade that arose from the problem of sewage disposal. The establishment of a sewer system was recognized as a matter of such large proportion that the financing could only be accomplished by an incorporated village.[7] This concern over sewage was doubtless caused by fear of typhoid fever, for there was an epidemic in 1907 with fifteen recorded cases and three deaths. The origin of the germ was never traced but samples of water and milk supplies were tested regularly by both local and New York City health authorities. Typhoid did recur in lesser incidence for many years but talk of a sewer system and village incorporation ceased.

The Katonah Board of Trade was extremely active in this decade, sincerely believing that the new Katonah had much to offer and ever advertising its attractions as a place in which to live and do business. We can judge its standing in the community when it promptly offered a reward of $1,000 for information leading to the apprehension of the person who in 1916, when war tensions were beginning, planted a bomb on the rear porch of the Frank Gumboldt Building. The bomb did only superficial damage; the culprit was never caught.

Katonah was deeply interested in politics on the local, state and national level. In 1907 the ebullient Teddy Roosevelt was in the White House and at the height of his popularity. Many things he did made news, such as his "trust-busting," his fight to acquire the land for the Panama Canal and the sending of the "Great

White Fleet" on its cruise around the world. Roosevelt had picked Taft as his successor and Katonah threw its support behind him. During the campaign a monster rally was held in a tent erected on Katonah Avenue, at which Chauncey M. Depew was the principal speaker. Taft was swept into office, and the night of the victory Katonah celebrated with a cavalcade of twenty motor cars led by J. Franklin Ryan. The cavalcade made several stops and at each stop Robertson T. Barrett would shout, "Are we strong?" and, "Did we win?", to be answered by a thunderous roar of approval.

The year 1912 was a tough one for the staunch Republicans of the town of Bedford. Teddy Roosevelt had bolted the party and was running under the Progressive banner. He had much support in the County, as did Wilson, and both Progressive and Democratic rallies were held in Katonah. When the votes were counted, however, Bedford stood with Pound Ridge and Cortlandt as the only three towns in Westchester County to go Republican.

In 1916 the Progressives had returned to the Republican fold and a Republican rally for the whole of northern Westchester was held at Katonah to aid in the election of Charles Evans Hughes. The effort bore fruit and the County went Republican by the largest pluralities in its history. It was in vain, for Woodrow Wilson was re-elected. Katonah soon put aside partisan feeling and stood staunchly behind Wilson in the war years which followed.

In the field of recreation there was much going on in this era. Two well organized sports in Katonah were tennis and baseball. The courts of the Katonah Tennis Club were across the tracks opposite the railroad station. In addition to providing healthful recreation for the local youth, the Club engaged in tournaments with teams from nearby villages, such as Mount Kisco and Brewster.

The local baseball club was known as the "Lakesides" and its home diamond was Lakeside Field (later called Gregory Field in honor of a player, Le Roy Gregory, who lost his life in World War I). This now forms part of the Saw Mill River Parkway. The Lakesides played a full schedule and were enthusiastically supported by the rooters. Usually the season would terminate on Labor Day with a monster clambake.

Boating on Katonah Lake and indeed on all the reservoirs was very popular. In 1907 there were 600 boats being used on "the Lake." [3] For a safe and sane July 4th celebration in 1910 a water carnival was staged as the main event. Boat races included Men's Canoe Race, double and single, Round Bottom Boat Race, double and single, and the same for flat-bottom boats. There was also a Ladies' Canoe Race, double and single, and a Double Canoe Race, lady and gentleman. In a competition for the best decorated boat the first prize was won by the Misses Josephine and Margery Van Tassel. In the fall of 1910 the use of canoes on the reservoirs was banned by the New York City Board of Water Supply, after two young men drowned when their canoe upset.

Winter brought much skating and sledding and there were indoor diversions as well. The Katonah Choral Club was well supported for many years. In 1909, when it was ten years old, after a winter of faithful practice it presented Mendelssohn's "Elijah" with young Reinald Werrenrath as guest soloist. Professor Hallam, still the leader of the group, also held an afternoon meeting each week in the Katonah school.

The first motion pictures came to Katonah in the summer of 1913.[8] They were shown out of doors in an open lot between Hoyt Brothers' store and Gorham's drugstore on the north side of The Parkway and later in Katonah Hall on Valley Road (now Fred's restaurant). Erected by Glenn Packer in the latter part of 1913, this "moving picture building" was twenty-three by fifty feet with hardwood floors, comfortable seats, and wide aisles. Mr. Packer's avowed purpose was to show the cleanest and best pictures. He planned to give two shows a week, and the building was available for dances and other entertainments on other than show nights. His program for the show of December 11, 1913, included: "Shipwrecked," "A Florida Romance," "Seeing Double," "Jean and her Family," and "His Undesirable Relatives."

One ambitious bit of entertainment deserves mention, the amateur circus staged by the Men's Club in September, 1913. Weeks, even months, of preparation went into it with its mock animals and elaborate tableaux. It was a great success and drew one of the largest crowds in years. *The Record* of that day stated that it "placed Katonah still more prominently on the map." As we look back over this decade, we realize that it was the aim of nearly all Katonah's citizens of that day to "put Katonah on the map" as a clean, decent and fine place in which to live, worship God and rear their families.

This chapter was written by Herbert Hendrickson, with help from Eleanor Hendrickson and Julia Mead.

References

Most of the information in this chapter has been taken from the Katonah newspapers. Certain specific references and those to other sources are given.

1. *Katonah Times,* Jan. 29, 1909.
2. *Ibid.,* July 17, 1907.
3. *Ibid.,* Aug. 9, 1907.
4. *Ibid.,* May 28[?], 1909.
5. Barrett, Elizabeth N. An informal Bible class. Katonah, 1958(?) MS. (In possession of Mrs. W. A. Kelly, Katonah. Copy at the Katonah Village Library)
6. New York Central System. Letter to Janet Doe, New York, Jan. 7, 1960. MS. (At the Katonah Village Library)
7. Katonah Village Improvement Society. Minutes. Jan. 11, 1907. MS. (At the Katonah Village Library)
8. Weist, Mrs. William G., Katonah. Oral communication.

Save WHEAT

Save SUGAR

Save MEAT

Save COAL

Save TELEPHONE SERVICE

BY saving telephone service, you help the Nation in its war program in several ways:

1. You help save CAPITAL that would be required for additions to the plant. The Govern...

From advertisement, N.Y. Telephone Company,
Katonah Record, September 13, 1918.

CHAPTER XVII
1917–1926

THE LACK of headline news concerning the war in Europe in the early 1917 issues of the *Katonah Record* astounds the present-day reader. Local affairs were headlined, rather than the impending disaster of World War I: the annual meeting of the Katonah Village Improvement Society; the need of care by motorists on the local highways; the honoring by the County Board of Supervisors of the memory of Admiral George Dewey; a joint entertainment planned by the Katonah Tennis Club and the Lakeside Baseball Team. The press was occupied with arousing interest in the proposed firehouse to be built next to Kellogg and Mead's where the library now stands. It was to be a tremendous edifice, large enough to house fire equipment, a library and an auditorium! On the social side, the Katonah Suffrage Club was producing an hilarious comedy entitled "A Box of Monkeys." Disaster-wise, a raging fire on Katonah Avenue had completely destroyed the L. W. Elliott building which housed the Blue Book Garage, and damaged the H. W. Kellogg apartment house. Only a short paragraph at the

bottom of a page noted that the Red Cross was to hold its regular
sewing meeting at the home of Mrs. George Nelson.

Where, oh where, was the European conflict and what was our
relation to it? On April 6, 1917, a headline stated that the Board
of Supervisors had named men to be in charge of defense and the
conservation of resources—*if needed*. On April 12th 350 men
from the township of Bedford met and volunteered to join the
Reserve Police Force. A few days later a mass meeting was held
in Mount Kisco to organize a Military Training Corps in northern Westchester. On April 20, 1917, President Wilson's declaration of war against Germany was printed in the *Katonah Record*.
The *North Westchester Times* of the same date told of the many
local people who viewed the Curtis biplane flown to Bedford
Country Club by Frederick Blakeman of the Aviation Corps, U.S.
Army. Community and county became organized with amazing
rapidity. On June 5th, men registered for the draft census, and by
June 11th, a complete military census was under way of every man
and woman between the ages of 16 and 50.

Now the press relegated local affairs to inside sheets. The first
page took on a new look. Patriotic poems, letters, essays appeared
"front and center" in every issue. The *"if needed"* organizers of
defense and the conservation of resources became essential, in a
pattern of organization repeated some twenty-four years later. The
Katonah Police Force Reserves was headed by Captain Franklin
Ryan, and later by George Hoyt. Three Liberty Loan Drives were
supported generously by the people of our village, with Katonah
going completely "over the top." Its quota of $81,500 in the second
drive was oversubscribed by $60,850. The creditable work of the
local Suffrage Club in the draft census and Liberty Loan Drives
brought praise from Senator Slater at a mass meeting at Katonah
High School in 1917. Hoarded pennies of piggy banks were exchanged at school for War Savings Stamps. "Four Minute Men,"
a branch of the Officers' Reserve Corps, delivered in that allotted
time authentic war information: George Covey, Robertson Barrett, and the Rev. George Barber served well in this capacity. Red
Cross workers prepared boxes for base hospitals in France, collected donations of phonographs, records and books for the boys,
and organized a Women's Motor Corps. On January 23, 1918, the
Katonah Record announced that registration of enemy aliens
would begin on February 4th.

Conservation of our resources became a major problem. School
children were encouraged to raise pigs, the purchase price being

defrayed by the Towns of Bedford and New Castle. The Westchester Committee of General Safety urged all good citizens to
start home gardens. A women's agricultural camp of volunteer
farmerettes was conducted on the Woodcock Farm in Bedford.
A Community Canning Club under Miss Esther King preserved
excess fruits and vegetables. On May 14, 1918, the "Victory Special," a food demonstration train, came to Katonah.

Although the pocketbooks of the 1918 ladies did not bulge with
the numerous ration books of World War II, conservation was
practiced in the community. Citizens were requested to keep their
autos idle on Sunday to save gas. In July, 1918, notice was given
that all outdoor lighting except street lights was to be turned off
Monday through Thursday. A government fuel-saving edict
closed all places of business other than food stores on Mondays
January 25 through March 25, 1918.

While the Katonahites were "keeping the home fires burning,"
many of the young people were seeing action overseas. Lt. Robert
E. Brady and Harvey J. Avery wrote home of their hazardous experiences on board the torpedoed troop ship "Tuscania." Avery's
letter of February 17, 1918, said in part:

> About 5:45 I was in the kitchen waiting for a pail of coffee,
> there was a heavy explosion in the front part of the ship, the
> lids flew off the stove, and pots of soup that were on it spilled
> over and caught fire. All the electric lights went out with the
> explosion and everything was pitch dark. I started to go down
> an alley that led to the deck, but as I started down the stairs
> I stepped on other men's heads, the alley was packed full, and
> a good many men must have been trapped down there. . . .
> The first one of our lifeboats was smashed, and the second
> was dropped into the water and smashed in lowering, and the
> same thing happened to the third. . . . Pretty soon another
> boat was lowered safely, and Eaves and one of the Lieutenants
> and I slid down the rope and landed in the lifeboat. By the
> time we got into the boat it was full of men and we had a
> hard time getting away from the ship as none of the men
> knew how to row; they would pull on the wrong oar and
> bring us right back to the ship. After awhile we got about a
> half a mile from the ship. . . .
> We had been rowing around for awhile when something
> black rose out of the water . . . We pulled on the oars and
> got away as fast as we could and at last it disappeared. I was

more frightened then than at any time. . . . They say that submarines have an unpleasant habit of taking men out of lifeboats and stripping off their life belts and clothes, and standing them on the deck of the submarine and submerging. . . .

We rowed around for about 2½ hours and at last a torpedo boat came along and picked us up. One of the bravest things I saw during the whole thing was when the Captain of the torpedo boat jumped into the icy water and rescued two men who were drowning. . . .

The boat landed us in a town in Ireland about the size of White Plains. We were taken in "Fords" to two of the best hotels in the town, and given a hot meal and put to bed and believe me, a good bed felt good. . . .[1]

Among Katonah's young people overseas was one woman. When in the summer of 1918, General Pershing asked for a small group of American women to serve with our army overseas, giving assistance supplied until then by the English W.A.C.s, Miss Helen M. Towey was one of this pioneer group. Through the late Dr. Katharine Bement Davis, formerly superintendent of the State Reformatory at Bedford Hills, Miss Towey heard of the group being formed and had only ten days after acceptance to undergo inoculations, have uniforms made and secure her complete outfit. This unit of fifty women with varied backgrounds, such as librarians, statisticians, and secretaries, went overseas in three groups and were attached to the office of the Chief Quartermaster, A.E.F., in Tours, France. Miss Towey sailed in August. She says:

It seemed exciting when we left New York on a little French boat with balloons overhead and the mosquito fleet of tiny boats protecting us. We were soon blacked out and after the third day a group of Polish men in French uniforms appeared up front. The story was that they were recruited in Canada. The tenth day we steamed into the harbor at Bordeaux and from then on were under military orders. . . .

There were the usual war shortages: no butter or sugar and very little meat. It seemed that one was always hungry and of course always broke, so the urchins begging chocolate and pennies at the barracks gate fared not too well. The usual reply to their pleas had to be, "pas chocolat—pas penny—pas chewing gum."

Due to her experience in statistics, Miss Towey was first assigned to the Salvage Department, Services of Supplies, and her final assignment was to the Payroll Division which handled expense and payroll accounts: "Even then, expense accounts were padded." Miss Towey remained overseas eight months and thereafter continued to work for a short time with that Division which was transferred to Washington.[3]

The Sullivan brothers of World War II fame had their counterpart in the five Noe brothers of Katonah who served their country with distinction in World War I: Peter in the Medical Corps; Cornelius and Fred in the Coast Artillery; Paul in the U.S. Navy; and Carl in the U.S. Army Tank Corps. Many other Katonah boys entered the service (see Appendix No. 30). Those who did not return were Corp. James Kelly killed in action in France, Sergeant Angelo M. Candee, LeRoy Gregory, Frederick B. Jones, and J. Stanley Russell.

November 11, 1918, saw the cessation of conflict in Europe, but it was the spring of 1919 before some of the boys were mustered out. A gala Welcome Home Celebration took place on May 31, 1919, planned and executed by a committee of which E. P. Barrett was chairman. The returning veterans were feted with an afternoon parade and speeches, band concert, dinner at the high school, and an evening entertainment to the accompaniment of heart-warming cheers from grateful and enthusiastic friends and neighbors. Peace had come once more to the world of Katonah.

The League of Nations was the burning issue preceding the 1920 elections. Warren G. Harding, Republican nominee, felt that America needed a return to normalcy, and the public responded by electing him to the presidency. We did not join the League and we rejected the World Court, but the period that followed was a far cry from normalcy. It was marked by national corruption and isolationism. Americans were war weary. They wanted to enjoy life and threw themselves with fervor into that era which has been dubbed the Jazz Age, the Flapper Age, the Golden Age of the Twenties. After the brief depression of 1921-22, there followed one of the greatest peace-time boom periods in the history of America.

Against this background, burning issues of the day were prohibition and women's suffrage. These had the support of zealous Katonah citizens. From 1913 to 1920 when the 19th Amendment became a reality, the local Suffrage Club had waged an untiring campaign. The first Katonah woman to vote was Mrs. Paul H.

Loizeaux who reached the polls at 6:02 that election morning in November, 1918.[4] Under the capable leadership of its presidents, Mrs. Oris Goan, Mrs. Ferdinand T. Hopkins, Jr., and Mrs. Eloise MacPhail, the Club flourished and grew to a membership of over one hundred. Of equal importance was the work of the Women's Christian Temperance Union. A petition urging the President to declare prohibition at least for the duration of the war had been taken to Senator Calder in Washington by Miss Irene Weir in 1917.

The impact of the rising automobile industry was felt on our village streets from the very beginning of this decade. In 1917 Fletcher Lent, unofficial greeter of Katonah, sold the last horse in his livery stable and switched to automobiles. The editor of the *Katonah Record* looked out his back window with a nostalgic sigh at the empty stalls. In 1920 the old watering trough at the junction of Bedford and Valley Roads was removed at the request of the Village Improvement Society officers. Said the *Katonah Record,* "It had long ago outlived its usefulness and was a distinct menace to auto drivers as no light has been placed thereon." Until 1920 cars were driven higgledy-piggledy along Bedford Road, the driver going on whichever side of the park he fancied. Then reason came to the traffic problem in the form of Officer Eich of the Bedford Town Police. He familiarized drivers with the new regulation: all village streets with parks in the center were to be one way on each side.

The farmer found the motor car an asset, but bemoaned the poor roads over which he had to travel. In 1921 the Katonah-Mount Kisco road was paved in concrete and hailed as a model road, twenty feet wide! Two years later Valley Road was paved. In January, 1926, Carl Rasmussen appeared driving a new Dodge for the Blakeen Farm Dairy and thus disappeared one of our old-time village fixtures, the mule team which had been faithfully on hand rain, shine, snow or blow. When the driver disappeared with a crate of milk bottles, the mules would calmly proceed to the spot where he would reappear. No car could ever do that!

Katonah kept abreast of the times with more than the motor vehicle. Listening to the wireless set was fast becoming a national pastime. H. C. Dexter and I. C. Racoosin enlisted members in their newly formed Radio Club in 1922. The movies became a stronger and stronger attraction. In 1918 Manager Glenn Packer built larger quarters on Katonah Avenue south of Valley Road where attractive prices of fifteen to thirty-five cents drew large audiences. Arthur P. Hill managed the theater from 1925 to 1929 when the new talking movies in Mount Kisco eclipsed Katonah's silent ones.

If there is one part of a community which reflects changes more vividly than any other, it is the business area. Old firms cease or take in or are taken over by newcomers. There were many such developments in Katonah during this decade:

1917   The Hoyt brothers after many years of success in both old and new Katonah retired. They transferred their merchandise business to the Country Service Corp. and their undertaking business to William H. Clark.

1919   Kelloggs and Lawrence succeeded Kellogg and Mead in the hardware business.

1921   The James Butler chain took over Doyle Bros. grocery in the building on the southwest corner of The Parkway and Katonah Avenue. Doyle Bros., like Hoyt Brothers, had been established in Old Katonah.

1921   F. W. Gorham, for forty years a Katonah merchant, retired from his drugstore on The Parkway.

1922   F. H. Lent sold his taxi service with space on the station platform, and thus resigned as Katonah's unofficial greeter. After several changes in ownership the space was procured in 1925 by James J. Towey, who had been running an independent service for several years with his brother John.[6]

1923   The Post Office moved from the Doyle Building to its present location in the Ryan Building.

1925   George Dickinson succeeded Parent and Wessell in the ice business.

In this decade, too, new enterprises were started:

1918   The Northern Westchester Bank opened its doors in what is now 135 Katonah Avenue. Seven years later it moved to its present building.

1920   The first chain grocery store, the A&P, came to our community.

1920   Jane Williams opened Katonah's first beauty parlor on The Terrace.

1921   Our first public phone booth was established in Morrison's Ice Cream Parlor.

1922 Stephen Strahota started his upholstery business at home.
1923 Liberatore Marchigiani established the first public bus
      service from our village. It ran to Pleasantville.

Besides the *Katonah Record,* a rather unusual newspaper with
wide outside circulation was published in Katonah from 1917 to
1925. This was *The Villager,* a literary periodical devoted to editorials and edited by Samuel Strauss, former treasurer of the *New
York Times* and publisher of the *New York Evening Globe.*

A new epoch in Katonah's business field was marked in 1920
when mechanics, plumbers and carpenters took part in its first
strike. Another innovation was the use of a voting machine for
the first time in the 1920 election. The voters were allowed to
practice on it beforehand!

Also in 1920, the Board of Supervisors approved a petition for
a fire district to include the territory within a radius of one mile
of Fire Headquarters. At a special meeting E. P. Barrett, John
Quick and George A. Teed were elected Fire District Commissioners, and Edward M. Fielder, Treasurer.

In December of that year the Executive Committee of the V.I.S.
discussed the matter of a new library building on the vacant lot
at Bedford Road and The Parkway and plans were shown. It was
thought that the building could be erected by popular subscription at an approximate cost of $15,000. Despite this, the building
was not put up at this time.

Until 1922 the water supply of the village was controlled by a
private company to which people paid a rent of twenty-five dollars a year. The Board of Trade began to agitate for the use of
water meters. A committee of the Board, made up of H. Z. Mayne,
D. W. Benedict, and C. F. Lawrence, secured the necessary signers
and presented the petition to the Town Board. House-to-house
canvassing raised the money to set up the water district. Water
meters were installed in 1925.[10]

The villagers were still so concerned with the need for a sewer
system that when the V.I.S. in 1922 considered a petition for
building a memorial hall, citizens protested that local sanitation
problems should take precedence over any such project. This plan
for a memorial hall, a tribute to the men and women of World
War I, was not carried out by the Village Improvement Society,
but was accomplished later by the Women's Civic Club. On May
30, 1924, the cornerstone of the Katonah Memorial House was
laid, and a copper plaque listing names of those who had served in

the War was placed on the building. A room was set aside for the use of the American Legion.

Other memorials were presented in this decade. A tree at the junction of Bedford and Valley Roads, hereafter to be used as the community Christmas tree, was dedicated to the late Joseph G. Miller, beloved citizen and former superintendent of highways. A Civil War memorial on Bedford Road north of the Parkway was presented to the V.I.S. by the McKeel Post G.A.R.

Changes came to Katonah, but some things remained constant. Cherry Street and Valley Road were still Meccas for coasters in the heavy winter snow. Ice was still being harvested on our ponds. The hurdy-gurdy man still heralded the coming of spring. The churches and school, though constant, were influenced by the changing times. As early as 1917, Superintendent George Covey addressed the Bedford Farmers' Club on the advantages of consolidation, and the 1923 joining of the Cantitoe and Katonah School Districts was another step in this direction. The village school of this decade was still on Bedford Road where the firehouse stands today. The published figures of the 1922 enrollment give us a picture of the school population at this time: Elementary, 213; High School, 131; St. Mary's, 121. The latter drew pupils from other regions as well as Katonah.

In 1919, during the incumbency of Father Martin A. Scanlan of St. Mary's parish, the Cruthers property on Valley Road was purchased for a parochial school. In 1921 the Knights of Columbus hut was moved here from Longacre Square, New York City, for an elementary school. The Sisters of Divine Compassion of White Plains came here to teach. The high school was added in 1924.[7]

Other schools were opened in this decade. In 1918, R. S. Fried took possession of the former Schmidt place on New Street for the Florence Nightingale School for Retarded Children, later renamed Bailey Hall for Dr. Pearce Bailey of Cross River.

In 1921, the Rev. William Finke founded Brookwood Labor College[2] on our present Cedar Road, just off Route 22 on the outskirts of Katonah. Faculty and students alike built buildings, cut wood, cooked meals, and did the many household chores, in addition to the normal school routine of teaching and learning. On occasion the public was invited to attend lectures on social problems, but, by and large, Katonah paid little heed to Brookwood and Brookwood to Katonah during its 16 years here.[8]

An influence on our religious lives was the evangelism that swept the country right after the war, particularly among the

Methodists. As in the revival of 1836, inspiring speakers came to Katonah. The Rev. John McKay of the Billy Sunday organization held mass meetings in a tent next to Kellogg and Mead's store in 1918. The Presbyterians thrilled to the testimony of mission men from the McAuley Water Street Mission. The fiftieth anniversary of the organization of the Katonah Presbyterian Church was observed for a week in 1917, culminating in Jubilee Day on November 17th.

The Episcopal congregation as a mission had held services in the old movie house and later in a storage building across from the present church. The latter was completed in 1923 and on December 16th dedicated as St. Luke's Chapel.

The First Church of Christ Scientist had its beginnings in Katonah in 1917 when Mrs. Grace Dubois driving around the region with a horse and carriage collected nine other members. Officially it was organized in 1919. The first formal meetings were held above the old Post Office.[9]

By 1925, St. Mary's Church was undergoing extensive alterations to increase its seating capacity. The building was extended toward the rectory, using the sacristy as a portion of the church proper. The local press commented, "It speaks well for a town when a church has to be enlarged."

Turning from the more serious aspects of daily living to the lighter side, we find the pleasures of Katonah's people to have been most respectable and dignified. Young people joined the Boy Scouts under the capable leadership of the Rev. J. P. Gillespie and the Camp Fire Girls, started some years before by Mrs. William R. Kellogg, now led by Mrs. William Britton. Serious minded youth belonged to the Junior Literary Society, a branch of the Seniors' Societas Orationis. Our local baseball team, the Lakesides, were playing games each Sunday on Gregory field across the lake. The Owl Athletic Association was formed to organize basketball.

The Tennis Club of the preceding era continued to function, as did McKeel Post, G.A.R. In 1923, two musical organizations came into being: the Choral Club led by Margaret Badgley for the Westchester County Music Festival, and the Fireman's Band directed by Professor Thornton of the Lincolndale Agricultural School. The V.I.S. planned concerts and dances and took charge of the community Christmas tree and the annual carol sings. An outstanding social event planned by this organization was the 1922 New Year's Eve party where the spirit of old Whitlockville was revived. A summer event of 1922 was a Street Fair and Carnival.

A new organization meeting frequently in Katonah was the Robert F. Crandall Post No. 129 of the American Legion. Although the group was chartered in 1922 in Bedford Hills, it was joined and supported by Katonah men, and many of its meetings were held in this village in the room at the Memorial House.

A continuation of an already existing group was the Women's Civic Club.[5] When the members of the Katonah Suffrage Club were satisfied that their objectives were to be gained by an amendment to the federal constitution, they changed the name of their organization in 1918 to the Women's Civic Club of Katonah. Their purpose was to aid women to obtain their full rights of citizenship, to inform themselves on problems of government, and to awaken in the members a keen sense of civic responsibility. Their first officers elected thereafter were:

President	Mrs. J. A. G. [Eloise] MacPhail
Vice-Presidents	Mrs. Edwin Tatham and
	Mrs. Henry D. Miller
Secretary	Miss Anna Van Tassel
Treasurer	Mrs. Elbridge A. Arnold

The Civic Club also interested itself in the welfare of schoolchildren. It purchased playground equipment for the school; it donated money towards milk during the lunch hour; it investigated the school's sanitary conditions. Its most ambitious enterprise of this decade, however, was the planning and completion of the Memorial House. The efforts of the women to raise funds for this tremendous project were symbolic of the spirit of Katonah.

In 1919 the Women's Civic Club and the Village Improvement Society jointly sponsored a Chautauqua, ten high class entertainments held during the week of July 18-22 in a large brown tent behind the Bedford Road schoolhouse. The 1919 Chautauqua included: the Del Mar Singing Quartet and Orchestra; Mr. Montaville Flowers, prominent American statesman; the Haskell Indian Band; Bruch, the Great Magician; Strickland Gillilan, humorist; and Louise McIntyre of·Battle Creek Sanitarium, an authority on the benefits of simple exercise. Inclement weather dampened the spirits of the spectators and the sponsoring organizations were obliged to make up the financial deficiency. But in the following two summers the Chautauquas proved most successful.

In the hilly regions east of Katonah village a less cultural and more athletic form of entertainment came into being during this decade. In 1924 the newly organized Goldens Bridge Hounds took over the fields and woods of Mt. Holly as part of their fox-hunting territory.

Under the sunshine of prosperity, this decade ended. Many of us were too little aware of the impending disaster that was to follow: a major depression and worldwide strife.

This chapter was written by Mabel Addis
with help in research by Helen Towey and Ella Weist.

References

Unless otherwise noted, information in this chapter has been taken chiefly from Katonah newspapers.

1. *Katonah Record*, Mar. 15, 1918.
2. *Ibid.*, June 10, 1927.
3. Towey, H. M. Service in the U. S. Army during World War I. Katonah, 1960. MS. (At the Katonah Village Library)
4. Women's Civic Club. Minute book. Katonah, Nov. 9, 1918. MS. (In possession of the Club)
5. *Ibid.*, 1918-date.
6. Towey, Miss Margaret. Katonah. Oral communication.
7. Lucid, R. G. *St. Mary's Parish Golden Jubilee, 1908-1958*. Katonah, 1958 (unpaged)
8. *Mount Kisco Recorder*, Nov. 19, 1937.
9. Meyerson, C. M. & Appleby, M. O'D. First Church of Christ, Scientist, Katonah, N.Y. Katonah, 1960. MS. (At the Katonah Village Library)
10. Bedford (N.Y.) Water District. Oral communication.

CHAPTER XVIII
1927–1937

THE YEARS 1927 to 1937 saw the Prohibition experiment repealed (1933) and a nation-wide economic depression run its course. The depression affected everyone in ways that depended on prior circumstance and habit. Everyone lived more sparingly; there were restless nights for persons with inventories, loans and payrolls to think about, and many were thrown out of work. There was local relief for those whose living was marginal, the pork and flour supplied by the welfare officer, Mrs. Josephine Green, supplementing unemployment checks. The two constant reminders to all, however, that this state of affairs was nation-wide and not local were the activities sponsored by the Work Projects Authority (WPA) and those of the Citizens' Conservation Corps (CCC).

on Bedford Road, Katonah Park
NEAR TELEPHONE OFFICE

From advertisement, *Katonah Record,* May 11, 1928.

The WPA worked on such projects as taking inventory of all local graveyards, indexing of the Town of Bedford minutes 1680 to 1702, and the widening of town roads. The CCC, made up of unemployed young men from all over the State, conducted reclamation and reforestation projects. In our neighborhood there was a semi-permanent camp in Pound Ridge, designated "Co. 210, Camp SP-9-Katonah," established in 1933 and active until 1941.[1]

Two important anniversaries took place in this decade. The 50th year of the Village Improvement Society was celebrated in October of 1928. Many former Katonah residents returned and letters of congratulation were received from others. Lord Exmouth, son of Henry E. Pellew, wrote recalling the first days of the Society when his father's interest in it had been such a vital one. At this celebration Robertson T. Barrett said:

> I venture to predict that Katonah will continue to grow, not merely in stature but in wisdom; that its parks and its shade trees, cared for lovingly, will become more attractive year by year; that its new library building will be built. I venture to become specific with regard to the latter prediction. I predict that this new library building will be completed so that we may celebrate, in 1930, the opening of Katonah's first public library by dedicating a new library worthy of the Katonah of today.[2]

Mr. Barrett's prediction came true. In January of 1929 a meeting was held to discuss the project. At this meeting Henry W. Kellogg read from a document of twenty-nine years before, proposing a town hall and library be built at a cost of $6,000 on a site on Bedford Road and The Parkway offered by the Syndicate. This was the location selected for the new library, and it was now given by the last remaining member of the Katonah Land Company, or Syndicate, Edward Percy Barrett, chairman of the Fund-Raising Committee. A total of $50,000 was raised, nearly every member of the community having a hand in it. Kerr Rainsford was selected as the architect, the Cameron Construction Company of New Rochelle was the builder, and George Green did the landscaping.[3]

In November of 1930 the books were moved from the old library building at 21 Edgemont Road. The removal was supervised by the Rev. George Benton Smith, and the cars were driven by Mrs. Claude Travis, Mrs. William Kelly, then Katharine Barrett, and Jacob H. Morrison.[4] On December 5, 1930, the new library building was dedicated and a tea was held from three to nine P.M. Those attending admired the reading rooms for adults and children on the main floor. The room above, now used as the Gallery, was intended for a museum of objects of local interest.[3]

The second anniversary was a Township one, Bedford's 250th birthday. This was one of fanfare and pageantry. The burning of Bedford Village in Tarleton's Raid during the Revolution was re-enacted on the green in Bedford Village. Among the British and American soldiers were members of the Katonah Fire Department. Katonah residents also took many other parts in this colorful pageant.[5]

Events of modern violence in Katonah were the two daring daylight robberies of the Northern Westchester Bank (now the County Trust Co.) in 1937. On Thursday, February 5th, occurred the first of these two robberies, netting Merl Vandenbush, then Public Rat No. 1, $17,626 (later recovered in full). Vandenbush and Anthony Rera, wearing mechanics' greasy overalls, and with faces grimy, strolled into the bank shortly after noon, pulled guns and herded employees into the vault, ordering them to lie face down on the floor. Vandenbush coolly scooped the cash into a paper shopping bag; Rera stood at the door and as customers entered, rushed them into the vault, ordering them to lie face down. The robbers as coolly left, drove over to Cross River Dam where they ditched their car (stolen, as it turned out) and transferred themselves and loot into the trunk compartment of a waiting car driven by George Rera. They got as far as Armonk only, where a road block had been set up in response to the police alarm which had gone out quickly all over the county. They were stopped by Patrolman William J. Hendricks. Sgt. John Hergenhan rushed to his aid and the bandits were captured exactly twenty-two minutes after the robbery. On March 16, Vandenbush and Anthony Rera were sentenced to prison terms of 45-70 years; the driver, George Rera, to a lesser term.

The second robbery, taking place shortly after noon on Friday, March 12th, shocked the community—the whole country, as a matter of fact—and was front page news in local, county, and New York City newspapers. The robbers in this case were not so quickly caught, nor was their identity immediately known. They were Robert Suhay, alias Rudolph Brinker, and Glen John Applegate, alias Gerald Lewis, alias Alfred Power, alias Lewis Moore, alias Frank Marvelle. This last was the name he used when purchasing a gun at a sporting goods store of Charles Niehaus, Dayton, Ohio.

Mrs. Robert L. Fowler of Katonah has written us a firsthand account of this second hold-up:

It was a nice spring day and as I remember it was the first day that my two sons, Bobbie and Harry were at home for the Easter vacation. My eldest daughter, Angela, the boys and myself decided to walk to Katonah to exercise ourselves and the dog which we took with us on a leash. When we got to the main street of town, we all separated to do various errands, agreeing to meet at the drug store in half an hour. Bobbie announced he was going to the bank to ask Mr. Fielder all about that hold-up which had taken place only [a few] weeks before. After a while, as he had not reappeared, Harry and I decided to go and look for him and hurry him along.

My impression on entering the bank was that it was empty except for a man on his knees in front of the safe. This all seemed rather odd, but I had no time to think much about it, as at this moment I felt something stuck into my back—on looking round, I saw a most unpleasant character with a sawed off shot gun. He said, "This is a bank hold-up. Keep quiet and get back there." I was then pushed toward the vault, and for the first time realized that this was no joke when I saw my son Bobbie, Mr. Fielder and several other people looking pale and frightened behind the bars. I joined them and to my horror saw that Harry and the dog still on a leash were being treated in the same way. Presently, as though this was not enough my daughter Angela came into the bank looking for us. When threatened with a gun, she laughed nervously and said, "You can't fool me; I know all about that hold-up last [month]—what is this, a movie"? The man said, "Keep quiet, sister, and step along or I'll knock your head off." So my daughter, looking puzzled and very scared, joined the rest of us.

A man with a felt hat well pulled down over his eyes stood in front of the vault and kept us covered with a revolver. Of the other robbers, one stood by the bank door to hold up anyone else who might happen in, and the third man collected the cash. By this time there were thirteen of us behind the bars in the vault.

When the robbers had collected all the loot, there ensued a

discussion among them as to whether they would shut the big iron door of the vault. If they decided to do this we all knew that we could only live a very few minutes. Mr. Fielder said, "If you close that door, you will be wanted for the murder of thirteen persons—but if you leave it open and go, I swear I won't press the alarm button until you are out of the bank." After what seemed an eternity but I suppose was only a short time, they decided to leave it open and go. It seemed so queer to be able to see out of the window the peaceful village street with people walking by, unconscious of what was happening to all of us.

As soon as Mr. Fielder sounded the alarm, there was great excitement, and everyone was so glad to see all alive. The robbers made a fast get-away with the cash and were only caught much later in, I think, Topeka, Kansas.

My children and I did not walk the four miles home as we had planned—we had had enough excitement for one day!

The westward flight of the robbers ended on April 16th in a little Nebraska town where they were captured by the local sheriff. A furious gun battle earlier in the day in Topeka, Kansas, had left a G-man dead. The fugitives were brought to trial in Topeka for his murder. The trial opened June 21, 1937, and ended June 25th with a verdict of guilty of murder in the first degree. President Edward M. Fielder and Teller Mrs. Mary A. Lent of the Northern Westchester Bank were among witnesses testifying that Suhay and Applegate were two who had robbed the bank on March 12th. On August 12, 1938, Suhay and Applegate paid for their crime. They were hanged at the Federal Penitentiary at Leavenworth, Kansas.[6]

Making smaller headlines, but still important in Katonah's life during this decade, were diversions of varied interest. In our new moving picture theater, behind Morabito's diner on Katonah Avenue, films shown starred Douglas Fairbanks, Harold Lloyd, Gloria Swanson, and other Hollywood celebrities. There were also special films, such as that of Charles Lindbergh in New York following his historic ocean flight.

Rivaling the movies in popularity were the amateur shows. There were no less than six groups offering plays and musicals. Of these, the Wildwood Players were the most prolific and are probably the best remembered. The CCC boys put on a minstrel show in September of 1935 and the American Legion presented a variety show in that same year. The Choristers were good enough to be invited to sing over the air on WOR. There were band concerts at home given by visiting organizations in the summer-time opposite the Post Office.

Amateur photography was popular, and there were frequent exhibits of camera pictures by amateurs, held in the gallery of the Katonah Village Library. We also had a whist club and a tennis club which continued to be popular in this decade. We had Fourth of July parades and fireworks, Labor Day field days, and circuses—never less than one a season. Beloved by the children was the itinerant organ-grinder who died in 1932. Katonah was famous for its good fishing. This was enjoyed by young and old. Scores of boats were on our reservoirs every summer and Isaac Waltons stood on all our bridges.

At Christmastime there was carol-singing around the village tree, and on April 12, 1936, the union Easter dawn services on Cross River Dam began, still important in our village life.

As the thirties drew to an end, we were a rather self-satisfied small community, reasonably prosperous and healthy. Disturbing reports came over our radios and through our newspapers: they concerned a man named Adolf Hitler. We disapproved of his actions, but he was an ocean away and not many of us believed yet that he would affect our lives and those of our children.

This chapter was written by Thomas H. Jameson with help in research by Elizabeth Bonny, Madelon Ryan and Julia Mead.

References

Unless otherwise noted, information in this chapter has been taken chiefly from Katonah newspapers.

1. Whitman, Mr. Will, Katonah. Oral communication.
2. *Katonah Record,* Oct. 26, 1928.
3. *Ibid.,* Dec. 5, 1930.
4. *Ibid.,* Nov. 21, 1930.
5. *Ibid.,* Oct. 10, 1930.
6. Mead, Julia A. The Northern Westchester Bank. Katonah, 1960. MS. (At the Katonah Village Library)

Well, folks, I s'pose you are all
anxious t~~~~~~how last V~~~~d~~

From the *Katonah Record*, September 16, 1943.

CHAPTER XIX
1938–1950

FROM THE TIME that France and Great Britain declared war on
Germany, none of us could longer remain insulated from the
disasters on the other side of the Atlantic. English children and
sometimes their mothers and nannies were visiting here "for the
duration." From September in 1939 we were actively involved in
war work. We worked for organizations such as "Friends of
France" and "British War Relief"; we helped the stricken
countries through our local branch of the American Red Cross.

We knew that, barring some miracle, we too would be drawn
into the war. On October 31, 1940, local Board No. 754 of
Selective Service opened on The Parkway in Katonah. During
most of the war years, the Board consisted of F. M. Godwin, B.
S. Litchfield and S. E. Weil, with Mrs. Clenidene S. Fowler,
chief clerk. It had jurisdiction of areas including Bedford, North
Castle, Pound Ridge, Lewisboro, Somers and North Salem. In
November 1940 it sent its first quota of inductees into the service—
all volunteers. During all the years it operated, it registered about
6000 men.[1]

256

Before October of 1940 several of our young men had enlisted
in the Canadian Air Force, and several of our World War I
veterans had gone back to active duty in the Army or the Navy,
or engaged in vital defense work. These World War I veterans
should never be forgotten. They stood between a country hur-
riedly preparing itself and very well prepared enemies. They
trained troops, they took over security, they constructed air bases.
Within a week of the declaration of war by the United States
some were in combat zones.

Like people in any other small eastern community, we heard
with horror of Japan's attack on Pearl Harbor. It came over the
radio as we were eating our Sunday dinners on December 7, 1941.
From then on, air raid precautions and disaster preparedness, and
relief courses were part of our daily lives. Men or women stopped
by to check on the number of our beds and blankets, in case they
were needed for evacuees from the city. Canteens and ambulance
corps were organized. Even the children were organized—Red
Cross "Victory Corps" were formed in schools. In the country
areas the older children became "messengers" to be sent out on
foot or by horse in case telephone wires should be cut.[2]

There were airplane spotters in the tower on the Robert Fowler
hill. There was a cannery organized in 1942. Everyone with a
plot of ground was urged to plant a "victory garden." Chickens
and a pig or two became members of most families living outside
the village limits.

We had gas-rationing by May of 1942, and general rationing
soon afterwards. We carried books of ration stamps wherever we
went. Like any small town we had suspected cases of black-
marketing, but not many. There was price control and most of
our merchants lived up to it honorably.

We had drives for bonds—seven of them—and drives for fats,
rubber, paper, and scrap metal. In May of 1944 Duffy's Bridge
over the railroad at the Old Dowburg Road Crossing was condemned. We believe it went for scrap.

In June of 1940 we had alien registration. All during the war we
had Italians and Germans living with us. Though we were at
war also with Italy, we did not regard Italians with the suspicion
that we felt for the Germans. "Nazi" was the word we used for
all Germans and much too often irresponsibly. "Communist"
was not yet a word of odium; the Communists were our valued
allies at this time, as we are now so apt to forget.

During the war our reservoirs were guarded and fishing

restricted. When an erroneous report came over the radio that German planes had passed Mitchell Field and were winging in our direction, we felt our reservoirs were their target.

These were hard years for families with relatives in the service, but in sharing work and fears we drew closer in community fellowship. By the war's end the term "hill topper" had fallen into disuse. It is now forgotten. Our worst fear in those days was that of finding our good friend, Miss Margaret Towey, unsummoned, at our door. It was she or a driver of her taxi company who brought bad news telegrams in person. They were never telephoned.

Katonah residents fought in every branch of our own services, in the British Army, in the Canadian Air Force and in the American Field Service. Some returned badly injured and some never returned. The "U.S.S. Fowler," D.E. 222, adopted by Katonah in 1944, was named in recognition of bravery for Robert Ludlow Fowler, III, one of our first local men to be killed. Lt. (J. G.) Fowler directed the course of the first torpedo believed to have sunk a Japanese warship.[3]

At last our men and women began coming home. We who had never left had taken prescribed courses in how to treat returning veterans "geared to killing" and "in need of rehabilitation." They were far better balanced than we were. It was months after we had celebrated V.E. and V.J. Days in our churches and in our village streets, however, before enough were back so that a celebration in their honor could be held. (For the names of those who served, see Appendix No. 30.) The Welcome Home party took place on the grounds of the Huntville Road school on June 29, 1946, and on this occasion the idea of a permanent War Memorial was born. There were many conflicting ideas as to what form it should take, but a park was finally decided on. Thirty-eight acres were acquired by purchase and seven by gift. Our old friend, the Katonah Land Company, in the person of E. P. Barrett gave the seven acres.

Money for construction work was raised by donation but not enough to turn the forty-five acres into a park. The spirit that has always moved Katonah citizens to work together for a common goal—whether it be tree-planting as in 1878 or moving an entire village to a new site as in the late nineties—spurred them on now. Lack of money was compensated for by loans of machinery, gifts of material and, most important of all, by thousands of hours of volunteer physical labor. In all there were ninety-eight different workers in the first season and nearly twenty-five hundred hours of labor given before the dedication on May 30, 1950.[4]

An aftermath of the war was a small rebellion here. With the rest of the country we believed in the aims of the U.N. and felt it was a shining hope for the future, but when there was a strong possibility that it might set up housekeeping at Cross River or Cantitoe, some of us fought it with letters, petitions and in the papers, feeling inhospitably but realistically that it would change our quiet country atmosphere into a sophisticated urban one. Others would have welcomed it heartily.

During our war years and made difficult by war shortage of material, a vast project was going on beneath us. The construction of the Delaware Aqueduct began in this area in 1938.[5] As in earlier years, New York City needed an ever increasing supply of water. This time it was not proposed to take it from us but from the tributaries of the Delaware River which would empty into the Rondout Reservoir in the Catskills, bringing it under us for a part of the eighty-five miles of Aqueduct which on this side of the Hudson would traverse Dutchess, Putnam and Westchester Counties to Hill View Reservoir in Yonkers.

The usual preliminary surveys had attracted little attention from most of us here. Our first real awareness came when Oscar C. Hays, division engineer, and Gilbert Nicoll, section engineer of the Croton Division of the New York City Board of Water Supply, took up residence in Katonah early in 1937.[6]

In May 1938 the contract for work in this section, including Shafts No. 13 and No. 14 and 30,600 feet of tunnel, was awarded to the Seaboard Construction Corporation for the estimated amount of $10,810,166.50.[5] A. A. McLaren, for Seaboard, moved to Katonah where he has made his home ever since. Shaft No. 13 was sunk on Route 35 a little below the Cross River Dam. Its location is under the red brick building which stands over it, housing machinery later installed. Shaft No. 13 is the drainage shaft for the twenty-one miles of tunnel[7] from the West Branch Reservoir near Carmel to the Reservoir in Valhalla. It lies at the lowest point of this section of the tunnel and can "unwater" it. A chamber at the top of the shaft contains, in addition to the unwatering equipment, the necessary connections through which water from the Cross River Reservoir may be introduced into the Aqueduct and other connections through which the local community may some day be supplied with water.[5]

Working conditions had changed since the earlier construction of Katonah's dams. Modern mechanical equipment obviated the army of laborers that had been required then. No shanties or "boarding-houses" went up, such as had been used at the approximate site of Shaft No. 13 some thirty years earlier when the Cross River Dam was built. Many men commuted daily by car. Others boarded or rented in the village. In contrast to the many acts of violence of the earlier days, only one, a stabbing, was reported in this district.[8] Unlike the building of our dams and reservoirs, the tunnel caused little inconvenience and aroused little antagonism. Easements were bought from those under whose land the tunnel was to pass and in cases where wells were affected by rock disturbance, settlement was made. The Board of Water Supply maintained its own police throughout the operation, and provisions concerning noise and discipline were rigidly enforced.

The West Branch-Kensico section was put into operation March 3, 1943. Water from the Delaware system was first delivered to New York City April 5, 1944, and regular operation from Rondout Reservoir to New York City was effected June 18, 1951.[9]

In the years of the war and those just preceding it, several groups were formed that did not last the decade. The Community Association, of which Rudolph S. Fried, director of Bailey Hall, was president, took over the Katonah Memorial House from the Women's Civic Club from the spring of 1941 to the fall of 1942. It promoted study groups and held excellent concerts and recitals under the direction of Mrs. Jonathan T. Lanman. Of equally brief duration were a boys' club, a girls' club and a teen-age canteen, all meeting at Memorial House. Another organization holding its meetings there took on a new status in this decade. Katonah members of the Robert F. Crandall Post of the American Legion established Katonah Post No. 1575 on September 5, 1946.

In line with the "Good Neighbor" policy, a class in Latin American culture, formed in 1941 by Mrs. Charles Durham and led by James Sherman, met at the Katonah High School. Twenty or more South and Central American women, in New York for a conference visited Katonah as guests of this class. They had lunch in our various homes and were interested in our children and housekeeping appliances. They were taken to the schools, the Library and Westfield State Farm.

In 1941 while Mrs. Amy Roberts was Librarian, the Library

held its first book fair. Since 1949 this has been an annual event.

The Thrift Shop opened in 1945. Mrs. Robert A. Chambers, then president of the Women's Civic Club, organized it as a means of support for the Memorial House. It has succeeded nobly in this purpose and has also provided an amusing and valuable exchange for belongings and ideas.

Our present flag-pole on The Parkway was dedicated in 1945. It was given us by Mrs. Samuel T. Armstrong in memory of her husband[10] and replaced the one brought down from Old Katonah which succumbed to splintering in 1943.

In 1944 Fowler G. Peck, the popular editor of our local weekly, the *Katonah Record*, died after thirty years of editorship. Robertson T. Barrett succeeded him and his editorials were brief masterpieces of philosophy, humor and insight. Among those subjects he chose for our attention were: the value of make-believe for children; one of the underprivileged—Abraham Lincoln; socialized medicine; jobs for veterans; inflation; labor unions; our part in the world's problems; and carrying the spirit of Christmas through the year.

A competitive news sheet, "The Mount Holly Road News," appeared briefly in the early winter of 1944 and Mr. Barrett gravely welcomed it to the ranks of journalism in his columns. Published by two nine-year-olds, it was in its way a reflection of our war years, dealing largely with the disappearance of fathers and cooks from the homes.[2]

After the war we grew by leaps and bounds. The school census taken in 1938 for Union Free School District No. 10[11] showed 363 children as being in public schools and 168 in private schools. When we moved from the public school on Bedford Road[12] to the one on Huntville Road in September, 1940, there were some who felt a new school of this size unwarranted. They were wrong. By 1951, District No. 10 enrolled 618 children.[13]

Increased population always brings problems that have to be met by new answers. One such answer was the development of the Northern Westchester Medical Group in 1945 by Dr. Robert E. Tschorn of Katonah who felt our doctors in general practice had entirely too much work and that specialists in particular fields should be brought into the community.

As this decade ended, our men were home again, and most of us had turned our eyes and thoughts back to our own hemisphere. The area of our attention, as was only natural, began to narrow to the near at hand. There was one among us, however, whose zest for adventure led her out into wider fields. From local papers we take the following:

1948, April 21, *Reporter Dispatch,* White Plains
ELEPHANT SHOPPING IN INDIA NEW EXPLOIT OF MRS. PARK. . . . In her fifties, a grandmother and one of the Nation's best-known animal sculptors, Madeleine Park is taking her new job in stride.

1948, May 5, *The Villager,* Bedford Village
Mrs. H. H. Park of Katonah left last week on the Queen Elizabeth for London. Her ultimate destination is India, where she will secure elephants and tigers for [Hunt's] American circus. Mrs. Park is well known for her internationally-recognized sculpture of wild animals.

Mrs. Park, whose death in 1960 ended a brilliant career, will always be remembered by the world-at-large as one of our most outstanding personalities.

This chapter and also Chapter 20 written by Janet Doe and Frances Duncombe with help in research by Julia Mead and Ella Weist

References

Unless otherwise noted, information in this chapter has been taken chiefly from Katonah newspapers.

1. Fowler, Mrs. Clenidene S., Katonah. Oral communication.
2. Duncombe, Mrs. Herbert S., Jr., Katonah. Oral communication.
3. Porcellian Club. *Porcellian Club in World War II.* Cambridge, Mass., 1948, pp. 46-48.
4. Doe, Janet. Katonah Memorial Park. Katonah, 1959. MS. (At the Katonah Village Library)
5. New York City. Board of Water Supply. *Annual report for 1938,* New York, 1939, v. 33, pp. 86-92.
6. Mead, Miss Julia A., Katonah. Oral communication.
7. New York City. Board of Water Supply. *The water sup-*

Courtesy of Miss Helen M. Towey

Among the first group of women in uniform to serve in World War I were these civilian employees in the Quartermaster's Corps of the Army. Miss Helen M. Towey, fourth from left, middle row, was one of 50 chosen to serve in it.

Courtesy of Carl J. Noe

The five Noe brothers in World War I. Left to right: Carl, Paul, Peter, Cornelius, Fred.

263

Katonah Village Library, dedicated December 5, 1930
Building is owned by the Katonah Village Improvement Society

Memorial House, dedicated November 11, 1925
to Katonah's veterans of World War I. Owned by the Women's Civic Club

Photo by Doris Kirchhoff

Huntville Road School, dedicated in 1940. Originally an elementary and high school, since 1956 it has been solely elementary.

Photo by Doris Kirchhoff

John Jay High School. Opened 1956 at Cross River for Union Free School District No. 1, Towns of Bedford, Lewisboro, North Salem and Pound Ridge.

Photo by
Mrs. William A. Kelly

Katonah Methodist
Episcopal Church, on
the corner of Edgemont
and Bedford Roads.
Services held in this
building since 1900.

Courtesy of
Ann Conlon

First Presbyterian
Church, present
building on same
property, in use
since 1900.

Courtesy of Ann Conlon

St. Mary's Roman Catholic Church which
was moved from Old Katonah to
Valley Road in 1899.

Photo by
Ralph E. Mayers

St. Luke's Episcopal Church, Bedford Road and Katonah Avenue. Services were first held in this building in 1923.

First Church of Christ, Scientist. Founded in 1917, the Church has held services in this building on Bedford Road since 1952.

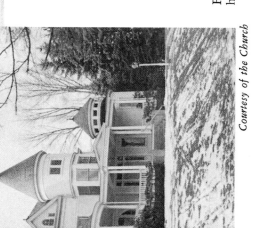

Courtesy of the Church

Present Firehouse on Bedford Road, erected 1958.

Second Firehouse, adjacent to first, erected 1927.

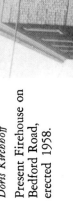

First Firehouse in New Katonah, erected 1899 on Katonah Avenue opposite Valley Road. Constructed in part from wood of original building in Old Katonah.

Photo by Doris Kirchhoff

Katonah Memorial Park, dedicated in 1950 to veterans of World War II.

Photo by Westchester County Publishers

Sidewalk show, sponsored annually since 1956 by the Katonah Gallery, features works
of local artists. This painting of the show is by James R. Thomson.

269

At Caramoor are held the June Music Festivals and other cultural events sponsored by the Walter and Lucie Rosen Foundation

These young people from many lands brought to this country by the Herald Tribune Youth Forum were guests in Katonah the spring of 1961

270

ply. New York, 1950, pp. 49-55.

8. *Mount Kisco Recorder,* Sept. 23, 1938.

9. New York City. Board of Water Supply, *1,820M. gal.,* New York, 1955, p. 24.

10. Katonah Village Improvment Society. Executive Committee. Minutes, May 29, 1945. MS. (At the Katonah Village Library)

11. Kellogg, Mr. William, Katonah. Oral communication.

12. Hasseltine, Mr. Erwin K., Katonah. Oral communication.

13. *Katonah Record,* Sept. 6, 1951.

He who ever strives upward, his
soul will be free. Goethe's *Faust*.

Tower of Katonah Village Library. Architect's drawing by Kerr Rainsford.

CHAPTER XX

1951–1961

THE FORTIES had brought many changes to Katonah. The fifties
brought even greater ones as the balance of population swung
from families who had lived and made their living in Katonah
for several generations to newcomers who established homes
here but worked elsewhere. In the early forties most of the
children in our public schools still came from Katonah's old
families. During the war years this situation began to change and
after the war began the influx of young couples who moved here
to give their children the benefits of country living combined
with good parochial or public school education. The number
of commuters by rail between Katonah and New York City
rose from 173 in 1940 to 272 in 1951. Of commuters to White
Plains and commuters by car to industries in neighboring townships, we have no record.

By 1950 we were holding double sessions in the Huntville
Road school. In 1952 consolidation was effected with Lewisboro
Union Free School District No. 1. Plans for enlarging the pupil
capacity of the combined district culminated in the building of
John Jay High School at Cross River. When this opened in 1956,
it was considered too large by some, but already more room

is needed and is being added. Sites for two new elementary schools were voted in May 1961. St. Mary's School was also feeling the pressure of increased attendance and on December 22, 1957, ground was broken for a new building. Although the great majority of Katonah's children attend either public school or St. Mary's, other schools do absorb some portion. Chief among these are Archbishop Stepinac High School in White Plains, Rippowam School at Bedford Center and the Harvey School on Route 22, Katonah.

In the interim between World War II and the close of the Korean War, despite the marked increase in the school census, some of our pupils on the high school level were dropping out. With large quotas needed to replace veterans overseas for whose return families and congressmen were clamoring, no boy felt sure of being able to complete his education without interruption. High school juniors and seniors, here as elsewhere, left school to "get it over with" by enlisting.

The Korean War had neither the build-up nor the sympathy of World War II. A summons to serve in that area was not greeted with a rush of patriotism. Our men did serve though. Several of these were veterans of World War II and one had served in the first World War also. Except to these men and their families, however, the war in Korea remained a hazy far-off struggle. Few now remember when it began and when it ended. There was no community welcome home for the men who took part in it and no plaque to give future generations their names. In Appendix No. 30 we have listed those men whom we have been able to discover.

In the Korean War years we were more acutely concerned with problems of community growth. We liked the new people who were moving in; they added much to our civic and intellectual lives but they filled to overflowing all our existing facilities. We had a Katonah Planning Commission, a Bedford Planning Board and a North Westchester Joint Planning Program to help us solve our problems. And always improvements in transportation, such as the Saw Mill River Parkway opened to Katonah in 1956, brought us still more people. Housing developments began to spring up, a few at first but soon too many to count.

To meet the demands of this expanding population each church and organization was forced to do its own expanding. The Methodist Church built a new parish hall in 1956.[1] The Presbyterian Church dedicated its new Educational Unit in 1957.[2] The

Episcopal Mission of St. Luke's grew into a church in 1958 and for additional space bought Mrs. Cassie Hoffman's house in 1959.[3] The Christian Science Church moved to larger quarters, buying the Judge Robertson house on Bedford Road in 1950.[4] St. Mary's Parish, comprising the church in Katonah and St. Matthias' Mission in Bedford Hills, added 300 families to its membership between 1945 and 1958,[5] and met the situation by increase in personnel and additional religious services.

The American Legion, Post No. 1575, accommodated a growing membership by first leasing and then buying in 1953 a building of its own on Route 22.[6] Katonah's all-volunteer Fire Department completed in 1958 a fine new firehouse on the old Bedford Road school property. The Library added more space by giving the children a room on the garden level. Among new local organizations formed to serve us were the Katonah Baseball Association in 1955 and the Lions Club in 1958. Reorganized was the Chamber of Commerce in 1953. Local units of county organizations, such as the Mental Health Association, the Business and Professional Women's Club and the Association for the Help of Retarded Children, also came into being during these years.

Of more than local or county importance in this last decade, Caramoor and the Katonah Gallery have gained widespread recognition. The Caramoor June Festival draws music-lovers to Katonah each summer, as the Gallery draws lovers of art throughout the year.

In the midst of our expansion and growth we were pleasantly reminded of our beginnings by the Township's 275th birthday in 1955. Descendants of several of the twenty-two men who settled Bedford in 1680 were present. Robertson T. Barrett's fine commemorative history of the Town of Bedford was published in connection with this anniversary.

Another and more personal anniversary was celebrated this same year, 1955, in Katonah. Three hundred of its citizens and former residents gathered at the Memorial House to pay affectionate respect to Simuel and Ida Pryor on their fiftieth wedding anniversary. Presents filled the House, tangible evidence that this honored Negro couple were "close to the heart of the community." Mr. and Mrs. Pryor's unfailing aid to those in need has made them beloved by all. In 1961 Mrs. Pryor was unanimously nominated by the Women's Civic Club for the Lane Bryant Award for outstanding volunteer community service. The nomination was seconded by the *Patent Trader* newspaper and Hill-crest Center for Children, and letters of endorsement were received from dozens of other organizations and persons.

All of the events of the middle 1950's were not of this pleasant and heartwarming nature. Some caused divergence of opinion. One in which the Katonah Village Improvement Society was concerned stemmed from events on the national scene when Senator Joseph McCarthy's influence claimed the attention of the American people. The Society scheduled events to which a local group and some individuals objected.[7] Among these were a film, "Report on the Middle East," showing the work of UNESCO and a lecture on the technique of the murder mystery. The charge was that the producer of the film and the lecturer were allegedly subversive. The Society went ahead with its program as planned.

The following year similar protests were made in an effort to prevent the showing of an educational film by the Katonah Village Library and the work of a Westchester painter by the Gallery, then a committee of the Village Improvement Society. The same sort of censorship was being attempted on many libraries, art galleries and schools throughout the county and in various parts of the United States. During an era when few individuals or organizations dared to stand by the principle of freedom of thought and speech, one of our oldest and most conservative organizations stood firm for this principle. Both of these events also took place.

Because this last chapter is in no sense literature for the present but a record for the future we should like to give a short description of what the people now living in and around Katonah are like. Our hope is that it may some day be as useful to later historians as the descriptions left of earlier generations of Katonah residents have been to the compilers of this history.

Politically, though the Democrats have gained some headway, we are still predominantly Republican. Since 1905, except for four years, Bedford's supervisor has been a Barrett. When Edward Percy Barrett retired from the office on December 31, 1953, after more than forty-four years of devoted service, his son, Douglas L. Barrett, succeeded him and was re-elected in 1955, 1957 and 1959. The members of the Town Board, the town clerk, and the superintendent of highways are also Republican. In the 1959 election, for the first time in fifty-four years, a Democrat was elected to town office, Justice of the Peace Albert V. Marchigiani.

From a civic standpoint, some of us are more alert than others, but it is seldom that any basic change in our living pattern is proposed without arousing strong feeling. This last year may well go down in local history as the "Year of Petitions." Major concerns bringing forth petitions addressed to Town, County and State have been zoning and highway construction.

The rezoning of 122 acres for Research-Office industrial use in a rural residential area adjoining John Jay's "Bedford House," brought first petitions and then suit by affected landowners against the Bedford Town Board. Dismissed by the County Supreme Court, this case is now being appealed.

A proposed relocation of Route 22 through Bedford caused storms of protest from opposing factions in the "Chestnut Ridge" and "Sells" route areas in the southern part of the township. Neither faction wanted the relocated route to run through its own territory. While this battle was at its peak, a proposed Inter-State Highway No. 87 was substituted for the controversial relocation. This, on the map, followed the Chestnut Ridge path but in the Katonah area departed from both Route 22 plans by swinging east and cutting through one of our newest residential areas. A meeting on the unpopular No. 87, held on Feb. 9, 1961, at the Fox Lane High School, Bedford, was attended by an estimated 900 persons. Area associations, which have been multiplying like rabbits during these last few years, were all represented. State and federal engineers listened for twelve hours to protests and reserved judgment. The third week in April we learned that Governor Rockefeller had signed a bill authorizing construction of 87 from White Plains to a point near Brewster. From the *Patent Trader* of April 20, 1961, we quote the following:

> According to the DPW [Department of Public Works] the description of the road is so general that the present path, which would take the road along Chestnut Ridge, could be changed if the DPW decided on another course.

We will not comment on this.

The three hearings on a Town Development Plan for Bedford, adopted March 28, 1961, were attended by more advocates of up-zoning than down-zoning. It would seem that at this time the wish to remain rural is strong in Katonah and in the township.

From a cultural standpoint, we are very conscious of our historic heritage. A treasured part of this heritage is "Bedford House," the home of John Jay, of whom we are justly proud. This beautiful house, containing much of its original furniture and a valuable collection of 18th century American portraits, was bought by Westchester County in 1958 from Jay's descendants. It was given as an historic monument by the County to New York State which has assumed responsibility for its renovation and operation as a museum. We have many professional artists, musicians and writers living in the community and many more who do excellent work on the non-professional level. There are several painting classes, music groups and a juvenile fiction workshop currently operating in Katonah. The widespread nature of our interests in other fields can be gauged from enrollment in our adult education and recreation classes. The courses most popular during the winter of 1960-61 were: Natural History, Bridge, Social Dance, Gym, Painting, Investments and Securities, and a seminar devoted to discussion of the National Purpose which drew fifty-eight participants.

We feel that the relationships formed during these last years between our community and young people from other nations have been of the greatest cultural value. In 1951, two foreign students visited our school and community for a two weeks' stay under the auspices of the *Herald Tribune* Youth Forum. Each year thereafter this beneficial association continued on a small scale until 1958. Since then our John Jay High School students have been hosts to the entire group brought over by the *Herald Tribune* during its final ten days. This year, visitors came from such far-off places as Lebanon, East Pakistan, Union of South Africa, Greece, Finland, Southern Rhodesia, Ceylon, Iceland, Thailand, Burma, Jordan, Ghana, Yugoslavia, Turkey, Vietnam, Nigeria, Singapore, Israel, Korea, United Arab Republic, India, Ethiopia, West Pakistan and Japan. There were others from France, Canada, Hawaii, Chile, Germany, United Kingdom, Denmark, Netherlands, Italy, Argentina, Norway and two, besides the Hawaiian, from the United States.[8]

Since 1958, the John Jay High School has participated in the student exchange program sponsored by the American Field Service. The first student to spend the school year here was Antonio Mattina, of Salerno, Italy. He lived with the William Kendall Clarkes. In 1959, Elin Mortensen, of Denmark, stayed with Mr. and Mrs. Lloyd Hardy and family. This year (1960-61) the Arthur Covey family are hosts to Ulrich Olderdissen of Frankfort, Germany. To provide funds for travel and incidental expenses, a thousand shares of $1.00 each were sold. As a result, one thousand members of the community own a part in this program. In exchange, students from John Jay have been abroad on the A.F.S. summer program. Elliott Gordon, class of 1960, visited Germany, and Thomas Evans, class of 1961, visited the Argentine. On their return, they had much to tell of interest. Through these two programs John Jay High School and the people of the community feel they are helping to promote world peace through understanding between young people of different nationalities.[8]

On an older level, a young couple from The Hague were invited to Katonah in 1961 by the members of the Presbyterian Church, not on a visit, but to make a permanent home. Until they are fully established, the Church is their sponsoring host. This also is proving a valuable aid in understanding between nations.

In the future someone may want to know how we of Katonah felt about juvenile delinquency and atomic energy, the issues which will always be linked with this era. Youthful lawbreaking is a matter of concern here as elsewhere, but we have had no teen-age gang warfare and we don't expect to. In the belief that lack of knowledge of the law and of the consequences of its breaking is prevalent among most young people, a course sponsored by the Westchester Committee of the National Council on Crime and Delinquency is currently being given at the John Jay High School. Although we have had a few individual acts of delinquency in and around Katonah, by and large we feel our young people are remarkably fine.

As for space travel, we were, of course, tremendously stirred by the Russian Sputnik, launched on October 4, 1957, but now most of us take satellites in our stride. On August 21, 1960, there were thirty-six man-made objects in orbit. "Echo," however, launched August 12, 1960, became a rather personal and familiar satellite while it was visible overhead. We went out into village streets or open fields and watched it with feelings of wonder and affection as it detached itself from star patterns at night and traveled the dark sky swiftly and alone. Dogs and monkeys have circled the world in outer space and returned. On April 12, 1961, Russia orbited the first man and brought him back alive, the trip around the world having taken an hour and 48 minutes. More than a little worried at the present time as to Russia's action or intended action in Laos, Cuba and the Congo, most of us applauded none-the-less President Kennedy's words of congratulation to Soviet scientists, as reported in the *New York World-Telegram*, April 12, 1961:

> The achievement by the U.S.S.R. in orbiting a man and returning him safely to ground is an outstanding technical accomplishment. We congratulate the Soviet scientists and engineers who made this feat possible. The exploration of our solar system is an ambition which we and all mankind share with the Soviet Union, and this is an important step toward that goal. Our own Mercury man-in-space program is directed toward that same end.

On May 5, 1961, when our own astronaut, Alan B. Shepard, Jr., made his successful flight into space in a Mercury capsule carried by a Redstone rocket, nearly everyone in Katonah shared in the experience by means of radio or television, either at the time or later. With Shepard they agreed, "Man, What a Ride!"

While the world of science rushes forward at a dizzying pace, in which we all share either as participants or spectators, our village of Katonah still retains restrictions and problems of the last century. No ink or glue can be manufactured in our business area. No liquor can be sold on former Katonah Land Company property. In 1878, the newly formed Village Improvement Society appointed a committee to seek ways of improved sanitation. Now, more than 80 years later, we still have no sewers!

Let us conclude by describing Katonah village in these good old days of 1961. Despite its growing size, about 4600,[12] it has managed to retain its "village" quality and so far has escaped the aspects of suburbia. Imitating "Peter Parley, Junior," that roving reporter of the eighties, let us too take "an annual walk around Katonah." In the 1883 issue of the *Feast of Lanterns*, he began:

> What we saw and what we heard. The depot . . . is the natural starting point of all explorers. Katonah is worth exploring. *There isn't another place exactly like it on the face of this round earth.*[9]

We agree completely.

The station from which this early explorer started is now a charming residence at 29 Huntville Road, moved there from Old

Katonah. Our second station, built to receive the first train stopping in New Katonah, also became a residence and was moved from its original site to one opposite St. Luke's Church.[10] So we shall begin from our third and present station.

What is this strange thing we find? A double paradox! Our railroad station no longer belongs to the railroad. Built in 1910[11] as necessary to our growing population, it was sold in December, 1958, as unnecessary to a traveling public many times as great! Space in the station is rented by the N.Y. Central Railroad, but it is no longer graced by a passenger-agent. Gone, too, are the schoolchildren who used to romp unadmonished through the premises. Gone are the gentlemen of leisure and their shaggy four-footed friend, who used to make it their club! Along the platform, parking spaces are leased to commuters by the owner, Arthur Towey, who conducts a taxi business. There is still a small park dividing Katonah Avenue here, trees above ground and village septic field below.

As we step across the park to the west side of the Avenue, we are greeted by a row of old friends. Most of these buildings went up at the time of the great move or were brought down from Old Katonah. This is also true on Valley Road, Edgemont Road, Bedford Road, and The Parkway. Some of the stores on the ground floors have recently undergone a plate-glass and chromium face-lifting, but above rise the same old gingerbread and turrets. Ugly? We like them!

The parks running in the center of Bedford Road and The Parkway are beautiful. Let anyone try and deny that. The saplings, "the size of buggy whips," that were planted in the late nineties are now of imposing height and dignity.

In our store windows, new things that we hasten to mention before they become obsolete are three-speed electric razors, electric-eye automatic exposure cameras, and stereophonic record-players. Toys are largely geared to the space age but the cuddly animals still survive. Summer shirts, skirts, pants and dresses are wash-and-wear. It will not be long now until the last electric iron is relegated to the Thrift Shop to be sold as an antique door-stop.

To find a hat, to find a hat! Oh, for "a love of a hat" such as Mr. Parley, Junior, found in Miss Crawford's window in '83! Alas, there is not a single real hat sold in all Katonah, only a wisp of veiling with a flower or bow perched on top, or a head covering of pleated plastic to be carried in the purse in case of rain.

Our markets: surely we **have come** to the peak in this department. For those who prefer to start from scratch, raw materials are still available, but the frozen ready-to-pop-in-the-oven meals are becoming cheaper and tastier every day. Or with still less trouble, one can exist on calory-metered liquids!

South of the main business block, we continue on to the new Shopping Center near the junction of Bedford Road and Katonah Avenue. This is really the last word: new buildings here and parking space galore. And in the parking space what are these automobiles that we see? Toys? No, real. Thrifty little foreign and domestic cars that run thirty to fifty miles on a gallon of gasoline.

As we take our annual walk, we meet quite a few residents who moved from Old Katonah. There is something that sets them apart as special; erect, alert and kindly. They are the invincible ones. Tolerant of today's foibles, but in matters of basic integrity preserving a firm front that it is well for us to understand and respect. In this last decade, we have lost a number of this "Old Guard" but their influence remains. Who will ever forget Miss Elizabeth Barrett, that high-spirited local saint whose interest in missions kept her in touch with every far corner of the globe and whose warm heart kept her in touch with every village need? Who will forget Mrs. Arthur Iselin, the last Jay of Bedford House to take part in community affairs? Who will forget Mrs. Gideon Avery (Marietta Holly), Mr. Bert Chapman, or Mr. Melville Allen? Or Mrs. Cassie Hoffman, who has left us for the wilds of Connecticut, or Miss Millie Smith, who left us for Riverdale?

With us, for which we are deeply grateful, are Mr. and Mrs. E. P. Barrett (Estella Travis), Mr. Robertson Barrett, Mrs. Albert Burt (Margaret Tompkins), Mrs. William Daniel (Jennie Reynolds), Mrs. Charles Mead (Emma Fisher), Mrs. Henry D. Miller (Elisabeth Dickinson), Mrs. Arthur Odell (Nellie Daniel), Mrs. Sidney Parker (Augusta Knapp), Mr. Robert Ryan, and the Misses Josephine and Margery Van Tassel.

We of the succeeding generation can never hope to equal them but as they drew their strength and wisdom from those who preceded them, we can try to do the same. We should like to pass on even a small part of their courage and ingenuity to those who follow us, that they in their turn may also hand it on: a pattern for all future generations in Katonah to follow with pride.

References

Unless otherwise noted, information in this chapter has been taken chiefly from local newspapers.

1. McGrath, Rev. Howard D. Katonah, N. Y. Oral communication.
2. Wollam, Mrs. Wendell G. 749 Roslyn Ave., Glenside, Pa. Oral communication.
3. Morton, Mrs. Hugh H. F. Fairfax, Vt. Oral communication.
4. Appleby, Mrs. Elmer D. Katonah, N. Y. Oral communication.
5. Lucid, Richard G. *St. Mary's Parish Golden Jubilee, 1908-1958.* Katonah, 1958 (unpaged)
6. Lucid, Richard G. The American Legion #1575 the Katonah Post. Katonah, 1959. MS. (At the Katonah Village Library)
7. *Westchester Spotlight* [issued by] the American Legion, Westchester County Committee on Un-American Activities. White Plains, N.Y., November, 1955, v. 1, no. 4.
8. Kanzler, Mr. Ernest V. Katonah, N.Y. Communication.
9. *Feast of Lanterns,* Katonah, Aug. 8 & 9, 1883.
10. Kelly, Mrs. W. A. Katonah, N.Y. Oral communication.
11. New York Central System. Letter to Janet Doe, New York, Jan. 7, 1960. MS. (At the Katonah Village Library)
12. Bedford (N.Y.) Town Clerk. Oral communication.

This history was completed March, 1961.

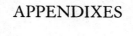

APPENDIXES

APPENDIX 1

First Indian Deed for Bedford Land, 1680

Stanford this twenty third day of december one thousand six hundred and eighty:

Witness these presentt that we whose names are under writen namly Catoonah Rockahway: Sepotah Iouis Tomacoppah Kakenand we doe for ourselves our heires Executors Administrators and asigns and for and in the behalfe of al other propriators of the land commanly caled the hoppground: we say we doe hereby sel Alinate asigne and set ouer from us our heirs executors Administrators and asignes for euer a certaine parsel of meddow and upland commanly called and known by the hoppground: which land lyes at the north end of Stanford bounds: as it is already bounded with markt trees: only the west line to be extended: southward til it shal meet with a southwest line drawn from three markt white oaks standing very neere together at the southeast corner of the sd land we the aboue named doe hereby sel alinat and asigne and set ouer from us and ours the land aboue specifyd with al the rights and priuiledges therunto belonging for euer unto Richard Ambler Abraham Ambler Ioseph Theale Daniel weed Eleazar slawson iohn Wescot Ionathan Pettit iohn Cross iohn Miler Nickolas Webstor Richard Ayres Wiliam Clark ionas Seely ioseph Stevens Daniel iones Thomas Pannoyer iohn Holms iunr beniamin Steuens iohn green senr david waterbery Sam weed ionathan Kilborn them their heires Executors administrators and asignes foreuer quiatly to posese and inioy without molestation by us or ours or any by our means or procurement moreouer we ye aboue mentioned Katoonah Rockaway Sepotah iouis Tohmacappah Pannaps Kakenand doe bargen and herby grant full liberty of timbor and herbedge for them and theire creatures upon our aiacent lands for euer and doe herby acknowledge to have receiued ful satisfaction for the land above sd in witnes of truth we have caused this bil of sale to be made and herto set our hands and seals the day and date aboue writen

Catoonah	( )	mark
rockaway	( )	mark
Sepatoh	( )	mark
iouis	( )	his mark
Tohmupoh	( )	mark
Pannaps	( )	mark
Kakenand	( )	mark

285

signed sealed & deliuerd in presence of us ioshua Knap David Waterbery Caco ( ) his mark poading ( ) mark
Stanford 23^{d} december 1680
Then paid unto ye indians specified in this within bil sale for this purchase as folows:

Twelve Indian cotes	— 09 — 0 — 0
Six blankets: ————	— 09 — 0 — 0
300: guilders wompan	— 16 — 0 — 0
two yard red brodcloth	— 02 — 5 — 0
Six yard red coton ———	01 —10 — 0
More by exspences ———	05 —01 — 6
Totals —————————	46 —16 — 6

The aboue bil of sale is acknowledged by the grantors the indians by
theire seueral names i say acknoledged before me.

Rich law Comis^{er}

Stanford december 23: 1680

Thus ends (?) writ (?)
Entered upon record 26 of Febr 1694/5
Abraham Ambler recdr.

(From the Town Clerk's record, Bedford (N.Y.) Town Book I, p. 129)

APPENDIX 2

Bedford. Minutes of Town Meetings, Excerpts, 1681-82

11th October
1681 . . .
6ly it is agreed by the propriators and by them concluded that notwithstanding what Inhabitants they shall: receiue into the hopground: yet they hold the full power in [t]heire own hands: of disposing lands: and the Inhabitants shall not haue any voice in disposing any lands
7ly it is voted that not any inhabitant they shall receiue into the sd hopground shall haue any power to sell Alinate or any other way dispose any land or lands that shall be layd out to him or them or any part of such lands without ye consent and abrobation of the propriators upon the pennalty of forfiting the said land unto the propriators:
8ly it is agreed that what Inhabitants they receiue they shall haue as great part in land and meadows as the propriators but forasmuch as part of the propriators lands is layd out already: the Inhabitants lots are to follow sucesiuely they paying fourty shillings a parson as purchas money in marchants pay between [t]his and march next ensuing and [t]heire proportion with us of what charge is already past and for future what charge shall be exspended . . .

29^h march
1682   by vote the propriators receiue Stephen Clason an Inhabitant w^h them according to ye order of receiueing Inhabitants . . .

18
Octob^r
1682   . . .
2^d wheras it [is] testifyed that Iohn Slason being one of ye propriators & hath sold his right in this place contrary to o^E order without consent of ye town therfore ye town taks ye sd right into [t]heire owne hands

(Taken from the Town Clerk's record, Bedford (N.Y.) Minutes of town meetings, 1680-1702)

287

APPENDIX 3

Indian Deed: Cohamung Purchase May 2, 1683

Witness thes presance yt we Catonah Sagamor e papiag his son Tanda-
qued Queraway e Chickheag we propriators of ye land e medow at
Cohamang haue for ourselues e ye rest of ye indians which are propriators of ye sd land e medow at Cohamung comanly so called haue
sold e by thes presance do sell alianat asigne e set ouer from us a euery
on of us e in ye name e Behalf of all other propriators of sd land e
medow at Cohamung e all our ayrs executors adminestrators e asignes
for euer unto ye proprietors of ye Town of Bedford in ye Colony of
Coneticut to them theyr ayrs executors administrators or asignes for
euer a sertain parsell of upland e medow all ready marked by us
Katonah Sagamor e Papiag. his son Tandaquid Queraway e Chickheag
unto ye propriators of Bedford e theyrs which sd land e medow lyeth
Southwest ioyning to ye bounds of Bedford and we do acknowledg
to haue reseued full satisfacktion for ye sd land e medow of the propriators of ye Town of Bedford e do promis e ingadge yt ye propriators
of Bedford shall quietly inioy e poses ye sd land e medow with out
molestation byus or any of ours foreuer as witness our hands in Bedford ye Second day of May 1683
    Thus under written

Katonah	his mark
Papiag	his mark
Tandaquid	his mark
Queraway	his mark
Chickheag	his mark

This aboue bill of seall signed e deliuered in ye presance of us
Iohn Green Iohn Baites Nicklous Webster
This aboue bill of seall is acknowledged by the granters each of them
before me—Abraham Ambler Comisioner in Bedford May 2th: 1683

(Taken from the Town Clerk's record, Bedford (N.Y.) Town Book I,
p. 115)

APPENDIX 4

Indian Deed: Simpkins Half Mile Square May 25, 1692

Bedford: This 25 of May 1692

Witness thes presance that we Cattonar Noname e Wappowaham e Wewanopeage e Chickheg e Pommeseecom we the propriatours haue sold e by thes presance doe giue grant bargen e set ouer unto Daniell Simkings of Bedford from us our ayrs executors e asignes a sertaine pees of land lying West of the bounds of Bedford to say half a mild squaire as it is allready marcked e layed out by the indians e me Daniell Simkings aboue said bounded as foloweth east by the bounds of Bedford e South by a broock coming ofe from the west ridges: e west e north as it is marcked we the aboue said proprietors doe set ouer the aboue pees of land unto aboue said Daniell Simkings him his ayrs executors administrators or asignes peasobly to posess with out any molestation by us our ayrs or asigns and we the aboue said indians haue reseued full satisfacktion for the aboue said land in witness of truth we the aboue said proprietors haue set to our hands in the day e date as aboue

the marck of Cattonah

the marck of Wappowham

The marck of Pummesecam

the marck of Noname

the marck of Chuckheag

the marck of Wewonapeage

Witnessed e deliuered in the presance of us   Stephen holmes   Iohn Brown his marck

Bedford May the 25: 1692: This aboue written bill of seall is acknowledged by the grantors before me   Ioseph Theall   Iustis of the peace Entered upon Record Febuary 28th 1698/9 by me Zachariah Roberts recorder Aprell the: 9: 1696 The town by a meiger vote doth order e grant to Daniell Simkings his purches of land ouer the broad broock west from the town bounds it shall be tacken in to the town Bounds e liable to pay if improved as other lands dew e to stand good to him e his for euer with out molestation from the town and entered upon record 28th of Febuary 1698/9 by me

Zachariah Roberts recorder

(Taken from the Town Clerk's record, Bedford (N.Y.) Town Book I, p. 139)

APPENDIX 5

Indian Deed: Cross's Vineyard July 24, 1700

This deed of seall made in the year one thousand seuen hundred: testifieth yᵗ I Catoonah Sagomore and cheef proprietor of yᵉ lands about Bedford haue formerly sold unto ye inhabitance of ye towne of Bedford a sertaine track of medow land e up land northerd from ye town: Ioyning to theyr first purches which track of land is bounded by a small brook east which runs neer ye west sid of potiticus path e west by Beuer Dam Riuer north by ye Cross Riuer and South by Bedfords land: this aboue named track of land I Catoonah haue sold from me e mine or any indien or indiens laying claime thereunto to ye inhabitance of Bedford for a ualiable considration in hand allready reseiued to my full satisfacktion therefore I Catoonah haue sold e do setouer this aboue said land for euer unto them e theyrs to poses and inioye in a free e full maner with all ye priuiledges there unto belonging e I doe ingadge for me e mine to them e theyrs that they shall inioy the same peasobly with out let or molestation from me or mine or any laying lawfull claime ther unto as witness my hand e seall this twenty fourth day of Iuly: 1700

Catoonah   his mark

Sined sealled e deliuered in the presance of us

beniamen hait
Abraham ffinch
Cakeep?
Toye beakeep   his mark
Rurohquosh   his marck

This bill of seall acknowledg by the grantor this: 25: of July: 1700 befor me Samuel Hait Iustice of peace
This aboue seale entred upon Record in Bedford Nouember 28ᵗʰ: 1700 by me Zachariah Roberts Recorder

(From the Town Clerk's record, Bedford (N.Y.) Town Book I, p. 141)

APPENDIX 6

Bedford. Town Meeting Minutes, Excerpts on New Purchase Oct. 4, 1700 and Nov. 3, 1701

Ocktobr 4th: 1700: The town by a meiger uote doth order the comitye to proseed with ye indiens about purchessing the lands westward of our town bounds & to new marck the old purches formerly bought of the indiens. . . .

Nouembr: 3th: 1701 the town by a maiger uote doth agree that the land westward of theyr first purches shall be payed by heads e euery head that payeth the indiens for it shall haue it euery one of them an equell share acording to what they pay and the town by a maiger uote doth chuse Zechariah Roberts senr Iohn Holmes iunr e Iohnathan pettit for theyr comitye e giueth them full power to tack caire in the towns behalf to see the indiens satisfied for the land they formerly bought of the indiens which is next of our first purches e euery man y^t hath land in ye town hath liberty to put in a head e they are to pay twenty shillings to ye purches e defray chardg

(Taken from the Town Clerk's record, Bedford (N.Y.) Minutes of the town meetings, 1680-1702, p. 40)

APPENDIX 7

Sale of Cross's Vineyard to John Dibell Mar. 2, 1701/02

At a legall town meeting March: 2th: 1701/2 The town by a meiger uote doth grant and sell to Iohn Dibell that purches of lands on the south sid of ye croos riuer called by ye name of crosses uinyard purches as the bounds stands in ye publick records page: 141: in ye record of Bedford for eighteen pounds three pounds in money e fiften pounds in indian pay yt is to say equifelent to money such pay as ye commitye ordreds to be bought: upon which considration we ye town do promis yt for we our selves e ours yt ye said Dibell he e his shall posess e peasobly inioye the same aboue sd granted premises—this aboue sd eighteen pounds the town hath reseued of ye aboue sd Iohn Dibell acording to bargen this 23 day of march 1702 and entred upon record by me Zechariah Roberts
record
the day e date as aforesaid

(Taken from the Town Clerk's record, Bedford (N.Y.) Town Book I, p. 152)

New Purchase, Confirmation of 1700 Contract Apr. 20, 1702

Thes may sertifie a bargen formerly made with katonah Sagamor e
other indians cheef propriators of ye lands about Bedford: Septembre
6ᵗʰ: 1700: for a sertaine track of land up land e medow land on ye west
side of Bedford: which land the indians hath sold to Bedford inhabitance: all the timber e feed on sd land twentye years before ye deate
here of and taken theyr paye to theyr full satisfacktion: there fore we:
katonah: and wackemane: trew proprietors of ye sd land with ye bounds
as foloweth namely to begin whaire Beuer dam riuer e cross riuer meets
e so to run on ye nor west side of a brook called miry brook e then to
run cross the hills west on yᵉ west side of cisqua medoʷ untill it meets ye
riuer called cisqua riuer e a great swamp and so to run up the brook
e by marked trees to the north end of Birum pond e so to ye south
end of cohamong pond e then to a great read oake tree formerly
marked by the indians for Bedfords suthermost bounds which stands
on the west sid of the west turn of meanous riuer this aboue sd land
we katonah e wackemane do sell from us e ouers for euer to ye inhabitance of Bedford to them e theyrs for euer to use inioye e posess ye same
peasobly for euer: e we do ingadge for us e ours to them e theyrs yt
they shall inioye ye same peasobly with out any let or molestation from
us or ours or any parson or parsons what sum euer laying claime there
unto e to free ye same from any bargen or seall or incumbrance what
sum euer before the seall here of: and we do own yt we have reseiued
our pay to our full satisfacktion for the aboue sd land as witness our
hands e sealls: thus under writen

Signed sealled e deliuered in   katonah   his mark
ye presance of us   wackemane   his mark
Zachariah Roberts
Iohn holmes
Cacaroca   his mark
mangakom   his mark
Arattom   his mark
Simon   his mark
This aboue sd bill of seall was acknowledged by ye granters
aprel: 20ᵗʰ : 1702 before Iames mot iustice of ye peace
and entred upon record aprell 23ᵗʰ: 1702 by me Zechariah Roberts re-
corder

(Taken from the Town Clerk's record, Bedford (N.Y.) Town Book I,
p. 160)

Dibell's Sale of Cross's Vineyard to Van Cortlandt Mar. 18, 1703

Be it known to all christian people where this deed of seall shall com greeting know ye y^t I Iohn Dibell of Bedford in ye countye of westchestar in ye prouence of new york in emerica for a ualiable considration in hand all ready reseued to my full satisfacktion haue sold e by thes presance doe sell alianate asigne e make ouer a sertain parsell of medow e upland in ye bounds of Bedford e bounded by Beuer dam Riuer westardly by Bedfords first purches with marked trees sutherdly eastwardly by a small brook which runeth in to ye croos Riuer and northerdly by the croos Riuer: this aboue sd land e medow thus bounded be it seuen hundred acres mor or less all with in sd bounds we Iohn Dibell e Mary Dibell doe sell alianate asigne e make ouer from us our ayrs executors administrators and asignes for euer: unto Mr Iacobus van Cortlandt of ye citye e prouence of new york unto him his ayrs executors administrators e asignes for euer with all ye rights titles priuiledges e apertanances what sum euer there to belongeth and I the sd Iohn Dibell doth ingadge for me e mine unto the aboue said Mr Iacobus van Cortlandt unto him e his for euer y^t they shall inioy ye same peasobly with out let or molestation from me or mine or any parson or parsons what sum euer laying lawfull claime there unto e to free ye aboue sd bargen from all encumbrances what sum euer befor ye seall here of as witness our hands e sealls march: 18th: 1703: and in the first year of hur magistyes Raigne Quen Anne

Iohn Dibell
Mary Dibell   hur mark

Signed sealled e deliuered in ye presance of us
Iohn Wascott
Hezeciah Roberts
Zachariah Roberts

March: 19th: 1703: This instant appeered befor me ye parsons of Iohn Dibell e mary Dibell his wife e acknowledged this aboue sd bill of seall to be theyr own uolentary ackt e deed I say befor me
Zachariah Roberts Iustice of peace

This aboue sd bill of seall entred in to the publick Record of Bedford aprell 6th: 1703: by me Zacha: Roberts Recorder

(Taken from the Town Clerk's record, Bedford (N.Y.) Town Book I, p. 167)

APPENDIX 10

Indian Deed, Land West of Bedford Bounds to Zachariah Roberts May 5, 1703

May 5th 1703 Catonah Sagomore and Wackamond for them selves
e in behalf of any other indians conserned haue sold to Zacha: Roberts
senr of Bedford all their land between Bedford bounds and Moscotah
Riuer which lyeth between Cisqua Riuer e ye Croos Riuer for seuerall
perticklers here after named
    10 peeses of eight: which is payed
    6 shirts
    4 Dazell cots
    2 blanckets
    1 brodcloth cot
    4 hatchets
    4 pound powder
    2 galons of rum
As witness our hands Catonah   his mark
                      Wackemand   his mark
This is ye truth of ye bargen test Zachariah Roberts Senr

Original deed in possession of Mr. & Mrs. Arnold S. Askin, Cross River
Rd., Katonah, N.Y. Deed unrecorded in Town Book.

APPENDIX 11

Indian Deed: Northwest Corner July 21, 1703

Witness thes presance y^t we Catonah Sagemor and Wockemone cheef proprietors of the lands about Bedford haue sold unto mr Iacobus uan Cortlandt of ye cityε e prouence of new yorck: e Zachariah Roberts senr of Bedford in ye county of Westchestor e in ye prouence of new yorck a sertain track of up land medow land e swamps all with in ye bounds here after named yt is to say: to Begin where Beuer dam Riuer e ye croos Riuer meets e So to run westwardly by Bedfords marked trees untill it coms to a ["white" overwritten] black oake tree marked upon a high hill e then to run west to Cisqua Riuer e then down sd Riuer untill it runs in to mescotah Riuer: e then to keep ye south side of Mescotah Riuer untill it meets the afore sd [Cross] Riuer e to keep the sd croos Riuer untill it meets ye aforesd Beuer Dam Riuer This aboue sd track of land thus bounded we Catonah e Wackemane: with all ye rights titles e priuileges ther unto belonging haue sold from us our ayrs or asignes e from any indian or indians what som euer laying any lawfull claime there unto: e we doe acknowledg that we haue re-seued all our pay for said land to our full satisfacktion Therefore we doe ingadge unto said mr Iacobus uan cortlandt of new yorck and Zachariah Roberts senr of Bedford yt they and theyrs shall inioy the the same peasobly for euer with out let or molestation from us or ours or any parson or parsons what Sum euer e to free ye same from all incumbrances what Sum euer before the seall her of as witness our hands e sealls this iuly 21th: 1703 in Bedford thus underwriten

Catonah   his mark
Wackemone his mark

Signed sealled e deliuered in the presance of us
   Nathan Clark
   Ioseph hunt
   Hezeciah Roberts
   Mashato   his mark
   Nequacom   his mark
   Wapapon   his mark
   Cacoporo   his mark
   Mantero   his mark
   Anhoock   his mark
iuly 21: 1703
This in stant appeered Before me the aboue said indians in ye pres-ance of all the witnesses e acknowledged ye aboue said seall of land

to be theyr uolentary ackt e deed befor me   Zachariah Roberts   Iustice
of ye Peace
This aboue sd Bill of Seall was entred in to the publick record of
Bedford Agust: 9th: 1703 by me Zacha Roberts recorder

(Taken from the Town Clerk's record, Bedford (N.Y.) Town Book I,
p. 170)

Indian Deed: Dibell Purchase Jan. 4, 1704

Witness these presance that we Catonah Sagomore e Wackemone cheef
proprietors of the land about Bedford haue sold and by these presance
doe sell alenate asigne e set ouer unt Iohn Dibell of Bedford in the
county of westchestar e in the prouence of new york a sertaine track
of upland meadow land e swamps all with in the bounds here after
named e Bounded By marked trees from one branch of Beuerdam Riuer
southward of ston hills e so to run westward of ston hill northward by
marked trees untill it meets with a brook coming out of ston hills and
so be bounded by sd brook untill it meets ye Cros Riuer e bounded by
the sd cros Riuer untill it meets a small brook and then bounded westward by Bedfords cros Vinyard purches e then bounded by Bedfords
first purches southwardly e eastwardly untill it meets the afor sd
branch which track of land thus bounded we catonah e wackemone for
us our ayrs e asignes doe sell from us e ours e from all other indian or
indians laying any law full claims there unto e haue sold the same to
the aboue sd Iohn Dibell to him his ayrs executors adminestrators e asignes for euer and doe acknowledg that we haue reseued
all our pay to our full satisfacktion therefor we doe ingadge for us
e ours to the sd Dibell him e his that they shall inioy the aboue sd land
with all the priuiledges there unto belonging for euer e to free the
aboue sd lands from any encumbrance what som euer befor the seall
here of as witness our hands e sealls this 4 day of ienewary: 1703/4:
e in the second year of hire magistyes raigne Quen Anne

Catonah	his mark
Wackemone	his mark
Mangocam	his mark

Signed sealled e deliuered in the presance of us

Iohn Miller
Iohn Thomson
Iohn Bartlet

David Holmes	his mark
Cacreco	his mark
Manaqui	his mark
Simon	his mark

This instant appeared before me the aboue named indians e acknowledged this aboue sd bill of seall to be theyr on uolentary ackt e deed
I say befor me Zacha Roberts iustice of the peace

This aboue bill of seall is entred upon public Record Febuery 13th: 1705 by me Zacha: Roberts Recorder

(Taken from the Town Clerk's record, Bedford (N.Y.) Town Book I, p. 181)

APPENDIX 13

Allotment of Land in the West [or New] Purchase Apr. 30, 1708

Bedford Aprill 30th: 1708:
A Record of the Draught of lotts of the West purchase as Laid into 50 Acrees Lotts

Number		Number	
1	John Copp	18	Robert Williams
2	Co^{ll} Jacobus Van Cort-land	19	Joseph Seely
		20	Abraham Wood
3	Jonathan and David Miller to Co^{ll} Court-land	21	Joseph Hunt
		22	Sarah Seely
		23	Zechariah Roberts Junr
4	Zachariah Roberts Junr.	24	Co^{ll} Jacobus Van Cort-land
5	Co^{ll} Jacobus Van Cort-land	25	Richard Holmes
6	Richard Wascott	26	Co^{ll} Jacobus Van Cort-land
7	Nathan Clark	27	John Copp
8	Jonathan Holmes	28	Hezekiah Roberts
9	Jonathan Miller	29	Cornelious Seely Junir
10	Zechariah Roberts Senr	30	Co^{ll} Jacobus Van Cort-land
11	Joseph Palmer	31	Co^{ll} Jacobus Van Cort-land
12	Daniel Jones	32	Joseph Holmes
13	John Holmes Junir	33	John Holmes Junr
14	John Wascott	34	Zechariah Roberts Senr
15	Co^{ll} Jacobus Van Cort-land	35	David Meed
16	John Miller	36	David Holmes
17	Peter Demilt & Richard Scoffield		

Entred Upon Record ye Day & Date above Said

P Me John Copp Town Clark

(Taken from the Town Clerk's record, Bedford (N.Y.) Town Book II, fol. 1^r)

Indian Deed: Northeast Corner Jan. 23, 1722

This indenture made this twenty third day of January in the ninth year of ye Reign of our souereign Lord George by ye grace of God of great Brittain FFrance e Ireland King Defender of ye faith etc and in ye year of our Lord Christ one thousand seven Hundred tweney two & Between Wackamawa and Teporineck and Mosess Indians natives & owners of ye land on ye north side of Cross River in ye bounds of Bedford in ye County of Westchester and Colony of newyork of ye one part and Joseph Seely of Bedford aforesd yeo^n of ye other part witnesseth that ye abovesd Wackamawa Teporineck & Mosses for & in Consideration of ye sum of twenty pounds Current money of newyork to them in hand paid By ye abovsd Joseph Seely at & before ye Ensealing and delivery of these presens and (?) Receipt whereof they doe hereby own & doe acknowledg themselves therewith satisfyed content and paid & whereat and wherefrom doe forever exonirat aquit and discharge ye abovsd Joseph Seely his heirs Ex^{cet} & adminst & every of them from every part and parsel thereof Have given granted alinated enfeofed confirmed conveyed Released assured Quited Claimed sold & made over and d̦e by these presence hereby cleorly and absolutely give grant alinate enfeof confirm convey release assure Quit Claim and make over unto ye abovsd Joseph Seely his heirs & assignes for Ever all that piece parcel or Lot of upland in ye bounds of Bedford aforesd being on ye north side of ye Cross River so called and bounded as followeth Easterly by a brook that runeth into sd River westerly by a brook yt runs to ye Cross River northerly by two black ash trees southerly by ye abovsd Cross River all which sd land as above bounded & expressed together with all & singular ye priviludegs & appurtinance Heridimments & Emoliments to ye same belonging or in any maner of way appertaining with all ye trees timber trees woods under woods standing or lying belonging to ye same of whom ye sd Wackumawa Teporinuk & Mosess their heirs Exec^t & admi^s to him ye said Joseph Seely his heirs & assignes to Have and to Hold for Ever ye same to be & remain to ye only proper use benefit & behoof of ye abovsd Joseph Seely his heirs and assignes for Ever and that ye abovesd Joseph Seely his heirs and assignes shall & may at all times for Ever hereafter have hold occupy possess & enjoy ye above received land and primisses as his & their own land of inheritance in fee simple freely & clearly discharged of & from all former gifts grants leases seales morgages dowrys Entails Judgments Executions or Expense or any other tithe or incumbrance whatsoever had made or comited at any time or times before ye ensealing & delivery of these presents and ye abovesd wackaman & Teporineck & Mosess for themselves their heirs Exec[t] & admin[ist] do covenant promiss grant & agree to and with ye said Joseph Seely his heirs Exec[t] & Admi[s] that they will warrant and forever defend ye same against any person or persons laying just claim to ye same by from or under them or either of them in Testimony whereof ye above persons to these presents have set their hands & seales [?]

ye day & year first above written

Wackamawa   his mark
Teporineck   his mark
Simon   his mark

Sealed & delivered in presence of
    John Westcote
    Andrew Mills
    Zac[h] Mills
    Simon   his mark
    Withams   his mark

Memorandom that on ye day & year within written ye within mentioned Wackamawa Teporineck & Mosess grantors to ye within deed appeared before Jonathan Miller Esq[r] one of his men[?] justices for ye keeping of ye peace for Westchester County assigned and did acknowledg ye within deed to be their verlingtary act & deed Tes- Jonathan Miller

This above deed recorded June ye 12 1727 per zac[h] Mills Clr

(Taken from the Town Clerk's record, Bedford (N.Y.) Town Book II, fol. 110-111)

APPENDIX 15

Explanatory Notes for Bedford Map, 1725 (p. 66)

This map is an attempt to show the development of the Town of
Bedford between 1680 and 1725 or thereabouts as recorded in early
deeds, highway records and other documents.

SYMBOLS

--- = Indian purchase lines within Township
··· = Indian purchase lines, by deed, extending beyond Township
     lines or cutting into them
    = Indian purchases   Δ = Mountains
    = Mills   □ = Highways

BEDFORD AS PURCHASED FROM THE INDIANS

(1) First Purchase, known as *Old* or *Hopp Ground Purchase* (see
App. 1), acknowledged at Stamford, Conn., Dec. 25, 1680, had
no identifiable boundaries by deed. In this 1725 map, western
boundaries are taken from manuscript of John Copp,[1] surveyor
for New (or West) Purchase, and northern boundaries from map
of Samuel Purdy (p. 000).

(2) *Cohamung Purchase* (see App. 3), May 2, 1683, gave to "ye proprietors of ye Town of Bedford in ye Colony of Coneticut" land
and meadow at Cohamung lying "Southwest joyning ye bounds
of Bedford." No definite boundary lines can be established for
this purchase. Because it was unaccounted for in division of
New Purchase land,[1] we feel the corner southeast of Highway
[2] and west of Old Purchase line was included in Cohamung
Purchase.

(3) *Simpkins Half Mile Square* (see App. 4), purchased May 25,
1692, by Daniel Simkings, was bounded "east by the bounds of
Bedford e South by a broock coming ofe from the west ridges."
In 1725 map, west and north boundaries of this purchase are taken
from east and south bounds of lots laid out bordering it in New
Purchase.[1]

(4) *Cross's Vineyard* (see App. 5) was sold to the inhabitants of
Bedford July 24, 1700. Boundaries in 1725 map are taken from
Purdy map (p. 000).

(5) *New* (or *West*) *Purchase* (see App. 8) was made Sept. 6, 1700,
by the inhabitants of Bedford. Boundaries in 1725 map are taken
from records of John Copp.[1]

303

⑥ *Northwest Corner* (see App. 11) was bought July 21, 1703, by Jacobus Van Cortlandt and Zachariah Roberts, Sr: Boundaries in 1725 map are made according to Purdy map (p. 000) and records of John Copp.[1]

⑦ *Dibell Purchase* (see App. 12), Jan. 4, 1703/04, made by John Dibell, was last Indian purchase in which name of Katonah appears on deed. Boundaries in 1725 map taken from Purdy map (p. 146).

⑧ *Northeast Corner* (see App. 14), purchased Jan. 23, 1722, by Joseph Seely, became property of the Town by quit claim 1736.[18] In Indian deed, a brook flowing into Cross River is given as eastern boundary.

Mills

① Webb's Mill, built by Joshua Webb after 1682 and before 1684,[23] was bought by Town in 1701[24] and granted to Jonathan Miller in 1723.[19] Currently known as Miller's Mill.

② Dibell's Mill, built and run for Town by John Dibell in 1705.[29] Currently known as Matthew's Mill.

③ Jonathan Miller's Mill, acquired by deed from Jacobus Van Cortlandt in 1713.[20]

④ Grist mill on Kisco Plain.[2]

Hills and mountains

Named prior to 1725:

▲1 Bates, His Hill [25]	▲3 David's Hill [21]
▲2 Bull Hill [3]	▲4 Noname's Hill [4]

Not named by 1725 so far as we know:

▲5 Aspetong	▲9 Muscoot Mountain (never included in Bedford bounds but marked here for direction point)
▲6 Guard Hill	
▲7 Indian Hill	
▲8 Mt. Holly	

Highways

Though subjected to alteration over the years, the following roads, recorded prior to 1725 or shortly thereafter, existed approximately in today's locations. Undoubtedly there were others, notably the "Vineyard Highway," that we have not been able to identify. It will be noted that a road is frequently "laid out" twice and at different widths. When this occurs, we believe the first laying-out may have been on paper only, followed by actual construction at the later date.

1. *Long Ridge Rd.* Marked out as "a cart way to ye hopground" Oct. 11, 1681.[26] Referred to as "road run east of Mianus River" in 1688.[27] From the first, the cartway continued as "the East Street"[32] to the Town common and "Bates His Hill."[25] This was a portion of our present Pound Ridge Rd.

2. *Rte. 22,* southwest from Bedford Village. Existed 1691 in Bedford Village area as the highway south of Bates's Hill.[33] Laid out in 1723, it began at house of Zachariah Mills and "so along ye South Side of Bates's hill keeping four rod wide along ye South Side of ye sd. Ridg of Hills till you come to Theales meadow e . . . till you cross both ye brooks yt: empty themselves in ye Meadow e from thence thro Comonk Valley e over Comonk brook till you come unto Comonk Ridge. So over ye sd. Ridge e thro Comonk broken Land till you come to Comonk Pond . . . till it comes to Ogdens Mill at Byram."[34] In division of land in New Purchase, southwest portion referred to as Cohamung Path.[5]

3. *Rte. 22,* north from Bedford Village to Cantitoe Corners; *Maple Ave.* to the point where, before the coming of the reservoirs, it ran to the Cross River. As Potiticus Path, Maple Ave. is mentioned in Cross's Vineyard deed of 1700 (see App. 5). Cantitoe Rd. is so named in 1704 grant to Thomas Wood of land "on the ridg on the east sid of Bever dam river South of Cross vinyard purches e west of cantito road."[30] Dec. 13, 1718, the whole extent was formally laid out from Bedford "northerly over ye Cross River to a fishing place called ye Falls."[35]

4. *Harris Rd.* from Bedford Center; *Cherry St.* as it runs from Harris Rd. towards Woods Bridge. Cherry St. portion referred to as the "Indian path which leads to Moschotach" in deed of 1705[38] and as Muscootah path in 1717.[39] David's Hill section of Harris Rd. referred to as "highway east" in 1705.[21] Section from Broad Brook to Cherry St. laid out by John Copp prior to 1726[2,3] (see Highway [15]). In late 1700's this route from Bedford Center to Croton River called "road that leads . . . to Vails Ford."[40]

5. *Guard Hill Rd.* Section running from Bedford Village to Clark Rd. referred to in 1704 as a highway crossing David's Brook north of Bates's Ridge.[31] A connecting link must have existed when Copp laid out New Purchase section prior to 1708 from the "east side of the Broad Brook Swamp at a place called Cohansey" to Kisco Brook as a "ten Rod Highway."[6] Dec. 10, 1718, the whole was described as "a Public Highway laid out beginning att ye Center of ye Town of Bedford near Justice Clausons & leads westward as ye road was partly cleared toward Hudsons River which sd road is 4 rods at narrowest and runs as far as Kisco River.[36]

6. *Clark Rd.,* portion from Guard Hill Rd. to Baldwin Rd.; *Baldwin Rd.* to South Bedford Rd.; *South Bedford Rd.,* portion from

Baldwin Rd. to Mt. Kisco. Western section of South Bedford Rd.
mentioned Apr. 7, 1702, in land grant by Town to "Cap peeter
mathews," as a highway southwest of Noname's Hill.[28] Between
1702 and 1726 Copp "laid out" as a ten-rod highway other sections
as a road "Southward of Nonames Hill antiently called Fred-
ericks Path." [4,7] Dec. 11, 1718, this route in its entirety was laid
out by the Town as "A Public Highway . . . to lead from a road
already laid out at a Bridge called ye Narrow Bridge and then
runs on ye East side of Daniel Hollys house & then westward as
the old road to Hudsons River; runns on the south side of Nonames Hill . . . and to runn sd. course untill it leads into the
road abovesd. near Kesco River." [36] We believe that to lead into
the "road abovesd.," Guard Hill Rd., [6] must have run north as
indicated and [5] run south from Hubbell's Cross Road as indicated. The route to Hudson's River could have been over Capt.
Merritt's Hill.

[7] *Bedford Center Rd.* to Broad Brook; *Broad Brook Rd.* Bedford
Center Rd. mentioned in 1705 deed as "highway south" of property south of David's Hill.[21] Broad Brook Rd. was Copp's third
10-rod highway in the New Purchase, laid out "Beginning at the
North East Corner Bounds of Vincent Simpkins half mile squair
so called by Broad Brook," running north 65° westerly to Kisco
Brook.[8] Laid out as a "Publick Road" in 1718 to "beginn at or
near ye house of Jonathan Miller, Junr; to lead westerly by . . .
Vincent Simkins swamp." [35]

Laid out between 1702 and 1708 in first division of New Purchase lots
as cross highways:

[8] *McLain St.,* south of Guard Hill Rd., between lots 12 and 13
on south side of highway at Cohansey, a 10-rod highway for
160 rods.[9]

[9] *West Patent Rd.,* from Guard Hill Rd. to Broad Brook Rd., west
of lot 17 on north side of highway at Cohansey and extending
to highway from "Vincents Corner 224 rods." [10]

[10] *Springhurst Rd.,* southern portion, between lots 27 and 28 on
north side of highway from Vincent Simpkins Corner.[11]

In second division of lots in New Purchase around 1725 Copp laid out:

[11] *Buxton Rd.; Babbitt Rd.,* portion running northwesterly over
Miery Brook towards Bull Hill. "At Broad Brook where Amawauk path so called Crosses the same," a highway to lot 32 and
thence "north westerly direct to a bridge made over Miery
brook." [3]

[12] *Haines Rd.,* Bedford Hills area. "On the westerly side of sd.
Bridge the sd. highway parts into two high ways, one passing

stil north westerly (under the South westerly part of Bull Hill) to the Indian line so Called, being the north westerly bounds of sd. New Purchase." [3]

13 *Cherry St.,* from Bedford Hills to Harris Rd. "Then again from ye afore mentioned Bridge, the other highway passes north easterly . . . to ye aforesd. Indian Line." [3]

14 *Babbitt Rd.* from Buxton Rd. east to Harris Rd. A road beginning at the "Southwest Corner of sd. Hendricks Lot [32] . . . and Continued the same Easterly along by southerly end of . . . No. 33, 34 & Extended sd. high way Easterly to a long Hollow." [3]

15 *Harris Rd.* (see also 4) from Babbitt Rd. to Broad Brook, from "a long Hollow, . . . laid out a high way a Cross Southerly to Broad Brook"; and *Harris Rd.* from Babbitt Rd. to present Cherry St., "and Northerly in sd. Hollow to & over Miery Brook, then turning in a Hollow Westerly up a Hill we continued sd. High way until where Turning Northerly we continued sd. High way to the Aforesd. Indian Line." [2,3]

16 *Springhurst Rd.* continued to Main St., Bedford Hills, as a cross road connecting lot 32, additional land and highway between lots 27 and 28. [2]

17 *South Bedford Rd.* between McLain St. and Town line. A cross road "from ye Pattent line by Kisco Plain beginning sd. high way at sd. line a little Northward of ye flowed Land occasioned by ye Dame made by ye Griss Mill there and marked out the same where the path now goes to ten rod high way" between lots 12 and 13. [2]

18 *Chestnut Ridge Rd.* Mentioned as a middle highway laid out as a dividing line for two tiers of lots in rough land 29 rods easterly of Woolsey's farm "where it begins from ye high way called Frederick's Path." [12,13]

19 *Succabone Rd.* from a point above Guard Hill Rd.; *Fox Lane* to Rte. 22. "A Drift or Highway Left between ye New Purchase and ye Old" used as an eastern boundary for part of lot 16 and for lots 4, 3, 2, 1 and continuing from the southeast corner of lot 1, southeasterly to Cohamung path or highway. [5,14,15,16,17]

Laid out by road commissioners about 1718:

20 *Old Post Rd.* from Bedford Village to the Stone Hill Rd.; the *Stone Hill Rd.* Described in 1718 as a "Public Highway . . . beginning in ye senter of ye Town of Bedford and leads eastward as ye road now lyeth tell it comes to Jonathan Millers Grist Mill, then running according to marked trees till it comes to the Colloney Line of Connecticute . . . four rods wide." [20,22,37] In 1719 mention is made of a road "Beginning att or near ye senter of ye Town . . . & to runn Easterly towards Ridgfield thorough ye Eastfield by ye House of John Wescote to keep in ye former way laid out . . . untill it leads through sd. fields & then to runn

as Ridgefield Road runns." [36] We believe this refers to the same
road, as John Wescote owned a home lot in that vicinity.[31]

21   *Middle Patent Rd.,* probably crossing over to the Banksville or
Greenwich Rd. via Hickory Kingdom Rd. Described in 1718 as
a "Public Highway laid out in sd. County; beginning at the road
at ye East end of Bedford near ye house of Richard Wareings and
runns as ye road is now marked out till it comes to ye Colloney
Line of Connecticut & leads to Horseneck [Greenwich] being four
rods wide in the narrowest place." [37]

References

1. Copp, John. Records of ye proprietors of that tract of land called the West Purchase in Bedford, 1740. MS. (Formerly collection of Nathaniel E. Stein, New York City, now property of Town of Bedford)
2. *Ibid.,* fol. 8ᵛ.
3. *Ibid.,* fol. 8ʳ.
4. *Ibid.,* fol. 6ᵛ.
5. *Ibid.,* fol. 12ʳ.
6. *Ibid.,* fol. 1ᵛ.
7. *Ibid.,* fol. 2ᵛ.
8. *Ibid.,* fol. 3ʳ.
9. *Ibid.,* fol. 2ʳ.
10. *Ibid.,* fol. 3ᵛ.
11. *Ibid.,* fol. 4ʳ.
12. *Ibid.,* fol. 7ʳ.
13. *Ibid.,* fol. 15ʳ.
14. *Ibid.,* fol. 18ʳ.
15. *Ibid.,* fol. 18ᵛ.
16. *Ibid.,* fol. 19ʳ.
17. *Ibid.,* fol. 19ᵛ.
18. Bedford (N.Y.) Town Book II, 1708-1741, fol. 137ᵛ. MS. (At Bedford Town House)
19. *Ibid.,* fol. 88ʳ, 113ᵛ.
20. *Ibid.,* fol. 41ʳ.
21. *Ibid.,* fol. 25ᵛ.
22. *Ibid.,* fol. 41ᵛ.
23. Bedford (N.Y.) Town Meeting Minutes, 1680-1702, p. 7, 14. MS. (At Bedford Town House)
24. *Ibid.,* p. 42.
25. *Ibid.,* p. 2.
26. *Ibid.,* p. 5.
27. *Ibid.,* p. 16.
28. *Ibid.,* p. 50.
29. Bedford (N.Y.) Town Meeting Minutes, 1702-1722, Mar. 5, 1704/05. MS. (At Bedford Town House)
30. *Ibid.,* Apr. 21, 1704.
31. *Ibid.,* Aug. 2, 1704.
32. Bedford (N.Y.) Town Book I, 1680-1704, p. 8. MS. (At Bedford Town House)
33. *Ibid.,* p. 10.
34. Westchester County. Road Commissioners. Record of highways. [New York?] 1714-1795, p. 2. MS. (At the Westchester County Clerk's Office, Court House, White Plains, N.Y.)
35. Westchester County. Division of Land Records. Deeds, Liber E, p. 225. MS. (At County Office Building, White Plains, N.Y.)
36. *Ibid.,* Liber E, p. 226.
37. *Ibid.,* Liber E, p. 224
38. *Ibid.,* Liber G, p. 491.
39. *Ibid.,* Liber G, p. 539.
40. Bedford (N.Y.) Town Book III, 1727-1882, p. 206. MS. (At Bedford Town House)

APPENDIX 16

Division of Land North of the Cross River May 28, 1736

We whose names are underwritten being Patentees of the Township of Bedford and Intending to Divide a Certain Tract of Land on the north side of the Cross river so Called and do bind & oblige our selves our parts in charge for the Dividing the said Land & do appoint Vincent Simkins Richd Holmes & John Holmes a Commitee to mannage both the laying out ye Land & siseing & agreeing with the Surveyor & to manage all as is proper & lawful or Convenient to do in & about the premises & if any of the pattentees refuseth to Joyn in sd Division that then we oblige our selves to pay as well our proportion of ye Charge of them that refuseth, as Witness Our hands this 28th day of May Anno Dom^e 1736

Zach: Mills
John Miller
John Holmes
//^{n} Richd Westcot
//^{l} Nathan Clark
David Miller
Jonath^n Holmes
Vincent Simkins
Saml Miller
Richd Holmes
Abner Miller
Hezekiah Roberts
Philip heirs
Will: Woolsey
Thos chambers
Danl Holly
Cornelius Seely
Richd Bouton
John Holmes [Clerk?]

(Taken from the Town Clerk's record, Bedford (N.Y.) Town Book II, p. 151)

APPENDIX 17

Allotment of Land South of the Cross River Apr. 22, 1737

The Drafts of that piece of Land in Bedford Township that Lyeth between ye old purchase e the Cross river so Called & easterly by ye Patent line & westerly by Spruce brook   Drawn this twenty Second Day of April—1737

	No.		No.
Richard Westcote	1	Stephen Clawson	16
Joseph palmer	2	David Holmes	17
Daniel Jones	3	Richard Ayres	18
Zachariah Roberts Junr	4	Richd Holmes	19
Jonathan Miller	5	David Miller	20
Vincent Simkins	6	Nathan Clark	21
Cornelius Seely Senr	7	John Miller Junr	22
John Holmes Junr	8	Obadiah Seely	23
John Westcote	9	Zachariah Roberts Senr	24
Thos Howard	10	John Copp	25
Peter Mathews	11	David Meed	26
John Holmes Senr	12	John Dibble	27
Co^{ll}. Courtlandt	13	Jonathan Holmes	28
Jeremiah Andres	14	Cornelius Seeley Junr	29
Joseph hunt	15		

John Holmes

(Taken from the Town Clerk's record, Bedford (N.Y.) Town Book II, p. 152)

Memorandum Concerning Allotments South of the Cross River
Apr. 24, 1737

Memorandum
That whereas we whose names are hereunto subscribed being chosen
by the pattentees of the Town of Bedford June ye 24th in the year
1737 [1736?] a Committee to lay Out & Divide among them a Certain
Tract of Land Containd within the Bounds and is that part of Bedford
Township as lyeth between the Old purchase & ye Cross River so
Called & W^d Tract is Bounded northerly by s^d Cross River Easterly
by the Line of s^d Bedford pattent southerly by the s^d Old purchase
& Westerly by a small brook Called the Spruce brook which runneth
into s^d Cross River, Accordingly we have with the assistance of Samuel
Purdy whome we have Employed to survey the same Laid said Tract
into Twenty Nine Lots according to the number of s^d pattentees—e
have Laid the same as Equally Quantity e Quality as we Could to the
best of Our judgment e on the day of the Date hereof the s^d Lotts
fairly drawn for e lott No. Eighteen was drawn for Philip Ayars on
the right of Richd Ayars and is Bounded Easterly by a highway by
Lott No. Seventeen Westerly by a highway Northerly by Lott No.
Nineteen e contains forty three acres & a half as witness our hands this
twenty fourth day of April 1737

No. 18

John Holmes
Richd Holmes
Vincent Simkins
John Holmes   Cl

(Taken from the Town Clerk's record, Bedford (N.Y.) Town Book II,
pp. 144-45)

APPENDIX 19

Bedford Township Freeholders of 1763

Nathan[l] Ingerson	Yeoman	Abraham WestCot	Yeom[n]
Nathan[l] Warring	Weaver	Ebenezer Ward	Merchant
Jacob Miller	Yeoman	Daniel Haight	Yeoman
Nathan Wood	Yeoman	John Silonan [Silkman?]	Yeoman
Michael Waring	Yeoman	Nathan[l] Clark	Yeoman
Daniel Mills	Yeoman	Tho[s] Maynard	Yeoman
Benjam[n] Miller	Yeoman	Ebenezer Miller	Yeoman
John Holms	Yeoman	Ezra Warring	Yeoman
Hezekiah Holms	Yeoman	Ephraim Warring	Yeoman
Joseph Holms	Cordwainer	John Maynard	Cordwainer
Daniel Miller	Yeoman	Daniel Newman	Yeoman
James Holmes	Yeoman	John Merrit	Yeoman
Stephen Holms	Yeoman	Daniel Smith	Yeoman
Justus Miller	Yeoman	Tho[s] Rustle	Weaver
John Miller	Yeoman	Lewis McDonold	Yeoman
Zebediah Mills	Yeoman	Abraham Caufeild	Weaver
John Forman	Blacksmith	Isaac Miller	Yeoman
James Lord	Taylor	Ebenezer Holms	Yeoman
Abraham Miller	Yeoman	Solomon Holms	Yeoman
Tho[s] Foreman	Yeoman	John Wescot	Yeoman
Andrew Mills	Yeoman	W[m] Hill	Yeoman
Isaac Holms	Yeoman	Encrease Miller	Yeoman
Jonathan Lyon	Yeoman	John Smith	Yeoman
Israel Lyon	Joiner	Joseph Caufeild	Yeoman
Gilbert Miller	Yeoman	David Mills	Yeoman
John Bull [Rall?]	Yeoman	James [R]aymond	Yeoman
John Elliot	Taylor	Joseph Clark	Yeoman
Sam[l] Trowbridge	Cordwainer	Ephraim [R]aymond	Yeoman
Jeremiah Caufeild	Yeoman	Moses Christy	Yeoman
William Frost	Weaver	William Woolsey	Yeoman
Benjam[n] Kniffin	Yeoman	Stephen Fowler	Yeoman
Cornelius Smith	Yeoman	Ebenezer Haight	Yeoman
Jeremiah Miller	Coopper	Frederick V Cortland	Yeoman
Zabulon Burchall	Yeoman	James Wright	MillWright
Silas Carpenter	Joiner	Daniel McDonold	Yeoman
Ezekiel Harris	Yeoman	Richar Woolsey	Yeoman
David Clark	Yeoman	Henry Dusunbury	Yeoman
Jonathan Miller	Yeoman	Caleb Sands	Yeoman
William Robinson	Yeoman	Thomas Bay	Mason

Joseph Owen	Yeoman	Samuel HoneyWell	Yeom[n]
Tho[s] Charteck	Yeoman	Elijah Bugby	Yeoman
Robert Knolton	Yeoman	W[m] Williamson	Yeoman
Nehemiah Lounsbery	Yeoman	Josua Mead	Yeoman
Zurabable Haight	Yeoman	Michael Basset	Yeoman
Jonathan Tyler	Yeoman	James Miller	Yeoman
Eli Seely	Yeoman	Silas Miller	Yeoman
Zebulen Crean	Blacksmith	John Dingee	Yeoman
Stephen Clark	Yeoman	Abraham Barritt	Yeoman
David Holms	Yeoman	Richard Honeywell	Yeoman
Abraham Higgins	Yeom[n]	Ammon Fowler	Yeoman
Samuel Barritt	Yeoman	Rich[d] Kitchum	Blacksmith
Marcus Mosman	Yeoman	Mathew Fontaign	Yeoman
Richard Searle	Yeoman	Nathan Caufeild	Yeoman
Ezekiel Griffin	Yeoman		

(Taken from: E. Marie Becker, The 801 Westchester County Freeholders of 1763, *New-York Historical Society Quarterly,* 1951, v. 35, pp. 283-321.)

APPENDIX 20

Bedford Petition for Help Against Raiders, 1777

Marauders in Westchester County
General Clinton Requested to Give Protection to the Town of Bedford
against Rogers' Rangers
To the Hon'le General Georg Clinton,
Commander in Chief of the Melitia of Westchester County, &c. &c.

We your Honours Petioners the Comitee of Bedford, Humbly
Sheweth that Bedford is now Becom a frontier against the Enemy in
Said County towards New York and towards the North Rivers and
the Drafts from the Mellitia that you ordered out for wise Ends are
Stationed Sixteen Miles below us and not Being now Likely to be
Numerous Enough to Streach from River to River and which Rivers
the Enemies are Masters, and there being a Sertain Company of Robers,
otherwise Called Rogers Rangers, that keep Conseald in Parts of
North Castle & Cortlandt Maner; Hardly a Night Pases but there is
Some Roberies Comitted or Some of our Good men Captivated and
Draged in a most Barberous maner to the Enemy; our Remaining
Mellitia has Been Obliged for Some time to watch Every Night of
which, Considering the Season of the year for Labour and Scarsity of
Labourers, they are much fetigued with s'd Dutty; therefore, and for
the Safty of the town and the Good People which have taken Refuge
here, we, your Petioners, humbly Pray that a Number of the Late
Drafts of about forty men, Including a Non Commissioner Comanded
by two Viglant oficers Be Stationed in and about Bedford to Gaurd
this Place and Detect those Robers; and in the mean time, Your
Petioners will Ever Pray for your Honour in the Execution of the
Great and Difficult task Comitted to your Care.
Bedford 9th May 1777.
Signed by Order of the Comittee,
Eben'r Ward, Chairman.
To B. General Clinton.

(Taken from: George Clinton, *Public Papers,* New York & Albany, 1899,
Military, v. 1, pp. 801-02)

314

Bedford. Town Meeting Minutes, Excerpt April 6, 1784
(The first town meeting after the Revolution of which record remains)

Bedford 7th April 1784
Philip Leek took the oath of office for Town Clark before James
McDonald Esqr
    Att an anuel Town Meeting held at the Presbyterian meeting House
in Bedford on the Sixth Day of April one thousand Seven hundred
and Eighty four for the Purpose of Choosing town officers for the
year Ensuing and to transact any other Bussiness Nessecary for the Day
Made Choice of
    Zebediah Mills moderator
also Philip Leek Town Clerk
Do Peter Fleming Supervizor
Do Lemuel Light Constable & Collector
    James McDonald Esqr his Surety
Made Choice of
    Philip Leek one of ye assessors
Do Richard Sackett one other
Do John Miller one other
Do Ephream Raymond one other
Made Choice of
    James McDonald⎫
  and Eli Tylor   ⎬ Commissioners of the Roads
  and Zebediah Mills⎭
Made Choice of
    Nathan Canfield Pounder or Usuel (?)
Made Choice of
    Henry Chorlick John Dinge Joseph Holmes & Benjamin Ambler
    Jonas Hoit & John Banks Senor John Woolsey & Joseph Owens
    Damage Prisers and fence Viewers any two of them to serve in
    any part of ye town
Made Choice of

Richard Sackett	Joseph Griffin
Israel Lyon	Henry Ruff
Josiah Mills	Celah Sarls
Benjn Hays	Silvenus Reynolds
Jesse Brush	Nehem^h Launsbery
Henry Clerk	James Arwin (?)
John Banks Juner	Silas Miller
David Holmes	Abm Holly

Joseph Miller	Jonathan Finch
Eli Seely	Samuel Palmer
Samuel Lyon Juner	Major Samuel Lyon
Joseph Rundle	Moses Crissey
Jacob Hoit	Joseph Owens
Elnathan Scoffield	Samuel Ambler
John Dingee	Gabriel Higgins

and Jabez Robertson for Highway masters

Made Choice of Ephream Raymond & James Raymond for Poor masters

Made Choice of Philip Leek & James McDonald Auditors of Acompts

Then Voted   that the Burying Ground be fenced in agreeable as it was Laid out for or Sett apart for Burying the Dead

Voted   that James McDonald Philip Leek and James Trowbridge be a Committee to superintend the work and see that it be Done

Voted that No Persons that have been Over to the Enemy Shall Come into town to Reside if Any have all Ready come in they are to be Imedietely Drove out

Voted   that Richard Sackett James Trowbridge Silvenus Raymond, John Banks Juner Capt Sentian Eli Tylor Gabriel Higgins John Miller ye 3rd Ezekiel Newman Cornelius Clark Abijah Holmes and Abram Holly be a Committee to carry the above Resolution into Execution

A True Coppy of the Votes

Philip Leek, Town Clerk

(Taken from the Town Clerk's records, Bedford (N.Y.) Town Book IV, 1784-1841, pp. 1-2)

APPENDIX 22

Census of Bedford, 1790

Name of Head of Family	Free white males of 16 years and upward, including heads of families	Free white males under 16 years	Free white females, including heads of families	All other free persons	Slaves
Smith, Isaac	2	3	3		
Worden, Gilbert	1		2		
Miller, Jeremiah	3	1	5		
Canfield, Nathan	1				
Miller, Jasper	1	1	6		
Newman, Zebulon	2	1	4		
Wright, Caleb	3	4	3		
Trenchard, John	1	1	1		
Wood, Silas	1	4	2		
Mills, George	1	1	2		
Elmer, Ichabod	1	2	2		
Smith, Stephen	2		2		
Smith, Simeon	1	2	3		
Lyon, Samuel, Junr	2	2	4		1
Brush, Jesse	2	1	6		
Mills, Titus	2	1	1		
Hill, Henry	5	2	2		
Hill, Caleb	1		4		
Miller, Enoch	2	5	4		
Miller, Samuel	1	5	1		
Miller, Ann	1		2		
Clark, Abel	3	2	1		
Robert, Sophia	1	2	2		
Kenedy, William	1		4		
Miller, Enos	1	4	4		
Wearing, David	2		4		
Clawson, David	1	2	2		
Miller, Nathaniel	1	1	1		
Wright, Gilbert	3	1	2		
Clark, Sarah			2		

NAME OF HEAD OF FAMILY	Free white males of 16 years and upward, including heads of families	Free white males under 16 years	Free white females, including heads of families	All other free persons	Slaves
Miller, Hezekiah	3	1	8		
Robertson, Jabez	2	1	6		
Robertson, William	1		3		
Westcott, Abraham, Senr	1	1	2		
Westcott, Ananias	1	2	7		
Westcott, Abraham, Junr	1	2	1		
Gregory, Daniel	2	2	5		
Brown, Halsey	1	2	3		
Dickinson, Arnold	4	4	7		
Smith, Noah	2	2	2		
Johnson, Josiah	1		2		
Mosher, John	1	2	2		
Wood, Stephen	2	5	3		
Armstrong, Edward	1	3	3		
Avery, James	1	1	2		
Dann, Ebenezer	1	2	7		
Holmes, Richard	1	2	4		
Miller, John	3		5		
Miller, Richard	1	5	4		
Holmes, Abijah	1	1	5		
Holmes, Peter	2	2	1		
Rundel, Joseph	1	1	1		
Haitt, Jonas	2	2	3		
Silkman, John	1	1	1		
Silkman, Daniel	1	6	2		
Clark, Amos	1	3	2		
Hoit, Daniel, Senr	1		1		
Hoit, Daniel, Junr	2	1	4		
Hoit, Thaddeus	3	2	2		
Hoit, Abraham	1	3	4		
Gregory, Aaron	1	1	4		
Rall, John, Senr	2	2	5		1
Gregory, Nehemiah	2		1		
Finch, Philip	1	2	4		
Hait, Jacob	1	2	2		
Hatter, John	1	1	1		
Holmes, Ann			3		

Name of Head of Family	Free white males of 16 years and upward, including heads of families	Free white males under 16 years	Free white females, including heads of families	All other free persons	Slaves
Higgins, Moses	2		1		
Higgins, Gabriel	2	3	4		
Higgins, Abraham	1		1		
Barret, Samuel	3	5	3		
Barret, Marcus	1	4	6		
Higgins, John	2	3	4		
Carhartt, John	1	5	4		
Griffin, Joseph	3	2	5		
Williamson, Marcus	1	1	2		
Smith, Samuel	1	1	1		
Moreman, Peter	3		3		
Light, Josiah	2	1	5		
Fowler, Ammon	1	3	4		
Haight, Nicholas	2	4	2	1	1
Griffin, Adam	3	4	3		
Griffin, Ezekiel	2	2	3		
Bugbee, Elijah, Senr	1	1	3		
Bugbee, Elijah, Junr	1	1	4		
Ketcham, Timothy	3	3	6		
Reynolds, William	1	2	1		
Reynolds, Jonathan	1	1	2		
Clark, Isaac	3	2	1		
Honeywell, Enoch	1	2	3		
Honeywell, William	1	2	3		
Rall, John, Jr	1	2	3		
Lounsberry, Henry	1	1	4		
Smith, Agnes	1		1		
Holmes, David	1	2	4		
Green, William	1	2	4		4
Ferguson, Thomas	1	3	3		
Harris, Ezekiel	1	5	2		
Smith, Gabriel	3	1	2		
Smith, William, Jr	1	1	2		
Holmes, Stephen	1	1	4		
Clark, Ruth		1	3		
Smith, William, Senr	1	2	1		
Conklin, James, Senr	1		2		

Name of Head of Family	Free white males of 16 years and upward, including heads of families	Free white males under 16 years	Free white females, including heads of families	All other free persons	Slaves
Clark, Daniel	1	2	2		
Clark, Nathan, Jr	2		2		
Lyon, Justus	2	4	4		
Light, Lemuel	4	1	6		1
Baxter, Phoebe			3		
Miller, Zephaniah	1		6		
Smith, Matthias	1	2	4		
Ferguson, Amey	2	2	4		
Weeks, Jacob	2	2	2		
Roberts, Amos	2	2	5		
Conklin, James	2		2		
Tyler, Eli	3	2	7		
Miller, Martha (wid° of Silas)	2	1	2		
Moreman, Marcus	2	3	3		
Dingee, Elijah	1	2	2		
Sarles, Thaddeus, Sen‍r	1	1	2		
Sarles, John	1	3	3		
Sarles, Willet	1		2		
Sarles, William	1		3		
Green, Stephen	1	2	2		
Sarles, Margaret			2		
Lounsberry, Jeremiah	1		3		1
Clark, Joseph	2	3	6		
Clark, Nathan, Sen‍r	2		3		
Raymond, Ephraim	1		5		
Raymond, Enoch	1	1	2		
Raymond, Thomas	1	2	2		
Raymond, John	1	2	2		
Hawxhurst, Thomas	1	4	3		
Cooley, John	2	2	5		
Smith, Deborah			1		
Fountain, Ezra	1		3		
Fountain, James	1	1	1		
Bettis, John	1	2	7		
Foreman, Aaron	1	1	2		
Combs, Solomon	2		1		
Seeley, Eli, Sen‍r	2		3		

Name of Head of Family	Free white males of 16 years and upward, including heads of families	Free white males under 16 years	Free white females, including heads of families	All other free persons	Slaves
Irwin, James	1	3	2		
Worden, George	2	1	3		
Woolsey, Stephen	1		2		
Marvin, Joseph	1	2	3		
Bonker, Oliver	1	2	1		
Sarles, Richard	1	5	1		
Tillet, Josephus	1	1	1		
Jones, Richard	1		1		
Owen, Joseph, Sen[r]	3	3	4		1
Owen, Joseph, Jun[r]	1	1	2		
Sarles, Seeley	2	4	3		
Charlick, John	2		4	1	1
Conklin, Ebenezer	1	1	1		
Sarles, Jeremiah	1	2	2		
Finch, Nathan	2	2	4		
Glover, John	1	5	6		
Hall, Samuel	1		3		
Sarles, James	2	3	4		
Miller, Isaac	2	2	4		
Mills, Thomas S.	1	1	1		
Williams, James	1	4	4		
Fleming, Peter, Esq[r]	1	1	5		2
Clark, Ichabod	1	1	2		
Westcott, Ezra	1	2	2		
Miller, Solomon	1		1		
Miller, Thaddeus	1	2	2		
Dann, David	1	1	1		
Dann, Hezekiah	1	1	2		
Raymond, Andrew	2		1		
Reed, Aaron	2	1	2		
Truslow, John	1	2	2		
Mills, Jonathan	1		1		
Mills, Joseph	1		2		
Bonker, John	1	3	3		
Hayes, Benjamin	3	1	2		5
Stephens, Joseph	2	1	1		
Holley, Jesse	2	1	6		2

NAME OF HEAD OF FAMILY	Free white males of 16 years and upward, including heads of families	Free white males under 16 years	Free white females, including heads of families	All other free persons	Slaves
Knoulton, Robert	1	2	3		
Organ, Cornelius	1	1	4		
Travis, Zebulon	1	1	2		
Seeley, Thaddeus	1	1	2		
Wright, Benjamin	1		1		
Zarr, Parker	1	1	1		
Brundige, Caleb	1	1	1		
Haight, Gould	1	1	2		
Brundige, Robert	3		2		
Schenck, John	1		1		
Creal, Emanuel	1	3	3		
Crissey, Moses	2	1	4		
Crissey, William	1	1	2		
Sarles, Thaddeus, Jr	1	4	3		
Clark, David	2	1	1		
Worden, Valentine	1	2	2		
Woolsey, John, Senr	1	1	3		
Woolsey, Jonathan	1		1		
Woolsey, John, Junr	1	2	5		
Seaman, Walter, Esqr	1	3	3		
Conklin, Jacob	1	1	4		
Palmer, Gilbert	2	4	2		
Woolsey, Thomas	1		1		
Woolsey, Joseph	2	3	5		
Sands, Caleb, Senr	3		1	2	
Sands, Caleb, Jr	1	1	1		
Sands, John	1		2		
Sands, Samuel	1	3	2		
Sands, Thomas	1	1	2		
Trowbridge, James	2	5	1		
Ranson, Henry	1		1		
Reynolds, Benjamin	1	1	2		
Miller, Drake	1		1		
Lyon, Israel, Senr	3	1	7		1
Lyon, Israel, Junr	2	6	3		
Matthews, Luke	1	3	1		
Finch, Jeremiah	1	2	3		

Name of Head of Family	Free white males of 16 years and upward, including heads of families	Free white males under 16 years	Free white females, including heads of families	All other free persons	Slaves
Ferris, Daniel	1	2	2		
Wood, Nathaniel	1	2	3		
Cooper, John	1		2		
Lyon, Jonathan	3		3		
Mills, James	1	2	5		
Holmes, Isaac	2		3		
Holmes, Elkanah	4	3	5		
Hayes, David	2	2	5	1	
McDonald, James	3	2	4		3
Hobby, Caleb	2	1	1		
Strang, John, Esqr	2	1	2		1
Mills, Andrew	2		4		
Worden, Joseph	1		2		
Worden, Ananias	2	2	2		
Forman, Thomas	2	3	8		
Newman, Elias	5	1	5		
Platt, James	1	1	1		
Neal, Samuel	1	2	1		
Tillet, John	1	3	2		
Daniels, Philip	1	1	1		
Mooney, William	1	1	1		
Bassett, Rebecca	2		5		
Bassett, Stephen	1	1	2		
Wilson, William	1	1	1		
Place, Uriah	1	4	4		
Banks, John, Junr	1	4	3		
Miller, Timothy	1	3	5		
Harris, Justus	2	2	6		
Williamson, William	1	4	4		
Mead, Joshua	1	5	2		
Belding, Benjamin	1	1	5		
St John, Moses	2		7		
St John, Abijah	1		1		
Day, David	2		2		
Patchen, William	1	1	1		
Denton, Alexander	1		3		
Denton, William	1	1	1		

Name of Head of Family	Free white males of 16 years and upward, including heads of families	Free white males under 16 years	Free white females, including heads of families	All other free persons	Slaves
Raymond, James, Senr	3	1	3		1
Raymond, James, Junr	1	2	2		1
Tyler, John	1	1	2		1
Boughton, Ira	2	1	2		
Mills, Dorothy			3		
Tyler, Jonathan	2		3		
Lounsberry, Stephen	2	2	3		
Tyler, Simeon	1	1	1		
Fountain, Samuel	1	1	4		
Haight, Major	2	1	3		
Dillingham, Henry	1	1	2		
Clark, Henry	3	1	2		
Haight, William	1	2	3		
Maynard, Stephen	1	2	3		
Lockwood, William	1	4	3		
Banks, John, Senr	1	3	6		
Merritt, John	1	3	3		
Holmes, James	1		2		
Newman, Joseph	3	3	4		
Miller, Jonathan	1	1	1		
Miller, Justina	2		4		
Miller, Ebenezer, Senr	2	3	4		
Miller, Benjamin, Jr	1	4	5		
Miller, Ebenezer, Jr	2		4		
Lounsberry, Gideon	1	4	3		
Maynard, John	1		1		
Dodge, Nathaniel	1	1	5	1	
Miller, Henry, Senr	2	3	11		
Farris, John	1	1	6		
Newman, Daniel, Jr	1	2	2		
Westcott, Caleb	1	2	4		
Newman, Daniel, Senr	2		4		
Smith, Daniel	4	1	2		
Miller, Benjamin (son of Wm)	1	1	2		
Miller, Cornelius	1	2	3		
Finch, Ezra	1	2	1		
Smith, Thomas	3		2	1	

Name of Head of Family	Free white males of 16 years and upward, including heads of families	Free white males under 16 years	Free white females, including heads of families	All other free persons	Slaves
Dickinson, Henry	1		2		
Lyon, Samuel, Jr	5	1	3		3
Mead, Elnathan	1	1	1		
Crissey, Isaac	1	1	1		
Sherwood, Samuel	1		2		
Holmes, Amey	1	1	1		
Pearse, Samuel	1	1	2		
Halsted, Thomas	2	3	2		
Halsted, William	1	2	1		
McLane, Daniel	2	1	4		
Palmer, Samuel	3	2	5		
Sheals, Mary	1		2		
Williamson, John, Jr	1		1		
Blake, William	1	2	2		
Carpenter, Wright	2	3	3		
Tripp, Sarah			4		
Deane, James	1		5		
Deane, Isaiah	1	2	2		
Farrington, Stephen	1	2	5		
Travis, Elisha	1	1	2		
Travis, Bartholomew	1		1		
Murphy, William	1		1		
Waterberry, Thomas	2	1	2		
Dingee, Emery	1	7	2		
Van Tassel, Stephen	1	2	2		
Dingee, John	2	1	4		
Barret, Abraham	1	4	4		
Barret, Bethuel	1		1		
Sarles, Lott, Esqʳ	3		6		
Lyon, Roger	2	3	3		
Reynolds, John	2	2	3		
Lyon, James, Jr	1		3		
Higgins, Ebenezer	1	3	4		
Campbell, James	3		2		
Campbell, John	1		1		
Holmes, Samuel	1	2	4		
Clark, Cornelius	2	3	2		

NAME OF HEAD OF FAMILY	Free white males of 16 years and upward, including heads of families	Free white males under 16 years	Free white females, including heads of families	All other free persons	Slaves
Pinkerton, James	3	2	2		
Bostwick, Robert	1	3	2		
Wheeler, Ebenezer	2	1	5		
Hamilton, Mercer	1	1	1		
Waterberry, Samuel	1	1	4		
Mills, Zebediah	3	3	3		
Hunt, Philip	1	3	2		
Hunt, Jonathan	1	3	4		
Ambler, Benjamin	2	1	2		
Sillock, Charles	1		2		
Harris, Abijah	1	1	2		
Holly, Abraham	1	1	2		
Bates, Elisha	1	1	3		
Bailey, Reuben	2	2	4		
Bostwick, Samuel	1	3	3		
Miller, Joseph	3		4		
Brown, Jacob	1	2	2		
Davenport, Revd John	1	1	4		
Elliot, Robert	3	2	3		
Reynolds, Jeremiah	1	1	1		
Miller, Abraham	1		3		
Elliot, Lewis	2		2		
Brown, Nathaniel	2	2	3		
Beyea, Peter	3	1	3		
Peck, Samuel	2	1	5		
Forman, Jacob	2	4	2		
Fisher, Joseph	1		3		
Wearing, Huldah	1		2		
Reynolds, Sylvanus	3	1	4		
Wood, Henry	1	1	3		
Gregory, Jekiel	1	3	3		
Sherwood, Abraham	1		2		
Miller, Hannah			2		
Ames, Henry	3	1	5		
Sackett, Richard, Esqr	3		3	6	
Ingersol, John	2		3		
Bostwick, Daniel	1		2		

Name of Head of Family	Free white males of 16 years and upward, including heads of families	Free white males under 16 years	Free white females, including heads of families	All other free persons	Slaves
Mills, Zephaniah	3	2	4		
Read, Samuel	1	1	2		
English, William	1	1	5		
Mills, John	1	2	6		
Holmes, Hezekiah	3	1	5		
Scofield, Henry	1		2		
Miller, Martha			2		
Miller, Benjamin, Junr	3	4	4		
Bostwick, John	1	2	5		
Seeley, Gideon	2	1	3		
Miller, Hakaliah	1	1	2		
Seeley, Stephen	1	1	2		
Holmes, Gilbert	1		3		
Miller, Henry, Senr	1		3		
Lyon, David	1	1	2		
Canfield, Abraham	5		4		
Hill, Jonathan	1		1		
Ambler, Jonathan	2		3		
Webb, Sylvanus	4	5	4		
Nicholson, Isaac	1	1	3		
Holmes, Joseph	2		1		
Seeley, Eli, Junr	1	2	1		
Williamson, James	1	4	4		
Merritt, Sylvanus	1	2	2		
Marshal, Caleb	1		1		
Hart, Abraham	1	1	3		
Merritt, Thomas	1		1		
Sackett, Richard	2	1	3		
Wearing, Joshua	3		3		
Pelham, John	1		1		
Hector, Frederick	1		2		
Lane, Jeremiah	1	3	4		
Lyon, John	1		3		
Laning, Daniel	1	1	2		
Smith, Ward	2	1	7		
Every, John	2	3	1		
Roe, John	1	1	1		

Name of Head of Family	Free white males of 16 years and upward, including heads of families	Free white males under 16 years	Free white females, including heads of families	All other free persons	Slaves
Miller, Caleb	3		4		
Collins, Daniel	1		1		
Sarles, Naomi	1	1	3		
Lyon, Moses	1	3	1		
Owen, Thomas	1		1		
Brown, Adonijah	1		2		
Ackley, Obediah	3	3	2		
Ackley, Caleb	1		1		
Charlick, Henry	1	2	4		
Chaterdon, Hannah		1	1		
Sutton, Ann			2		
Williamson, John	1	4	2		
Canfield, Isaiah	1	2	3		
Worden (Widow)	2		2		
Clark, Samuel	1	2	2		
Clark, Silas	1		3		
Osborn, Deborah			3		
Hartford, Peter	2	2	1		
Miller, Abigail			3		
Quameno				4	

(Taken from: Heads of Families, Bedford Town, New York. In: U.S. Census. 1st, 1790, v. 7, pp. 195-96.)

APPENDIX 23

Bedford. Highway Assessment List, 1797, Excerpts

[District No. 7, Croton Lake Rd. adjoining Cherry St.]

	Days' [Work]		Days' [Work]
Eli Tyler P Master			
Roger Lyon	4	Abraham Barrett	4
Reuben Forguson	1	John Dingee	3
James Lyon	4	Peters Dingee	2
John Haight	4	Eli Tyler	4

[District No. 8, Cherry Street, south end which became present Harris Rd.]

Nicholas Haight [*Pathmaster*]			
David Haight	6	Elijah Buckbee Junr	2
David Olmsted	3	John Harris	1
Abigail Banks	3	Ammon Fowler	5
Elijah Buckbee	7	Nicholas Haight	9

[District No. 11, Cantitoe, Maple Avenue area]

Silvanus Reynolds P Mas			
Nathaniel Brown	9	Gerrard Green	7
Adonijah Brown	1	Arnold Dickerson	6
Annias Westcoate	2	John Nicholds	2
Jeremiah Reynolds	5	Silvanus Reynolds	6
John Townsend	2	Tyler Reynolds	2
Daniel Gregory	2		

[District No. 12, Mt. Holly, in the vicinity of Holly Branch Rd.]

Isaac Hoyt P Master			
Jones Hoyt	5	Lewis Newman	2
Caleb Utters	2	Daniel Hoyt	4
Daniel Silkman	7	Isaac Hoyt	4
Amos Clark	5	Abraham Hoyt	5
John Newman	2		

[District No. 15, Cantitoe, south towards Matthew's Mill]

Annias Westcoate P Master			
William Robertson	9	Abram Westcoate	3
Jabez Robertson	3	Ebeneazer Dann	4
Hezekiah Miller	7	Drake Miller	2

Days' [Work]		*Days' [Work]*	
Cornelius Miller	4	John Sherwood	3
John Dannolds	2	Thomas Westcoate	3
Abraham Sherwood	3	Daniel Sherwood	5
Daniel Sherwood Jun[r]	3	Richard Miller	2
Stephen Sherwood	3	Annanias Westcoate	6

[District No. 18, Cherry St., north end to the Croton River]
John Bassett P Master

Timothy Ketchom	8	Ezekiel Ketcham	3
Joshua Oysterbanks	5	Ebeneazer Redfield	5
Ezekiel Buckbee	4	Adams Wakeman	6
Thomas Davis	3	Caziah Wakeman	6
Samuel Smith	5	Isaac Clark	7
John Thorpe	3	John Rundal	2
Stephen Bassett	3	Jonathan Reynolds	2
John Bassett	6		

[District No. 21, along old Rte. 22 and east of present railroad, north
    to Lewisboro line]
Thomas Purdy P Master

Thomas Purdy	6	Stephen Newman	4
Robert Reynolds	4	Jesse Dickerson	4
Daniel Newman	2	Robert Purdy	2
Daniel Newman Jun[r]	3	Moses Smith	5
Aaron Smith	5	Jacob Smith	1
Thomas Smith	12	Noah Smith	7
Mag[r] Sam Lyon	14	William Miller Esq[r]	4
Henry Dickerson	3	Samuel H. Miller	2

[District No. 24, Mt. Holly area]
Jacob Hoyt P Master

Jacob Hoyt	8	Peter Hartford	3
Joseph Newman	5	Giddeon Seely	3
Jonathan Newman	2	Caleb Jones	2
Jonah Holly	5		

[District No. 27, Harris Rd. up to and including Beaver Dam Rd.]
Moses St. John P Master

Moses St. John	7	Abner Miller	3
Gabriel Smith	8	Ezekiel Miller	2
William Williamson	6	Joseph St. John	2
Valentine Worden	4	Robert Reynolds	2
James McDonald	2	Jesse Smith	2

	Days' [Work]		Days' [Work]
Ezekiel Harris	7	Gabriel Smith Junr	4
Abijah Harris	4	James Platt	2
William Smith	3	Willm Smith Junr	4

(Taken from the Town Clerk's record, Bedford (N.Y.) Town Book IV (unpaged))

APPENDIX 24

Bedford. Division of School Districts Aug. 27, 1813, Excerpts

We David Olmsted Benjamin Isaacs and Aaron Read, being appointed Commissioners to superintend and manage the concerns of the Schools in the Town of Bedford and to divide said Town into suitable and convenient number of Districts and being duly Qualified to execute the trust reposed in us as Commissioners in conformity to the Statute in that case made Passed the nineteenth day of June one Thousand Eight hundred and twelve Do make, constitute and appoint the following School Districts designated in manner following (Viz) . . .

The fifth District beginning at Harts Mills so called thence westerly and Northerly by the Highway to the Brick Church, thence from the Baptist Church up the Highway leading to Cherry St. to the foot of the hill South and near the House of Moses St. John also from said Baptist Church westerly passing by the School House to the foot of the hill west and near the house of Thomas Woolsey sr.(?) Also beginning at the road East of Elisha Clarks and running northerly by Roger Lyons to and including the House of Eli Tyler containing all the Inhabitants residing on said roads as above described which said Inhabitants shall constitute one District and shall be known and distinguished by School No. 5.

The Sixth District beginning at the Bridge at Governor Jays Millpond and running southerly to the Brick Church including the road leading to Govr Jays and the road leading to Jesse Peck and the road leading to John and Samuel Collyers, then beginning at the head of the Lane by Sylvanous Reynolds running Easterly including the house now occupied by Abram Powell to Jeremiah Reynolds, thence Southerly down the road to Beaver Dam River bridge near Willet Wordens house including Stephen Smith thence from said Jeremiah Reynolds Eastward with the road to Cross River road near Abijah Holmes thence down said road by said Holmes to the house occupied by John Williams son of James Williams including said house and also from said Abijah Holmes Northerly up said Road to Poundridge Line including the house of Joseph H. Reynolds containing all the Inhabitants residing on said Roads as above described which said Inhabitants shall constitute one District and shall be known and designated by School No. 6.

The seventh District beginning at Salem line a little North of Joshua Oysterbanks and running down Cherry Street passing by Nicholas Haights & Joseph Griffin Junr to a small House on the hill late the Property of Gilbert Griffin deceas'd including the house of Lucretia Clark, then beginning at the road leading to Mountpleasant near Platt Bennetts and running westerly on said road to the brook west of Enoch Honeywell then beginning at the road a little South of James Banks and running Southerly by Elijah Buckbee' to and including Moses St. John including the Crossroad leading by Daniel Parks to the old School House and from said Moses St. John North Easterly through his farm to Beaver Dam river thence down said River to Cross River still down said Cross river to Salem line and with s^d Salem line westerly to the first mentioned road near s^d Joshua Oysterbanks comprehending all the Inhabitants residing on said roads on the within described Premises which said Inhabitants shall constitute one District and shall be known and distinguished by No. 7.

The Eighth District beginning at the Bridge near Governor Jays Mills, then running Northerly by Benjamin Miller to Salem line and as far west as to include Abel Mead and Zadock Mead, then beginning again at the first mentioned road near the bridge and running Easterly by Lyman Cook to Salem line, then beginning at the Crossroad leading Eastward passing by Jonah Holly, Eastward to said Salem line including all the Inhabitants residing on said roads which said Inhabitants shall constitute one District and shall be known and distinguished by No. 8.

The Ninth District beginning at the Brook in the Road west and near Enoch Honeywell, and running westerly to Croton River, thence down said River to York Town line, thence southerly by Bedford town line untill it comes opposite the foot of the hill in the Road a little North of Joseph Greens, thence to extend Eastwardly to the foot of the hill a little East of Elisha Mosemans house, thence Northerly to the East end of John Ferris's House still Northerly including Ebenezer Mosemans to the Place of beginning comprehending all the Inhabitants residing on said Road or on said Premises which said inhabitants shall constitute one District and shall be known and distinguished by School No. 9.

The Tenth District being but a half District beginning on the road on the line of Govr Jays farm a little South of John Lyons House and running Notherly to Salem line by the Road, thence westerly said Salem line to Cross River, thence by Cross River, to Beaverdam River, thence up said Beaverdam River to Govr Jays farm, thence Easterly by said Jays farm to the first mentioned Road including all the Inhabitants on said Road and within said Premises which said Inhabitants shall constitute one half District in connection with a part of a District in

South Salem and shall be known and distinguished by School No.
10. . . .

Completed this 27th day of August 1813
           By David Olmsted
           Benjamin Isaacs
           Aaron Read

Recorded this 31st day of August 1813
           Benjamin Isaacs Town Clerk

(Taken from the Town Clerk's record, Bedford (N.Y.) Town Book III,
Back Section, pp. 7-11)

APPENDIX 25

Lower Salem (N.Y.) Highway Assessment List, 1823, Excerpt

Dis[trict] No. 24 [Whitlockville]:

	[Days' work]		*[Days' work]*
Aaron Whitlock	2½	Jacob Dickinson	5½
Joseph Banks	4½	William Davenport	2
Noah Smith Jun	1	Stephen Purdy	1
John B. Whitlock	7½	Benjamin Miller	1
Norman W. Miller	1	Londy Sarles	1
Magnus Nadee	1½	William Smith	1

(From Town Clerk's record, Lower Salem (N.Y.) Book of Records 1784-1831, p. 191. MS. In possession of the Westchester County Historical Society, White Plains, N.Y.)

APPENDIX 26

Bedford. Highway Assessment List, 1833, Excerpts

[District] No. 22 [Matthew's Mill to Cantitoe Corners]

[Days' work]		[Days' work]	
Henry Robertson P. Master	10	John Miller	6
William Miller	11	Cornelius D. Miller	1
Hezekiah Miller Est.	6	Polly Smith	1
Alexander Higgins	1	Walter Hull	1
Aaron Smith	1	Jarvis Hull	1
Nicholas Horn	1	David Hull	1
Gilbert Miller	1	Gideon W. Waite	1
Huey Wescott	2	Hackaliah Miller	3
Embra Farrington	1	Ananias Wescott	6

[District] No. 32 [Cantitoe Corners and running north on Maple Ave.]

Abraham Powell P. Master	22	Stephen Genung	1
Jared Powell	1	James Roe	1
Dickinson Powell	1	William Sarles	1
Amos Newman	6	Henry Sension	1
Jared Green	15	Martin Knapp	1
Jared Green Jun[r]	1	John W. R. Miller	1
Israel Green	1	Hannah Dickinson	22

[District] No. 33 [Cantitoe Corners and running west on present Rte. 22]

Oliver Green P. Master	6	Alexander Peck	1
William Jay	72	Jesse Peck Jr.	1
Walter S. Lyon	16	Abraham Wescott	1
Sally Lyon	13	Robert Wilson	1
Stephen Wescott	6	Knapp S. Park	1
Jesse Peck	7½	Jarvis Bouton	1½
Daniel Park	4	Aaron Mills	1

[District] No. 34 [Harris Rd. from Bedford Rd. south past Reformatory]

David Haight Jr. P. Mast.	1	James Park	4
David Haight	7	William Lyon	5½
Caleb Haight	3	Stephen Lyon	1
James Haight	1½	Lewis & Laura Brown	4
William W[m]Son	8		

[*District*] *No. 36* [Harris Rd. & Cherry St. from Bedford Rd. to Croton Lake Rd.]

[*Days' work*]			[*Days' work*]
William Fowler P. Mast.	18	Gilead Buckbee	14½
Weeden Fowler	1½	Edward Sutton	1
James Banks	3	Joseph Sutton	1
Abigail Banks	3½	Martin Nash	1
Ebenezer Mead	3	Willet Holmes	[blank]
William Ketchum	2½		

[*District*] *No. 38* [Western portion of Croton Lake Rd. & part of Haines Rd.]

George W. Campbell P. M.	1	John Bates	4½
John Ferris	5	Asberry Elliott	6
Punderson Ferris	1½	John Bassett	4
Willet Sutton	8	Benajah Miller	1
James Sarles	1	Sarah Hains	8

[*District*] *No. 43* [Cherry St. from Croton Lake Rd. to Whitlockville Rd.]

Norman W. Miller P.M.	3	Abel A. Manroe	1
Moses Marshall	3	Joseph Reynolds	3
Jeremiah Trowbridge	6	Nathaniel Miller	3
Henry Haight	6	William Elliott	4½
John J. Banks	2	Benjamin Miller	1
Ephraim Know[l]ton	8	Joseph P. Hart	1
Alfred Wood	6	James Hadley	1
Jerred Daniels	1		

[*District*] *No. 45* [Cherry St. from Whitlockville Rd. to Croton River]

David Olmsted P. M.	4	Franklin Stedman	1
Seth Shove	1	Floyd Tucker	2
Ira Walker	1	Eli T. Dingee	2
Charles Bassett	1	Peter Dingee	6

[*District*] *No. 46* [Whitlockville Rd. from Cherry St. to Cross River]

Aaron Gregory P. M.	3	William Wood	5
John Hops	1	Samuel Benedict	1½
Banks Newman	2½	Obadiah Akerly	1
Floyd Tucker Junr.	1	Lewis Reynolds	1
Daniel Tucker	2	Squire Wood	19
Jeremiah Miller	1	John B. Wood	3
Noah Smith	5½	John Husen	1

[*District*] *No. 47* [Rte. 22 from Jay St. to Lewisboro line]

[*Days' work*]   [*Days' work*]

Moses Smith P. M.	14½	Elias Newman	2½
Thomas Purdy	12	Isaac Newman	3
Aaron Smith	13	Elisha Reynolds	6
Daniel Smith	1	Samuel H. Miller	8½
Henry Dickinson	8	Eunice Newman	3
William Newman	3		

[*District*] *No. 48* [Rte. 35 from North Salem Rd. to Holly Branch Rd.]

Stephen Clark P. Master	7	Miron B. Silkman	2
Elias Hait	8½	Isaac Hait	11½
John Silkman	5	William Todd	1½
Aaron Silkman	13	Daniel Hait	8

[*District*] *No. 49* [Mt. Holly Rd. from North Salem Rd. east and then
north to Lewisboro line]

Stephen Todd [P. M.?]	15	Daniel Bouton	1
David Silkman	4½	James Newman	9
Stephen Holly	2	Clark Newman	1
Jonah Holly	9	Jesse Hait	7
John Holly	1	Saml. Hait	8

[*District*] *No. 50* [North Salem Rd. from Hoyt's Mill to Lewisboro
line]

John Banks P. M.	4	James Miller	8
Edward Banks	4	Seth Miller	1
James Hoyt	1½	Abijah Miller	1
John Merritt	5	George Hatter	1
David Merritt	3	Rhoda Collyer	2
John Merritt Jr.	5	Jesse Smith	2
Zadock Mead	9	John Hallock	5
Coley Reynolds	1	Sension Reynolds	1
Alva Miller	6	Anna Banks	1½
Cyrus Miller	1	James Newman Jr.	1

(Taken from the Town Clerk's record, Bedford (N.Y.) Town Book IV,
unpaged)

Bedford. Military Roll, 1855

Adams, James H.	50	Hait, Elias G. jr	50	Reynolds, Henry C.	50
Archer, William	50	Hull, Walter	50	Reynolds, Ira	50
Avery, Elisha	50	Hallett, Benjamin	50	Reynolds, George	50
Avery, Seth	50	Holly, Nathan	50	Reynolds, William	50
Abott, William D.	50	Hoyt, Seth	50	Reynolds, Edwin	50
		Haight, Caleb	50	Reynolds, D. Merritt	50
Bates, George	50	Hubbell, Zadoc	50	Reynolds, Willett F.	50
Barrett, Dennis	50	Haight, David	50	Ruscoe, George W.	50
Burgess, John	50	Holmes, George	50	Reynolds, Stephen	50
Banks, William H.	50			Raymond, Bennett	50
Benger, Samuel	50	Johnson, Nehemiah	50	Raymond, George W.	50
Betts, Henry H.	50	Johnson, Milton	50	Reynolds, Augustus	50
Barrett, James P.	50	Jones, Rufus	50		
Benedict, Moses S.	50	Jones, Rufus K.	50	Sutton, James H.	50
Bumsted, Jotham	50			Sutton, Leonard	50
Barrett, Elias M.	50	Knox, John	50	Slawson, Joseph	50
Barrett, Giles	50	Keeler, Elie	50	Stedwell, William	50
		Keeler, Henry L.	50	Sarles, Albert	50
Clark, William H.	50	Knowlton, Stephen T.	50	Sarles, William	50
Collyer, Warren	50	Knowlton, Van buren	50	Sherwood, Charles	50
Collyer, John A.	50	Knowlton, Robert	50	Sherwood, William H.	50
Culliver, Edward	50			Sutton, Walter	50
		Lyon, Newman C. jr	50	Selick, Horace	50
Dickinson, Charles	50	Lyon, William	50	Smith, Henry W.	50
Dickinson, Nathaniel	50	Lyon, Walters S. jr	50	Sutton, Francis	50
Dickinson, Jesse	50	Lyon, Ferris J.	50		
Dorsey, James	50			Trowbridge, Isac L.	50
Dickinson, Arnell F.	50	Mills, Andrew	50	Timberman, John	50
Dean, Joseph	50	Mills, John	50		
Daily, Edward	50	Mead, Benjamin	50	Underhill, Henry	50
		Miller, Alfred	50		
Finch, James	50	Miller, Henry	50	Williams, S.	50
Finch, William	50	McCord, Mark	50	Williams, Isac	50
Ferris, Andrew	50	Miller, Hezekiah	50	Williams, Francis	50
		Merritt, Norman	50	Worden, William H.	50
Green, John	50	Merritt, James	50	Worden, George	50
Green, Oliver jr	50	Miller, Harvey S.	50	Woodcock, John P.	50
Green, Cyrus	50			Wescott, John	50
Gunion, William	50	Newman, Stephen P.	50	Wescott, William	50
Griffin, Albert	50	Newman, William jr	50	Wood, William jr	50
Green, William J.	50	Newman, Benjamin	50	Wickware, Charles	50
				Woolsey, Martin	50
Harford, Charles	50	Palmer, Henry	50		
Hait, Isac N.	50	Pendor, George C.	50	Zar, Robert	50
Howe, John A.	50	Polean, George	50	Zar, William H.	50
Harris, George W.	50	Putney, Cornelius	50		

The undersigned assessors of the town of Bedford in the County of Westchester being severally sworn say that they have made strict and diligent inquiry to ascertain the names of all persons required to be enrolled as liable to military duty by the laws of the United States residing in said town of Bedford that the roll hereto annexed is as, near these deponents can ascertain a correct roll of all persons residing in said town who are liable to be enrolled.

Winthrop Raymond
Charles G. Betts
Stephen H. Miller   Assessors

subscribed and sworn before me this 28th and 30th day of August 1855

Jabez Robertson Justice of the Peace

(Forms a small MS. book at Bedford Town House)

APPENDIX 28

Restrictive Covenant for Residential Land in New Katonah

The party of the second part for the party of the second part and the heirs and assigns of the party of the second part hereby convenants and agrees to and with the parties of the first part that neither the party of the second part nor the heirs or assigns of the party of the second part will erect or cause or permit to be erected any building upon the property hereby conveyed costing less than $ —— nor within fifteen feet of the street on which said building fronts or any building other than a dwelling house within sixty feet of the line of the street on which said lot fronts or any slaughter house or any manufactory of gunpowder soap candles starch glue varnish vitriol ink or turpentine or any structure for tanning dressing or preparing skins hides or leather or any brewery distillery or bone boiling establishment cattle yard or hog pen and will not permit upon the premises hereby conveyed the vending or selling of any alcohol liquors wines ales or beer except for medical purposes or any other dangerous noxious noisy or offensive trade employment or establishment whatsoever and will not use said premises nor cause or permit the same to be used for any business purposes whatsoever or for any purposes other than strictly private residence nor support keep or permit upon said premises any swine vicious dog or poultry of any description that the party of the second part shall commence to build a dwelling house on said premises within one year from the delivery of the deed for the same And it is understood and agreed that the stipulations aforesaid are to apply to and bind the heirs executors administrators and assigns of the respective parties.

(Excerpt from deed of the Katonah Land Company to Harry Z. Mayne, Oct. 12, 1899. In: Westchester County. Div. of Land Records. Deeds. Liber 1542, pp. 163-66. MS. At County Office Building, White Plains, N.Y.)

Buildings in Old Katonah Moved to New Katonah

Building	Location in old villages	Location in New Katonah	No. on Maps pp. 144-45
Avery, Alfred F.	River Rd. & Main St.	Oak Hill (burned)	24
Avery, Charles. Hardware Store	Railroad Ave., West	50 The Terrace	12
Benedict, Joseph	The Dowburg Rd.*	55 Valley Rd.	31
Benedict, Moses	The Dowburg Rd.	5 & 7 Edgemont Rd. & Katonah Ave.	32
Brundage, Leemon	West side of present Woodsbridge Rd.	Greenville Rd.	49
Carpenter, Dr. W. J.	River Rd.	18 Anderson Rd.	25
Chapman, Dr. J. F.	River Rd.	22 The Terrace	27
Cox's Mill (formerly Wood & Whitlock's)	Whitlockville	St. Mary's Church & E. P. Barrett barn (wood used for both)	36
Deacon, Henry	West side of present Woodsbridge Rd.	22 Edgemont Rd.	51
Dexter, Philip	East side of present Woodsbridge Rd.	41 North St.	56
Drugstore	Main St.	113 Katonah Ave.	16
Firehouse	North St.	Katonah Ave. (torn down in 1959)	18
French, John	West side of present Woodsbridge Rd.	24 Woodsbridge Rd.	52
Gorham, F. W.	South St.	95 Edgemont Rd.	45
Green, Alsoph. Hotel	Railroad Ave., West	35 Anderson Rd.	13
Haight, Phebe	Whitlockville	121 Bedford Rd.	35
Hait, Isaac	Old Cross River Rd.	New St.	None
Hallett, John W.	West side of present Woodsbridge Rd.	99 Edgemont Rd.	50
Hitt, Edgar Blacksmith Shop	Railroad Ave., West	26 Valley Rd.	10
Horton, Wallace	Railroad Ave., West	Summit Rd.	11
Hoyt, Albert	Railroad Ave., East	Congdon Lane	3
Hoyt Brothers Furniture Store	Railroad Ave., East	79 & 81 Edgemont Rd.	4
Hoyt, James	Main St.	48 The Parkway	23
Hoyt, Samuel B.	"The Cut" (Deer Park Rd.)	23 Bedford Rd.	7
Hoyt, Zeno	Railroad Ave., East	128 Bedford Rd.	6
Hubbard, Oliver	Anderson Ave.	2 Anderson Rd.	43

* The Dowburg (or Dahlberg) Road is labeled "Croton Ave." on a contemporary map.

Building	Location in old villages	Location in New Katonah	No. on Maps pp. 144-45
Jaycox, Charles	Anderson Ave.	Anderson Rd.	42
Jones, Seth	West side of present Woodsbridge Rd.	33 North St.	54
Kellogg, Henry	Railroad Ave., East	12 The Terrace	1
Lent, Fletcher	Railroad Ave., East	13 Edgemont Rd.	2
Lyon, Albert	South St.	36 The Terrace	48
Lyon, Jere	Church St.	29 Katonah Ave.	46
Lyon, Thomas	Main St.	26 Anderson Rd.	21
Methodist Church (old)	Whitlockville	Lumber used to build 16 Anderson Rd.	37
Methodist Parsonage (old)	Whitlockville	Anderson Rd.	39
Methodist Parsonage	Anderson Ave.	8 Bedford Rd.	44
Miller, Lewis	Palmer Ave.	4 Valley Edge	28
Parent, Henry	The Dowburg Rd.	37 Wildwood Rd.	34
Parent, Henry	The Dowburg Rd.	36 Anderson Rd.	33
Presbyterian Manse	River Rd.	31 Bedford Rd.	26
Purdy, Daniel	"The Cut" (Deer Park Rd.)	Congdon Lane	8
Purdy, Ebenezar	Railroad Ave. & Main St.	Greenville Rd.	14
Railroad Station	Railroad Ave.	27 & 29 Huntville Rd.	9
Ray, George	South St.	8 Anderson Rd.	47
Reading Room	Railroad Ave., East	21 Edgemont Rd.	5
Reynolds, Frank	[Cross River, N.Y.]	101 Edgemont Rd.	None
Ritchie, Romaine. Barber Shop	Main St.	121 Katonah Ave.	20
Robertson, W. H. House	North St.	85 Edgemont Rd.	19
Robertson, W. H. Barn	North St.	Edgemont Rd. between The Parkway & Greenville Rd.	17
Rogers, Mary	East side of present Woodsbridge Rd.	119 Valley Rd.	55
Searles, Horace	River Rd. & The Dowburg Rd.	Valley Rd. (St. Mary's School on site)	30
Silkman, Myron	Main St. & Railroad Ave.	11 Nightingale Rd.	15
Smith, Thomas S.	Palmer Ave.	79 Edgemont Rd.	29
Travis, Bernard (part of House)	Church St.	North side of Anderson Rd. (torn down)	40
Tuttle, James	Whitlockville	69 Anderson Rd.	38
Van Tassel, W. P.	West side of present Woodsbridge Rd.	22 Woodsbridge Rd.	53
Whitlock, Huldah	East side of present Woodsbridge Rd.	37 Edgemont Rd.	57
Wickware, Dr. C. E.	Main St.	12 Bedford Rd.	22
Williams, James	Anderson Ave.	10 Bedford Rd.	41

Katonah's War Veterans, 1776-1953

Our Men in New York Regiments during the Revolution

This list is made up of men shown by land deed or highway assessment list to have lived around the time of the Revolution in our Cherry Street, Cantitoe or Mt. Holly areas, or along Route 22 between Cantitoe and the Lewisboro line. Their placement in New York regiments is from information in *New York in the Revolution* issued by the New York State Comptroller's Office, Albany, 1898. Undoubtedly we have omitted some names and made other errors. No attempt has been made to place our men in regiments of other states, though some did serve in such. Except where rank is given, all are enlisted men.

	Home	Westchester County Militia	The Line
Banks, John	Harris Rd. or Mt. Holly	2nd Regt.	
Brown, Adonijah	Cantitoe	3rd Regt. 4th Regt.	
Brown, Adonijah, Jr.	Cantitoe	4th Regt.	
Brown, Nathaniel	Cantitoe	3rd Regt. 2nd Regt. Land Bounty Rights	1st Regt.* Additional Regt.*
Clark, Daniel	Mt. Holly	2nd Regt.	
Clark, Isaac	Mt. Holly & Cherry St.	1st Regt. 2nd Regt. Enlisted & lieut. 3rd Regt. Enlisted & ensign	
Clark, Nathaniel	Mt. Holly	2nd Regt.	
Dann, Ebenezer	Cantitoe	2nd Regt. Land Bounty Rights	
Dannolds, John	Cantitoe		4th Regt.
Davis, Thomas	Cherry St.		4th Regt.
Dingee, Emery	Croton Lake Rd.	2nd Regt.	
Dingee, John	Croton Lake Rd.	2nd Regt.	
Dingee, John, Jr.	Croton Lake Rd.	2nd Regt.	
Dingee, Samuel	Croton Lake Rd.	3rd Regt.	
Gregory, Daniel	Cantitoe	2nd Regt.	
Hait (Hoyt), Abraham	Mt. Holly	2nd Regt. 3rd Regt.	
Hait, Daniel	Mt. Holly	1st Regt. 2nd Regt. Land Bounty Rights	

* We are in doubt about placement here.

	Home	Westchester County Militia	The Line
Hait (Hoit, Hoyt), Jacob	Mt. Holly	2nd Regt. 3rd Regt. 4th Regt. 4th Regt. Land Bounty Rights Assoc. Exempts	
Hait (Hayt), Jacob, Jr.	Mt. Holly	4th Regt. Land Bounty Rights	
Hait, Jonas	Mt. Holly	2nd Regt. Land Bounty Rights	
Hait, Phineas (Phinahas)	Mt. Holly	1st Regt. 2nd Regt. Land Bounty Rights	
Harris, Abijah	Harris Rd.	2nd Regt.	4th Regt.
Harris, Ezekiel	Harris Rd.	2nd Regt.	
Harris, John	Harris Rd.		2nd Regt.
Harris, Justis	Harris Rd.	2nd Regt. Capt.	
Harris, Robert	Harris Rd.	2nd Regt.	
Harris, William	Harris Rd.	2nd Regt.	
Hartford, Peter	Mt. Holly	3rd Regt. 4th Regt.	
Ketchem, Timothy	Cherry St.	(Dutchess Co.) 5th Regt. Land Bounty Rights*	
Lounsbury, Gideon	Mt. Holly	4th Regt.	
Lyon, Roger	Mt. Holly	2nd Regt.	
Lyon, Samuel	Route 22	2nd Regt. 3rd Regt. Assoc. Exempts	
McDonald, James	Harris Rd.	2nd Regt. Qtmster. 3rd Regt. Levies (Weissenfels)	Artillery Regt.*
Maynard, Stephen	Mt. Holly	2nd Regt.	
Mead, Joshua	Cherry St.	1st Regt. 2nd Regt. 3rd Regt.	
Merritt (Merret), John	Mt. Holly	2nd Regt.	
Miller, Abijah	Harris Rd.	2nd Regt.	
Miller, Abner	Harris Rd.	2nd Regt. Land Bounty Rights	
Miller, Benjamin	Route 22 or Mt. Holly	2nd Regt. Land Bounty Rights 4th Regt. Land Bounty Rights	4th Regt.
Miller, Cornelius	Cantitoe	2nd Regt.	
Miller, Ebenezer	Mt. Holly	2nd Regt. 3rd Regt.	
Miller, Hezekiah	Cantitoe	2nd Regt. Enlisted & Lieut. 2nd Regt. Land Bounty Rights Lieut.	
Miller, Increase	Mt. Holly	2nd Regt.*	
Miller, Richard	Cantitoe	2nd Regt.	
Miller, Timothy	Harris Rd.	2nd Regt. Ensign	
Miller, William	Route 22	2nd Regt.*	4th Regt.*
Newman, Jonathan	Mt. Holly	1st Regt. 2nd Regt.	

* We are in doubt about placement here.

	Home	Westchester County Militia	The Line
Osborn, John	Hoyt's Mills	4th Regt. Levies (Pawling) 1st Regt. 2nd Regt. 3rd Regt. Levies (Pawling)	
Platt, Jonathan	Cherry St.		4th Regt. Capt.
Price, Nathaniel	Cherry St.		Artillery Regt.
Purdy, Thomas	Route 22	2nd Regt.	
Rall (Rull), John	Hoyt's Mills	1st Regt.	
Robertson, William	Cantitoe	Levies (Graham & Willett) *	Artillery Regt.*
Rundal (Rundle, Rundell), John	Cherry St.	4th Regt. 2nd Regt. Land Bounty Rights	
St. John, Moses	Harris Rd.	2nd Regt. Enlisted & Capt. 3rd Regt.	
Seely, Giddeon	Mt. Holly	4th Regt. Land Bounty Rights	
Sherwood, Daniel	Cantitoe	Levies (Malcom)	
Sherwood, John	Cantitoe	(Dutchess Co.) 6th Regt. Land Bounty Rights*	
Sherwood, Stephen	Cantitoe	3rd Regt. Land Bounty Rights	
Silkman, John	Mt. Holly	2nd Regt.	
Silkman, John, Jr.	Mt. Holly	2nd Regt. Land Bounty Rights	
Smith, Daniel	Route 22	2nd Regt. 3rd Regt.	
Smith, Gabriel	Harris Rd.	2nd Regt. Land Bounty Rights	
Smith, Jacob	Route 22	3rd Regt. Land Bounty Rights	1st Regt.*
Smith, Jesse	Harris Rd.	2nd Regt.	2nd Regt.*
Smith, Moses	Route 22		4th Regt.
Smith, Noah	Route 22	2nd Regt.	
Smith, Samuel	Cherry St.		4th Regt.
Smith, Thomas	Route 22	2nd Regt. Land Bounty Rights	
Smith, William	Harris Rd.		4th Regt.
Townsend, John	Cantitoe	(Dutchess Co.) 3rd Regt.* 7th Regt.*	
Westcoate (Wescot), Abram	Cantitoe	2nd Regt.	
Westcoate (Wescot), Annanias	Cantitoe	2nd Regt.	
Williamson, William	Harris Rd.	2nd Regt.	
Wood, William	Cherry St.		4th Regt. Surgeon's mate †
Worden, Valentine (Voluntine)	Harris Rd.	2nd Regt.	

* We are in doubt about placement here.

† Heitman, F. B. *Historical register of officers of the Continental Army*, Washington, D.C., 1893, p. 443.

Civil War Monument
The Parkway and Bedford Road, Katonah

East Side:

IN MEMORIAM

Capt. James McKeel, Capt. John W. Sweetman, and members of Co. A, 4th N.Y. Vol. Heavy Art'y who enlisted from Katonah, N.Y., to serve during the Civil War of 1861-1865.

James C. Bogan	J. T. Lockwood
Franklin Dingee	James H. Lyon
Oscar L. Dearborn	Robert A. Reynolds
Leonidas E. Gallahue	Leonard H. Secor
Edgar Hitt	Clark See
Rufus Hitt	Emerson See
Patrick Hughes	Harrison Totten
B. F. Lockwood	Starr V. Totten

Albert Tucker
Dedicated May 30, 1914
Erected by Private J. T. Lockwood of Co. A. 4th N.Y. Vol. Heavy Art'y

West Side:

IN HONOR OF
OUR FRIEND
Hon. William H. Robertson
and our comrades

Major Theodore Price	4th N.Y. Heavy Art'y
Captain James McKeel	4th N.Y. Heavy Art'y

and

Charter members of McKeel Post No. 120 Grand Army of the Republic

Jeremiah T. Lockwood	Co. A	4th N.Y. Heavy Art'y
Edward A. Teed	Co. A	4th N.Y. Heavy Art'y
Clark See	Co. A	4th N.Y. Heavy Art'y
Edgar Hitt	Co. A	4th N.Y. Heavy Art'y
Purdy Quick	Co. L	4th N.Y. Heavy Art'y
Abram S. Knapp	Co. I	4th N.Y. Heavy Art'y
Edwin S. Folsom	Co. B	1st N.J. Volunteers
Edgar B. Newman	Co. F	48th N.Y. Volunteers
Samuel S. Austin	Co. B	6th N.Y. Heavy Art'y
Charles Fisher	Co. D	6th N.Y. Heavy Art'y
Enoch H. Avery	Co. D	6th N.Y. Heavy Art'y
Webster L. Hull	Co. A	6th Conn. Volunteers
Charles H. Corbyn	Co. H	170th N.Y. Volunteers
C. Ward Varian	Co. E	165th N.Y. Volunteers

James A. Tuttle   Co. D 2nd N.Y. Cavalry
Jeremiah B. Turner   Receiving Ship "Vermont"
Erected by McKeel Post No. 120, S. N. Y. G. A. R.
Dedicated May 30, 1923

Civil War Dead

The Rev. W. F. Brush, in a Decoration Day address at the Katonah
Methodist Episcopal Church, listed the following Civil War soldiers
from this area who were no longer living.

Katonah Cemetery

James Sniffen	Albert Tucker
John Carson	John Austin
Jeremiah Austin	Benj. Ballard
Jeremiah Lockwood	Wright Ferguson
John Smith	Gilbert Totten
Mead Silkman	William Johnson

George Briggs

Buried in the South

This list includes men from a wider area than our own.

James Lyon	Alonzo Gallahue
Daniel Cox	James Muller
Jesse Hoyt	Peter Dolan
James Brown	Chauncey Totten
Frank Dingee	John Jones
Charles Dingee	John Smith

Joseph Ferguson

(Taken from: Rev. W. F. Brush, "Decoration Day at Katonah." *The
Recorder*, Mt. Kisco, June 8, 1888)

Katonah's World War I Veterans

Allen, Charles M. Sergeant, 9th
Co., 4th Regt. France.
Allen, Frederick M. Lieutenant.
Allen, Michael.
Annin, William E., Jr.
Armstrong, Donald. Major.
Armstrong, Francis T. Major.

Avery, Harvey J. Corporal, me-
chanic.
Bailey, Pearce. Colonel.
Benedict, James A.
Bonar, James F.
Bossie, Louis.
Brady, Robert E. Lieutenant.

Brink, Willard. Corporal.

* Candie, Angelo M. Sergeant, Co. E, 1st Bn., U.S.T.C. Died Nov. 1, 1918, Waco, Tex.

Cervoni, Louis.

Conner, Lewis A. Colonel.

Connolly, Richard.

Coster, Gerald Holsam.

Di Amandi, Agustino.

Di Bella, Giuseppi.

Dingee, Harold M.

Felice, Antonio.

Fincke, Rev. William M.

Forbes, Henry H. Captain.

Forshay, Howard J.

Fowler, Clenidene S.

Fowler, Robert L. Lieutenant.

Fowler, W. Hoyt.

Franklin, William B. Captain, U.S.N.R.F.

* Gregory, Le Roy. Co. L, 105th Inf., 27th Div. Killed in France Oct. 18, 1918.

Gribble, Lawrence P.

Griffin, Benjamin H.

Gumboldt, Frank W., Jr. Lieutenant. College Park, Md.

Haight, Charles L.

Hallett, George J. Sergeant.

Hunt, Cornelius.

Hunt, J. Ramsay. Major.

* Jones, Frederick B. U.S.N.R.F. Died Sept. 27, 1918, at Great Lakes Training Station, Ill.

Jones, George C. Corporal.

Kellogg, William R. Corporal.

* Kelly, James J. Corporal. Co. B., 105th Inf., 27th Div. Killed in France Oct. 16, 1918.

Kelly, John W.

Kennedy, Roland B. Tank Corps, 303 Bn., Co. C. England.

King, William. Corporal, Tank Corps 714. France.

Kniffen, Charles P.

Kniffen, Francis J.

Latella, Carmelo.

Latella, Dominick.

Lione, Antonio.

MacPhail, J. A. Garfield. Lieutenant.

Marler, Arthur. Sergeant, 21st Co. Sandy Hook, N.J.

Marler, George B. Chief Mechanic, B. Bn., 57th Art.

Matteson, Clayton P.

Miller, Valentine.

Noe, Carl J. Tank Div. France.

Noe, Cornelius. Sergeant, B. Bn., 43rd Art., CAC. France.

Noe, L. Frederick. B. Bn., Art. RAR. France.

Noe, Paul A. Ch. Elec., U.S.N. Sub. Base, New London, Conn.

Noe, Peter, Jr. Lieutenant. New Haven, Conn.

Odell, Bradford I.

Okie, Reginald W.

Ostrander, Edward F. A Co., 5th Field Sig. Corps. France.

Parker, Wilbur S.

Poole, William A.

Renzivillo, Camelo.

Reynolds, Frank. 304 Supply Co. France.

Reynolds, Stephen B.

Richardson, Allen B. N.A.C. Lieutenant.

Richardson, David W. R.A.F.

* Russell, J. Stanley. 32nd Sq., Avio Div. Died Mar. 25, 1918, Waco, Tex.

Ruxton, William V. C. Captain.

Santori, Stefano.

Schaefer, E. Paul. Corporal, 348 Inf.

Schaefer, J. Albert. Sergeant, 26th Co., 7th Bn.

* Gold star men.

Schaefer, Theodore K. Sergeant,
    Quartermaster Corps.
Searles, Wallace B.
Sheehan, Frank.
Towey, Helen M.
Towey, Matthew R. Merchant
    Marine.
Travis, Clarence J. M.D.N.A.
    Base Hospital No. 23.
Travis, Howard C. D Co., 24th
    Engineer Corps.

Turnure, Percy R. Major.
Vuotto, Costanzo. Corporal.
Weeks, Kenneth T. Corporal,
    Supply Train 427. France.
Whitall, Thomas Wistar.
Whitman, Harold C. Major.
Will, Alexander A. Sergeant.
Will, William M. Corporal.
Williams, Frederick H. Captain.
Woodcock, Waldorf.
Wright, Oliver D. Corporal.

Those Who Served in World War II

ARMED FORCES

Abbey, Francis O.
Allen, Fred M., Jr.
Allmond, Benjamin
Allmond, Francis
    Edwin
Andersen, Rolf
Angot, Emile Paul, Jr.
Archer, Raymond O.
Archibald, Donald S.
Armstrong, Donald
Armstrong, Francis
    Tuttle
Avery, Charles W.
Bailey, Frank T.
Baker, Mary Louise
Bals, Robert
Barber, William
Barker, David, Jr.
Barker, James M.
Barker, William E.
Barrett, Donald P.
Barrett, Ione P.
Barrett, Laurence N.
Barry, Doris V.
Barry, John William
Barteaux, Leon Ernest,
    Jr.
Becker, Lloyd S.
Becker, Roger H.
Beckley, Leonard C.
Beekman, Gerardus
Beekman, Robert S.
Bellamy, Gayer D.
Bernardo, John

* Bernardo, Pompei M.
Bittner, Warren John
Blackley, William
Blazek, Edward M.
Bonar, James
* Booth, Jasper W.
Booth, Leonard V.
Booth, William Joseph
Brady, James W.
Brandenburg, Julius
Brown, David, Jr.
Brown, William J.
Brundage, Merritt L.
Buckley, Alfred J.
Buckley, James P., Jr.
Bunce, Arthur J.
* Buonassissi, Michael
Bunn, Charles E.
Burt, Albert J.
Burt, Julian
Busch, John F.
Carmel, Edwin
Carmel, Harry
Chambers, Ridgely W.
Choupin, Jean
Christian, Arthur T.
Christian, Edward J.
Christian, Joseph D.
Clarke, Richard W.
Clarkson, George
    Stanley
Cloherty, Henry
    Joseph
Coffin, Sanford

Collins, Fred W.
Congdon, Donald M.
Congdon, Willard D.
Coster, Edward L.
Covey, Arthur R.
Covey, Edwin B.
Cranston, T. Andrew
Crowell, Harry B.
Cullen, Charles J.
Cullen, George A.
Curley, Thomas J.
Dale, Francis R.
Daniel, Robert
Davis, Jeffrey T.
DeLena, Alexander
DeLena, Ralph M.
* Diamanti, Albert
Dingee, Edward J.
Dolicker, Joseph Pat-
    rick
Duffy, Vincent
Dugan, Patrick J., Jr.
Duncombe, Herbert
    S., Jr.
Durkin, John L.
Durkin, Joseph J.
Eisenhauer, James F.
English, William H.
Ferguson, Arthur E.
* Ferguson, Charles, Jr.
Ferguson, Robert J.
Ferris, Anthony M.
Ferris, Arthur L.
Fiacco, Arthur J.

* Gold star men.

Fiacco, Thomas N.
Finlayson, Walter A.
Fish, Leonard T.
Fish, Wilbur B.
Forsythe, Thomas, Jr.
Foulke, Donald
Foulke, G. Brion
Fowler, Clenidene S.
Fowler, Harry W.
Fowler, Robert C.
* Fowler, Robert L., III
Frankel, Stephen B.
French, Harry J.
Fuchs, Joseph J.
Ganung, Daryl R.
Ganung, Edwin T.
Ganung, Leon E., Jr.
Garfunkel, Arthur T.
Garfunkel, Richard H.
Gazaldini, Anthony
  Joseph
Genett, Ernest F.
Gerardi, August J.
Gerardi, Joseph P.
Gerardi, Lawrence S.
Gould, Allen E.
Grant, Jerome
Grant, Robert
Green, Robert
Hall, Leonard H.
Hammond, Donald K.
Hancock, Douglas D.
Hancock, Phillip H.
Harder, George E., Sr.
Harper, Harry H., Jr.
Hayes, Donald B.
Healy, Joseph P.
Helmes, Bruce P.
Helms, Irving L.
Hennion, William D.
Hickok, Margaret E.
Hilbert, Webb, Jr.
Holmes, John C.
Hope, Charles M.
Hopkins, David
Holly, LeRoy G.
Housted, Niles L.
Hunn, Kenneth L.
Hunt, James Ramsay,
  Jr.
Iemolo, Ross
Iglehart, Lewis M.
Igoe, Thomas
Iselin, Arthur, Jr.

Iselin, William Jay
Johnson, Jack F.
Johnson, Robert, Jr.
Johnson, Robert C.
Jones, James
Jones, Paul S.
Joyce, Roland L.
Kallback, Bertil
Kellogg, Donald R.
Kellogg, Douglas E.
Kellogg, Richard H.
Kellogg, Robert W.
Kelly, Michael F.
Kelly, William A.
Kirk, John M.
Knapp, LeRoy C.
* Knudsen, Ellwood B.
Knudsen, John W.
Kobin, William
Lammers, William H.,
  Jr.
Lawrence, James F.
Lazzaro, Dominick
Lent, Sheldon F.
Leone, Joseph
Leone, Thomas
Litchfield, Edward S.
* Lorzer, Douglas D.
Lundgren, Andre
MacDonald, Elizabeth
MacVicar, Thomas C.
Maddock, John D.
Maddock, Joseph D.
Maddock, Richard J.
Maher, Gerald P.
Matteson, Kenneth E.
Mayer, Allan J.
Mazzola, Sabatino W.
McCagg, Louis B.
McGarry, William P.
McHale, Patricia L.
McLaren, James A.
McLaren, Thomas A.
Mederos, Thomas S.
Melahn, Charles R.
Miller, Burton
Miller, H. Ralcey
Miller, J. Gilson
* Miller, John J., Jr.
Milson, Daniel
Moffat, John
Moore, Bruce A.
Morabito, Anthony P.
Morabito, Frank J.

Morabito, Salvatore
Morgan, Joseph
Nash, Harold
Neff, Horace R.
Nelson, George H.
Nicoll, Thomas B.
Nieters, John M.
Noe, L. Fred
Noe, Paul A.
Noe, Paul A., Jr.
Oberle, Vincent
O'Boyle, Edwards C.
O'Connor, John F.
O'Connor, William J.
Odell, Bradford
O'Leary, Frank P.
O'Leary, John T.
O'Leary, Mathew L.
* Olmstead, Barnes
Olmstead, Helen P.
O'Sullivan, Mounty F.
Paddock, Ralph L., Jr.
Paddock, Robert B.
Paddock, William A.
Park, H. Halsted, Jr.
Parker, Joseph W.
Parks, Elton, Jr.
Pecora, Dominick
Pecora, Lewis
Pedersen, Arthur Paul
Phelan, Edward W.
Phelan, Raymond
  Bruce
Pianforini, Alexander
  J.
Pianforini, Louis P.
Pike, Albert H., Jr.
Pippet, John R. B.
Pope, Thomas M.
Price, Alan M.
Price, Hugh R.
Prigge, Charles L.
Puret, Frank
Quaintance, Richard E.
Raneri, Philip
Ray, Frederick G.
Ray, Robert W.
Reagan, Philip
Reagan, Richard
Roberts, Bernard R.
Robertson, Henry
Rogers, Clarence A.
Rogge, John R.
* Rosen, Walter B.

* Gold star men.

Santore, Albert W.
Santore, John Paul
Sawicky, Joseph Edward
Scallon, James J.
Schaus, Willard
Schermerhorn, Harold C.
Shilling, Warren
Shilling, William
Schmitt, William J.
Schutte, Stephen R., Jr.
Scofield, John R.
Scully, Donald T.
Seelig, George H.
Shepherd, David G.
Shepherd, William E.
Sherman, James J.
Silkman, John G.
Sitzer, Albert F.

Smith, Baldwin D.
Smith, Joseph L.
Smith, Walter E.
* Stapleton, James P.
Stephenson, Robert E.
Thomas, Ralph D.
Thompson, John M.
Towey, Arthur
Towey, David A.
Towey, Edward J.
* Towey, Joseph M.
Towey, Walter J.
Traber, Cornelius E.
Travis, Harold J., Jr.
Twidy, Richard
Virtuoso, Clement J.
Virtuoso, Dominick
Vogler, George F.
Vogler, Louis
Vogler, Robert A.
Vogler, Wilbert M.

Wallgren, Harry A.
Wallgren, Herbert F.
Wallgren, Roy K.
Warner, Benjamin T.
Webb, Frank
Weissgarber, Michael
Wells, John Joseph
Wesche, Carl D.
Wiesner, Alexander J.
Whitman, Clarence, II
Wiggins, Harold B.
Will, Robert M.
Willets, Claudia S.
Wilson, G. Gordon
Wilson, Leonard M., Jr.
Wilson, Robert
Woyak, Edward
Yodice, Ralph P.

AIR TRANSPORT COMMAND
Barrett, Robertson T., Jr.

AMERICAN FIELD SERVICE
Duncombe, Sydney
Litchfield, Philip A.

RED CROSS FIELD SERVICE
Helmes, Charles T.

OFFICE OF STRATEGIC SERVICES
Alexander, Henry C.

MERCHANT MARINE
Dubuque, Joseph
Fiacco, Carmen
Horne, William

Katonah Men in Service during the Period of the Korean War

Blair, Capt. M. Douglas[K]
Duncombe, David
Duncombe, Col. Herbert S., Jr.[K]
Edwards, Frank
Fisher, Samuel
Foulke, Donald[K]

Fowler, Charles
Fowler, Robert[K]
Fowler, William[K]
French, Harry F.[K]
Ganung, Robert[K]
Graydon, Col. Charles Wood
Hart, Donald F.[K]

Herbert, Daniel, Jr.[K]
Hibbard, Peter[K]
Noe, Paul, Jr.[K]
Ruger, Lt. Col. John W.
Silkman, Richard P.[K]
Towey, James, Jr.

* Gold star men.
[K] = served in Korea or adjacent waters.

APPENDIX 31

Periodicals Published in Katonah, 1872-1961

The periodicals are arranged in order of their first publication. If one is continued under another title, that title follows it immediately. Asterisks separate the titles of periodicals which were not connected in any way.

Feast of Lanterns. Katonah, N.Y.
V. 1, no. 1–v. 1, no. 10 (?). 1872 (?) –Sept. 1-2, 1887 (?).
Published at intervals of one to four years by the Ladies' Aid Society of the Methodist Episcopal Church in connection with their fair.
Carried church and village news and history, poems, essays, advertisements.
A further, single issue was published July 14, 15, & 16, 1927.

* * * * *

Katonah Sentinel. Katonah, N.Y.
Aug. 20, 1873–April 17 (?), 1874.
A local newspaper, published by O. H. Miller and Wm. A. Miller.
Continued as: *The Recorder.*

The Recorder. Katonah, N.Y.
V. 1, no. 1–? April 24, 1874–1897.
Continuation of: *Katonah Sentinel.*
Wm. A. Miller and J. T. Lockwood, editors and proprietors; W. N. Stewart, publisher.
In 1878 Lockwood sold his interest to Miller and retired. June 3, 1881, the paper moved to Mt. Kisco, the *Mt. Kisco Courier* merged with this, and title became *The Recorder and Mt. Kisco Courier,* with Wm. A. Miller as editor and proprietor.
Continued as: *Mount Kisco Recorder.*

* * * * *

Katonah Advertiser. Katonah, N.Y.
V. 1, no. 8, Thursday, Nov. 5, 1874 (the only issue found).
Everett Benedict, editor, publisher and proprietor.
A two-leaf sheet giving brief editorials, news items, and advertisements.

* * * * *

Blue Light. Katonah, N.Y.

No. [1]–9. Aug. 9, 1876–July 30, 1884.

Published annually under the auspices of the Ladies' Aid Society of the Presbyterian Church in connection with their fair.

Carried church and local news, recipes, essays, poems, advertisements.

* * * *

Katonah Times. Katonah, N.Y.

V. 1, no. 1–v. 31, no. 24. 1878–Nov. 5, 1909.

Published weekly by Woolhiser & Austin. Taken over in 1894 by Robert D. Knapp, who was editor and proprietor through Dec. 31, 1908. Sold in January, 1909, to Will H. Chamberlain who became publisher, editor, and proprietor. *Croton Falls News and Folio* and the *Croton Valley Times* merged in this, the latter in 1901.

Continued as: *North Westchester Times.*

Croton Valley Times. Katonah, N.Y.

1890–1901.

Published by Woolhiser and Austin. Merged with the *Katonah Times.*

North Westchester Times. Katonah, N.Y.

V. 31, no. 25–the present. Nov. 12, 1909–the present.

Continuation of: *Katonah Times.*

Published weekly by Will H. Chamberlain, editor and proprietor. Beginning v. 36, no. 32, Jan. 16, 1914, moved to Mt. Kisco. In 1917 sold to A. A. Norton.

* * * *

Katonah Record. Katonah, N.Y.

V. 1, no. 1–v. 37, no. 41. May 15, 1913–Jan. 26, 1950.

Published weekly by the Katonah Publishing Corp.: Frank E. Perley, president, treasurer, editor; Fowler G. Peck, secretary and general manager. Peck became editor 1914–44. Robertson T. Barrett was president and treasurer 1914–19. George H. Covey was president and treasurer 1919–42. J. Gilson Miller joined the staff in 1923 and was office manager 1945–53. Robertson T. Barrett became secretary, treasurer and managing editor 1944–49.

David M. Wilde and Scudder M. Parker bought the paper in 1949.

Continued as *The Record.*

The Record. Katonah, N.Y.

V. 37, no. 42–v. 45, no. 30. Feb. 2, 1950–Sept. 27, 1956.

Continuation of: *Katonah Record.*

Parker, Wilde, and Miller staffed the paper through July, 1953.

Bought by Carll Tucker, Jr., of the Patent Press, Inc., July 31, 1953. Victor Salvatore became editor and Peter D. Brundage, associate editor.

With v. 45, no. 22, Aug. 2, 1956, the paper moved to Mt. Kisco.

Continued as: *Patent Trader*.

* * * * *

The Villager. Katonah, N.Y.

V. 1, no. 1–v. 8, no. 400. April 28, 1917–June 6, 1925.

Published weekly by Samuel Strauss, president, Kate Parsons, secretary.

Carried only editorials and essays, and was used as reference material in college courses.

Public Schools of Katonah, 1812-1961

Our present school system had its beginning in 1812 when the Township of Bedford accepted the State's offer of aid in establishing and maintaining common schools and agreed to share equally in the expense. Of the eleven Bedford school districts set up in 1813, Nos. 6, 7, 8, and 10, with approximately the same boundaries, are included in today's Union Free School District No. 1. Our first combination with Lewisboro dates back to 1813. District No. 10 was designated a "½ district." The other half, adjacent to it, was across the Salem (now Lewisboro) line. A further combination with Lewisboro in 1836 joined part of District No. 7 (Cherry Street) with half of Salem District No. 11 (Whitlockville).

One-room schools were operating in all four of our local districts by 1814. New schools came into being as population in newly developed areas called for them. The schoolhouse on Silkman's Corners in Whitlockville was established in 1836. In 1862 a school in Old Katonah was also established. In 1883 a large two-room school built on Palmer Ave., midway between the two villages, took the place of both the earlier schools.

The first school of New Katonah, a two-story edifice, opened Jan. 2, 1895, replaced the Palmer Ave. school which burned in 1893. In anticipation of the move from Old Katonah, it was located on North St. It served twelve years and was succeeded by the much larger school on Bedford Rd., known as Union Free School District No. 10 of Bedford, Lewisboro and North Salem, which opened in April 1907. This school included two years of high school which was raised to four, giving our children for the first time high school education in their own district. Districts in the three townships shared in the high school program, but either kept their own elementary schools open or contracted with District No. 10 to educate their grade children.

Cherry Street had annexed itself to District No. 10 in 1905. Gradually the other common school districts in our area and the Goldens Bridge and Herman Chapel districts of Lewisboro also were annexed. Mt. Holly, for many years a contracting district, was the last to join, in 1950. In 1940 a new and still larger grade and high school on Huntville Rd. succeeded the Bedford Rd. school.

Meanwhile, in Lewisboro, seven districts (one including part of Pound Ridge) had been joined to form Union Free School District No. 1. Their new elementary school in South Salem opened in 1939.

In 1952 Lewisboro District No. 1 and our District No. 10 effected consolidation as Union Free School District No. 1, Towns of Bedford, Lewisboro, North Salem and Pound Ridge. In 1960-61 this District educated 1775 children. There are two elementary schools in the District, the one at South Salem and the school on Huntville Road, converted entirely to this purpose. The John Jay School, opened Oct. 1, 1956, in Cross River, is the only high school. Sites for two additional elementary schools, one in Vista and one east of Goldens Bridge, were voted by the District on May 3, 1961.

GENEALOGIES AND BIOGRAPHIES

GENEALOGIES AND BIOGRAPHIES

Listed in this section are families living in Katonah and its vicinity before the move to the new village in 1897. The list is not complete. It omits many prominent families on which material has been unavailable. For help on the families included we are indebted to their present-day descendants. Prepared over a period of three years, these genealogies may not in all cases record births, deaths and marriages that have occurred during this interim. No additions or corrections have been made later than February, 1961.

We have used the following abbreviations wherever possible without confusion:

b. = born	mar. = married, married to
d. = died	mos. = months
d.y. = died young	unmar. = unmarried
dau. = daughter	yrs. = years.

The small numbers above names denote generations, not necessarily from the first member of the family in America but from the first through whom we can trace a clear line to the present.

References to sources have been omitted to save space. They will be found, however, with the longer versions of these same families' records in notebooks at the Katonah Village Library and at the Westchester County Historical Society Library in White Plains, N.Y.

The Allen Family

ALVAH S. ALLEN,[2] b. June 14, 1823, son of BAILEY ALLEN[1] of North Salem, married Phebe Jane Reynolds of Bedford, N.Y., dau. of Joseph and Ann (Fuller) Reynolds, Sept. 29, 1843. Their three sons were: LEVI[3] (1844-1846); JOSEPH BAILEY;[3] and CHARLES H.[3] Mr. Allen was killed in a fall from a building on which he was working as carpenter June 3, 1852. He is buried in Cat Ridge Cemetery, North Salem, as is his son, LEVI.[3] Mrs. Allen married 2nd Roberts Purdy Dec. 19, 1859. They had twins, Georganna and George F. Purdy, b. May 29, 1861, at North Salem. In 1872 the family moved to Katonah, living on the east side of the railroad near the dry bridge at Whitlockville Depot. Georganna married Elbert Mercene Green. Their daughter is Jennie Elizabeth Adkins of Salisbury, Md. George F. Purdy married June 7, 1882, Charlotte S. Brown. He worked on their land, at Lyon Brothers store in Katonah, at Elliott's Livery Stable, and later with his half-brother, JOSEPH ALLEN,[3] at carpenter work, building a home at 38 The Terrace and another at 17 Hillside Ave. Their daughter is Mrs. Harriet Jane Barrell, 44 Huntville Rd.

JOSEPH BAILEY ALLEN,[3] b. July 21, 1846, worked on the family farm and later followed his father in the carpenter trade. He married Sara Eliza Green (1849-1922) Dec. 30, 1867. After moving to Katonah he worked as Superintendent for Henry E. Pellew and later for Clarence Whitman, who bought the Pellew home, "Katonah's Wood." On May 11, 1887, the Allens bought a hilltop farm of 63 acres from Jacob C. Buckley, south of Old Katonah, west of the tracks, and next to the Knowlton property. Mr. Allen was on the Sidewalk and Street Committee for the Village Improvement Society for the new village, and a fireman. He and his wife were members of the Presbyterian Church. They were parents of: MELVILLE JOSEPH;[4] AND LYDIA J.[4] About 1898 he built two new homes for his family and son overlooking the village on Terrace Heights. The original little Red House, the oldest in Katonah village (now owned by Lewis and Mildred Hasbrouck), had become too small. Mrs. Allen died in 1922 and Mr. Allen, July 15, 1932. They are buried in Union Cemetery, Bedford.

MELVILLE JOSEPH ALLEN,[4] b. Jan. 7, 1869, worked with the stone masons on many of the foundations for the New Katonah homes. He married June 30, 1891, Wilhelmina Stuart Wood (see Wood genealogy). Their children were: CHARLES MELVILLE[5] AND FLORENCE BEATRICE.[5] They lived on Terrace Heights, at Cantitoe in 1901, and in 1913 bought a farm in Maryland. In 1918 they moved to White Plains, and returned to Katonah after Mr. Allen's mother's death to live with his father on Terrace Heights. MELLVILLE JOSEPH[4] was a building contractor. Mrs. Allen, d. Nov. 15, 1946, and Mr. Allen, d. Aug. 2, 1956, are buried at Union Cemetery, Bedford.

CHARLES MELVILLE ALLEN,[5] b. June 25, 1893, attended the Katonah school and was a sergeant in the Army in World War I. He married, June 12, 1920, Madeleine Purdy of Croton Falls. Mr. Allen had his own garage in his large red barn on Terrace Heights, next to where they lived. There were no children. Mr. Allen died July 24, 1956, and is buried in Ivandell Cemetery, Somers. Mrs. Allen lives at 50 The Terrace.

FLORENCE BEATRICE ALLEN,[5] b. Apr. 9, 1897, married Aug. 15, 1925, Stirling F. Ashley (1897-1956) at White Plains. She died in Farmington Falls, Me., Feb. 22, 1954. Both are buried in Bedford Union Cemetery. They left one daughter, VIRGINIA RUTH ASHLEY,[6] b. Aug. 23, 1927, married Feb. 7, 1948, to Arthur W. Porter, Jr., at Portland, Me. Their children are: DANIEL ARTHUR,[7] b. May 28, 1949; JEFFERY ALLEN,[7] b. July 31, 1950; ROBERT ASHLEY,[7] b. Dec. 18, 1953; LAWRENCE ANDREW,[7] b. Apr. 30, 1955; JUDITH ALTHEA,[7] b. June 4, 1956; and MICHAEL ANTHONY PORTER,[7] b. Jan. 12, 1959. The Porter family lives at Farmington Falls, Me.

CHARLES H. ALLEN,[3] b. May 18, 1849, in North Salem, married in 1868 Emaline Sprague (1854-1913). They had 6 children: WILBUR;[4] MARY JANE;[4] EVA JOYCE;[4] SARAH;[4] FRED;[4] and CARRIE.[4] CHARLES[3] died May 8, 1927, at Bethel, Conn.

WILBUR ALLEN,[4] b. Mar. 24, 1869, married Grace Ridge and had dau. MANERVA.[5]

MARY JANE ALLEN,[4] b. Mar. 26, 1871, married Henry Lynch Apr. 4, 1891.

EVA JOYCE ALLEN,[4] b. Mar. 17, 1873, married Robert Taylor and moved to Waterville, Conn. Their sons: HOWARD E.[5] and LEROY TAYLOR.[5]

SARAH ALLEN,[4] b. Mar. 19, 1879, married in October, 1903, William E. Currid. Their children: CHARLES;[5] MARGUERITE;[5] STANLEY;[5] LAURENCE;[5] JACK;[5] ALLEN;[5] FRANCIS;[5] and JOSEPH CURRID.[5]

FRED ALLEN,[4] b. Aug. 11, 1883, married June 14, 1905, Grace Osborn. Their children: FLORENCE;[5] GENEVIEVE;[5] LEWIS;[5] and GEORGE.[5]

CARRIE ALLEN,[4] b. Oct. 23, 1885, married June 26, 1905, Arthur Osborne. Their children: MARION;[5] MYRTLE;[5] and MINNIE OSBORNE.[5]

Compiled by Madeleine Purdy Allen.

The Avery Family

The Averys came from Connecticut into Westchester, settling in Pound Ridge and Cross River. ENOCH AVERY[1] was an enlisted man in the Westchester County Militia, serving in the 4th Regiment under Col. Thaddeus Crane. Dec. 5, 1765, he married Dorcas Wolsey at Poughkeepsie and they made their home in Cross River, now part of the Pound Ridge Reservation. They are buried in the family plot near their home, which is still standing. Their children were: SALLY,[2] mar. John, son of Enoch Piatt; RUTH,[2] mar. John Harford; NANCY,[2] mar. Enos Mead; ELISHA;[2] WILLIAM;[2] and STEPHEN.[2] ENOCH [1] married 2nd, at 80 yrs., Miss Hoyt, and they had one daughter.

ELISHA AVERY,[2] b. 1771, d. Mar. 7, 1832, married 1st Miss Harris and 2nd Anna Scofield, who died Jan. 16, 1839, at 64 yrs. Their children were: ANTHA M.,[3] mar. Isaac Lyon; ANNER,[3] mar. Wakeman Wood; LAURA A.,[3] mar. Thaddeus Keeler; SERENA,[3] mar. Joseph Hanford; ALFRED,[3] mar. Anna M. Keeler; ENOCH,[3] mar. Lucy Wood; LYDIA,[3] mar. Michael

Scofield; ALANSON,[3] mar. Jane Ann Olmsted; and MARY,[3] mar. Joseph Wood.

ALFRED AVERY[3] (1796-1846) married Anna Maria Keeler, dau. of Major Jeremiah and Huldah (Hull) Keeler. Their two daughters were: HARRIET ANN,[4] mar. John C. Holmes of Cross River; and HULDAH MARIA,[4] mar. John Burr Whitlock (1822-1890) (see Whitlock genealogy).

ENOCH AVERY[3] (1798-1884) and his wife, Lucy Wood, were parents of 5 children: CHARLES WOOD;[4] GEORGE,[4] mar. Amy Brown; SARAH ANN,[4] mar. Aaron Burr Whitlock (see Whitlock genealogy); ELISHA LEMUEL;[4] and ENOCH BURR,[4] mar. Lydia Newman, dau. of William and Phebe Merritt Newman of Mt. Holly. ENOCH[3] was a colonel in the New York Militia, and by profession a building contractor. After the death of his first wife Sept. 20, 1853, he married Miss Chloe Merritt. He died Mar. 29, 1884.

ALANSON AVERY[3] (1802-1837), b. in Cross River, d. in Monmouth, Ill., married Jane Ann Olmsted, daughter of Silas and Jane A. (Westervelt) Olmsted. Their children were: ANNA MARIA,[4] mar. Edward Waite; SILAS OLMSTED,[4] mar. Julia Ellis; NANCY JANE,[4] mar. David N. Chichester; and ALFRED FRANKLIN.[4] ALFRED F. AVERY,[4] b. Oct., 1, 1836, in Cross River, married Ophelia Jane Todd (1841-1922) (see Todd genealogy). They traveled a great deal. They lived in a very large house on the River Road in Old Katonah and ran a boarding-house. He was interested in the lens factory and Jim Cox's grist and lumber mill. He moved the Wickware house from the Triangle to Bedford Rd. in New Katonah, where he lived while he built the "Cobbles." He was very active in the new village. Mrs. Avery enjoyed writing and wrote our first small book on Katonah in 1896. She also had a small Bible school in Greenville. They had 2 children: WESTERVELT[5] (1890-1890); and MYRTILLA[5] (1868-1959). Myrtilla was educated locally, at Blair Academy, and at Wellesley College. She taught languages at the Lacrosse, Wis., High School and at Albany Girls' School. She was director of Farnsworth Art Museum at Wellesley College for twenty-five years. She was the author of two books on art, and was a member of the Medieval Academy of America and the Archaeological Institute of America. Dr. Myrtilla Avery held degrees from Wellesley, the University of the State of New York and Radcliffe. Unmarried, she died at her home, 425 West 23rd St., New York City, at 90.

CHARLES WOOD AVERY[4] (Enoch,[3] Elisha,[2] Enoch[1]), b. Aug. 27, 1822, married 1st Anna G. Whitlock (1826-1871) and they had one daughter, SARAH ESTHER[5] (1847-1897), unmar. He married, 2nd, Emily Smith, daughter of Noah and Grace (Miller) Smith, Jr., of Whitlockville. They had one son, ARTHUR SMITH,[5] b. in Old Katonah, Oct. 4, 1876. CHARLES W.[4] ran a hardware store on Railroad Ave. which he sold to Henry Kellogg. He died in Old Katonah in 1886. Mrs. Emily Avery and ARTHUR[5] moved into New Katonah and lived at 80 Edgemont Rd. ARTHUR[5] received his education on Palmer Ave. and at business school in New York City. Sept. 1, 1906, he married Marjorie Ash of Carthage, N.Y., a Katonah kindergarten teacher. He worked for Clairville Benedict and was in the funeral business with William H. Clark in Katonah. Later he went into business for himself in his home and barn on Edgemont Rd., continuing until his death in 1952. ARTHUR[5] and Marjorie were parents of one son, CHARLES WOOD AVERY,[6] b. Sept. 13, 1918, in the Mt. Kisco hospital, who attended Katonah High School and transferred to Exeter for his last two years, graduating in 1936. He attended Amherst College, transferred to the University of North Carolina, then was with the Dramatics Workshop in New York City. He served for 4½ years in World War II with the Special Services, several years in Europe, having joined on April 15, 1941.

ELISHA LEMUEL AVERY[4] (Enoch,[3] Elisha,[2] Enoch[1]) married Chloe Esther Whitlock (1833-1885), daughter of Thaddeus and Nancy Gregory Whitlock of Whitlockville. They lived in the Horace Todd place at Rte. 22 and Todd Rd. and later moved to the Whitlock homestead in Whitlockville. ELISHA[4] worked in his uncle's store. He died in January, 1881, and Chloe, Apr. 3, 1885, leaving 2 sons, 3 young daughters, and her mother who was over 80. The children attended the red school house on David Silkman's corner and later the Palmer Ave. school. After the death of Mrs. Avery, the girls moved to Goldens Bridge. Children born to ELISHA[4] and Chloe were: ANNETTA[5] (1861-1861); AARON BURR[5] (1863-1932), mar. Sue Montross; ENOCH THADDEUS,[5] b. Aug. 25, 1864; CARRIE W.,[5] who mar. Wilson H. Crane and lived in Brewster; GEORGIANA[5] (1872-1886); and ELLA ETTA.[5] ENOCH T.,[5] b. on the old Todd place, spent his boyhood in Whitlockville. About 1888 he moved into the B. Travis house on Main St., Old Katonah, and worked for Whitlock who had bought out the Chadeayne and Lyon Store. He moved to Croton Falls to take over the operation and supervision of "Elmhurst," the farm of the Hon. Odle Close. He married Loretta S. Griffin (1865-1941). They had one son, HENRY ELISHA[6] (1889-1889). ENOCH[5] and his sister, ELLA AVERY,[5] presently make their home on Prospect St., Brewster, a wonderful couple.

WILLIAM AVERY[2] (Enoch[1]) married Ruth Piatt. They had 12 children: HARVEY;[3] ELIZABETH,[3] mar. Nathaniel Reynolds; NEHEMIAH,[3] mar. Judah Miller; HENRY,[3] mar. Hannah Reynolds; SUSAN,[3] mar. John Miller; NANCY,[3] mar. Stebbins Adams; DORCAS,[3] mar. Alfred Green; HULDAH[3] mar. Abram Matthew; ISAAC,[3] mar. Jemmia Smith; WILLIAM;[3] EMMELINE,[3] mar. David Waterbury; and RUFUS.[3]

HARVEY AVERY,[3] b. in South Salem Nov. 5, 1792, married Nancy Reynolds (1791-1879). They made their home on Old Post Rd., Cross River, and had: ELIZABETH;[4] RUTH;[4] POLLY ANN;[4] HARVEY WILLIAM;[4] and OLIVE.[4] HARVEY WILLIAM[4] married Caroline Reynolds, dau. of Gideon Reynolds of Cross River. Their children were NANCY ELIZABETH,[5] mar. Wilbur Hunt; GIDEON HARVEY;[5] JULIA,[5] mar. John C. Hull; ANNA TODD;[5] MARY JANE;[5] and CAROLINE OLIVE,[5] mar. Dr. William H. Stowe (1842-1915) of Cross River. GIDEON HARVEY[5] married in 1874 Marietta Holly, dau. of Jonah Holly (see Holly genealogy). They moved to the Holly homestead where Mr. Avery farmed the place. Their 3 children, MARY ALETTA;[6] HARVEY JONAH;[6] and HOLLY GIDEON,[6] attended Mt. Holly school and later, school in Katonah. HARVEY[6] ran an auto shop on Katonah Ave. until he retired to the homestead. HOLLY[6] has a bee business on the farm and is noted for his honey. He is active in the Farmers' Club.

Mrs. Douglas L. Barrett (MARGARET G. FOWLER[6]) is a descendant of RUFUS AVERY[3] (Julia Gorham;[5] Charlotte Avery;[4] Rufus;[3] William;[2] Enoch).[1] She resides on Harris Rd., Katonah, with her husband and daughter, MARGOT L. BARRETT.[7]

STEPHEN AVERY[2] (Enoch[1]), b. 1773 in Cross River, d. Mar. 31, 1848, married Nancy Benedict (1777-1849). They were parents of NOAH;[3]

ORREN;[3] NANCY;[3] HULDAH;[3] WOLSEY;[3] DAVID;[3] and LEWIS.[3] DAVID[3] married 1st Sally Heatherington and 2nd Mary Ann Seymour by whom he had: ELBERT,[4] a butcher in South Salem; CORNELIA,[4] mar. Marcus Knapp; JENNIE,[4] unmar.; and SARAH IDA,[4] mar. Leander Mead. SARAH[4] and Leander Mead had 3 children born in Cross River: CHARLES GRANT;[5] DAVID R.;[5] and IDELLA,[5] mar. Eugene Mead Hill. CHARLES G.,[5] a partner in Kellogg & Mead, a hardware store on The Parkway, married Emma Fisher (see Fisher genealogy). DAVID RUTHERFORD MEAD,[5] b. in Cross River Oct. 30, 1876, married Alsina Benedict (see Benedict genealogy).

Compiled by K. B. Kelly.

The Barrett Family

SAMUEL BARRETT,[1] of Wethersfield, Conn., settled at Vredeland, afterwards Westchester, Mar. 16, 1656. He married 1st Hannah Betts (1639-1686). They lived in Lower Yonkers and had one son, JOHN.[2] SAMUEL[1] married 2nd Leiah. He died before Dec. 28, 1691.

JOHN BARRETT[2] married Martha and they had 2 sons: SAMUEL;[3] and ABRAHAM.[3] JOHN,[2] collector of Lower Yonkers in 1713, died before Oct. 23, 1722.

ABRAHAM BARRETT[3] married Martha Holmes. They had 5 children: JOHN BARRETT,[4] their eldest, b. 1720, removed to the Manor of Cortlandt.

SAMUEL BARRETT[3] removed to Bedford in 1681, one of the first to join the original settlers. He married Jemima and they had: JOHN;[4] ABRAHAM;[4] SAMUEL;[4] JAMES;[4] JONATHAN;[4] JOSEPH;[4] ISAAC;[4] and MARY.[4] SAMUEL's[3] will was probated Sept. 13, 1759.

SAMUEL BARRETT[4] married Mary Moseman. Their 4 sons were born on Broad Brook Rd., Bedford. MARCUS[5] and REUBEN[5] moved to Carmel, Putnam County. JESSE[5] never married and SAMUEL[5] remained in the family home, which remained standing until it burned in 1914.

At 21 yrs., in February, 1776, SAMUEL BARRETT[5] enlisted as a private in the Westchester Militia under Capt. Hezekiah Gray, Col. Thomas's regiment. In 1777 SAMUEL[5] was under Capt. Marcus Moseman, his uncle. Capt. Hezekiah Gray was killed and his wife and 4 children managed a tavern across the road from SAMUEL's[5] house. In 1778 SAMUEL[5] married the widow Abigail (Waterbury) Gray (1743-1805), dau. of David and Mary (Sturges) Waterbury. They had 4 sons, all born in Bedford, 3 buried in Buxton Cemetery: JOSEPH;[6] FREDERICK;[6] JESSE,[6] d. at sea; and PHINEAS.[6] In October, 1832, SAMUEL[5] asked for and received his pension as acted upon by Congress June 7, 1832. He died Dec. 10, 1844, aged 89 yrs., 8 mos.

JOSEPH BARRETT[6] (1779-1863), a farmer, married Deborah St. John Dec. 24, 1799. He was very active in the Bedford Presbyterian Church. He died at 83 yrs., 6 mos. JOSEPH[6] and Deborah had 11 children: ASENETH;[7] JONATHAN SMITH;[7] ABIGAIL;[7] ELOISE;[7] MOSES ST. JOHN;[7] JESSE;[7] RUFUS KING;[7] ANNA;[7] EMILY;[7] CLARISSA;[7] and PHEBE.[7]

FREDERICK BARRETT[6] (1781-1856) married Polly St. John, sister of Deborah. They lived on the Bedford-Pound Ridge road and had 8 children.

Sons, HIRAM[7] and HARVEY,[7] were local farmers. HERBERT ST. JOHN BAR-
RETT[9] (1875-1933) (Frederick,[8] Hiram,[7] Frederick,[6] Samuel,[5] Samuel,[4]
Samuel,[3] John,[2] Samuel[1]) owned and lived in the homestead. He was
killed by a hit-and-run driver in front of Bedford Court House Dec. 22,
1933. His widow and only child, SHIRLEY ST. JOHN BARRETT,[10] sold the
farm. SHIRLEY[10] is now MRS. ERNEST FREDERICK KRUG, JR.,[10] and lives in
New York City.

FREDERICK IRVING STARBUCK,[10] head of Young and Halstead in Mt.
Kisco, is a grandson of JOSEPH BARRETT MOGER,[8] who in turn was a grandson of FREDERICK[6] (1781-1856).

PHINEAS BARRETT[6] (1787-1857) married Sally Palmer and had sons:
SAMUEL;[7] STEPHEN;[7] GEORGE WASHINGTON;[7] BENJAMIN FRANKLIN;[7] SAM-
UEL H.;[7] and ISAAC NEWTON;[7] and 5 DAUGHTERS.[7] They owned a large
farm on Hook Rd. and helped lay out and build Girdle Ridge Rd. in
1852, connecting their farm and Cantitoe Corners. Their homestead is now
owned by A. Ross Jones.

GEORGE WASHINGTON BARRETT[7] left Bedford in 1835 for New York City.
He was very active in the antislavery movement. He was one of ten to
organize the New York Republican Club and was a great admirer of
Horace Greeley. He is buried in Buxton Cemetery, Bedford. One of his
sons, GEORGE PHINEAS,[8] was a banker and his great-grandson, OSCAR R.
BARRETT, JR.,[10] is an insurance broker in New York City and a resident
of Bronxville. OSCAR[10] is very interested in Bedford and its history and
is a member of the Founders of the Patriots, Sons of the Revolution, and
the Bedford Historical Society. He has two grandsons who carry on the
family names, JOHN[12] and SAMUEL BARRETT,[12] and a granddaughter, ABI-
GAIL BARRETT BOWER.[12]

BENJAMIN FRANKLIN BARRETT[7] (1831-1907) married Sarah Shove, dau.
of Dr. Seth Shove of Cherry St. After their marriage they lived in their
home on Cherry St., now owned by John Rogge. She taught school and
they had one son, SETH BARRETT,[8] who was a wonder on electrical and
telegraph equipment.

MOSES ST. JOHN BARRETT[7] (1809-1865) married 1st Elizabeth Mary
Edwards Nexsen in the Presbyterian Church in Bedford Village May 11,
1835. They had: ELIAS;[8] ELIZABETH;[8] and JOSEPH.[8] MOSES[7] married 2nd
Sarah Newell from Ossining and they had: HARVEY;[8] GEORGE;[8] MOSES;[8]
and EDWARD NEWELL.[8] EDWARD,[8] a graduate of Lafayette College in
Easton, Pa., wrote for a New York paper, and farmed as a hobby. He
married Elizabeth K. Hunt, dau. of Charles A. Hunt of Katonah (see
Hunt genealogy). No children.

JOSEPH BARRETT[8] (1840-1910) attended Bedford Academy and graduated from Lafayette College in 1861. Feb. 13, 1867, he married Emma
Robertson, dau. of Henry and Huldah (Fanton) Robertson, in the Baptist
Church, Bedford Center. They lived at Cantitoe in the Robertson homestead. He was a farmer, school commissioner, supervisor of the Town
of Bedford, and cashier of the New York Custom House. From Cantitoe
they moved to Cross River Rd. and Rte. 22, and when the City took
this property, they built in 1898 a new house on Edgemont Rd., now
owned by the Presbyterian Church. He was a student of local history and
wrote chapters on Bedford, New Castle and North Castle for Scharf's
History of Westchester County, 1886. He was interested in the Village

Improvement Society, Choral Club, Farmers' Club, and was treasurer of the Women's Reformatory. He was superintendent of the Presbyterian Sunday School for many years, elder for 31 years, and attended the General Assembly in Portland, Ore., representing our local church. He was deliberate, thoughtful, kind, and his judgment was most accurate. Mrs. Barrett acquired her political interests early from her supervisor father and the successful career of her brother, Judge William H. Robertson. She had a deep interest in all local people, faith in the joy of living, and her influence was great. She died in her Katonah home at 92 yrs. Nov. 16, 1933. Children of JOSEPH[8] and Emma Barrett were: ELIZABETH NEXSEN;[9] HENRY R.;[9] WILLIAM G.;[9] EDWARD P.;[9] and ROBERTSON T.[9]

ELIZABETH NEXSEN BARRETT[9] attended school at Cantitoe and Bedford Academy and was a graduate of Blair Academy in Blairstown, N.J. She spent her life in Katonah, living for others, with humility and unselfishness, working untiringly for a better community and world. She was a brilliant writer and noted pen acquaintance. She had great interest in the Presbyterian Church and foreign missions. She taught Sunday School until she was 85. She held many offices in the District Nursing Association, was president of the Village Improvement Society, helping to build the new library, and was active in the Red Cross. She did enough personal welfare work to be remembered for many generations and was always the first to welcome a new family into the village with a plate of cookies. She had great force and warmth and gave encouragement to all. She died on her 91st birthday, Nov. 17, 1958.

HENRY R. BARRETT[9] (1869-1940), educated at the Cantitoe school, Bedford Academy, Blair Academy, and Lafayette College, was admitted to the bar in 1892 and joined the law office of his uncle, William H. Robertson. He was a power in Republican politics in Westchester County for almost 50 years. Among offices held in White Plains were: director of the Citizens Bank, president of the Publishing Company of the *Daily Reporter,* counsel for 20 years to the sheriff of Westchester County, and president of the Chamber of Commerce. He was a member of the Delta Kappa Epsilon Club, Elks Club, Westchester Hills Golf Club, and Sons of the American Revolution. He lived in Katonah for the first 30 years of his life and then in White Plains for 40 years as one of its leading citizens. In December, 1900, he married Anna Parker. Their children were: HENRY R., JR.;[10] EMILY;[10] DONALD;[10] IONE;[10] and DOROTHYANNA.[10] After his wife's death in 1914, the children came to their grandmother's home and grew up in Katonah. He married 2nd in 1925 Mrs. Elizabeth Endriss.

HENRY ROBERTSON BARRETT, JR.,[10] a White Plains lawyer, married Lillian E. Daniel in 1929. Children were: HENRY ROBERTSON BARRETT, III,[11] b. 1931, also a lawyer in White Plains; and JEAN ELIZABETH,[11] who mar. John B. Dolan and has children, SUZANNE ELIZABETH,[12] b. 1956, CATHERINE ANN,[12] b. 1958, CAROLYN LOUISE,[12] b. 1959, and JOHN PETER,[12] b. 1960.

EMILY EUNICE BARRETT[10] married Elmer Jamison Gray. They live in Detroit. Their dau., ELIZABETH ROBERTSON GRAY,[11] married Robert Dean Allison. Their son is ROBERT GRAY ALLISON,[12] b. 1959.

DONALD P. BARRETT,[10] unmar., lives in White Plains. His twin, IONE P. BARRETT,[10] known as "Jill," has law offices on Katonah Ave., Katonah.

DOROTHYANNA BARRETT[10] married Edwin Kellogg Bertine (1897-1960). Their children are: JOAN BARRETT BERTINE,[11] who mar. Roy Edwin

Olson II and has children, SANDRA LEE,[12] b. 1959, and CHERYL ANN OLSON,[12] b. 1960; and PETER EDWIN BERTINE,[11] a lieutenant, J.G., in the U. S. Navy stationed in Hawaii.

WILLIAM G. BARRETT[9] (1873-1933) lived in Katonah until World War I. He married in Old Katonah in 1897 Ella Maude Williams, dau. of James H. and Elizabeth Miller Williams. Their 6 children were: MARGARET;[10] JOSEPH;[10] MARIAM;[10] JAMES;[10] WILLIAM;[10] and ELIZABETH.[10] All were born in Katonah. He was elected school commissioner in 1899 and register of Westchester County in 1901, and was interested in the Y.M.C.A. and Lions Club in White Plains.

MARGARET BARRETT[10] married 1922 David Field Griffen. They made their home in Katonah 1947-1958. Their only child, MARGARET NEXSEN GRIFFEN,[11] b. 1932, lives in New York City.

JOSEPH WILLIAM BARRETT[10] (1899-1956) married Gladys Stocum of Bedford Hills, who makes her home in Miami, Fla. Their sons are: RICHARD WILLIAM,[11] who lives in Washington, D.C., with wife Shirley C. Patterson and sons, CHRISTOPHER JOSEPH,[12] b. 1949, PATTERSON HALL,[12] b. 1953, and ROBERT WILLIAM,[12] b. 1958; and PHILIP GERARD,[11] a paratrooper in World War II, who is married to Joyce A. Christian, and has dau. BEVERLY JOY,[12] b. 1948. They live in Bedford Hills and he is in the advertising business in New York City.

MARIAM BARRETT[10] married Paul William Miller, an insurance broker. They make their home in Rye, N.Y. Their only child, DONALD BARRETT MILLER,[11] married in 1959 Joan Marie Griffen and is associated with the American Felt Co., Glenville, Conn. They live in Port Chester, N.Y.

JAMES HENRY BARRETT,[10] mar. Katharine Brown, lives in N.Y. City. Their daughters are: LINDA JEAN,[11] an actress; and KATE ROSS,[11] who is teaching in England.

WILLIAM HURD BARRETT[10] was with the 11th Airborne in World War II. He married Mary Grace Filkins, a former French teacher in Katonah High School. They live in Newark, N.Y.

RACHEL ELIZABETH BARRETT[10] makes her home in Greenwich Village in New York City.

EDWARD PERCY BARRETT,[9] b. at Cantitoe June 25, 1875, received his early education in our local schools. Admitted to the bar in 1900, he joined the Robertson & Barrett law firm, later known as Barrett & Buckbee. In 1916 he opened his own law offices in Katonah and still is active. He was supervisor of the Town of Bedford for 45 yrs., retiring at 78. He was a leader of the Bedford Republican Party, resigning in 1959. He was an old-fashioned down-to-earth farmer. In World War I he raised enough food to run a canning factory on his farm on Cherry St. He still keeps and cultivates his own garden on Huntville Rd. He has helped and operated a number of side businesses, among them: a woodworking mill in White Plains; a gas-producing electric plant on Katonah Ave.; the electric plant on Bedford Rd.; Country Service Store; Northern Westchester Electric Co.; and Sports Store. He has fine local Indian relic and mineral collections. He worked on the Building Committee of the Katonah Village Library, and was a moving spirit in the Katonah Memorial Park Association. Mr. Barrett is known as the dean of the County Republican politicians. In November, 1901, he married Estelle A. Travis, daughter of

Byron and Margery Putney Travis. They built a home at 27 Bedford Rd., where their children, DOUGLAS LANGLEY,[10] b. 1902, and EMMA ROBERTSON BARRETT[10] (1906-1907) were born. In 1907 they built at 51 Bedford Rd. Here KATHARINE ELIZABETH BARRETT[10] was born. A son, EDWARD P. BARRETT, JR.[10] (1915-1915), was born at the farm on Cherry St. Mr. and Mrs. Barrett now reside on Oak Hill, having celebrated their 58th anniversary. DOUGLAS L. BARRETT,[10] Supervisor of the Town of Bedford, his wife, Margaret G. Fowler, and daughter, MARGOT LOUISE BARRETT,[11] live on Harris Rd. KATHARINE E. BARRETT[10] married William A. Kelly, a building contractor, and they live on Oak Hill with children: DAVID AUSTIN,[11] b. June 24, 1938, and KAREN ELIZABETH KELLY,[11] b. Aug. 15, 1944. Their son, EDWARD WILLIAM KELLY,[11] b. Aug. 27, 1935, married Madelyn Sue Weisenbarger of Lima, Ohio, June 26, 1960. They make their home in Pound Ridge.

ROBERTSON T. BARRETT,[9] b. at Cantitoe, attended local schools, Blair Academy, and Lafayette College. He was admitted to the bar in 1909. After a sample of law with his brothers, he turned to writing. He was editor of the *Yonkers Daily News,* then joined American Telephone & Telegraph Co. in 1921 until his retiring age. In 1913 he married Mabel Backus and they had: WALDO,[10] d.y.; LAURENCE;[10] ROBERTSON T., JR.;[10] and ADELAIDE.[10] Mrs. Barrett died in 1943. He remarried in 1944 Frances J. Weber. After his retirement they ran the *Katonah Record* for a time. Mr. Barrett wrote a book to commemorate the 275th year of the Town of Bedford in 1955. He has devoted his time to the Fire Department, Presbyterian Church, Village Improvement Society, and the Westchester County Historical Society. He was president of the Bedford Historical Society and historian of the Town of Bedford. LAURENCE NEXSEN[10] is head of the English Department and dean of curricula at Kalamazoo College, Kalamazoo, Michigan, where he lives with his wife, Ruth C. De Yoe, and children TIMOTHY DE YOE,[11] b. 1950; LAURENCE MICHAEL,[11] b. 1953; and BARBARA CHASE BARRETT.[11] ROBERTSON T. BARRETT, JR.,[10] is an air captain with a Texas company. He married Margaret Sloat, daughter of Clifford H. and D. Barbara Schultz Sloat of Katonah. Their children are: MARTHA ELIZABETH,[11] b. 1942; ROBERTSON SLOAT,[11] b. 1943; JOHN DAVID,[11] b. 1945; and BRUCE EDWARD,[11] b. 1948. ADELAIDE E.[10] is married to Dr. Geoffrey A. Corson of Dauphin, Pa. They have: ALAN BARRETT,[11] b. 1952; LINDA BELL,[11] b. 1954; BARBARA ELIZABETH,[11] b. 1956; and MARGARET ANNE CORSON,[11] b. 1958.

Compiled by K. B. Kelly.

The Benedict Family

THOMAS BENEDICT,[1] b. 1617 in Nottinghamshire, sailed from England in 1638. He settled first in the Massachusetts Bay Colony where he married Mary Bridgum. In 1640 the couple moved to Southold, L. I., thence to Jamaica, and in 1665 to Norwalk, Conn. In 1684 Thomas helped "plant" the town of Danbury. There were 5 sons and 4 daughters. The girls mar-

370

A HISTORY OF KATONAH

ried into the Olmsted, Slawson, Beebe and Wood families. Until the 7th generation, the line of THOMAS BENEDICT[2] (through whom one branch of our local Benedicts descends) lived in Norwalk and New Canaan.

SAMUEL BENEDICT[7] (Joseph,[6] Samuel,[5] Samuel,[4] Thomas,[3] Thomas,[2] Thomas[1]), b. Dec. 25, 1794, and his wife, Harriet Town, came to make their home in Whitlockville. All their children were born there: JOSEPH[8] in 1828; ELIZABETH[8] in 1829; and twins, MOSES SMITH[8] and AARON[8] in 1832.

JOSEPH BENEDICT[8] (1828-1896) lived on the Dowburg Rd., east of Whitlockville. He married Mary E. Goldey. Children were: CHARLES S.,[9] b. 1856; JULIA A.,[9] b. 1858; JOSEPH G.[9] (1860-1868); HARRIET G.,[9] b. 1869, who mar. Walter S. Flint and had children, MARION,[10] b. 1896, and LAURENCE BENEDICT FLINT,[10] b. 1901; and JOSEPHINE,[9] b. 1878. CHARLES SUMNER BENEDICT[9] was a noted doctor in New Rochelle. He married Hannah A. Leaycraft. They had: HELEN S.[10] (1888-1903); SUMNER L.,[10] b. 1889; and DOROTHY H.,[10] b. 1898. The old Joseph Benedict home was moved and is now the home of the Catholic priests on Valley Road.

AARON BENEDICT[8] (1832-1862) married Eliza Worden and raised his son and 3 daughters in Bedford and High Ridge, Conn. He was killed in the Civil War.

MOSES SMITH BENEDICT[8] (1832-1897), called Smith, stayed in Whitlockville, living on the Dowburg Rd. next to JOSEPH.[8] He married Julia, dau. of John Burr and Rachel Whitlock, and they had 3 sons and 3 daughters: ADA,[9] b. 1855, drowned in 1862; ELIZABETH[9] (1859-1884); and JULIA AUGUSTA[9] (1866-1949), unmar.; EVERETT[9] (1854-1911), mar. Susie Chichester, no children; DEWITT CLINTON,[9] b. 1863; and CRESWELL,[9] b. 1869, who mar. Elizabeth S. and ran the Benedict store in Mt. Kisco until his death in 1920. MOSES SMITH[8] had a jewelry store in Whitlockville Station in 1858. He advertised watches, clocks, gold chains, lockets, rings, spectacles, pens, silver, thermometers, brushes, note paper, fishing tackle, clock repairs, powder flasks, game bags, melodeons & accordions tuned, music books, soap, perfumery and bachelor's hair dye. He was appointed postmaster in 1861 by President Lincoln, a position he held until 1873. He died in 1897. His old home was moved and is now on the corner of Katonah Ave. and Edgemont Rd. belonging to William Doyle.

DEWITT CLINTON BENEDICT,[9] b. July 13, 1863, spent his life in Whitlockville and Katonah. He helped survey for the Cross River Reservoir and carried on his father's store. He was a member of the Fire Department and on the School Board, a trustee of the Methodist Episcopal Church and its treasurer for 17 years, on the Board of Directors of the Northern Westchester Bank and active in the Village Improvement Society. He married Grace Dale Smith, dau. of Emmett Smith of Banksville. Their children were: CAROLYN JULIA,[10] b. 1900; CLINTON SMITH,[10] b. 1901; CLARENCE WHITLOCK,[10] b. 1903; WALTER EMMETT,[10] b. 1904; GERTRUDE,[10] b. 1907; and DONALD BANKS,[10] b. 1910. All were born and raised in New Katonah and lived years in the house now belonging to Dr. Edward J. Gallagher. DEWITT[9] died in February, 1932. Mrs. Benedict carried on the store with the help of her children until her death in 1937, after which it was sold to Charles Raneri. The Benedict store served the community for over 100 years.

CAROLYN JULIA BENEDICT,[10] graduate of Arnold College, married Melvin Darke Engle in 1923. Their daughter, ELIZABETH BENEDICT ENGLE,[11] b. in Winthrop, Mass., is married to William R. S. Kennedy, Jr. CAROL BENEDICT KENNEDY,[12] b. Jan. 26, 1959, is their only child. Mr. and Mrs. Engle live in Allentown, Pa.

CLINTON SMITH BENEDICT,[10] a civil engineer, graduate of Rensselaer Polytechnic Institute, worked on the Delaware Aqueduct. Part of the time he was assigned to Shaft 13, just west of Cross River Dam, thus working near the same spot where his father had surveyed nearly 50 years previously. He has been interested in the Skating Club, Tennis Club, Boy Scouts and Lions Club. He was treasurer of the Methodist Church for 8 years and chairman of the Building Committee of the Parish House. He is well known in the engineering field and connected with the Federal Aviation Agency. He lives on High St., Katonah, with his wife, Lois Trimble, a former teacher and a successful writer in many fields, whom he married in October, 1928. Their son, CLINTON SMITH, JR.,[11] b. Nov. 20, 1929, graduated from Katonah High School in 1947. He joined the Air Force in 1950 and married Peggy McCuistion Nov. 8, 1953. Their children are: BARBARA LOIS,[12] b. Aug. 23, 1954; STEVEN RUSSELL,[12] b. June 15, 1956; KATHRYN,[12] b. Dec. 6, 1958; and WILLIAM WARREN,[12] b. Feb. 5, 1960. CLINTON S., JR.,[11] is a technical representative for the General Electric Co., working from the laboratory in Ithaca, N.Y.

CLARENCE WHITLOCK BENEDICT,[10] known as "Gus," a chemical engineer, graduate of R. P. I., was an outstanding athlete in our local schools, at college, and in town sports. He married Edna Bohren Nov. 28, 1934, and lives on Quarter-Mile Rd., Armonk. Gus is president of the Electro-Plating Service, Inc., in White Plains. He belongs to the Whippoorwill and Winged Foot Golf Clubs and is vice-president of the U.S. Golf Association. He and Edna have sons: BRUCE WHITLOCK,[11] b. 1937; and STUART EDWARD,[11] b. 1940. Bruce graduated June 5, 1960, from St. Lawrence, a versatile athlete, member of the varsity football team and named Williamson Little All-American. Stu was named all-county football guard from Pleasantville High School and was one of the top junior golfers in the county. He attends Colgate University.

WALTER EMMET BENEDICT[10] married Mary Elizabeth Gore Nov. 12, 1942, and they have one daughter, MARY GORE,[11] b. July 14, 1943. A mechanical engineer, graduate of R. P. I. with a master's degree, WALTER E.[10] lives with his family in Newton, Pa., and is superintendent of the Trenton plant of Congoleum Nairn.

GERTRUDE BENEDICT,[10] a graduate of Drew Seminary, lives in Stamford, Conn. She still has interests in Katonah, and owns the house at 99 Edgemont Rd. occupied by the Lawrence Kurutz family.

DONALD BANKS BENEDICT[10] is a graduate of the University of Michigan, with degrees of B.S. and M.S. in chemical engineering. He is vice-president of Union Carbide Corporation and has charge of its 5 chemical and plastic divisions. He married Winifred Thornhill and they live in Chappaqua. Their children, all born in Charleston, W.Va., are: DAVID BANKS,[11] b. 1939, grad. Horace Greeley, now at Lehigh University and on the varsity basketball team; ROBERT THORNHILL,[11] b. 1941, grad. Horace Greeley and on their varsity basketball team, now at Stevens Institute of

Technology; JANE ELLEN,[11] b. 1944, now at Emma Willard School; and HELEN ELIZABETH,[11] b. 1946, now at Horace Greeley.

* * * * *

JOHN BENEDICT,[2] son of THOMAS,[1] married Phebe Gregory and they had 9 children. Son, JOSEPH,[3] moved to Ridgefield, Conn. JOSEPH'S[3] son, JOSEPH,[4] b. in Norwalk, 1708, moved from Ridgefield to South Salem, settling near the village of Cross River. He was a justice of the peace. He had 3 wives and 23 children; however, most of them died young. LEWIS BENEDICT[5] (1754-1827), son of JOSEPH[4] and Lydia, married Jemima Newman and they had 9 children. He served in Delevan's dragoons.

LEWIS BENEDICT[6] (1791-1855), son of LEWIS,[5] had a son, JEREMIAH BENEDICT,[7] b. 1821, who made his home in Banksville. JEREMIAH[7] had sons: LEWIS C.[8] (1856-1864); ARTHUR PALMER,[8] b. 1858; and WILLIAM E.,[8] b. 1868. ARTHUR P.[8] and WILLIAM E.[8] bought homes at 38 and 40 The Terrace. ARTHUR P. BENEDICT[8] married Ida Mead and they came to Katonah with their children: MARY ALMIRA;[9] LEWIS ARTHUR;[9] and ANNA LOUISE.[9] MARY ALMIRA[9] married Wilfred Gerlach of Port Chester. ANNA LOUISE,[9] very active in the Presbyterian Church, married Henry Austin of Mahopac Falls, who died in 1958. They had no chilrdren.

LEWIS ARTHUR BENEDICT[9] makes his home at 26 Hillside Ave. He is a retired banker, having been with the Fifth Avenue Bank of New York. He is treasurer of the building fund for the Presbyterian Parish House. LEWIS ARTHUR[9] has one daughter, GLADYS MAY,[10] by his 1st wife, May Kennedy, daughter of Charles and Castella (Totten) Kennedy of Katonah. GLADYS MAY[10] married Irving Helms of Katonah and has 2 daughters: ANN BENEDICT,[11] b. 1944; and JANICE LYNN HELMS,[11] b. 1952. Mrs. Helms is a kindergarten teacher in the Katonah Elementary School and lives on Croton Lake Rd. with her daughters. LEWIS A. BENEDICT'S[9] 2nd wife was Harriet Eudora Russell, also a direct descendant from THOMAS BENEDICT.[1] She was born in South Salem, dau. of Marianna Webster and John Russell and granddaughter of HARRIET BENEDICT WEBSTER[8] (Jesse,[7] Solomon,[6] Solomon,[5] Amos,[4] Benjamin,[3] John,[2] Thomas Benedict[1]). Graduating from Katonah High School and Oneonta Normal School, she taught in Hillsdale and Briarcliff but made her home in Katonah with her mother. She and LEWIS A. BENEDICT[9] built their home at 26 Hillside Ave. She was very active in the Presbyterian Church and held various offices of importance. She died in 1954. After her death, Mr. Benedict married 3rd Mrs. Jessie Cornwall, former librarian of Katonah.

WILLIAM E. BENEDICT,[8] son of JEREMIAH,[7] b. in Banksville, came with his wife Susan Howard and son HOWARD[9] to Katonah in the early 1900's. HOWARD[9] married and made his home in Hawthorne where he died leaving one married daughter, SHIRLEY.[10]

NANCY BENEDICT,[6] daughter of LEWIS[5] and Jemima, married Stephen Avery. Their son was DAVID AVERY.[7] DAVID'S[7] daughter, IDA AVERY,[8] married Leander Mead (see Avery genealogy). Their sons, CHARLES G.[9] and DAVID R. MEAD,[9] both lived in Katonah. CHARLES G. MEAD[9] married Emma Fisher (see Fisher genealogy).

DAVID R. MEAD,[9] a building contractor, married ALSINA EUDORA BENEDICT[9] (LeRoy,[8] Jesse,[7] Solomon,[6] Solomon,[5] Amos,[4] Benjamin,[3] John,[2] Thomas Benedict[1]). Mrs. Mead's parents lived between Ridgefield and South Salem and she attended the Conservatory of Music in Danbury. The DAVID MEADS[9] were parents of two daughters: BERTHA EUDORA;[10] and IDA AVERY.[10] Mr. Mead died in 1954. Mrs. Mead lives on Terrace Heights in the last home he built.

BERTHA EUDORA MEAD,[10] b. at 37 Hillside Ave., grew up in Katonah, graduating from high school in 1922. After a summer course at Columbia College, she entered the New York Training School for Teachers, preparing for the New York City school system. Upon graduating, she was given a tenure of office which she held through 35 yrs. of teaching, retiring in 1959. She married 1st Arthur Saxton and, after his death in 1955, married 2nd Oscar Damm. They live in Pelham and she has no children.

IDA AVERY MEAD,[10] b. on her grandmother's farm in Ridgefield, Conn., moved into the Mead's new home at 69 Valley Rd. in November, 1907. She graduated from Katonah High School in 1926 and from New Paltz Teacher's College in 1929. She married John Lee Dorsett of Atlanta, Ga., in August, 1931. He is a partner in Clark Associates and they live at 35 Huntville Rd. Their only child, JOHN DAVID DORSETT,[11] married in 1958 Mary Elizabeth Egan, dau. of George and Mary (Leonard) Egan of Lincolndale. He joined his father in the funeral business. They have a son, GEORGE LEE DORSETT,[12] b. Mar. 9, 1960.

* * * * *

CLAIRVILLE EZRA BENEDICT, born 1864, descendant of JOHN BENEDICT,[2] married Mrs. Adelaide Jordan, daughter of Rev. Horace W. Bolton. She was a professional singer and he an engineer. They lived in the stone house on Rte. 100 north of Somers.

* * * * *

MRS. CHARLES M. ALLEN (Madeleine Purdy), of 50 The Terrace, is a descendant of the Benedicts through Thomas,[1] James,[2] Thomas,[3] Thaddeus,[4] Peter,[5] Eli Star,[6] Rev. Victor W. Benedict,[7] a Baptist minister in Danbury, whose daughter, Ella Frances Benedict,[8] married Fred A. Purdy. Mrs. Allen has no children and has made her home in Katonah since her marriage. She attended school in Katonah graduating from our High School (see Allen genealogy).

Compiled by Lois T. Benedict and K. B. Kelly.

The Birdsall Family

Members of the Birdsall family lived in Peekskill, N.Y., as early as 1735, when Daniel was born there. TIMOTHY BIRDSALL[1] was born in Peekskill. He and Abigail Birdsall were the first to settle in the Town of Bedford. Abigail married John Banks and is buried in Buckbee graveyard, off Harris Rd. TIMOTHY[1] married Esther Haight, dau. of David and Elizabeth (Wetmore) Haight of Bedford (see Haight genealogy). After Esther's early death, Mar. 26, 1807, Timothy moved back to Peekskill and later to Michigan where he died. Their only child was JAMES HAIGHT BIRDSALL.[2]

JAMES HAIGHT BIRDSALL,[2] b. Jan. 14, 1807, was left with his grandparents, Mrs. & Mrs. David Haight, and grew up on that part of Cherry St. now known as Harris Rd. He married in South Salem Sept. 23, 1829, Sarah Wood Loder (1810-1896), dau. of Jared and Nancy (Green) Loder of Cross River. JAMES[2] became associated with his brothers-in-law, Loder Brothers, noted dry goods merchants, and he and Sarah moved into New York City where all the children but the youngest were born. In 1854, he bought his home, "Terrace Hill," on Harris Rd. and shortly thereafter moved back to Katonah. The property, part of the present grounds of Bailey Hall, extended from Harris Rd. north to the present village. The house had been built by Nicholas Haight in 1845. The twelve children of JAMES[2] and Sarah Birdsall were: STEPHEN BUXTON[3] (1830-1831); BENJAMIN LODER[3] (1832-1834); ELIZABETH JANE,[3] b. 1833; CATHERINE ANN[3] (1835-1835); twins AURELIA[3] (1836-1841) and CORNELIA[3] (1836-1836); POLLY ANN AMANDA,[3] b. 1838; SARAH AURELIA,[3] b. 1842; OLIVER HOLBROOK[3] (1843-1846); CYRUS LODER,[3] b. 1846; JEREMIAH[3] (1849-1849); and LOUISE WARNER,[3] b. 1856. The family attended St. Matthew's Church, where James was a warden 1862-1886. JAMES[2] and Sarah are buried there as are their 12 children.

CYRUS LODER BIRDSALL[3] (1846-1915), unmar., was a florist for over 40 years. His greenhouses were at his home, Terrace Hill, and he was well known by all in that area. He was a gentle, kindly man, a great reader and a lover of music. In 1879, he became owner of 30 acres of the Birdsall property when it was deeded to him, and the remaining 3 acres in 1894. In his later years, he lived there with his sisters, Sarah and Louise. He died July 7, 1915, in Katonah.

SARAH AURELIA BIRDSALL,[3] b. June 16, 1842, never married. She died in Katonah at the family home in September 1901.

LOUISE WARNER BIRDSALL,[3] after the death of the other members of her family moved from the big house to her cottage on the three acres of land deeded her in 1895, which lay on Cherry St. and both sides of Bedford Rd., through which Muddy Brook ran. She lived there until her death Jan. 10, 1937. This property was taken by the Parkway. The homestead was sold to Dr. Fried of Bailey Hall, who had the house, barn and outbuildings torn down.

POLLY ANN AMANDA BIRDSALL,[3] b. Aug. 2, 1838, married Andrew Colvin and they made their home in Mt. Vernon, N.Y., where their 3 children were born: HELEN;[4] ARTHUR;[4] and FLORA McDONALD COLVIN.[4] POLLY[3] died Mar. 9, 1913, and is buried in St. Matthew's.

ELIZABETH JANE BIRDSALL,[3] b. Sept. 30, 1833, married James Benezett Warner (1823-1901) Sept. 23, 1850. She died June 29, 1925. They were parents of 3 children: ALICE;[4] WILLIAM SMITH;[4] and WILFRED HAIGHT WARNER.[4]

ALICE WARNER[4] (1852-1929) married William Steel Beckley (1850-1926). They were parents of: LEONARD WARNER[5] (1877-1945); WILLIAM STEEL, JR.[5] (1881-1950); and ALICE BECKLEY,[5] b. 1883.

LEONARD WARNER BECKLEY[5] was the organist at St. Matthew's Church from 1923 to 1945. He married Marion Beatty Crawford and had children: ADELE CRAWFORD,[6] b. 1906; and LEONARD CURRY,[6] b. 1913. ADELE BECKLEY[6] married 1st Charles Hoffman and 2nd John Wetzel. She had two daughters: JOAN MARION HOFFMAN,[7] b. 1928; and LUTITIA JANE

WETZEL,[7] b. 1936. LEONARD CURRY BECKLEY[6] married Vera Forrest McCarthy.

WILLIAM STEEL BECKLEY, JR.,[5] married Edythe May Bostwick (1882-1958). Their son, WILLIAM STEEL BECKLEY, III,[6] married Marguerite Ridge and has a daughter NANCY ELLEN BECKLEY,[7] b. 1942.

ALICE BECKLEY[5] married Theodore A. Taylor, Jr. (1883-1931). Their children are: ALICE,[6] b. 1919, mar. Gifford Appleby Acker; MARJORIE BECKLEY,[6] b. 1923, mar. James Harold Keeler, Jr.; and THEODORE AUGUSTUS TAYLOR, III,[6] b. 1925, mar. Bertha Alene Waith. Mr. & Mrs. Acker live in Hawthorne, N.Y., and have children: BARBARA ALICE,[7] b. June 11, 1951; GIFFORD A., JR.,[7] b. Oct. 29, 1953; CYNTHIA ANN ACKER,[7] b. Aug. 17, 1955. The Keelers live in Rowley, Mass., and have children: JAMES HAROLD, III,[7] b. December 16, 1948; KATHRYN ANN,[7] b. Oct. 1, 1951; RICHARD BECKLEY,[7] b. May 30, 1953; and DAVID ALAN KEELER,[7] b. Feb. 19, 1956. Mr. & Mrs. Taylor live in Rochester, N.Y., and have children: GARRY EDWARD,[7] b. Jan. 1, 1950; MARCIA ALENE,[7] b. Apr. 27, 1951; and DEBORAH ALICE TAYLOR,[7] b. June 10, 1952.

WILLIAM SMITH WARNER,[4] b. 1854, married Leonora Emily Beckley. Their only child, EMILY WARNER,[5] married Kenneth J. Boedecker. Their son, KENNETH J. BOEDECKER, JR.,[6] b. 1927, married Margaret Gardner. Their children: KENNETH J., III;[7] and CHARLES GARDNER BOEDECKER.[7]

WILFRED HAIGHT WARNER[4] (1872-1930) married Thelma Lord Hall, b. 1874.

Compiled by Alice Beckley Taylor (Mrs. Theodore Taylor), Warehouse Lane, Rowley, Mass.

The Brundage Family

The Brundage family is an old one in the Townships of Bedford and North Castle, settling many years ago in the Chestnut Ridge area. SOLOMON BRUNDAGE[1] is mentioned on the Bedford highway assessment list of 1833 as of there, and his name and that of his wife, Esther, appear on a mortgage of 1831, owners of property in Bedford on Chestnut Ridge.

JAMES FOUNTAIN BRUNDAGE[2] (1819-1900), son of Solomon and Esther, was a farmer. He lived on Prospect Hill, Chestnut Ridge, now part of the Arthur Butler property. He married Sally Ann Daniels (1822-1896) and they had 4 daughters: MARY E.,[3] HELEN ELIDA,[3] ESTHER E.,[3] ANNIE M.;[3] and 4 sons: WILLIAM H.,[3] ROBERT J.,[3] HERMAN B.,[3] and LEEMON R.[3] JAMES F.[2] died at the home of his daughter, Mrs. Charles Keeler of Norwalk, Conn., in 1900 and is buried in Middle Patent Cemetery, North Castle.

LEEMON R. BRUNDAGE,[3] b. 1840 on his father's Chestnut Ridge farm, married Mary Cornelia Sarles, dau. of Stephen and Esther Sarles of Taylor's Corners, Bedford Village. They moved to Old Katonah about 1869 where he was a maker of shoes for S. O. Arnold until shoes began to be manufactured in volume by machinery. He then was school tax collector and took charge of the pumping station in New Katonah. Mr. and Mrs. Brundage belonged to the Methodist Church, where he was a trustee and sexton for 12 yrs. He died in October, 1902, leaving his wife and one son, LEEMON MERRITT.[4] He is buried in Oakwood Cemetery, Mt. Kisco.

LEEMON MERRITT BRUNDAGE,[4] b. at Taylor's Corners, Bedford, married Anne Agnew Barclay, dau. of Henry Barclay of New York City and sister of Mrs. Lewis Miller. LEEMON M.[4] was bookkeeper for Hoyt Brothers and manager of the Katonah Silk Mill until he moved to Denver, Colo. Later he returned east and settled in Norwalk, Conn., where he worked for Vanderhoef Bros., hat manufacturers. He was partner in the Mutual Hat Company and mayor of Norwalk when he died in 1911. His wife had died in Norwalk Jan. 15, 1902, leaving her husband and one son, JAMES HOYT.[5]

JAMES HOYT BRUNDAGE,[5] b. Apr. 22, 1892, in Denver, married Hildred Scofield. They had one son, MERRITT LEE BRUNDAGE,[6] who was educated in our Katonah school and died unmarried. Mr. and Mrs. Brundage live on Greenville Rd., Katonah, in the house built by his grandfather in 1874 south of old Katonah and moved west to its present location.

Compiled by F. R. Duncombe.

The Buckbees of Cherry Street

ELIJAH BUCKBEE[4] (John,[3] John,[2] Richard[1]), son of JOHN[3] & Abigail (Hunt) Buckbee, was one of the earliest and perhaps the first settler in our south Cherry St. area of Bedford Township. In 1750 he bought 50 acres of land "laid out to John Holmes in the last Division" and another 55-acre lot "East Northerly of said parcel of land afore mentioned and a highway, North Westerly by the Indian Line." For this property, which included the land now owned by Douglas L. Barrett, he paid 738 pounds. ELIJAH[4] was described in the deed as "of Courtlandt's Manor." ELIJAH,[4] b. 1717, married Abigail Vail (1720-1795). Their children were: EZEKIEL;[5] JOHN;[5] SAMUEL;[5] ELIJAH;[5] PHEBE;[5] and ELIZABETH.[5]

EZEKIEL BUCKBEE[5] (1737-1804) married Eunus. Their children, as mentioned in the will of ELIJAH,[4] were: EZEKIEL, JR.;[6] EUNUS,[6] mar. Nathaniel Bayley; CHARLOTTE,[6] mar. John Bassett; SAMUEL;[6] and JOHN.[6]

JOHN BUCKBEE[5] (1742-1809) married Mary Hyatt and maybe Sophia. SAMUEL BUCKBEE[5] (1769-?) married Sarah. Their children were: PHILIP;[6] DANIEL;[6] SAMUEL;[6] SARAH;[6] MARY;[6] and PHOEBE.[6]

PHEBE BUCKBEE[5] married Ebenezer Purdy.

ELIZABETH BUCKBEE,[5] in a letter to her father dated April 2, 1783, signed herself "Elizabeth Harriss" and wrote that her husband had been taken prisoner March 14. She is believed also to have been at some time the wife of Harmon Montross with children: Sarah, b. about 1770, mar. Joseph Halstead; Elizabeth, b. about 1772, mar. Randolph; and Stephen, b. about 1775. The will of ELIJAH BUCKEE[4] leaves bequests to: Stephen Montross; Sarah, mar. to Joseph Halstead; Elizabeth Randolph; and Annoter Randolph "to give her education."

ELIJAH BUCKBEE, JR.,[5] b. July 13, 1759, married 1st Anna Ketchum, dau. of Timothy and Hannah Ketchum, at Christ Church, Salem, Dec. 12, 1782. Their children were: ELIZABETH,[6] b. 1783; ABIGAIL,[6] b. 1785;

HANNAH[6] (1788-1793); GILEAD[6] (1790-1875); ELIAS[6] (1795-1797); and PHOEBE[6] (1797-1799). Anna died in 1799 and ELIJAH[5] married 2nd Nancy Charlick. His will filed in the Town of Eastchester in 1830 mentions his wife Nancy, daughter ABIGAIL HOLMES,[6] granddaughters ANN HOLMES,[7] PHEBE SMITH.[7] Although the will of ELIJAH[4] bequeathed the remainder of his farm, after a plot 3 rods square should be set aside for a burying place, to his sons, JOHN[5] and ELIJAH,[5] it appears to have been Elijah who lived in the homestead. ELIJAH[5] died on Feb. 23, 1830.

ELIZABETH BUCKBEE,[6] b. June 6, 1783, married Jotham Smith and had one son, ISAAC SMITH.[7]

ABIGAIL BUCKBEE,[6] b. Nov. 13, 1785, on Cherry St., married Willet Holmes, son of David and Sarah Holmes. Their only child was DAVID HOLMES[7](1804-1826).

GILEAD BUCKBEE,[6] b. June 15, 1790, died at the homestead Nov. 24, 1875. He married Nov. 15, 1821, Sarah Rundle (1802-1886), dau. of John and Elizabeth (Keeler) Rundle of North Salem. Mrs. Buckbee was a devout Christian, a member of the Methodist Episcopal Church. Their home was a preaching place and many prominent men stopped there. Both are buried in the family burying-ground near their home. They were the parents of ANNA GRACE.[7]

ANNA GRACE BUCKBEE,[7] b. July 25, 1830, in the Cherry St. homestead, married Jotham Smith Holmes, who ran the large farm until they sold it in 1900 and moved into Bedford Hills. Mrs. HOLMES[7] died Dec. 9, 1903, after a long illness, leaving her husband and 5 children: MARTIN;[8] MORRIS;[8] SARAH;[8] BELLE;[8] and FLORENCE HOLMES.[8] EMMA C. HOLMES,[8] another daughter, had died Apr. 15, 1901, at 54 yrs. They are buried in Oakwood Cemetery, Mt. Kisco. BELLE HOLMES,[8] unmar., had a musical education and taught many local children the piano. FLORENCE HOLMES,[8] unmar., taught school in Tarrytown.

MORRIS BUCKBEE HOLMES,[8] b. Oct. 27, 1869, married Abbie E. Rockwell June 28, 1919. At nineteen he went to Brewster where he worked at the grocery store of Ganung and Hazelton. After 7 years there, he went to New York City and worked on the waterfront. Later he became a salesman in a shoe store, then on the road for Endicott Johnson. He opened and ran his own shoe store in Mt. Kisco until he retired in 1930. Mrs. Holmes died Dec. 5, 1949. MORRIS[8] died July 30, 1959, at his home on Burbank Ave., Bedford Hills. Two daughters survive: MRS. OLIVIA HOLMES VAN WAGNER,[9] Mustato Rd., Katonah; and MRS. GRACE HOLMES HAIGHT[9] of Dixon, Calif.; and three grandchildren, ALLEN,[10] DOUGLAS,[10] and DEBORAH HAIGHT.[10]

Compiled by F. R. Duncombe.

The Carpenter Family

WALTON JAY CARPENTER[2] who practiced medicine in Old and New Katonah descended from an English family that came to New England in the 17th century. His father, CHARLES B. CARPENTER,[1] married Rachel White. WALTON JAY[2] was born in Duanesburgh, Schenectady County,

N.Y., Sept. 11, 1852, from where he removed with his family to Illinois 4 years later. They returned to Duanesburgh after two years. At fifteen WALTON JAY[2] entered the Delaware Literary Institute. Later he taught school, after which he attended Union College. There was a term of medical preparation under Dr. Alfred L. Loomis of New York and in the fall of 1875 he entered the Medical Department of the University of the City of New York, graduating in 1877.

Dr. Carpenter's first practice was at Round Hill, Conn., but he came to Katonah in 1878. He married there Apr. 30, 1884, Anna Lavinia Green, daughter of Alsoph Green (see Green genealogy) and they were parents of WALTON T. CARPENTER,[3] b. Sept. 30, 1886. Anna L. Carpenter died in 1898 and Dr. Carpenter married Mrs. Ella Dean of Bedford Village in 1900. She died in 1907 and he married Mrs. Charlotte Truesdell Hoyt, widow of Robert Hoyt. Dr. Carpenter was active in the planning and construction of the Northern Westchester Hospital where he performed many operations for his own patients and also for those of other doctors throughout northern Westchester. He was president of the Board of Education of the Katonah School District and an active supporter of the Village Improvement Society. He was a member of the Methodist Church of Katonah and also a member of the following: Masonic Organization, Kisco Lodge 708, Croton Chapter 202, and Crusade Commanding 56.

WALTON T. CARPENTER[3] graduated from the Katonah High School and attended the Holbrook Military Academy in Ossining, N.Y., for 3 years. After his graduation from Yale University in 1908 he established the Carpenter Ice Cream Company of White Plains, of which he was president until his retirement in 1951. Mr. Carpenter resides at 88 Sterling Ave., White Plains, N.Y.

Compiled by W. T. Carpenter, 88 Sterling Ave., White Plains, N.Y.

The Collyer Family

THOMAS LANGLEY COLLYER,[2] b. Aug. 22, 1742, in Minbury, Devonshire, England, son of JOHN[1] and Margery (Langley) Collyer, came to America in 1769 and settled in Weston, Conn. He brought with him a carding machine, said to be the first in this country. He married 1st Abither Hawley, by whom he had a son, THOMAS LANGLEY, JR.,[3] b. Jan. 7, 1776. Abither is buried in Connecticut. THOMAS[2] married 2nd Elizabeth Wakeman, widow of James Hill. They had 5 children, all born in Weston: MARGERY LANGLEY;[3] MARY;[3] MOSES WAKEMAN;[3] SAMUEL;[3] and JOHN.[3] THOMAS[2] married 3rd Catherine Bennett (1751-1812), widow of Elephlet Wakeman. They had no children. THOMAS[2] moved from Weston to Bedford, N.Y., probably because of the water power. His mill stood where Matthew's Mill stands today, and he died in the little house above the mill. He helped select the site for St. Matthew's cemetery and was the first to be buried in it.

MARGERY LANGLEY COLLYER[3] (1780-1810) married Capt. Hull Fanton, a carpenter from Weston, Conn. Their children were: ELIZABETH WAKEMAN,[4] mar. Thomas Merwin; ANN,[4] mar. Thomas F. Lawrence; HULDAH

HILL,[4] mar. Henry Robertson (see Robertson genealogy); THOMAS LANG-LEY,[4] who mar. twice and had 7 children; SARAH,[4] mar. Myron Silkman (see Silkman genealogy); and JOHN COLLYER FANTON,[4] brought up by his uncle, John Collyer.

MARY COLLYER[3] (1781-1866) married Gabriel Smith, Jr. (see Smith Family of Katonah genealogy). MOSES WAKEMAN COLLYER[3] married Betsey Lyon. Sons were: STEPHEN;[4] SAMUEL;[4] and JOHN.[4] SAMUEL COLLYER[3] (1787-1827) married Sarah Trowbridge. Son was JAMES THOMAS.[4]

JOHN COLLYER[3] (1789-1831) married Rhoda Smith, dau. of Mercy and Jesse Smith of Bedford. Their children were: WARREN;[4] ELIZABETH J.;[4] DELIA;[4] AUGUSTA ANN;[4] JOHN ADDISON;[4] and THEODOSIA[4] (1830-1906), mar. Daniel Merritt Miller of Whitlockville (see Miller genealogy).

WARREN COLLYER,[4] b. Dec. 21, 1813, owned a large farm near Hoyt's Mills. Soon after the completion of the Harlem Railroad he moved into Katonah and opened a hotel near the station. In 1878 he sold the hotel and returned to his farm, where he died May 8, 1880. He was a bachelor and a frank and honest friend. He accumulated a goodly fortune which he left to his brother, J. ADDISON COLLYER,[4] also a bachelor, and to two sisters, Mrs. E. J. Purdy and Mrs. D. M. Miller. His pallbearers were: Jonah Holly, James F. Merritt, Stephen Holly Miller, Isaac N. Hait, Dr. Charles E. Wickware and J. D. Powell. He is buried in St. Matthew's cemetery.

ELIZABETH J. COLLYER[4] (1815-1902) married in Bedford, February, 1843, Ebenezer Purdy (1819-1906). They owned a large house on Railroad Ave. and Main St. in Old Katonah, which they sold to Dr. Carpenter who had it moved to the hill on the east side of Greenville Rd. (Aires Pinto now owns this house.) Mr. Purdy owned and ran a store on Railroad Ave. next to his home. Mr. and Mrs. Purdy also owned a farm on Goldens Bridge Rd. (The house on this farm is now owned by Philip de Young.) The Purdys were the parents of: ELECTA J.[5] (1845-1898), mar. Uel Todd Bailey; ELIZABETH J.[5] (1847-1929), who lived in Katonah 81 years and died at her home on Bedford Rd.; and ELLA J. PURDY[5] (1849-1916), mar. Dec. 13, 1876, Daniel J. Smith of Katonah (see Smith Family of Katonah genealogy).

DELIA COLLYER[4] (1818-1850) married Cyrus Miller; no children.

AUGUSTA ANN COLLYER[4] (1820-1865) married Wright Beyea of Katonah and had ADAGETTIA BEYEA.[5]

Collyer descendants living in Katonah or nearby are: EDWARD P. BARRETT[6] and ROBERTSON T. BARRETT[6] (Emma Robertson[5]); ADELLA FANTON[6] of Danbury, Conn. (Thomas C.,[5] John Collyer Fanton[4]); RHODA BENEDICT LAWRENCE[7] (Hannah Dickinson,[6] Elizabeth Robertson[5]); ELIZABETH DICKINSON MILLER[7] (Arnell Dickinson,[6] Elizabeth Robertson[5]); EMILY SPARKS CLARK[7] (William Clark,[6] Joseph Clark,[5] Elizabeth Smith,[4] Mary Collyer[3]); LORRAINE CLARK GIBSON[7] of Bedford Hills (Frederick Clark,[6] Joseph Clark,[5] Elizabeth Smith[4]); GERTRUDE SMITH SMITH[7] (Elizabeth Bailey,[6] Electa Purdy[5]); ELLA D. MILLER[8] (Elizabeth Dickinson Miller[7]); JAMES F. LAWRENCE, JR.,[9] and RANDALL G. LAWRENCE[9] (James F. Lawrence,[8] C. Fayette Lawrence,[7] Hannah Dickinson[6]); MARGERY LANGLEY VAN NORDEN[7] (M. Augusta Horton,[6] Margery V. Silkman,[5] Sarah Fanton[4]); ESTELLE TRAVIS BARRETT[7] (Margery Langley Putney,[6] M. Antoinette

Silkman,[5] Sarah Fanton[4]); RUTH HOLMES HALL[7] of Katonah and JOHN
CLARK HOLMES[7] of Pound Ridge (John R. Holmes,[6] Marietta Robertson[5]);
DOUGLAS LANGLEY BARRETT[7] and KATHARINE BARRETT KELLY[7] of Katonah
(see lines Edward Percy Barrett and Estelle Travis Barrett); MARGOT L.
BARRETT[8] (see Douglas L. Barrett); EDWARD W. KELLY,[8] DAVID A. KELLY[8]
and KAREN E. KELLY[8] (see Katherine Barrett Kelly); IONE P. BARRETT[7]
(Henry Barrett,[6] Emma Robertson,[5] Huldah Fanton,[4] Margery Collyer,[3]
Thomas Collyer,[2] John Collyer[1]).
    Compiled by K. B. Kelly.

The Daniel Family

ALFRED F. DANIEL[1] (no relation to the Daniels family and spelled without the "s") moved to Cherry St. July, 1866, from New York City, where
he was born of English parents. He married 1st Dec. 1, 1863, Ellen Crummey, dau. of Alexander and Jane Crummey, b. Oct., 25, 1843, in New
York City, d. in Katonah Dec. 2, 1890. ALFRED F. DANIEL[1] was superintendent of the large Anderson Farm, which ran from Valley Rd. to
Whitlockville Rd. and east from Cherry St. to the new village. He and
his family lived in the present Ross house on Cherry St. and later in the
house now taken down across from the Anderson main house. The chil-
dren of ALFRED[1] and Ellen were: ELIZABETH;[2] WARD;[2] SUSIE;[2] ALFRED C.;[2]
WILLIAM J.;[2] ABBY;[2] SADIE;[2] J. EASTMAN;[2] ELLEN;[2] and HARRIET.[2] Mr.
Daniel married 2nd Nettie, a nurse. When Mr. Anderson sold his farm,
the Daniels moved into New Katonah and owned the present Arthur
Towey house on Katonah Ave. Mr. Daniel was a water inspector for
New York City, testing our water each day. He was also sexton for the
Presbyterian Church. He died Apr. 5, 1922. Mrs. Nettie Daniel lived in
Katonah until her death June 10, 1936.

ELIZABETH DANIEL[2] married 1st Charles L. Hathaway, by whom she had
4 children, who all died young. Mr. Hathaway died July 19, 1901. She
married 2nd Albert Odell of Goldens Bridge. She died Feb. 6, 1949.

WARD DANIEL[2] died at 18 yrs. and his sister, SUSIE DANIEL,[2] at 10 yrs.

ALFRED CARPENTER DANIEL[2] was a blacksmith in Old Katonah where
he worked for Edgar Hitt and also in New Katonah. He married Jan.
26, 1900, Mrs. Cassie Hitt Barton, dau. of Edgar Hitt (see Hitt genealogy),
and they had one son, ALFRED DANIEL[3] (1900-1918). After the fire of May,
1902, they lived in Mel Allen's cottage on The Terrace and later built
a new home at 66 Bedford Rd. Mr. Daniel died June 20, 1913, and Mrs.
Daniel later married Frank Hoffman.

WILLIAM JOHN DANIEL[2] (1872-1931) attended Cherry St. School and
at 15 yrs. started in the carpenter trade. He married, June, 1896, Jennie
Reynolds, dau. of Robert A. (called Dick) and Henrietta Greene Reynolds,
and granddaughter of Phoebe W. Daniels of Cherry St. Jennie, born on
Cherry St., attended school there. William, a contractor when New
Katonah was being built, finished his own home, 37 Hillside Ave., Mar.
25, 1898, and they moved right in with their only child, MILDRED LEONE.[3]
He built homes for George Attride, Oliver Green and James Ford on

Highland Ave.; George Ray, Herbert Chapman on The Terrace; Alfred C. Daniel and Dr. F. H. Williams on Bedford Road; Peter Gruber on Cottage Place and James H. Williams' store on Katonah Ave., presently William Phelp's drug store building. He built Martin Mead's home and Mead Memorial Chapel on Mead Street, Waccabuc, and remodeled the Howe home into the present Waccabuc Country Club. He also built the Goldens Bridge Methodist Church in 1902. He was a member of Jr. O.U.A. Mechanics and of Katonah Fire Department. Mr. and Mrs. Daniel sold their home on Hillside Ave. and built a new one at 6 Ashby Place, now owned by Dr. Edwin T. Iglehart. Later they moved to Alexandria, Va., where Mr. Daniel died in 1931. Mrs. Daniel now lives in Katonah. MILDRED L. DANIEL,[3] b. 1897 in Katonah, graduated from Katonah High School and married Raymond Keller of Wilton, Conn. She died July, 1921.

ABBY DANIEL[2] married Mr. Schmelter of Mt. Kisco. They had two children: EDWIN[3] and ELLEN LOUISE SCHMELTER.[3] LOUISE[3] married Frank Allmond and their two sons are: FRANCIS EDWIN;[4] and BENJAMIN ARTHUR ALLMOND.[4] The Allmonds lived in Mt. Kisco and Katonah and then moved to Middletown, N.Y. FRANCIS EDWIN ALLMOND,[4] b. Dec. 30, 1921, graduated from Katonah High School June, 1939. He enlisted in the U.S. Navy Sept. 17, 1940, trained at Newport and Mare Island, Calif., and was on a sub-chaser during World War II. He is married and has 2 children. BENJAMIN ARTHUR ALLMOND,[4] b. Feb. 9, 1925, graduated from Katonah High School in 1943. He was in the Navy July 23, 1943, trained at Great Lakes Center and progressed to Signalman 3rd Class. He served in the Philippines and Pacific. He married Sept. 29, 1956, Evelyn Abrams and they make their home in Suffern, N.Y., with their child.

SADIE DANIEL,[2] unmar., makes her home with her sister, HATTIE,[2] in Ossining.

JOHN EASTMAN DANIEL,[2] b. on Cherry St., 1878, married Apr. 26, 1901, Lucy Evelyn French (1878-1942), dau. of John H. and Phoebe (Reynolds) French of Katonah. He was a carpenter and they made their home in Katonah. Children were: EVELYN[3] (1904-1904); WILLIAM JOHN,[3] who lives on Katonah Ave. and is associated with Kelloggs & Lawrence; BLANCHE D.;[3] and ROBERT.[3]

BLANCHE DANIEL,[3] graduated from Katonah High, married Oct. 15, 1932, Paul Stephen Jones, son of William Stephen Jones of Bedford Hills. Mr. Jones served in the Navy in World War II and has his own business, Wesco Gas Service, Inc. The Jones live at 34 Pleasant St. and are parents of: MARJORIE HELEN[4] and DAVID PAUL JONES[4] who attends John Jay High School. MARJORIE H. JONES[4] graduated from Katonah High June, 1954, and from Green Mountain College, 1956. She married Kenneth Alan Ball, son of Clifford R. Ball of Needham, Mass., Apr. 12, 1958, in Katonah's Presbyterian Church. They live in Westwood, Mass., with sons: DAVID ROSS;[5] and GREGORY ALAN BALL.[5]

ROBERT DANIEL[3] married Doris Mason, dau. of George Mason of Katonah. They make their home in Purdy's Station and are parents of NANCY,[4] who mar. Raynor Weisnecker and lives in Carmel with 2 children: CAROL,[5] b. 1944; and JAMES,[5] b. 1950.

ELLEN DANIEL,[2] called Nellie, married Arthur Odell. They lived in South Salem and Cross River. After Mr. Odell's death, she moved to 5 Edgemont Rd., Katonah. The Odells had 6 children: ERNEST;[3] EDNA,[3] who mar. Ruben Wood and lives in Vista with 8 children; ELLEN,[3] who mar. George Seelig and has 4 children; RUTH,[3] who mar. Ralph Lostocco and lives in Danbury, no children; HELEN;[3] and DOROTHY ODELL,[3] who mar. Thomas Bradsell and lives in Florida with their 2 sons. ERNEST ODELL,[3] mar. Margaret Burt, dau. of Margaret Tompkins and Albert J. Burt of Katonah, died June 4, 1937, leaving her with 7 small children (see Tompkins genealogy).

HARRIET DANIEL[2] married Charles French of Mt. Kisco. They were parents of: GEORGE,[3] who mar. and lives in Ossining; WILLIAM,[3] who mar. and lives in Mt. Kisco; IRENE,[3] d. y.; SADIE[3] and GLORIA FRENCH,[3] who live with their mother in Ossining, as does their aunt, SADIE DANIEL.[2]

Compiled by K. B. Kelly.

The Daniels Family of Katonah

JARED DANIELS[1] lived at Cherry St. on the West Rd., now called Croton Lake Rd., in the square house presently owned by Norman Randell. He was a farmer, married to Sarah Monroe. Three of their children were: SARAH WHEATON;[2] PHOEBE W.;[2] and JOHN.[2] Another son may have been George Daniels (1832-1877), mar. Bessie Reynolds, dau. of George and Anna (Norton) Reynolds. JOHN DANIELS[2] was living at Cherry St. when he was exempted from service in the Civil War, but later married and moved to Stamford, Conn.

SARAH WHEATON DANIELS,[2] b. at Cherry St. in 1817, married in 1840 Obadiah Ackerley (1819-1883), a shoemaker of Whitlockville. She died Oct. 25, 1882, of shock from fire in the drugstore in Old Katonah. SARAH[2] and Obadiah Ackerley were parents of: ESTHER,[3] mar. Edgar B. Newman (see Newman genealogy); MRS. WILLIAM H. BARKER;[3] and GEORGE ACKERLEY,[3] d. Feb. 15, 1907.

PHOEBE W. DANIELS,[2] b. at Cherry St., Jan. 25, 1821, married Nov. 28, 1839, John L. Reynolds (1819-1901) (Joseph, Jonathan, 3 Johns, Jonathan, John Reynolds). They lived in the square house in which she was born and were parents of 12 children: WILLIAM HENRY[3] (1840-1912), mar. Susan A. Barrett; FRANCES,[3] b. Aug. 12, 1842, who mar. Amaziah Totten and was the great-grandmother of GLADYS BENEDICT HELMS,[6] presently living on Croton Lake Rd.; ROBERT A.[3] (1844-1924), a carpenter of Cherry St., who mar. Henrietta Greene and has dau. MRS. WILLIAM J. DANIEL[4] of Bedford Rd., Katonah; SARAH E.[3] (1846-1909), mar. David William Olmstead Jan. 8, 1869; CAROLINE[3] (1848-1848); OPHELIA[3] (1850-1850); PHOEBE,[3] b. 1851, mar. John H. French (see French genealogy); ABIGAIL,[3] b. Oct. 30, 1854, mar. Charles Green of Katonah; JOHN S.[3] (1857-1906), mar. Margaret Ryan in 1874; ALBERT L.[3] (1859-1859); CASSIUS J.,[3] b. 1860, who married and lived in Yalesville, Conn.; and GEORGE B. REYNOLDS[3] (1864-1910), mar. Rhoda Dingey.

Compiled by K. B. Kelly.

The Deacon Family

EDWARD DEACON[1] (1828-1881) and his wife Amelia lived in Old Katonah on the present Woodsbridge Rd. Their children were: JOHN Q.;[2] SETH;[2] MARCUS C.;[2] WEBSTER;[2] MARY A.;[2] and HENRY B.[2]

JOHN Q. DEACON[2] (1851-1879) ran a fish and oyster store on Railroad Ave., Old Katonah.

SETH DEACON[2] was a printer. He married Anna Way Bruise and they had one dau., KATHERINE.[3] The family moved to Millerton, N.Y. Mrs. Deacon died Oct. 10, 1902, from malaria followed by typhoid fever. Mr. Deacon died from the same cause on Nov. 28, 1902.

MARCUS C. DEACON,[2] b. 1861, lived only four years.

WEBSTER DEACON[2] was the station-master in Mt. Kisco. His wife Mary Alice, dau. of Charles Van Tassel, died in March, 1959, at 88 yrs.

MARY A. DEACON[2] married Carpenter B. Wheeler in October, 1892.

HENRY B. DEACON[2] was chief clerk for Lyon Brothers' store on Railroad Ave. in Old Katonah. He had the agency for Victor Talking Machines with FIAT records—best in Buffalo Fair—in December, 1901. He lived with his mother and when their land was taken by New York City, they moved their home around the corner to Edgmont Rd. Mr. Deacon ran a grocery store in his home in New Katonah for many years. He married Jan. 6, 1890, at 22 yrs. Edith Wright, dau. of William Wright, a carriage painter in Old Katonah. She was only 17 yrs. at the time of her marriage. They had no children and their last home was on Katonah Ave. in the large house which Harold Park tore down to have space for his new gas station. Mr. Deacon is well remembered walking his small white dog.

Compiled by K. B. Kelly.

The Dickinsons of Cantitoe

ARNELL (sometimes written ARNOLD) DICKINSON[1] (1721-1791) came from North Castle where his "earmark" was recorded in 1736, and bought land at Cantitoe in 1773 from William Axtell and his wife, Margaret De-Peyster, granddaughter of Jacobus Van Cortlandt. He married 1st Deborah Carpenter (1724-1751) and 2nd in 1753 Mary Akerly by whom he had ARNELL,[2] b. 1772. In the family Bible which bears the inscription "March 27, A.D. 1753, Arnell Dickinson, his book" there is an entry, "John Dickinson was born July (paper torn here). My mother was born on September 18, and in the year 1692 and departed in May 6, 1758."

ARNELL DICKINSON[2] (1772-1832) married Hannah Frost (1783-1862) of Goldens Bridge. She brought with her and planted on her wedding day a pine tree which grew to tremendous height and became a well-known land mark. The stump still stands on the northeast corner of Cantitoe Corners, the present Sharp property. They had 3 children: ISAAC FROST,[3] who died at 12 yrs.; PATIENCE MARIA,[3] mar. Samuel Knapp; and ARNELL FROST.[3]

ARNELL FROST DICKINSON[3] (1818-1867) was a boy of 14 when his father died. He assumed the responsibility of the property at Cantitoe, which he inherited. He farmed the place profitably and became known as a scientific farmer as well as a public spirited citizen, active all his life in local affairs. In spite of the demands of the farm, he held many public offices: president of the Farmers' Club, secretary of the Temperance Society, commissioner of highways, trustee of the school of Cantitoe, postmaster at Cantitoe, Bedford town supervisor, member of the Assembly at Albany and superintendent of the poor. In this last office he instituted a major and much needed reform, the registering of orphans sent to the almshouse. ARNELL[3] married Elizabeth Ann Robertson, dau. of Henry and Huldah (Fanton) Robertson, Oct. 18, 1852, at her home at Cantitoe. (see Robertson genealogy). Elizabeth was a teacher qualified to instruct in common schools. She walked every day from her home at Cantitoe to Mt. Holly, receiving a salary of two dollars a month. They were parents of 3 children: ELIZABETH[4] (1864-1953), mar. Jacob Burdett; HANNAH[4] (1853-1936); and ARNELL FROST, JR.[4] (1858-1946).

HANNAH DICKINSON[4] married James Fayette Lawrence (1846-1909), son of Cyrus and Mary Elizabeth (Howe) Lawrence of South Salem, Jan. 6, 1876. All the children were born in South Salem. Twins, a boy and a girl, died at birth in 1877. ELIZABETH LAWRENCE,[5] b. June 29, 1878, is now Mrs. Ebenezer Albert Wood of Peekskill (see Wood genealogy). ANNA META LAWRENCE,[5] b. Mar. 24, 1880, died Sept. 30, 1897. WALTER ARNELL LAWRENCE,[5] b. May 9, 1882, died in Brooklyn. CYRUS FAYETTE LAWRENCE,[5] b. Oct. 1889, died in September, 1960. RHODA BENEDICT LAWRENCE,[5] b. Dec. 10, 1896, lives in New York City.

CYRUS FAYETTE LAWRENCE[5] (1889-1960) moved to Katonah in 1912 and took a position with Kellogg and Mead. Upon Mr. Mead's death in 1918, the business became known as Kelloggs & Lawrence, Inc. Oct. 22, 1918, Mr. Lawrence married Anna Janet Ramage of Yonkers. A member of the Katonah Presbyterian Church since 1912, he served as a trustee and elder 35 years. With the Y in World War I, he was a member of Katonah Fire Department from 1914 on, and its president for 25 years. He was a charter member of the Katonah Rotary, past president and secretary for over 25 years. He had a lifelong interest in the Christian Endeavor movement, and was active in the Katonah Board of Trade, Village Improvement Society and Red Cross. FAY[5] was educated in South Salem public schools and Chappaqua Mountain Institute. Mrs. Lawrence joined the Presbyterian Church here in 1919, served as president of the King's Daughters, the Ladies' Aid Society, and the Women's Civic Club. They had one son, JAMES FAYETTE LAWRENCE.[6]

JAMES FAYETTE LAWRENCE[6] (1920-1959), b. in Katonah on Nov. 23, 1920, graduated from Katonah High School June, 1939. He attended Hamilton College and expected to graduate in 1943 but enlisted Aug. 8, 1942, and was inducted Feb. 25, 1943. He was a staff sergeant in the Air Branch of the Army, serving in New Guinea and Leyte. He married Charlotte E. Ganun, dau. of Edwin E. Ganun of Mt. Kisco, Dec. 8, 1943. JAMES[6] joined the Presbyterian Church in 1934, served as deacon and trustee and was president of Westchester County Christian Endeavor

Union. He was a member of Katonah Post American Legion; secretary, Katonah Chamber of Commerce for five years; member of Katonah Fire Department from 1946; and associated with Kelloggs & Lawrence. He died in action while serving as Fire Chief Oct. 6, 1959. JAMES[6] and Charlotte had two sons: JAMES FAYETTE,[7] b. Dec. 31, 1944; and RANDALL GANUN,[7] b. Sept. 24, 1947. Both boys attend John Jay High School.

ARNELL FROST DICKINSON[4] (1858-1946) married Julia E. Miller (1861-1926), dau. of Daniel Merritt and Phebe C. (Wildey) Miller of Whitlockville (see Miller genealogy). He built a large new home across from his father's at Cantitoe and ran a large farm. He was road commissioner in 1901 and for many years after. Their children were: ELISABETH MILLER;[5] ARNELL FROST[5] (Dec. 7, 1884-1945), mar. Susan Reynolds, no children; GEORGE WARREN[5] (1889-1952), mar. Laura Josephine Martin (1889-1941) of Purdys, no children; and THEODOSIA COLLYER.[5]

ELISABETH DICKINSON,[5] b. June 1, 1883, married Henry Decker Miller (1876-1930) in 1902. They bought the old Zeno Hoyt building which had been moved from Old Katonah to Bedford Rd., south of Huntville Rd. where Mrs. Miller now lives in the cottage. They were parents of: JULIA[6] (1903-1914); ELLA D.,[6] b. 1904; HENRY ROBERTSON[6] (1906-1925); GEORGE L.[6] (1909-1960); and DONALD DICKINSON MILLER[6] (1914-1916). Mrs. Miller was one of the leading spirits in the fight for women's suffrage. She was an original incorporator and is a charter member of the Women's Civic Club and a member of the Bedford Farmers' Club. Before and during World War II she was very active in Red Cross work, also the first woman ever nominated for a member of our school board. ELLA D.[6] lives at home and works at the Roosevelt Veterans Hospital at Montrose, N.Y.

THEODOSIA COLLYER DICKINSON,[5] b. at Cantitoe Aug. 3, 1891, married in 1917 Frederick Murdock Allen of Peekskill, N.Y. She was very active in local affairs. She died June 19, 1929, after a long illness, leaving one son, FREDERICK MURDOCK ALLEN, JR.[6]

FREDERICK MURDOCK ALLEN, JR.,[6] b. May 21, 1920, in Katonah, graduated from Katonah High School June, 1937, made his home with his aunt, Mrs. Henry Miller. He continued his education at Rensselaer Polytechnic Institute in Troy where he graduated in 1941 as a metallurgical engineer. He worked for Ludlow Valve Company until he enlisted in the Navy in January, 1944. He was trained at Notre Dame University and saw duty in the Atlantic. He married Virginia Whitfield of Virginia and they are parents of: BARBARA JEAN,[7] b. 1946; and RICHARD FREDERICK,[7] b. December, 1950. They live in Wilmington, Del., where Mr. Allen works for the DuPont Company.

Compiled by Alma R. Crane, F. R. Duncombe, and K. B. Kelly.

The Doyle Family

MICHAEL DOYLE[1] arrived in New York City in 1847 from County Wicklow, Ireland. He married Mary McFarland in Londonderry in 1834.

They were the parents of JAMES DOYLE,[2] who came to work for John Jay at Bedford House in 1852.

JAMES DOYLE[2] (Jan. 1, 1835-June 27, 1888) married in 1861 Catherine A. Towey (1835-1902). They lived on the southeast side of Cantitoe Corners in a house since moved back and now the first on Girdle Ridge Rd. Later they lived on the Cross River Rd. south of Hoyt's Mills. JAMES[2] was a farmer and interested in horticulture. He and his wife are buried in Pleasantville, N.Y. They were parents of 5 children, all born in Katonah: WILLIAM J.;[3] THOMAS J.;[3] M. FRANCIS;[3] MARY;[3] and DAVID A.[3]

JOHN DOYLE[1] was a brother of MICHAEL[1] and an uncle to JAMES.[2] He came to Old Katonah to work for Edgar Hitt as a blacksmith. He had been very successful in California before losing all in a tidal wave and coming to Katonah.

Doyle Brothers, the 4 sons of JAMES,[2] owned a large house and green-houses in the Cross River valley, east of Old Katonah, and started a florist business there in 1888. When New York City took the land, they moved their home, now owned by Michael Vuotto, across to its present site on Deer Park Rd. This move was completed Oct. 18, 1901. Mrs. Doyle, MARY,[3] M. FRANCIS[3] and DAVID[3] moved into the redecorated home in January, 1902. In the fall of 1897, Doyle Brothers contracted to set out some of the trees for the new village of Katonah. The *Katonah Times* of May 20, 1898, stated, "A large number of trees set out last fall are now leafing out and they most all survived." Doyle Brothers bought 5 lots on Bedford Rd. and Valley Rd. from the Katonah Land Company in May, 1901, to establish a residence and greenhouses. In New Katonah the brothers, WILLIAM,[3] FRANCIS,[3] and DAVID,[3] bought the southwest corner building on Katonah Ave. and The Parkway from Edgar Hoyt. There they ran a grocery and florist business until 1921. These Doyle Brothers also bought the last houses in Old Katonah, the Jere Lyon and Moses Benedict houses, and placed them on Katonah Ave. at Edgemont Rd. running south. These 3 buildings are still owned by WILLIAM J. DOYLE, JR.[4]

In 1906 WILLIAM[3] and DAVID A. DOYLE,[3] with William and E. P. Barrett, formed the Bedford Hills Company. They bought land where the Town House now stands and developed it as the Bedford Hills Park. In so doing they were instrumental, with Mr. Seth Low, in changing the name of the village from Bedford Station to Bedford Hills. The Company dissolved in 1959 when the last lot was sold.

WILLIAM J. DOYLE,[3] born in the house on Cantitoe Corners Oct. 3, 1863, attended Katonah schools. When 22, he founded the family florist business, opening stores in both Katonah and White Plains. He was an authority on horticulture, winning many cups and prizes as a horticulturist and writer. In New Katonah he was appointed collector of taxes for Bedford in April, 1900, replacing Herbert L. Merritt, and was reappointed the following year. He became deputy sheriff of Westchester County in 1901 and sheriff thereafter. He married Jan. 15, 1902, Lida Farrell of White Plains. WILLIAM J.[3] and Lida Doyle were parents of: WILLIAM J.;[4] and JOHN FRANCIS DOYLE,[4] both born at the Doyle Homestead on Deer Park Rd. JOHN FRANCIS[4] died at about 1 yr. In 1906 the William J.

Doyles bought from E. P. Barrett his home at 27 Bedford Rd. They made their home here and also in White Plains, always returning to Katonah for the summer. Mr. Doyle's latter years were devoted exclusively to real estate. He died July 22, 1933, and his wife, May 29, 1929.

THOMAS J. DOYLE,[3] b. Feb. 15, 1866, was a member of the Deer Park family business. In the new village he left his brothers and started a barber shop on Katonah Ave. in the John French building (now the Marion Shop). This he sold in April, 1898, to William Robertson, who moved the business up to Edgar Hitt's building where he added pool and billiard tables to it. TOM[3] then opened a cash grocery store and contracted for a new building 4 stories high next to Benedict's. This is now owned by the Misses Zimmerman. In January, 1902, he opened a house-painting, paper-hanging and interior-decorating business with William H. Blanchard, in addition to his grocery business. He married Elizabeth Doyle of Red Hook and they built a home at 34 Bedford Rd. Later they moved to New York City for a while where THOMAS[3] was a health officer. He died at the Deer Park homestead where his brother FRANCIS[3] resided. The THOMAS DOYLES[3] had no children. Mrs. Doyle spent her remaining years at her home, 34 Bedford Road.

MICHAEL FRANCIS DOYLE,[3] b. July 24, 1868, was a member of Doyle Brothers and ran the store until it closed in 1921. He was postmaster of Katonah from June 5, 1912, until September, 1913, and again from Nov. 21, 1918, until April, 1925. He married Jennie Bedell of Katonah, dau. of Ella and Abram Bedell. They had one child who died at birth. Mr. Doyle died in 1938 and Mrs. Doyle died later at her home on Deer Park Rd.

MARY DOYLE,[3] unmar., the only daughter of JAMES[2] and Catherine Doyle, was born July 19, 1876. She had a good education and became a schoolteacher, dying while still young.

DAVID A. DOYLE,[3] b. Feb. 22, 1878, Katonah educated, joined his brothers in business. He was elected November, 1901, superintendent of the poor of Westchester County, and Jan. 7, 1907, was appointed postmaster of Katonah, resigning in favor of his brother, M. FRANCIS,[3] in 1912. Oct. 8, 1910, at Saratoga, the N.Y. Association of Postmasters was founded, at which time DAVID A. DOYLE[3] was elected vice-president, representing the 3rd Class post offices. He married Marie O'Brien and bought the James Hoyt house in Old Katonah, which was moved in one piece to 48 The Parkway and now belongs to Mrs. Mary Maher. The DAVID DOYLES[3] had one dau. who died in her 6th year.

WILLIAM J. DOYLE, JR.,[4] son of WILLIAM[3] and Lida Farrell Doyle, moved from the Deer Park homestead into Katonah in 1906. He attended schools in Katonah and White Plains, graduated from Lafayette College, Easton, Pa., and received his law degree from Fordham University. He is an attorney and a large real estate owner in Katonah. Sept. 1, 1936, he married Dorothy Gallaway, dau. of Mr. & Mrs. Wm. H. Gallaway of White Plains. They built a new home on Mustato Rd. and reside there with dau., SHARON,[5] and son, WILLIAM J. III.[5]

Compiled by K. B. Kelly.

The Eastman Family in Katonah

The Eastman family descended from Roger Eastman, who emigrated from England in 1638. DR. JOHN HUSE EASTMAN[2] was born at Sandy Hill, now Hudson Falls, N.Y., July 22, 1849, the son of JOSEPH BARTLETT[1] and Mary (Huse) Eastman. JOSEPH B. EASTMAN[1] was pastor of Sandy Hill Presbyterian Church and soon after, the family moved to Windsor, near Binghamton, where he was principal of Windsor Academy.

JOHN[2] attended Windsor Academy and Amherst College. He graduated in 1869 with Phi Beta Kappa. He belonged to Psi U fraternity. In order to earn enough to go into the ministry, he joined the Knox College, Galesbury, Ill., faculty as a professor in Latin and Greek. It was several years before he entered Union Seminary, New York, for theological training. While an undergraduate there, he supplied the Katonah Presbyterian Church, his first visit being Apr. 30, 1875. He graduated May 10, 1875, and was ordained and installed in Katonah July 8, 1875, at which time there were 14 members belonging to the church. In three years there were 83 members and 98 the fourth year.

"Dominie" Eastman was a force for good in our community. Under his guidance and remarkable power, spirit and influence, much progress was achieved in our Presbyterian Church; also in the Village Improvement Society and its Library. He took great pride in the village and even helped lay the wooden sidewalks. He had a whimsical good nature and enjoyed his fellow men. Dr. Eastman preached in Katonah from 1875 to Apr. 20, 1895. He then accepted the Presbyterian parish at Pottsville, Pa., but his extraordinary gift for letter-writing kept him in touch with his many Katonah friends.

JOHN EASTMAN[2] married Lucy King. Their two children were born in the Presbyterian manse: ELIZABETH;[3] and JOSEPH B.[3] Mrs. Eastman died a few years after their move to Pottsville. JOHN EASTMAN[2] received a Doctor of Divinity degree from Amherst College in 1899. He resigned as pastor of Pottsville in 1915, retired with his children to Winchester, Mass., and died of a cerebral hemorrhage Nov. 9, 1917.

ELIZABETH EASTMAN[3] never married and after their father's death made a home for herself and her brother on Cathedral Ave., Washington, D.C. She died there at 77 yrs. around 1956. Miss Eastman went to France during World War I to work in a YWCA canteen at Chaumont. She belonged to the American Association of University Women and the Cosmopolitan Club of New York and was active in the Common Council for American Unity, devoted to assisting immigrants.

JOSEPH B. EASTMAN[3] at the time of his death Mar. 15, 1944, was director of the Office of Defense Transportation. Born in Katonah in 1883, he graduated from Amherst College in 1904 and attended Boston University Law School for a year. In Boston he was associated with South End House on an Amherst scholarship; he was secretary of the Public Franchise League and active in the financial operations of the New Haven Railroad. Justice Louis Brandeis recommended Mr. Eastman to President Wilson who named him a member of the Interstate Commerce Commission in 1919, a position in which he continued under Presidents Harding and

Hoover. In 1933 President Roosevelt appointed him Federal Co-ordinator of Transportation. Mr. Eastman was a key member of the United States war machine. Justice Brandeis remarked of him: "Joe Eastman has more interest in public service and less in his own career than any man I have ever known." Mayor La Guardia, of New York, described him as "one of the ablest heads of departments in the entire country because he knew his job so well, kept his feet on the ground, was so well balanced, looked for results and not headlines, worked and did not talk." Mr. Eastman had many friends in Katonah. He gave the address at the 50th anniversary of the founding of the Katonah Village Improvement Society here in October, 1928.

Compiled by K. B. Kelly.

The Fisher Family

CHARLES FISHER[1] was born in New York City Jan. 3, 1839. Soon after his birth his father, captain of a sailing vessel, was lost at sea. His mother died in 1841 leaving CHARLES[1] and his older sister SUSAN,[1] then 14 years old. The children lived with Mr. & Mrs. George Vance and CHARLES[1] attended Cooper Union, a school for orphan boys.

SUSAN FISHER[1] married David Mills of New York, who died leaving her with 5 small children: JESSIE;[2] CHARLES;[2] SUSAN;[2] GEORGE VANCE;[2] and ANNIE MILLS.[2]

CHARLES FISHER[1] moved to Somers and lived with Mr. & Mrs. Edmund Hallock on their farm. He enlisted in the Civil War in 1862 at 23, eventually becoming a second lieutenant in the 6th N.Y. Heavy Artillery Regiment. Sept. 28, 1865, in New York City he married Catherine Lena Austin of Somers, daughter of Elias and Jane Austin. He did various kinds of work in various places. In Katonah he was with the American Lens Mfg. Company, and was also a painter and a farmer. The Fishers lived at various times in half of Warren Whitlock's house in Whitlockville, in Ephraim Knowlton's farm on Cherry St., in the old Allen house, now 50 The Terrace, in the Joseph Allen house in Old Katonah and in Sarah Shove Barrett's house on Cherry St. CHARLES[1] died Apr. 25, 1922, his wife, Catherine, Feb. 3, 1922. They were parents of: JANE ELIZA;[2] EMMA AUSTIN;[2] CHARLES HALLOCK;[2] and HOWARD KITCHING.[2]

JANE ELIZA FISHER,[2] b. in Whitlockville July 31, 1870, married late in life Arthur T. Vaux Aug. 26, 1939. He died in 1941 and she returned to Katonah to live with her sister, Mrs. Charles G. Mead, where she died, Feb. 18, 1955.

EMMA AUSTIN FISHER[2] was born Sept. 1, 1872, in Greenpoint, L.I. Her parents returned to Whitlockville when she was about 6 months old. She attended the Whitlockville school under Seeley Lounsbury and Ida Birdsall, and the Cherry St. school under Sarah Horton, Sophie Kellogg, Sarah S. Barrett, Richard Carr and Ella Mills. After finishing, she did practical nursing and took care of children. On Jan. 5, 1898, she married Charles Grant Mead (Oct. 16, 1873-June 7, 1918), son of Leander and Sarah Ida (Avery) Mead of Cross River. They were the last couple to be married in the Presbyterian Church in Old Katonah. They lived in White Plains four years, Mr. Mead being with Fowler & Sellars' hardware store. They then came back to Katonah where for the last 16 years of his life Mr. Mead was a partner of Henry W. Kellogg in his hardware store, under the firm name of Kellogg & Mead. Mr. & Mrs. Mead were very active in the Presbyterian church. They had 3 children: EMMA BEATRICE;[3] JULIA ADAMS;[3] and LEANDER AUSTIN MEAD.[3]

CHARLES HALLOCK FISHER,[3] b. in Whitlockville July 12, 1875, never married and made his home with his parents until his death in Bedford Hills Sept. 9, 1916. He was a gardener.

HOWARD KITCHING FISHER,[2] b. on Cherry St. Jan. 2, 1884, died in the "flu" epidemic Dec. 1, 1918, in Bedford Hills. He lived with his parents, was in the taxi business and a clerk in Adams' store in Bedford Hills.

EMMA BEATRICE MEAD,[3] b. in White Plains Sept. 27, 1899, came to Katonah when very young, and was graduated from the Katonah High School. She was active in town affairs, in the Presbyterian church, in the County Christian Endeavor Society, and in the Choral Club. She was with the Northern Westchester Bank for many years and died March 22, 1949.

JULIA ADAMS MEAD,[3] b. in White Plains Oct. 29, 1900, lives with her mother at 73 Valley Rd., Katonah. She is currently treasurer of the school district, chairman of the Historical Committee of the V.I.S., and works in White Plains with the Westchester Children's Association.

LEANDER AUSTIN MEAD,[3] b. in Katonah July 27, 1907, married in St. Mark's Church, Mt. Kisco, Oct. 9, 1937, Marion Sebeth Andrews, daughter of Dr. Frederick and Mrs. Emma (Sebeth) Andrews of Mt. Kisco. Their daughter, DOROTHY JULIA MEAD,[4] was graduated from the Fox Lane High School in 1960, and now attends Plattsburg State University.

Compiled by Janet Doe and K. B. Kelly.

The Fowlers of Cherry Street

HENRY FOWLER[1] came from London to Roxbury, Mass., about 1652. His son, JOSEPH FOWLER,[2] moved to Eastchester, N.Y., and thence to North Castle. Joseph's wife was Hannah Guion. AMMON FOWLER,[3] son of JOSEPH[2] and Hannah, was born in North Castle around 1736. He married 1st Mary Weedon, and she and their son, WEEDON,[4] were baptized July 23, 1761. After Mary Weedon's death, AMMON[3] married Phoebe Haight, widow of Abraham Kipp and daughter of Samuel Haight of Philipse Manor. Phoebe already had a son, Abraham Kipp, Jr. To AMMON[3] and Phoebe were born: REBECCA,[4] b. 1776, mar. Moses Smith in 1797; WILLIAM,[4] b. 1778; HANNAH,[4] 1780-1780; MARY,[4] b. 1783, mar. John Griffen; JAMES H.,[4] b. 1785; SOPHIA,[4] b. 1788, who died at 5 yrs.; and GILBERT.[4] AMMON[3] bought his land on Cherry St. in 1762. He was included in the freeholders' list of 1763 as of Bedford; however, the town records of North Castle for 1773 list him as an overseer of roads in that Township, so it is evident that he didn't move to Bedford as a resident until after that date, or that he returned temporarily to North Castle on the death of his father in 1773. He was a Quaker and took no active part in the war.

WEEDON FOWLER[4] remained a Loyalist during the Revolution and some time prior to 1782 he migrated to St. Johns, New Brunswick, with his father's younger brothers, HENRY[3] and JAMES FOWLER.[3] WEEDON[4] died around 1784 leaving his wife, Elizabeth Sherwood, and several small children, one named AMMON.[5]

WILLIAM FOWLER,[4] b. 1778, married Esther Taylor in 1803 and to them were born: SOPHIA,[5] b. 1803; WEEDON,[5] b. 1807; HENRY H.,[5] b. 1813; and SARAH,[5] mar. John Banks.

WEEDON FOWLER,[5] b. 1807, married Miss Trowbridge in 1829 and they made their home on Cherry St. He was a farmer and sent his milk to New York City to sell. He was an active Presbyterian in Old Katonah. He often drove Rev. J. H. Eastman to Amawalk to preach. He was a man of few words. He died in March, 1898, at 91 yrs., leaving sons: AMMON;[6] JAMES H.;[6] and HENRY H.[6]

AMMON FOWLER[6] farmed the Cherry St. homestead. He married Sarah Bumstead of Bedford Center. They had no children. AMMON[6] sold the farm and moved into the village of Katonah where he died in 1919.

JAMES HENRY FOWLER[6] (Weedon,[5] William,[4] Ammon,[3] Joseph,[2] Henry[1]), b. on Cherry St., moved to Carmel and had 4 sons: ELLSWORTH;[7] EDWARD;[7] J. EDSON;[7] and WILLIAM H.;[7] and one daughter, CLARA.[7]

ELLSWORTH[7] married Edith M. Townsend and raised his family in Carmel. J. EDSON'S[7] son, EDSON FOWLER,[8] and his family live today in Brewster. EDSON'S[8] only child, CHARLES,[9] was born in February, 1937. He has completed his military service and is now attending college.

When New Katonah was being settled, WILLIAM H. FOWLER[7] of Carmel and his wife, Esther Sloat (dau. of Charles Sloat of Cherry St., Katonah) bought the property at the head of The Parkway. He built a fine home and carpenter shop and moved in, in January, 1900. WILLIAM[7] was a building contractor and very active in the development of the new homes. In 1900 he built two houses of his own on Edgemont Rd., using lumber from the old village homes and the old Methodist Episcopal Church, which he had bought for $455. He took the old Parent homestead down and rebuilt it for Harry Mayne, now "Wildwood." He bought land from Samuel Hoyt and built a new home on its site on Deer Park Rd., now belonging to Mrs. James F. Lawrence. His last owner-built home was on Cherry St. and Glenridge Rd., recently owned by the Merz family. He married 3 times and had 4 sons and 2 daughters. By Esther he had: CARRIE,[8] who died in infancy; CLENIDENE SLOAT,[8] b. May 4, 1896; WILLIAM HOYT,[8] b. Dec. 5, 1898, who served in World War I, and died in his early forties; ALICE,[8] who died while attending school in Katonah; and CHARLES MILTON,[8] b. 1909. Mrs. Esther S. Fowler died May 23, 1910, age 40 yrs. By his 2nd wife, Alberta Ganung, WILLIAM[7] had a son, DONALD FOWLER,[8] b. December, 1920. By his third wife, Ida Cox Taylor, there were no children. After the war WILLIAM H.[7] was joined by his sons CLENIDENE[8] and CHARLES MILTON[8] in the building business, known as William H. Fowler and Sons. WILLIAM HOYT FOWLER[8] did not stay in Katonah. Fowlers presently living on the original Fowler land on Cherry St. are CLENIDENE[8] and C. MILTON.[8]

CLENIDENE SLOAT FOWLER,[8] b. in 1896, married Caroline Schulz in 1920.

Clen served in two wars: in the Navy in World War I and with the 13th Naval Construction Battalion in World War II. They have 2 sons: ROBERT C.;[9] and WILLIAM E.[9]

ROBERT C. FOWLER,[9] b. 1922, graduated from Katonah High School 1940, and served with the 3rd Marine Division in World War II and with the First Marine Division in Korea. He is married to Mary M. Bullock and they make their home in California.

WILLIAM EDSON FOWLER,[9] b. 1932, graduated from Katonah High 1949, and served with an Infantry Division in Korea. He married Barbara Anne Haberle and they live in Somers with daughter MARGARET JEAN,[10] b. Nov. 17, 1955, and son STEPHEN EDSON,[10] b. Oct. 19, 1959.

CHARLES MILTON FOWLER,[8] b. 1909, attended Katonah High School. He married Mabel Burt of Katonah and they live on Hickory Rd. They are parents of: CHARLES MILTON, JR.;[9] RICHARD HOYT;[9] and PRISCILLA ANN.[9]

CHARLES MILTON FOWLER, JR.,[9] b. Nov. 10, 1930, graduated from Katonah High School 1948, served in the Korean War, and married Barbara Lane in 1955. Their children are: BRYAN LANE,[10] b. Feb. 27, 1956; and CHRISTOPHER MARTIN,[10] b. Oct. 8, 1958.

RICHARD HOYT FOWLER[9] graduated from Katonah High School 1955. He then studied art and now works in New York City and lives at home.

PRISCILLA ANN FOWLER,[9] b. Dec. 10, 1939, graduated from Katonah High School. She married Richard Dickens, son of Merwin and Helen Dickens of Lake Waccabuc, in 1957. They make their home at Lake Waccabuc with their 2 sons: RICHARD SCOTT,[10] b. May, 1958; and JEFFREY SAMUEL DICKENS,[10] b. July 17, 1960.

Compiled by F. R. Duncombe and K. B. Kelly.

The French Family of Katonah

JOHN HENRY FRENCH,[2] son of JOHN[1] and Polly (Perkins) French, b. 1852, came to this country in 1865. He married Apr. 22, 1872, Phoebe Reynolds (1851-1924), dau. of John J. and Phoebe (Daniels) Reynolds of Cherry St. JOHN[2] was a cobbler and worked with S. O. Arnold in Old Katonah and with his son, Elbridge Arnold, in New Katonah, a total of fifty years. Sept. 26, 1902, he succeeded Leemon Brundage as collector for the Katonah Board of Education. When New York City took their home on Bedford Rd. in May, 1900, they bought and moved into a building (present Marion Shop) on Katonah Ave., where Mrs. French ran a 5- & 10-cent store on the first floor and they lived above. She closed the store after World War I. Both died in 1924. They were parents of 5 children: CHARLES HENRY;[3] MARY;[3] LUCY EVELYN;[3] JOHN WINFIELD;[3] and GROVER C. FRENCH.[3]

CHARLES HENRY FRENCH,[3] b. 1873, married Daisy Emma Light, adopted dau. of Martin Todd. They lived in Katonah, Croton Falls, Jersey City, and Mill Plain, Conn., and were parents of: CLARENCE;[4] GRACE MAY;[4] twin girls,[4] d. y.; CLARA;[4] HAROLD;[4] and EDNA,[4] whose twin brother d. y. The girl twins were born Nov. 30, 1900, in Jersey City. Mrs. French brought them to visit in Purdy's Station where they got cholera and died in August, 1901. CLARENCE FRENCH[4] (1893-September, 1960) lived in Danbury and had 3 children. GRACE MAY FRENCH,[4] b. 1895, married Stanley Baker and lives in Croton Falls. There are no children. CLARA FRENCH,[4] b. Sept. 1, 1902, at Bayonne, N.J., mar. Anthony Chorsky, lives in Croton Falls with 4 children. HAROLD FRENCH,[4] b. 1904, lives in Croton Falls with 4 children. EDNA FRENCH,[4] b. 1912, mar. James Coffey, lives in Danbury with son, WALTER COFFEY.[5]

MARY FRENCH[3] (1875-1957) married Eugene Field Louden, son of William A. and Phoebe (Miller) Louden of Greenwich. He was associated with Young & Halstead and they lived in Mt. Kisco, where their 2 daughters were born, HELEN MAY[4] and DOROTHY AUGUSTA LOUDEN.[4] They moved to Katonah when the girls were young and made their last home at 34 North St. Mr. and Mrs. Louden both died in 1957. HELEN MAY LOUDEN[4] married William James Travis, son of James C. and Elizabeth (Graham) Travis of Katonah (see Travis genealogy). They have no children and lived in Katonah until he retired from the Telephone Company and they moved to Largo, Fla.

DOROTHY AUGUSTA LOUDEN,[4] educated in Katonah, married John A. Lang, a carpenter from Switzerland. They live at 84 Huntville Rd., Katonah. Their 2 children are HELEN LOUDEN[5] and JOHN A. LANG, JR.,[5] HELEN L. LANG,[5] graduated from Katonah High in June, 1950, married Robert Shannon of Eastchester, N.Y. They made their home in Rochester and now live in Medfield, Mass. They are parents of 3 girls: ELIZABETH FRENCH;[6] BARBARA;[6] and JENNIFER LANG SHANNON.[6] JOHN A. LANG, JR.,[5] was active in Scouts and graduated from Katonah High in 1955. He is now a carpenter, fireman, and very interested in the Sportsmen's Club. He married May 9, 1959, in the Katonah Methodist Church, Robyn Glenn, dau. of Walter J. and Dorothea Glenn of Cherry St. JOHN[5] served two years in the Army, stationed at Fort Belvoir, and was separated from the Army July 9, 1959. They have dau. ALLISON LANG,[6] b. 1960.

LUCY EVELYN FRENCH[3] (1878-1942) married John Eastman Daniel (1878-1931) Apr. 26, 1901 (see Daniel genealogy).

JOHN WINFIELD FRENCH,[3] b. Sept. 30, 1880, married 1st Margaret Dowd (1881-1906) of Sharon, Conn., Feb. 7, 1901. Their daughter is DOROTHY MAY FRENCH.[4] He married 2nd Carrie Mason by whom he had twins, LAURA MASON[4] and HARRY JOHN,[4] b. in Mt. Kisco Nov. 24, 1907. JOHN W. FRENCH[3] was a painting contractor. The last home he built was on the corner of Edgemont and Greenville Rds., where he died in 1949. DOROTHY MAY FRENCH[4] was married July 29, 1922, in the Katonah Methodist parsonage to Harry Elwood Oakley, son of Frederick and Sophie (Heilmier) Oakley of White Plains. He has been a driver for H. H. Park, Inc., 35 years. They have no children and live on Greenville Rd.

LAURA MASON FRENCH[4] graduated from Katonah High, married Feb. 20, 1932, James Eisenhauer of Pennsylvania. They built a home at 84 Huntville Rd. He was transferred to California where they now live. Their daughter, JUDITH EISENHAUER,[5] b. May 10, 1940, married Emile Allan Pelletier June 25, 1960. HARRY JOHN FRENCH[4] is the Katonah postmaster and lives on Valley Rd. He married Sept. 20, 1930, Gladys Ruggles, dau. of Charles Henry and Effie C. (Hoyt) Ruggles of Katonah. Their son, HARRY JOHN FRENCH, JR.,[5] was born Sept. 16, 1932. He graduated from Katonah High School June, 1950, entered the U. S. Navy and served during the Korean War 1950-1953 as a gunner's mate. He married Lois Grimason of Waccabuc. Their children are: LOUISA,[6] b. July 23, 1954; and PETER FRENCH,[6] b. Nov. 27, 1955. HARRY[5] was employed as an RFD mail carrier in the Katonah Post Office when he was killed in a car accident Jan. 27, 1957. Mrs. French and children are living in Rumson, N.J.

GROVER CLEVELAND FRENCH[3] was born in 1884. He spent his youth in Katonah, worked for the Juengst factory in 1902 and later was a painter. He married Grace Merritt of White Plains and they had: IRMA;[4] WALTON;[4] RICHARD;[4] CHARLOTTE;[4] RUTH;[4] and CHARLES.[4] They spent most of their life in Mt. Kisco and White Plains where he died about 1955. Mrs. French lives in Hawthorne, as does CHARLES[4] and his family of 4 children. CHARLOTTE[4] at one time lived with her aunt, Mrs. Eugene Louden, and attended the Katonah school. She married and has two children.

Compiled by K. B. Kelly.

The Gorham Family of Katonah

FREDERICK W. GORHAM[10] was a Mayflower-descendant through three persons who came to this country on that vessel: JOHN TILLEY,[1] his daughter ELIZABETH TILLEY,[2] and JOHN HOWLAND,[2] whom she later married. The Gorham line leads back: Henry Gorham;[9] David Gorham;[8] Jabez Gorham;[7] Jabez Gorham;[6] Joseph Gorham;[5] Jabez Gorham;[4] Desire Howland,[3] mar. John Gorham; John Howland,[2] mar. Elizabeth Tilley;[2] John Tilley.[1]

FREDERICK GORHAM[10] came to Katonah from Bethel, Conn., in 1882 and opened a drugstore in the old village, first on Railroad Ave., and later on Main St. In 1884 he married Eliza Blakeslee, dau. of Joseph and Eliza Bishop Blakeslee in Bethel, Conn. They bought the old public school house on South Rd. in Old Katonah and made it into their home. The house is now situated at 95 Edgemont Rd. When the village moved, Mr. Gorham built at 25 The Parkway. Here they lived and he had his drugstore. Later they built on Terrace Heights. He retired from business in 1921.

He was at one time president of the Board of Education; also president of the Board of Trade, and served on the Executive Committee of the Katonah Village Improvement Society. He was the first contributor to the Building Fund for the present Library building. Known for his photography, Mr. Gorham took many views of the new village of Katonah.

Mrs. Gorham supervised the publication by the Village Improvement Society in 1900 of "Sketches and Views of Old and New Katonah." The Gorhams both were active in the Presbyterian Church.

A daughter, HELEN,[11] born to them in the old village, married R. Benson Ray, son of George S. and Florence Warren Ray of Katonah (see Ray genealogy).

Compiled by Alma R. Crane and K. B. Kelly.

The Green Families

Many families with the name of Green have settled in and around Katonah. It is probable that all descended from JOHN GREEN[1] and Joanne Tattershall who came from Salisbury, England, to Boston in 1635.

JOHN GREEN[5] (Barlow,[4] Peter,[3] John,[2] John[1]) b. in Warwick, R.I., 1731, d. 1798, moved to North Castle, N.Y., in 1774. He and his wife, Amy Hawxhurst of Oyster Bay, L.I., were parents of: JOHN;[6] SAMUEL;[6] ISAIAH;[6] JARED;[6] OLIVER;[6] ISRAEL;[6] DEBORAH,[6] mar. Thomas Green; FANNY,[6] mar. John Palmer; and MARY,[6] mar. Hopkins. In the Quaker Cemetery at Amawalk lie: I. Green, d. 1848 (or 9) aged 55; Jared, d. 1839, aged 82; Caroline, date unreadable; Jemima, d. 1850, aged 83; Jared, Jr., d. 1834, aged 44; Oliver (Feb. 15, 1788-Oct. 1862); Betsey (Feb. 11, 1794-Aug. 2, 1851); and another Betsey.

JARED GREEN[6] (1757-1839) owned 185 acres of land in 1837 as recorded in town books of Bedford. JARED GREEN, JR.[7] (1790-1834) we believe was the son of JARED.[6] PHEBE GREEN[7] (1802-1883) was probably a daughter of JARED.[6] PHEBE[7] married William Wood, son of Squire Wood (see Wood genealogy).

OLIVER GREEN[7] (1788-1862) who lies buried in the plot with JARED[6] and Jemima (dau. of Arnell and Mary Ackerly Dickinson) we believe is their son. OLIVER[7] married Betsey Holly, daughter of Jonah and Lydia Banks Holly (see Holly genealogy). A son was JARED HOLLY GREEN.[8]

JARED HOLLY GREEN,[8] d. Feb. 26, 1891, aged 75 yrs., 8 mons., 26 days, is mentioned on a map of 1862 as a merchant of Bedford Village. In town assessment records, 1878-83, he was assessed $6,670 and owned 152 acres on Maple Ave. This land extending to the Cross River is now owned by Mrs. Paul Sturtevant. JARED HOLLY[8] married Susan Weeks (1817-1893), a Quaker from Amawalk. They had daughters but no sons.

OLIVER GREEN[8] (1829-1882), related to JARED HOLLY GREEN[8] and possibly a brother, lived next to him on Maple Ave. to the south, near Cantitoe, and in 1879-83 owned 112 acres of land assessed at $3,800. He was the 1st secretary of the Bedford Farmers' Club, and is buried in Kensico Cemetery. He married Armenia Hoyt. Their children were: EVELYN;[9] and OLIVER WENDELL.[9]

OLIVER WENDELL GREEN,[9] b. on Maple Ave., married in June, 1900, Josephine Brown and moved into a new home on Highland Ave., the first house built on the hill. Mr. Green was a salesman for Schrafft's in New York. Resigning due to poor health, he became road commissioner for the Town of Bedford. After his death in 1936, Mrs. Green became head of the Welfare Department of the Town of Bedford. Mr. and Mrs. Green were very active in village affairs and the Methodist Church. Their children were: OLIVER WENDELL, JR.;[10] and GRACE,[10] who mar. Baldwin Smith in May, 1934, and lives on Huntville Rd. Mr. Smith is chairman of the English Department at the John Jay High School.

OLIVER WENDELL GREEN, JR.,[10] married Marjorie Harmon of Somers. They lived in Katonah until several years ago when they moved to Somers. He works for Brady-Stannard in Brewster. Their children are: OLIVER WENDELL III,[11] b. Sept. 30, 1935; and NANCY,[11] b. May, 1946.

OLIVER WENDELL GREEN III[11] married Kathleen Prandoni. They have a daughter, MELANIE ANN,[12] b. July 31, 1960, in Germany.

* * * * *

Descended from JOHN GREEN[1] (Caleb,[7] Samuel,[6] John,[5] Barlow,[4] Peter,[3] John,[2] John[1]), SAMUEL FOWLER GREEN[8] farmed his homestead in Somers, later taken for the reservoirs, and also the farm lands now used by Lincoln Hall. SAMUEL'S[8] sons, EDWARD S.[9] and CALEB C.,[9] were the founders of Green Bros.' store in Goldens Bridge.

EDWARD S. GREEN,[9] b. 1863, moved from Goldens Bridge to Pawling, N.Y. He died at Daytona Beach, Fla., 1940. He and his wife, Julia Brady, had one son, CLARENCE K.,[10] who was brought up in Katonah but now resides in Goldens Bridge with his wife, Eliza Silkman Hunt. Their only son, ROBERT EDWARD GREEN[11] is in the gravel business and is justice of the peace in the town of Lewisboro. Born Mar. 21, 1927, he graduated from Katonah High School and served in the U. S. Navy during World War II. June 19, 1949, he married Helen Ann Young from Red Bank, N.J. They are parents of: ROBERT EDWARD, JR.,[12] b. 1950; RICHARD DAVID,[12] b. 1952; SUSANNE ELIZABETH,[12] b. 1958; and CYNTHIA LEIGH,[12] b. 1960.

CALEB C. GREEN,[9] b. Aug. 1, 1861, lived in Goldens Bridge until his death June 7, 1921. He married 1st Dec. 11, 1889, Sarah Ella Thorn and after her death in 1895, married 2nd Elizabeth Healy, the mother of his children: RALPH[10] (1900-1902); HAROLD HEALY,[10] b. 1902; HELEN[10] (1904-1906); MARION;[10] and GEORGE WALDO.[10] HAROLD H.,[10] married to Beatrice Denton of Pawling, carries on the family store in Goldens Bridge. GEORGE W.[10] married Helen Colyer of New York City and they are parents of: LYNDA;[11] MARION;[11] and PHYLLIS.[11] They now reside on Pleasant St., Katonah.

* * * * *

Descended from JOHN GREEN[1] also was HACKALIAH GREEN[8] (John,[7] Samuel,[6] John,[5] Barlow,[4] Peter,[3] John,[2] John[1]). HACKALIAH GREEN[8] (1815-1888) and his wife, Huldah Vriedenburg, lived on the Cross River in Whitlockville. Their son was OSCAR[9] who married Marion Green. OSCAR[9] and Marion were parents of CLIFFORD[10] (1890-1960); ETHEL,[10] b. 1891, who married William Kellogg; and ALICE,[10] b. 1893, who married Elliott Kellogg (see Kellogg genealogy).

* * * * *

Descended from JOHN GREEN[1] (Emma Nelson Green,[8] Israel,[7] Samuel,[6] John,[5] Barlow,[4] Peter,[3] John,[2] John[1]) was KATHRYN GREEN LOUNSBURY[9] who married George Nelson, great-grandson of Gen. William Green and Martha Archer. Sons of George and KATE NELSON[9] were: HARRY[10] and GEORGE NELSON,[10] who grew up in Katonah. Their last home is now owned by Dr. Tschorn and used as a medical center.

* * * * *

HERMAN GREEN[1] (1804-1898), a prosperous farmer in Goldens Bridge, owned property now belonging to Mrs. Richard C. Bondy. It was for him that Herman Chapel was named, the small Methodist church on North Salem Rd. which stood on land now owned by Mr. and Mrs. Edwin Patrick. His wife, Mary, died Oct. 12, 1879, at 79 yrs. Both Herman and Mary are buried in Ivandell Cemetery, Somers. Their son,

BYRON GREEN[2] (1831-1881), lived on the farm with his wife, Sarah Halstead. They had 2 daughters: MARION[3] and FLORENCE[3] (Flora). FLORENCE[3] married Daniel H. Todd and ran the homestead farm. MARION[3] married OSCAR GREEN,[9] son of Hackaliah and Huldah Green. MARION GREEN[3] spent most of her life in Katonah after her husband's death. She was a wonderful woman, organist in the Methodist, Presbyterian, and Episcopal Churches. She was a charter member of St. Luke's Episcopal Church, Katonah. She died Dec. 20, 1954, at 87 yrs. Her granddaughter, MRS. WILSON HINKLEY,[5] lives in her old home on Edgemont Rd.

* * * * *

Green families other than those we can trace back to JOHN:[1]

THADDEUS K. GREEN[1] (1788-1862) and his wife, Nancy, had sons: ALSOPH;[2] STEPHEN[2] of Pound Ridge; and WILLIAM[2] of North Castle.

ALSOPH GREEN[2] (1834-1885) lived in New Castle until 1870 when he came to Katonah and bought the hotel which he called "The Green Hotel." In 1879, ALSOPH[2] owned a good deal of property. He had 2 children: ANNA LAVINIA[3] ("Venie"), who married Apr. 30, 1884, Dr. Walton J. Carpenter (see Carpenter genealogy); and THADDEUS K.[3] THADDEUS[3] continued to run the Green Hotel and when the City took the land, he moved it to Bernard Travis' orchard, which became known as Greenville. The hotel still stands, Teddy's Lakeside Inn. The sons of THADDEUS[3] were ROBERT[4] and OLIVER.[4]

WILLIAM GREEN[2] of North Castle, son of THADDEUS[1] and Nancy, had a daughter, CAROLINE E.,[3] b. 1866, who married Charles Avery Whitlock of Katonah, son of Aaron Burr and Sarah Ann Avery Whitlock (see Whitlock genealogy).

* * * * *

GEORGE GREEN,[1] owner of the Metropole Hotel in New York City, bought many acres in the Cross River valley above Hoyt's Mills and built a large home and stock farm. He married 1st Susan Putney, daughter of Old Katonah's first merchant, David, and they had one son, JOHN.[2] After Susan's death, he married 2nd her cousin, Estella Putney Hadden, who disliked hotel-living, so they stayed in Katonah. They had twin sons, LEROY[2] and GEORGE,[2] d. y. On the farm they had 350 horses at a time, pigs, chickens and cows. There was a large club house with all kinds of games and a bowling alley. Through Mr. Green's farm, many folks came to Katonah to make their homes, John, Valentine, Mary and Peter Miller, and William King. Mr. Green was a wonderful host and generous man. After his death, the farm was sold in January, 1897. JOHN GREEN[2] went back to New York. He married Derando Mayo, daughter of actor Frank Mayo. LEROY GREEN[2] made his home with the John H. Truesdells and entered Holbrook Military Academy in 1902, with Walton T. Carpenter, Thomson Dean and James Benedict. LEROY[2] later moved to Hawaii, where he lived with his wife, Dorothy, and daughters, VALERIE[3] and ELEANOR.[3] VALERIE[3] married a doctor and lives in Phoenixville, Pa., and has a son. ELEANOR[3] became a doctor, married a doctor, and lives in Hawaii.

* * * * *

HENRY GREEN[1] married Hannah Knapp and had children: CHARLES;[2] and SARAH ELIZA.[2]

CHARLES GREEN,[2] b. 1852, married Abigail E. Reynolds. They were parents of 7 children and lived on The Terrace, Katonah. Daughter ELLA A.[3] was the mother of BARNES OLMSTEAD,[4] who was in the march of Bataan and later died in a prison camp. IDA E.,[5] d. 1960, married William Pinchbeck and they had sons: JOSEPH;[4] WILLIAM ELMER;[4] and FRANK,[4] who graduated from Katonah High School and now lives on Crompond Rd., Yorktown, a grandparent. MARTHA[3] married Lars Pederson. Both have died, and PAUL PEDERSON,[4] their only son, educated in Katonah, married, lives upstate. ELMER[3] married 3 times but left no children. PHEBE[3] married Howard Dakin of Mt. Kisco.

SARAH ELIZA GREEN[2] married Joseph Bailey Allen, son of Alvah S. and Phoebe Allen of North Salem. They moved to Katonah and had 2 children: LYDIA JANE;[3] and MELVILLE JOSEPH ALLEN[3] (see Allen genealogy).

Compiled by F. R. Duncombe and K. B. Kelly.

The Haight Family of Old Cherry Street

The early spelling of this name was Hoit, Hait, Hoyt or Haight. The first known Haight in this country was SIMEON (or SIMON) HAIGHT,[1] who came from England in 1628 or 1629. He landed in Salem, Mass., and moved south to settle finally in Rye, N.Y., in 1678. His great-grandson, JONATHAN HAIGHT[4] (Samuel,[3] Nicholas,[2] Simeon[1]), moved to North Castle. Jonathan's son, DAVID,[5] married as his second wife Abigail Purdy. Their son, DAVID,[6] b. at Purchase about 1748, married Elizabeth Wetmore, b. at Rye, 1750, dau. of James and Elizabeth (Abraham) Wetmore. James Wetmore, a Quaker and a Tory, moved to Canada during the Revolution or shortly thereafter and died in New Brunswick in 1790.

DAVID HAIGHT[6] and Elizabeth Wetmore Haight came to Bedford and made their home on old Cherry St. (now Harris Rd.) and Bedford Rd. at the present site of the home of Mrs. Reginald Vockins. Their ten children were: ABIGAIL;[7] JAMES;[7] SUSANNAH;[7] ELIZABETH;[7] ESTHER;[7] ALTHEA;[7] CALEB;[7] MARY;[7] DAVID;[7] and LAVINIA.[7] DAVID[6] died Sept. 3, 1836, and Elizabeth, June 10, 1843. They are both buried in St. Matthew's churchyard, Bedford, N.Y.

ABIGAIL HAIGHT,[7] b. 1770, married John Harris and they lived in Canada where she died in 1852.

JAMES HAIGHT,[7] b. 1773, was a vestryman at St. Matthew's Church, Bedford, 1824-1839, 1844-1845, 1846-1853. He never married and died in 1866.

SUSANNAH HAIGHT[7] married Garret Williamson and they lived in Chenango Forks, N.Y. Their grand-daughter was SUSAN MILLER WILLIAMSON,[9] dau. of E. M. WILLIAMSON.[8]

ELIZABETH HAIGHT,[7] b. in Rye, married Elias Miller and lived in Chenango Forks, N.Y.

ESTHER HAIGHT,[7] b. in Rye, 1782, married Timothy Birdsall of Peekskill (see Birdsall genealogy).

ALTHEA HAIGHT,[7] b. 1783, in Rye, died unmar. at 82 yrs., 7 mon., Apr. 1, 1866.

CALEB HAIGHT[7] married 1st Betsey Whitlock, dau. of Thaddeus and Grace (Burr) Whitlock (see Whitlock genealogy), and 2nd, Maria Jackson. He was overseer of highways in 1832, 1836, 1837 and 1860. He was vestryman for many years at St. Matthew's Church. Their children were: BETSEY;[8] NICHOLAS;[8] CALEB;[8] and JOHN.[8] He owned 84 acres of land adjoining that of Abigail Banks.

MARY HAIGHT,[7] known as Polly, was born 1787. She married Phineas Hoit and their son, DAVID HOIT[8] (1819-1885), married Catharine Lyon (1826-1909), dau. of William and Rachel (Robertson) Lyon (see Lyon and Robertson genealogies). Catharine Lyon Hoit lived on the homestead with her sister Betsey Lyon. Charles Herbert Lyon, son of their brother, John Addison, inherited it from Catharine.

DAVID HAIGHT,[7] b. 1790, married Deborah Battey (1790-1835) and their children were: JAMES;[8] THOMAS B.[8] (1820-1844); DAVID;[8] MARY LAVINIA[8] (1825-1864); and AUGUSTA ANN,[8] who died unmar. May 30, 1871, at 43 yrs. DAVID[7] was mentioned as a weaver in September, 1817.

LAVINIA HAIGHT,[7] b. 1791, married Moses Marshall (see Marshall genealogy).

NICHOLAS HAIGHT[7] (John,[6] David,[5] Jonathan,[4] Samuel,[3] Nicholas,[2] Simeon[1]), b. 1760, married Jemima Halstead (1763-1807), dau. of Lt. Ezekiel Halstead, who served in the Revolution. NICHOLAS[7] was pathmaster of Cherry St. Road District in 1797 and lived on Harris Rd. (then part of Cherry St.). He died May 16, 1818, at 57 yrs., 8 mos., and 20 days. In August, 1819, his farm was auctioned off. Heirs were Benjamin, Halstead E., Henry, John, Nicholas, Warren, Abigail, wife of Jotham Smute, Mary, Elizabeth, Christine Augusta Grant and James Grant Haight. NICHOLAS[7] and Jemima are buried in the Haight Cemetery beside the railroad tracks in Bedford Hills.

HENRY HAIGHT,[8] b. 1785, heir of NICHOLAS,[7] married Sophia (1793-1877) and lived on Cherry St. in the present Robert Ross house. He owned a wool-carding and fulling mill at his home. He was vestryman at St. Matthew's 1854-1855. He died Dec. 3, 1855, and is buried in St. Matthew's Cemetery.

Compiled by Alice Beckley Taylor and F. R. Duncombe.

The Hait Family of Mt. Holly

This family is known as Haight, Hait, Hoit, and Hoyt. SIMON (SIMEON) HAIT[1] or Hoyt was mentioned in 1629 as of Charlestown, Mass. His son, BENJAMIN HAIT,[2] b. in Windsor, Conn., 1644, married twice. JONAS HAIT,[3] his son, b. 1679, married Sarah Smith of Stamford, Conn., in 1705.

DANIEL HAIT,[4] b. Aug. 17, 1706 (Jonas,[3] Benjamin,[2] Simon[1]), married Jemima Lounsbury in 1731. In 1740 he sold his lands in Stamford to his uncle, Benjamin, and is recorded in 1741 as a Bedford freeholder. DANIEL[4] and Jemima were parents of 10 children: DANIEL,[5] b. 1731; ISRAEL,[5] b. 1733; JEMIMA,[5] b. 1735; SARAH,[5] b. 1736; ELIZABETH,[5] b. 1738; JONAS,[5] b. 1740; ABRAHAM;[5] JACOB,[5] b. 1748; HANNAH;[5] and PHINEAS.[5]

DANIEL HAIT[5] married Martha Smith and they had 10 children, all born in Bedford: MARY,[6] b. 1758, mar. Enos Weed in 1784 at Salem; EZRA,[6] b. 1759; SARAH,[6] b. 1761, mar. Elisha Sheldon; MARTHA,[6] b. 1763, mar. Peter Sherman at Salem; ISAAC,[6] b. 1765; ELIZABETH,[6] b. 1767, mar. Joshua Hobby; ALETHA,[6] b. 1770, mar. Elisha Palmer; LYDIA,[6] b. 1772, mar. Ebenezar Hobby; DANIEL[6] (1773-1778); and DAVID[6] (1777-1778).

ISRAEL HAIT[5] married Joanna Holmes. They had 9 children: THADDEUS,[6] b. 1761; ISRAEL;[6] JOHN;[6] ABIJA;[6] AMOS;[6] JAMES;[6] HANNAH;[6] JEMIMA;[6] and HULDA.[6]

JONAS HAIT[5] married Mary Lewis and their 7 children were: LEWIS;[6] STEPHEN;[6] SAMUEL;[6] ELIAS,[6] b. 1781; EUNICE,[6] mar. Stephen Newman (see Newman genealogy); BETHIAH,[6] who mar. Isaac Hait and had son, MARTIN HAIT,[7] b. 1803, who mar. Emeline Wright and lived in Bedford; ABIGAIL,[6] b. 1808, mar. William Todd.

ABRAHAM HAIT[5] and wife, Keziah, had 6 children: PRUDENCE,[6] mar. Elisha Clark of Bedford; REBECCA,[6] who mar. Lyman Gregory; PHINEAS,[6] mar. Mary; DANIEL,[6] b. 1787, mar. Phoebe Lyon; ELIJA,[6] lost at sea; KEZIAH,[6] who mar. John Gray. PHINEAS[6] and DANIEL[6] stayed in Bedford.

JACOB HAIT,[5] b. 1748, married Anne Bishop, b. 1750. Their 5 children were: SOLOMON,[6] b. 1781; CLARA,[6] b. 1783 or 1785, mar. Benjamin Benedict of Lewisboro; JESSE,[6] b. 1786, mar. Sarah Clark in 1828; SAMUEL,[6] b. 1792, mar. Catherine Howe; and ANNE,[6] b. 1794, who mar. Silas Reynolds and lived in Somers. JESSE[6] and SAMUEL[6] stayed in Bedford.

ABRAHAM,[5] JONAS,[5] ISRAEL,[5] JACOB,[5] and PHINEAS[5] all served in the 2nd Regt., Westchester County Militia, during the Revolution.

On the highway assessment list of 1797 for Bedford, ISAAC HOYT[6] (Hait) was pathmaster and JONAS,[5] ABRAHAM,[5] JACOB[5] and DANIEL[5] were all listed in the same district (Mt. Holly area).

ISAAC HAIT,[6] b. 1765 (Daniel,[5] Daniel,[4] Jonas,[3] Benjamin,[2] Simon[1]), married 1st Abigail Ayers, by whom he had a son DANIEL HAIT,[7] b. 1801; and 2nd BETHIAH,[6] daughter of JONAS[5] and Mary Hait, by whom he had MARTIN.[7] ISAAC,[6] Abigail and BETHIAH[6] were buried in the Mt. Holly graveyard, as were also a Betsy and Hattie Hait, and removed at the coming of the Cross River Reservoir. Other Haits buried there were Daniel, Sarah, Martin, John, Mary, Warren Hait and Sarah his wife, Elias Hait and Esther his wife, Jessie Hait, Kate Hait, Annie Hait, Jacob Hait.

ELIAS HAIT,[6] son of JONAS[5] and Mary, inherited his father's farm on Mt. Holly in 1816. He and his wife, Esther, were parents of WEBSTER H. HAIT,[7] b. 1813, mar. Eliza Pullen. He was a merchant. ELIAS GRANT HAIT,[8] b. 1824, son of WEBSTER[7] and Eliza, mar. Cathy Haight Reynolds and went by the Haight spelling. In 1862 they lived on Cross River Rd. in the last house in Bedford (now owned by Oliver Barbour).

DANIEL HAIT[7] (Isaac,[6] Daniel,[5] Daniel,[4] Jonas,[3] Benjamin,[2] Simon[1]) (1801-1856) married Harriet Todd (1799-1898). Their son, ISAAC N. HAIT,[8] b. 1837, married Alathea Merritt Lyon, dau. of Newman Clark and Alathea (Merritt) Lyon of Bedford (see Lyon genealogy). He was a farmer and they spent most of their years in the old homestead, which he sold to George Green. Mr. Hait moved to New York City but returned and bought a place in South Salem where he died March, 1907. ISAAC[8] and Alathea's children were: HARRIET TODD[9] (1863-1870); ALATHEA

Louisa,[9] b. 1865; EMILY VIRGINIA,[9] b. 1874; IDA MAY,[9] b.1879, d. 1945 in Douglas, Ariz.; and JAMES MERRITT HAIT[9] (1878-1932).

EMILY VIRGINIA HAIT[9] married Sept. 12, 1900, GEORGE LINUS HOYT[8] (1874-1956) (Stephen,[7] Jared,[6] Stephen,[5] Jonas,[4] Benjamin, Jr.,[3] Benjamin,[2] Simon Hoyt[1]) of South Salem. They made their home on Oscaleta Rd., the Hoyt family home since 1802. Their three children: JAMES DUDLEY;[10] ALATHEA PRIDHAM,[10] who mar. Spencer Collin Dec. 6, 1957, and resides on Oscaleta Rd.; and MILLICENT BELL HOYT,[10] who mar. Christian Meyer in August, 1941, and lives in Ardsley, N. Y. The daughters have no children. GEORGE L. HOYT[8] married 2nd Apr. 7, 1951, Christine Loos, who makes her home at Truesdale Lake.

J. DUDLEY HOYT,[10] b. Apr. 8, 1904, married Mary Alice Myers of Millerton, N.Y., June 30, 1932. He owns his own garage business in South Salem. Their only child, RODGER STEPHEN,[11] b. Apr. 29, 1934, graduated from Katonah High School in 1951, from Cobleskill in 1953, and from Kansas State, 1957. In 1954 RODGER[11] married Janet Brower of Cedarhurst, L. I. They live in Ithaca, N.Y., where he is with the New York State Breeders Association. Their 2 children are: CYNTHIA LYNN,[12] b. Apr. 22, 1957; and STEPHEN RODGER,[12] b. Dec. 21, 1958.

JAMES MERRITT HAIT[9] married Belle Silvey. Their children are: ROSWELL NEWTON,[10] living in Whippany, N.J., HELEN,[10] mar. Kenneth M. Williams, living in Carbondale, Pa.; MORTIMER,[10] residing in Madison, N.J., with wife, Jane, and sons MORTIMER, JR.,[11] and BRADFORD;[11] KATHRYN;[10] and JAMES MERRITT, JR.,[10] who lives in California.

Compiled by F. R. Duncombe and K. B. Kelly.

The Hanford Family

JACOB WALLACE HANFORD,[1] b. in North Salem, Nov. 4, 1814, later lived in Sodom near Brewster and moved in 1839 to Whitlockville. He was a cabinet-maker and furniture-dealer, and for many years in the undertaking business; this he sold to Samuel B. Hoyt in 1858. After this sale he bought the old Whitlock factory and manufactured felloes (rims) for wheels. He married Betsey Whitlock (see Whitlock genealogy), dau. of John Burr and Rachel (Olmsted) Whitlock of Whitlockville. There he owned many plots of land and lived, some of the time, west of the village where the Croton and Cross Rivers joined. To JACOB[1] and Betsey were born 3 children: CHARLES EDGAR;[2] HOBART;[2] and FRANCES ELIZABETH.[2] Mrs. Hanford, b. Jan. 29, 1819, in Whitlockville, died Oct. 21, 1873. She was very active in the Methodist Episcopal Church. Mr. Hanford died in December, 1890, after a long illness. He was survived by his daughter, his sons having died before him.

CHARLES EDGAR HANFORD,[2] b. Feb. 6, 1843, married Mary Emma Kipp July 8, 1868, and died before 1874.

HOBART HANFORD,[2] b. April 8, 1847, married Henrietta Griffin. They were parents of one son, HENRY GRIFFIN HANFORD,[3] b. in April, 1875, in Hyde Park, Pa.

FRANCES ELIZABETH HANFORD[2] (Nov. 9, 1853-Feb. 26, 1920) married William A. Miller (1852-1883), son of D. Merritt and Mary Ann (Hoyt) Miller. Frances was a devoted member of the Methodist Episcopal Church and was organist of the Church in Old Katonah. FRANCES[2] and William A. Miller were the parents of one daughter, VIDA HOYT MILLER[3] (1878-1936) (see Miller genealogy).

Compiled by K. B. Kelly and Madelon Ryan.

The Hitt Family of Old Katonah

One of the popular personalities in Old Katonah was EDGAR HITT[2] (called Bobbie), son of HIRAM[1] and Clarissa Jessup Hitt.

Born in Somers, Oct. 23, 1833, he came to Katonah in 1871. He served in the Civil War in the 4th Regt. Heavy Artillery and was at the theater in Washington the night Lincoln was shot. Shortly before that he had been married and when the war was over he and his wife lived for a time in Pound Ridge.

In Katonah he was well known as a wheelwright, blacksmith and inventor. Among his inventions was a "Tire Upsetter," a device for tightening the metal rim of a wheel.

The Hitts had 2 daughters. The elder, CASSIE,[3] b. 1872, married Thomas Barton in 1888 and had one daughter by him. The other DAUGHTER,[3] born in 1874, married William Hanlon and moved to Connecticut. They had 10 children.

CASSIE HITT[3] married 3 times, her 2nd husband being Alfred Daniel, Jr., by whom she had a son who died at 18. Cassie's 3rd husband was Frank Hoffman, by whom she had no children.

EFFIE BARTON,[4] daughter of Mrs. Hoffman's first marriage, married Joseph Collyer. Effie and Joseph had one son who died at 18.

Mrs. Hoffman, long identified with Old and New Katonah and a contributor of reminiscences to this book, sold her house on Bedford Rd. in 1959 to St. Luke's Church and has gone to live with her daughter in Newtown, Conn. She is missed for her unfailing neighborly kindness towards all.

Compiled by K. B. Kelly.

The Holly Family of Mt. Holly

JOHN HOLLY[1] (1618-1681), b. in England, came to America in 1630 with his two brothers. In 1642 he bought land in Stamford from William Newman. He was an important citizen: marshal, collector of customs and excise, deputy, and selectman. He married Mary and they had 8 children. ELISHA HOLLY[2] (1658-1719), next to the youngest child of JOHN,[1] married Martha Holmes, dau. of Stephen. ELISHA[2] was an auditor and justice and represented Stamford at the Assembly in Hartford. ELISHA[2] and Martha were the parents of 10 children. Their eldest son, ELISHA HOLLY[3] (1687-1752), married Rebecca Bishop in January, 1715, and they had 8 children. DANIEL HOLLY,[3] cousin of ELISHA,[3] lived in Bedford around 1717 with his 2nd wife, Abigail Clawson.

STEPHEN HOLLY,[4] son of ELISHA[3] and Rebecca, was born in Stamford in 1728. He married 1st Hannah Marshall in 1751, who was the mother of REBECCA,[5] who married Joseph Benedict and lived in South Salem. STEPHEN[4] married 2nd in 1765, Lois Mead of Greenwich. He spent some of his life in the Manor of Cortlandt, probably around South Salem. His will was probated Feb. 8, 1771, in Stamford. Lois was left guardian of their children: STEPHEN;[5] ISAAC;[5] JONAH;[5] and HANNAH.[5]

JONAH HOLLY[5] (1767-1844), the first of the name to settle on our present Mt. Holly Rd., was pathmaster there in 1795. He married Lydia Banks (1773-1859), dau. of John and Elizabeth Banks of the same area. JONAH[5] and Lydia were parents of: STEPHEN;[6] JOHN B.;[6] LOIS;[6] BETSEY;[6] and DEBORAH.[6]

STEPHEN HOLLY[6] (1803-1868) married Polly Banks (1794-1872) of Greenwich Way, now called Banksville. They lived on Mt. Holly Rd. in the house presently owned by his great-grandsons, HARVEY[9] and HOLLY AVERY.[9] STEPHEN[6] and Polly were parents of JONAH[7] (1824-1898) and BENJAMIN[7] (1830-1851). STEPHEN[6] and his brother, JOHN,[6] were active in the Cross River Baptist Church. JOHN B. HOLLY[6] (1804-1876), son of JONAH[5] and Lydia, married Deborah R. LOIS MEAD HOLLY[6] (1796-1866) married Alvah Miller and lived on Mt. Holly (see Miller genealogy). BETSEY HOLLY[6] married Oliver Green and lived on Cantitoe Rd., the present Maple Ave. (see Green genealogy). DEBORAH HOLLY[6] (1799-1857) never married. All of JONAH[5] and Lydia's children except Betsey were buried in the neighborhood graveyard now under the Cross River Reservoir and were removed to Union Cemetery, Bedford. BETSEY[6] is buried in Amawalk Quaker Cemetery.

JONAH HOLLY[7] (Stephen,[6] Jonah,[5] Stephen,[4] Elisha,[3] Elisha,[2] John[1]) b. in the Mt. Holly homestead, married Mary Benedict (1833-1928), 7th child of Jesse and Esther (Keeler) Benedict, who lived on the South Salem-Ridgefield road. For her, JONAH[7] built a large home at the top of the hill at the sharp corner on Mt. Holly Road. This burned and they moved down into STEPHEN's[6] house. JONAH[7] was a pillar in the Cross River Baptist Church. He was a well-to-do farmer of many acres with a hobby of fine horses. JONAH[7] and Mary's children were: MARIETTA;[8] and STEPHEN J.[8]

MARIETTA[8] (1854-1950) married Gideon Harvey Avery (1852-1928) of Cross River Nov. 4, 1874 (see Avery genealogy). They made their home with her parents. MARIETTA[8] loved music and taught music to many of the neighborhood children. They were parents of: ALETTA MARY[9] (1876-1949); HARVEY JONAH,[9] b. in 1889; and HOLLY GIDEON AVERY,[9] b. 1898. The children attended the Mt. Holly School and came into Katonah for advanced courses. HARVEY[9] for many years lived in Katonah and was in the auto business. HOLLY[9] remained on the farm and specialized in bees and honey. The brothers live in the homestead and have never married.

STEPHEN J. HOLLY[8] (1864-1922), son of JONAH[7] and Mary, married

Julia Garrison (1873-1947) of New York. They lived in the house now occupied by Mr. and Mrs. John Hyatt Choate on Mt. Holly. Their children were: EUNICE MAY,[9] b. 1893, who mar. Robert Waite of Pound Ridge and had no children; LEWIS J.;[9] HOWARD STEPHEN;[9] ALICE MARIETTA;[9] ESTHER BENEDICT;[9] and LEROY GARRISON.[9]

LEWIS J. HOLLY[9] (1897-1954), a painting contractor, married Myrtle Osterberg of Cross River. They made their home on Old Shop Road, Cross River, where Mrs. Holly still lives. They were parents of one son, LEWIS REYNOLDS.[10] Born in 1939, LEWIS[10] was president of his Senior Class of 1957 at John Jay High School and is now attending Marietta College, Ohio, as a pre-medical student. He is the only male Holly of the 10th generation left to carry on the family name in this area.

HOWARD STEPHEN HOLLY,[9] b. 1901, married Annie Whitman. They are parents of AUDREY,[10] b. 1939; and NAN,[10] b. 1940.

ALICE MARIETTA HOLLY,[9] b. 1904, married Clarence R. Moore. Their daughter, DORIS EUNICE MOORE,[10] b. 1922, married Harold Reynolds and they are parents of 5 children: GRAHAM,[11] b. 1947; RAEMONDE ALICE,[11] b. 1949; GARRISON,[11] b. 1954; LUCINDA[11] and ALEXANDER REYNOLDS,[11] twins, b. 1958.

ESTHER BENEDICT HOLLY,[9] b. 1907, married Clinton Tripp. They have 2 daughters: ARLENE VIRGINIA,[10] b. 1928; and SHIRLEY ROBERTA TRIPP,[10] b. 1930. ARLENE VIRGINIA TRIPP[10] married Leonard Briggs and they have 2 children: LYNN ESTHER,[11] b. 1949; and RANDAL LEONARD BRIGGS,[11] b. 1952.

LEROY GARRISON HOLLY[9] (Stephen,[8] Jonah,[7] Stephen,[6] Jonah,[5] Stephen,[4] Elisha,[3] Elisha,[2] John[1]), b. on Mt. Holly Rd., 1911, married Barbara Reynolds.

* * * * *

Other Hollys who appear in Bedford town records in the late 1700's are Abraham and Jesse. An Abraham is mentioned as a brother of Stephen in 1771. Jesse Holly at one time owned a great deal of land including the mill on the Cross River, later one of those called Hoyt's Mills.

Compiled by F. R. Duncombe.

The Hopkins Family

Although the Hopkins family has never actually resided in Katonah, its members have long been so closely identified with it in social, civic and business life that we have come to think of them as ours.

STEPHEN HOPKINS[1] sailed from England with his family in 1620 on the "Mayflower" and settled in Plymouth, Mass. Son, GILES,[2] by his first wife, came also on the "Mayflower" and married Catharine Wheldon of Yarmouth. STEPHEN[3] (1642-1718/19), b. at Yarmouth, married 1st Mary Myrick. Their son, JOSEPH[4] (1688-1771), b. & d. in Harwich, married Mary Mayo. JOSEPH[5] (1715-1762) married Mary (Mercy) Berry. They removed to Putnam County, N.Y., then Dutchess, and joined in 1749 the church of Rev. Elisha Kent. Capt. SOLOMON,[6] b. Harwich 1739, d. in Putnam 1792, was commissary general of Dutchess County during the

Revolution. He married Elizabeth Crosby believed to be the sister of Enoch. JEREMIAH,[7] b. near Carmel 1762, d. there 1829, married Thankful Stone about 1783. He was a major of Militia. NATHANIEL[8] (1797-1860) married Theresa Travis.

FERDINAND TRAVIS HOPKINS,[9] b. at Lake Mahopac about 1832, lived in Putnam County on the family farm until, aged 21, he sought work in New York City. His 1st employment was with Brooks Bros., men's clothiers. In 1878 he brought the farm in Somers where his son still resides. FERDINAND T.[9] had by his 1st wife: NATHANIEL[10] and FRANCES;[10] and by his 2nd wife, FERDINAND T., JR.[10] He died June, 1920, having been for many years a member of the Presbyterian Church in Katonah.

FERDINAND T. HOPKINS, JR.,[10] b. 1879, also a member of our Presbyterian Church, was president of the Northern Westchester Bank in Katonah and associated actively in Katonah affairs. He and his 2nd wife, Myrtle Kennedy, have children: JEAN TRAVIS,[11] b. May 7, 1920; and FERDINAND TRAVIS, III,[11] b. Apr. 12, 1923. Both of them spent much time in Katonah while growing up.

FERDINAND T. HOPKINS, III,[11] married Elinor White Kuchler Oct. 16, 1948. They have one child, FERDINAND TRAVIS HOPKINS, IV,[12] b. May 14, 1950, and live in Somers.

JEAN TRAVIS HOPKINS[11] married Charles E. Drexler July 9, 1949. Their daughter is MARJORIE JEAN DREXLER,[12] b. Mar. 12, 1953. The Drexler family lives in Setauket, L.I.

Compiled by F. R. Duncombe.

The Edgar Hoyt Family

Descended from SIMEON (SIMON) HOYT,[1] the first of this family to come to America from England, the line of EDGAR HOYT[8] came down through Simeon's son Benjamin (Cyrus,[7] Benjamin,[6] Benjamin,[5] Jeremiah,[4] Benjamin,[3] Benjamin,[2] Simeon.[1])

EDGAR HOYT[8] was born in South Salem Nov. 12, 1858, the son of CYRUS,[7] b. 1812, and his wife Hannah McCaull Hoyt, b. 1818. The grandparents of Edgar were BENJAMIN HOYT, JR.,[6] b. 1779, and Betsey Northrup, whose names are the earliest written in the family Bible owned by this branch of the family. EDGAR[8] married Bertha Lawrence (1862-1958), dau. of Edward and Jane (Brady) Lawrence of South Salem, and they were parents of MARTHA HOYT[9] and LOUISE HOYT.[9] In Old Katonah, Edgar worked for Mr. Wescott. When the village moved, Mr. Hoyt's was the first new place of business to be erected and was known as the "Pioneer House." It still stands on the south corner of Katonah Ave. and The Parkway. On the first floor of the Pioneer House, Mr. Hoyt operated a restaurant and sold baked goods. The restaurant was so popular with traveling men that they often planned stops at Katonah because of its excellent service. Later this business was sold to Frank W. Hoyt who continued to operate it until Doyle Brothers bought the building.

MARTHA HOYT,[9] b. July 22, 1893, married Lloyd Bedford Cox, b. June 1, 1892. Mr. and Mrs. Cox make their home in Bedford Hills, where during the last years of her life, Mrs. Bertha Hoyt lived with them. The children of Mr. and Mrs. Cox are: MARTHA LOUISE;[10] and LLOYD BEDFORD COX, JR.[10]

MARTHA LOUISE COX,[10] b. Jan. 7, 1924, is Home Service Adviser for the Public Service Electric and Gas Co. of New Jersey. She lives in Trenton, N.J.

LLOYD BEDFORD COX, JR.,[10] b. Feb. 15, 1930, is in the real estate and insurance business with his father in Bedford Hills and lives in Bedford Village. Aug. 10, 1957, he married Eleanor Hope Jeffers of Syracuse, N.Y. Their daughter, HOPE ELIZABETH COX[11] (Betsy), was born Dec. 4, 1959.

LOUISE HOYT,[9] b. July 16, 1895, married Lester Hazen King and moved to Rowayton, Conn.

Compiled by F. R. Duncombe.

The Zeno Hoyt Family

ZENO HOYT,[8] b. in Litchfield County, Conn., Aug. 20, 1807, lived in the old village of Katonah. He was a descendant of the SIMON (SIMEON) HOYT,[1] Hait, or Haight, who came from England to settle in Charlestown, Mass., in 1629. ZENO HOYT[8] (Isaac,[7] Jesse,[6] Abner,[5] Daniel,[4] Zerubbabel,[3] Walter,[2] Simon[1]) married 1st Emily Hunt and 2nd, Sophia A. Dingee, dau. of Eli F. and Phebe Dingee of Bedford. ZENO[8] and Sophia Hoyt were parents of: EMILY,[9] mar. Daniel Griggs of New York City; JESSE;[9] and SETH.[9] The Zeno Hoyts lived in a large house just east of the railroad tracks, on land purchased in 1852 from Elisha Reynolds. Moved from Old Katonah, this house now stands near Bedford Rd. at the south end of present Katonah and belongs to Mrs. Henry D. Miller. ZENO[8] held many public offices, including poormaster, constable and officer of the County Court. As constable he always had a room ready in the basement where tramps and transients were welcome to spend the night if it were not being occupied by a prisoner waiting transportation to jail. His wife would feed these men supper and breakfast. Zeno died Jan. 22, 1875, and Mrs. Hoyt, in September, 1898, at 79 yrs.

JESSE HOYT,[9] b. 1841, enlisted, aged 20, May, 1861, in Co. A, 27th N.Y. Regiment. He served as private for two years and was in the battles of Bull Run and Antietam. He died at Hagerstown, Md., of typhoid fever.

SETH HOYT,[9] b. in Bedford Township July 14, 1844, married Sarah J. Scott, daughter of Lewis and Julia A. Scott of Greenwich, Conn., Mar. 6, 1865. They were the parents of 2 children: FREDERICK ZENO,[10] b. 1870; and EFFIE CLARA.[10] FREDERICK ZENO[10] died unmar. Aug. 20, 1920.

EFFIE CLARA HOYT,[10] b. 1876, married Charles Henry Ruggles of Ridgefield, Conn., Oct. 31, 1897. They made their home at 108 Valley Rd. in a large house across from our present St. Mary's School. Mr. Ruggles died Sept. 6, 1934, and Mrs. Ruggles lived on in their home until her death Jan. 3, 1954. They were the parents of: MABEL HOYT;[11] and GLADYS V. RUGGLES.[11]

MABEL HOYT RUGGLES,[11] b. in Old Katonah Aug. 22, 1898, married

July 3, 1919, Charles E. Ferguson of Davis, Indian Territory, Oklahoma. He served in the Navy on transport duty in World War I. He was a devoted church member and deacon for many years, a carpenter by trade. He died at his home on Valley Rd. Oct. 9, 1958. Their 2 sons were: CHARLES E., JR.;[12] and ARTHUR EARL FERGUSON.[12]

CHARLES E. FERGUSON, JR.,[12] b. Feb. 18, 1921, served in World War II in the 104th Infantry Band and was killed in action Jan. 10, 1945. His parents arranged a High School Band award in Charles' honor, which is given yearly.

ARTHUR EARL FERGUSON,[12] b. Dec. 20, 1923, graduated from Katonah High School in 1941. He served in World War II in the 311th Infantry, 78th Infantry Division, and was awarded the Purple Heart and Croix de Guerre from the French Government. ARTHUR[12] married Charmain Mooring of Eureka, N.C., Apr. 7, 1946. They are parents of 2 children: ARTHUR EARL, JR.[13] b. Apr. 9, 1947, at Cobleskill, N.Y.; and DONNA FRANCES,[13] b. Oct. 19, 1959.

GLADYS V. RUGGLES,[11] b. in Katonah Nov. 2, 1907, graduated from Katonah High School. She married Harry John French Sept. 20, 1930 (see French genealogy).

Compiled by K. B. Kelly.

The Hoyts of Hoyt Brothers, Hoyt's Mills

The early spelling of this name was Hoyt, Hait, Haight and Hoit. SIMON or SIMEON HOYT[1] came from England to Charlestown, Mass. A son was JOSHUA.[2] A grandson, JOSHUA,[3] married Mary Pickett and one of their children was JAMES HOYT.[4] JAMES[4] married Mary Waterbury and had a son WATERBURY HOYT,[5] who married Lavinia. They lived in South Salem, where their son, JAMES,[6] was born Feb. 17, 1801.

JAMES HOYT[6] (Waterbury,[5] James,[4] Joshua,[3] Joshua,[2] Simon[1]) moved to Bedford about 1820. He married Elizabeth Banks, dau. of Jonathan Banks of Banksville. They lived for a time on the Mt. Holly farm of James F. Merritt. Around 1843 they bought the property on the Cross River later known as Hoyt's Mills. They were parents of: ALBERT;[7] SAMUEL B.;[7] JAMES E.;[7] SETH S.;[7] EMILY;[7] MARY A.;[7] CLARA N.;[7] ELIZABETH;[7] and MATILDA.[7]

SAMUEL B. HOYT,[7] unmarried, lived with his sisters, ELIZABETH,[7] EMILY[7] and MATILDA M.,[7] on present Deer Park Rd. by "The Cut," across the road from his business. New York City didn't take his home but he was given money for devaluation of land when they took the village away from in front of him. He moved his home in one piece and had it placed near the flag-pole at 23 Bedford Rd. He died in New Katonah in 1903.

SETH S. HOYT,[7] b. on Mt. Holly Dec. 25, 1831, lived at Hoyt's Mills from 1843 on and eventually took over the business from his father. He married 1st Sept. 19, 1865, Hannah M. Howe (1834-1888), dau. of Jeremiah Howe of North Salem. He modernized the old mill only to have it taken by New York City. He built anew on Katonah Ave. next to the railroad, the most complete mill in the Harlem Valley, a building 30x60 feet and three stories high, with 30-horsepower gasoline engines for operating the plant. He married 2nd Armenia Newman Green, widow of Oliver Green of Maple Ave., Katonah. She died in 1906. His son, GEORGE HOYT,[8] who was in partnership with his father, married Elizabeth Ferris, dau. of James and Mima Jane (Putney) Ferris. They lived at 51 The Parkway. After GEORGE HOYT's[8] death Dec. 17, 1933, his widow married George Daily and lived for many years in Katonah. She sold her home to Dr. Adams and died in Harrison, N.Y., Mar. 23, 1959, at 89 years.

JAMES E. HOYT[7] (May 31, 1839-1891) at 16 yrs. started working in David Putney's store at Whitlockville Station. He left after a year to clerk in Purdy's Station and later to be with William A. Moore. He returned to Putney in 1858 only to join William Banks' store at New Castle Corners in 1862. In 1865 JAMES,[7] with his brother ALBERT,[7] joined David Putney in a partnership, as Putney and Hoyt Bros. Putney retired the next year and SAMUEL B.,[7] JAMES E.,[7] and ALBERT HOYT[7] formed Hoyt Brothers' general store, furniture and undertaking business. JAMES[7] married 1st Matilda Kirby, dau. of Leonard Kirby of Kirbyville, who died Oct. 12, 1879. In 1881 he was elected superintendent of the poor of Westchester County. After Mr. T. C. Adams resigned in December, 1887, JAMES[7] was appointed supervisor of the Town of Bedford and was reelected for another term. He married 2nd Aug. 2, 1887, Mrs. Elizabeth King Crandall of Binghamton, sister of Mrs. J. H. Eastman. He died at 52 yrs., leaving no children.

ALBERT HOYT,[7] b. Nov. 25, 1841, a member of Hoyt Brothers in Old Katonah, married Augusta Light, who died May 28, 1922. He bought and brought the James Hoyt house from Old Katonah and had it placed at 48 The Parkway, where he died Jan. 1, 1907. They had two children, ROBERT[8] and JAMES A. HOYT,[8] who are buried in Oakwood Cemetery, Mt. Kisco.

MARY ANNA HOYT[7] married Daniel Merritt Miller (1822-1890), son of Norman W. and Deborah Gregory Miller of Whitlockville, Sept. 27, 1823 (see Miller genealogy). She died in June, 1853, aged 30 yrs.

CLARA N. HOYT[7] (Feb. 8, 1836–Mar. 18, 1868) was the first wife of Joseph O. Brady, who ran a meat market in Old Katonah. After her death he married twice more and moved his market to New Katonah. CLARA HOYT BRADY[7] left 3 sons: SAMUEL HOYT[8] (Dec. 26, 1865–Apr. 20, 1888); ELMER E.,[8] who mar. Dec. 29, 1886, Annie E. Chadeayne, dau. of John Chadeayne, and lived in Katonah and then Stamford, Conn., and had one daughter, FLORENCE BRADY[9] of 41 Valley Rd., Stamford; and JOSEPH BRADY.[8]

JOSEPH BRADY,[8] a baker in the old village, took over his father's meat market in the new village. He married in 1878 Harriet E. Miller, dau. of Hurd L. Miller. They celebrated their golden anniversary in Katonah in 1928. After he retired, he devoted much time to his flowers, sending small bouquets into the city by commuters to the needy children of New York. He died June 21, 1939, at their home, 42 Bedford Rd. JOSEPH[8] and Harriet Brady were parents of: ROBERT E.;[9] and LOUIS S.[9] ROBERT,[9] unmar., a pianist and never strong, who lived with his mother until her death in 1943, then moved to New York City where he died in 1951. He is buried in Union Cemetery, Bedford. Louis S. Brady[9] became a successful banker in New York City. He married Ethel MacPherson (1882-1939). They lived 1st in Katonah on Mustato Rd., then moved to Scarsdale where Mrs. Brady died Jan. 7, 1939. Mr. Brady remarried and moved to Hillsdale, N.Y., where he died in 1958, and is buried in Union Cemetery. The children of Louis S.[9] and Ethel Brady were: Harriet;[10] Emily;[10] and George.[10] Harriet[10] married Sherwood Bonney. They live in Scarsdale, N.Y. Children: Kent;[11] and Jean Bonney.[11] Emily[10] married William Feeney. They live in Pleasantville, N.Y., and have children: James[11] and Louis Feeney.[11] George[10] married Elizabeth Kingsbury. They live in Greenwich, Conn., and have children: Robert Douglas;[11] and Georgia.[11]

Matilda M. Hoyt[7] taught at the Mt. Holly School and sang in the choir of the Methodist Episcopal Church. She died Jan. 7, 1903, at 68 yrs. and is buried in Oakwood Cemetery, Mt. Kisco.

The Hoyt Brothers' Building, erected 1897 at The Parkway and Katonah Ave., New Katonah, was 65x90 ft., had 3 floors, basement and attic, steam heat with acetylene gas, a very modern building. Here Samuel[7] was in charge of undertaking, James A.,[8] of the business end, and Robert[8] of furniture, carpets and upholstering.

James A. Hoyt[8] married in 1897 Grace Bowman, dau. of Dr. S. L. Bowman, pastor 1890-1892 of the Katonah M. E. Church. He spent his life in Katonah, greatly interested in local affairs and the store. In November, 1901, he bought a lot from Daniel J. Smith next to Wendell Green. In 1902 when the bodies were being moved from our local cemeteries, he was an agent for Kensico Cemetery. He died Apr. 24, 1922. Mrs. Hoyt lives at 45 Park Ave., Bloomfield, N.J.

Robert Hoyt,[8] b. in Old Katonah in 1870, graduated from the Katonah school and after one year at preparatory school entered Columbia University. There he took civil and mechanical engineering, graduating in 1892. He worked for the City on the new Croton Dam and was also a member of Hoyt Brothers. In 1905 he left the store and was appointed county register of maps in White Plains, where he continued till his death from typhoid fever Mar. 27, 1907. He and his wife, Charlotte Truesdell Hoyt, dau. of John W. Truesdell, had one child: Charlotte,[9] b. 1904. In 1902 he built a new home at 25 Bedford Rd. Mrs. Charlotte Truesdell Hoyt married 2nd Dr. W. J. Carpenter (see Carpenter genealogy). Charlotte Hoyt[9] married Dudley Child and they had two children, born in Troy: James;[10] and Dale Child.[10] Their last known home was outside of Philadelphia.

Compiled by K. B. Kelly.

The Hunt Family

Charles A. Hunt,[1] b. Dec. 25, 1830, believed the son of Harvey Hunt of North Salem, grandson of Isaac, and great-grandson of Gilbert Hunt, came to Katonah from Patterson, N.J. He used to drive through this region with his old horse, "George," and a two-seated rig loaded with large family Bibles for sale. He was an artist, painting landscapes in oil.

Katonah's beauty may have attracted him; he bought the Kincaid house and the farm that ran from Cherry St. to Bedford Rd., south of present Huntville Rd. and extending to the present Vockins' place on Harris Rd. He did not farm it for a livelihood but wanted a place to bring up his family. Mr. Hunt had married twice: children by his 1st marriage were: ELIZABETH;[2] CHARLES AUGUSTUS;[2] CATHERINE;[2] and FRED L.[2] Those by his 2nd wife, who came to Katonah with him, were: MARY;[2] and AGNES.[2] The three youngest attended Cherry St. school. Mr. Hunt died in Katonah Oct. 3, 1893.

ELIZABETH HUNT,[2] a landscape painter like her father, married Edward Newell Barrett (half brother of Joseph Barrett), a writer for New York papers. They lived on McLain St., Bedford Hills, and retired to Sweetbriar, Va. After Mr. Barrett's death in 1934, she returned to Katonah to live with her sisters at 8 Huntville Rd. until they moved to California, where ELIZABETH[2] died in her 94th year June 26, 1956, leaving no issue.

CHARLES AUGUSTUS HUNT,[2] b. May 30, 1865, a widower with an infant son, CHARLES A. HUNT, JR.,[3] when the family arrived here, married 2nd in 1897, Annette Vrooman (1870-1953) of New York City and was employed by the Railway Express Company there. CHARLES AUGUSTUS[2] and Annette, parents of CORNELIUS DONALD[3] and HARVEY KISSAM,[3] lived in many Katonah houses. They built the house at Sunrise Ave. and Bedford Rd., the present Polly Quincy house on Jay St., and the small house against the hill on Glenridge and South Rd., where he died June 3, 1950, and where Mrs. Hunt lived until she moved to California, where she died. Both are buried in Bedford Union Cemetery.

CHARLES AUGUSTUS HUNT, JR.,[3] married an out-of-town girl and had no children.

CORNELIUS DONALD HUNT[3] graduated from Katonah High School and Rensselaer Polytechnic Institute in Troy. He had his own blueprinting business in White Plains and married Margaret Goreth there. They are parents of: CHARLES AUGUSTUS III;[4] MARGARET;[4] and ELIZABETH KISSAM.[4] They lived on Hook Rd. until after the war, when they moved to Hillsdale, N.Y. MARGARET[4] married Donald Bailey of Marblehead, Mass., and they live in New Orleans, La. ELIZABETH KISSAM[4] married William Davidson of Union, N.J., Aug. 16, 1958, and they live in Elizabeth, N.J. CHARLES AUGUSTUS III[4] married Mary Byron of Gloversville, N.Y., and they live in Wolcott, Conn.

HARVEY K. HUNT,[3] b. June 10, 1903, graduated from Katonah High School and R.P.I. He worked in White Plains, then in Philadelphia where he met his wife, Arnellen. They had one SON[4] and moved to California when he was transferred to the West Coast.

CATHERINE HUNT,[2] known as Kate, with her sisters and her brother Fred, after their father's death built a home and called it "Sunset Hill," now owned by Bailey Hall. She went to Sweet Briar and eventually to Culpepper, Va. She never married. In Katonah she was an organizer and original member of the Women's Civic Club.

FRED LIVINGSTON HUNT,[2] b. 1874, bought houses in the old village and had them moved down to the Hunt land. He had the honor of building and owning the largest number in the new village and in 1898 rented his places for $8.00 a month. He owned the old depot, which he placed on the lane to his old home, where it is now 29 Huntville Rd.; the Myron

Silkman home on Nightingale Rd., the Daniel Purdy house by "The Cut," which he placed in back of Charles Robertson's home (131 Bedford Rd.); the Zeno Hoyt residence which he made into a three-family house, now belonging to Mrs. Henry D. Miller on Bedford Rd.; the present house at 121 Bedford Rd. and the one in back on Congdon Lane. He also bought the old Isaac Hait house when the Cross River Reservoir was made and lived in it off New St. It has recently been owned by Schuyler Bradt. Mr. Hunt married Lillian Agnes Cook, daughter of Harvey T. Cook. Their children were: Lockwood;[3] Robert;[3] Priscilla;[3] Julian;[3] Jean;[3] and Marshall.[3] Their last home was the present James Beardsley home on McQueen St. The Fred Hunts bought a farm in Wingdale, N.Y., and moved there with their children. Lockwood[3] and Julian[3] are now successful furniture-makers in Wingdale: Country Furniture, Inc. Mr. Hunt died Jan. 14, 1945, in Dover Plains, N.Y. Mrs. Hunt died Feb. 21, 1946, in Greenville County, S.C.

Mary I. Hunt,[2] raised in Katonah, was married June 30, 1902, to Morton S. MacQueen of Philadelphia in the family home, "Sunset Hill," by the Rev. A. R. Teal. Mr. MacQueen was in the hardware business and they moved to Philadelphia where Mrs. MacQueen died, leaving three small girls: Elizabeth;[3] Alberta;[3] and Milleretta MacQueen.[3] The three girls returned to Katonah to live with their aunts. Elizabeth MacQueen[3] graduated from Sweet Briar College. She married Harry Lounsbury Nelson, son of George and Kathryn G. (Lounsbury) Nelson of Katonah. They lived at 51 Bedford Rd., where their two sons were born: Harry Lounsbury, Jr.,[4] Jan. 23, 1928; and Peter MacQueen Nelson,[4] Jan. 29, 1931. The boys are married with children of their own. Harry and Elizabeth Nelson[3] moved to San Marino, Calif., and often visit Katonah. Alberta MacQueen,[3] graduate of Sweet Briar, married Louis O. DeRonge and lives in West Hartford, Conn., with their son. Milleretta,[3] graduate of William and Mary College, married Harry Chandler and they make their home in Virginia Beach, Va. They have a married daughter.

Agnes Hunt[2] lives in Pasadena, Calif. She was very active in our local affairs. She still owns part of the old farm, in back of Arthur Covey's and off of McQueen St., beside James Beardsley's home.

Compiled by K. B. Kelly.

The Jay Family

Augustus Jay,[1] b. in La Rochelle, France, Mar. 23, 1665, was the third son of Pierre and Judith (Francois) Jay. His grandfather, Jean Jay, was a tallow chandler and his father, Pierre Jay, a rich merchant. Augustus[1] completed his commercial education in England, and because of the persecution of the Huguenots, he fled from France, arriving in New York City in 1697. Oct. 28, 1697, he married Anna Maria Bayard, dau. of Balthazar Bayard, a prominent merchant. Augustus[1] sought no governmental posts, but contented himself with a flourishing trade. The Augustus Jays had a son, Peter,[2] and 4 daughters: Judith,[2] mar. Cornelius van Horne; Mary,[2] mar. Peter Vallette; Frances,[2] mar. Frederick van Cortlandt; and ANN JAY,[2] d. an infant. AUGUSTUS JAY[1] died Mar. 10, 1751.

PETER JAY,[2] b. in New York Nov. 3, 1704, after two years of commercial education in England joined his father in business in 1724. Jan. 20, 1728, he married Mary Van Cortlandt, daughter of Jacobus Van Cortlandt of Yonkers, and they had 7 sons and 3 daughters. In King George's War PETER JAY[2] was one of the commissioners for the defense of the colony. He was alderman of New York and an elder of Trinity Church. Upon his retirement he settled at his country home in Rye, N.Y., in 1746. He died Apr. 17, 1782.

JOHN JAY,[3] the 8th child and the 6th son of PETER[2] and Mary Jay, b. in New York City Dec. 12, 1745, spent his boyhood in Rye. He graduated from Kings College in 1764 and, entering the law office of Benjamin Kissam, received his law license in October, 1768, at 23 yrs. Apr. 28, 1774, he married Sarah Livingston, dau. of Gov. William Livingston, at "Liberty Hall," the Livingston home at Elizabeth Town, N.J.

JOHN JAY[3] was a member of the First and Second Continental Congresses in 1774 and 1775. While still a member of the latter, he was absent from its sessions in the summer of 1776 attending the Provincial Congress of New York, and thus lost the opportunity of signing the Declaration of Independence. However, he drafted the resolutions which authorized the New York delegation to sign. In 1777 he was chairman of the committee which drafted the New York State constitution, and he became first chief justice of the State. In 1778 he returned to the Continental Congress and became its president.

From 1780 to 1784 Jay was in Spain and France working for peace with England. He returned and that autumn became Secretary for Foreign Affairs. He took an active part in the movement for the ratification of the constitution, contributing five articles to *The Federalist*. When Washington was elected president of the new government, Jay was appointed Chief Justice of the Supreme Court, which position he held from September, 1789, to June, 1795. In 1794 he was sent to England to negotiate a treaty to clear up some of the serious differences between the two nations. The treaty was signed in September, 1794, and is known as the Jay Treaty.

On Jay's return from England in the spring of 1795, he found that he had been elected governor of New York State. He planned to retire from public life in 1798, but was re-elected governor, and it was not until the spring of 1801 that he was able to carry out his long planned retirement in Bedford, Westchester County. By the will of PETER JAY,[2] JOHN[3] inherited first choice of his mother's share of Jacobus Van Cortlandt's Bedford lands. By 1801 JOHN JAY[3] owned 750 acres in Bedford at Cantitoe, henceforth his home. John Jay's retirement was saddened by the death of his wife, Sarah, May 28, 1802, at Bedford House after only a few months' residence. He spent his remaining 28 years at Bedford, supervising his farm and keeping open house for his old friends and his country neighbors. It was on the piazza at Bedford House that John Jay told the aspiring novelist, James Fenimore Cooper, his son William's classmate, the story of an anonymous secret agent for the American side in the Revolution; and from this story Cooper wrote *The Spy*. JOHN JAY[3] died at Bedford May 18, 1829, and is buried in Rye. The children of John and Sarah Jay were: PETER AUGUSTUS[4] (1777-1843), who mar. Mary

Rutherford and remained in Rye; Susan[4] (1780), b. and d. in Spain; Maria,[4] b. 1782, mar. Goldsborough Banyar; Ann,[4] b. 1783 in Paris; William[4] (1789-1858); and Sarah Louisa[4] (1792-1818).

William Jay,[4] b. in New York City June 16, 1789, graduated from Yale in 1808 and studied law. Sept. 4, 1812, he married Hannah Augusta McVickar, dau. of John McVickar, a merchant of New York City. Their children were: Anna,[5] b. 1813, who married Rev. Lewis P. Balch; Maria B.,[5] b. 1815, mar. John F. Butterworth; John[5] (1817-1894); Sarah Louisa,[5] mar. Alexander McWhorter Bruen; Eliza,[5] b. 1823, and Augusta B.,[5] b. 1833, who were the successive wives of Henry Edward Pellew (see Pellew genealogy). Eye trouble caused William Jay[4] to abandon his profession and retire to his father's estate at Cantitoe. He threw himself with energy into agricultural pursuits. He perfected his skill in grafting and budding, and was particularly successful with peaches, cherries, pears and plums. He raised horses from imported stock and Merino sheep. William[4] and his father planted many of the trees under which we drive on Maple Ave. and along Jay St. He was appointed a judge of Westchester County in 1818 by Gov. DeWitt Clinton, a post which he held until 1843. He was very active in the antislavery movement, in the Temperance Society, and in the Episcopal Church. He was a founder of the American Bible Society. Judge Jay and Augusta McVickar Jay together made Bedford House a happy center for family and friends. The judge died Oct. 14, 1858.

John Jay II,[5] b. June 23, 1817, was graduated from Columbia College in 1836 and admitted to the bar in 1839. He also was active in the abolition movement and was bold and outspoken in his opposition to slavery. In 1869 he was appointed by President Grant to be United States Minister to Austria, a post which he held until 1875. He married June 23, 1837, Eleanor Kingsland Field, dau. of Hickson Field of New York City. They were parents of 6 children: Eleanor,[6] mar. Henry Grafton Chapman; William,[6] mar. Lucie Oelrichs; Mary,[6] mar. William Henry Schieffelin; Augusta,[6] mar. Edmund Randolph Robinson; Anna,[6] mar. Gen. Hans Lothar von Schweinitz in 1873; and John Jay,[6] d. y. John[5] inherited Bedford House from his father, and it was there that the children grew up. After their marriages they returned for the summer holidays with their families. John Jay[5] died May 4, 1894. His wife, Eleanor, survived him by many years, making her home with her daughter, Mary Jay Schieffelin[6] in New York. Dying in 1910, she was buried from Bedford House in St. Matthew's churchyard beside her husband.

William Jay II,[6] b. in New York City Feb. 12, 1841, graduated from Columbia College in 1859. He served with distinction in the Civil War, taking part in the battles of Chancellorsville and Gettysburg. In 1867, Col. Jay was admitted to the bar and practised law for many years in New York, as head of the firm of Jay and Chandler. June 12, 1873, he married Lucie Oelrichs of New York. Their children were: Julia[7] (1879-1890); Eleanor[7] (1882-1953); and Dorothy[7] (1887-1889). The Jays had a house in New York but maintained Bedford House as their summer home. Col. William Jay[6] died Mar. 28, 1915.

Eleanor Jay,[7] b. at Bedford House Oct. 11, 1882, was married at St. Agnes' Chapel, New York, Nov. 29, 1904, to Arthur Iselin, a banker, son of William E. and Alice (Jones) Iselin, of New York. Mr. and Mrs.

Iselin had 4 children: DOROTHY,[8] b. Sept. 22, 1905, who mar. Guy Paschal of Washington and had 3 children; WILLIAM J.[8] (1908-1951), who mar. Fanny Humphreys of Mt. Kisco and lived in Greenville, S.C., with their 5 children; ELEANOR,[8] b. June 3, 1910, who mar. 1st Thomas Mason and had a dau. HOPE MASON,[9] b. May 13, 1936, and 3rd mar. Cactus Wanny Wade with whom she now lives on the 4W Ranch, Libby, Mont.; and ARTHUR ISELIN, JR.,[8] b. May 23, 1916, at Bedford. ARTHUR, JR.,[8] married Cornelia Wheelright of New Hampshire. Their children are: VIRGINIA;[9] GEORGE;[9] DOROTHY;[9] NINA;[9] and PETER J. ISELIN.[9] They live in Nelson, N.H.

Mrs. ELEANOR JAY ISELIN[7] inherited Bedford House from her father Col. William Jay. After his death in 1915 she made her permanent home there. She took an active part in all community affairs. For years she was chairman of the Flower Committee of the Altar Guild of St. Matthew's Church, where in the cemetery she now lies buried with so many of her Jay ancestors. She was a trustee of the Rippowam School, president of the Katonah Women's Civic Club, and active in the Village Improvement Society. She opened her home frequently to meetings of the Bedford Historical Society, Bedford Garden Club, and the Bedford Farmers' Club. She was interested in public affairs, particularly woman's suffrage, and was a strong Republican.

In 1923, Mrs. Iselin added a fireproof wing to Bedford House to safeguard its valuable portraits, mementoes, and historical documents. Mr. Iselin died in May, 1952, and Mrs. Iselin, Nov. 5, 1953. ARTHUR ISELIN, JR.,[8] and his family were the last descendants to make Bedford House their home. VIRGINIA[9] and GEORGE ISELIN[9] attended Katonah Elementary School and John Jay High School for a few years. PETER JAY ISELIN[9] was born at this time. Jay descendants living in the neighborhood are: WILLIAM JAY SCHIEFFELIN III,[9] great-grandson of MARY JAY SCHIEFFELIN,[6] who lives with his family on McLain St., Mt. Kisco; and MRS. MARY SCHIEFFELIN BROWN,[8] wife of Charles S. Brown and granddaughter of MRS. SCHIEFFELIN,[6] who lives in the St. John Cottage at Cantitoe.

Compiled by Mary S. Brown.

The Kellogg Family of Katonah

HENRY WARD KELLOGG[3] was born in South Salem, N.Y., Feb. 27, 1858, son of GARDNER J. KELLOGG[2] and Maria Raymond, and grandson of JASON[1] and Catherine (Miller) Kellogg. JASON[1] (1790-1860), it is believed, was born in Stamford, Conn., and moved to South Salem. He and his wife, Catherine (1798-1856), are buried in South Salem churchyard. GARDNER J. KELLOGG[2] was a farmer and very active in Salem town affairs.

HENRY WARD KELLOGG,[3] educated in the Salem district school, at the age of 15 secured a position with Hoyt Brothers' general store at Old Katonah, where he worked 7 years. Next he was clerk at Mead's Hotel, Waccabuc, N.Y., and then spent 8 years as an inspector in the Custom House of New York City. In June, 1887, he returned to Katonah and bought out Charles Wood Avery's hardware store on Railroad Ave. and added plumbing and heating to the business. He moved his house to 12 The Terrace, New Katonah, in June, 1898, and built a new store on The Parkway. Mr. Kellogg aided greatly in the development of the new village. He was a progressive and practical business man with great ability. He served as a justice of the peace for six years and was postmaster. He was a Mason, a Royal Arcanum, and belonged to the Methodist Episcopal Church. Oct. 11, 1881, he married Cordelia Ann Elliott, b. Dec. 30, 1858, dau. of William Asbury and Sarah M. (Ward) Elliott. The Elliotts lived on Croton Lake Rd. off Cherry St. for several generations. Their old homestead was taken by the City and moved across the road, now on the south side. Mr. and Mrs. Kellogg became the parents of 3 children: LAURA BROOKS;[4] ASBURY ELLIOTT;[4] and WILLIAM RAYMOND.[4]

LAURA BROOKS KELLOGG,[4] b. June 6, 1883, was educated in our local school and Jamaica Normal School. She married Willard B. Fisher Oct. 14, 1903, and they had 2 children: HAROLD MORRIS;[5] and HELEN KELLOGG FISHER.[5] Mrs. Fisher died in October, 1957. Dr. Fisher retired and died in 1959 on Greenville Rd., Katonah. HAROLD M. FISHER[5] is an optometrist in Mt. Kisco and New York City. He married Mildred Lewless and they have 2 daughters: MABEL FRANCES,[6] b. 1937; and BARBARA ANN FISHER,[6] b. 1941. HELEN K. FISHER[5] married George W. Sarles, son of George C. Sarles of Bedford Hills. They reside in Bedford Hills and he is with the Bedford Hills Concrete Products Corporation. Their 2 sons are: PETER GEORGE,[6] b. 1938; and ROBERT ALLAN SARLES,[6] b. 1941. PETER SARLES[6] is a clerk with Kelloggs and Lawrence.

ASBURY ELLIOTT KELLOGG[4] was born at the Elliott farm on Croton Lake Rd., Aug. 25, 1886. He graduated from New Katonah's first public school and went to high school in White Plains. He carried on the family firm, now known as Kelloggs and Lawrence, Inc. He married Alice Marion Green, dau. of Oscar and Marion Green, Apr. 18, 1914, and they have 5 children: DONALD;[5] MARGARET;[5] MARION;[5] RICHARD;[5] and JANICE.[5] Mr. Kellogg is a Republican, a Methodist, and a member of the Fire Department. He and Mrs. Kellogg live at 136 Valley Rd.

DONALD RAYMOND KELLOGG[5] is president of Kelloggs and Lawrence. He married Apr. 19, 1941, Eleanor Sloat, dau. of Clifford Sloat of Katonah. They reside on Kelly Circle and have 5 children: PATRICIA ELEANOR,[6] b. Jan. 5, 1943; DONALD RAYMOND, JR.,[6] b. Feb. 4, 1944; ALAN ELLIOTT,[6] b. Dec. 14, 1946; JANE ELIZABETH,[6] b. Oct. 7, 1948; and JEFFREY HOLLAND,[6] b. Nov. 21, 1955.

MARGARET JEAN KELLOGG[5] married Wilson Cornelius Hinkley, who is with the New York Central Railroad. They live on Edgemont Rd. and have 3 sons: RONALD EDGAR[6] and RAYMOND WILSON,[6] twins b. Dec. 28, 1949; and WILLIAM CHESTER HINKLEY,[6] b. Nov. 25, 1954.

MARION KELLOGG[5] married Francis Owen Abbey, who was born in England and lived in Peekskill. They reside on New St. and have 3 sons: DENNIS OWEN,[6] b. Dec. 20, 1943; ROBERT ELLIOTT,[6] b. July 28, 1947; and JOHN FRANCIS ABBEY,[6] b. Oct. 3, 1950. Mr. Abbey is with the Bowery Savings Bank in New York City. He is an enthusiastic fisherman.

RICHARD HALSTEAD KELLOGG,[5] a member of the family firm, married Mary Joselyn, daughter of Charles and Nellie Joselyn of South Salem. They live at 12 Elm Rd. and have 2 daughters: BARBARA ALICE,[6] b. Oct. 4, 1951; and NANCY BURGESS,[6] b. May 20, 1953.

JANICE LUCILLE KELLOGG[5] married Lindsay Price Northam of Cross River. They live in Red Hook, N.Y., and have 5 children: LINDSAY PRICE, JR.,[6] b. Sept. 28, 1946; JUDITH LOUISE,[6] b. Oct. 9, 1948; ELIZABETH ANN,[6] b. Feb. 11, 1952; MARION JEAN,[6] b. May 2, 1955; and ELLEN KELLOGG,[6] b. Feb. 24, 1958.

WILLIAM RAYMOND KELLOGG,[4] b. Oct. 16, 1888, educated locally and at White Plains, graduated from Amherst and Columbia Law School. He is an attorney-at-law in Katonah, and has always been interested in our schools. He was president of the Board of Education for many years. He married Oct. 19, 1918, Ethel Green, dau. of Oscar and Marion Green, and they reside at 56 The Terrace. They have 3 sons: DOUGLAS ELLIOTT;[5] ROBERT WILLIAM;[5] and DAVID HENRY KELLOGG.[5]

DOUGLAS ELLIOTT KELLOGG[5] married Joan Hill, dau. of Samuel and Arleen Hill at Fryeburg, Maine. They live in Newtown, Conn., and have 4 children: LINDA CAROL,[6] b. Aug. 31, 1952; RANDOLPH WEBSTER,[6] b. Feb. 8, 1956; LISA ANNE,[6] b. Oct. 8, 1958; and DIANE ELIZABETH,[6] b. Dec. 9, 1959. He works for the Foredom Electric Company in Danbury, Conn.

ROBERT WILLIAM KELLOGG[5] married Marya Alice Steele, dau. of Frederick and Olga Steele of Boston. Robert is a guidance director with the Yorktown School District. They live in Yorktown and have 3 sons: CHRISTON STEELE,[6] b. July 31, 1951; HOLLIS ABBOTT,[6] b. July 17, 1953; and BRADFORD HALSTEAD,[6] b. July 26, 1955.

DAVID HENRY KELLOGG[5] married Sylvia Park, dau. of Harold H. and Madeleine (Fish) Park of Katonah, May 26, 1951. He is with Mosby Engineers, Sarasota, Fla., where they live with their 3 sons: STEPHEN WESLEY,[6] b. June 20, 1953; PETER GREGORY,[6] b. Nov. 26, 1954; and SCOTT JEFFREY,[6] b. Mar. 22, 1960.

HENRY WARD[3] and Cordelia (Elliott) Kellogg had 45 offspring, 22 of whom are living in Katonah.

Compiled by K. B. Kelly.

The Knapp Family

ROBERT D. KNAPP,[2] editor of the *Katonah Times* from 1894 to 1910 was born near Ithaca, N.Y., Dec. 23, 1867, one of 12 children of CYRUS[1] and Helen Knapp, he was brought up on the family farm. Milk in those days was 2 cents a quart and potatoes, 25 cents a bushel, but CYRUS[1] managed to send 10 of his 12 children to college. ROBERT[2] graduated from Cortlandt State Normal College. For a while thereafter he worked in Staten Island as a bookkeeper. Then, coming to Katonah to visit Mr. Stanton, principal of our school, he was told that the printing office and paper were for sale and encouraged to buy the business. He secured a loan from the Farmers and Drovers Bank of Somers.

Mr. Knapp was at one time president of the Board of Education in Katonah and worked with George H. Covey, then school commissioner, for our first four-year high school. In 1910, after leaving Katonah, Mr. Knapp was elected district superintendent of schools for the 4th Supervisory District of Westchester Co., comprising the Towns of Cortlandt, Yorktown, Somers and North Salem. This position he held until 1937, resigning because of age limitation. During his term of office he had established the following Central Rural School Districts: North Salem, Somers, Yorktown, Shrub Oak, Hendrick Hudson and the Consolidated District of Croton-on-Hudson. By this means he had abolished every one-room school in northern Westchester and caused to be built 12 new schools including 6 high schools. This was a State record unmatched by any other district superintendent.

In the old village of Katonah Mr. Knapp lived opposite the railroad station. In the new village he built the house now owned by Judge Gallagher, adjacent to the Saw Mill River Parkway. Selling it in 1910, he moved to Purdys Station, where he now resides.

ROBERT D. KNAPP[2] married 1st Mabel Holden in 1895. There were two children, both born in Katonah: ROBERT DWIGHT, JR.,[3] b. June 8, 1902; and RUTH FRANCES,[3] b. Jan. 31, 1907. Mabel Holden Knapp died Oct. 6, 1941. Mr. Knapp married 2nd July 4, 1944, Maud Taylor Schrenkeisen who died Mar. 17, 1950, leaving no children.

ROBERT DWIGHT KNAPP, JR.,[3] married Vera Roser and they live at 39 Crestmont Ave., Yonkers, N.Y. He is at present superintendent of the State Board of Underwriters.

RUTH FRANCES KNAPP[3] married Philip O'Malley and they reside at 205 Davis Ave., White Plains, N.Y. With an M.A. degree, she is a teacher and supervisor of French in the White Plains school system.

Compiled by F. R. Duncombe.

The Lyon Family, Katonah Branch

THOMAS LYON,[1] b. in England, 1631, died in Greenwich, Conn., 1690. His son, JOHN,[2] born in England, 1655, died in Rye, N.Y., 1736. John's grandson, ROGER LYON[4] (1715-1797), was a captain in the Westchester Militia. He lived near Byram Lake, North Castle, and was said to have entertained General Washington after the Battle of White Plains. ROGER[4] was blind in his old age with a remarkable memory. He had 9 children: ROGER;[5] JOSEPH;[5] SARAH;[5] DANIEL;[5] JOHN;[5] GILBERT;[5] JUSTUS;[5] GLORIANNE;[5] and SAMUEL.[5]

ROGER LYON, JR.,[5] (1736-1824) died in Bedford and is buried in Buxton Cemetery. He married Phebe (1735-1817) and they had 4 children. Son JAMES[6] (1761-1850) married in 1785 Martha Banks and they had 8 children: JAMES, JR.;[7] KNAPP;[7] DEBORAH;[7] NEWMAN CLARK;[7] PHEBE;[7] ISRAEL;[7] MARY;[7] and BANKS.[7]

JAMES LYON, JR.[7] (1800-1869) married 1st Maria Quereau (1801-1828) in 1824 and had PETER.[8] He married 2nd Charity Gedney (1799-1848) in 1831. They had: HARVEY[8] (1832-1906); PHEBE,[8] b. 1835; ALBERT,[8] b. 1837; WILLIAM,[8] b. 1839; JAMES HENRY,[8] b. 1841. JAMES[7] moved to western New York State and is buried there. ALBERT[8] married Casseline Robinson (1849-1917) but had no children. He was a wheelwright in Old Katonah with a wagon-shop at the very end of Railroad Ave. He lived on South

Rd. near the churches. When his home was taken by the City, he bought the building back at auction in 1898 and had it moved to 34 The Terrace. He was known as "Princy" Lyon and had only one good eye. He died in New Katonah in 1922 and both he and his wife are buried in Union Cemetery. WILLIAM[8] married Lucretia Merritt (1837-1904). JAMES HENRY[8] was killed at Petersburg, Va., while serving in the Artillery during the Civil War.

NEWMAN CLARK LYON[7] (1796-1890) married Alathea, dau. of Nathaniel and Deborah Honeywell Merritt. He was on the Town of Bedford military roll in 1855. They had 11 children: WILLIAM EDWARD,[8] b. 1819; MERRITT,[8] b. 1820; NATHANIEL MERRITT,[8] b. 1823; HENRY A.,[8] b. 1825; HENRY,[8] b. 1827; JAMES MERRITT,[8] b. 1830; SARAH JANE,[8] b. 1831; ANN MATILDA,[8] b. 1832; NEWMAN C.,[8] b. 1834; NATHANIEL,[8] b. 1835; and ALATHEA MERRITT,[8] b. 1839. NEWMAN[7] and his wife and many of the children are buried in Buxton Cemetery, Bedford.

SARAH JANE LYON[8] (1831-1921) married Stephen Holly Miller (see Miller genealogy).

SAMUEL LYON[5] (1747-1819), known as "Major Lyon," son of Capt. ROGER,[4] was a private in the Westchester County Militia, 2nd Regt., under Col. Thomas Thomas. He married 1st Mary Lounsberry (1747-1793) and 2nd Elizabeth Fleming (1767-1855) and had 4 children: JOHN;[6] SARAH;[6] MARY;[6] and SAMUEL, JR.,[6] who spent his life in North Castle. SAMUEL[6] married Rosalinda Fowler and they had 10 children. JOHN[6] (1770-1820) married in 1790 Sarah (Sally) Smith (1770-1854), dau. of Samuel Smith. They had 8 children: WALTER SMITH;[7] ALFRED;[7] MARY;[7] THOMAS SMITH;[7] LORETTA;[7] ISAAC DICKINSON;[7] SAMUEL;[7] and JOHN ADDISON.[7]

WALTER SMITH LYON,[7] b. 1791, was a minister and farmer and owned a large farm on Jay St. which he sold to George Todd sometime before his death Oct. 13, 1867. This property now belongs to the Harvey School. He married Betsey Booth (1796-1842), dau. of Hezekiah Sanford, Nov. 25, 1814, and they had: ANTOINETTE,[8] b. 1816; THOMAS SMITH,[8] b. 1818; SARAH,[8] b. 1820; MARY,[8] b. 1823; LOUISA SANFORD[8] and LOUISE SMITH,[8] twins, b. 1826; CAROLINE,[8] b. 1828; BETSEY,[8] b. 1830; WALTER SANFORD,[8] b. 1833; and JOHN AHAZ,[8] b. 1835.

THOMAS SMITH LYON[8] (1818-1900), b. on Jay St., owned in 1850 a farm next to his father's, now the Legion property. He was in the coal and lumber business in Old Katonah and owned and lived in the house, now at 15 Edgemont Rd., which was moved to New Katonah by Fletcher H. Lent. He was one of the group to start the Katonah Fire Department. In 1862 he is listed as a merchant of Somers. He died at the home of his son-in-law, Constant Whitney, at Yorktown in December, 1900. He and his wife, Calista B. Haight, are buried in the Lyon Cemetery on Jay St.

The REV. WALTER's[7] daughter, MARY LYON[8] (1824-1912), married John Jay Wood (1821-1884), son of Stephen Wood of Croton Lake Rd. Their 10 GREAT-GRANDCHILDREN[12] are mentioned in the Wood Family chronicle.

JOHN ADDISON LYON[7] (1816-1891) married June 11, 1850, EMILY ROBERTSON LYON,[7] dau. of William and Rachel Lyon, his second cousin, and they had 2 sons: CHARLES HERBERT;[8] and IRVING ADDISON,[8] b. 1858. CHARLES HERBERT[8] (1854-1938) married Ella Calkins who died in 1912.

Both are buried in Union Cemetery. There were no children. IRVING[8] was a banker and lived in Paris, France.

JUSTUS LYON[5] (1744-1815) married Sarah Ferris and they had: JUSTUS, JR.;[6] HANNAH;[6] SARAH;[6] BETSEY;[6] WILLIAM;[6] JOHN;[6] STEPHEN;[6] and FERRIS.[6]

JOHN[6] and WILLIAM[6] of Bedford and STEPHEN[6] who lived on the premises in Sing Sing were partners in a lumber-market, store and ship-building dock with a sloop in 1818. JOHN[6] married Catharine, dau. of Elias Quereau and they had 9 children.

WILLIAM LYON[6] (1783-1840) married Rachel Robertson (1785-1872), dau. of Jabez and Rachel Robertson of Cantitoe. Both are buried in Union Cemetery. They lived on his father's homestead and had 9 children: STEPHEN,[7] b. 1810; WILLIAM H.,[7] b. 1812; HARVEY,[7] b. 1815; BETSEY,[7] b. 1818, d. y.; HENRY,[7] b. 1821; BETSEY,[7] b. 1824; CATHARINE,[7] b. 1826; FERRIS,[7] b. 1828; and EMILY ROBERTSON,[7] b. 1831.

STEPHEN LYON[7] (1810-1898) married Jan. 1, 1834, Amanda A. (1814-1847), dau. of John and Sarah Mills Miller of Bedford. They lived on Jay St. where Beaver Dam Rd. begins and had 5 children: JOHN MILLER,[8] b. 1834; WILLIAM PENN,[8] b. 1837; JERE MILLER,[8] b. 1841; STEPHEN E.,[8] b. 1843; and AMANDA A.,[8] b. 1846. Three years after the death of his first wife he married Amy Ann Wheeler (1815-1897). They adopted Emma Lyon, who died March 19, 1958, at 102 yrs., 9 mos. Stephen was postmaster at Cantitoe from April 15, 1845, until the office was discontinued Feb. 18, 1846.

JAMES MILLER LYON[8] (1834-1902) lived on his father's farm and Nov. 11, 1859, applied to the Highway Department of Bedford, asking that they build Beaver Dam Rd. He married Sarah J. Clifford (1838-1881). Both are buried in Union Cemetery. They had no children.

WILLIAM PENN LYON[8] (1837-1908) married Mary Ann Sniffin (1837-1893) Sept. 16, 1874, at Round Hill, Conn. They lived in his father's homestead and had 2 children: MABEL,[9] b. 1876, mar. George S. Robinson; and STEPHEN D.[9] WILLIAM PENN[8] was a member of the Baptist Church of Bedford for 38 years. In January, 1867, he and his brother, JERE,[8] bought out John Burr Whitlock's store and made a success of it. They ran a general store, stable and undertaking establishment. PENN[8] kept the store and JERE[8] was the bookkeeper. In July, 1901, PENN[8] bought the George W. Horton place at Amawalk consisting of 185 acres which he intended to occupy and farm. Active in the Village Improvement Society, PENN[8] was a man of good sense, strong convictions and an honored citizen. He died very suddenly of a heart attack.

JERE MILLER LYON[8] (1841-1908) married Susan Robertson (1841-1924), dau. of B. Rumsey and Lydia Miller Robertson of Cantitoe Rd. They had no children. He died with a fortune of $100,000 gained as a Katonah merchant. JERE[8] was a wizard at math. and could add two columns, one with each hand, at the same time. He was an eccentric character and kept a wallet stuffed with 600 four-leaf clovers he had gathered, and believed they brought great luck.

STEPHEN D. LYON[9] (1882-1929), born at the homestead on Jay St. and Beaver Dam Rd., grew up in Katonah and entered the undertaking business, Lyon and Hartnett, in White Plains. He married Elsie Miller, dau.

of Horace Miller of Bedford, June 1, 1904, and they had 2 daughters: BEATRICE;[10] and RUTH.[10] BEATRICE[10] married Earl N. Thorpe, an internationally known sculptor, who died in February, 1951. Mrs. Lyon and Mrs. Thorpe and her two sons live on Old Mamaroneck Rd., White Plains.

FERRIS LYON[7] (1828-1878) married Sarah, dau. of William Williamson. They lived on the south end of Beaver Dam Rd. and were devoted Baptists. Sarah, an invalid for a number of years, died Nov. 1, 1898. Both are buried in Union Cemetery. They had 6 children: WILLIAM HENRY;[8] MARY EMILY;[8] CAROLINE;[8] STEPHEN;[8] CONANT S.;[8] JEANETTE.[8]

WILLIAM HENRY LYON,[8] b. July 30, 1856, taught school in Bedford Center near the old Baptist Church and in Bedford's stone school house (now the Museum) from 1873 to '76. Then he went into the sale of oil with Swan & Finch, which turned into Standard Oil. He retired in 1925. He had a wooden leg caused by a fall from a moving train between Bedford and Katonah in his early days. He sold the family homestead to New York State for a reformatory for women, now Westfield. WILLIAM[8] belonged to the Bedford Baptist church, Bedford Farmers' Club and Mt. Kisco National Bank. He was under sheriff of Westchester County and a staunch Democrat. Sept. 14, 1918, he married Mrs. Jennie Fields Ferris in New York City. He died on his 88th birthday in 1944 in White Plains. Both are buried in Union Cemetery. They had no issue.

CONANT S. LYON[8] had many Katonah friends and visited often at John Truesdell's. He was in the silk-importing business on 34th St., New York City. In July, 1927, he married Helen Thompson and they made their home in Crestwood. He died in Bronxville Aug. 9, 1945, in his 75th year, leaving no children.

CAROLINE LYON[8] (1861-1953) married Dr. Leonard K. Knox. They made their home in White Plains and were parents of 2 sons: GEORGE LYON KNOX[9] (1890-1944) who mar. Violet Stewart and had dau. BERNICE,[10] b. 1907, mar. and living in Jackson Heights; and JOHN KNOX,[9] b. 1891, mar. and living in Miami, Fla.

JEANETTE C. LYON,[8] b. on Beaver Dam Rd., married Sept. 21, 1904, in New York City Arthur M. Cornell (1878-1932) of Brooklyn. They made their home in Bedford Hills and had 2 daughters, ALICE DOROTHY[9] and PHYLLIS LYON CORNELL.[9] Art Cornell was a sportsman and an enthusiastic trout fisherman. He learned of Katonah through its streams and in 1903 became manager of the Katonah Lighting Company. He served for 16 years until the company was absorbed by the Associated Gas & Electric Corporation. He then established the Northern Westchester Company, a corporation dealing in electrical supplies and electrical work. Later he added the Katonah Flower Shop with cut flowers and a greenhouse in the present Zimmerman building and worked there until his death, Dec. 14, 1932. He belonged to the Katonah Rotary Club and Katonah Fire Department. He is buried in Oakwood Cemetery. Mrs. Cornell, known as "Nettie," lives in their house at Bedford Hills.

ALICE DOROTHY CORNELL[9] graduated from the Katonah High School and Elmira College. She married Chester L. Dexheimer Feb. 20, 1932, of Bedford Hills where they live. He is an office central foreman and has been with the telephone company for 36 years. They have 2 children:

CHESTER LeRoy, Jr.,[10] b. 1934, called "Roy"; and PHYLLIS DEXHEIMER,[10] b. 1941.

ROY DEXHEIMER[10] graduated from Bedford Hills High School and Hobart College where he was an English Education major and won the Walter H. Durfee Award for outstanding senior. He married June, 1957, Betsy Hacker, dau. of Dean Louis M. Hacker of Columbia University, in New York City. He served 2 years in the Army and is teaching English in Irondequoit High School in Rochester, N.Y. PHYLLIS DEXHEIMER[10] graduated from Fox Lane High School and is attending State University Teachers College in Potsdam, N.Y.

PHYLLIS LYON CORNELL[9] graduated from Katonah High School, attended Mt. Holyoke College and graduated from Packard Business School. She married July 12, 1941, Harold V. O'Brien of Milford, Conn., at St. Mark's Church, Mt. Kisco. They live on Bedford Rd., Bedford Hills, with Mrs. Cornell and their daughter, MAUREEN,[10] b. 1948. PHYLLIS[9] works for *Reader's Digest* and Mr. O'Brien for Brooks Dairy.

Compiled by K. B. Kelly.

The Marshalls of Cherry Street

DAVID MARSHALL[1] of old Stephentown, present Somers, married Anne Haight and they were parents of WILLIAM MARSHALL.[2] WILLIAM[2] married Sophia Brown of Bedford. His will was written Jan. 19, 1797, and proved Feb. 7, 1797. He left to his wife, Sophia, one third of his estate; to his daughters, ANNE,[3] CHARLOTTY,[3] SOPHIA,[3] and BETSEY,[3] one third equally divided; and one third to his son, MOSES.[3]

Sophia Brown Marshall of Bedford dated her will Mar. 13, 1828, and it was proved Oct. 23, 1828. She named children: ANNA BAKER;[3] CHARLOTTE BAYLEY;[3] SOPHIA BANKS,[3] wife of John; MOSES MARSHALL;[3] and SALLY MARSHALL;[3] as well as Hiram Coffin.

MOSES MARSHALL,[3] a saddler, had a harness shop on Cherry St. For years after his death, cards bearing his name were occasionally seen on the underside of a saddle-flap. He married Lavinia Haight, b. 1791, dau. of David and Elizabeth Wetmore Haight (see Haight genealogy).

Compiled by Alma R. Crane and F. R. Duncombe.

The Meads of Mt. Holly

ABEL MEAD[1] was born in Connecticut on July 7, 1752. His original ancestor in this country was William Mead, b. about 1600 in England. William settled in Stamford, Conn., in the spring of 1641, coming from Wethersfield. It is believed he arrived in Massachusetts on the "Elizabeth" in 1635. ABEL[1] served in a Connecticut regiment during the Revolution and his musket is still owned by his family. He married Phoebe Reynolds and at that time bought the Lounsbury farm on Mt. Holly Rd. and present Rte. 35. ABEL[1] died Aug. 29, 1833, and his farm was inherited by his son ZADOC.[2]

ZADOC MEAD,[2] b. May 3, 1775, on the Mt. Holly farm, died Aug. 18, 1833. He was a private in the war of 1812. He married Nancy Knapp (1815-1898). Their only son was BENJAMIN.[3]

BENJAMIN MEAD,[3] b. Dec. 25, 1815, on the homestead, married Mary Waterbury. He died Dec. 23, 1898, just short of his 83rd birthday. Their son was WILLIAM BENJAMIN.[4]

WILLIAM BENJAMIN MEAD[4] (Benjamin,[3] Zadoc,[2] Abel[1]) b. Nov. 28, 1867, married Cassie Tompkins of Chappaqua and they had one daughter, DOROTHY MAY.[5] Mr. Mead farmed his Mt. Holly land until he sold it in 1910 to Dr. and Mrs. J. Ramsay Hunt. Thereafter the Meads lived for a short time in Bedford Center and then bought a home on Valley Rd., Katonah. The Meads were very active in the Presbyterian Church until 1947 when they moved to New Jersey. Mr. Mead passed away at the home of his daughter and son-in-law Aug. 11, 1957, at Fair Haven, N.J. Mrs. Mead is making her home with her daughter in New Jersey.

DOROTHY MAY MEAD,[5] b. Aug. 2, 1909, on Mt. Holly Rd., was the fifth generation to live on the farm. She graduated from Katonah High School in June, 1926, and from New Paltz Teachers College in 1929. She taught on Long Island where she met her husband. She married Harold Heaton Elting June 30, 1934, in the Katonah Presbyterian Church. They are parents of 2 daughters: NANCY MAY,[6] b. Dec. 10, 1935; and JOANNE ELTING,[6] b. Jan. 27, 1940.

Compiled by K. B. Kelly.

The Merritt Families of Katonah

JOHN MERRITT,[2] son of JOHN[1] and Sarah (Miller) Merritt of English descent, b. Feb. 18, 1788, purchased a farm on Mt. Holly. He married Hannah Gregory (1791-1878), dau. of Stephen and Chloe (Fillow) Gregory of Somers. They were parents of: RUTH ANN,[3] b. 1812, wife of Jacob Timberman; PHEBE,[3] b. 1815, wife of William Newman (see Newman genealogy); JOHN,[3] b. 1819, d. at 8 weeks; JAMES FILLOW,[3] b. 1820; CHLOE,[3] wife of Enoch Avery (see Avery genealogy); NORMAN,[3] b. 1823; and CAROLINE,[3] b. 1826, unmarried. JOHN MERRITT,[2] a farmer, died at his home in August, 1856.

JAMES FILLOW MERRITT,[3] b. on Mt. Holly, May 7, 1820, married Lucy Ann Whitlock, dau. of John Burr and Rachel (Olmsted) Whitlock (see Whitlock genealogy) in 1846. They were parents of: JOHN BURR;[4] and ELLA,[4] who married Isaac W. Turner. ELLA[4] and Isaac Turner lived on Mt. Holly in the present Grimshaw house on North Salem Rd. and had no children. He was supervisor of the Town of Bedford.

NORMAN MERRITT,[3] b. on Mt. Holly, Dec. 8, 1823, married 1st in October, 1852, Hannah Maria Washburn (1835-1873), dau. of Ezra and Clorinda (Merritt) Washburn. They made their home in Goldens Bridge and their children were: CLORINDA WASHBURN[4] (1855-1922), who married

Nov. 18, 1874, George Erwin Todd, b. 1844, and lived on Cherry St. (see Todd genealogy); CAROLINE[4] (1858-1922), who married Elbert Todd and also lived on Cherry St.; and two babies who died young. NORMAN[3] and his son-in-law, George E. Todd, owned the Lyon farm on Jay St. presently owned by Harvey School. NORMAN[3] married 2nd June 3, 1874, Mary Ann Washburn. Their two children were: RHODA;[4] and NORMAN, JR.[4]

JOHN BURR MERRITT,[4] son of JAMES[3] and Lucy Merritt, was born on Mt. Holly, Oct. 30, 1849. There he ran the farm and lived until January, 1916. He married Phoebe Cornelia Teed of Somers. Their only child was ELLA MAUDE,[5] born at the farm in 1880. She married Jan. 15, 1901, Simeon Brady, in Goldens Bridge Sept. 26, 1875, son of Edward and Julia (Todd) Brady. Their home was on Rte. 100, Somers, a large farm, which now includes the golf course and The 19th Hole. Mrs. Brady was for many years town clerk of Somers. Their 2 children were: SIMEON,[6] b. May 7, 1902; and LUCY M. BRADY,[6] b. May 16, 1903, wife of Stephen Brown of Somers.

SIMEON BRADY[6] was born in Somers and attended Katonah High School, Mohegan Military Academy and Peekskill Military Academy. He was in the auto sales and garage business, Brady-Stannard, in Brewster, and was killed in an auto accident. He married Katherine Tooumey who died in 1957. Their only child, CAROL ANN,[7] married Kenneth Stuart Brown, June 3, 1951. They live in California with their 4 children: MICHAEL SIMEON;[8] PETER EDWARD;[8] DEBRA ANN;[8] and CHRISTOPHER BROWN,[8] b. Aug. 1, 1960.

ANTHONY M. MERRITT[1] (1785-1846), a cousin of JOHN MERRITT,[2] lived locally and married Rhoda Gregory (1793-1880), dau. of Stephen and Chloe (Fillow) Gregory, a sister of Hannah Gregory Merritt. Their children were: CLORINDA;[2] REBECCA JANE;[2] and STEPHEN.[2] CLORINDA,[2] b. 1809, married Ezra Washburn, b. 1801, of Somers. Their children were: ANTHONY MERRITT;[3] HANNAH MARIA,[3] who married her cousin, Norman Merritt, son of John and Hannah (Gregory) Merritt; and RHODA ANN WASHBURN,[3] b. 1837, who married 1st John S. Frost and, 2nd, Elbert Todd, a dentist, son of Abraham Todd. REBECCA JANE MERRITT[2] married Abner White of Danbury. STEPHEN MERRITT[2] died at 30 yrs., apparently unmarried.

ABRAHAM MERRITT[1] and LEVI MERRITT[1] were brothers, born in Ossining. Abraham came to Katonah as a foreman for Henry Pellew around 1886. He married Mary Jane Searles, daughter of Leonard A. Searles (see Searles genealogy).

Compiled by K. B. Kelly.

The Miller Families

JOHN MILLER,[1] b. circa 1609 in England, was of the Wethersfield, Conn., colony. In October, 1642, he received from the Town of Stamford, Conn., as did the other settlers from Wethersfield, "five acres, house lot and marsh and upland." Inventory of his estate recorded in 1665 shows that he left

3 sons, JOHN,[2] JONATHAN[2] and JOSEPH.[2] His widow married 2nd Obadiah Seeley.

JOHN MILLER,[2] granted land in Stamford in 1667 and proposed a freeman in 1669, was one of the 22 original proprietors of Bedford in 1680. In 1697, the names John, Jonathan and Joseph, were on the patent granted to Bedford from Connecticut. JOHN[2] had 5 children: SARAH;[3] JOHN,[3] mar. Mary Holmes; JONATHAN,[3] mar. Sarah Holmes; MARY,[3] mar. Richard Holmes; and DAVID.[3]

JONATHAN MILLER[3] and Sarah Holmes, mar. in 1690-91, had 11 children: JONATHAN,[4] b. 1691, d. one month; JONATHAN,[4] b. 1692; JOHN,[4] b. 1694; STEPHEN,[4] b. 1696; SAMUEL,[4] b. 1698; SARAH,[4] b. 1700; RACHEL,[4] b. 1703; NATHANIEL,[4] b. 1705; INCREASE,[4] b. 1707; EBENEZER,[4] b. 1709; and BENJAMIN,[4] 1711-12. These names are repeated in later generations of Millers, indicating though not proving a common ancestor.

EBENEZER MILLER[4] had a son, DEACON EBENEZER,[5] b. circa 1736, who mar. a granddaughter of John Westcote. By this marriage children were: KEZIA,[6] mar. Benjamin Banks; DEBORAH,[6] mar. Jonathan Newman; and JONATHAN[6] (1765-1848), mar. Rachel Banks (1768-1833). JONATHAN[6] and Rachel Miller were parents of ALVAH[7] (1797-1852) who married Lois Holly (see Holly genealogy) and lived on the south end of Mt. Holly Rd. until his death. ALVAH[7] and Lois (Holly) Miller were parents of STEPHEN HOLLY.[8]

STEPHEN HOLLY MILLER[8] (1823-1905) married Sarah Jane Lyon (1831-1921), dau. of Newman Clark Lyon and Alathea Merritt (1797-1885). A farmer, he was also very active politically: town assessor 24 yrs., commissioner of highways 31 yrs., court crier 11 yrs., deputy sheriff, census marshall and School District trustee, 35 yrs. He joined the Bedford Baptist Church at 76 yrs. He and his wife lived on Mt. Holly Rd. in the present Frank McKown house, leading a very social life. They had 6 children: ALVAH[9] (1855-1931); EMMA JANE[9] (1853-1938); CYRUS[9] (1859-1936); STEPHEN, JR.[9] (1865-1872); LOIS ADELIA[9] (1866-1942); and ARTHUR[9] (1869-1921) who mar. Julia Tracy and had children, TRACY[10] and ROBERT HOLLY[10] of Montclair, N.J.

ALVAH MILLER[9] married Phebe A. Sutton. They had 6 children: NATHANIEL LYON,[10] b. 1879, now of Ridgefield, Conn.; MARGUERITE AUGUSTA[10] (1881-1951); MABEL LORRAINE[10] (1889-1953); SARAH ISABEL[10] (1890-1894); ALVAH LAWRENCE[10] (1894-1950); and CYRUS W.[10] (1896-1951). Son of ALVAH LAWRENCE MILLER[10] is ALVAH LAWRENCE, JR.[11] Sons of CYRUS W. MILLER[10] are: ALLEN M.,[11] b. 1926; and SERGE,[11] b. 1933, who has son, CYRUS WILLIAM,[12] b. 1958.

LOIS ADELIA MILLER[9] married Lewis Frost Ferris, son of Anthony Merritt Ferris. They lived on Deer Park Rd., Katonah, and had children: MARIE,[10] mar. Oliver U. Todd; GENEVIEVE[10] (1895-1896); ANTHONY MILLER;[10] HARRIET EWEN,[10] graduate of Barnard College; and ARTHUR LEWIS FERRIS[10] who married Charlotte Ham and has dau. HELEN MARIE FERRIS.[11] Mrs. Todd and her sister, HARRIET E. FERRIS,[10] live north of Katonah on Old Rte. 22 opposite Todd Rd.

ALFRED W. MILLER,[10] grandson of STEPHEN HOLLY MILLER,[8] is in the publishing business in New York and writes sports articles under the name of "Sparse Gray Hackle."

Living also in the Mt. Holly area in the early 1800s, related to ALVAH[7] and descended from JOHN,[1] the family of INCREASE MILLER (1766-1854), owned many acres on the North Salem Rd. both in Bedford and across the Salem (now Lewisboro) line. The father of INCREASE was Stephen, d. 1780. Stephen and wife Mary (1726-1822) had children: INCREASE; STEPHEN, JR.; SAMUEL; and REBECCA. In 1823 INCREASE MILLER and wife, Hannah, sold for "one cent lawful money of the United States of America" to the trustees of the Methodist Church property on which to build what became known as "Herman Chapel." The deed provided land be reserved for the erection of a school and for a family burying ground. In this ground on Increase Miller Rd., Lewisboro Township, lie Mary Miller, widow of STEPHEN; Hannah (d. 1852, ae. 77), wife of INCREASE; INCREASE: SAMUEL (1798-1835), son of INCREASE; and STEPHEN MILLER, JR. (1793-1850). In the same group of graves lie Rebecca Merritt (1755-1830), possibly the dau. of STEPHEN MILLER, and Amelia Hoyt (1802-1844), possibly the dau. of INCREASE. Probable sons of INCREASE were: Anson M. Miller, to whom INCREASE gave the right to "pass with oxen . . . through my lands" in 1840, and Nathaniel, to whom INCREASE deeded his land "for love and affection" in 1853 and who in return leased it back to INCREASE for $1.00 during his lifetime and agreed to furnish him with clothing and board.

WHITLOCKVILLE MILLERS

BENJAMIN MILLER,[4] b. 1711, son of JONATHAN,[3] was probably the Benjamin who owned property on the Cross River where his son WILLIAM[5] operated a gristmill. WILLIAM MILLER[5] (1734-1818), mar. Mary (1743-1816), was one of our first judges. He had a wooden leg. His sons were: SAMUEL H.;[6] and BENJAMIN H.[6]

SAMUEL H. MILLER[6] (1775-1859) was born in what later became Whitlockville and was owner of 20 acres there in 1837. He married Deborah Olmsted, dau. of Major David, in 1797, and they were parents of GEORGE WASHINGTON[7] (1799-1870); MARY[7] (1801-1838); and JOHN ADAMS[7] (1804-1876).

JOHN ADAMS MILLER[7] married Charity B. Merritt, dau. of Nathan Merritt of New Castle, in 1831. In 1837 JOHN A. MILLER[7] sold 114 acres of land to Gideon Reynolds. Much of this became the village of Old Katonah. JOHN[7] and Charity were parents of: MARY B.;[8] HENRY,[8] Captain in Co. B, 6th Heavy Artillery, July 22, 1863–Dec. 18, 1864, killed in action; and JOSEPH O.[8]

MARY B. MILLER[8] married Francis Carpenter. MRS. LESTER J. REYNOLDS[10] of Kinderhook, N.Y., is her granddaughter.

JOSEPH OWEN MILLER[8] (1841-1902), b. in Whitlockville, left home in 1862 to clerk for Whitlock, Avery & Co. in Croton Falls. Later he left there also to clerk at the Court House in White Plains. He married Elizabeth Wright Oct. 12, 1861. They had a son, d. infant, and 5 daughters. The family moved to Mt. Kisco where Mr. Miller was village president several terms. He was a justice of the peace and county register 1884-1887. Under President Cleveland he was inspector of Chinese immigration. In 1900 he was elected supervisor of New Castle. Dying Nov. 29, 1902, he left his wife and daughters: MRS. STEPHEN VAN TASSEL[9] of Mt. Vernon;

JOSEPHINE[9] (Mrs. B. E. Smythe of Mt. Kisco); ADDIE;[9] LULU;[9] and AUGUSTA[9] (Mrs. C. R. F. Green).

LULU MILLER[9] married Joseph E. Merriam, supervisor of Bedford. Their children were: GEORGE FRANKLIN[10] (1907-1941); JOSEPH E., JR.[10] (1913-1956) who mar. Hazel Moliero, and had children, SANDRA MERRIAM,[11] b. 1937, who mar. Quentin Harvell and has children, RICHARD,[12] b. 1957, and MICHAEL HARVELL,[12] b. 1959, and JOSEPH EDWIN MERRIAM, III,[11] of Bedford; and JEAN MERRIAM,[10] who mar. Gordon Gale Gorham, son of George R. and Katherine Gale Gorham, and had dau. GALE MILLER GORHAM,[11] b. 1940, who mar. 1957 Donald Edward Daggett and has dau. DEBORAH JEAN DAGGETT,[12] b. Sept. 13, 1958. Children of AUGUSTA MILLER[9] and Dr. Green of Peekskill were: ROBERT MILLER;[10] ALICE GREEN DUGAN[10] of Peekskill; HELEN,[10] mar. Hobart Stout; THURSTON GREEN;[10] and MAUDE GREEN LANE[10] of Peekskill.

BENJAMIN H. MILLER,[6] son of WILLIAM,[5] married 1st a daughter of Thaddeus Whitlock. Among grandchildren mentioned in the will of Thaddeus was NORMAN.[7]

NORMAN W. MILLER[7] (1799-1862), b. in Whitlockville, a hatter by trade, married Sept. 20, 1821, Deborah Gregory (1803-circa 1884), dau. of Stephen and Chloe (Fillow) Gregory. Their children were: DANIEL MERRITT;[8] ANN ELIZABETH;[8] SMITH;[8] MARY;[8] and CHLOE SALOMA.[8]

DANIEL MERRITT MILLER[8] (1822-1890), a dealer in horses, was an active member of the Methodist Church in Whitlockville and Old Katonah. He married 1st Sept. 27, 1823, Mary Ann Hoyt, a dau. of James and Elizabeth (Banks) Hoyt, who died June, 1855. Their sons were: NORMAN HOYT,[9] (1847-1853); and WILLIAM ARTHUR.[9] DANIEL[8] married 2nd Sept. 6, 1858, Phebe C. Wildey (June 2, 1836-Aug. 19, 1865) by whom he had: JULIA E.;[9] MARY A.;[9] and GEORGE WILDEY.[9] In December, 1869, he married, 3rd, Theodosia Collyer (1830-1906), dau. of John and Rhoda (Smith) Collyer, who was a devoted mother to his children.

WILLIAM ARTHUR MILLER[9] (Dec. 21, 1852-Sept. 6, 1883) was educated locally, then at Fort Edward for 2 yrs. and at Packard Business College. He founded in 1873 the *Katonah Sentinel,* Katonah's first locally published paper, which became the *Recorder* in 1874. He was very active in the Fire Department and Village Improvement Society, was clerk of the Board of Supervisors of Westchester County, and in 1882 passed an examination for Custom House service, after which he became a night inspector. Sept. 27, 1876, he married Frances Elizabeth Hanford, dau. of Jacob Wallace and Betsey (Whitlock) Hanford. William died suddenly of "malarial typhoid fever," Sept. 6, 1883, leaving his wife and a 5-yr.-old daughter, VIDA HOYT.[10] VIDA[10] was a musician of rare talent, being a master of the organ and piano, and possessed a fine voice. She was organist for a time in the Methodist Church in both Katonahs and also in the Presbyterian Church in New Katonah. Born in Old Katonah Oct. 29, 1878, she died in New Katonah July 22, 1936. She married May 2, 1900, J. Franklin Ryan of Danbury, who became a local justice of the peace. He is an influential citizen and business man. They had one daughter, MADELON RYAN,[11] who lives with her father on Orchard Lane, Katonah.

JULIA E. MILLER,[9] b. Apr. 2, 1861, married Arnell Frost Dickinson, son of Arnell F. and Elizabeth Ann (Robertson) Dickinson of Cantitoe (see Dickinson genealogy).

MARY A. MILLER,[9] known as "Mollie," was a very popular schoolteacher on Palmer Ave. in Old Katonah before she married Lafayette L. Long of Buffalo. She died Oct. 31, 1922, leaving 3 sons: MERRITT M.,[10] WARREN W.,[10] and HARRY H. LONG[10] of Buffalo.

GEORGE WILDEY MILLER[9] (1863-1894), unmar., died suddenly at 31. He was in the general trucking business in New York City with a local friend, Stephen S. Chadeayne. A Republican and tax collector of the Town of Bedford, he was a favorite in all circles, social and business.

SMITH MILLER,[8] b. 1826, married in 1851 Julia A. Clark (1830-1924), dau. of Nathan, a farmer. They lived on the top of Mt. Holly and later in Mt. Kisco, where he died Nov. 4, 1894. They were parents of 3 children: LEWIS H.;[9] FRANCIS C.;[9] and EDITH.[9]

LEWIS H. MILLER,[9] b. Oct. 9, 1852, was locally educated and then attended business college. He began at 15 yrs. as bookkeeper for Hoyt Brothers in Old Katonah and continued in business in Katonah for 72 years. After his association with Hoyt Brothers he went into the real estate and insurance business, with his office in the Benedict Building. He had charge of the sale of lots for the Katonah Land Company. He was a member of the Fire Department, active in the Methodist Church, ran on the Prohibition ticket in November, 1898, for county register and for member of Assembly in 1900. He married in 1880 Margaret E. Barclay (1857-1938), dau. of Henry of New York City. They built several beautiful homes here in New Katonah: one now owned by Harold H. Park on Bedford Rd.; another at 27 The Terrace; another now owned by Mr. Marcus on Mustato Rd. His homes were always show places and in good taste.

The Lewis Millers were the parents of two daughters, LUELLA C.[10] and HENRIETTA M.[10] Both girls attended our local school and then went to high school in New Rochelle, living with our ex-principal, Mr. Tryon. They later studied at Drew Seminary in Carmel. LUELLA[10] attended advanced music courses at Syracuse University from September, 1902, graduating in 1906. The following year she married Edwin T. Iglehart, who for many years was a professor of Literature and Bible and Historical Theology in Japan. Their 9 children attended school in Katonah when in this country. Children are: FERDINAND C.,[11] mar. Martha S. Jennewine, one son; MARGARET B.,[11] unmar.; NANNIE S.,[11] mar. Clarence A. Parker; NETTIE M.[11] (twin of Nannie), mar. Dr. Walter E. Lawrence, 3 sons, 2 daus.; JULIA M.,[11] mar. John S. Marden, 2 sons; EDWIN T., JR.,[11] unmar.; LUELLA JEAN,[11] mar. Dr. Lloyd McDaniel, 3 sons; LEWIS M.,[11] mar. Marylin Steurnagel, one son, one dau.; CHARLES S. IGLEHART,[11] mar. Jane MacAlpine, 2 sons. Dr. and Mrs. Iglehart live on Ashby Place, Katonah, as does EDWIN T., JR.[11] They are active in the Methodist Church.

FRANCIS C. MILLER[9] (1855-1929) married Henrietta Dean (1852-1922). They lived in Mt. Kisco. Daughter, ELSIE,[10] b. July 4, 1876, mar., lives in Mt. Vernon. EDITH[9] (1867-1955), unmar., taught school and lived in Mt. Kisco.

ANN ELIZABETH MILLER[8] (1824-1856) married George Quick. Their children were: DAVID BERNARD,[9] b. 1842; AUGUSTUS SMITH,[9] b. 1844; DEBORAH ANNA,[9] b. 1846; CATHERINE OPHELIA,[9] b. 1847; NORMAN MILLER,[9] b. 1850; and MARY JANE QUICK[9] (1856-1857). Most of the children lived near Tarrytown, N.Y.

MARY MILLER[8] (1829-1889) married William Levi Travis (see Travis genealogy).

CHLOE SALOMA MILLER,[8] b. 1839, married in 1858 Jasper Stimas, a farmer in Tarrytown. Their children were: HARRIET LOUISA;[9] MARY OPHELIA;[9] JAMES HENRY,[9] b. 1864; HANNAH ANN,[9] b. 1865; JASPER MILLER,[9] b. 1868; and WILLIAM ARTHUR STIMAS,[9] b. 1877.

* * * * *

HURD L. MILLER[1] (1823-1910), a veteran of the Civil War, and his 1st wife, Mary Hoyt (1819-1899), lived in Old Katonah. Children were: LOUIS;[2] RACHEL ELIZABETH;[2] MARY FRANCES;[2] and HARRIET.[2] LOUIS,[2] an actor, had a daughter, CLARA,[3] who was raised by her aunt, Mrs. Joseph Brady. CLARA[3] became an actress and died in Africa. RACHEL ELIZABETH[2] married in 1872 James H. Williams (1845-1910). Mr. Williams, b. in Pennsylvania, learned the harness-maker's trade in Brewster. He had a harness-shop on Railroad Ave. in Old Katonah and a home in back of the Presbyterian Church there, now moved to 10 Bedford Rd. In the new village in 1901 he built at 131 Katonah Ave. Here he made his home and conducted his business. Their 2 children were: CLARENCE WILLIAM WILLIAMS,[3] mar. Gertrude Green, whose only child, HARVEY JAMES WILLIAMS,[4] lives in White Plains; and ELLA MAUDE WILLIAMS,[3] mar. William George Barrett (see Barrett genealogy). HURD L. MILLER[1] married 2nd in February 1901, Mrs. Elizabeth Peck (1848-1927), mother of Fowler Peck, former owner and editor of the *Katonah Record*.

MARY FRANCES MILLER[2] (1852-1925) married William H. Spendley (1845-1927). Their only child was EDNA SPENDLEY,[3] mar. late in life.

HARRIET MILLER[2] 1854-1943) married Joseph Brady (1852-1939) (see Hoyt Brothers genealogy).

Compiled by K. B. Kelly and F. R. Duncombe, with assistance from Alma R. Crane.

The Newman Families of Katonah

It is probable that all our local Newmans descended from William Newman, b. in England, who lived in Stamford, Conn., in 1642 where he sold land that year to John Holly (see Holly genealogy). William had brother John, wife Elizabeth, and children: Thomas; Daniel; John; Elizabeth; and Hannah. Thomas died in 1659 leaving wife Mary and children: William; and Catherine. Daniel, a freeman in 1670, died 1695, leaving wife Sarah. A later Daniel was on the Bedford freeholders' list of 1763 and the tax list of 1779.

Newmans in the northeast corner of Bedford near Cross River in the late 1700's were JOSEPH[1] and STEPHEN.[1]

JOSEPH NEWMAN[1] and his wife, Patience, had: TIMOTHY;[2] JOHN;[2] JONATHAN;[2] DAVID;[2] JOSEPH;[2] JAMES;[2] RACHEL R.;[2] PATTY,[2] wife of John Finch; PATIENCE BOUTON;[2] and a son-in-law, Henry Clark. All of these are mentioned in his will, probated 1820, witnessed by Jonah Holly. Patience Newman signed the original articles of faith of the Cross River Baptist Church in 1789.

JAMES NEWMAN[2] (1782-1863) married Clarissa (1787-1851). They joined the Cross River Baptist Church in 1840.

BANKS NEWMAN[3] (1806-1844), son of JAMES[2] and Clarissa, married Nov. 7, 1827, Sarah Reynolds, the 14th child of James and Abigail Knapp Reynolds of Cross River. BANKS[3] died in 1844 leaving his wife with 6 children: CLARISSA;[4] JAMES H.;[4] ELIAS;[4] RACHEL;[4] CHARLES W.;[4] and EDGAR BANKS.[4]

JAMES H. NEWMAN,[4] b. June 19, 1833, was raised by a Reynolds uncle and in December, 1854, went to Illinois to live. There he married Cynthia A. Hayden and raised 2 sons: CLARK E.[5] (1866-1920); and ORRIS H.[5] (1870-1894).

ELIAS GILBERT NEWMAN,[4] b. Oct. 24, 1834, married Mary E. Cooper in 1859. They had: MARY A.[5] (1869-1889); and ALBERT EUGENE[5] (1860-1892), who married Minnie Lotspike. He was an editor in Tennessee and left no children.

CHARLES W. NEWMAN,[4] b. Sept. 7, 1838, raised by a Reynolds uncle, served 3 years in the Civil War in the 133rd Regt., N.Y. Volunteers. He married Adeline A. Waterbury May 13, 1867, and they had: ADDIE AUGUSTA,[5] b. 1869, unmar., who lived in White Plains; ELLA FRANCES[5] (1873-1916) who mar. Brewster Boyd and had RODERICK BREWSTER BOYD,[6] May 29, 1906; EDGAR BANKS,[5] b. 1870, who mar. Linnie B. Wadsworth and had CHARLES WADSWORTH,[6] Aug. 5, 1894.

EDGAR BANKS NEWMAN,[4] b. July 1, 1842, reared by a Reynolds uncle, enlisted in the Civil War in the 48th N.Y. Volunteers. He was color-bearer in the Battle of Olusta, Fla., and was wounded in the knee, taken prisoner and was in a Jacksonville, Fla., hospital. He reported being well treated. After returning home, he had his right leg amputated. He married May 17, 1871, Esther Ackerly of Whitlockville and they had 3 children: CLARA,[5] b. 1871, d. infant; LEONARD ACKERLY;[5] and WILLIAM EDGAR.[5] EDGAR[4] was a Custom House officer. In 1901 he was night clerk at the Barge Office in New York City. The Newmans lived on Main St. in Old Katonah and when the village moved, built a beautiful new home at 55 Bedford Rd.

LEONARD ACKERLY NEWMAN,[5] b. 1873, run over by a train, died July 26, 1891, at 18 yrs.

WILLIAM EDGAR NEWMAN,[5] b. in Old Katonah in February, 1877, was a very popular youth. He married Charlotte Bedell in 1904. He was a salesman with Merwin Kniffin, grocer in White Plains; with Morse & Rogers, shoes, in New York City; and last, with Kelloggs and Lawrence on The Parkway. WILLIAM EDGAR[5] and Charlotte Bedell Newman had one son, EDGAR BEDELL.[6]

EDGAR BEDELL NEWMAN[6] unmar., was born Oct. 12, 1912, on Valley Rd., Katonah, in the house now owned by Mrs. C. F. Lawrence. For some years he ran a small greenhouse business at his home on Deer Park Rd.

* * * * *

STEPHEN NEWMAN[1] (1771-1813) married Eunice Hait who lived in the Mt. Holly area near the Cross River. Apparently they moved to Carmel but were back in Bedford by 1797 and mentioned in a highway assessment list for District 17 which ran along present Rte. 22. Daniel Newman and

Daniel Newman, Jr., were also in this district. Here they lived on the E. J. Purdy farm in the house presently owned by Philip de Young. A Stephen Newman was an ensign in Lt. Col. Joseph Benedict's Regt., Westchester County Militia, 1808, and became a lieutenant in 1814. We do not know if he was related to STEPHEN.[1]

AMOS NEWMAN,[2] son of STEPHEN[1] and Eunice, b. Nov. 2, 1797, married Phebe Powell Jan. 4, 1826, and they lived for 25 yrs. with her parents, the Abraham Powells of Cantitoe. About 1851 they bought the Thomas S. Lyon place on Jay St., the present Legion property and in 1862 built the large home which burned about 1952. They had many children, but only STEPHEN[3] lived. AMOS[2] died Mar. 1, 1880. Mrs. Newman, b. in 1801, died in 1885.

STEPHEN NEWMAN[3] married Clarissa Lounsbury, dau. of Phineas of Bedford, and died on his wedding journey at Niagara Falls Oct. 22, 1867, at 35 yrs., 5 mos., and 15 days. Clarissa lived on with her husband's parents and in 1893 owned over 160 acres. She later married Dr. Jared Green Wood, a widower, of the Cherry St. Wood family (see Wood genealogy). It was with Dr. and Mrs. Wood that Simuel Pryor made his home and grew up in Katonah.

WILLIAM P. NEWMAN[2] (1802-1872) married Sept. 3, 1834, Phebe Merritt, b. July 25, 1815, dau. of John and Hannah (Gregory) Merritt. WILLIAM[2] and Phebe were baptized at the Cross River Baptist Church. They were parents of: BENJAMIN;[3] GILBERT;[3] JULIA;[3] LYDIA ANN;[3] and DAVID B.[3] (1839-42).

BENJAMIN B. NEWMAN,[3] b. Mar. 5, 1837, married Sept. 22, 1865, Mary E. Halstead, dau. of Isaac Halstead. They lived in North Salem with their 5 children: MATILDA,[4] b. 1867; HARRIET,[4] b. 1870; ISAAC,[4] b. 1872; GEORGE B.,[4] b. 1874; and JULIA A.,[4] b. 1876.

GILBERT B. NEWMAN,[3] b. June 29, 1838, married Oct. 10, 1865, Cornelia M. Silkman, b. 1844, dau. of Aaron D. and Emily Newman Silkman. They had sons: AARON D.;[4] and FRANK FLETCHER.[4]

AARON D. NEWMAN,[4] b. Dec. 10, 1868, lived in Cross River, and married Agnes Giles, dau. of the Baptist minister there. They moved to Washington, D.C., and raised 2 children: DOROTHY[5] and LAWRENCE.[5] Both AARON[4] and Agnes are buried in Cross River. They had celebrated their golden wedding Oct. 12, 1942, in Washington. DOROTHY[5] married Gerald Ward Brooks and lives in Illinois. They had 2 daughters. LAWRENCE[5] married but has no children. His present home is in Chevy Chase, Md.

FRANK FLETCHER NEWMAN[4] married Grace Dorsey and lives in Baltimore. They had 6 children.

JULIA A. NEWMAN,[3] b. 1844, married Frank Fletcher, b. 1836, a Baptist minister, Jan. 1, 1867. They had: WILLIAM NEWMAN;[4] LOREN;[4] GILBERT N.;[4] and IDA A. FLETCHER.[4]

LYDIA ANN NEWMAN,[3] b. 1846, married Jan. 1, 1862, Enoch B. Avery (1836-1869), son of Col. Enoch Avery. They lived in Cross River. Daughters were: LUCY J.;[4] and LYDIA ANN AVERY[4] (see Avery genealogy).

Compiled by K. B. Kelly.

The Olmsted Family of Katonah

RICHARD OLMSTED,[1] b. England in 1607, arrived in this country on the ship "Lion" in 1632. He was an original proprietor of Hartford, Conn., constable in 1646 and representative in the General Assembly 1653-1679. He died November, 1684.

JOHN OLMSTED,[2] son of RICHARD,[1] baptized at Hartford 1649, married 1st Mary Benedict and 2nd, in 1695, Elizabeth, widow of Thomas Gregory.

JOHN OLMSTED, JR.,[3] son of JOHN[2] and Elizabeth, b. 1700, married Mindwell Sherwood. They had 10 children. One son was DAVID,[4] b. in Ridgefield, Conn.

DAVID OLMSTED,[4] b. about 1755, moved to Bedford around 1790. He owned and lived in the present Arthur Bernhard house near Quick's Lane on Cherry St. He married 1st Mary Whitlock (1755-1817) (see Whitlock genealogy). DAVID[4] was a representative to the General Assembly. He was a corporal in the Revolution in 1775; sergeant in Capt. Benedict's Company in 1776; saw service along the Hudson June 3rd as Captain in a Connecticut Company; as major he crossed the Delaware with Washington and fought at Trenton and Princeton. Major DAVID OLMSTED[4] was constable in Bedford, inspector of elections 1803-1807 & 1815-1822, and school commissioner in 1813. Children of DAVID[4] and Mary Olmsted were: Rachel,[5] bapt. in Weston, Conn., mar. John Burr Whitlock in 1808 (see Whitlock genealogy); DEBORAH,[5] mar. Samuel H. Miller (see Miller genealogy); DAVID, JR.,[5] b. 1791; JOHN;[5] JESSE;[5] WILLIAM;[5] CHLOE[5] (1790-1845), mar. Augustine Banks, son of John and Abigail (Birdsall) Banks; BETSEY,[5] who also married into the Banks family; and SOPHIE,[5] unmar. DAVID OLMSTED[4] after the death of his wife, Mary, married 2nd Sarah, who survived his death in 1824.

Compiled by K. B. Kelly.

Pellew of Cantitoe

Henry Edward Pellew did not live in this area for very many years but he left such a lasting impression on the community that he is always considered as belonging to it.

He was born in Canterbury, England, Apr. 26, 1828, and died in Washington, D.C., Feb. 4, 1923. Educated at Trinity College, Cambridge, he received his B.A. degree in 1850. He was one of the founders of Keble College, Oxford. He served on the boards of Feltenham Industrial School and other institutions, and was connected with various London hospitals and charities.

Oct. 5, 1858, he married at Bedford, N.Y., Eliza, daughter of William Jay. They returned to England to live. Three children were born, two of whom predeceased him, and one became the seventh Viscount Exmouth. Dec. 22, 1869, his wife died.

May 14, 1873, Pellew married Augusta Jay, Eliza's sister, at the American Legation in Vienna, Austria, where her brother, John Jay, was the U.S. Minister. Since marriage with a deceased wife's sister was at the time against English law, subsequent to his second marriage, he moved with his family to the United States, purchasing from W. H. Schieffelin the place called "Katonah's Wood" at Cantitoe which was originally part of the Jay estate. Mr. Pellew took an active interest in Katonah affairs and was a leading spirit in organizing the Katonah Village Improvement Society in 1878, serving as its president from that date until 1891 when he moved to Washington. Mr. Pellew was also president of the Bedford Farmers' Club for several years while he lived at "Katonah's Wood," where, about 1874, a daughter was born to the second Mrs. Pellew.

Compiled by F. R. Duncombe.

The Pronay Family

The first Pronay to move into the Township of Bedford was JOHN PRONAY[1] who was born in Budapest, Hungary, Dec. 25, 1859, and settled in Old Katonah in 1889. He became an American citizen Oct. 20, 1894, and married Elizabeth Klingstein (July 4, 1875-Dec. 5, 1933) Dec. 25, 1894. John was a tailor and furrier in Old Katonah, and played the violin in the local orchestra. In moving his business to New Katonah, he opened his first shop there where the Becker Flower Shop is now. He died Feb. 9, 1912. He and his wife had 3 children: KATHREAN C.,[2] b. Aug. 29, 1895; CORNELIUS J.,[2] b. Nov. 1, 1897 (the first child born in New Katonah); AGNES F.,[2] b. Apr. 9, 1908.

KATHREAN C. PRONAY[2] married in 1916 John J. Miller of Katonah, and died in January, 1947. They had two children: JOHN J., JR.,[3] b. 1921; and BARBARA C. MILLER,[3] b. 1925. JOHN J. MILLER,[3] a Navy electrician, died 1942, the first local boy killed in action in World War II. BARBARA C. MILLER[3] married in 1947 John W. Gullen of Waccabuc. They have children: JOHN;[4] and GEORGE GULLEN.[4]

CORNELIUS J. PRONAY[2] worked for a year or so when about 13 in Morrison's bakery. He attended school but managed to put in week-day hours from 4:30 a.m. to 8:30 a.m. and from 3:30 p.m. to 10 p.m. On Saturdays he worked from 6 a.m. to 11 p.m. His salary was $3.00 a week and whenever one of the regular bakery drivers was sick, Cornelius had to take his route and miss school. Later on he got a job helping the stationmaster, during his high school years.

In later years Mr. Pronay became a painting and decorating contractor. In 1922 he married Vera I. Munsell of Tarrytown. He was president of the Board of Trustees of the Katonah Presbyterian Church, secretary of the Katonah Fire Department and Board of Fire Commissioners. At present he is secretary of the Katonah Fire Department Benevolent Association. The 2 children of CORNELIUS J.[2] and Vera Munsell Pronay are ELIZABETH E.,[3] b. 1923, and CORNELIUS J., JR.,[3] b. 1926.

ELIZABETH E. PRONAY[3] married Harold Muckler of Pleasantville in 1948. They have two daughters, JANET[4] and JUDY MUCKLER.[4]

CORNELIUS J. PRONAY, JR.,[3] is a teacher and unmarried.

AGNES F. PRONAY[2] became a florist and bookkeeper. In 1932 she married C. Everett Becker of Katonah and they are owners of the Florist Shop on The Parkway. Mr. and Mrs. Becker have sons: WARREN H.,[3] b. 1932; and LOWELL E.,[3] b. 1938.

WARREN H. BECKER[3] married Martha Leasure of New Haven, Conn. They have: DIANA,[4] b. 1957; and GEORGE,[4] b. 1960.

LOWELL E. BECKER,[3] unmar., was in the U.S. Air Force and now is in merchandising in Washington, D.C.

Compiled by Janet Doe and F. R. Duncombe.

The Ray Family

ROBERT RAY[1] came to America from Ireland. He married in 1850 Susan Anna Sloat, dau. of Budd Flower and Susannah (Wright) Sloat, a direct descendant of Jan Jansen Slot, who came from Holland about 1650. Their children were: ROBERT,[2] b. 1851; WILLIAM,[2] b. 1854; FRANCES,[2] b. 1857; and GEORGE S.,[2] b. 1860, in New York City.

GEORGE S. RAY[2] (1860-1931) married Florence Warren (1866-1960), dau. of Benson and Sarah Ganung Warren of Somers, N.Y. They came to Old Katonah from Purdy's Station in 1888 and lived on South Rd. He was employed by Hoyt Brothers. They lived between the churches and the old village on the west side of the Cross River. Their only son was ROBERT BENSON.[3] They boarded with L. H. Miller after the village moved and in August, 1898, the Rays prepared plans and built a home at 32 The Terrace. Mr. Ray was a member of the Fire Department and they were members of the Methodist Episcopal Church.

R. BENSON RAY[3] graduated from the Katonah school. He married in 1920, Helen Chapman Gorham, "Mayflower" descendant, dau. of Frederick W. and Eliza Blakeslee Gorham of Katonah (see Gorham genealogy). Mr. Ray served on the Board of Education 1942-1954 and was president for two years; was organist in the Presbyterian Church for many years; and served as treasurer and member of the Executive Committee of the Village Improvement Society. He retired in 1951 as vice-president of the Bowery Savings Bank. Mr. and Mrs. Ray live at 25 Hillside Ave., Katonah. Mrs. Ray is past regent of Enoch Crosby Chapter, D.A.R., and has been very active in the Presbyterian Church. They had sons: ROBERT WARREN,[4] b. Mar. 13, 1923; and FREDERICK GORHAM,[4] b. Apr. 1, 1925.

ROBERT WARREN RAY[4] graduated from Katonah High School in 1942. He enlisted in the U.S. Army in 1944 and served in the Pacific campaign. He graduated from the Agricultural and Technical Institute, Delhi, N.Y., in 1947. In 1949 he married Lois Alta Wilson, dau. of Hobart and Lillian Wilson. Children are: FREDERICK WILSON,[5] b. July 31, 1951; and HELEN MARIE,[5] b. Dec. 2, 1958. They make their home at Delhi.

FREDERICK GORHAM RAY[4] graduated from Katonah High School in 1943. He enlisted in the U.S. Navy, May 28, 1943. He attended Union and Harvard Colleges under the SV-12 service; graduated from the Wharton

School of Finance at the University of Pennsylvania. He was discharged from the Navy in 1947 as lieutenant, J.G., in the Supply Corps. In 1958 he attended the Graduate School of Banking at Rutgers University. He joined the Northern Westchester National Bank and is a vice-president attached to the Chappaqua bank. He married in 1950 Anne Louise McLaren, dau. of Arthur and Louise Ligon McLaren. They live at 6 Devoe Place, Chappaqua, with their 2 children: PETER GORHAM,[5] b. May 31, 1953; and KAREN LOUISE,[5] b. Apr. 4, 1956.
Compiled by K. B. Kelly.

The Robertson Family

The Robertsons, of Scottish descent, came to the Massachusetts Bay Colony in the early years. In Fairfield County, Conn., there are recorded deaths of: Samuel, Aug. 9, 1674; Samuel, Jr., Apr. 2, 1698; and John. July 14, 1737, and Apr. 13, 1742, WILLIAM[1] bought land in Greenwich which he sold Feb. 16, 1743, to Jabez Sherwood.

WILLIAM ROBERTSON[1] came to Bedford in 1744, purchasing a house and 100-acre farm from Daniel Merritt. The house was on one side of Cantitoe Rd. and the farm on the other, running through to Hook Rd. His eldest son was born in Connecticut, 2 more sons and 5 daughters in Bedford. In 1763 he was on the Bedford freeholders' list. He died in 1786 and is buried in Wescott Cemetery.

JABEZ ROBERTSON[2] (1744-1832), son of WILLIAM,[1] had one daughter by his 1st wife, Polly, and she married Enos Canfield. JABEZ[2] married 2nd in 1784, Rachel Lounsbury. Their children were: RACHEL,[3] mar. William Lyon; CATHERINE,[3] mar. Peter K. Buxton; BETSY,[3] mar. Terah Miller; JABEZ;[3] HENRY;[3] and LAWRENCE.[3] HARRY[3] and LARRY[3] were twins, one born in November and one in December, 1791! JABEZ[2] lived on the homestead where, the night of July 2, 1781, part of the French Army commanded by Rochambeau is said to have camped.

JABEZ ROBERTSON, JR.[3] (1787-1872) married Betsey Smith in 1815. He taught school several winters and worked his father's farm in summer. JABEZ[3] and Betsey lived in her home at Bedford Center, now owned by H. Cushman, and Jabez started a store near the Baptist Church. He was justice of the peace for over 50 years. He was town clerk 1831-1857 and School Commissioner 1824-1843. A leading member of the Baptist Church, he was a gentle, affectionate family man, a dignified and accurate business man. JABEZ[3] and Betsey had 8 children, one of which was WILLIAM N.[4]

LAWRENCE ROBERTSON[3] (1791-1848) married Sally Dykeman. They had 2 daughters and 2 sons. One, HEZEKIAH D.[4] (1826-1870), a merchant, was at different times superintendent of schools and Supervisor of the Towns of Bedford and Pound Ridge. He was a Whig, then American Party, and afterwards Republican. He was a member of the State Senate 1859-1861.

HENRY ROBERTSON[3] (1791-1881) married in 1821 Huldah H. Fanton (1801-1891), dau. of Hull and Margery Collyer Fanton (see Collyer genealogy). HENRY[3] and Huldah lived on the Robertson homestead and had one son, WILLIAM,[4] and 4 daughters: ELIZABETH;[4] SARAH;[4] MARIETTA;[4] and EMMA.[4] HENRY[3] had a good local education, taught school for several years, kept a store in Bedford and in Bedford Center with his brother, JABEZ.[3] For more than 30 years before the railroad came, he ran a market wagon. Between 1830 and 1850 he was supervisor of the Town of Bedford. In 1845 he let Col. Enoch Avery use his north meadow on Cantitoe for "general training." He was connected with the Bedford Baptist Church for over 50 years. He and his wife celebrated their golden wedding in 1872. Children of HENRY[3] and Huldah (Fanton) Robertson were: WILLIAM HENRY[4] (1823-1898); ELIZABETH ANNE[4] (Mar. 4, 1826-July 19,1905); SARAH LOUISE[4] (Oct. 30, 1827-June 13, 1849); MARIETTA LOUNSBURY[4] (Jan. 9, 1840-Jan. 24, 1926); and EMMA HASELTINE[4] (Nov. 30, 1841-Nov. 16, 1933).

ELIZABETH ANNE ROBERTSON[4] married Arnell F. Dickinson Oct. 18, 1852 (see Dickinson genealogy).

SARAH LOUISE ROBERTSON[4] married James Tyler Sherwood in 1846. Their one child died December, 1848. Sarah Louise was brought home from the west in a rocking chair in a freight car because she wanted to die at Cantitoe.

MARIETTA LOUNSBURY ROBERTSON[4] married John C. Holmes as his 2nd wife and had a son JOHN ROBERTSON HOLMES[5] (1869-1943).

EMMA HASELTINE ROBERTSON[4] married Joseph Barrett at Bedford Center Baptist Church Feb. 13, 1869 (see Barrett genealogy).

WILLIAM HENRY ROBERTSON,[4] b. on the Cantitoe farm, attended Union Academy in Bedford Center, now the home of Dean Virginia Gildersleeve of Barnard College. He taught school in Bedford and Lewisboro, then studied law in the office of Judge Robert S. Hart in Bedford and was admitted to the bar in 1847. In 1865 he married Mary E. Ballard, dau. of the Hon. Horatio Ballard of Cortlandt County, and in 1869 he built a home in Old Katonah. In New Katonah he built a house at Bedford Rd. and The Parkway where he resided until his death. Offices held by WILLIAM H. ROBERTSON[4] were: 1848, assemblyman, reelected; 1853, state senator; 1845, superintendent of schools, supervisor of Town of Bedford for 4 terms; 1855, county judge, twice re-elected (12 years); 6 years inspector of the 7th Brigade of New York; 1860 and 1864, member of the Electoral College, voting for Lincoln; 1866, representative to the 40th Congress; 1872, 2nd term as state senator for 10 years, last 8 years as president *pro tem* of that body; 1880, a delegate from N.Y. State at the National Convention in Chicago; 1881, collector of the port of New York, appointed by President Garfield; 1865-1876 and 1880-1884, for 15 years a member of Republican State Committee. Judge Robertson was a political success. He had a strength of personality, sincere courtesy, wonderful legal and business ability, unusual common sense and thorough self-control.

The Robertson name has gone. Issue of the family now living in our locality are: Edward P. and Robertson T. Barrett; James Fayette Lawrence, Jr.; Randall G. Lawrence; Mrs. Henry D. Miller and Ella Miller; Ione Barrett; Douglas L. Barrett; John C. Holmes; Mrs. Arthur Cornell; Philip G. Barrett; Mrs. Chester Dexheimer; Mrs. Harold O'Brien; Mrs. William Kelly; Mrs. Leonard H. Hall.

Compiled by K. B. Kelly.

The Searles Family

LEONARD ACKERLY SEARLES,[1] b. 1816, lived on Croton Lake Rd. By his 1st wife he had: HORACE;[2] and MARY JANE.[2] His 2nd wife was the widow of Palmer Gureau. LEONARD[1] died in 1888, was buried in old Katonah Cemetery and removed to Oakwood Cemetery in Mt. Kisco.

HORACE SEARLES[2] married 1st Susan Ann Farrington. Their children were: EDWARD;[3] ELOISE;[3] and AGNES.[3] He married 2nd Eliza Margaret Bloomfield (July 11, 1850-Jan. 1925). They were parents of: ANNA EDWINA;[3] and WALLACE.[3] Mr. Searles was a general contractor and teamster and dug many of the cellars for the homes in New Katonah. He owned a large home on the Dowburg Rd. in Old Katonah, which the second Mrs. Searles ran as a boarding house. She was generous and kind and saw something good in everyone. In March, 1898, HORACE[2] purchased a new lot toward upper Valley Rd. and to it moved their house. It was completed by Aug. 26, 1898, and could hold 40 boarders. It closed as a boarding-house soon after Mrs. Searles' death in January and Mr. Searles' death in September, 1925, but was owned by the family thereafter. It was bought by St. Mary's Church around 1957 and torn down to make room for their new elementary school.

EDWARD SEARLES[3] married and moved to Peekskill where he owned a music store. His children were: HARRY;[4] KENNETH;[4] LUCY;[4] MARGERY;[4] GRACE;[4] and MORLEY.[4] All still reside in Peekskill.

ELOISE SEARLES,[3] called "Lou," taught school in New Rochelle and married John Stephenson of that place, living there until they moved to Great Barrington, Mass. A daughter, ELOISE STEPHENSON,[4] was born June 18, 1900. Mr. Stephenson embarked in the carriage business in Massachusetts in September, 1900. His grandfather had invented the horse-car in New Rochelle for New York City. Mr. and Mrs. Stephenson returned to Katonah and rented a house at 10 Bedford Rd. and subsequently bought at 77 Valley Rd. He was in the paint business and very active locally. ELOISE SEARLES STEPHENSON[3] died August, 1920, at their camp at Lake Waccabuc. Mr. Stephenson and his 2nd wife, Etta Stephenson, built on Sunrise Ave. where he died July, 1954.

ELOISE STEPHENSON,[4] graduated from Katonah High School and from New Rochelle School of Nursing, accepted a position in the Women's Hospital in Flint, Mich. There she met John D. Morgan, whom she married Feb. 25, 1927. He was connected with Buick Motor Co. and they made their home in Flint. The Morgans were parents of: HELEN,[5] who mar. Fred Thompson, and has 2 children; and JAMES MORGAN.[5] Mr. Morgan and son JAMES[5] both died in 1953. Mrs. Morgan visits Katonah to see her relatives and many friends.

AGNES SEARLES[3] married 1st Charles Miller and 2nd Dr. Collard, a physician at Sing Sing Prison and in private practice at his home address, 31 Spring St., Ossining; no children. She died at the home of her sister, MRS. F. H. WILLIAMS,[3] 26 Bedford Rd., Katonah, July, 1948.

ANNA EDWINA SEARLES[3] attended Katonah schools. She has always been very active in the Methodist Church. She married, Feb. 21, 1901, Dr. Frederick Harold Williams, who came to Katonah in October, 1899, from Millerton, N. Y. Their children were: HAROLD GORDON[4] and MARGARET

ELEANOR WILLIAMS.[4] Graduated from Philadelphia Dental College in 1898, Dr. Williams was a skilled dentist, practicing until 1953. He started practice in the Van Tassel building. Then in January, 1903, Dr. and Mrs. Williams moved to their own home at 26 Bedford Rd., with room for his dental office. Her father, HORACE SEARLES,[2] dug the cellar and William Daniel was the contractor. Dr. and Mrs. Williams were very active in the town's social life and interested in its growing. He was a veteran of World War I, a captain in the 151st Machine Gun Battalion, 42nd Division. He served as dentist for Bedford's Reformatory; was a member of Mt. Kisco F. and A.M. Lodge 708; a member of the Katonah Fire Department for more than 50 years; and a member of the American Legion. He died Jan. 28, 1960, at 81 yrs.

MARGARET ELEANOR WILLIAMS[4] graduated from Maryland College, Washington, D.C., in 1937. During the war she worked for 4½ years in Lutherville, Md., and at present lives at home and works at the *Reader's Digest*.

HAROLD GORDON WILLIAMS[4] attended school in Katonah and Rutgers Preparatory School. He married in 1939 Helen Gildea, daughter of John Gildea of Croton Lake Rd. She died soon after and he married 2nd Margaret Hoy of Washington, D.C. They are parents of: BETTY LOU,[5] a John Jay graduate, 1959, attending Rochester School of Nursing; and MARSHA LOIS,[5] b. 1950. GORDON[4] is the proprietor of the Katonah Motor Sales. He and his family make their home at 152 Bedford Rd.

WALLACE SEARLES,[3] b. in Old Katonah in 1894, was a local baseball player and active in town affairs. He married Ruth Shoens, who was teaching school in Katonah. A graduate of Philadelphia Dental College, he took over Dr. Williams' practice for 6 months during World War I and then joined the service and was in Europe a year. They made their home in Ossining and had one daughter, ELIZABETH.[4] When he died Mrs. Searles returned to her teaching. ELIZABETH (BETTY)[4] married Samuel Dunlap and they live in Johnstown, Pa., with their 5 children: RANDALL;[5] RICHARD;[5] ALEXANDRA RUTH;[5] ELIZABETH;[5] and RUSSELL DUNLAP.[5]

MARY JANE SEARLES,[2] b. in Yorktown, Oct. 13, 1836, married Abraham Merritt Oct. 13, 1859, in the Methodist Episcopal Church. They moved to the town of Bedford in 1870. Their children were: LYDA;[3] EDNA;[3] and HERBERT LEONARD MERRITT.[3] Mr. Merritt was superintendent for Henry Pellew at which time they lived in the "Stone House" on Cantitoe. Mrs. Merritt died at her home at 12 The Terrace in January, 1903. Mr. Merritt died at the home of his son-in-law on Edgemont Road.

LYDA MERRITT[3] (1861-1939) married Fletcher Hedding Lent (1852-1929), b. in Ashley Falls, Mass., son of Rev. Isaac H. Lent. In Old Katonah they lived on the east side of the railroad in a large house between Albert Hoyt's and the Chadeayne Bldg. When the village was moving they bought the Seth Shove house on Cherry St. In June, 1898, they advertised for sale the house consisting of 22 rooms and 13 acres of land. They moved their own house from the old village to 15 Edgemont Rd. Mr. Lent was in the livery business and in the new village built a large barn in back of his home. In August, 1900, it was news when he harbored an auto in his stable for two days. In 1901 he secured the contract for carrying mail to Cross River, Boutonville, Lake Waccabuc and South Salem for four years. The Lents had one of the first phonographs in town and let it out for parties. Their 2 sons were: ROBERT HOYT[4] and FLETCHER HOBART LENT.[4]

ROBERT H. LENT,[4] b. in Old Katonah, was very active in local baseball and a member of Katonah Fire Department. He married Orpha White who retired February, 1958, after 32 yrs. as clerk at Bedford Hills Post Office. They make their home at 145 Valley Rd. and are parents of SHELDON FLETCHER,[5] b. Oct. 23, 1918, and graduated from Katonah High School in 1937. SHELDON FLETCHER LENT[5] married Apr. 12, 1941, Nina Bernardo, daughter of Pompeius and Maria (Primavera) Bernardo of Croton Lake Rd. He entered the Army in September, 1942, while he was working for the Katonah Lumber, Coal and Feed Company. The Sheldon Lents are the parents of: JUDITH;[6] STEPHEN;[6] and NINA MARIE.[6] They have built a new home on Valley Rd. next to Mr. Lent's parents. Mrs. Lent is employed in the office of the assessors at Bedford Town House. SHELDON[5] is employed by Westfield State Farms in the Supply Dept.

F. HOBART LENT,[4] b. on Cherry St., attended Katonah schools. He married in 1922 Mary Edna TenEyck, who graduated from Syracuse University with a music and art major. Mrs. Lent is a piano instructor, teaching our local children. They make their home at 19 The Terrace. Mr. Lent was elected Bedford town tax receiver in 1933 and has been reelected ever since. Their only child, SUZANNE TENEYCK,[5] graduated from Katonah High School in June, 1945, and from Syracuse in 1949. She married Gilbert R. Anderson, son of Irvin Anderson of Kentucky, at the Lent winter home in St. Petersburg, Fla. They live in Fort Worth, Tex., with their two children: SUSAN RAE,[6] b. Sept. 11, 1952, and MARK STUART ANDERSON,[6] b. Jan. 3, 1954. Mr. Anderson is a partner in a sheet-metal and air-conditioning company.

EDNA MERRITT[3] was the librarian in Old Katonah. She married William Lent, son of James Lent, a stone mason in Katonah, and no connection of the Lent family above. William was a plumber by trade and they lived on Huntville Rd. They had no children.

HERBERT L. MERRITT,[3] b. in Katonah, married Mary Eleanor Scofield, dau. of James and Mary (Carr) Scofield of Old Katonah. He worked for Henry Kellogg and then went into partnership in the plumbing and heating business on Katonah Ave. with George Teed. He was receiver of taxes for the Town of Bedford and postmaster from Apr. 23, 1923, to 1929. Mr. and Mrs. Merritt built a home at 9 The Terrace in 1908 where Mr. Merritt died in July, 1940, and Mrs. Merritt in August, 1956. Their only child, DORIS,[4] graduated from Katonah High School. She worked in the Katonah Post Office, New York City Water Department, and has been employed in the office of Dr. Edward J. Gallagher, 59 Valley Rd., for several years.

Compiled by K. B. Kelly.

The Shove Family of Cherry Street

DR. SETH SHOVE[3] (1805-1878), b. in Warren, Conn., was the son of LEVI[2] and Abigail Weed Shove, who came to Warren from Danbury,

Conn., where the family had lived since emigrating from England among the first settlers in the New World. His grandfather, the Rev. Seth Shove[1] (1667-1735), was the first minister in Danbury and is buried in the old churchyard there. Dr. Shove[3] received a common school and academic education in Warren and Goshen. Of a studious disposition, he showed an interest in medicine from an early age. His father was a farmer and Seth, next to the youngest of 11 children, could count on little financial help, so he taught school in Warren, in Kent and in Fishkill, studying under local doctors until he had saved enough money to enter the Medical Department of Yale College, from which he was graduated in 1829.

After receiving his degree he made a tour on horseback looking for a favorable place to settle and start his practice. He visited New York and neighboring towns in Long Island and finally rode north through Westchester County. Stopping at the house of Dr. Joshua Bowron in Newcastle, he learned of an opening in the neighborhood and rode on to Squire Wood's in Cherry St., who said to the young man: "This is the place for you; it is the hub of a thriving community." Dr. Shove settled in Cherry St. in August, 1829, and practiced there throughout his long life, driving miles in every kind of weather, charging 50 cents a visit and 2 dollars for delivering a baby.

Nov. 17, 1829, he married Irene Pulford of Warren. In 1837 they built the house in which they spent the rest of their lives (now owned by L. E. Hayes). Dr. Shove was a member of the American Medical Association, president of the Medical Society of the County of Westchester for two terms, and one of the organizers and first president of the Croton Medical and Surgical Union which usually held its meetings in Katonah. In 1837 he was surgeon in the local militia regiment under Col. A. H. Lockwood. He showed civic interest in the Franklin Society of which he was an original member.

Dr. and Mrs. Shove had 5 children, only 2 of whom grew to maturity.

Sarah Shove[4] became a teacher and married Benjamin Franklin Barrett. They had son, Seth Shove Barrett[5] (see Barrett genealogy).

Irene Shove[4] studied medicine and was skilled in delivering babies. She and her husband, Dr. J. Francis Chapman, had sons, Charles Francis[5] and Herbert Shove Chapman.[5]

Dr. Charles Francis Chapman[5] (1868-1933) graduated from the College of Physicians and Surgeons in 1890. He practiced a short time with his father and then opened an office in Mt. Kisco. He married Ella J. Whitlock (see Whitlock genealogy). They had no children.

Herbert Shove Chapman[5] (1871-Dec. 28, 1946) married May Jackson of Mt. Kisco in 1898. They made their home in Katonah at 26 The Terrace where Mrs. Chapman still lives. Mr. Chapman commuted for over 47 years to the North British Mercantile Insurance Co. in New York City. He was a well loved member of the community; his hobbies were painting and horticulture.

Dr. and Mrs. Shove had taken into their home her nephew, Charles E. Wickware, whom Dr. Shove trained as a dentist. Dr. Wickware married Nancy Ambler of South Salem. They had three children: Ella (Mrs. George Ketchum of New York); Addie (Mrs. Horace Todd—see Todd genealogy); and Charles, who settled in Waterbury, Conn.

Compiled by Christina Rainsford and K. B. Kelly.

The Silkman Family

JOHN SILKMAN,[1] b. 1720 in the Palatinate, left Rotterdam on the ship "Harle," which reached Philadelphia Sept. 1, 1736. Protestants suffering persecution in the Palatinate had been invited to settle in Penn's "Woodlands." Silkman did not remain there long but came to Greenwich, Conn., in 1740, where in 1745 he married Mercy Rundle, dau. of Abraham and Rebecca (Mead) Rundle. During the colonial wars, 1739-1748, he served on a privateer, and was badly burned in an explosion. In 1748 he bought his first piece of land in Bedford near Cross River and from time to time added more until his farm consisted of 200 acres. He built his home in 1751, which still stands on Rte. 35 and Holly Branch Rd. Here were born his 6 daughters and 3 sons: DANIEL;[2] JACOB;[2] and JOHN, JR.[2] Dec. 29, 1761, he is recorded as selling one sound and well Negro boy called Caesar, aged 12 yrs., for 60 pounds to Lewis McDonald. In 1763 he was included in the freeholders' list for Bedford of those worth 60 pounds or more. In the Revolution, though 6 yrs. over the draft age, he enlisted as a private in the 2nd Regt., Westchester County Militia. He was a member of Col. Budd's regiment Sept. 10, 1776, and Col. Thomas' regiment Feb. 7, 1783. He sold supplies to the State of New York and rented to the State a four-ox team with which he transported them. His son, JOHN, JR.,[2] was in the same regiment. JOHN[1] is listed in the U.S. census, 1790, as the head of a family; in the 1800 census, as a member of his son DANIEL's[2] family. July 5, 1794, he bought of Nathaniel Reynolds a plot of land in the Cross River burying ground in which he laid to rest his wife, Mercy. He died in 1805.

DANIEL SILKMAN[2] married in 1782 Joanna Brundage (1764-1820), dau. of Joseph and Joanna (Lyon) Brundage, a descendant of John Winthrop, founder of the Massachusetts Bay Colony. Before their marriage they built on the farm a home now owned by George Aarons. DANIEL[2] and Joanna had 6 sons and one daughter: JACOB;[3] JOHN;[3] DANIEL;[3] JOSEPH;[3] DAVID;[3] AARON;[3] and JOANNA.[3] DANIEL[2] inherited the family farm as his brother, JACOB,[2] never married and JOHN, JR.,[2] had only a daughter. DANIEL[2] was a farmer all his life and lived only in the two houses. He died suddenly Apr. 21, 1804, at 47 yrs.

JACOB SILKMAN[3] (1784-1865) went into the carpenter and lumber business. He married Elizabeth Sutherland of Salem and they were parents of: MYRON BRUNDAGE;[4] DAVID M.;[4] AARON BURR;[4] SARAH ANN;[4] DANIEL;[4] ALMIRA;[4] and JOSEPH.[4] JACOB[3] was school commissioner of District No. 13 in 1820. He moved to Scranton in 1839 where he died in August, 1850.

JOHN SILKMAN[3] married Mary Polly Hitchcock of Pound Ridge and ran the family farm. In 1821 he succeeded his brother as school commissioner. Children of JOHN[3] and Mary were: WILLIAM;[4] CHARLES HENRY;[4] DAVID;[4] THOMAS H.;[4] JOHN HITCHCOCK;[4] ELIZA H.;[4] ELETHEA H.;[4] and CAROLINE E.[4]

DANIEL SILKMAN[3] (1787-1856) married Sarah Bailey and lived in Somers. He was a drover; bought and sold cattle. Their only child, JAMES BAILEY,[4] a graduate of Yale and a lawyer, married Harriet Van Cortlandt Crosby.

They were parents of: Julia;[5] Emilie;[5] Elizabeth;[5] and Theodore H.,[5] who was surrogate of Westchester County 1900-1906 and the grandfather of Mrs. Gordon McCulloh[7] of Rye.

Joseph Silkman[3] married Sarah Mead of Cross River. They had no children.

David Silkman,[3] d.y. Joanna[3] married Allen Hobby.

Aaron Silkman[3] ran part of the family farm and married Susanna Dickson. They were parents of: Wright;[4] Aaron D.;[4] and Joanna Brundage,[4] mar. Griffen Miller. Aaron[3] and wife Susanna are both buried in Cross River cemetery.

Myron Brundage Silkman,[4] son of Jacob,[3] a carpenter, engaged later in the lumber and coal business. Born 1807 on the farm, he built a home there, but in 1850, built a new home on Main St. in Old Katonah, where he lived until his death in 1884. He was a justice of the peace from 1853 until his death and one of the justices of sessions during a period of 8 years. He was very active in local affairs and in the Methodist Church. He married Sarah Fanton of Weston, Conn., sister of Mrs. Henry Robertson. They had 2 daughters: Margery V.;[5] and Marie Antoinette.[5] Margery[5] married James E. Horton and they had: Frederick;[6] Sarah;[6] Anna Silkman;[6] and Mary Augusta Horton.[6] The entire family was active in the Methodist Church, school affairs and the village library. Margery L. Van Norden[7] of New York City is the daughter of M. Augusta Horton[6] and Howard Van Norden. The Hortons lived in the Main St. house in Old Katonah and built at 9 Bedford Rd. in New Katonah. Marie Antoinette[5] (1836-1868) married Cornelius Putney. Her only grandchild is Mrs. Edward P. Barrett[7] of Katonah.

David M. Silkman[4] married Laura Hoyt and they lived in Whitlockville. On his property stood the little Red School House. Their 3 children were: John;[5] James H.;[5] and Mead S.,[5] d.y. The family plot is in Oakwood Cemetery.

Aaron Burr Silkman,[4] b. on the family farm, moved to Scranton and Providence, Pa., with his parents and younger children. He married twice and had 4 daughters and one son, Edward J.[5] This branch of the family lives in Baltimore and Charleston.

William Silkman[4] (1807-1874), son of John,[3] was the 1st postmaster of "Whitlocks," established July 14, 1832. He continued from Nov. 10, 1832, when it became "Whitlockville," to Mar. 15, 1840. William[4] was a hatter until he closed shop and went to Scranton, where he completed his cousin Aaron's house about 1849. This house is now a branch of the Scranton library called the Silkman House Library. William[4] and his wife, Mary Jane Bailey, had 8 children. Eltinge Silkman La Bar,[7] William's[4] great-grandson, of Hawley, Pa., possesses numerous family papers.

John Hitchcock Silkman[4] was the 2nd postmaster of Whitlockville. He was a storekeeper in Somers and in Milwaukee, Wis. He returned east twice a year for his merchandise. He married Rachel Jane Hobby of Bedford and had 4 children.

Wright Silkman,[4] son of Aaron,[3] was a farmer on the family farm. He married the Methodist minister's daughter, Catharine Keeler. Their daughter, Joanna Emily,[5] married DeWitt Clinton Reynolds of Cross River and had 14 children. Aaron Keeler Silkman,[5] their son, married

Cornelia Todd, dau. of Martin and Sally (Lawrence) Todd. They were parents of: GEORGE;[6] EVELYN;[6] WRIGHT;[6] AARON;[6] MARTIN TODD;[6] and ETHELYN.[6]

GEORGE SILKMAN[6] married Bethenia Grumman of Pound Ridge. They were parents of JOHN GRUMMAN;[7] JULIA BERTHA;[7] GEORGE LESLIE;[7] and CLARENCE OAKLEY.[7] JOHN G.[7] married in 1906 Elizabeth Dawson and had 2 daughters. After her death, he married Mary Shanley. They lived on Nightingale Rd. and had 3 children: JOHN GRUMMAN, JR.,[8] who mar. Anna Cecile Dwyer and has JOHN GRUMMAN III,[9] and MARY;[9] GEORGE BURKMAN,[8] who mar. Hilda May Warfield and has GEORGE BURKMAN, JR.,[9] HOWARD JOHN,[9] and LINDA MAY;[9] and ANNA SILKMAN,[8] who mar. Robert E. Denley and has JOHN JOSEPH,[9] ROBERT EDWARD[9] and JUDITH DENLEY.[9] Mrs. John G. Silkman sold the Nightingale Rd. home in 1960 and moved to Florida. ANNA[8] and her family who lived with her mother moved to Goldens Bridge. JULIA[7] married Peter Demgar and lived in Sayerville, N.J. GEORGE L.[7] married Emma Elizabeth Davenport and lived in Patterson with children ELSIE[8] and GEORGE DAVENPORT.[8]

EVELYN SILKMAN,[6] dau. of AARON KEELER SILKMAN,[5] married John Silkman Hunt. They were parents of 6 children: MILDRED;[7] CORNELIA TODD;[7] ELIZA SILKMAN;[7] EDITH;[7] WILLIAM EDGAR;[7] and ELBERT PURDY HUNT.[7] MILDRED[7] and WILLIAM[7] make their home in Pleasantville. ELBERT[7] lives in Florida. CORNELIA[7] married Bradford Odell. They live on Grandview Ave., Katonah, and are parents of: DOROTHY IRENE;[8] BRADFORD, JR.;[8] and DONALD ELBERT ODELL.[8] DOROTHY IRENE ODELL[8] married Arthur Pinori and they live in Goldens Bridge with children: DONNA;[9] and PETER PINORI.[9] BRADFORD ODELL, JR.,[8] of Valley Rd. married Eleanor J. Ritchie and has: JEANNE;[9] and SUSAN ELIZABETH ODELL.[9] DONALD ELBERT ODELL[8] married Anne McGill. They live in Glenns Ferry, Idaho, with 2 daughters.

ELIZA SILKMAN[7] married Clarence Green (see Green genealogy).

WRIGHT SILKMAN[6] (1871-1959), son of AARON K.,[5] married Mary Hawley. They lived in Mill Plains and had: HAWLEY WRIGHT;[7] ALFRED WINFRED;[7] and RUTH ANITA.[7] They all married and had families.

AARON SILKMAN[6] was a veterinarian in New York City. He married Pheella Rossell and their only child, HORTENSE E.,[7] lives in Brooklyn.

ETHELYN SILKMAN[6] married Charles A. Anderson of Norway and lived in Goldens Bridge. Their children were: CHARLES H.;[7] HELEN C.;[7] and MARJORIE E. ANDERSON,[7] who died in 1955 leaving her husband and a daughter, PATRICIA ANN ROTENBURG,[8] of Mt. Kisco. CHARLES[7] married Olive Seymour and had one son, JOHN CHARLES ANDERSON,[8] who attended Katonah High School and served 3 years in Germany with the Army. Jan. 30, 1960, he married Mary Ann Plevka of Lake Waccabuc in St. Luke's Church, Katonah. HELEN,[7] a Katonah High graduate, married Percy Keene. They reside in Mt. Kisco and have 2 sons: DONALD EDWARD,[8] who mar. Ethel Natt and has dau. DEBORAH LYNN,[9] b. 1956; and PERCY CARTER KEENE.[8]

MARTIN TODD SILKMAN[6] (1877-1957), a farmer, was a very large land owner on Todd Rd. in Lewisboro. He married Lulu Reynolds of Cross River. Their children were: MARTIN REYNOLDS;[7] HELEN CORNELIA;[7] and MABEL TODD.[7]

HELEN CORNELIA SILKMAN[7] graduated from Drew Seminary, Carmel,

N.Y. She married Albert W. Ritchie of Purdys. Until Mr. Ritchie's death in 1957, they lived on Todd Rd. with sons: DOUGLAS ALBERT;[8] and DONALD TODD RITCHIE.[8] Mrs. Ritchie and sons now reside at 29 Hillside Ave. in Katonah. DONALD[8] attends John Jay High School. DOUGLAS,[8] who graduated in 1960, was awarded: $500 from the Katonah Rotary Club; the American Legion award for leadership and scholarship; the Bausch and Lomb award for excellence in science; and a scholarship at Clarkson College which he now attends.

MABEL TODD SILKMAN[7] married George V. Austin, Jr., of Yonkers. They live at 16 Elm Rd., Katonah. Their children are: GEORGE V., III;[8] JEAN ANN;[8] and MARILYN TODD AUSTIN.[8] The older two attend John Jay School and Marilyn attends Katonah School.

MARTIN REYNOLDS SILKMAN,[7] a builder, married Gladys Prigge of Katonah. They live on Todd Rd. Their only child, RICHARD PRIGGE,[8] graduated from Katonah High School in 1950 and served 4 years in the U.S. Navy. He married Beatrice Martinez of Bedford Hills in August, 1959. They reside in their newly built home on Todd Rd. and have a son, JOSEPH RICHARD,[9] b. Sept. 28, 1960.

Compiled by K. B. Kelly.

The Smith Family of Katonah

DANIEL SMITH[1] (1720-1796) was a freeholder in the Town of Bedford owning sixty pounds or more in 1763. Upon his death he left a wife, Mary, and sons: DANIEL;[2] GABRIEL;[2] DENTON;[2] THOMAS;[2] CALEB;[2] WARD;[2] JOHN;[2] and JAMES;[2] and daughters: MARY;[2] and HANNAH GREGORY.[2] DANIEL[1] is buried in St. Matthew's Cemetery. DANIEL[1] or DANIEL[2] was in Col. Thomas' 2nd Regt., Westchester County Militia.

Either DANIEL[1] or DANIEL[2] bought many acres from 1773 to 1794 from Hezekiah Roberts, Samuel Benedict and Augustus Van Cortlandt. Much of this land lay on or near old Rte. 22 and lay along the Beaver Dam and Cross Rivers. In the year 1850 both Moses and Aaron Smith (probably descendants of Daniel) lived in houses on this acreage.

Moses, who had married Rebecca Fowler, dau. of Ammon, lived on the northeast corner of Rtes. 35 and 22 (now owned by N.Y.C. Water Supply). This was subsequently owned from 1860 by his son, Daniel, who sold it around 1891 to Joseph Barrett.

Aaron lived on Rte. 22 near Jay St. in the house now owned by William Paddock. Aaron, b. 1772, died in 1856. His wife, Polly, died in 1848. They are buried in St. Matthew's. On Aaron's death his son, Joseph Smith, took title to the house. Daniel Joseph Smith, son of Joseph and Mary Smith, subsequently sold this property to John Robertson Holmes.

Daniel J. Smith, b. in Katonah Nov. 26, 1849, was educated locally and at Chappaqua Mountain Institute. He was a farmer, a charter member of the Katonah Fire Department, and its financial secretary for 30 years, also assessor of the Town of Bedford for several terms. Dec. 13, 1876, he married Ella J. Purdy (Nov. 2, 1849-Jan. 18, 1916), daughter of Elizabeth Collyer and Ebenezer Purdy of Katonah. When New Katonah grew, he developed part of his land, now Highland Ave., and built a new home at the end. Daniel Joseph died at the home of his daughter on Edgemont Rd. after a long illness Mar. 26, 1931. Their only child, Elizabeth, b. Nov. 19, 1890, married Elbert Washburn in Danbury, Apr. 4, 1928. They sold their home and left Katonah. Mr. Washburn has died and Elizabeth lives in New Jersey. They had no children. Daniel J. left, besides his daughter, a sister, Sarah E. Sutton of Chappaqua, and a brother, Charles, of Chicago. Daniel J. is buried in Kensico Cemetery.

Another Katonah Smith kin is Miss Emily S. Clark of Bedford Rd. Her father, William Henry Clark (1873-1948), was the son of Joseph Smith Clark and Mary Whelpley, the grandson of Elizabeth Ann Smith (1820-1898) and Truman P. Clark. Elizabeth was the daughter of Gabriel Smith, Jr., and Mary Collyer and granddaughter of Gabriel Smith (1729-1819) and Jemima (1734-1822).

Compiled by K. B. Kelly.

The Smiths of Whitlockville

NOAH SMITH, JR.[2] (1794-1861), son of NOAH,[1] married Grace Miller (1805-1882), believed the granddaughter of Benjamin Miller. They lived on present Whitlockville Rd. halfway up the hill on the east side and were one of the very first families in the new settlement. They had 12 children: HARVEY WOOD[3] (1824-1885); LUCY AMELIA[3] (1825-1842); HARRIET[3] (1827-1844); SARAH AMELIA[3] (1829-1830); MARY C.[3] (1830-1910); WINFIELD[3] (1832-1833); CHARLES S.[3] (1834-1855); CHARLOTTE M.[3] (1836-1907); EMILY,[3] b. 1838; HENRY C.,[3] b. 1840; HESTER[3] (1841-1842); and NANCY JANE,[3] b. 1844.

NOAH[2] was a partner in the firm of Whitlock and Smith. After this discontinued, he built and operated a store across from his home on Whitlockville Rd., where his son, HARVEY,[3] joined him in the firm of N. Smith and Son. Later NOAH[2] built a new store across from Whitlock's store and turned the old one into a house, in which HARVEY[3] lived after his marriage. NOAH[2] was on the committee which bought land for a Methodist Episcopal church from John B. and Rachel Whitlock in 1837. NOAH[2] and his wife, Grace, were buried in the Old Katonah Cemetery and thence removed to Oakwood in Mt. Kisco.

HARVEY WOOD SMITH[3] married Oct. 4, 1848, Amelia Eliza Sparks (1827-1855), dau. of the Rev. Thomas and Elizabeth Maria (Granger) Sparks of Whitlockville. They had 3 children: JANE LOUISA,[4] who married Seth Canfield and had daughters, SARAH,[5] ANNIS,[5] and BETH CANFIELD,[5] and sons, LAWRENCE,[5] THOMAS,[5] and LeROY CANFIELD;[5] THOMAS SPARKS[4] (1851-1942); and HARRIET[4] (1852-1855). Mrs. Amelia Smith died Aug. 28, 1855. HARVEY[3] married 2nd June 8, 1858, Laura Marsh who was teaching school in Katonah. The dau. of the Rev. C. and Eunice Emelie (Camp) Marsh, she was born at Warren, Conn., Dec. 25, 1832. Their 9 children were: EUNICE EMILY[4] (1859-1947), unmar., a bookkeeper and nurse; CHARLES SIDNEY;[4] HELEN AMELIA[4] (1863-1939), called "Ella," who mar.

William P. Hynard of Baldwin Place and had no children who lived; MARY FRANCES;[4] SARAH GRACE[4] (1868-1902), who mar. twice but had no children; EDWARD MARSH[4] (1866-1875), who drowned on Christmas in the Cross River; HARVEY LEIGH;[4] LUCY GERTRUDE;[4] CAROLINE EDNA[4] (1875-1957), called "Caddy" and later, "Edna," unmar., buried at Attleboro, Mass. HARVEY WOOD SMITH[3] carried on an extensive dry goods and groceries business with his father in Whitlockville. After the railroad came, he opened a store on Main St. in Old Katonah. In 1879 he established a cut-shirt business. He brought the shirts from New York City and had the ladies of Katonah sew them, after which the completed shirts were returned. Thus he helped many ladies to own their own sewing machines. He retired from business thereafter. His health failing, he died Feb. 12, 1885, leaving his widow and 9 children.

CHARLOTTE M. SMITH,[3] dau. of NOAH[2] and Grace, unmar., spent her life in Whitlockville and Katonah. EMILY SMITH[3] married Charles Wood Avery (see Avery genealogy). HENRY C. SMITH[3] made his home in Stonington, Conn.

EUNICE EMILY SMITH[4] and CHARLES SIDNEY[4] went to Attleboro, Mass., to work for their uncle, Charles Marsh, in the jewelry business. After HARVEY's[3] death the rest of the family moved there also, to live on LeRoy St.

THOMAS SPARKS SMITH,[4] b. in Whitlockville, September, 1851, married in 1878 Matilda Lounsbury (1857-1931), dau. of Seely and Catherine E. (Cox) Lounsbury. He was a tinsmith with Charles Avery's hardware store and later with Henry Kellogg. When the City sold the Old Katonah houses, he bought one on Palmer Ave., had it taken down and moved to Edgemont Rd. in the new village. It now belongs to Everett Becker. Mr. and Mrs. Smith lived there and later, at the time of Mr. Smith's death, over E. A. Arnold's shoe store on The Parkway. THOMAS SPARKS[4] and Matilda Lounsbury Smith had children: CHARLOTTE AMELIA;[5] CELIA;[5] and THOMAS HERBERT.[5]

CHARLOTTE AMELIA SMITH,[5] known to her many friends as "Millie," is interested in local affairs and active in the Methodist Episcopal Church.

CELIA SMITH[5] (1882-1956) married C. Arthur Heuss, a druggist in Yorktown, where they lived with their only child, CHARLOTTE HEUSS,[6] who is a guidance director in the Yorktown School District. Mrs. Heuss returned to Katonah after her husband's death in 1942 and lived with her sister, MILLIE SMITH,[5] for several years until her own death.

THOMAS HERBERT SMITH[5] (1892-1933) worked for the N.Y. Central Railroad. He lived at home, unmar.

CHARLES SIDNEY SMITH[4] (1861-1935), called "Sidney," married Annie Wheaton and had one son, BYRON WHEATON.[5] SIDNEY[4] was a jewelry valuer and then undertaker before moving to North Hollywood, Calif., where he died and was buried in Glendale, Calif. He had no grandchildren.

MARY FRANCES SMITH[4] (1864-1930), called "Frank," married William E. Coles. They lived in Attleboro, Mass., and had one son, CHESTER ERNEST COLES.[5]

HARVEY LEIGH SMITH,[4] b. Whitlockville Mar. 30, 1870, married Lue Mae McCastline of New York. He was boys' director at the Y.M.C.A. in Brooklyn, N.Y. He had a cerebral hemorrhage while speaking in New Haven at a banquet to raise money for Y.M.C.A. work and was buried from the home of his sister, LUCY,[4] in Attleboro, Mass., June 6, 1910.

HARVEY LEIGH[4] and Lue Mae Smith had daughter, GRACE McCASTLINE,[5] who mar. William Waite and has 2 children.

LUCY GERTRUDE SMITH,[4] called "Tillie," b. Apr. 21, 1872, married Joseph M. Seagrave June 27, 1895. She died in Massachusetts Dec. 30, 1955. The Seagraves had one daughter, ROSAMOND HELEN SEAGRAVE,[5] who married Roland H. Patch, lives in Storrs, Conn., and has no children.

Compiled by K. B. Kelly.

The Todd Family

CHRISTOPHER TODD,[1] b. 1616 in West Riding, Yorkshire, England, married Grace Middlebrooks and they came on the "Hector" to Boston, June 26, 1637. They were parents of 6 children. CHRISTOPHER,[1] a farmer, miller and baker, died in New Haven, Conn., Apr. 23, 1686.

SAMUEL TODD,[2] a son b. 1645, married Mary Bradley, Nov. 26, 1668. He too was a miller and baker. Their son, JONAH TODD[3] (1684-1730), b. in New Haven, married Hannah Clark. Their only child, ABRAHAM TODD[4] (1710-1772), graduated from Yale in 1727 and married Hannah Dickerman Nov. 30, 1727. Ordained in 1733, he was a pastor at Greenwich, Conn. ABRAHAM[4] and Hannah had children: MEHITABEL;[5] LOIS;[5] JONAH;[5] ABRAHAM;[5] HANNAH;[5] OLIVER;[5] MARY;[5] and MABEL,[5] mar. Allen Mead of Greenwich, Conn. ABRAHAM[5] and OLIVER[5] and their wives moved to South Salem, N.Y., when the British took Greenwich.

OLIVER TODD[5] (1748-1814) married Lydia Close in 1768. He served in Col. Crane's regiment in the Revolution. He and Lydia are buried in the Todd homestead plot, Rte. 100. Their children were: FANNIE,[6] mar. Dr. Gilbert Reynolds; IRA,[6] who mar. Rebecca Gilbert and was a farmer in South Salem; HULDAH,[6] mar. John Brady; and UEL.[6]

UEL TODD,[6] b. May 2, 1782, in South Salem, married 1st Laura Mead, dau. of Col. Enoch Mead; 2nd, Jane (Baker) Teed; and 3rd Betsey (Baker) Purdy. In 1812 he moved into the house on Whitehall Corners, Rte. 100. He had 14 children by his 3 wives, among them HARVEY MEAD[7] and OLIVER UEL.[7]

HARVEY MEAD TODD[7] (1803-1881) lived on Rte. 100 and Plum Brook Rd. He was a director of the Farmers and Drovers Bank in Somers, where so many of Katonah's people dealt. He ran a large farm and earned a large fortune. He married Esther Warren Nelson and they had 4 children.

OLIVER UEL TODD,[7] b. Oct. 5, 1805, married Dec. 10, 1832, Hester Jane Green. They lived in the homestead at Whitehall Corners on about 250 acres situated on the turnpike. Immense droves of cattle and sheep on their way to the city markets found ample accommodations there and it became a noted hostelry. In 1849, his records report 11,000 head of cattle at 8¢ per night; 16,000 head of sheep at 1¢ per night. OLIVER UEL[7] died in 1880. His only child, MARY OPHELIA,[8] married James T. Green and died without issue. When the City took Katonah, the Parent family moved into the Todd homestead.

ABRAHAM TODD,[5] b. Dec. 21, 1738, in Greenwich, Conn., died 1797. He married Lydia Husted Aug. 24, 1757, and soon after moved with his brother to present Todd Rd. about three miles east of Goldens Bridge. A farmer, he served in the Revolution under Lt. Col. Joseph Benedict and Col. Thaddeus Crane. ABRAHAM[5] and Lydia were parents of 5 children, one of them ABRAHAM.[6]

ABRAHAM TODD,[6] b. Feb. 23, 1762, died Dec. 10, 1842. He was a farmer and married Deborah Seeley. Children were: ALICE;[7] ABRAHAM;[7] BETSEY;[7] MABEL;[7] JONAH;[7] and MARTIN.[7]

ABRAHAM TODD[7] (1788-1847) married Apr. 7, 1814, Maria Wescot. He was a farmer in Lewisboro and they had 11 children. One, ABRAHAM HARRISON TODD,[8] b. June 17, 1819, married Jan. 9, 1839, Mary A. Horton, dau. of Daniel and Susan (Rockwell) Horton of Putnam County. They had: OPHELIA JANE;[9] GEORGE E.;[9] SUSAN M.;[9] HORACE H.;[9] and HENRY,[9] d.y.

OPHELIA JANE TODD,[9] b. May 4, 1841, married Sept. 12, 1866, Alfred Franklin Avery, son of Alanson and Jane Ann (Olmsted) Avery of Cross River (see Avery genealogy).

GEORGE E. TODD [9] (1844-1909) married in 1874 Lennie U. Merritt, dau. of Norman and Hannah (Washburn) Merritt of Goldens Bridge. He was a farmer and lived on Cherry St. His large home, partly torn down and remodelled, is the present home of A. Patti. His ice pond is known as Todd's Pond. GEORGE[9] and Lennie had 7 children born in New York City and Katonah: SUSAN;[10] CAROLYN M.;[10] GEORGIANA;[10] GEORGE E.;[10] CHARLES S.;[10] MARION;[10] and ELEANOR.[10] CAROLYN M.[10] married Bruce K. Conover and they lived at her parents' home with their 2 children before moving to Buffalo. Mr. Todd had one of the show places of Katonah and entertained lavishly.

SUSAN M. TODD,[9] b. 1850, married in 1878 Samuel H. Everett. They lived in New York City and had 4 children. Their daughter, SUSAN EVERETT,[10] married J. Willis Clark. Her son, JOHN WILLIS CLARK, JR.,[11] lives in Mt. Kisco.

HORACE H. TODD,[9] b. Nov. 19, 1848, married in September, 1881, Adelaide W. Wickware, dau. of Dr. Charles E. and Nancy (Ambler) Wickware of Old Katonah (see Shove genealogy). HORACE[9] and Adelaide Todd made their home between Goldens Bridge and Katonah, on a large farm running east on present Todd Rd., formerly Weeks St., and west to the Croton River. Their 3 children were: ELLA,[10] b. 1882; ABRAM HORACE,[10] b. 1888; and OLIVER UEL[10] (1890-1950). The sons ran the farm after their father's death. ABRAM HORACE[10] never married. OLIVER UEL[10] married Marie Ferris of Katonah, dau. of Lewis and Lois Adelia (Miller) Ferris, who continues to live on the farm.

MARTIN TODD[7] (Aug. 7, 1803–Aug. 11, 1885) married Sept. 5, 1837, Sallie Lawrence. He was a farmer on Todd Rd., Lewisboro, and they raised their 4 children on the homestead: WILBUR;[8] JULIA;[8] GEORGE;[8] and CORNELIA.[8]

JULIA TODD[8] (1841-1915) married in 1859 Edward B. Brady of Goldens Bridge. They were parents of 12 children. LUCY BRADY BROWN[10] of Somers (see Merritt genealogy) is a granddaughter, and ROBERT GREEN,[11] justice of the peace of Lewisboro, is a great-grandson (see Green genealogy).

GEORGE TODD[8] ran the homestead and never married.

CORNELIA TODD[8] (1845-1923) married Aaron K. Silkman, son of Wright and Catherine (Keeler) Silkman (see Silkman genealogy).

WILBUR TODD[8] (1839-1910), a farmer in Goldens Bridge, married in 1874 Emma F. Newman and was the father of 6. One son, JOSEPH TODD,[9] b. 1881, married Dec. 10, 1904, Harriet Isler. He had a farm on Todd Rd. at the corner of North Salem Road. JOSEPH[9] and Harriet Todd had 10 children: LOUISE;[10] JULIA;[10] MARGERY;[10] SARAH;[10] GEORGE;[10] AMELIA;[10] EDITH;[10] ALICE;[10] JOHN;[10] and MARTIN.[10] MARTIN TODD[10] graduated from Arnold College, and joined the Katonah High School faculty in 1949. Coach Martin Todd is now with the John Jay School. He and his wife have 4 children: SALLY;[11] SUSAN;[11] JOSEPH;[11] and MARTIN.[11]

Compiled by K. B. Kelly.

The Tompkins Family

SEARING FOWLER TOMPKINS,[2] son of GABRIEL TOMPKINS[1] and Mary Fowler, was born in Tarrytown, N.Y., around 1820. On Dec. 31, 1872, he and his wife, Annette, bought of Jacob C. Buckley and his wife, Mary S., thirty acres of land in what became New Katonah. This included The Terrace, part of Bedford Rd. and Terrace Heights. The house is now owned by Louis E. Hasbrouck. Mr. Tompkins ran the farm for family use. By his first wife, Joanna Bassett (1824-1863), he had 6 children: SARAH,[3] b. July 19, 1847, who mar. Mr. Furman and had one son; MARY ELIZABETH,[3] b. Oct. 30, 1853; CAROLINE V.;[3] ASALINE,[3] b. Sept. 13, 1857; MINNIE,[3] b. Apr. 1861; and WILLIE,[3] b. Feb. 5, 1863. SEARING[2] married 2nd Annette Carson (1843-1913), b. in Scarsdale, dau. of Jacob and Margaret (Townsend) Carson. Children of Searing and Annette were: MAUDE;[3] and MARGARET TOWNSEND.[3] Buckley owned the farm again by Feb. 19, 1886, and Tompkins moved into Old Katonah around March, 1886. He died about 1893.

CAROLINE VALENTINE TOMPKINS,[3] b. June 20, 1856, married in February, 1880, John Quick (1858-1932), a shoe manufacturer, son of Amos Purdy Quick. John and Carrie had children: ADRIAN LEON;[4] ANNIE;[4] AMOS PURDY[4] (1892-1894); and CARRIE V. QUICK[4] (1889-1889). CAROLINE TOMPKINS QUICK[3] died Jan. 13, 1913. John Quick married 2nd Oct. 22, 1915, Mary W.

ADRIAN LEON QUICK,[4] b. Jan. 11, 1881, in New York City, was a New York furniture-dealer until he retired to Katonah in 1949. He married 1st Alice Tompkins and 2nd Regina Adderson. He had no children. He died on Quick's Lane at 77 yrs. June 5, 1958.

ANNIE QUICK,[4] b. in New York City Dec. 23, 1884, was a shoe stylist associated with her father. She married Robert Dickinson (1878-1944) Feb. 2, 1909. They had no children. Mrs. Dickinson died on Quick's Lane Oct. 5, 1959.

MAUDE TOMPKINS,[3] b. on Terrace Heights Mar. 23, 1875, attended school on Cherry St. and Palmer Ave. She married Ernest P. Hockley and they lived in Bedford Village and had 2 children: ANNE HOCKLEY,[4] who married Joseph Hocter and had sons JOSEPH[5] and WILLIAM HOCTER;[5]

and WILLIAM P. HOCKLEY,[4] who married Hilda Carlson and lives in Bedford with their daughter, HILDA ANN HOCKLEY.[5] Mrs. MAUDE T. HOCKLEY[3] died March, 1960, at the home of her daughter, ANNIE (HOCKLEY) HOCTER,[4] of Fort Pearce, Fla. Mrs. Hockley was a member of St. Matthew's Episcopal Church, Bedford. She was survived by two grandchildren and three great-grandchildren.

MARGARET TOWNSEND TOMPKINS,[3] b. on Terrace Heights June 14, 1878, attended school at Cherry St. and Palmer Ave. She married Albert Jesse Burt and they were the parents of 9 children: VIOLA;[4] LILIAN;[4] ALBERT,[4] b. December, 1899; WILTON,[4] b. 1901; MALCOLM;[4] MARGARET,[4] b. 1907, who mar. Ernest Odell and is a widow; MABEL;[4] JULIAN;[4] and ADRIAN LEON BURT,[4] b. 1912. Mrs. Burt lives on High Street with Viola, Albert, Adrian, and Margaret.

VIOLA BURT,[4] b. January, 1897, married James E. Ludlam. They were the parents of JAMES E.[5] and BARBARA MARION LUDLAM.[5] Mrs. Ludlam assisted for many years in Gumboldt's store. JAMES E. LUDLAM,[5] b. 1919, married Lee Gatley and lives in Monroe, N.Y. with children: THOMAS WILLIAM,[6] b. Sept. 16, 1941; ROGER JAMES,[6] b. Sept. 28, 1942; and PAMELA LUDLAM,[6] b. May 28, 1949. BARBARA MARION LUDLAM,[5] b. 1920, graduated from Katonah High School and married E. Paul Angot. They live on Quick's Lane with their only child, BARBARA SUSAN ANGOT,[6] b. July 12, 1947. Mr. Angot is a partner with Walter Raith in one of Katonah's leading markets, "Walt & Paul's," 93 Katonah Ave., an I.G.A. store. SUSAN[6] attends John Jay High School.

LILIAN BURT,[4] b. January, 1899, married Peter Lehneman and they had one daughter, MARION LEHNEMAN,[5] who came to Katonah and lived with her grandmother, Mrs. Albert J. Burt. She graduated from Katonah High School June, 1950, and worked for the N.Y. Telephone Company. She was living with her cousin, Mrs. Paul Angot, when she married June 4, 1953, in Roanoke Rapids, Va., John Francis Kelly, son of James and Katherine (Fitzgerald) Kelly of Mt. Kisco. They make their home at 82 Valley Rd. with their children: KATHLEEN LOUISE,[6] b. August, 1957; and JOHN FRANCIS KELLY, JR.,[6] b. Mar. 6, 1959.

MALCOLM S. BURT,[4] b. 1904, married Winifred Sweeney, dau. of James Sweeney of Katonah. They are the parents of: MALCOLM JAMES;[5] ROBERT,[5] b. July 10, 1930, unmar.; WINIFRED JOAN;[5] BARBARA;[5] CAROL;[5] DOROTHY;[5] EDWARD J.;[5] and WILLIAM ADRIAN.[5] They have made their home in Katonah and Mt. Kisco. At present, they live on Katonah Ave. in Katonah. The children have all attended Katonah schools at times.

MALCOLM JAMES BURT,[5] b. June 11, 1929, graduated from Katonah High in 1949 and from Bowling Green State University, Ohio, in 1953. He married Adabelle Dolores Werdann, called "Ginger," of New York City. Their children are: STEVEN,[6] b. Nov. 20, 1957; and MARY ELIZABETH,[6] b. Feb. 26, 1958.

WINIFRED JOAN BURT,[5] b. Nov. 3, 1931, married in St. Francis' Church, Mt. Kisco, January, 1953, Anthony Acquisto, son of Charles Acquisto of Mt. Kisco. They are parents of: PAMELA,[6] b. Dec. 10, 1953; ANTHONY, JR.,[6] b. Jan. 10, 1956; and THOMAS ACQUISTO,[6] b. Nov. 5, 1958.

BARBARA BURT,[5] b. Dec. 26, 1932, married Frank Gatto. They are parents of: CATHERINE,[6] b. Dec. 30, 1956; BARBARA ANNE,[6] b. Jan. 16, 1958; and FRANCIS GATTO,[6] b. Jan. 29, 1960.

CAROL BURT,[5] b. Aug. 17, 1936, married Lloyd Hulse. Their children are: DEBRA,[6] b. Mar. 28, 1956; ELIZABETH,[6] b. July 31, 1957; and PATRICIA HULSE,[6] b. Aug. 13, 1959.

DOROTHY BURT,[5] b. Nov. 10, 1937, unmar., lives at home with her family. She works for the Telephone Company.

EDWARD JOHN BURT,[5] b. Nov. 27, 1939, unmar., works for the Katonah Post Office.

WILLIAM ADRIAN BURT,[5] b. Nov. 24, 1941, joined the U.S. Air Force. He had his basic training at Lackland Air Base in Texas and went on to the Technical School for Supply Specialists in September, 1959. He is still in the service.

MABEL BURT,[4] b. 1908, married Charles Milton Fowler, son of William (see Fowler genealogy).

JULIAN BURT,[4] b. 1910, married Hazel Harrison and they live on Highland Ave., Katonah, with their children: GEORGIANNA,[5] b. Sept. 1, 1945; JANICE,[5] b. Feb. 10, 1948; LYNN,[5] b. May 31, 1953; PETER,[5] b. Nov. 24, 1955; and MARY ELLEN,[5] b. Mar. 11, 1960.

Compiled by Viola Ludlam and K. B. Kelly.

The Towey Families of Katonah

MARTIN TOWEY,[2] son of JAMES[1] and Margaret Towey, b. in 1853 near Ballaghaderreen, County Mayo, Ireland, was the eldest of the family. Coming to the United States in 1871, he settled in Katonah and worked on the John Jay farm. His aunt, MRS. CATHERINE TOWEY DOYLE,[1] wife of James, lived at Cantitoe Corners, and another aunt, JANE TOWEY KELLY,[1] was the wife of Michael Kelly of Mt. Holly. MARTIN[2] sent for his brothers, MICHAEL,[2] PATRICK,[2] and THOMAS TOWEY[2] to come to this country.

MARTIN[2] married in St. Joseph's R.C. Church in Croton Falls in February, 1874, Annie Horkins. Born in Carracastle, County Mayo, Ireland, she had arrived in the United States on the "Queen" of the National Line in 1871. They made their home on Weeks St., now Todd Rd., in Lewisboro, living in the present McCagg house and in the house farther along on the corner. They were the parents of: MARGARET;[3] JAMES;[3] MARTIN;[3] MARY;[3] ANNA;[3] and HELEN.[3] About 1892 they bought a home south of Hoyt's Mills in the Cross River valley. In October, 1898, he bought a lot, at 13 The Terrace, where William Fowler built their home. MARTIN[2] died in 1919 and Mrs. Towey in 1940.

MARGARET TOWEY,[3] b. in Bedford 1875, married Francis Rogers. They had no children. She died in Katonah in 1926.

JAMES TOWEY[3] (1877-1950), b. on Weeks St., married Minnie Donohoe. They had 2 sons: JAMES, JR.,[4] who died in New York City aged twelve; and FLOYD[4] who married but had no children. JAMES[3] and FLOYD[4] both died in Danbury.

MARTIN TOWEY, JR.,[3] b. in Lewisboro 1879, married Margaret Louise Bryant. Their son, ROBERT TOWEY,[4] is married and living in Columbus, O., but has no children. MARTIN[3] died in Totowa, N.J., in 1936.

MARY TOWEY[3] was born on Weeks St., now Todd Rd., in 1882. She worked as an occupational therapist in the Manhattan State Hospital, New York City, spending most of her life in Katonah. She never married and died in her home on The Terrace in 1943.

ANNA C. TOWEY,[3] b. on Weeks St., now Todd Rd., in the present McCagg house in 1885, spent many years as a teacher in New York City schools. She was one of 6 to graduate from our local school June 27, 1902. She graduated from Potsdam Teachers College and received her B.S. from Columbia University. She died in Katonah in 1955, unmarried.

HELEN M. TOWEY,[3] b. in Lewisboro, 1887, graduated from our local school and the Miller School of Business in New York City. She worked as private secretary to Prof. Henry Marion Howe in Bedford Hills and was in World War I, serving her country in France with the Army Quartermaster Corps. She worked for many years as office manager of the National Committee for Mental Hygiene in New York City, commuting from Katonah. She was active in the Choral Society, V.I.S., and is a charter member of the Women's Civic Club. Miss Towey, retired, lives at 13 The Terrace.

MICHAEL TOWEY,[2] son of JAMES[1] and Margaret, b. in Ireland, settled in Katonah and married Winifred Towey, sister of the Michael Towey who worked for a while with Aaron B. Whitlock. Winifred also had two Towey sisters who worked for Mrs. M. A. Woodcock of Bedford Village in 1902. MICHAEL[2] worked for Judge Robertson and later was Katonah's one-man police force, being elected constable for many years. In September, 1898, he purchased property in New Katonah and built a house there at 10 Ashby Place. Winifred died and he married 2nd Bridget. He lived in Katonah until his death. He had no children.

PATRICK TOWEY,[2] son of JAMES[1] and Margaret, came to the United States from Ireland as a boy of 12. He lived with and worked for Daniel J. Smith, attending our local school. He married Margaret Dempsey and they were the parents of: MARY;[3] JOHN;[3] JAMES;[3] MARGARET;[3] ANN;[3] and ELIZABETH.[3] PATRICK[2] bought a home near Hoyt's Mills. His house burned to the ground June 15, 1900. He then bought William Daniel's house on Hillside Ave. and Huntville Rd. and later built a home at 62 Bedford Rd. on land which he had purchased in October, 1898. His three youngest daughters still reside there. Mr. and Mrs. Towey and MARY[3] died in Katonah.

JOHN E. TOWEY[3] was born and educated in Katonah. He and his brother JAMES[3] bought out Fletcher Lent's taxi business which they continued to operate throughout their lives. JOHN[3] married around 1919 Winifred M., b. in Ireland June 15, 1892. They lived at 165 Katonah Ave. Their children, VIRGINIA,[4] PATRICIA[4] and ARTHUR[4] were educated at our local schools. VIRGINIA,[4] mar. James Donovan, lives in Port Chester with their 3 children. PATRICIA[4] married Alfred Burke, and lives in Yorktown with their 2 children. ARTHUR[4] served in the U.S. Army and is the present owner of Katonah's only taxi service. Recently he purchased from the New York Central their station building and property. ARTHUR[4] has married twice. By his first wife, Mrs. Betty Cooper Towey, he has JUDITH,[5] and by Mrs. Lorraine Towey, MARTIN.[5] Mr. and Mrs. Towey live at 165 Katonah Avenue. JUDITH[5] married David Gerardi of Katonah. TISHA SELENE GERARDI[6] was born Jan. 22, 1961.

JAMES J. TOWEY,[3] son of PATRICK[2] and Margaret, bought the Hillside Ave. house from his father. He also owned 36 Bedford Rd. He married Lavina Slavin of Horseheads, N.Y., and they had children: MARY LOUISE;[4] and JAMES J., JR.[4] JAMES TOWEY[3] died Jan. 23, 1954. Mrs. Towey, a nurse, has been with Bryn Mawr College in Pennsylvania, Four Winds in Cross River, and last year retired after 10 years with Westfield State Farms hospital in Bedford Hills. She lives at 36 Bedford Rd.

MARY LOUISE TOWEY[4] graduated from Mater Misericordiae Academy, Merion, Pa., Good Counsel College, White Plains, and received an M.A. from Columbia University. She was on the John Jay faculty as a teacher of social studies before her marriage in December, 1957, to George Godwin Mekeel. Mr. and Mrs. Mekeel live at 37 Hillside Ave. with sons, GEORGE NILES,[5] b. Dec. 15, 1958; and DANIEL DELMAR MEKEEL,[5] b. Dec. 22, 1960. Mr. Mekeel recently bought Augustine Healy's store on Katonah Ave.

JAMES J. TOWEY, JR.,[4] graduated from St. Mary's in Katonah, served two years in the U.S. Army, and is with Glasser Brothers of Bedford Village. He married May 30, 1958, Ida L. Bocchino, of Croton Falls. They make their home at 36 Bedford Rd. with their daughters: MARGARET ANN,[5] b. Mar. 12, 1959; and KATHLEEN,[5] b. Oct. 12, 1960.

MARGARET,[3] ANN[3] and ELIZABETH TOWEY[3] are unmarried and live at 62 Bedford Rd. MARGARET[3] for many years worked with her brothers in the Towey Taxi Company and was later with the *Patent Trader* newspaper. ANN[3] is with the Katonah branch of New York City Water Department. ELIZABETH[3] is with Westfield State Farms in Bedford Hills.

THOMAS TOWEY,[2] youngest son of JAMES[1] and Margaret Towey, went to work for Ferdinand Hopkins in Somers when he came from Ireland. He married and had 4 children: JAMES JOSEPH;[3] THOMAS;[3] ELIZABETH;[3] and ANNIE.[3] Both girls married men by the name of Bassett. THOMAS[3] married but had no children.

JAMES JOSEPH TOWEY[3] worked for Mr. Hopkins and married Elizabeth Wuest. They had 9 children. EDWARD JAMES,[4] b. May 8, 1911, mar., no children, lives in Pennsylvania. THOMAS,[4] unmar., lives at home on Rte. 100 and works for the New York City Water Department. FLORENCE[4] lives at home and is employed by Grand Union in Mt. Kisco. JOSEPH MARTIN,[4] b. Nov. 3, 1916, graduated from Katonah High School June, 1938. He worked for the Katonah Lumber Company and entered the Air Force in September, 1942, serving in Hawaii, Australia, New Guinea and Leyte. Mar. 8, 1944, he married Rosé Bernardo. He was killed on a bombing mission over the Philippines Nov. 28, 1944. WALTER JOHN,[4] b. Jan. 18, 1919, graduated from Katonah High School in 1937, entered the armed forces Jan. 14, 1942. He lives, unmar., in New York City. DAVID ARTHUR,[4] b. Aug. 18, 1921, unmar., lives in Somers. MYRTTE[4] married John Lally. They make their home in Goldens Bridge and have 2 sons. MARTHA,[4] unmar., works for a dentist in Mt. Kisco. ALMA[4] married Joseph Moravick. They live in Lincolndale with their 4 children. EDWARD JAMES,[4] WALTER,[4] DAVID,[4] and JOSEPH[4] were all in World War II.

* * * * *

There also arrived from the same county in Ireland two brothers, JOHN[1] and MICHAEL TOWEY,[1] who settled in Cross River. JOHN TOWEY,[1] a farmer and horse-dealer, married Ann Slavin and had a farm on present Rte. 35, near Mead Street. They had one son, Martin, who died. The farm was inherited by a nephew, JOHN TOWEY.[2]

MICHAEL TOWEY[1] married Anna B. Casey and they were parents of: MARY;[2] JOHN;[2] ANN;[2] MATTHEW;[2] JOSEPH;[2] and THEODORE.[2] MICHAEL,[1] a farmer, lived near Herman Chapel on Todd Rd., Lewisboro, but the children bought a lot on Hillside Ave., Katonah, and built a home now owned by Edward Hunter.

MARY TOWEY[2] married Leon E. Ganung and lives on Glenridge Rd. Mr. Ganung, an electrician, died in September, 1956. They had children: OLIVIA;[3] ELIZABETH;[3] BEATRICE;[3] LEON E., JR.;[3] ROBERT;[3] and AUDREY GANUNG.[3] OLIVIA[3] married Gerald Way and they live in Stamfordville, New York. ELIZABETH,[3] mar. Fred Collins, lives in Daytona Beach, Fla. BEATRICE,[3] mar. William Butler, lives in Croton Falls. LEON E. GANUNG, JR.,[3] b. Apr. 20, 1926, joined the Marines Mar. 17, 1944, and served in California, Guam and Iwo Jima. A plumber, he lives in Bedford Hills with wife, Elizabeth Pasquale, and daughter, BETTY LEE GANUNG.[4] ROBERT GANUNG[3] graduated from Katonah High School, 1946, did well in school baseball and joined the Philadelphia Athletics Farm Team. He married Josephine De Sole of Mt. Kisco and they built a new home on Jay St., Katonah, where they live with their 3 children: DONNA JEAN,[4] b. 1954; ROBERT, JR.,[4] b. 1956; and STEPHEN TOWEY GANUNG,[4] b. Oct. 9, 1957. Bob is an electrician with Hammond Electric in Mt. Kisco. AUDREY GANUNG[3] married William Ernest Waterbury, who is with the *Reader's Digest*. They live on The Parkway with their 2 children: DEBORAH;[4] and WILLIAM E. WATERBURY, JR.[4]

JOHN TOWEY[2] was a plumber by trade. His 1st wife died in Cross River and he married 2nd Helen Nash, a cashier with the New York Telephone Company in Mt. Kisco. They live at 42 The Terrace.

ANN TOWEY,[2] unmar., lives in New York City.

MATTHEW R. TOWEY[2] was very active in local affairs. He worked with the Boy Scouts and was a member of Rotary and of the Fire Department, of which he was chief from 1928 to 1932. He was a foreman for the New York Telephone Company and was with them for 42 years. He married Mary Clancy of Peekskill, also with the Telephone Company. They built a home on New St., where Mrs. Towey resides. He died in December, 1959, at 62 yrs.

JOSEPH TOWEY[2] was a very good steam-fitter. He has left Katonah and is married and living in Hollywood, Fla.

THEODORE N. TOWEY,[2] educated in Katonah and graduated from Fordham University, married Irene Koterba of Katonah. They lived on Orchard Rd. until transferred to Cincinnati, O. He is with the Long Lines of the Telephone Company. They are parents of 2 daughters born while living here, JOAN[3] and MAUREEN.[3]

JOAN TOWEY[3] graduated from Cornell, studied a year at the University of Oslo, Norway, under a Fulbright Scholarship, and received her M.A. from the University of Michigan. While studying for her doctorate in English Literature at Cornell, she married Aug. 8, 1959, in Our Lady's Chapel on the Cornell campus, Thomas Patrick Mitchell, son of Prof. James Mitchell of Galway, Ireland. They are living in Ithaca, N.Y.

MAUREEN TOWEY[3] graduated from the University of Michigan and is a speech therapist in California.
Compiled by K. B. Kelly.

The Travis Families of Katonah

Travis is a French family name. Through Garret Travis and his wife, Catharine, who lived in Rye in 1705, are descended our many different Travis families.

WILLIAM LEVI TRAVIS[1] (1826-1866) came to Whitlockville and married Mary Miller (1829-1889), dau. of Norman W. and Deborah (Gregory) Miller. He was a harness-maker. Around 1850 they moved into New York City when he became a Central Park policeman. Later the family returned to Katonah and subsequently moved to Dobbs Ferry. Children were: JOHN LEVI;[2] STEPHEN GREGORY MERRITT;[2] WILLIAM JEWITT;[2] MARY GEORGIANA;[2] NORMAN;[2] and WILLIS MILLER,[2] unmar.

JOHN LEVI TRAVIS,[2] b. in Judge Jay's stone house at Cantitoe, July 25, 1847, attended school locally until the family moved to Dobbs Ferry. He married Emma Fields.

STEPHEN G. M. TRAVIS[2] (1849-1941), a farmer in Dobbs Ferry, married in 1873 Phillippine Kunther. A granddaughter is MARGARET KING TRAVIS,[4] wife of John Irving Lane, Jr., of Pleasant Valley, N.Y.

WILLIAM JEWETT TRAVIS,[2] b. Aug. 26, 1850, married 1st Mary Elizabeth Hotchkiss and 2nd, Ruella Messiter. Children were: ARTHUR L.;[3] FRANK HOTCHKISS;[3] WILLIAM JEWETT, JR.;[3] FLOYD;[3] RALPH MESSITER;[3] and HAROLD.[3] WILLIAM J.[2] was a saddler in Dobbs Ferry but returned to Katonah when he retired. Living first on The Terrace, he died at his home at 52 Sunrise Ave. in 1934.

HAROLD TRAVIS[3] lived at 29 Bedford Rd., Katonah, with his wife, Melissa Mitchell, and children, HAROLD MITCHELL[4] and RUELLA.[4] RUELLA[4] graduated from Katonah High School and married James Curtiss, a lawyer. They and their daughters, MARTHA[5] and RUELLA CURTISS,[5] live in Glenrock, N.J. HAROLD MITCHELL[4] was with the Air Force in World War II. He married Hortense Menichelli of Croton Falls and they live on Daisy Lane, Croton Falls, with son, HAROLD MITCHELL, JR.,[5] b. Oct. 8, 1947. HAROLD[3] and Melissa Travis are living in Ridgewood, N.J.

* * * * *

JOSHUA TRAVIS[1] and wife, Sarah, lived in Yorktown, where he died Aug. 2, 1804. STEPHEN TRAVIS[2] (1789-1854), one of their 11 children, moved to North Salem and Somers and married Aug. 31, 1809, Phebe Bouton (1790-1863), dau. of Avery and Sarah (Keeler) Bouton of Ridgefield, Conn. They had 13 children: FLOYD;[3] SARAH E.,[3] d.y.; LEWIS;[3] LEONARD;[3] ELISHA;[3] BERNARD;[3] JESSE;[3] JOHN;[3] MARY;[3] SERENA;[3] JAMES;[3] and JOSEPH.[3] Most of them were well known in Katonah. LEWIS TRAVIS[3] (1810-1901) had a farm in Goldens Bridge. He married Nancy Nichols (1812-1902) and they were parents of: JAMES H.;[4] FLOYD;[4] STEPHEN;[4] FRANCINA;[4] PHEBE;[4] MARTHA;[4] and SARAH ELIZABETH.[4] FLOYD TRAVIS[4]

(1842-1923), after the death of his 1st wife, Kate Davenport, married Margaret (Benjamin) Travis (1854-1927), widow of BERNARD TRAVIS.[3] They bought the house at 55 Bedford Rd. where they lived at the time of his death.

BERNARD TRAVIS[3] (1819-1891), mar. Eliza Ann Harris (1820-1883) from upstate New York, owned a large millinery establishment in New York City. He bought the James Clark place and 43 acres between Whitlockville and Old Katonah, also land from Alfred Wood, Gideon Reynolds, Daniel Miller, William Robertson and Jesse Dingee around September, 1863. His home was one of the show places in Whitlockville and his hobby, trotting horses which he raised and raced. BERNARD[3] and Eliza Ann Travis had sons: GEORGE W.,[4] d. at 1 yr.; CHARLES EDWIN;[4] and BYRON ALDBERT.[4] BERNARD TRAVIS[3] married, 2nd, Aug. 7, 1884, Margaret J. Benjamin of Carmel (1854-1927).

CHARLES EDWIN TRAVIS[4] (1854-1905) spent his youth in Old Katonah. He married Jennie Smith Buckhout (1854-1949), daughter of Isaac C. and Emma (Moses) Buckhout, Nov. 13, 1877. He owned and operated a newspaper in Mt. Kisco at one time. Later this family moved to White Plains. Their children were: AUGUSTA B.;[5] GEORGE ELLIOT[5] (1880-1881); LEROY WINFIELD;[5] and ROBERT HOYT.[5] AUGUSTA B. TRAVIS[5] lived in Katonah and White Plains. Now retired, she makes her home in Harrison, N.Y.

LEROY W. TRAVIS,[5] b. in Katonah Nov. 5, 1881, attended our school and Chappaqua Mountain Institute and graduated from White Plains High School. He was employed by the New York Central for 45 years. His last 18 years were spent in Buffalo where he had been transferred. He married March 10, 1906, Ella Jane Jones (1880-1948), dau. of Thomas and Mary Louise (Mead) Jones of Somers. They lived in Katonah for 25 yrs. on Mustato Rd. and at 81 Edgemont Rd. Their only child, DOROTHY LEROY,[6] b. in Katonah Mar. 2, 1907, graduated from Katonah High School and Skidmore College. She was a physical education teacher in Schenectady and is still associated with the schools there. She married Byron H. Proper Apr. 16, 1954. They have no children.

ROBERT HOYT TRAVIS,[5] b. June 18, 1891, in Goldens Bridge, now resides on DeKalb Ave., White Plains, a retired photographer. He married Sept. 5, 1916, Mildred Laurena Boyce, dau. of Isaac and Ellen Boyce of White Plains. Daughters are: MARION ELLEN;[6] and NORMA JUNE.[6] MARION E. TRAVIS[6] served during World War II with the American Red Cross in Europe. She married Dec. 31, 1955, Edward Thomas Broadhurst, Jr. They live in White Plains with their son, EDWARD THOMAS BROADHURST III,[7] b. 1957. NORMA JUNE TRAVIS[6] was with Time, Inc., until her marriage to William Michalec Sept. 18, 1949. He is with the General Precision Laboratory in Pleasantville, where they live. Children are: SARAH BOYCE,[7] b. 1954; JAMES VACLAV,[7] b. 1956; and ANNE AUGUSTA MICHALEC,[7] b. 1959.

BYRON ALDBERT TRAVIS[4] (Bernard,[3] Stephen,[2] Joshua[1]), b. July 30, 1857, attended the private school for boys in Somers. He married Margery Langley Putney (1858-1880), dau. of Cornelius and Marie Antoinette (Silkman) Putney of Katonah. His wife died at 22 yrs., leaving him with a baby daughter, ESTELLE ANTOINETTE.[5] BYRON[4] died Sept. 9, 1888.

ESTELLE A. TRAVIS,[5] b. in Katonah in her grandfather's home by the millpond, attended school at Palmer Ave. before moving into New York City. She returned summers and holidays to stay with her aunt, Mrs. James Horton, and married Edward Percy Barrett Nov. 27, 1901 (see Barrett genealogy).

* * * * *

ANSON STRATTON TRAVIS[2] (1871-1936), son of JOSEPH[1] and Mary (Sloat) Travis of Union Valley, came to Katonah to clerk in Hoyt Brothers' store. He married in 1893 Augusta Mary Robertson (1875-1951), dau. of Charles Frederick and Calista A. (Dean) Robertson of Katonah. June 10, 1898, he purchased from his brother-in-law, William Robertson, a barber business formerly belonging to Romaine Ritchie. He sold this to Frank Gumboldt, who had run the business for him. He was employed by the N.Y. Central Railroad for 36 years. ANSON[2] and Augusta Mary Travis were parents of CLAUDE ROBERTSON,[3] b. in Brewster Dec. 19, 1901.

CLAUDE ROBERTSON TRAVIS,[3] b. 1901, married Vivien Arlene Waite, dau. of Ernest P. and Sarah Jane (Weed) Waite of Bedford, Sept. 29, 1922. He was a technical engineer with Electrical Research Products. They made their home in Crestwood, N.Y., before moving to 81 Edgemont Rd., Katonah, in June, 1935. Mr. Travis died in 1943. Their daughter, DIANE ROBERTSON,[4] b. Apr. 2, 1935, graduated from Katonah High School in 1953 and attended Beaver College in Pennsylvania. She married Aug. 6, 1957, William Lawrence Momsen, son of Richard Paul and Dorothea (Harnecker) Momsen of Rio de Janeiro, Brazil, and Cross River, N.Y. Their son is WILLIAM TRAVIS MOMSEN,[5] b. July 26, 1958, in Alameda, Calif.

* * * * *

JOHN TRAVIS[1] (1774-1867) of Somers married Elizabeth (1769-1852). Two of their children were: WILLIAM T.,[2] mar. Betsey Flewellin (1795-1872); and JAMES ROBERT.[2]

JAMES R. TRAVIS,[2] b. Jan. 25, 1804, married Aug. 13, 1825, Susan Gorle (1808-1874). A farmer and shoemaker, he died Aug. 8, 1889, in Somers. Their 7 children were: MARY JANE[3] (1829-1882), mar. a Putney; ESTHER,[3] who mar. Samuel Gale and died Feb. 23, 1834; WILLIAM,[3] d. in November, 1867; ELIJAH[3] (1839-1842); GEORGE B.;[3] JOSIAH COCK,[3] d. in 1836; and EDMUND JAMES.[3]

GEORGE B. TRAVIS,[3] b. Aug. 22, 1830, lived in Amawalk, and married Anne M. Gale of Amawalk. They were parents of: LEWIS;[4] JAMES C.;[4] and GEORGIA,[4] d.y.

LEWIS TRAVIS[4] married Anna Purdy and they had one daughter, GRACE.[5]

JAMES C. TRAVIS,[4] b. in Amawalk 1866, a farmer and painter, married Elizabeth Graham (1864-1909). They had 7 children: twins, CLARENCE J.[5] and HOWARD C.;[5] CORA;[5] SUSAN;[5] GEORGIA;[5] WILLIAM J.;[5] and RAYMOND G.[5] Selling their farm to New York City, they moved to the corner of Anderson Rd. and Greenville Rd., Katonah. LEWIS[4] lived next door for a while and there was an open lot between, for the horses. Later they moved to the east end of Anderson Ave. where Mrs. Elizabeth Travis died.

CLARENCE J. TRAVIS,[5] b. in Amawalk, 1888, attended school in Katonah and worked for Kellogg & Mead. Joining the Army in World War I, he was in the Medical Corps, M.D.N.A. Base Hospital. After the war he returned to Germany for 3 yrs., working in the hospitals there. He never married and worked in our veteran hospitals. Retired now, he lives in Bath, N.Y.

HOWARD C. TRAVIS,[5] b. in Amawalk 1888, was in the 24th Engineer Corps in World War I, and was a linesman with the Pennsylvania Railroad. He is married and now lives in Chicago.

CORA L. TRAVIS,[5] b. 1890, was a nurse. She married Johnston Adgate and they had children: JOSEPH;[6] and JANET ADGATE,[6] mar. Eugene Clark.

SUSIE K. TRAVIS,[5] b. 1892, married William Keon. They live in White Plains. Children are: JUNE KEON,[6] who mar. Stephen Martnike and lives in Stamford with their 2 daughters; and WILLIAM KEON, JR.,[6] mar. and lives on Shelby Rd., Valhalla, with children: LINDA,[7] b. 1943, and WILLIAM KEON III,[7] b. 1949.

GEORGIA ANNA B. TRAVIS,[5] b. 1896, married May 1, 1915, in New York City Harold Reynolds, b. June 22, 1894, son of Franklin Eli and Mary (Frye) Reynolds of Cross River. He ran a blacksmith-shop on the northwest corner of Greenville Rd. and Edgemont Rd. Their children were: BARBARA,[6] b. Feb. 25, 1916; and HAROLD REYNOLDS, JR.,[6] b. Jan. 10, 1918. Mr. Reynolds died in Katonah Sept. 2, 1918. Mrs. Reynolds married 2nd Ted Dittrick and they live in White Plains. BARBARA REYNOLDS[6] married LeRoy Holly (see Holly genealogy). HAROLD REYNOLDS, JR.,[6] married Doris Moore. They live in Miami, Fla., with their 5 children.

WILLIAM J. TRAVIS,[5] b. on Rte. 35, Amawalk, in 1897, moved to Katonah with his family but left in 1916 for 7 yrs. He joined the Telephone Company and was a linesman, construction foreman, construction superintendent and construction engineer. He married Helen M. Louden, dau. of Eugene F. and Mary (French) Louden in 1922. Living first in Mt. Kisco, they moved to North St., Katonah. In 1958 after his retirement, they sold their home and moved to Largo, Fla. They have no children.

RAYMOND G. TRAVIS,[5] b. in New York City, 1902, married May Barry of Boston. They live in Canaseraga, N.Y., and he is with the U.S. Forestry Service. Their children were: RAYMOND, JR.;[6] PHILIP;[6] AUDREY;[6] HAROLD;[6] and WALTER.[6]

EDMUND JAMES TRAVIS[3] (James R.,[2] John[1]), b. Dec. 1, 1832, was a farmer in Amawalk, living on Rte. 35 where the Amawalk spillway is at present. He married Charlotte Bedell (1834-1914) Jan. 18, 1852. Their sons were: EUGENE IRWIN;[4] and ANDREW FISHER.[4]

ANDREW FISHER TRAVIS,[4] b. in Amawalk June 27, 1862, farmed his land but was a carpenter by trade. He married Jeanette L. Griffen (1864-1932) of Amawalk. After selling the farm to New York City, they came to Katonah and lived on Croton Lake Rd. and also on Anderson Ave. for a short while. They moved a great deal, living in Peekskill, North Salem, and Mt. Kisco. Children were: HERBERT[5] (1890-1890); FRANCES B.,[5] b. 1891; JAMES EDMUND,[5] b. 1892; HERBERT GRIFFEN,[5] b. 1895; CHARLOTTE BEDELL,[5] b. 1897; CHARLES IRWIN,[5] b. 1899; and LENA,[5] b. 1902. ANDREW[4] died on Greenville Rd., Katonah, at the home of his son, JAMES,[5] June 29, 1944. All are buried in Amawalk Quaker Cemetery.

FANNY B. TRAVIS,[5] b. 1891 in Johnsville (now called Wicopee), Dutchess County, N.Y., married Frank Nolan of Danbury, Conn. She lives in Lake Secor.

JAMES EDMUND TRAVIS,[5] b. also in Johnsville in 1892, is a carpenter. He married Sept. 30, 1916, Anna Louise Akin of Danbury, dau. of James J. and Hattie (Kittle) Akin. They lived in North Salem for 11 yrs. before building in 1927 at 2 Greenville Rd., Katonah, where the old Reynolds blacksmith-shop stood. Later they moved to Bedford for 7 yrs. and returned to their present home on Terrace Heights. They have no children.

HERBERT G. TRAVIS,[5] b. in Peekskill, 1895, married Susan Finney. They live in Salem Center with their only child, ALICE.[6]

CHARLOTTE B. TRAVIS,[5] b. in Amawalk in 1897, married in 1915 Robert Payne of Bethel, Conn., a carpenter. They have lived in Katonah at times. In 1926 they moved the old Reynolds blacksmith-shop over one lot and made it into a home at 4 Greenville Rd. Their children, SHIRLEY,[6] ROBERT H.[6] (1918-1944), and THOMAS WHITNEY PAYNE,[6] all attended school in Katonah. Their last home was on Hickory Rd. They now live in Florida.

SHIRLEY PAYNE,[6] b. Jan. 14, 1917, in Bridgeport, is a graduate nurse with degrees from McLean Hospital, Boston, New York University, and St. Vincent's. She studied mental health at Boston University. At present she is associated with a hospital in Springfield, Mass.

T. WHITNEY PAYNE,[6] b. in Mt. Kisco Oct. 6, 1926, married Virginia Hazzard of Patterson where he is a truck driver. They are parents of: T. WHITNEY, JR.,[7] b. Jan. 25, 1952; TONI,[7] b. 1953; PATTI,[7] b. 1956; and LORI ALLYN,[7] b. Aug. 10, 1959.

C. IRWIN TRAVIS,[5] b. in Amawalk 1899, married Ruth Doughty. They have one son, LEONARD,[6] who lives at Salt Point, N.Y.

LENA TRAVIS[5] (1902-1932), b. in North Salem, married Albert Post of Fishkill Plains, N.Y. Their children were: ROBERT;[6] WALLACE;[6] and BETTY POST.[6] Mrs. Post is buried in Quaker Cemetery, Amawalk.

Compiled by K. B. Kelly.

The Van Tassel Family of Katonah

JOHN VAN TASSEL[1] was descended from Petrus Van Tassel of the Island of Texel and John Van Tassel of the Netherlands. JOHN[1] was a soldier of Capt. Gilchrist's Company Mar. 15, 1739. He also served in the Revolutionary War during its entirety. He and his wife, Mary Bartine, lived in Yonkers. He is buried in Sleepy Hollow Cemetery, Tarrytown.

STEPHEN VAN TASSEL,[2] son of John and Mary Bartine Van Tassel, was born in Yonkers. He enlisted in the Revolutionary War at Tarrytown in May, 1776, Capt. Laden's Company. He was in the battle of White Plains at Chatterton Hill. He re-enlisted under Capt. Sybert Archer in the Dutchess County Militia, 6th Regt., and under Capt. Gilbert Dean with the 1st Regt. of Westchester County Militia. He was taken prisoner in April, 1780, and spent 11 months and five days confined in Old Sugar House Prison in New York City. He married Mary de Revere of Yonkers and they moved to Somers. Their home still stands on Rte. 100, owned by Mr. F. T. Hopkins and occupied by Mr. Webster Keefe. They raised their 10 children at the farm: BENJAMIN,[3] b. 1789; STEPHEN, JR.,[3] b. 1791;

ABRAHAM,[3] b. 1793; LAVINIA,[3] b. 1796; SARAH,[3] b. 1797; JACOB,[3] b. 1799; RACHEL,[3] b. 1800; HANNAH,[3] b. 1804; ELIZABETH,[3] b. 1805; and WILLIAM,[3] b. 1807. STEPHEN[2] and Mary are buried in the Todd Cemetery on Rte. 100, Somers.

STEPHEN VAN TASSEL, JR.,[3] married Elizabeth Baxter, dau. of David and Hannah (Osborn) Baxter of North Salem. They made their home in North Salem and were the parents of 4 children: WILLIAM PETTIT;[4] DAVID;[4] EMILY;[4] and HARRY.[4]

WILLIAM PETTIT VAN TASSEL[4] (July 16, 1822–Aug. 14, 1894) married Oct. 15, 1845, Caroline Maria Mead (1820-1890) of South Salem. They moved into Old Katonah in 1867. He was a veterinary and wholesale produce merchant. WILLIAM[4] and Caroline lived on the road from Old Katonah to Bedford, now Woodsbridge Rd. They were the parents of 7 children: ANDREW MEAD;[5] JOSEPHINE;[5] GEORGE;[5] GERARD;[5] CHARLES CONKLIN;[5] ANNA ELIZABETH;[5] and CAROLINE VAN TASSEL,[5] d.y.

ANDREW MEAD VAN TASSEL[5] was born in North Salem July 11, 1846, and came to Old Katonah with his father in 1867. Jan. 24, 1871, he married Ella R. Bennett, daughter of Diron Harrison Bennett of Branchport, N.Y., and they made their home on Main St. next door to the meat market he operated. He also ran a slaughter-house and was a commission merchant. He was on the school board in Old and New Katonah. ANDREW[5] and Ella were parents of 5 children: ELIZABETH O.;[6] GEORGE ANDREW;[6] twins, HABBERT[6] and JOSEPHINE;[6] and MARGERY HORTON.[6] GEORGE[6] died at 13. HABBERT[6] died in June, 1878, at 20 months. When in 1897 New York City took their home, the Andrew Van Tassels moved their store to New Katonah. This building still stands on Katonah Ave. and Valley Rd. presently owned by Eli Antonecchia. In 1898 Mr. Van Tassel added a new barn and icehouse next to the store. However, he lost these in the big Katonah fire of May 30, 1902. Mrs. Van Tassel died Mar. 27, 1901, at 49 yrs. Mr. Van Tassel died June 14, 1914. Both are buried in Oakwood Cemetery, Mt. Kisco.

CHARLES CONKLIN VAN TASSEL,[5] b. 1859, married Martha Elizabeth Young in 1885. They had 5 children: CHESTER BURROUGHS;[6] ETHEL[6] (1888-1914) HOWARD[6] and ARTHUR[6] who died as infants; and WALTER NIELD.[6] From 1936 until his death in 1947, Mr. Van Tassel lived in Katonah in the old Albert Lyon place, 36 The Terrace.

ANNA ELIZABETH VAN TASSEL,[5] unmar., lived in her father's home on Bedford Rd., now 22 Woodsbridge Rd., until she sold it in May, 1901. She taught school and then was employed by the Railroad in Grand Central, Mt. Kisco and Yonkers Park. Miss Van Tassel, b. July 14, 1861, died Aug. 31, 1925.

ELIZABETH OPHELIA VAN TASSEL,[6] dau. of ANDREW,[5] b. in Old Katonah July 28, 1872, married at her home on Katonah Ave. in the new village June 21, 1900, Walter Trumble Chace of Walton, N.Y. Mr. Chace had come to Katonah and worked as a plumber for Henry Kellogg. They set up housekeeping at 10 Bedford Rd. Mr. and Mrs. Chace had 2 daughters: ELLA LOUISE;[7] and MARTHA JEANETTE CHACE.[7] Mrs. Chace died Jan. 11, 1912. Mr. Chace has retired after being associated with Kellogg's for 57 years and resides at his home, 79 Valley Rd.

ELLA LOUISE CHACE,[7] b. in New Katonah Apr. 7, 1902, graduated from Katonah High School and New York State College for Teachers in Al-

bany where she majored in English and library work. She was librarian
in Peekskill High School and is now assistant librarian at the Katonah
Village Library. July 7, 1928, she married William Godfrey Weist, son of
Charles and Laura (Lancaster) Weist of Peekskill, N.Y., and lived in
Pleasantville for 11 years, before moving back to Katonah. Sons are: WIL-
LIAM G. WEIST, JR.,[8] b. July 6, 1931; and ANDREW MERWIN WEIST,[8] b.
Feb. 1, 1935.

WILLIAM G. WEIST, JR.,[8] graduated from Katonah High School in June,
1949, from Amherst College in 1953, and received his master's degree in
geology from the University of Colorado in 1956. He married Sept. 8, 1956,
Patricia Ruth Jones, daughter of Lloyd T. and Marion Murphy Jones of
Colorado Springs, Colo. She is a graduate of the University of Colorado,
majoring in music. WILLIAM, JR.,[8] is with the U.S. Geological Survey in
Denver. They live in Arvada, Colo.

ANDREW MERWIN WEIST[8] graduated from Katonah High School in June,
1953. He served in the Army, spending 18 months in Germany, and later
graduated from Clarkson College in Potsdam, N.Y.

MARTHA JEANETTE CHACE[7] graduated from Katonah High School and
trained at Vassar Brothers Hospital, Poughkeepsie, N.Y. She married
Dec. 22, 1944, Harry J. Nairn. Since the death of her husband in 1956
she has returned to her nursing profession. She lives at Oregon Corners,
Putnam County, N.Y.

JOSEPHINE VAN TASSEL[6] and her twin brother HABBERT,[6] d.y., children
of ANDREW,[5] were born on Sept. 23, 1876. She graduated from the Katonah school, and went into the newspaper office of the Katonah Times,
working there until Mr. R. D. Knapp sold the paper. She collected news,
wrote stories and set type. Mr. Knapp considered her one of his most valuable assistants. She attended the McAvoy Private School for Teachers in
Cortland and taught in a number of our local schools including Cantitoe,
Mt. Holly, Bedford Hills and North Salem. In 1918 she became agent at
the Bryn Mawr Park railroad station where she officiated for 27 years
and substituted in other stations. She has been prominent in the Women's
Civic Club, the Katonah Choral Club and the local Chautauqua. During
her 60 and more years of membership in the Presbyterian Church she has
served as president of the Ladies' Aid, taught Sunday School and been
active in Christian Endeavor.

MARGERY HORTON VAN TASSEL,[6] dau. of ANDREW,[5] was born in Katonah
Sept. 28, 1878. She graduated from the Katonah school. After a lapse of
years she attended McAvoy's Private School for Teachers in Cortland for
5 summers, and received a New York State life license to teach. For 22
years she taught in local schools, Mt. Holly and Cantitoe among others.
Her last position was in the Jennie Clarkson Home where she taught for
5 years. She has always been actively interested in the D.N.A. and has
been treasurer of the Katonah Branch for 30 years. She was census enu-
merator of the school district for 23 years. After many years of active service in the Women's Civic Club, she was made an Honorary Member.
At the present time she is parliamentarian for that organization. Throughout her more than 60 years' membership in the Presbyterian Church she
has taught in Bible School, shared in the activities of the women's work,
and been a leader in the Young People's Society of Christian Endeavor.

The Misses Josephine[6] and Margery Van Tassel[6] live at 10 Bedford Rd.

Compiled by K. B. Kelly.

The Whitlock Family

The Whitlocks, for whom the now submerged little village of Whitlockville on the Cross River and the Croton River was named, came from Fairfield County, Conn. Joseph,[3] b. 1718, was the son of Thomas[2] and grandson of John Whitlock.[1] Joseph Whitlock[3] and his wife, Mary Jarvis, had 4 children: Rachel,[4] b. 1742; Thaddeus[4] (1749-1823); and twins, Joseph[4] and Mary,[4] b. 1755. All were baptized at Westport, Conn. Mary Whitlock[4] married David Olmsted and they moved to Cherry St. (see Olmsted genealogy).

Thaddeus Whitlock[4] married at Westport in 1775 Grace Burr (1753-1840), dau. of John and Grace (Bulkley) Burr and granddaughter of Daniel and Mary (Jennings) Burr. About April, 1792, they moved into that part of Salem, N.Y., later known as Whitlockville. Their children were: Aaron,[5] b. 1777; Mary,[5] b. 1780, wife of Squire Wood (see Wood genealogy); John Burr,[5] b. 1787; all baptized in Westport; and Betsey Whitlock[5] (1793-1814) b. in Salem, N.Y., wife of Caleb Haight (see Haight genealogy). Apparently, as indicated in the will of Thaddeus,[4] there was a 3rd daughter, "first wife of Benjamin Miller."

Aaron Whitlock[5] married Esther Ketchum, who died Feb. 6, 1866, at 84 yrs., 10 mos. Their 2 children were: Thaddeus[6] (1803-1871); and Saloma[6] (1810-1852).

Thaddeus Whitlock,[6] b. in Whitlockville, and Nancy Gregory (1805-1894), dau. of Stephen and Chloe (Fillow) Gregory, were married Oct. 16, 1823, in Somers by Rev. Ezra Fountain. Thaddeus[6] was town overseer of highways in 1832, '36, '37, and '60. Thaddeus[6] and Nancy were parents of 6 children: Aaron Burr[7] (1824-1904); Artemas;[7] Anna Gregory,[7] mar. Charles Wood Avery (see Avery genealogy); Silas;[7] Chloe Esther[7] (1833-1885), mar. Elisha Lemuel Avery (see Avery genealogy); and Thaddeus Haight[7] (1835-1876).

Aaron Burr Whitlock,[7] b. in Whitlockville, ran a store there and later in Croton Falls and Somers. Feb. 11, 1848, he was married to Sarah Ann Avery (1828-1885), dau. of Col. Enoch and Lucy (Wood) Avery, by Rev. Lorin Clark in Cross River. They belonged to the Methodist Church in Purdy's. Aaron married 2nd Addie J. Smith of Catskill. Children of Aaron Burr[7] and Sarah Whitlock were: Eveline,[8] b. 1849; Caroline Lee,[8] b. 1852, who mar. William Thacker and had children, Emily,[9] Walter Burr[9] and Stephen G. Thacker;[9] George Burr[8] (1856-1858); Charles Avery,[8] b. 1859; William[8] (1862-1862); Walter Burr,[8] b. 1864; Sarah Avery,[8] b. 1867, who mar. Morey W. Smith of Catskill, moved to Tarrytown and had 6 children, Frances,[9] Marjorie,[9] Dorothy,[9] Eleanor,[9] Morey, Jr.,[9] and Kathryn Smith;[9] and Lucy Jeanette Avery,[8] b. 1868, mar. A. Vail Smith. Lucy[8] and Vail lived in Croton Falls and Brewster with children: ISABEL;[9] WHITLOCK;[9] EVALENE;[9] A. VAIL, JR.;[9] MOREY;[9] and LAWRENCE W. SMITH.[9]

CHARLES AVERY WHITLOCK,[8] b. June 7, 1859, married Mar. 4, 1885, Caroline E. Green, b. 1866, dau. of William H. Green of North Castle. They lived in the old Whitlock homestead in Whitlockville. He worked at night in the round house in Croton Falls and had a bicycle repair and steamfitting shop on the old farm. When they had to leave the farm, they took lumber from the old shop and rebuilt it in Mt. Kisco, where he continued bicycle repairs. Their 2 children were: WALTER GREEN,[9] b. 1888, and MILDRED AVERY,[9] b. 1891. Both attended New Katonah's first new school. MILDRED[9] married in 1914 A. Leroy Banks of Mt. Kisco and they had: EVELYN VIRGINIA[10] (1914-1914); and CLIFFORD LEROY BANKS,[10] b. 1916. CLIFFORD BANKS[10] married Jean E. Colville and they have sons: ROBERT JOHN;[11] and PETER DONALD BANKS.[11]

WALTER GREEN WHITLOCK,[9] b. in Whitlockville Jan. 16, 1888, married Oct. 21, 1909, in White Plains Clara O'Connor, b. May 23, 1889, in Bedford Hills, dau. of Thomas and Elizabeth (Scott) O'Connor. They moved to Tilly Foster in 1945 where Mrs. Whitlock died Feb. 25, 1959. Their children were: WALTER GREEN, JR.,[10] b. 1919; CHARLES AVERY[10] of New York City; AARON BURR,[10] b. 1927, of Tilly Foster; and EILA CAROLINE,[10] mar. Edward Fernandez. The Fernandez' operate a soda fountain in the Mt. Kisco Pharmacy and are parents of RODERICK FERNANDEZ.[11]

WALTER GREEN WHITLOCK, JR.,[10] b. in Mt. Kisco, married Alice Correa. They live in Danbury with sons: CHARLES[11] and WALTER GREEN III.[11]

WALTER BURR WHITLOCK[8] (1864-1945), a farmer, lived in Somers. He married Mar. 20, 1888, at Purdy's, Frances C. Smith from Catskill. They had children: ADA JEANETTE,[9] b. 1891, who mar. Frederick Davis and had GEORGE W.,[10] WALTER WHITLOCK,[10] ERIC W.,[10] and RICHARD DAVIS;[10] and AARON BURR,[9] who mar. Ina L. Humason and had son, AARON BURR, JR.,[10] b. Oct. 13, 1918.

ARTEMAS WHITLOCK,[7] b. in Whitlockville, married Sarah Ann Tucker. They lived in Highbridge, N.Y., and had 7 children. One, JAMES S. WHITLOCK,[8] died in Croton Falls at 25 yrs. while a clerk in T. H. Whitlock's store. Another was ANNA G.,[8] mar. S. Allen Kennard of Brooklyn and West Somers.

THADDEUS HAIGHT WHITLOCK,[7] b. in Whitlockville, married Laura A. Hanford, dau. of Joseph and Serena (Avery) Hanford. Their children were: ODLE CLOSE,[8] b. 1860, who mar. Mary Birdsall and had sons, ODLE CLOSE JR.,[9] and LESTER;[9] ARTHUR,[8] b. 1865, who had son HAROLD;[9] and MABLE,[8] b. 1874, who mar. Francis Bedient and had dau. LEONA MAY BEDIENT.[9]

JOHN BURR WHITLOCK[5] (1787-1863) was five when his family settled in Salem. He was an ensign in 1810 and a lieutenant in the War of 1812. He was instrumental in organizing and building a Methodist Church in Whitlockville and gave the land for the cemetery. He was inspector of schools in 1833, overseer of highways in 1835 and for many years thereafter. He was a partner of Squire Wood in a store and mill and other enterprises. Jan. 14, 1808, he married Rachel Olmsted, b. May 16, 1786, dau. of Mary Whitlock and David Olmsted. They had 8 children: WARREN[6] (1808-1883); ELIZA[6] (1811-1837), mar. Wright M. Beyea; DANIEL DELEVAN[6] (1813-1834); MARY[6] (1816-1871), mar. Daniel Parent; BETSEY[6]

(1819-1873), mar. Jacob W. Hanford (see Hanford genealogy); JOHN BURR, JR.,[6] b. 1822; LUCY ANN,[6] b. 1824, mar. James Fillow Merritt (see Merritt genealogy); and JULIA AUGUSTA,[6] b. 1829, mar. Moses Smith Benedict (see Benedict genealogy).

WARREN WHITLOCK,[6] b. Nov. 7, 1808, lived in Whitlockville all his life. He was a member of the original Cherry Street Class before the organization of the Methodist society, charter member when it was organized in Whitlockville, and helped build the first church there. He married Amanda (1811-1861), and they had 5 children: MARY ELIZABETH[7] (1834-1895); DANIEL DELEVAN[7] (1839-1893); RACHEL LAVINIA,[7] mar. James Sniffen of Englewood, N.J.; HENRY,[7] d. 1853; and a daughter[7] who married George Hanford.

DANIEL DELEVAN WHITLOCK,[7] b. in Whitlockville, lived after his marriage in Pleasantville and New York. He beloged to the 48th Regiment, New York Volunteers. His children were: DANIEL D., JR.;[8] and ELLA,[8] wife of Dr. Charles F. Chapman of Katonah and Mt. Kisco.

JOHN BURR WHITLOCK, JR.,[6] b. Jan. 22, 1822, in Whitlockville, mar. Jan. 1, 1846, Huldah Maria Avery, b. June 1, 1830, dau. of Alfred and Anna Maria (Keeler) Avery of Cross River. JOHN BURR[6] was employed in his father's store in Whitlockville, but about 1858 bought out a business in Old Katonah, which he later sold to Lyon Bros. In 1899 he built a residence which he sold to A. F. Avery. He built another near the railroad bridge, which was his home for the last 20 years of his life. After retiring from mercantile pursuits, he held for many years a position in the Custom House in New York City and usually spent his winters in the City. In 1875 he became a member of the Katonah Presbyterian Church. He died suddenly in 1890. His home was moved when the reservoir came and it now stands on the northeast corner of Edgemont and Bedford Rds. JOHN BURR[6] and Huldah Whitlock were parents of 2 daughters: ANNA MARIA,[7] wife of Clark W. Tileston and mother of CARLOS H.,[8] PASTORIA,[8] and HENRY TILESTON;[8] and HARRIET AVERY,[7] who married 1st in New York City, June, 1877, John Daniel Lewis (1856-1882), son of Samuel A. and Sophia (Phillips) Lewis. HARRIET,[7] blessed with a beautiful soprano voice, was well trained and appeared professionally in New York City and throughout the country. She married 2nd Feb. 1, 1889, in Windsor, Canada, Edward Strakosch, while both were appearing with the Clara Louisa Kellogg Opera Company. Her children were: SAMUEL ALEXANDER LEWIS,[8] b. Apr. 11, 1878, educated and raised in Katonah, d. unmar. in Phoenix, Ariz.; and HAZEL STRAKOSCH,[8] b. Oct. 11, 1892, who attended school in Katonah. She married three times and has one daughter, CHLOE.[9]

Compiled by F. R. Duncombe and K. B. Kelly.

The Whitman Family

CLARENCE WHITMAN,[8] who came to live at Katonah in 1891, was descended from JOHN WHITMAN[1] who emigrated from England prior to 1638 and settled in Weymouth, Mass. His son, REV. ZECHARIAH,[2] b. Weymouth, 1644, graduated from Harvard in 1668. In 1670 he married 1st Sarah

Alcock, b. about 1650, who died 1715. Their son, JOHN[3] (1688-1772), married Mary Graves of Charlestown. Deacon JOHN,[4] b. Sept. 21, 1717, married Mary Foster. In 1761 the family emigrated to Nova Scotia on the sloop "Charming Molly." JOHN,[5] b. in Stowe, Mass., 1753, accompanied them. He married Elizabeth Rice, also b. in Stowe. They settled at Round Hill, Annapolis County. ELNATHAN[6] (1785-1868) married 1st Eleanor Spurr, who died 1824. They lived at Round Hill and he represented Annapolis County 1836-1840 in the Provincial Parliament. JOHN,[7] b. 1814, son of ELNATHAN[6] and Eleanor, spent his boyhood on the farm in Nova Scotia and then entered upon a mercantile life. He married June 24, 1841, Rebecca Cutler (1820-1874). They moved to Cambridge, Mass., about 1865, and later to Staten Island, N.Y.

CLARENCE WHITMAN[8] (June 17, 1847–May 14, 1931), b. in Nova Scotia, married in 1875 Mary Hoppin Morton, dau. of Marcus Morton, Chief Justice of Massachusetts. In 1876 he founded, with his brother EBEN,[8] the firm of E. C. and C. Whitman, textile commission merchants, which he continued after his brother's death as Clarence Whitman and Co. In the summer of 1891, because a higher altitude was recommended for his wife, he brought the family from Staten Island to "Katonah's Wood" at Cantitoe Corners which he purchased the next year, remodeling the house of Henry Pellew and raising fine Guernsey cattle. Always taking a keen interest in countryside and village, when the old village of Katonah was forced to move, Mr. Whitman was instrumental in securing a new site and the services of B. S. and G. S. Olmstead, the country's foremost landscape architects, to lay out the new village. It was he, also, who as chairman of the Tree Planting Committee of the Village Improvement Society saw to the planting of the first trees. Mr. Whitman was vestryman and warden of St. Matthew's Church for 25 yrs. CLARENCE[8] and Mary Hoppin (Morton) Whitman were parents of: CLARENCE MORTON,[9] b. 1877; ARTHUR McGREGOR[9] (1879-1880); HAROLD CUTLER,[9] b. 1883; ESMOND,[9] b. 1886; and GERALD,[9] b. 1890.

CLARENCE MORTON WHITMAN[9] (Feb. 15, 1877–Sept. 7, 1936), a graduate of Harvard 1899, married Nov. 19, 1903, Eleanor Motley, b. Sept. 28, 1884. They had children: CLARENCE II;[10] PETER MORTON;[10] and H. MOTLEY.[10]

CLARENCE WHITMAN II,[10] b. Jan. 1, 1905, a graduate of St. Paul's School 1923, Harvard College 1927, and Harvard Business School 1929, married Carol Whitman, a 2nd cousin, about 1940. In World War II, he was a lieutenant-commander in the Navy. Children are: C. LAWRENCE,[11] b. 1941; and BRADFORD,[11] b. 1943. They live at 150 East 72nd St., New York.

PETER MORTON WHITMAN,[10] b. Nov. 19, 1909, a graduate of St. Paul's 1928 and Harvard 1932, married Elizabeth Blodget Apr. 27, 1934. Mr. Whitman is vice-president of Johnson and Higgins, New York. Children are: ELEANOR M.,[11] b. Nov. 6, 1936, who mar. James B. Laughlin, Sept. 7, 1956 and has LAURA B. LAUGHLIN,[12] b. Jan. 29, 1959, and TIMOTHY WHITMAN LAUGHLIN,[12] b. Dec. 7, 1960; ELIZABETH,[11] b. Aug. 19, 1938, a graduate of Vassar 1960; PETER M., JR.,[11] b. July 1, 1942, now at St. Paul's School, class of '61; and CLAIRE SANFORD,[11] b. Feb. 15, 1949. The PETER M. WHITMANS[10] live at Bedford Hills, N.Y.

H. MOTLEY WHITMAN,[10] b. Dec. 29, 1912, educated at St. Paul's, married Henrietta Tjaarda of Amsterdam, Holland. Their children are: HENRI MORTON;[11] and LUCIA P.[11] They live at 150 East 72nd St., New York.

HAROLD CUTLER WHITMAN,[9] b. August, 1883, attended St. Mark's School and Harvard and was a major in the U.S. Army in World War I. Jan. 2, 1906, in Panama, he married 1st Georgia Fargo Squiers (1886-1942), dau. of the Hon. Herbert G. Squiers and Helen Lacey Fargo. Like his father, HAROLD C. WHITMAN[9] has interested himself in community affairs. He is past-president of the Village Improvement Society and of the Bedford Golf and Tennis Club, and has served 7 yrs. as town councilman and 23 yrs. as vestryman and warden of St. Matthew's Church, Bedford. HAROLD CUTLER[9] and Georgia (Squiers) Whitman had children: HAROLD CUTLER, JR.,[10] b. 1907; JOHN SQUIERS[10] (1908-1956); GEORGIA MARY,[10] b. 1910; ROBERT,[10] b. 1912; HELEN MORTON,[10] b. 1914; and MARIE JOSEPHA CLARE,[10] b. 1923. Mrs. Whitman died Oct. 7, 1942. Feb. 17, 1945, Mr. Whitman married 2nd in Bermuda Edna W. Jardine, b. about 1892 in Nottingham, England, dau. of Sir Ernest Jardine, Baronet.

HAROLD CUTLER WHITMAN, JR.,[10] b. New York City, Nov. 13, 1907, attended St. Mark's School and Harvard and served in the 29th Infantry Div., U.S. Army 1945-1949. He married 1st Ruth Malone in Bedford Village in 1930 and had son HAROLD C. III,[11] b. Aug. 2, 1931, at Providence, R.I., who married Aimee Dupuis May 25, 1960, at Greenwich, Conn. HAROLD C., JR.,[10] married 2nd Joan Howard Dec. 30, 1946. Their children, born at Salisbury, Md., are: ESMOND PHILIP,[11] b. June 20, 1951; and ISABEL,[11] b. Mar. 16, 1957. The family now lives at Parsonsburg, Md.

JOHN SQUIERS WHITMAN,[10] b. Nov. 22, 1908, in Providence, R.I., died July 7, 1956. He attended Mohonk School and Franklin and Marshall College and served in the Canadian Black Watch during World War II. He married Florence C. Meyer Oct. 8, 1935, at Norwalk, Ohio, and had children: HERBERT GOLDSMITH SQUIERS,[11] b. Dec. 10, 1936, in Montreal; JOHN ALBERT,[11] b. Apr. 5, 1939; and GEORGIA ELIZABETH,[11] b. May 22, 1940. All live in Montreal.

GEORGIA MARY WHITMAN,[10] b. July 4, 1910, in Providence, R.I., attended Miss Porter's School at Farmington, Conn., and the Naum Los Art School. She married Nov. 19, 1954, in Bedford Village Col. E. H. Mitcham, and is now living in Middlebury, Vt.

ROBERT WHITMAN,[10] b. Aug. 31, 1912, at Ashton, R.I., attended Lenox School, Lenox, Mass., and Cornell College of Agriculture. He served in the U.S. Air Force 1942-1945. He married Doreen Kerr-Jarrett Jan. 7, 1947, at Montego Bay, Jamaica, B.W.I. Their children are: IAN MONTCRIEF,[11] b. October, 1947; JESSICA MARY,[11] b. Nov. 3, 1951; DEBORAH DOREEN,[11] b. July 4, 1952; and CHRISTINE CUTLER,[11] b. 1959. They live in Leesburg, Va.

HELEN MORTON WHITMAN,[10] b. Nov. 2, 1914, at Ashton, R.I., attended Miss Porter's School and the Lowthorpe School of Landscape Architecture. She now lives at Salem Center, N.Y.

MARIE JOSEPHA CLARE WHITMAN,[10] b. New York City July 17, 1923, married Samuel Clarendon Myer, March, 1945, at Bedford. Their children are: GEORGIA MADELINE,[11] b. 1952; VIRGINIA CATHERINE,[11] b. 1953; and JOSEPHA MARIA MYER,[11] b. 1957. The Myers make their home in Sausalito, Calif.

GERALD WHITMAN,[9] b. New York City Feb. 6, 1890, a graduate of St. Mark's 1908 and Harvard 1912, married June 14, 1916, Eleanor Taft, b. July 24, 1894, at Providence, R.I., dau. of Robert and Alice Grinnell Taft. The GERALD WHITMANS[9] were parents of: ROBERT T.,[10] b. Apr. 9, 1917, a graduate of St. Mark's 1934 and Harvard 1938, who as a lieutenant of the U.S.N.R. was lost in sinking of the cruiser "Indianapolis" July, 1945; ELEANOR,[10] b. 1918; GERALD, JR.,[10] b. 1920; FREDERICK GRINNELL,[10] b. 1922; and ALICE,[10] b. 1924.

ELEANOR WHITMAN,[10] b. Aug. 6, 1918, at Bristol, R.I., married Dr. Robert Watkins June 20, 1940. They live in Pittsford, N.Y. Their children are: GEORGIA MARY,[11] b. Apr. 30, 1941; ROBERT, JR.,[11] b. Feb. 5, 1943; WILLIAM TAFT,[11] b. Aug. 8, 1944; GERALD LAWRENCE,[11] b. Apr. 20, 1948; and KATHERINE GREENOUGH WATKINS,[11] b. Jan. 2, 1951.

GERALD WHITMAN, JR.,[10] b. Jan. 20, 1920, at Providence, R.I., a graduate of St. Mark's 1938 and Harvard 1942, was a lieutenant in the U.S.N.R. in World War II. He married Barbara VanNorman of Springfield, Mass., June 12, 1942. They live in New Britain, Conn. Their children are: PETER VANNORMAN,[11] b. 1944 at Norfolk, Va.; PAMELA LEIGH,[11] b. 1946 at Greenwich, Conn.; LYNN ROBSON,[11] b. 1947, at Greenwich; ROBERT T.;[11] and SANDRA HOPKINS,[11] b. 1950 at Wareham, Mass.

FREDERICK GRINNELL WHITMAN,[10] b. June 13, 1922, at Providence, R.I., attended St. Mark's School in 1942 and was a lieutenant in the U.S. Army, World War II. He married Katherine Chalmers in Riverton, N.J., 1953. They now live in Darien, Conn. Their children are: WILLIAM WALLACE,[11] b. June 14, 1954; FREDERICK G.,[11] b. May 18, 1956; and SUSAN TAFT,[11] b. Aug. 9, 1959.

ALICE WHITMAN,[10] b. Nov. 11, 1924, at Providence, married Norris H. Sailer of Metuchen, N.J., at Ashville, Me., July 30, 1955. They live on RD 2, Lebanon, N.J. Their children are: EDWARD NORRIS,[11] b. Aug. 6, 1956; JAMES ESMOND,[11] b. Aug. 11, 1957; and ELEANOR WHITMAN SAILER,[11] b. Nov. 26, 1958.

Compiled by F. R. Duncombe.

The Wood Family

Sons of EDMUND WOOD,[1] coming from England in 1635, started the large Wood family in America. They settled in Massachusetts, Connecticut, Long Island, and later in Westchester. One of these sons was JONAS.[2] JONATHAN,[4] grandson of JONAS,[2] was buried in Wilton, Conn., in 1732. JONATHAN's[4] grandson, OBEDIAH WOOD,[6] and his wife, Anne Roe, were admitted to Christ Church in Salem, N.Y., in 1754. OBEDIAH's[6] brother, EBENEZER WOOD[6] (1731-1824), married Rachel Lockwood. EBENEZER[10]

(Eben A. Wood) married in 1902 Elizabeth Lawrence, dau. of James F. Lawrence and sister of C. Fayette Lawrence. They resided in Peekskill with their son, LAWRENCE.[11] Mrs. Wood still lives there, visiting Katonah often.

WILLIAM WOOD[7] (1756-1825), son of OBEDIAH[6] and Anne Roe, lived in Cross River next to the cemetery, and about 1794 moved to Cherry St. He became a surgeon's mate with the 4th New York Regiment in August, 1777, for a year.

SQUIRE WOOD[8] (1782-1858), only child of WILLIAM[7] and Abigail Smith Wood, bought 46 acres of land on Cherry St. from John Thorpe in 1805. He married 1st Apr. 1, 1800, Mary Whitlock (1780-1827), dau. of Thaddeus and sister of John Burr Whitlock. They had 7 children: ALFRED;[9] LUCY;[9] HARVEY;[9] WILLIAM;[9] JOHN BURR;[9] JULIA;[9] and SQUIRE.[9] SQUIRE,[8] a partner in Wood and Whitlock's store on Cherry St., was a captain in the 38th Regt. Militia and in 1826 was the 1st postmaster of Cherry St. After Mary Whitlock Wood's death, SQUIRE[8] married 2nd Mary Tyler in 1829.

ALFRED WOOD[9] (1801-1875) lived in the Cherry St. homestead. He married Electa Fountain, dau. of Jerusha Fountain of Yorktown, and they had 5 sons and 3 daughters. TYLER[10] and JULIA[10] died young. HOSEA,[10] WILLIAM,[10] JAMES[10] and HARVEY[10] all walked to California in the Goldrush of 1849. HARVEY[10] married Marinda Gee in California and they raised 3 children there. WILLIAM[10] and JAMES[10] also remained out west but neither married.

HOSEA WOOD[10] returned and ran the family farm. He married Agnes J. Wright of Quebec in 1860. She taught school in Old Katonah, Cherry St., and Cantitoe. They had a son, d.y., and 3 daus.: EDITH;[11] DELE;[11] and WILHELMINA.[11]

WILHELMINA WOOD[11] (1865-1946) married in 1891 Melville J. Allen (see Allen genealogy). Neither EDITH[11] nor DELE[11] married. ALFRED WOOD[9] had sold his Cherry St. farm to James W. Anderson in 1872 and bought a small farm on Beaver Dam Rd. next to the bridge. He died there in 1875 and HOSEA[10] in 1898.

WILLIAM WOOD[9] (1807-1885) married Phebe Green, daughter of Jared, and had 6 sons: JARED GREEN;[10] WILLIAM ELY;[10] JOHN BURR;[10] EZRA;[10] SAMUEL GARDNER;[10] and OLIVER GREEN.[10] They lived on Whitlockville Rd. in the present Gifford house. JARED GREEN WOOD[10] (1835-1902) was a student of Dr. Seth Shove's in 1861 and became a doctor. He was a surgeon in the Civil War and later practiced in Brewster. He married 1st Mary A. Pardee (d. 1884), dau. of Harrison Pardee of Croton Falls, and they had: EDWARD MORRIS;[11] and CLARA.[11] In 1896 he married 2nd Clarissa Lounsbury, widow of Stephen Newman (see Newman genealogy) and practiced in Brewster and in Katonah, living on Rte. 22 on the present Legion property.

WILLIAM ELY WOOD[10] (1837-1914) married Lydia Lawrence and lived in Stamford, Conn. They had 2 sons and 4 daughters. JOHN BURR WOOD[10] (1838-1898) married Marie Jacquenium. They had 2 daughters and one son, FRANKLYN E.[11] (1868-1944), a well known local taxidermist, sportsman and merchant with stores in Bedford Hills and Mt. Kisco. He is survived by 2 daus., MARJORIE[12] and MARIE.[12]

SQUIRE WOOD, JR.,[9] (1815-1892) was Cherry St. postmaster from 1836 until the office was discontinued Apr. 15, 1837. Later he moved to Somers, buying the S. Reynolds place on Rte. 139. He had children: MARTIN;[10] SAMUEL H.;[10] and CORNELIA.[10] CORNELIA[10] married Henry Hoffman and they lived on Croton Lake Rd. and also on Cherry St. in the present Ross house. He boarded New York City horses, bringing them from New York to Sing Sing by boat and walking them to the farm. CORNELIA[10] and Henry Hoffman had BERT[11] and CLARA.[11] CLARA[11] married, June 19, 1889, Irving Elliott. BERT[11] married and lived in White Plains. SAMUEL H.,[10] b. in the Wood home on Cherry St., taught in the Cherry St. and Haines Rd. Schools. Later he was in business in New York City and lived on Edgemont Rd. He had two wives and two children: ELLA OSBORNE,[11] who died of pneumonia Mar. 10, 1907, at 23; and SQUIRE S. WOOD.[11] Squire,[11] at one time lived with grandfather SQUIRE[9] and walked from Somers to school at Palmer Ave. SAMUEL[10] died Dec. 29, 1907. SQUIRE S.[11] married and moved to New York City.

The 2nd son of EDMUND,[1] EDMUND[2] (1578-1662), had a grandson, JEREMIAH WOOD[4] (1641-1709) of Long Island, through whom the James Wood family of Wood Rd. descends.

Compiled by K. B. Kelly.

The Wright Family

WILLIAM BURNETT WRIGHT[2] (1844-1922), the son of JAMES WRIGHT[1] of Mount Pleasant, married Helen Briggs Tice in Peekskill where they had children: ALMINA;[3] WILLIAM F.;[3] EDITH;[3] GEORGE;[3] ALAN;[3] and HELEN B.[3] In 1885 WILLIAM B.[2] and family moved to Old Katonah, making their home above the drugstore on Main St. He had a carriage, sleigh, and wagon paint-shop on Railroad Ave. In November, 1898, they moved to Fred Hunt's house on Nightingale Rd. recently owned by Mrs. John Silkman, and later moved to a house on old Rte. 22 at the present entrance to Cedar Rd.

ALMINA WRIGHT[3] married Randolph White. Their daughter, ETHEL WHITE,[4] married Reinhardt Prigge of White Plains. Mr. Prigge worked with the New York Central Railroad and died at their home on Cherry St. Mrs. Prigge now resides at 36 Greenville Rd. Their children were: HELEN,[5] d.y.; GLADYS;[5] DOROTHY;[5] CHARLOTTE;[5] and CHARLES PRIGGE,[5] b. in Katonah at 7 The Terrace. GLADYS[5] married Martin R. Silkman (see Silkman genealogy). DOROTHY[5] married Harold T. Gavitt and lives in Mt. Kisco. Their son, ROBERT HAROLD GAVITT,[6] is working for his master's degree at Brown University. CHARLOTTE[5] married William J. Barber of Ireland and lives at 38 Greenville Rd. Their 3 children are: WILLIAM J., JR.;[6] CHARLOTTE ANN;[6] and JEANNE BARBER.[6] CHARLES PRIGGE[5] married 1st Margaret Beach, by whom he had: CHARLES, JR.;[6] and BARBARA JOAN PRIGGE,[6] who mar. Mar. 6, 1960, Peter Morrison, son of Guy Morrison of Katonah and lives at "Caramoor." CHARLES PRIGGE[5] married 2nd Elizabeth Dazell by whom he had: JANICE;[6] DONALD;[6] and BRUCE.[6] They live in Connecticut.

WILLIAM E. WRIGHT[3] married Margaret Boyle and had no children. They lived in New York City where he was head decorator with the old Belmont Hotel.

EDITH WRIGHT[3] (1876-1952) married Henry Deacon of Katonah (see Deacon genealogy).

GEORGE T. WRIGHT[3] (1878-1945) married Marion McNeil of Bedford Village. He was in business with his father, WILLIAM.[2] In the May, 1902, fire, GEORGE WRIGHT[3] lost his stock of paint and brushes. There were about a dozen wagons in the shop at the time being painted. Parts of a few were saved but most were destroyed. George, or "Shorty," as he was known, was a talented musician. Shorty Wright's Band played at all the public and private dances. He is well remembered as a real friend to many. GEORGE[3] and Marion's children were: twins, ELEANOR,[4] d.y., and AILEEN;[4] LUCILLE;[4] and GEORGE T. JR.,[4] who is stationed at Corpus Christi, Tex., with the U.S. Navy. AILEEN[4] married Thomas Brennan and lives in Bedford Hills. Their 2 children are: GEOFFREY GEORGE[5] and EILEEN BRENNAN.[5] LUCILLE[4] married Severio Genovese and lives near Mahopac Falls. Their children are: JOHN ANTHONY;[5] SANDRA;[5] DEBORAH;[5] and JAMES GENOVESE.[5]

ALAN WRIGHT[3] married Irene Schelhouse and died leaving FRANCES;[4] and WILLIAM B.,[4] who lives in Norwalk with his family.

HELEN B. WRIGHT[3] (1883-1957) married Thomas Martin Wade, son of James Wade of Amenia June 24, 1903. Mr. Wade, a telegraphist, came to Katonah in 1902 to become our freight agent. He joined the original police force of the Town of Bedford when it was organized July 1, 1909, and was killed on duty in May, 1925. Their children were: GEORGE THOMAS[4] (1905-1906), b. on Rte. 22, Katonah; MARION AILEEN;[4] ADELE KATHERINE;[4] and HELEN LOUISE WADE,[4] born in Bedford Hills.

MARION A. WADE[4] married Leon Arcellus Stoddard, son of Leon A. Stoddard, principal of Katonah High School (1915-1918), and Emma Waful. L. Arcellus Stoddard is associated with the County Trust Company. Their only child, PATRICIA ANN STODDARD,[5] graduated from Katonah High School in 1952 and from State University Teachers College at Geneseo, N.Y., in 1956. She is with *Cue Magazine* as an editorial assistant and lives with her parents at 85 Huntville Rd.

ADELE K. WADE[4] married 1st Rowland F. Archer. Their son, THOMAS ROWLAND ARCHER,[5] graduated from John Jay High School in 1958, is in Texas with the Air Force. She married 2nd Tharpe C. Jones of Bridgeport. ADELE[4] and her daughter, DEBORAH DEE JONES,[5] live at 36 Greenville Rd. She is an assistant department manager at Macy's in White Plains.

HELEN L. WADE[4] married Andre Nils Lundgren of Sweden. They are parents of: LINDA ANDREA,[5] who graduated from John Jay High School and married June 25, 1960, James V. McManus, a teacher at Katonah Elementary School; ANDRE, JR.,[5] who attends John Jay; and THOMAS WADE LUNDGREN.[5] The Lundgrens live in Goldens Bridge.

Compiled by K. B. Kelly.

ERRATA

CORRECTIONS

P. 3 par. 4, L. 3:
    1723 instead of 1722

Page 3, Line 4:
    Delete "(which included Windsor, Hartford and Wethersfield)"

P. 38, L. 6,
    1723 instead of 1722
    also L. 5 from bottom
    Oct. 4, 1703 instead of 1702

P. 40, L. 1:
    1723 instead of 1722

P. 40, par. 2 L. 15:
    5,200 acres instead of 4,393

P. 41, par 4, L. 5:
    1743 instead of 1748

Page 52
At the time of publishing KATONAH THE HISTORY OF A NEW YORK VILLAGE AND ITS PEOPLE in 1961, the true date and story of Bedford's burning was unknown to us. For generations historians had given the date as July 2, 1779, and attributed the act to Colonel Tarleton on his way back to Mile Square after his raid on Pound Ridge. For those reading this 1978 reprint of KATONAH we would like to correct this misconception by the following:

delete and the burning of Bedford Village lines 4 and 5
insert between lines 23 and 24

Just nine days later on July 11, the village of Bedford was burned to the ground by a mounted party of more than four hundred men. Some were British, some were Hessians and some

470

were those Westchester tories known as "the Refugees". By mid-morning only one house was left standing.

Reference: THE BURNING OF BEDFORD July, 1779, by Dorothy Humphreys Hinitt and Frances Riker Duncombe, published by the Bedford Historical Society, 1974

P. 70, add at bottom:
"Now the home of L. E. Hayes."

P. 97, L. 10 from bottom:
"Herman Chapel" should read "Hermon Chapel." (Although the Chapel is spelled "Herman" in some sources, "Hermon" appears to be the more accepted spelling.)

P. 120, L. 3:
Dowburg Road" should read "Dowberg (or Dahlberg) Road".

P. 147, Legend:
prepared in 1743, instead of 1748

P. 211 insert between lines 27 and 28
"This garage was taken over by Harold H. Park in 1909. Here, Mr. Park sold Maxwells, Haynes, Overlands and Buicks and started the first gasoline business in Katonah."

Reference: Robertson T. Barrett
Katonah Record, Dec. 25, 1947

P. 223, in description of "Katonah area about 1907," L. 8:
"Muscoot Dam" should read "'Croton Dam"
L. 9–10:
Delete "Katonah had to move again"

P. 228, back row, 3rd from left:
"Louis Haight" should read "Lewis Haight"

P. 286, bill of sale—more by expences—08—01—6, instead of 05—01—6 Total "46—16—6" is correctly transcribed but is incorrectly computed in the original. The right sum should be inserted following the transcription: "45—16—6"

P. 301, title:
1723, instead of 1722

P. 304, L. 3:
"p. 000" should read "p. 146–47"

L. 27:
"△9 Muscoot Mountain" should read "△8 Muscoot Mountain"

L. 30:
"△8 Mt. Holly" should read "△9 Mt. Holly"

P. 316, L. 18:
"Silvenus Raymond" should read "Silvenus Reynolds"

P. 343, Robertson house:
87 Edgemont Rd., instead of 85

P. 352:
Add to names of men serving during the Korean War:

Allmond, Benjamin	Kammerer, John
Barrie, Arthur	Kellogg, David
Benedict, Clinton, Jr.	Morrison, Grant
Blum, John	Odell, Donald
Corlett, Richard	Suda, Robert
Consentino, Aldo	Williams, Richard
Ganung, Thomas	Wilson, Donald
Hilbert, Samuel	Winter, Norman

P. 366, L. 8:
"FREDERICK" should read "FRED"

L. 10:
"FREDERICK[6] (1781–1856)" should read "JOSEPH[6] (1779–1863)"

P. 381, L. 14:
"They had two children" should read "They had 4 children: IRENE[3], b. & d. 1904; DOROTHY[3] (1909–21);"

L. 18:
"to Middletown, N. Y." should read "to Suffern, N. Y."

L. 21:
"has 2 children" should read "has 3 children"

L. 4—5 from bottom to read:
"NANCY[4], who mar. Raynor Weisnecker and lives in Carmel; CAROL[4], b. 1944; and JAMES[4], b. 1950"

P. 390, par. 2:
Charles Hallock Fisher,[2], instead of [3]

P. 396, L. 2—5 from bottom:
Delete "It was for him that Herman Chapel was named,

the small Methodist church on North Salem Rd., which
stood on land now owned by Mr. & Mrs. Edwin Patrick."

P. 399, par. 5, L. 7:
Jotham Smith, instead of Smute

P. 401, L. 21:
"Kenneth M. Williams" should read "Kenneth McWilliams"

P. 403, line 8 should read:
of Elisha[5] b. march 1755; and Rebecca[5] b. July 1752 mar.
1773, Joseph Benedict in Christ Church in Salem.

P. 403, line 10 should read:
of his life in the Manor of Cortlandt, probably between Cross
River and Waccabuc.

P. 403, line 15 delete:
of the same area.

P. 408, par. 2, L. 1:
James E. Hoyt[7] (May 31, 1839–1890) instead of 1891

P. 410, L. 5—7:
"Mr. Hunt had married twice . . . and AGNES[2]." should
read "Mr. Hunt had 6 children: ELIZABETH[2]; CHARLES
AUGUSTUS[2]; CATHERINE[2]; FRED L.[2]; MARY[2]; and AGNES[2]."

P. 419, L. 36:
"In July, 1901, PENN[8] bought" should read "According
to the *Katonah Times,* July 5, 1901, PENN[8] then bought"

P. 423 L. 12:
"In Goldens Bridge" should read "born in Goldens Bridge"

P. 424, L. 22:
Add "and ALFRED[8]."
L. 4 from bottom:
"STEPHEN HOLLY MILLER[8]" should read "ALFRED MILLER[8]"

P. 425, par. 2, L. 1:
Benjamin Miller[4] b. 1712, not 1711

P. 425, L. 8:
"Herman Chapel" should read "Hermon Chapel"

P. 430, L. 16:
"Later" should read "in 1888"

P. 444, L. 5:
"Mr. Washburn has died and Elizabeth lives" should read
"They live"

P. 446, lines 20 and 21 should read:
of Greenwich, Conn. In 1769, Abraham[5] and Oliver[5] bought
land in Cortlandt Manor in the present Todd Road—Mt.
Holly area of Lewisboro, three miles east of Goldens Bridge.
At that time Abraham already owned adjacent property.

P. 446, line 26 change first two words to read: present Town of
Lewisboro.

P. 446. line 27 change South Salem to present Lewisboro.

P. 447 line 1, change soon after, to sometime later.

P. 447, line 20 insert
in present Katonah, after Cherry Street

P. 452, L. 27—29:
These lines should read: "He married and had 6 chil-
dren: JAMES JOSEPH[3]; THOMAS[3]; ELIZABETH[3], mar. George
Bassett; ANNIE[3], mar. Edward Bassett; MARGARET[3]; and
WINIFRED[3]."

L. 38:
"1944" should read "1941"

L. 4 from bottom:
2nd half of line should read: "They live in Lincolndale
with their 6 children: JOSEPH[5]; MARY[5]; JANE[5]; ANN
MARIE[5]; DAVID[5]; and JOAN CATHERINE MORAVICK[5]."

P. 467, L. 41:
"1896" should read "1888"

P. 481, last name in list:
"Fennell" should read "Fennel"

P. 490, L. 2 from bottom through P. 491, L. 2 should read:
"in Katonah, which had started holding services in 1911
in the old firehouse on Katonah Ave. St. Luke's moved to
the hall across the street from the present church in
October 1915 and became an official mission under the
Rev. Henry Chamberlaine, rector of St. Mary the Virgin
in Chappaqua. In 1917, Canon H. Adye Prichard of St.
Mark's, Mt. Kisco, assumed charge"

P. 494, L. 1:
after "information on" insert "most of"

P. 503:
  "Herman Chapel, 97" should read "Hermon Chapel, 97, 425"

P. 509 Newman, Edgar B.:
  add p. 347

ORGANIZATIONS

The brief sketches found in this section are condensed from more detailed accounts filed in the Katonah Village Library.

American Legion

Katonah Post No. 1575 of the American Legion was founded Sept. 5, 1946. Prior to its formation many Katonah veterans belonged to the Robert F. Crandall Post No. 129 at Bedford Hills which covered this area. The first commander was John O'Leary. For meetings and activities the Legion had the use of the Memorial House and its facilities, as one room in that building had been set aside for the Legion as far back as 1924. In 1953, with the help of the Katonah community-at-large, through individual donations and non-interest-bearing loans from various organizations and individuals, the Legion was able to purchase "Idlewood," a former resort-hotel property on Rte. 22. It opened its swimming pool and wading pool to residents and set up swimming and diving classes for local children. Other services to the community are the Christmas party for Katonah youth, begun in the 1940's, and leadership in Memorial Day services at the flag-pole and veterans' graves. Membership in the Katonah Post has grown from 100 in 1946 to 200 in 1959.

American Red Cross

In 1881 Clara Barton obtained the consent of the government for the organization of the American Red Cross. The Spanish-American War of 1898 gave the impetus for the widespread organization of auxiliary units throughout the country. Auxiliary No. 20, covering fourteen towns and villages of northern Westchester, was formed on June 21, 1898, at the home of Mrs. Henry Marquand of Mt. Kisco. Prominent among the first officers were a number of Katonah members: Mrs. William Chandler Casey, Mrs. James Lounsbery, Mrs. William Jay, Mrs. Clarence Whitman and Mrs. William H. Robertson. The original purpose of the organization had been to supply nurses, clothing, food and books to the armed forces. When peace was declared, this group had the vision to see that expert nursing care and disaster relief should be carried on both at home and abroad. A home nursing program was constituted as the District Nursing Association of Northern Westchester (see page 480). In 1910 the auxiliary became a full-fledged chapter of the American National Red Cross. Under the pressure of World War I, the Chapter started first aid classes, launched a successful War Fund Drive, organized a Motor Corps, and under the leadership of Mrs. George Nelson conducted regular sewing classes.

During World War II the Chapter again became very active with Mrs.

Henry D. Miller, Mrs. L. A. Alliger, and Mrs. Henry Alexander as successive chairmen. The working committees included First Aid, Home Service, Canteen, Bandages and Dressings, Blood Bank and Disaster Relief. Nurses' aides and "Gray Ladies" were trained, and courses of instruction in first aid and home nursing were offered to the public. A Junior Red Cross was established in the local school.

At the present time the Katonah Chapter of the Red Cross is under the leadership of Elizabeth A. Odell and Seymour W. Strong. The Home Service Committee continues to be active, and extensive plans to re-activate other areas are under consideration.

Association for the Help of Retarded Children, Inc.

The Westchester Chapter of the Association for the Help of Retarded Children was formed at a meeting in the Mount Vernon Public Library on Apr. 12, 1949. Its purpose is "to help the mentally retarded regardless of age, race, creed or color—wherever they may be." The Chapter is financed by voluntary contributions and fees from various projects.

The accomplishments of the Westchester Chapter include the establishment of the Westchester School for Retarded Children in Pelham Manor; special classes in Chappaqua, Mount Kisco, Valhalla, Yonkers, Port Chester, North Pelham and Katonah; recreation groups for teen-agers in Mamaroneck, Mount Vernon, Yonkers and White Plains; a Sheltered Workshop in White Plains to train for jobs in industry; a Diagnostic and Guidance Clinic at Burke Foundation in White Plains. A special class was organized in our area in 1956 by Mrs. Harold Walker and Mrs. Simuel Pryor of Katonah, and Mrs. Thomas McCallum and Mrs. William Bertkau of Bedford. In 1958 the class was moved from Bedford Village to the Presbyterian Church in Katonah. The class has an enrollment of nine children and is supported by five organizations as well as individual contributions.

Bailey Hall

Bailey Hall, a private school for mentally retarded boys, was founded in 1912 in Riverdale, N.Y., as the Florence Nightingale School. It moved to Harris Rd., Katonah, in 1919. In 1932, the School was incorporated, and the name officially became Bailey Hall in honor of Dr. Pearce Bailey, resident of Katonah, a noted neurologist and a founder of the New York Neurological Institute. The original founders of the school were: Dr. Rudolph S. Fried, graduate of Prague University; Miss Sara Weinberger, former superintendent of Montefiore Hospital in Pittsburgh; and Miss May Jean Robins, special student at the University of Pennsylvania for the Education of Mentally Retarded Children.

The purpose of the school is to find out what a boy is capable of doing, and to help him to learn to do it as well as he can. The methods used include: educational training plus industrial training, plus supplying the chemical needs of each student by individualized feeding for efficiency. The present (1960) director is Miss May Jean Robins, assisted by Charles Murphy. The school enrollment is limited to 35 pupils between the ages of 12 and 22.

Boy Scouts

The first Boy Scout troop in Katonah was organized around 1919 (exact date unknown because of destruction of records at the James Fenimore Cooper Council headquarters). Dr. James P. Gillespie, the Presbyterian minister, was the first scoutmaster. Since 1930 the Rotary Club has acted as sponsor. Membership has risen from around twenty boys at the start to around ninety in 1959. In this time thirteen boys have attained the rank of Eagle Scout, and the troop has won many ribbons in competition, including blue ribbons at the last eight Muscoot district camporees. Two boys have represented the Washington Irving Council at Albany and in England, respectively, Walfred Scofield in 1957 and Reed Hilliard in 1959.

Business and Professional Women's Club

The Business and Professional Women's Club of Upper Westchester was accepted by the National Federation of Business and Professional Women's Clubs Mar. 14, 1958. The local group was an outgrowth of the White Plains Business and Professional Women's Club, which acted as sponsor. The first president was Doris Kirchhoff; Catherine Gillette has followed her for two one-year terms. The Club is not an active service organization but is for the development of women's business and professional careers, and for helping women to go ahead in their careers. Membership covers Pleasantville, Chappaqua, Mount Kisco, Croton Falls, and Pound Ridge, as well as Katonah. Present membership totals twenty-five and they meet for dinner the third Tuesday of each month. Oct. 22, 1960, they were hostess-club for District 9, entertaining twenty-five other Clubs in the area from as far away as Poughkeepsie for an all-day district meeting.

Caramoor

Caramoor, the endowed estate of Walter and Lucie Rosen, lies three miles east of Katonah on Girdle Ridge Rd. and is the scene of the annual Caramoor Concerts early each summer. The house was completed in 1939 and contains a dining room and period bedrooms transported intact from great houses in Italy, England and France, predominantly baroque. The

Music Room, large enough to seat several hundred people, has early-16th-century carved-walnut ceilings.

The present Caramoor Concerts, sponsored by the Walter and Lucie Rosen Foundation, grew out of the late Mr. Rosen's activity as a founder of the Friends of Music in Westchester. (Mr. Rosen died in 1951.) Until the erection of the outdoor Venetian Theatre, concerts and short operas were given in the Music Room or in the enclosed Spanish courtyard. The outdoor theatre, designed by the Viennese architect, Frederick Keisler, was completed in 1958 to accommodate the increasing metropolitan audiences. Caramoor is also host to persons and organizations who come to view the art collection, largely Venetian Renaissance, and the magnificent formal gardens and lawns.

District Nursing Association

The DNA of Northern Westchester County was born of the work of Ellen Morris Wood, a Spanish-American War nurse. Starting as Red Cross Auxiliary No. 20, it was reconstituted Nov. 15, 1898, as the District Nursing Association. After Miss Wood's death in 1900, a memorial fund permitted the organization to hire its first nurse. The first Katonah Branch was organized on May 7, 1901, with Mrs. Rouse Babcock, chairman. Previously Katonah had been represented in the county organization by Mrs. William Jay, a vice-president, and Mrs. James Lounsbery, as treasurer. Mrs. William H. Robertson served from 1898 to 1924 in various capacities. Miss Elizabeth N. Barrett served as Branch chairman from 1902 until 1921 and from 1934 until 1942. She was a director until 1952 and honorary director until her death in 1958. Miss Margery Van Tassel has served as treasurer from 1923 to the present.

Before the advent of welfare agencies, the District Nurses took over family welfare during home emergencies, but clinics and nursing instruction and services have been standard service from the start. The work of the Katonah office was transferred in 1953 to the present central office in Mt. Kisco. Special emergencies in which the Association served have been the Chappaqua cyclone of 1904, the typhoid epidemic of 1907, the polio epidemic of 1917 and influenza of 1919.

First Church of Christ, Scientist, Katonah, N. Y.

The First Church of Christ, Scientist, began with informal readings of lesson-sermons by a group gathered by Mrs. Grace Dubois in 1917. It was recognized as a Christian Science Society in 1919 and admitted as a branch of the mother church in Boston in 1929. Services were held in a building on The Terrace from 1931 to 1948, in the Memorial House from 1948 to 1952, and thereafter in the present Bedford Rd. building purchased in 1950. The Reading Room, until 1960 maintained in the church quarters, subsequently opened at 135 Katonah Avenue.

First Presbyterian Church, Katonah, N. Y.

The first service, followed by others, which led to the establishment of the First Presbyterian Church of Katonah, was held in Avery Hall May 2, 1871. Sunday, Nov. 17, 1872, the new Church was organized with seven members. Persons actively engaged in the project were John M. Cornell, Dr. J. F. Chapman, Thomas Kincaid, Edward S. Folsom and A. F. Avery. In 1874 a new building was completed and dedicated on December 21, the cost of the site, building and furnishings being a little over six thousand dollars. The first pastor, Rev. John H. Eastman, was ordained and installed July 8, 1875. In 1892 the Sunday School room was enlarged and space provided in the church for the pipe organ, still in use, the gift of George Green.

The period from 1895 to 1900 was one of transition as the property occupied by the church was acquired by the City of New York. A temporary chapel, erected in New Katonah, was first occupied in February, 1898. A new building of Brewster granite was begun in 1899 and occupied July 9, 1900. The manse, next to the church, had been moved intact from the old village where it had been built in 1880.

Ministers serving the Church were:

Rev. John H. Eastman	1875-1895
Rev. Will A. Babbitt	1895-1900
Rev. Arthur R. Teal	1900-1903
Rev. Andrew D. Reid	1903-1906
Rev. William T. Bartlett	1907-1909
Rev. George P. Payson	1910-1915
Rev. James P. Gillespie	1916-1921
Rev. James Cromie	1922-1928
Rev. Ernest C. Potter	1929-1951
Rev. Wendell G. Wollam	1951-1961
Rev. Justus J. Fennell, Jr.	1961-

The need for additional facilities brought about in 1951 the purchase of premises at 29 Hillside Ave. for use as a manse, the old manse to be used as a Church House. The increasing need for more facilities for Christian education resulted in an addition to the church building at a cost of more than one hundred thousand dollars. This was dedicated Apr. 20, 1958. In 1959 the manse on Hillside Ave. was sold and the property formerly owned by Miss E. N. Barrett, adjoining the church property, was purchased to replace it, thus including all the buildings in one desirable property.

The church is serving a growing community and has a membership of more than four hundred. During the years it has been served by ten pastors. It is represented abroad by Miss Alice H. Schaefer who went from the church as a missionary in 1923 and is now serving in Hong Kong. Miss Schaefer was the first woman to be ordained an elder in this church. David C. Young, now studying at Union Theological Seminary, will be the first from the church to enter the ministry.

Girl Scouts

Girl Scouting in a permanent form reached Katonah in 1948. Earlier troops had been started in the late 1930's but had disbanded. Their leaders were Miss Marie Rosso, Miss Nina Bernardo, Mrs. Paul Noe, Mrs. Walter Raith, and several Sisters at St. Mary's. The new start was made by Sister Mary Jerome with 52 girls. Mrs. Albert Melahn showed energy and devotion in helping with the girls and interesting other women, including Mrs. Walter B. Dudley, Mrs. Theron L. Beacom, and Mrs. Claude Hisky.

In 1950, Mrs. Thomas Jameson became the first Neighborhood Chairman, her function necessitated by the growing number of troops. In the eyes of the national Girl Scout organization, Katonah was a *Lone Troop,* with an unchartered pioneer form of Scouting in which a locality sinks or swims on its own. Locally there were too few resources to fulfill Scouting's purpose, "to help girls become happy, confident and useful citizens." The national organization favored the association of neighborhoods into councils, and in 1953 a Study Committee was at work. Mrs. Margot Crouch, Mrs. Dudley, and Mrs. John Baur were active members. In 1956 the Northern Westchester Girl Scout Council was chartered, with an office in Mt. Kisco, a professional executive director and secretaries. From the first, Katonah women were active on the Board of Directors, including Mrs. Dudley, Mrs. Baur, Mrs. Harold M. Fisher, Mrs. Mortimer Cohen, and Mrs. Irving Sadai.

In terms of the girls in the troops, the Council has brought more camping and other varied programs, better trained leaders, and stimulating chances to meet other Scouts, even as far away as the Colorado Roundup. Also, it has helped girls find more ways to help their own communities. Ingenious girls and devoted women have made Scouting a real part of Katonah. The extraordinary hold this organization has on those who serve it promises lasting benefit and even greater growth for the future.

Great Books Discussion Group

A Great Books Discussion Group was formed at Katonah Village Library in the fall of 1956 with twenty-five participants, under the leadership of C. Hartley Grattan. Now going into its fifth year, the group, part of the nationwide program of adult liberal education of the Great Books Foundation, meets every two weeks for stimulating around-the-table conversation and members are encouraged to interpret and evaluate the readings.

Harvey School

Harvey School is a nonprofit educational corporation founded in 1916 by the late Dr. Herbert Swift Carter and established as an elementary school by the late Herbert Swift Carter, Jr. It is a combination boarding-day school, accommodating 125 boys who are preparing for the secondary boarding schools. Leverett T. Smith has been headmaster since 1939. The life and the work, the atmosphere and the environment are dedicated to boys 9 to 13 years old, grades 4 through 8. Originally located at Hawthorne, New York, Harvey moved to Katonah in 1959, where the school now occupies 78 acres of the former Sylvan E. Weil estate on Rte. 22. The original estate house provides for administrative offices, library and faculty apartments. New buildings housing dining-room, common room and kitchen, and new school building containing study hall and 10 classrooms, all of fireproof construction, join the main building. Removed by several hundred yards are two new fireproof dormitories, housing 64 boys and 8 faculty.

Katonah Baseball Association

The Katonah Baseball Association is an informal organization conceived by John Mueller, John Ruger and Arthur Covey, to sponsor and promote baseball for the young people of Katonah. From its beginning in 1955, the Association has provided Little League baseball for boys 8 to 12 years of age, Babe Ruth baseball for boys 13 to 15, and Connie Mack baseball for boys 16 to 18. Its funds are from solicited contributions and have been devoted to providing proper equipment, supervision, insurance and playing facilities.

Katonah Chamber of Commerce

The Chamber of Commerce is an outgrowth of the Board of Trade, the body associated with the organization of the new town in 1898. The Chamber was reorganized in 1953, four years after its constitution was adopted, under the leadership of Eli Antonecchia. The Chamber of Commerce has been responsible for the decoration of the town at Christmas time; for measures taken to keep the town clean; and for help in regulating automotive traffic and parking.

Katonah Gallery, Inc.

The Katonah Gallery got its start from an exhibition and sale of original art organized in November, 1953, by Mrs. Paul Brouard. It was formally opened in June, 1954. In 1956 the Gallery became incorporated. Its officers ceased to be a committee of the Katonah Village Improvement Society, but constituted themselves a rent-paying body to the parent organization. The annual fund drive for Friends of the Gallery began in that same year, 1956, as did the Annual Sidewalk Show and the Art Lending Service, organized by Mrs. Philip DeYoung. There are 22 members of the Gallery Committee, each of whom is responsible for an exhibition during a fifteen-month period. The Advisory Board numbers five. A paid secretary has been employed since 1958. The Gallery has sponsored lectures, tours, and classes in art appreciation.

Katonah Memorial Park Association, Inc.

The Katonah Memorial Park Association grew out of a Committee on Permanent Memorial in connection with the Welcome Home Day for veterans of World War II, July 29, 1946. It was incorporated Sept. 5, 1947. The land, forty-five acres, was acquired by purchase and by gift of E. P. Barrett (from the Katonah Land Company) after a fund drive that realized more than $40,000. The initial work, roads, grading, planting, building of shelter and playgrounds, was accomplished by 2500 hours of volunteer work during August and September, 1949, much of it, then as now, contributed by Paul A. Noe, conceiver and chief promoter of the original Welcome Home Day.

Under the successive chairmanships of C. H. Gifford, A. Elliott Kellogg and Dr. Robert E. Tschorn the Park became a reality and was formally dedicated on Memorial Day in 1950, the chief addresses being given by Lieutenant-Governor Joe R. Hanley and Supreme Court Judge William F. Bleakley. A thousand each of spruce and hemlock seedlings were set out in 1950 and 1951. The Summer Program of the Recreation Committee of the Town of Bedford was begun in 1952 at the Park. The tennis courts were completed by 1955, the Little League diamond in 1960, and funds for a swimming pool is an objective. Annual expenses of the Park are met by dues of the membership and other contributions.

Katonah Methodist Episcopal Church

In the late 1700's and early 1800's an itinerant Methodist, the Rev. Peter Moriarty, and his associates began holding services at Cherry St. Here they continued to be held until in 1836 two prayer meetings, one at Cherry St. and one in the new schoolhouse at Whitlockville, were attended by two zealous Methodist Episcopal laymen from Peekskill. These meetings, of great spiritual power, resulted in the "Great Revival," as it was called, and led to the building and dedication of the Whitlockville Methodist Episcopal Church Dec. 2, 1837. The Bedford Circuit supplied preachers to this Church until 1865 when the Whitlockville Church became a separate charge with its own pastor, Rev. E. B. Otheman. In 1872 Rev. Thomas LaMonte, father of the noted financier, Thomas W. Lamont, became pastor. Shortly thereafter it was decided to move the church to the east into the new center which was developing nearer to the railroad station. The cornerstone was laid in 1874 on the new site west of the Cross River, and the edifice of the Katonah Methodist Episcopal Church was completed in 1875. Here the congregation worshipped until the removal of the village to its present site.

March 28, 1900, the present Church on Bedford Rd. was dedicated. Need for additional facilities resulted in the building of a parish hall in 1956.

*Pastors who served the Church while it was part
of the Bedford Circuit were:*

Rev. Alonzo F. Silleck and Rev. George L. Fuller	1836-1837
Rev. Nathan Rice and Rev. William H. Bangs	1838
Rev. Robert Travis and Rev. J. L. Dickerson	1839-1840
Rev. Jesse Hunt and Rev. James H. Romer	1841-1842
Rev. Charles F. Pelton and Rev. J. K. Still	1843
Rev. Charles F. Pelton and Rev. D. B. Turner	1844
Rev. D. B. Turner	1845
Rev. Bradley Sillick and Rev. Thomas Sparks	1846
Rev. Thomas Sparks and Rev. Uriah Messiter	1847
Rev. Loren Clark and Rev. George W. Knapp	1848
Rev. Loren Clark and Rev. Joseph Elliott	1849
Rev. Loyal B. Andrus and Rev. Francis Donnelly	1850-1851
Rev. William Stilwell and Rev. Henry B. Mead	1852-1853
Rev. John A. Sillick and Rev. Clark Fuller	1854
Rev. Samuel M. Knapp and Rev. W. Stevens	1855-1856
Rev. Aaron Hunt	1857-1858
Rev. Thomas Edwards	1859-1860
Rev. A. C. Gallahue	1861-1862
Rev. J. C. Nichols	1863-1864

Pastors appointed after the Church became a charge by itself were:

Rev. Edwin B. Otheman	1865-1866
Rev. J. Chester Hoyt	1867-1868
Rev. William M. Chipp	1869-1871
Rev. Thomas LaMonte	1872-1874
Rev. Edmund Lewis	1875-1878
Rev. Philip Germond	1878-1881
Rev. Richard Wheatley	1881-1883
Rev. William S. Winans, Jr.	1884-1887
Rev. Wilbur F. Brush	1888-1890
Rev. Dr. S. L. Bowman	1890-1892
Rev. David H. Hanaburgh	1893-1897
Rev. Eli Quick	1898-1900
Rev. Osmon P. Hoyt	1901-1903
Rev. W. McKendree Darwood	1904-1906
Rev. Robert H. Kelley	1907-1908
Rev. Andrew M. Gay	1909-1913
Rev. Augustus A. Walker	1914-1915
Rev. George E. Barber	1916-1921
Rev. Robert L. Ross	1922-1927
Rev. George Feare	1927-1929
Rev. George Benton Smith	1930-1941
Rev. D. George Davies	1942-1946
Rev. M. Douglas Blair	1947-1950

Rev. Clarence W. Hunter   1951-1953
Rev. Ivan F. Gossoo   1954-1960
Rev. Howard Dixon McGrath   1961-

Katonah Parent Teacher Association

The Katonah PTA, with membership in the National Congress of Parents and Teachers, was organized in 1936 as an outgrowth of agitation for a new and safer school than the wooden structure on Bedford Rd. Mrs. Horace Bump was its first president. Its activities in behalf of the old school (1936 to 1938) were the providing of hot soup lunches and, for such as could not afford them among the student body, eye-glasses. During World War II the PTA supplied workers to the volunteer cannery at Bedford Hills two days a week. One year when paid cafeteria help could not be found it supplied volunteer help there, too. The present college scholarship fund was inaugurated after the war. On the building of the John Jay High School, the organization divided itself and became two separate bodies to serve the two schools, elementary and high.

Katonah Rotary Club

The Rotary Club was organized in 1929, under the sponsorship of the Pleasantville Rotary Club, and chartered as Rotary International No. 3101. J. Franklin Ryan was its first president. One of the Club's first projects was the promoting of mail delivery in Katonah. Since 1930 it has been sponsor of the Boy Scout troop. When the new high school building (now Katonah Elementary School) was built in 1938, the Club installed and operated a bowling alley in one of the rooms in the school basement. This activity, until conversion of the bowling room to school use in the crowded fifties, netted the club $5000, and the income has been used toward the scholarship award of the Club given at commencement. The Club has also raised money for its scouting activities by selling Christmas trees. Among gifts of the Club to Katonah are the four signs at the approaches to the village. Present membership is 31; meetings are held at Rock Gate Restaurant Tuesday evenings at quarter past six.

Katonah Village Improvement Society

The idea of forming a Village Improvement Society was first brought up at the annual meeting of the Bedford Farmers' Club in 1878 by Henry E. Pellew. The group was organized as the Katonah Village Improvement Association and Mr. Pellew was elected its first president at the first meeting, October 21, that same year. The purposes of the association were to improve the sanitation, safety and sightliness of the village, and to advance the cultural life. Mr. Pellew was assisted by five vice-presidents and an executive committee of fifteen, out of a total membership of thirty-nine. The Society was incorporated under its present name in 1886. In 1880 a reading room, forerunner of the Library, was opened in space rented in a private dwelling. Various village organizations soon began to use it for meetings.

After the move to the new village site, one of the chief concerns of the Society, besides promoting cultural activities such as library facilities, concerts, lectures, exhibitions and book fairs, was for many years the upkeep of the boulevarding on Bedford Rd., on The Parkway and near the railroad depot, all on lands owned by the Katonah Land Company. The Town of Bedford took over their maintenance in 1958, when it acquired these lands.

The present Executive Committee of the Society numbers nineteen and from this Committee nine are on the Board of Trustees of the Library. The Society acts as a fund-raising body for the Library, the two having been legally separated in 1952. In 1954 the Society fathered a second organization, the Katonah Gallery, which was chartered as an independent corporation in 1956. Other activities of the Village Improvement Society include support and maintenance of the building that houses the Library and the Gallery, lighting of the village Christmas tree, caring for the flag-pole, providing meeting rooms for various village organizations, and promoting interest in the village and its history through the activities of the Historical Committee. Executive Committee meetings are held at the Library the third Monday of each month, except for a summer recess; and the annual meeting of all members is in November.

Katonah Village Library

Until 1880 there was no public reading room or library in the old village of Katonah. The Farmers' Library and Reading Room, attempted in 1854, had not materialized. When the Katonah Village Improvement Society was formed in 1878, a library was one of its goals. A room was found on Railroad Ave. east of the station. By December, 1880, it had opened with a total of 400 volumes donated by friends and supplemented by books loaned by the State Library. A Library Committee of nine, appointed from the Executive Committee of the Village Improvement Society, was usually headed by a minister. Need for money to buy more books, for more shelving, for more room to house the shelves resulted in activities both cultural and money-raising: annual lecture courses, concerts, a debating society, and a literary society. Village organizations used the reading room for meetings.

During the first two years men of the Village Improvement Society took turns at the library desk evenings. Increased service necessitated hiring a librarian, or "curator," paid $6.00 a month, and a janitor at $4.00. Coal for the stove and kerosene for lamps came to $25.00 a year. A second reading room was added. In 1883 people other than members of the Society could have library cards for $1.00 a year and take out books for ten cents a week. By 1885 there was a printed catalog.

Katonah loved its library. The list of donations is impressive: loyal Society members gave $15.00 to $100.00 annually; Hoyt Brothers paid a third of the monthly rent of $15.00; matting for the floor was given, also a locust hitching post; other friends put up window boxes and planted shrubs and flowers by the front porch. By 1887 an amusement room, rented out for the sale of ice cream in summer, was used in winter for chess and for a weekly painting class; in it the Young Men's Christian Union held prayer meetings.

In December, 1896, application was made to register the Library under the State Board of Regents. The new status was granted on the eve of the village's move to its new site. During this period suggestion was first made that the Library be free-of-charge to public school pupils. Although Katonah moved during the summer of 1897, the Library did not re-open until October, 1898, on its new foundation at 21 Edgemont Rd. A new librarian and the chairman of the Library Committee began a card catalog of the book collection, classifying it according to the Dewey Decimal System. July 13, 1908, the Board of Education of Union Free School District No. 10 included in its budget $100.00 for the Village Library, thus making library service free to the public. Within the year, both readers and books circulated jumped 2,000 above the previous year's figures; schoolchildren from within and outside the District were the largest users.

In the new village a large lot had been set aside at Bedford Rd. and The Parkway as a future library site. By 1920 the need for a larger building was imperative, but nothing was done until 1928, when Mr. Clarence Whitman and Mr. E. P. Barrett backed a fund-raising campaign, realizing $50,000. Plans were drawn by Mr. Kerr Rainsford, and the building was opened in 1930.

In 1952 came the momentous steps of separation from the K.V.I.S. and incorporation as an association library, one supported partly by a sponsoring organization and partly by public funds. This made it possible to enroll in the State Pension Plan the Library staff, which by now consisted of a full-time librarian, an assistant, and part-time helpers.

Consolidation and centralization of local school districts were occurring. Katonah's School District No. 10 consolidated in 1952 with Lewisboro (see Appendix No. 31). The enlarged District was unwilling to assign tax money collected from the whole District to Katonah's Library which served only part of the District. Therefore in 1954 tax-collection for Bedford libraries was transferred from the school districts to the Town of Bedford. The Katonah Village Library has remained an association library, and its trustees continue to be elected from members of the Village Improvement Society's Executive Committee.

The Library now contains 17,000 volumes and circulated over 54,000 books in 1960, as compared to 25,000 in 1950. It has an active children's room with its own librarian. Its reference facilities, used by students and professionals in all fields, are greatly enhanced through its membership in the Westchester Library System, making available material in other County libraries. As from its earliest days, the Library remains a most important center of cultural activity.

Librarians

Miss Viola Devoe	1882-1883
Miss Frankie Smith	1883-1884
Miss Maude Green	1884-1890
Miss Edna Merritt	1891-1896
(Library closed for moving.)	
Miss Augusta Horton	1898-1903
Miss Antoinette Horton	1903-1905
Miss Matilda Ryan	1906-1919
Miss Agnes Hunt	1919-1927
Mrs. Emma Howe	1927-1929
Mrs. Amy Roberts	1930-1947
Mrs. Jessie Cornwall	1947-1955
Mrs. Eleanor Hendrickson	1955-

Katonah Volunteer Fire Department

The Katonah Fire Department was organized as the result of the fire that destroyed a large part of Old Katonah in November, 1874. Shortly thereafter three companies were formed and thirteen men of the community made themselves responsible for procuring and paying for an engine and adequate length of hose, and for erecting a suitable building to house this equipment. Their first firehouse, on North St., was ready for occupancy July 1, 1875.

In 1899, after the move to the present village, the Department was incorporated as Katonah Fire Department. The Katonah Land Company had presented it with a lot on Katonah Ave. opposite Valley Rd. Here a new building was erected, using part of the original firehouse brought down from Old Katonah.

In 1920, the Katonah Fire District was established, giving tax support to the Department. In 1927 a new brick firehouse was put up next to the wooden one. In 1935 the Department became a member of the Fire Chiefs Emergency Plan, which integrates the fire-fighting power of all county fire departments through the control center in White Plains. The Volunteer and Exempt Firemen's Benevolent Association was formed in 1939, providing numerous benefits.

When the former public school grounds on Bedford Rd. became available in the 1940's, by public referendum the Fire District was able to purchase it for one dollar. In 1958 the present firehouse was completed there at an approximate cost of $225,000. It houses about $100,000 worth of equipment.

Lions Club of Katonah

The Lions Club was organized in February, 1958; the official charter was received in April. Under its president, Marty Armato, it performed the following community services in its first year: sale of brooms for the benefit of the Blind Home, curbing of the Bedford Rd. sidewalk bordering the Library corner, conducting of the yearly fund-raising campaign for the Boy Scouts, and sponsorship of the 'Teen Canteen. Since then, a project for the planting of new trees and shrubbery in the center strips on Bedford Rd. has been begun. During the spring of 1960, azaleas and dogwood were set out, starting in the boulevarding at the Methodist Church corner and extending half way through the next block to Valley Rd. Membership in the Club now totals 28. Meetings are held twice a month at the 19th Hole Restaurant.

Mental Health Association of Westchester County
Northern Westchester Committee

The Northern Westchester Committee of the M.H.A. was organized in the fall of 1955, after a series of preliminary meetings initiated by Mrs. Paul Noe of Katonah. The first officers of the newly formed committee were: Mrs. Barbara Faubel, general chairman; Mr. Charles Combs, vice-chairman; Mrs. Paul Noe, 2nd vice-chairman; Rev. Ivan Gossoo, recording secretary; Mrs. John Tintera, corresponding secretary; Mrs. Dominick Antonelli, treasurer. The M.H.A., with its local committees, is maintained by memberships, contributions, and fund-raising benefits. Any resident of the townships of Bedford, Lewisboro, Pound Ridge, Somers and North Salem may become a member of the M.H.A. by the payment of annual dues of $3.00. The business of the M.H.A. is vested in an Executive Board which meets regularly eight months a year at the Katonah Library.

The accomplishments of the Northern Westchester Committee of the M.H.A. since its beginning have included: publication in the *Patent Trader* of articles dealing with mental health; the provision of speakers and films for various PTA groups and other organizations; an exhibit and open house held in the Presbyterian Educational Building; a series of public meetings; teacher seminars sponsored jointly by the M.H.A. and B.O.C.E.S.; and adult education courses at John Jay High School.

St. Luke's Episcopal Church

Early records show that members of the Episcopal Church in Katonah were organized as St. Mark's, Katonah, as early as 1855 and were for the most part under the care of the clergy of St. Matthew's Church, Bedford. From 1867 to 1887 St. Mark's, Katonah, was listed in the *Living Church Quarterly and Annual*. Apparently this church disbanded soon afterwards. An effort to revive it was made by John Jay II in a codicil dated 1888 to his will, but on his death the legacy was by error applied to St. Matthew's in Bedford Center. The error was discovered by the vestry of St. Matthew's in 1961 who turned over the fund's use to St. Luke's Episcopal Church in Katonah, which had started holding services in the early 1900's. In 1916, Canon H. Adye Prichard of St. Mark's, Mt. Kisco, assumed charge of the little mission with services held in a hall across the street from the present church.

The cornerstone of St. Luke's Church building, at the junction of Bedford Rd. and Katonah Ave., was laid Oct. 15, 1921. The architect was Hobart Upjohn. The first services were held there Dec. 9, 1923. Although St. Luke's had a succession of vicars, it remained a part of St. Mark's, Mt. Kisco, until May 17, 1944, when it was received as an organized mission of the Diocese of New York. Three years later, being free of debt, the church was consecrated. In January of 1958 St. Luke's became a self-supporting parish, and on April 20 of that year, the Rev. Hugh H. F. Morton, who had been vicar since 1952, was instituted as the first Rector.

Clergymen serving St. Luke's were:

Canon H. Adye Prichard of St. Mark's Church, Mt. Kisco, in charge of the mission	1916-1944
James Winchester Hyde, locum tenens	1944
Rev. Arnold M. Ross, vicar	1945
Rev. Percy L. Johnson, vicar	1945-1947
Rev. Gerwyn J. Morgan, vicar	1948
Rev. George French Kempsell, Jr., vicar	1949-1952
Rev. Hugh H. F. Morton, vicar	1952-1957
and rector	1958-1961
Rev. Richard Bowman, rector	1961-

St. Mary of the Assumption Roman Catholic Church

In 1890 a Roman Catholic church was erected at the south end of Old Katonah on a hill overlooking Cross River. The simple Gothic style building, 40 by 70 feet, contained beams from an optical factory in Whitlockville. This was a mission to St. Joseph's parish, Croton Falls. Previous to this time Sunday Mass was said in the hall of Green's Hotel, Old Katonah. This church was moved to its present site on Valley Rd., Katonah, purchased in 1899 by Rev. Philip A. Meister, pastor of St. Joseph's. Rev. William S. Murphy, who had succeeded Father Meister, opened St. Mary's which continued as a mission until 1908 when it was made a separate parish with a mission in Bedford Hills. The first pastor of the new parish was Rev. C. J. Crowley.

A large residence, formerly the home of Joseph Benedict in the old village, was purchased from the N.Y. Department of Water Supply. This building, to serve as a rectory, was moved to 55 Valley Rd. and placed over a hall seating 300, thus providing a parish center for many activities, plays, lectures, dances, etc. The second pastor, Rev. Martin A. Scanlan, served seventeen years during which time major renovations were made to the little 1890 church. The pastors of St. Mary's have been:

Rev. Cornelius J. Crowley	1908-1918
Rev. Martin A. Scanlan	1918-1935
Rev. Thomas F. Temple	1935-1944

Rev. Charles J. McCabe   1944-1947
Rev. John J. Dalton   1947-1950
Rev. John T. Halpin   1950-1955
Rev. John G. Leuchs   1955-

In addition to their duties in St. Mary's parish, which includes the mission of St. Matthias in Bedford Hills, the priests of St. Mary's serve as chaplains at Westfield State Farm.

St. Mary's School

St. Mary's School on Valley Road was begun in 1921 as a new activity for the parish of St. Mary of the Assumption. The school opened for four grades and was dedicated as St. Mary's Grammar School by Archbishop Patrick J. Hayes. The building, itself, had already had an interesting history. It had been the famous K. of C. Hut on Longacre Square in New York City, a meeting place for soldiers during the first World War. When moved to Katonah and put on its new site on Valley Rd., the former hut was easily remodelled for its new role as Katonah's parochial school. Adjacent to it, the former Hawthorne House was adapted as a convent for the Sisters of the Divine Compassion, who staffed the school. By 1924 an auditorium-gymnasium and four new classrooms were added, and by 1930 a high school was functioning in enlarged quarters. The simple hut with the letters K. C. serves also as a memorial to two parish boys: James Kelly, killed in action in France in 1918, and Angelo Candie, who died in camp the same year.

In 1958, the Golden Jubilee of the parish, a new grammar school was erected on the site of the old Searles boarding house just east of the school on Valley Rd. The modern school contains eight classrooms, a large auditorium-gymnasium, cafeteria, and principal's and health inspection rooms. The original buildings are now used for the enlarged high school.

Superiors of St. Mary's School:

Sister Mary Berchmans   1921-1927
Sister Mary Cecelia   1927-1930
Sister Mary Anna   1930-1936
Sister Mary Raymond   1936-1942
Sister Mary Gregory   1942-1948
Sister Mary Evangelista   1948-1951
Sister Mary Gonzaga   1951-1957
Sister Mary Evangelista   1957-

Sportsmen's Club

The Sportsmen's Club of Northern Westchester was founded Nov. 14, 1944, and incorporated in 1945. The first president was Asahel Waite.

For four years meetings were held in the old firehouse, next to the Bank. In 1948 the organization was given its present meeting place in Memorial House. That same year it broadened its membership to include junior members, and began the annual Pan Fish Derby, open to all children.

The regular seasonal work of the Club has been bird-feeding, raising and liberating of pheasants, trapping of vermin, planting of berry trees and grain for animal provender, and the cleaning and stocking of streams. It has offered fly-tying classes, stocked a Sportsmen's Bookshelf in the Library annually, since 1948; made gifts of subscriptions to *The Conservationist* to local schools, and published its own magazine, *The Creel*. Politically, the Club has worked for deer control; for more restrictions on out-of-state hunting and fishing; against licensing of all firearms; against restrictions on the sale of ammunition. During World War II and the Korean War the Club sent a mimeographed newsletter to local men in the Services. It now sends *The Creel* to all local men in the Services. Present membership of the Club is 310, 54 being Juniors. Meetings are held the third Tuesday evening of every month.

Women's Civic Club

The Women's Civic Club of Katonah was an outgrowth of the Katonah Suffrage Club founded in 1913. After women won the vote, the name was changed to its present one, its object being to provide a strong program for an educated electorate and to back such projects for social betterment as the Children's Court, hot lunches and recreational facilities at the school. Through the influence of the Club a woman was placed on the School Board. The Club was incorporated in 1923. The dream of a permanent building to serve as Club headquarters and as a community house for the village was realized in 1925 when the present Memorial House was dedicated on Armistice Day, money for the purchase of the property and erection of the building having been raised by public and private subscription and by a nucleus of war stamps and bonds saved for a war memorial. The building is a memorial to the men and women of Katonah who served in World War I. A room was set aside for the use of the American Legion which they used until 1952 when they rented property on Rte. 22 and then acquired it in 1953.

To provide a permanent source of income for maintaining the building and for the increased activities of the Club the Thrift Shop was opened in 1945. In 1941 the Memorial House was rented to a newly formed Community Association whose purpose was to coordinate the various village activities, but after a year's trial period, the Association felt they could not renew the rent. The faith and farsightedness of a few members brought the Club through these difficult war years. It now has a membership of 160, a budget of $7,000, 14 active committees, and a monthly program for the members. The Memorial House is used free by many organizations and is available for rental for private and community affairs.

Defunct Organizations

Information on the following defunct organizations will be found on file in the Katonah Village Library:

Baseball League
Brookwood Labor College
Camp Fire Girls
Chautauqua
Choral Club
Christian & Missionary Alliance
Community Association
Eidswold (World War II)
G. A. R.

Katonah Bowling Association
Katonah Tennis Club
League of Women Voters
Wildwood Players
Woman's Christian Temperance Union
Women's Suffrage
Young Men's Christian Association

INDEX